JOHN ARBUTHNOT

The History of John Bull

JOHN ARBUTHNOT

The History of
John Bull

EDITED BY
ALAN W. BOWER
AND
ROBERT A. ERICKSON

OXFORD
AT THE CLARENDON PRESS
1976

Oxford University Press, Ely House, London W. 1

GLASGOW NEW YORK TORONTO MELBOURNE WELLINGTON
CAPE TOWN IBADAN NAIROBI DAR ES SALAAM LUSAKA ADDIS ABABA
DELHI BOMBAY CALCUTTA MADRAS KARACHI LAHORE DACCA
KUALA LUMPUR SINGAPORE HONG KONG TOKYO

ISBN 0 19 812719 7

© *Oxford University Press 1976*

*Printed in Great Britain
at the University Press, Oxford
by Vivian Ridler
Printer to the University*

FOR

RHINA AND LIISA

PREFACE

We love to see the Subject unfolding it self by just Degrees, and breaking upon us insensibly, that so we may be kept in a pleasing Suspence, and have Time given us to raise our Expectations, and to side with one of the Parties concerned in the Relation. I confess this shews more the Art than the Veracity of the Historian, but I am only to speak of him as he is qualified to please the Imagination (Addison, *The Spectator*, 2 July 1712).

THE prospective editor of the *John Bull* pamphlets faces an unusual challenge. Almost everyone has some idea of 'John Bull' as the cartoon symbol of the English people; almost no one has read the original political allegory which brought John Bull to life, although the work was extremely popular in the heated party atmosphere of 1712. The central character of the allegory will strike a chord of memory in many readers: he is a sturdy 'plain-dealing' merchant infatuated with the practices of the 'Gentlemen of the Long Robe', and he pretends to the role of Lawyer to his entire neighbourhood. With a new wife and a new perspective he gradually comes to his senses, realizing that the lawyers have nearly destroyed his substance: he pulls himself together, withdraws from his disastrous legal campaigns, and learns to manage his own affairs. This personification so captured the imagination that William Hazlitt's *Character of John Bull*, written a century later, reads as though it was conceived as a severe but faithful précis of Arbuthnot's original. However, we hope it will appear in the following pages that the *John Bull* pamphlets are so intricately and vitally a part of the texture of their *own* time that, if only for this reason, they are worth our consideration.

The prospective reader of *John Bull* encounters a peculiar combination of an engaging surface with a continually echoing and elusive network of references beneath. There is no denying that the complexity of historical allusion here is daunting, and it may be well to remember, in reading the history of John Bull, the literal meaning of the term from which the words 'story' and 'history' are both derived, ἱστορία, 'a learning by inquiry'. As the *John Bull* pamphlets retell the history of Europe from 1698 to 1712 in terms of a neighbourhood chat, John Bull himself undergoes a process of gradual learning by inquiring into his own past: he 'comes to his senses' by telling his own story. Indeed one of Arbuthnot's achievements in *John Bull* is the skill with which he shows England arriving at a mature sense of political awareness after a period of furious political conflict. An 'allegorical' effort is required of the reader if he is to share with John this passage from bewilderment to clarity. But we need not regard 'allegory' ('a speaking otherwise') as simply a trope in which a second meaning is to be read beneath and concurrent with the narrative surface. In good allegory much is happening, and our effort of interpretation must be itself an 'unfolding of the subject' on several levels at once, not the quickly exhausted game of carrying out a series of one to one equations. Arbuthnot collaborated with history, the inexhaustible story-teller, in creating his pamphlets; we as his readers must collaborate with the story and with history; but there is a unique pleasure to be derived, in Ellen Leyburn's words, from 'the indirection which compels the search of the imagination and its consequent leap into the significance of . . . allegorical satire'.

Arbuthnot, like the hero of his pamphlets, has been ill served by his friends, for critics have too often merely nodded at his work with a passing superlative as they pursued their interests in his contemporaries: in consequence the *John Bull* pamphlets are neither readily accessible nor generally understood in all their allusive subtlety, despite the agreement among commentators that they constitute one of the liveliest and most ingenious political allegories in English literature. We have therefore attempted to set an annotated text firmly within its historical background. The editorial matter is, inevitably, extensive; but the text is too delightfully buoyant to be submerged by even our explication.

If this edition succeeds in presenting a *History of John Bull* whose complexity of reference is recoverable by the modern reader, much of the credit must be given to the mentors and colleagues who encouraged us through the early drafts and guided us from the bottomless pit of allusion. Raymond Brett, David Foxon, William Frost, Frank Gardiner, James Johnson, John Kenyon, Roger Lonsdale, Maynard Mack, Graham Midgley, James Sutherland, and Rachel Trickett laboured in the manner of kind-hearted evangelists over our endeavours. Any heresies or inaccuracies which they could not persuade us to eschew are of course our own. Angus Ross and Patricia Köster allowed us to use their as yet unpublished but invaluable work on Arbuthnot. John Bull was less fortunate in his friends, but was lucky enough to find a patient, encouraging, and uncomplaining wife: we were doubly blessed. We owe further debts of gratitude to the staffs of all the libraries listed in our bibliographical appendix, and to Wilmarth S. Lewis and Lord Rothschild who allowed us access to works from their private collections. A joint project, especially a transatlantic one, must always present considerable difficulties; but the Universities of Hull and of California at Santa Barbara gave generous practical and financial aid, as did the Leverhulme Foundation Trust in the form of a travel grant which enabled us to spend a summer together in work on the manuscript.

A. W. B.
R. A. E.

CONTENTS

LIST OF SHORT TITLES

Unless otherwise stated, all works cited were published in London.

Annals	Abel Boyer, *The History of the Reign of Queen Anne, Digested into Annals*, 11 vols., 1703–13.
Beattie	Lester M. Beattie, *John Arbuthnot Mathematician and Satirist* (Russell & Russell, New York, reprint, 1967).
Canting Crew	'B.E.', *A New Dictionary of the Terms Ancient and Modern of the Canting Crew, in its Several Tribes of Gypsies, Beggars, Thieves, Cheats, &c.*, 1699.
Canting Dictionary	*A New Canting Dictionary: Comprehending all the Terms, Antient and Modern, Used in the Severall Tribes of Gypsies, Beggars, Shoplifters, Highwaymen, Foot-Pads, and all other Clans of Cheats and Villains*, etc., 1725.
Carstens	Patricia Carstens (now Köster), 'Political Satire in the Works of Dr. John Arbuthnot', London University Ph.D. thesis, 1958.
Churchill	Sir Winston Churchill, *Marlborough, His Life and Times*, 2 vols. (Harrap & Co., 1947).
Colvile	*A Miscellany of the Wits Being Select Pieces by William King, D.C.L., John Arbuthnot, M.D., and other Hands*, ed. Kenneth N. Colvile (Philip Allan & Co., 1920).
Coombs	Douglas S. Coombs, *The Conduct of the Dutch: British Opinion and the Dutch Alliance during the War of the Spanish Succession* (Martinus Nijhoff, for the University College of Ghana, The Hague & Achimota, 1958).
Defoe, *Review*	*Defoe's Review Reproduced from the Original Editions*, ed. Arthur W. Secord, 23 vols. (Columbia Univ. Press, for the Facsimile Text Society, New York, 1938).
Dickson	Peter G. M. Dickson, *The Financial Revolution in England: a Study in the Development of Public Credit 1688–1756* (Macmillan, London; St. Martin's Press, New York, 1967).
Dictionary of Proverbs	*A Dictionary of the Proverbs in England in the Sixteenth and Seventeenth Centuries . . . Found in English Literature and the Dictionaries of the Period*, ed. Morris P. Tilley (Univ. of Michigan Press, Ann Arbor, 1950).
DNB	*The Dictionary of National Biography*, ed. Sir Leslie Stephen and Sir Sidney Lee, 22 vols., 1949–50.

EP	*The Evening Post.*
FP	*The Flying Post.*
Hawkesworth	*The Works of Dr. Jonathan Swift, D.D., Dean of St. Patrick's, Dublin...*, Volume V, ed. John Hawkesworth, 1754.
History of Utrecht	*The History of the Treaty of Utrecht. In which is Contain'd, a Full Account of All the Steps Taken by France, to Bring the Allies to a Treaty during the War, and by that Means to Divide Them,* 1712.
Holmes	Geoffrey S. Holmes, *British Politics in the Age of Anne* (Macmillan, London; St. Martin's Press, New York, 1967).
Key	(William Wagstaffe ?), *A Complete Key to ... Law is a Bottomless-Pit,* etc., 6 edns., 1712–13.
London Past and Present	Peter Cunningham, *A Handbook for London, Past and Present* (Murray, 1850).
London Spy	*The London Spy by Ned Ward,* ed. Kenneth Fenwick (Folio Society, 1955).
LP	*The London Post.*
OED	*The Oxford English Dictionary,* ed. James A. H. Murray and others, 13 vols. (Clarendon Press, Oxford, 1933).
PB	*The Post Boy.*
PM	*The Post Man.*
Pope, *Poems*	*The Poems of Alexander Pope: a One-Volume Edition of the Twickenham Text,* ed. John Butt (Methuen & Co., 1965).
PPB	*The Protestant Post Boy.*
Scott	*The Works of Jonathan Swift, D.D., Dean of St. Patrick's, Dublin . . .,* Volume VI, ed. Sir Walter Scott (Edinburgh, 1814).
Scouten	*A Bibliography of the Writings of Jonathan Swift,* ed. A. H. Scouten (Univ. of Pennsylvania Press, Philadelphia, 1963).
Spectator	*The Spectator,* ed. Donald F. Bond, 5 vols. (Clarendon Press, Oxford, 1965).
Swift	*The Prose Writings of Jonathan Swift,* ed. Herbert Davis, 14 vols. (Basil Blackwell, Oxford, 1939–63).
Swift, *Contests*	*A Discourse of the Contests and Dissensions between the Nobles and the Commons in Athens and Rome with the Consequences they Had upon Both those States,* ed. Frank H. Ellis (Clarendon Press, Oxford, 1967).
Swift, *Journal*	*Jonathan Swift, Journal to Stella,* ed. Sir Harold Williams, 2 vols. (Clarendon Press, Oxford, 1948).

Swift, *Poems*   *The Poems of Jonathan Swift*, ed. Sir Harold Williams, 2nd edn., 3 vols. (Clarendon Press, Oxford, 1958).

Swift, *Tale*   *A Tale of a Tub to which is Added the Battle of the Books and the Mechanical Operation of the Spirit*, ed. A. C. Guthkelch and D. Nichol Smith, 2nd edn. (Clarendon Press, Oxford, 1958).

Tatler   *The Tatler*, ed. George A. Aitken, 4 vols. (Duckworth, 1898–9).

Teerink   *The History of John Bull for the First Time Faithfully Reissued from the Original Pamphlets, 1712, together with an Investigation into its Composition, Publication and Authorship*, ed. Herman Teerink (H. J. Paris, Amsterdam, 1925).

Trevelyan   George M. Trevelyan, *England under Queen Anne*, 3 vols. (Longmans, 1930–4).

Tryal   *The Tryal of Dr. Henry Sacheverell, before the House of Peers, for High Crimes and Misdemeanors; upon an Impeachment . . . Published by Order of the House of Peers*, 1710.

Works   *The Life and Works of John Arbuthnot, M.D., Fellow of the Royal College of Physicians*, ed. George A. Aitken (Clarendon Press, Oxford, 1892).

THE JOHN BULL PAMPHLETS

PUBLICATION AND RECEPTION

1712 was a year of acrimonious political debate. The War of the Spanish Succession had seen the armies commanded by the Duke of Marlborough destroy, in one decade, the threat of Bourbon hegemony which had hung over Europe for two generations. Louis XIV had sued for an ignominious peace and Queen Anne was willing to accept his offers; but she presided over a European alliance which grew ever more factious in proportion to its success and she ruled over a divided kingdom. The war, and the peace negotiations at Utrecht, had exacerbated the bitter divisions between the Whig and Tory parties;[1] and no matter how non-partisan a man might have wished to be, he was with the Tory government if he supported the peace, and he was with the Whig opposition if he agreed with the allied demands for a resumption of hostilities.

At least he could claim to make a reasonably well-informed choice. Polemics of every description poured from the London presses during the first half of the year, among them five pamphlets from the printing-house of the Tory bookseller John Morphew which allegorized the war against France as John Bull's lawsuit against Lewis Baboon. The first, *Law is a Bottomless-Pit*, was published on Tuesday, 4 March; the second, *John Bull in his Senses*, on Monday, 17 March; the third, *John Bull still in his Senses*, on Wednesday, 16 April; the fourth, *An Appendix to John Bull still in his Senses*, on Friday, 9 May; and the last, *Lewis Baboon Turned Honest, and John Bull Politician*, on Thursday, 31 July.[2]

The popularity of this Tory satire can be gauged by the many 'editions' of the pamphlets and of the *Key* to their allegory[3] (for example, the first pamphlet appeared in six London 'editions', an Edinburgh 'reprint', and a Dublin piracy), and by the volume of

[1] See Holmes, pp. 68–74.

[2] For the full titles and publication details see the bibliographical appendix.

[3] These were, in the main, reimpressions rather than editions. The *Key* ran to six 'editions'. The first and second provided a gloss on pamphlets I to III: the third and fourth added notes on IV and the *Story of the St Alb[a]n's Ghost*. The fifth contained a gloss on all five pamphlets, as did the sixth (published in 1713) which also added a *Key* to the *History of Prince Mirabel*.

Whig criticism they provoked. On 14 April the *Medley* argued its anti-Tory case with an 'affadavit' signed by John Bull, and on 24 April the *Protestant Post Boy* included the pamphlets in a list of the most notorious Tory 'manufactures' which would be destroyed by the proposed tax on paper:

> *No* Conduct *now must rise from* Fairy-ground;
> *No dull* Tom Double, *or* John Bull *appear*
> *To make us what in Truth we never were.*

The same newspaper devoted large sections of its next two issues (26 and 29 April) to angry and wayward explication of the allegory; and even the *Flying Post*—less given to editorial elaboration—was moved to comment on 3 May: 'I wonder that the Examiner should be such an ungrateful Calf as to forget *that his Father John Bull is still in his Senses,* and that Law is a Bottomless Pit; but perhaps he was afraid of dropping into it from the Triple tree.' Whig polemicists attacked 'the *Rage*' of party in 'the *Conducts* and the *Bulls*',[1] and—assuming the allegory to be the work of Swift—condemned it as a treasonable expression of anti-war sentiment by the leading Tory propagandist. One wrote with heavy irony, 'The worthy Author of a *Tale of a Tub* and *John Bull* . . . will, I hope, very suddenly gratifie the Public with a more ample *Eulogy*' of Louis XIV.[2]

One of the Tory pamphleteers who dutifully took up the defence continued the satirical allegory of the Duke of Marlborough as the dextrous attorney, Humphrey Hocus: 'we have seen . . . the Hocus's . . . carrying all before them, and charming almost the whole Country',[3] and Charles Leslie castigated the Duke as one who 'Ruins poor *John Bull.* . . . And Magnifies his Allies'.[4] Yet another Tory paid the pamphlets the compliment of imitation in the story of 'Bonenetto' ('Benenato' or Prince Eugene) and 'the impregnable Fortress of Ecclesdon' ('Ecclesdown' or Dunkirk).[5] A Whig writer paid a similar if unintended compliment in an elaborate five-part 'answer' to *John Bull* which followed the allegorical scheme and the structural outline of the original but which succeeded only in demonstrating its

---

[1] *History of Utrecht,* p. 172.

[2] *French King Vindicated* (1712), p. 45: see also *Who Plot Best* (1712), p. 20.

[3] *Exhortation to the Love of Our Country* (1712), p. 5.

[4] *Salt for the Leach* (1712), p. 8.

[5] *Prince Eugene not the Man you Took Him for* (1712). Claude Bruneteau has drawn our attention to a similar imitation in a dialogue between Nic. Frog and two kinsmen concerning '*the Hardships intended against* John' and submitted to the *Examiner,* 15 May, by 'the famous Sir *Humphrey Polesworth*'.

own imaginative and literary inferiority.[1] Presumably *Law not a Bottomless Pit: or, Arguments against Peace* (advertised in the *Supplement*, 2 April 1712) was even less successful, for no copy seems to have survived. *John Bull* has survived, partly because contemporaries regarded it as more than a series of five ephemeral pamphlets to be forgotten with their topical concerns.

ALLEGORICAL ANTECEDENTS

Lester M. Beattie realized that the genesis of the allegory of *John Bull* cannot be traced to any single source:

> The real framework is the lawsuit, war pictured as a process of litigation, a formula capable of varied use. . . . The author's shrewdness is attested by his picking up a fable close to the homely interests of life and yet not too simple to sustain an unfolding situation of some intricacy. But Arbuthnot did not invent the formula. Periodical literature of the time which he cannot have missed contains hints which seem to have dropped down into his mind and lain waiting till he had need of them.[2]

But Beattie's assertion that Arbuthnot could neither have identified nor consulted his disparate raw materials is more open to question. It is at least possible that Arbuthnot's choice of the lawsuit 'formula' was determined by a conscious resolve to challenge its common employment in Whig polemic. It is of course true that the progress from actual war to figurative law was contextually and even phonetically logical: 'The Reason is plain, War and Law having so near a Correspondence . . . we must allow the Men of Law are Men of War, and have something in them Synonymous to a Soldier; particularly that tho' they are not raised by the same Steps, they may be Ruin'd by the same Method, for Peace would undue them all.'[3] Only a few days before the publication of the first *John Bull* pamphlet on 4 March 1712, the whiggish *Protestant Post Boy* for 1 March had recounted a tale of a farmer who unwisely terminated his lawsuit against an aggressive neighbour, and had drawn an unequivocal moral:

> *Since without* Spain, *for which Thou'st fought,*
> *Thou must be Ruin'd on the spot;*
> *. . . a* Bad Peace *is worse by far,*
> *Than all the Miseries of War.*

---

[1] The five pamphlets were *A Postscript to John Bull, A Continuation of the History of the Crown-Inn, A Farther Continuation of the History of the Crown-Inn, An Appendix to the History of the Crown-Inn,* and *The Fourth and Last Part of the History of the Crown-Inn,* all published in 1714.

[2] Beattie, pp. 74–5.   [3] Defoe, *Review,* 7 Oct. 1707, iv. 406.

Beattie discussed a number of such analogues from, for example, Leslie's *Rehearsal*, Defoe's *Review*, and Ned Ward's *Nuptial Dialogues* (1710); and without materially affecting his argument it would be possible to detail others more directly applicable to Arbuthnot's allegory from polemics such as Defoe's *Worcestershire-Queries about Peace* (1711). But it is difficult to accept that Arbuthnot was not in some way consciously stimulated by two other Whig allegories not considered by Beattie: another tale from the *Protestant Post Boy*, and an earlier pamphlet, *Seldom Comes a Better: or, a Tale of a Lady and Her Servants* (1710).[1]

There are clear comparisons to be drawn between the narration of Lewis Baboon's activities[2] and the opening paragraphs of this Whig pamphlet:

THERE is a certain *Great Man*, that has an Estate sufficient to content any one besides himself, much advanc'd in years, but from his very Youth exceedingly litigious: In his Nature so injurious and oppressive, that for above fifty years he has not so much as suffer'd *his own Tenants* to live with any sort of Ease; but contrary to his Leases and most solemn Engagements, and his own Interest, he has almost beggar'd them all, and made them *meer Slaves*. . . .

There being no *One* near him that could *singly* be a Match for him, the whole Neighbourhood, bordering upon him, have rais'd a *Joint-Stock* to oppose him: and there being a *very Good and Wise Lady* that lives near him, and has a fine large *Mannor*, divided from *His* only by *a broad River*, and who had been as ill us'd by *him* as any of the rest; by common Consent they agreed, about *Eight Years* since, to exhibit a *Bill in Chancery* against *him, to reduce him to the antient Bounds of his Mannor, and settle the same*: and at their general Request *this Lady* undertook to carry on *the Suit* in her own name and theirs.[3]

The allegory soon descends into a crude eulogy of the 'Chief Steward' (Godolphin) and an attack on the Lady's (Tory) enemies. Yet there are very interesting correspondences between this Whig satire and *John Bull* in points of detail such as the description of Sacheverell as '*a busy, forward, pragmatical Parson*';[4] and although it would be foolish

---

[1] In his *Checklist of the Writings of Daniel Defoe* (Bloomington, 1960), J. R. Moore tentatively attributed this pamphlet to Defoe. But it is highly improbable that in 1710 Defoe would have described Harley, his employer, as 'a cunning Fellow, a Pettifogger, and of a very ill Character, that never was true to any Cause he ingag'd in' (p. 6).

[2] See *John Bull*, 6: 13–27.   [3] *Seldom Comes*, pp. 3–4.

[4] Ibid., p. 5; cf. *J.B.* 27: 14–15.

to attach too much significance to such parallels, it is clear that the Whig version of the lawsuit allegory was ripe for reversal. Even if Arbuthnot had not seen this variation on the theme it seems unlikely that he was unaware of another, in the form of a letter from '*John Grub*, Malster' to the *Protestant Post Boy* for 23 February 1712— only nine days before the publication of his first pamphlet concerning the lawsuit of John Bull, clothier.

You mun know that I have been long entangled in a joint Law-Suit against one *Dobson* the Miller [Louis XIV], a plaguey, crabbed, peevish old Fellow, who is perpetualy Wrangling and Jangling with all his Neybours far and near. Now, that we might the better deal with him, my Neybour *Derrick* the, *Button-Maker* [the Emperor], my Cousin *Clinch*, the *Cheese-Factor* [the Dutch], and some more on's, enter'd into Bonds, not to lay down the Cudgels till we had made old *Dobson* return us all our own, and find sufficient Security for his good Behaviour for the Future. We cast him at *Common-Laaw* some Years agoe. . . . We have now had him in *Chancery* about 9 Terms, and have got the better of him in several *Hearings*; and are in fair Way of getting a *Decree*, whereupon he has several Times offer'd to come to Composition, which our Councel still advis'd us against . . . so that when all his Tricks fail'd, what do's me, this Old *Fox*, but go's underhand and wheedles with Cousin *Bob Scribble* [Harley], my Clerk in Court . . . [who] turn'd Cat in Pan, and betray'd the Cause; he first persuaded me to change my Councel [Marlborough, relieved of command in 1711] . . . then he . . . says I shall be undone if I don't make a Composition . . . and calls my Neybour *Derrick* and the rest of my Friends a Parcel of Rogues, tho', I believe, they are as Honest Men as any under the Sun. Now I have shew'd the Offers he has made me to . . . most of the Head Gentry of the Cuntry [the Whig Junto], who all tell me that he's a shuffling old Raskal, and designs only to Trick me as he did formerly . . . and say, they have it from my *Old Council*, That if I will but stand it another Term or two, we shall certainly have a Decree for Possession of the whole Estate.

There are so many direct parallels with Arbuthnot's *John Bull* in these idiomatic sentences that it is tempting to make insupportable claims for this polemic letter as a source. It is, however, certain that when Swift, in his celebrated portrait of Marlborough as Crassus, wrote, 'Cowardice in a Lawyer is more supportable than in an Officer of the Army',[1] he did so in the sure knowledge that his readers were conversant with the correlation of war and law in Whig polemic. Whether or not Arbuthnot was consciously stimulated by

---

[1] *Examiner*, 22 Feb. 1710, iii. 96.

such antecedents, they certainly provided more than mere 'hints'
on which a Tory reply might be formulated.

THE AUTHORSHIP AND HISTORY OF THE TEXT

When the *Protestant Post Boy* for 26 April 1712 dismissed the ironic
suggestion that the pamphlets were 'Publish'd . . . by the Author of
the NEW ATALANTIS' (Mary de la Riviere Manley)[1] and identified
Swift, in the persona of Sir Humphry Polesworth, as the narrator of
John Bull, it was voicing a common opinion:

> one who Midwife's *John Bull into his Senses* ought not to be out of her own.
> This puts me in Mind of a Pamphlet which goes by that Name, written by a
> Gentleman whose Hands are *Swift* to do Mischief . . . tho' said to be publish'd
> by that vertuous Gentlewoman . . . . this amazing Performance . . . has [so]
> put upon People's Understandings, as to get into a Reputation with the
> whole Faction.

Any Tory satire which 'got into a Reputation' would be attributed
to Swift by men who had learned to fear his political writings, and
neither Swift nor Arbuthnot made any public attempt to confirm or
deny the common opinion. Indeed, true to their practice of anonymity, they maintained and savoured a discreet silence, even among
their friends. On 4 August 1712 Peter Wentworth wrote to his
brother about the rumours that Bolingbroke had left secretly for
France to negotiate with Louis XIV:

> The conjectures thereupon are various, some think that Lewis Baboon . . .
> is shuffling off from what he had promised for the Allies. . . . The fourth part
> of John Bull [i.e. the fifth and last pamphlet] is come out, wch I suppose my
> Lady will send you . . . I have heard this part much commended. but in my
> poor opinion I think the humour flags and does not come up to the two first,
> tho the Author is the same, who I din'd with t'other day and by his friend's
> sly commendation of the admirable banter, and his silence, 'twas plain to me
> he had a secreet pleasure in being the reputed Authour.[2]

Both Swift and Arbuthnot were at Windsor on this date and had
been there for some days.[3] The editor of the Wentworth papers was
correct in attributing *John Bull* to Arbuthnot, but he may well have

---

[1] See the title-pages of the last three pamphlets.

[2] *The Wentworth Papers, 1705–1739*, ed. J. J. Cartwright (1883), p. 294.

[3] Arbuthnot was in attendance on the Queen. For Swift's movements during the
first week of August 1712 see *The Correspondence of Jonathan Swift*, ed. Harold Williams
(Oxford, 1963–5), i. 305.

been wrong in identifying him as the 'reputed Authour' in this anecdote. As a 'sly friend' Arbuthnot was fond of practical jokes at the expense of Swift, who was not unused to being identified by Arbuthnot as the author of the mischievous doctor's own creations.[1] Yet in a letter to Stella on 10 May 1712 Swift protested, 'I hope you read John Bull. It was a Scotch Gentleman a friend of mine that writ it; but they put it upon me',[2] and Pope, who had no axe to grind, said quite categorically in 1735, 'Dr. Arbuthnot was the sole writer of *John Bull*'.[3]

The authorship of the *John Bull* pamphlets remained a subject of contention for over two centuries, and in 1925 Herman Teerink used his edition to argue an ingenious case for Swift. This occasioned a flurry of scholarly dispute[4] until, in 1935, Lester M. Beattie refuted the proposition in a detailed examination of the evidence provided by Teerink.[5] There is no need here to reconsider the case so expertly sifted by Beattie but there may be some value in an *ad melius inquirendum* which takes into account the textual history of the allegory and the vexed question of eighteenth-century copyright. Quite simply, much of the confusion over authorship has arisen because *John Bull* appeared in so many editions of Swift's works. A full textual history would therefore require a largely irrelevant formal history of the Swift canon and we make no pretence to such an ambitious project. What follows is an abbreviated survey of the four main stages in the publication history of *John Bull*.

1. *The Early Miscellanies*

After 1712 the first significant publication was a collected edition of the pamphlets which appeared on 24 June 1727 in the second volume of *Miscellanies in Prose and Verse*, by Pope, Swift, Gay, and Arbuthnot,[6]

[1] *Works*, pp. 39–40.
[2] *Journal to Stella*, ed. Harold Williams (Oxford, 1948), p. 532.
[3] Joseph Spence, *Observations, Anecdotes, and Characters of Books and Men*, ed. J. M. Osborn (Oxford, 1966), i. 57.
[4] Teerink was supported by E. J. Morley in *Year's Work*, vi (1925), 220, A. W. Secord in *American Historical Review*, xxxii (1927), 357, and by W. Michael in *Contemporary Review*, cxliv (1929), 314–19. E. Pons took issue with his attribution in *Revue Anglo-Americaine*, iv (1927), 354, as did T. F. Mayo in *PMLA* xlv (1930), 274.
[5] Beattie, pp. 36–74.
[6] 'The First Volume' and 'The Second Volume' were published on 24 June, and a third, entitled 'The Last Volume' on 7 Mar. When another was published on 4 Oct. 1732, it appeared as 'The Third Volume'. See the note on publication in Scouten, p. 5.

under the title *Law is a Bottomless Pit. Or, the History of John Bull.*
Publish'd from a Manuscript found in the Cabinet of the Famous Sir H.
Polesworth, in the Year 1712. In the preface to the first volume Pope
and Swift wrote 'The second . . . will consist . . . of several small
Treatises in Prose, wherein a Friend or two are concerned.' *John*
Bull also appeared in the second volume of further editions of the
Miscellanies in 1731 and 1733.

The *Miscellanies* text of the pamphlets was in two parts, the first
comprising the first two pamphlets, abridged in places but expanded
at certain points, and the second the remaining three pamphlets
similarly treated. The preface to the fifth pamphlet, expanded by a
brief historical introduction, was made to serve as a general preface;
cryptic footnotes were added to explain those basic allusions that
were no longer topical; and a postscript of chapter headings for a
non-existent continuation of the allegory was appended.[1] In consequence this text made significant alterations to the structure and
the content of the satire.

2. The Faulkner Editions

In 1735 Arbuthnot died in London, and in Dublin George Faulkner
published a four-volume edition of the *Works* of Swift which did not
include *John Bull* but did contain much that had previously appeared in the *Miscellanies*. Faulkner was, of course, safe from the legal
wrath of the London booksellers who owned the English copyright
of the *Miscellanies* and whose inability to agree on a full and accurate
edition of Swift was, he claimed, his original stimulus.

Swift's protestations of the little interest he took in Faulkner's venture,
even of unwillingness to countenance it, of his readiness to leave the affair
largely to his friends, were but parts of the disguise behind which throughout
life he hid connexion with his own writings. The set of *Miscellanies* corrected
in his own hand, which happily has survived,[2] was almost certainly in
Faulkner's hands while he was engaged in assembling material for the first
four volumes of his edition of the Dean's *Works*.[3]

In the corrected *Miscellanies* 'Most of the annotations are of the
type that an author makes when revising for a new edition, i.e.

---

[1] This was not the spurious 'History of John Bull, Part III' published in various
editions of the *Miscellaneous Works of the Late Dr. Arbuthnot* after 1750.

[2] In the library of Lord Rothschild.

[3] Harold Williams, *The Text of Gulliver's Travels* (Cambridge, 1952), pp. 93–4.

minor textual corrections and changes in punctuation', and although *John Bull* is not marked as the work of Arbuthnot it comprises the bulk of the second volume, which contains only a few small pieces by Swift and 'is scarcely annotated at all'.[1] It seems that Swift had no intention of claiming the allegory as his own by including it in the Dublin *Works*, for it did not appear in any of Faulkner's editions from the initial four volumes of 1735 to the final twenty volumes of 1771. 'It is true that when the *Miscellanies* was reprinted in 1736, with a warning to the reader that pieces not marked with an asterisk were not by Swift, *John Bull* was in fact so marked; but as the asterisk was missing from *A Tritical Essay upon the Faculties of the Mind*, a piece certainly by Swift, the distinction is obviously untrustworthy.'[2]

Since a suspect reprint was no match for Faulkner's *Works*, a further reprint was quickly forthcoming.

After Motte's death (1738) the principal owners of the copyright of Swift's works in England were his partner and successor Charles Bathurst (with Gilliver) and Charles Davis (with Woodward), who had already experienced, and continued to feel, the result of Faulkner's competition. . . . No doubt induced by their rival's success they resolved to co-operate . . . for the reprint of Swift's works, and the outcome was the *Miscellanies*, sm. 8vo, 1742.[3]

There were thirteen volumes in this reprint, with *John Bull* and three other prose pieces by Arbuthnot listed under his name in *The Third Volume by Dr. Arbuthnot, Mr. Pope and Mr. Gay*. The attribution is all the more impressive since

There is clear evidence not only that Pope directed this edition, but that his warm friends George and Anne Arbuthnot, the Doctor's son and daughter, were consulted about what should and what should not be included. George Arbuthnot was more than thirty years old when his father died in 1735. That in a matter of such moment John Arbuthnot should have allowed an impression unfair to Swift to remain permanently fixed in the minds of his own family is utterly beyond belief.[4]

In 1751 the *Miscellanies* were again published in London, in a new format and expanded by a further volume, with volumes I–VII as the *Works* and VIII–XIV as the *Miscellanies* of Swift.[5] The sixth volume contained *John Bull*, but the allegory was still unequivocally signified to be 'by Dr. Arbuthnot'.

[1] *The Rothschild Library; a Catalogue of the Collection . . . formed by Lord Rothschild* (reprinted 1969), i. 367.   [2] Beattie, p. 57: see also Scouten, p. 28.
[3] Scouten, p. 65.   [4] Beattie, p. 58.   [5] Scouten, p. 82.

3. *The Copyright Disputes*

Printing began in 1755 on a new edition of Swift's *Works* prepared for the London trade by John Hawkesworth. It was to appear in various formats and sizes during the next few years,[1] and all versions were to include *John Bull*. As Thomas Sheridan complained to William Strahan on 5 June 1784, this was a series of editions 'thrown together in the most irregular undigested form'.[2] He proposed a new edition; but as John Nichols observed:

A material obstacle in respect to the then existing state of Literary Property, as far as it related to Copyright (a right still held sacred by every respectable Bookseller), prevented *my* undertaking at that period a regular Edition of Swift. Strange as it may appear, the actual property in the Dean's Writings was then vested in no less than FIVE different sets of Proprietors. . . . Of the Twenty-five Volumes *Five* only were my exclusive property, and an *eighth* share of *Six* others, which had been purchased by Mr. Bowyer and myself; and any proposal for an amalgamation was constantly opposed by some of the other proprietors, particularly Mr. Bathurst, who possessed an exclusive right to *Six* of the Volumes.[3]

Sheridan persuaded all parties to settle their differences, and his seventeen-volume edition of Swift's *Works* was published in 1784.[4] In the preface to the second volume he warned that,

The 17th and last volume, consists of Martinus Scriblerus, John Bull, and various other Pieces in prose and verse, published in Pope's Miscellanies. As these Pieces are admirable in themselves, and as it is well known that Swift had a great share in some of the most capital, tho' according to his usual practice, he never claimed any, but let his friends Arbuthnot and Pope enjoy the whole reputation as well as profit arising from them; and as these have always made a part of Swift's Works, where only they are now found collected, it was thought proper to add this volume to the rest.

In other words, volume seventeen was a sort of appendix which was primarily designed to maintain intact the whole copyright claim to those contents of the *Miscellanies* not by Swift. It is ironic that Sheridan, who was the first editor to suggest that Swift 'shared' the composition of *John Bull* with Arbuthnot, was also the first to omit the preface, which, it has been argued, may have been Swift's only significant contribution to the allegory.[5]

---

[1] See Scouten, pp. 80–3.

[2] John Nichols, *Illustrations of the Literary History of the Eighteenth Century* (1817–58), v. 395.   [3] Ibid. v. 394.

[4] See Scouten, p. 119.   [5] See Beattie, pp. 164–6.

John Nichols himself undertook the revision of Sheridan's work at the request of the other sharers in the copyright.[1] The result was a new nineteen-volume *Works* (with *John Bull* again in the seventeenth volume) which ran through four different editions between 1801 and 1810.[2] But Nichols's manifest pride in his achievement received a rude shock when, in 1814, Sir Walter Scott's edition of Swift was published in Edinburgh:[3]

having made a solid breakfast on John Dryden, [Scott] conceived the idea of a pleasant dinner and supper on Jonathan Swift; which, from the entertainment I had prepared, he found a task of no great difficulty . . . he very soon, by a neat shuffling of the cards, and by abridging my tedious annotations . . . presented to the Booksellers of Edinburgh an Edition somewhat similar to mine.[4]

This was grossly unfair to Scott, even allowing for the fact that it was the righteously indignant outburst of a rival frustrated by a series of legal decisions against the principle of perpetual copyright. Indeed, Scott's *John Bull* exemplifies the intelligent work he had put into the whole project. True, he followed Nichols's 1808 text,[5] and he reprinted many of the notes from the earlier edition, but here the resemblances ended. Scott had no personal stake in the English copyright and his only reason for printing *John Bull* was its literary merit.

AMONG the pieces usually published in Swift's works, of which he is not the author, there is none which can bear comparison with the 'History of John Bull'. It is not only a satire original in its outline, but the exquisite simplicity, brevity, and solemnity of the narrative, is altogether inimitable. . . . Dr. Arbuthnot, author of this excellent *jeu d'esprit*, is well known as the intimate and confidential friend of Swift, Pope and Gay. With the disadvantage of northern birth and education, he wrote a pure English style, although it may be remarked that he sometimes calls in the aid of national idiom, where he conceives it will add force to his picture. Lewis Baboon is for example termed a 'false loon', and the whole character, conduct, and language of Sister Peg is traced with a Scottish pencil.[6]

Scott was also the first editor to attempt recovery of the 1712 text,

[1] Nichols, v. 396.   [2] See Scouten, pp. 129–32.
[3] Ibid., p. 138.   [4] Nichols, v. 396–7.
[5] See L. H. Potter, 'The Text of Scott's Edition of Swift', *Studies in Bibliography*, xxii (1969), 240–55.   [6] Scott, vi. 235.

for although he printed the text of Nichols's 1808 edition—itself based on the various editions which followed the 1727 *Miscellanies* text—he reintroduced the original pamphlet divisions and restored the preface to its rightful place before the fifth pamphlet, working from the 1712 Edinburgh reprint of the pamphlets. In addition he made some attempt to find parallels among literature contemporaneous with *John Bull*, and he quoted from histories such as Abel Boyer's *Annals* or polemics such as *The Dutch Better Friends than the French*, 1713. In fact he was the first editor to consider the allegory worthy of serious textual and critical attention.

4. *Modern Editions*

Thomas Roscoe has the dubious distinction of being the last editor to print *John Bull* in a *Works* of Swift (published in 1841). By the late nineteenth century it was generally accepted as the work of Arbuthnot and, on rare occasions, printed separately as such. There has, however, been some variation in the actual text chosen by subsequent editors. The principal modern editions may be tabulated as follows.

1883   An edition by Edward Arber, who preferred an expurgated version of the 1712 text for *An English Garner*. George A. Aitken supervised a reprint of this edition in 1903.

1889   Henry Morley printed the 1727 *Miscellanies* text for *The History of John Bull* in the 'Cassell's National Library' series.

1892   George A. Aitken also chose the 1727 text for his edition in *The Life and Works of John Arbuthnot*.

1920   K. N. Colvile followed the 1727 text for *A Miscellany of the Wits*.

1925   Herman Teerink 'reissued' the 1712 pamphlets in an edition which sought to prove that *John Bull* was the work of Swift.

It must, of course, be admitted that Swift, Pope, Bolingbroke, or indeed any member of the Tory circle may have collaborated to a greater or lesser degree with Arbuthnot during the composition of the pamphlets. It is certain that we shall never know what happened when the Tory wits met to discuss their literary ventures over a good dinner and a few bottles of claret in Arbuthnot's rooms at St. James's. Yet the informed evidence all points one way. John Arbuthnot was the author of the *John Bull* pamphlets.

THE TEXT OF JOHN BULL

Herman Teerink's contention that Swift wrote *John Bull* may have been misguided, but the ingenuity and enthusiasm of his argument did Arbuthnot studies a notable service by reawakening scholarly interest in the allegory. His edition also implicitly posed the question of copy-text when he 'reissued' the original pamphlets in preference to the text which first appeared in the 1727 *Miscellanies*. Clearly the substantive changes of the 1727 text moved some considerable way from the author's original intention; but if these could be proved the result of authorial revision, the 1727 text would have to be taken into account as an independent witness.

The *Miscellanies* project was planned during Swift's stay in England in 1726. Pope took on the responsibility for the editing, and Swift, on his return to Dublin, began to assemble pieces for inclusion. On 15 October he reported to Pope, 'I am mustring as I told you all the little things in verse that I think may be Safely printed,¹ but I give you despotick Power to tear as many as you please.'² It was a convenient arrangement, as Pope, 'with Homer and Shakespeare off his hands . . . was free to enter into new fields'.³ Moreover 'In the publication of his own writings Pope was wont to exercise constant care, and he would not be less meticulous if entrusted with the writings of a friend for whom, of all his contemporaries, he held the highest regard.'⁴ The two friends worked quickly, and on 5 December Swift again mentioned the verses he had selected, with a parenthetical jibe at Pope's editorial fussiness: 'Since you have receiv'd the verses, I most earnestly intreat you to burn those which you do not approve, and in those few where you may not dislike some parts, blot out the rest, and sometimes (tho' it may be against the laziness of your nature) be so kind as to make a few corrections, if the matter will bear them.'⁵

There are few surviving letters written by Arbuthnot during the later months of 1726, but what correspondence is extant suggests that he was busy enough with his own many and varied activities, though he was conversant with the *Miscellanies* project. In late October Pope was recovering from an illness, complicated by injury,

---

¹ In the 'Last Volume' of the *Miscellanies*.
² *The Correspondence of Alexander Pope*, ed. G. Sherburn (Oxford, 1956), ii. 408.
³ B. Dobrée, *Alexander Pope* (1951), p. 81.
⁴ Williams, *The Text of Gulliver's Travels*, p. 71.
⁵ Pope, *Correspondence*, ed. Sherburn, ii. 420.

during which the doctor attended him. On 5 November Arbuthnot wrote to Swift:

Gay has had a little feaver, but is pretty well recoverd; so is Mr Pope. We shall meett at Lord BolingBrokes on Thursday in town, at dinner, & Remember yow. . . . I had the honor to see Lord Oxford, who askd kindly for yow, & said he would write to yow. if the project go's on for printing some papers [i.e. the *Miscellanies*], he has promisd to give Copys of some things, which I beleive cannot be found else wher.[1]

Edward Harley, upon the death of his father Robert in 1724, succeeded as Lord Oxford and came into possession of the great Harleian library which was to be especially useful to the Scriblerians in the compilation of their *Miscellanies*. Oxford took seriously the task of collecting pieces for his library, but when in late 1726 he asked Arbuthnot for copies of some brief verses, he received a harassed apology from the busy doctor: 'It was not possible for me at this Time to send the Ballad but your lordship shall have it ther are a hundred incorrect Copys of it about town. . . . I happen to be so unlucky as to have twenty things to do at this moment, else your lop should have had the ballad.'[2]

   On 8 December 1726 Pope asked Oxford to return to London and mentioned the *Miscellanies* to him, apparently for the first time: 'I want you for many reasons; & among the rest, to hear what you say of a Book called Gullivers Travels; and to desire you to lend us, John Bull &c. for a good End, in order to put together this winter many scatterd pieces of the same kind, which are too good to be lost.'[3] Why is there no mention of *John Bull* in any of the letters written by Arbuthnot between the time when the *Miscellanies* were first mooted early in 1726, and 18 February 1727 when Pope reported to Swift that the first two volumes were in print? Why did Pope not ask Arbuthnot rather than Oxford for *John Bull*? Perhaps the author had not bothered to keep copies of his celebrated polemics? Does the 'us' in Pope's letter refer to himself and Arbuthnot, to the other Tory wits, or is it simply a form of authorial plural? There is no evidence to provide answers to such questions.

   [1] Angus M. Ross, 'The Correspondence of Dr. John Arbuthnot, first Collected together and Edited, with a Biographical Introduction, Notes and a Dissertation' (Cambridge Univ. Ph.D. thesis, 1956), p. 489.
   [2] Arbuthnot to Oxford, 16 Nov. 1726. Ross suggests that the piece in question was 'perhaps the ballad on Molly Lepell' by Pulteney, Chesterfield, and Arbuthnot, which the doctor enclosed in another letter to Oxford on 23 Nov. ('Correspondence', pp. 493–9).   [3] Pope, *Correspondence*, ed. Sherburn, ii. 421.

We know that Arbuthnot was supposed to share the burden of
editing the περὶ Βάθους for 'The Last Volume' of *Miscellanies* (published on 7 March 1728), and in a letter probably composed in
January of that year Pope complained to Swift: 'The third Volume
of the Miscellanies is coming out post now, in which I have inserted
the Treatise περὶ Βάθους I have entirely Methodized and in a manner
written, it all, the Dr grew quite indolent in it, for something newer,
I know not what.'[1] From what we know of the doctor it is not unreasonable to postulate that he reacted in a similar manner to any
editorial labour expected of him apropos of the previous volume.
Arbuthnot was the only Tory satirist to marry and raise a family,
and it seems unlikely that this dedicated physician, whose 'imagination was almost inexhaustible, and . . . at anybody's service, for . . .
he did not care what became of it', would have relished the editing
of his five occasional pamphlets fifteen years after their first publication, particularly as he was reputedly so careless of his writings
'that his sons, when young, have frequently made kites of his
scattered papers of hints which would have furnished good matter
for folios'.[2] Certainly such charming reminiscences concern the
Arbuthnot of Pope's *Epistle* and anecdotal legend; but while we must
suspect some nostalgic distortion in them, it is an undeniable fact
that the composition of *John Bull* was a unique spate of pamphleteering for a man who was always more concerned with his profession
and personal relationships than with his literary reputation: 'Not
being in the least jealous of his fame as an author, he would neither
take the time nor the trouble of separating the best from the worst;
he worked out the whole mine, which afterwards, in the hands of
skilful refiners, produced a rich vein of ore.'[2] Of course this general
account of Arbuthnot's attitude to his literary works is of little
value as evidence. But it does suggest a possible explanation for
another matter of historical fact: there is not a shred of external
evidence to suggest that Arbuthnot revised his pamphlets for the
Miscellanies edition. Indeed, what scraps of evidence survive point
to the conclusion that Pope did the job.

Internal evidence also suggests an editor other than the author,
the changes made in the 1727 text falling into five principal categories.

[1] Ibid. ii. 468.
[2] From Lord Chesterfield's 'character' of Arbuthnot, *The Wit and Wisdom of the
Earl of Chesterfield*, ed. W. Ernst-Browning (1875), p. 319.

1. *The Continuous Narrative*

Any editor might have been tempted to fashion a continuous *History of John Bull* which would be aesthetically and even physically more attractive than the original pamphlets. Inconvenient passages such as the preface to the third pamphlet and phrases such as 'in my last part' were emended as necessary. Such changes were not seriously prejudicial but it is difficult to make sense of the bipartite division of the text. The second part contains the last three pamphlets, dividing the allegory where the original departed from its treatment of the European war to concentrate on the historical background. It thus includes the fourth pamphlet, the *Appendix*, the very name of which is enough to suggest how unhappily it sits with the third and fifth pamphlets to form a continuous narrative. In fact, only the first and last pamphlets were predominantly concerned with foreign affairs, and no bipartite division would be satisfactory. Any attempt to give the pamphlets coherence within a subdivided or chronological format would have involved a complete reworking of the text. The occasional emendations without the necessary drastic revision could only be attributed to Arbuthnot on the grounds that they reflect his careless attitude towards his literary creations— the very grounds on which it could be argued, conversely, that he was unlikely to have undertaken revision in the first place.

2. *The Footnotes*

Signposting the topical satire of 1712 was an obvious necessity in an edition published fifteen years later. William Wagstaffe was the putative author of the *Complete Key* to the 1712 pamphlets,[1] but he had died in 1725, and the two sets of annotations provided by the *Key* and the 1727 edition of the *Miscellanies* are far too brief to provide evidence of anything except Tory bias.

3. *The Censoring of Personal Satire*

The largest single change effected in the 1727 text was the omission of the last chapter of the first pamphlet which attacked the Tory turncoat Nottingham, alias Don Diego Dismallo the Conjurer. The most logical explanation for this omission seems to be that the dramatic-dialogue form of this chapter (a form used frequently in the

---

[1] See *Dictionary of Anonymous and Pseudonymous English Literature* (*Samuel Halkett and John Laing*), ed. J. Kennedy, W. A. Smith, and A. F. Johnson (1932–4).

later pamphlets, and there retained by the 1727 editor) was considered inappropriate after a sequence of twelve narrative chapters. If the editor was determined to remove the personal attack on Nottingham, why did he not also omit the satirical destruction of Don Diego in the fourth pamphlet? Admittedly he there dropped 'Dismallo', a transparent allusion to the nickname 'Dismal' Nottingham; but an intelligent reader of 1727 would have had no difficulty in identifying the intended victim from a passage of satire which is a far more pointed condemnation of Nottingham's actions than the omitted earlier parody of his sententious oratory. It would be folly to seek logical reasons for all the editorial changes in the 1727 text, for Nottingham was not the only character left, like Jack in the allegory, neither reprieved nor decently hanged. In the ninth chapter of the first pamphlet the Duke of Somerset was pilloried as 'Signior Cavallo, an Italian Quack' in a satire which captured his arrogant stupidity. Yet in the 1727 text 'Signior Cavallo' was replaced by 'some quacks'. Since the only justification for the interlude was the expressly personal attack on Somerset it was a debilitating change. The Duke of Marlborough was also treated less harshly in 1727. For example, the intrigue between '*Hocus* [Marlborough] and *Frog* [the Dutch] . . . to throw the Burden of the Law-Suit' on John became the stratagem of 'the Tradesmen, Lawyers and *Frog*'.[1] The cumulative effect of such changes is to reduce the stature of Hocus as the cunning manipulator of Bull's domestic enemies.

Equally prejudicial is the censoring of personal satire against the Duchess of Marlborough. In the twelfth chapter of the first pamphlet there is an hilarious parody of the stormy final interview between the Duchess and Queen Anne when Mrs. Hocus berates Mrs. Bull. In 1727 the speech was retained, but as the outburst of one of the tradesmen (i.e. a Whig). It lost little of its broad humour, but it lacked the satirical edge of the original. A critic would have to place a great deal of emphasis on Arbuthnot's reputation for carelessness to argue that he would have so diluted his satire. In addition, the changes in question are too systematic, if occasionally puzzling. This again might be a clue to the editor's identity, for Pope not only remained on friendly terms with the Duchess of Marlborough but also never sought to offend influential personages unless his conscience or his art demanded that he should. No political end would have been served by reprinting every detail of the attack on the

---

[1] *J.B.* 18: 12–13.

Marlboroughs in 1727, and, as David Foxon has pointed out to us, in comparisons between Pope's manuscripts and his printed satires there is a good deal of evidence that he censored his personal attacks in a manner very comparable with the emendations to the satire of *John Bull.*

4. *Additions to the Satire*

There is a significant number of interpolations of new material into the 1727 text. The most substantial additions are those which elaborate satiric points or facilitate penetration of the allegorical disguise. Nothing could be more harmful to pamphlets written with a fine sense of pace and witty indirection. In the tenth chapter of the first pamphlet Mrs. Bull braves the wrath of her recalcitrant husband to tell him that he will never realize his dream of becoming a lawyer: '*John* heard her all this while with patience, 'till she prick'd his Maggot, and touch'd him in the tender point; then he broke out into a violent Passion, "What, I not fit for a Lawyer".'[1] The 1727 text inserted twelve lines of tautological elaboration between Mrs. Bull's statement and John's violent retort. In the original his anger is dramatic: in the 1727 text it is anti-climactic. It seems unlikely that Arbuthnot would have so jeopardized the character he had been at such pains to establish in the preceding chapters.

5. *The Correction of Accidental Errors*

When Angus Ross examined the peculiarities in Arbuthnot's use of English he noted that, unlike most of the doctor's correspondents, who wrote in a manner close to the norms of contemporary printing, Arbuthnot 'shows a singular disregard for punctuation, capitalization, or any indication of sentence division'.[2] We do not suggest that there is a direct relationship between private letters and published works, but it is interesting that the original *John Bull* pamphlets were marked by unusual eccentricity in the three respects noted by Ross, and that the great majority of the 1727 emendations were concerned with their rationalization. Arbuthnot also habitually doubled medial and final consonants,[3] a usage which occurs in the original pamphlets, for instance in 'Cudgell', 'Linnen', or 'accute'. The 1727 text emended 'Cudgell' to 'Cudgel' in one instance, but

---

[1] *J.B* 17: 2–4.   [2] Arbuthnot, 'Correspondence', p. 832.
[3] Ibid., pp. 839, 848–53.

retained the original spelling in others; and it preferred 'Linen' to 'Linnen' twice in its version of the first pamphlet, but retained the original spelling on its third appearance. Similarly, the Scots doctor's 'accute' (retained by the 1712 Edinburgh reprint) was emended to 'acute' in the 1727 London text. But any comparative analysis is atrophied by the inconsistency of the revisions. Some obvious misprints such as 'Suecess' were corrected, but others, such as 'Quean', were left to the editors of later editions; some obvious infelicities such as dittographies were removed, but others were not; and some of the changes made in 1727, such as 'too' to 'se' or 'Soup' to 'Soupe', defy explanation as the decisions of an editor.

Perhaps the most significant failures of the 1727 text in its movement towards the correction of accidental errors are to be found in the idiomatic passages. The London 1712 editions printed two lines of the pidgin English quack announcement by Ptschirnsooker (Bishop Burnet) as: 'this White Powder from *Amsterdam,* and the Red from *Edinburgh,* but the chief Ingredient', when, to be consistent, they should have read: 'dis White Powder . . . de Red . . . de chief'.[1] The 1712 Edinburgh reprint made the necessary changes, but the 1727 text reprinted the inconsistent version. Similarly, in the speech of Peg (the Scots people), the 1727 text twice retained 'mun' (for may), and yet twice anglicized 'auld' to 'old', while the Edinburgh reprint retained all the dialectal usages.[2] It is ironic that the Edinburgh text, for all its failings, made relatively few (if logical) changes, but no concerted attempt to rationalize the far less important (if eccentric) punctuation and spelling of the original pamphlets. True, the 1727 text did have its successes, perhaps significantly in its handling of the more formal rhetoric of Frog's letter to Bull, Habakkuk's deception of Jack, or the lament for declining Grubstreet. In all of these the tone was maintained by the more regular use of, for example, archaic participles. Certainly the 1727 *John Bull* is more consistent in terms of physical presentation, but, for all its emendations, it is not a particularly good text in many other respects.

In short, although both external and internal evidence are inconclusive, it seems that someone, probably Pope, went through the pamphlets making a number of significant if unhelpful changes and a few historical annotations, and that the rest was left to the printer William Bowyer.[3] Bowyer, ordinarily a capable and respected

[1] *J.B.* 68: 30–1.   [2] *J.B.* 54: 34–55: 25.
[3] See J. D. Fleeman, in *The Times Literary Supplement,* 19 Dec. 1963, p. 1056.

professional, did full justice neither to himself nor to the text in the case of *John Bull*.

It is obviously necessary to distinguish between manuscript re-visions, and emendations to a printed text which has already been partly normalized by the printer; but there may be a clue as to what happened to *John Bull* in 1727 from an altogether different source, in the shape of a fragment of the *Memoirs of Scriblerus* discovered by George Sherburn among Pope's scrap papers.

The first draft of the passage is in the handwriting of Arbuthnot and super-imposed on it are drastic alterations in the hand of Pope. Later one or the other, probably Pope, produced a third version which was the one finally to appear in print ... the extreme illegibility of the manuscript as the result of Pope's editing and the fact that both he and Arbuthnot made corrections and changes in their versions suggest either that Pope took the trouble to copy the page for the benefit of the person who was to make the fair copy for the press, or that, desiring to make the further changes that appear in the printed version, he was simply driven to using a clean sheet.[1]

The passage concerns Indamora's debate with herself over Martin's love for her Siamese twin sister, and, in Arbuthnot's version, shows a more esoteric name-finding, more of a sense of psychological struggle on the part of a young woman who contemplates the actualities of married life, a more vivid prose style, and over all a strong sense of the all too human ironies of the twins' inextricable condition. But even from this short fragment it is clear that Pope's first concern was with the presentation of Arbuthnot's original. One section by Arbuthnot,

if Tryphena will never any more see Martin—Martin must never more bless the eyes of Tabitha. but why do I say wretched since my Rival can never enjoy my lover without me, the pangs that other lovers feel

was revised by Pope to read,

if Tryphena must never more see Martin—Martin must never more bless the eyes of Tabitha. Yet why do I say wretched since my Rival can never enjoy my lover without me? the pangs that others feel

and appeared in the printed version of 1741 as,

if Lindamira must never more see Martin, Martin shall never again bless the

---

[1] *Memoirs of the Extraordinary Life, Works and Discoveries of Martinus Scriblerus*, ed. C. Kerby-Miller (New Haven, 1950), pp. 364–5.

eyes of Indamora: Yet why do I say wretched? since my Rival can never possess my Lover without me. The pangs that others feel.[1]

Kerby-Miller argues that Pope primarily contracted and refined the work of his collaborators[2] (mainly Arbuthnot); but the 1727 text of *John Bull* shows both pruning and addition, sometimes for no apparent reason. If Pope had gone to work on the allegory as he did on the whole Double Mistress episode, it would have been considerably cut down. Perhaps he was more respectful of work that had already appeared in print to popular acclaim. Yet if one compares the *Scriblerus* alterations and changes with the texts of *John Bull*, it is as though the 1727 text had reached the second stage of relative formal purity, and had progressed to the third stage in isolated instances. The 1727 text was a rough job. Probably a batch of the original pamphlets, marked with marginal deletions and revisions, was sent to William Bowyer. The correction of accidentals was the normal business of the printer, but he (and the editor) did not pay it enough attention, probably on the erroneous assumption that the work had already been done satisfactorily in the first printing of the pamphlets.

The *Scriblerus* fragment also highlights another failing of the 1727 text in relation to the 1712 pamphlets, which was implicit in our discussion of the 1727 emendations: it is not only invalid as an independent witness, but also inferior as literature. Kerby-Miller wrote of the *Scriblerus* manuscript: 'there is a rich burlesque tone and an easy movement in Arbuthnot's version which makes it preferable to Pope's highly condensed revision and in some ways more successful than the polished version that was finally published.'[3] The same might be said of the *John Bull* texts. Gone in 1727 is the flavour of an older spelling ('shreveled' for shrivelled, 'stiffled' for stifled, 'whither' for whether, 'cursying' for curtsying, 'choul' for jowl, 'poinant' for poignant). Changed too are such vulgar phrases as 'there wants', 'many a black and blue Gash and Scars', 'as I hop'd to be sav'd'. People no longer 'talk Politics', they 'talk of Politicks'; '*Paul*'s' is now '*St. Paul*'s'; beggars are no longer 'randy'. Lewis Baboon, 'it is the cheatingest, contentious Rogue upon the Face of the Earth', is now merely 'the most cheating, contentious Rogue'. And when Sir Humphry on occasion indulges in a hard word, 'contranitent'

---

[1] *Memoirs of Scriblerus*, ed. Kerby-Miller, p. 368. [2] Ibid., pp. 364 ff.
[3] Ibid., p. 365.

becomes 'contrary'. Corrections such as '*Comets fiery Tale*' to 'Tail' destroyed puns;[1] and emendations such as the omission of 'Loyal' from Mrs. Bull's 'Loyal Heart', which removed vital allusions,[2] suggest that the sense of decorum which guided the editor or proofreader was of a kind unresponsive to the text.

If Pope was responsible for the major changes made in 1727, it is no reflection on either his art or Arbuthnot's polemics to admit that he was not really at ease in the good doctor's less refined world of political pamphleteering.

[1] *J.B.* 94: 32 n.   [2] *J.B.* 40: 13–18 n.

CONTEXTS

AN ALLEGORICAL SATIRIST

WE tend to see Arbuthnot in the mind's eye as part of an illustrious company, as a member of the Scriblerus Club, as a public servant, and less as an 'individual'. Swift rears darkly above his time, Pope has emerged as a complex critic of his age, but Arbuthnot exists for us as he seems to have existed for most of his contemporaries—a witty, cheerful, self-effacing adjunct to Augustan life. 'By all those who were not much acquainted with him', wrote Chesterfield, 'he was considered infinitely below his level; he put no price upon himself, and consequently went at an undervalue.'[1] From those who knew him best, however, we receive a picture of hyperbolic goodness: Arbuthnot was 'a perfectly honest man' (Swift), possessing all the 'genuine marks of a good mind' (Pope), with 'Candor, Generosity, & good sense' (Lady Mary), in sum 'the best conditioned creature that ever breathed' (Erasmus Lewis).

Perhaps Arbuthnot's character eludes the modest estimate of posterity and the eulogies of friends, and only a delicate but knowing irony, like Swift's in a letter to Pope, can do justice to the rare quality of goodness which the doctor expressed in the whole course of his life:

Mr. Lewis sent me an Account of Dr. Arbuthnett's Illness which is a very sensible Affliction to me, who by living so long out of the World have lost that hardness of Heart contracted by years and generall Conversation. I am daily loosing Friends, and neither seeking nor getting others. O, if the World had but a dozen Arbuthnetts in it I would burn my Travells but however he is not without Fault. There is a passage in Bede highly commending the Piety and learning of the Irish in that Age, where after abundance of praises he overthrows them all by lamenting that, Alas, they kept Easter at a wrong time of the Year. So our Doctor has every Quality and virtue that can make a man amiable or usefull, but alas he hath a sort of Slouch in his Walk. I pray god protect him for he is an excellent Christian tho not a Catholick and as fit a man either to dy or Live as ever I knew.[2]

In the wave of anti-Episcopal feeling which swept Scotland after

---

[1] *The Wit and Wisdom of the Earl of Chesterfield*, ed. W. Ernst-Browning, p. 320.
[2] Swift, *Correspondence*, ed. Harold Williams, iii. 104 (dated 29 Sept. 1725).

the deposition of James II, the Revd. Alexander Arbuthnot of Kincardineshire lost his living, and John, his eldest son, left home to seek his fortune. He resided for a time in London with a woollen-draper, then studied medicine at Oxford, and finally took his doctor's degree at St. Andrews on 11 September 1696. After returning to London, Arbuthnot made a name for himself in scientific circles with his amusing and learned critique of Woodward's theory of the deluge, and a few years later he published his more practical *Essay on the Usefulness of Mathematical Learning*. These efforts helped earn his election to the Royal Society in 1704, and the following year he was appointed 'Physician Extraordinary to the Queen . . . in consideration of his good and successful services perform'd as Physitian to his Royal Highnesse'—that is, to Prince George, whom Arbuthnot may have treated at Epsom.[1] By 1710 Arbuthnot had been admitted to the Royal College of Physicians and was Physician in Ordinary to Queen Anne. Swift referred to him, in his *Journal* entry for 8 December 1711, as 'the Queen's favorite physician'.

When the *John Bull* pamphlets appeared in 1712, Arbuthnot was forty-five years old, settled in his ways and outlook, a man of achieved prominence in the milieux of science and the court. His professional and social walks of life were combined in his service to the Queen in her perpetual illness and to those who moved about her. His success, however, was tempered by his own frequent attacks of stone and fever, and the loss, as he tells Swift in 1713, of six of his children. 'I know by Experience, that the best cure [for grief] is by diverting the thoughts.'[2] Perhaps Arbuthnot's *gourmandise* and fondness for gaming were such diversions, but Swift had a nobler interpretation of his friend's behaviour: 'you are a Philosopher and a Physician, & can overcome by Your Wisdom and your Faculty those Weaknesses which other men are forced to reduce by not thinking on them.'[3]

The tone of Swift's letters to Arbuthnot is, as Angus Ross has observed, that of discourse 'with a valued and beloved equal', and their mutual correspondence provides an interesting contrast between two kinds of satirical temperament.[4] On the one side Swift,

---

[1] Arbuthnot, 'Correspondence', ed. Ross, p. 34.

[2] Ibid., p. 264 (Nov. 1713). Referring to the Arbuthnot–Swift, Arbuthnot–Pope collections of letters, Ross notes, 'These . . . place Arbuthnot in an important position in the earliest complete exchange of familiar letters between a group of literary men, which survives . . . in the original MSS' (p. 859).

[3] 16 June 1714, Swift, *Correspondence*, ii. 36–7.

[4] Arbuthnot, 'Correspondence', p. 865.

physically withdrawn from the centre of court affairs for much of his life, is the impatient, combative satirist attacking his victims with all the means at his disposal, from modest proposals to burning-glasses to practical jokes, always eager to impose his satiric hegemony on the course of history, domestic or national; on the other side stands Arbuthnot, all his professional life a Londoner, and until 1 August 1714 an important presence in the court, yet remarkable for having (in Swift's words) 'a Mind so degage in a Court where there is so many Million of things to vex you'. Arbuthnot brought to his daily life, to court politics, to 'history', the same professional combination of detachment and compassion that he had learned as the most trusted physician of a dying queen. His temper of philosophical equanimity was based on a wary scepticism, an ironic 'Theory of human virtue', which, after the Queen's death, took this form: 'I have an opportunity calmly & philosophicaly to consider That treasure of vileness & baseness that I allwayes beleived to be in the heart of man, & to behold them exert their insolence & baseness every new instance instead of surprising & greiving me, as it dos some of my friends, really diverts me, & in a manner improves my Theory.'[1] For Arbuthnot, so sardonic and yet at the same time so compassionate, 'history' and human nature are in a continual conspiracy to create the materials for, and even the patterns of, satire, without much active assistance. Arbuthnot's kind of satire is rooted even more firmly than Swift's in the verifiable texture of history, the written record; and his letters and works testify to the enormously diverse stuff of his reading. He was fascinated not so much by the baseness and folly of mankind as by the manifold satiric patterns human nature evolves in history. Behind *John Bull* is a mind that posits, 'Events will take their course. History will unfold its own absurd drama—will satirize itself—with only a little allegorical help from me.' But here again Arbuthnot would have been characteristically modest. We have tried to show in this edition that he devoted considerable care and skill to the making of *John Bull*, and the fate of his hero to some degree belies the cynicism of the kind doctor's 'Theory of human virtue'.

BACKGROUND 1698–1712

... The most ingenious and humorous political satire extant in our language, Arbuthnot's History of John Bull.

Lord Macaulay in the *History of England*

[1] Arbuthnot, 'Correspondence', p. 469 (17 Oct. 1725).

Discussion of the *John Bull* pamphlets as satire entails a review of the historical events to which they allude. This is no easy task: even a well-informed contemporary of Arbuthnot would have been hard pressed to explain many of the allusions in the work. The chief points of reference are, however, obvious enough, and we have in the following pages outlined chronologically those clusters of events with which the allegory is primarily concerned. This introductory discussion of the period is quite selective, but for the sake of intelligibility we have tried to strike a balance between history as seen by Arbuthnot's contemporaries and as it appears in retrospect. From the point of view of an Englishman living in 1712, the two major events during most of this span of time were Marlborough's—and the Whigs'—war with France and Spain on the Continent ('The War of the Spanish Succession'), and the career of the Godolphin war ministry at home.

1. *Partition and Alliance, 1698–1701*

In 1697, after a series of wars, the Treaty of Ryswick brought at least a temporary peace to the states of Europe. The French king, Louis XIV, who had initiated wars of conquest since 1667, was left with an impoverished nation, and he and his people seem sincerely to have desired peace. Now the prominent political question for the statesmen of the Maritime powers (England and Holland[1]), France, and the Austrian Empire was what to do about Charles II of Spain. This king, who reigned over a rich and far-flung empire including much of the Netherlands, the West Indies, and South America, was a dying invalid and would have no issue. There were three claimants to the Spanish throne, the young Prince Philip of Bourbon, Duke of Anjou and grandson of Louis; Charles, youngest son of the Habsburg Emperor Leopold I; and Joseph Ferdinand, Electoral Prince of Bavaria.

---

[1] Names and titles applied at this time to the people of the Netherlands require some clarification. In 1581 the seven northern provinces of the Netherlands, led by the major province, Holland, revolted from Spanish rule. The independence of this 'nation', the 'United Provinces', was formally recognized in 1648; its people were the Dutch, and the state (the modern kingdom of the Netherlands) was variously referred to as the Dutch Republic, or as the States-General (after the title of its governing body), or simply as Holland. The province of Flanders (corresponding to Holland) was, and still is, a synonym for the whole area. Cf. I. F. Burton, *The Captain-General: the Career of John Churchill, Duke of Marlborough, from 1702 to 1711* (1968), pp. 202–3 n.

France was the great rival in trade of the Maritime powers. If the Spanish empire were to fall under French domination, the English and Dutch carrying-trade would be disastrously reduced, England's national security would be threatened by French occupation of the Spanish Netherlands, and Holland itself would be exposed to Louis's armies stationed at her borders.[1] Louis well knew that a Bourbon king of Spain would arouse not only the antagonism of William III of England and the States-General of Holland, but that of the Austrians and many minor princes of Europe as well. Yet he wished to prevent the passing of the Spanish empire to a Habsburg. After a series of highly secret discussions, William and Louis signed a Partition Treaty at The Hague recognizing Joseph Ferdinand's right to most of the Spanish empire. The Emperor naturally enough refused to honour the treaty, but William and Louis had preserved the 'balance of power'. Neither Charles II nor any English minister was let into the secret of these negotiations, though the indignant Spanish nobles, aware that something was 'hatching beyond the Pyrenees', induced Charles to make a will naming Joseph Ferdinand heir to the entire inheritance.[2] Hardly four months after the will was signed, however, the boy-prince of Bavaria died. Now the self-styled arbiters of European politics, with the approval of Holland, felt called upon to devise a Second Partition Treaty. It is no wonder that Arbuthnot chose to burlesque these manœuvres as a surveying expedition on the grounds of a hapless nobleman. Louis, in a genuine effort to avert war, consented to let the Habsburg prince, Charles, have most of Spain and its possessions, but Leopold refused this offer in the hope of getting the whole. Matters finally came to a head when the Spanish nobles, who would accept a French (or even a Habsburg) king before dismemberment of their possessions, prevailed upon Charles to sign a second will bequeathing the entire Spanish inheritance to the Bourbon prince. Failing Louis's acceptance of these terms for his grandson, the empire was to go to the Austrian Charles.

Louis was now faced with a dilemma. On the one hand, he could accept the will and risk a second war with Austria and the Maritime powers; on the other, he could refuse the will, stand by the Second Partition Treaty, and watch Spain devolve to the Habsburgs. Whether he accepted the will or not, he would have to fight in order to keep the possessions promised him under the treaty. In November 1700 Louis decided to accept the Spanish bequest, thereby breaking

[1] See Trevelyan, i. 123.   [2] Ibid., i. 126.

his agreement with the other partitioners. The Grand Monarch then launched upon a series of audacious and aggressive actions (culminating in the proclamation of 'James III' as King of England) which solidified the anti-French sentiment of the Maritime powers and Austria into the Treaty of Grand Alliance, whereby England, Holland, and Austria pledged their mutual support. Leopold of Austria no longer expected to win the whole Spanish empire for his son Charles, and at this time 'neither England nor Holland were ready to fight on those terms, though they changed their minds two years later'.[1] The Treaty of 1701 accepted Philip V as King of Spain as long as the crowns of France and Spain were never united, and demanded certain territories for the House of Austria, of which the Spanish Netherlands was to 'serve as a dyke, rampart and barrier' to protect the United Provinces from France. In effect, the Allies agreed to drive France out of Italy and the Spanish Netherlands. All these machinations set the stage for a war in which John Churchill, Duke of Marlborough, proved himself one of England's greatest generals.

2. *Marlborough, Godolphin, and the War*

From his early years, Churchill exercised a 'judicious foresight' in money matters which laid 'the foundation of his immense fortune'.[2] He was to demonstrate this quality throughout a richly rewarded (and miserly) life, despite his imprudent marriage to the volatile Sarah Jennings, attendant to the Princess Anne, in 1677. The marriage delayed Marlborough's military advancement, but he had a chance in the 1690s to distinguish himself in battles against Louis XIV, his old patron in the Dutch wars. When Anne became Queen in 1702, he was made Captain-General of the forces, and his wife, the Queen's loyal but domineering companion, was given important Household offices.

Marlborough, at fifty-three a veteran of siege and diplomacy, saw himself succeeding to William's role as leader of the Protestant forces of Europe. He would carry on 'William's war' under his own command, but 'he could not be sure of money for the war unless a financier in full sympathy with his extensive plans were in control of the national purse'.[3] That financier was Sidney Godolphin, a diligent and dextrous civil servant who had transferred himself from James to William as smoothly as had Churchill, his friend and kinsman by marriage. The office of Lord Treasurer was at this time the prime

[1] Trevelyan, i. 145–6.   [2] Churchill, i. 60.   [3] Trevelyan, i. 186.

ministerial post of England, and in this capacity, under William, Godolphin had sufficiently demonstrated his skill at raising money from Parliament for war against the French. Marlborough in fact made his serving as commander-in-chief of the allied armies in 1702 conditional upon Godolphin's leadership of the ministry. Trevelyan notes that the 'Godolphin Ministry', which governed England from 1702 to 1710, 'derived its coherence not from party loyalty, but from the family alliance of Marlborough and Godolphin and their agreement on public affairs'.[1] By 1712 it would be a natural, and merciless, allegorical step to represent this alliance as an illicit union between John Bull's extravagant first wife and his unscrupulous 'attorney general', 'Hocus'.

Anne's first ministry was a coalition of moderate to extreme Tories; the Junto, a small group of Whig lords (led by Somers, the lawyer, Halifax, the financier, and 'Honest Tom' Wharton, the campaign manager), whom the Queen could not abide, were excluded. In the early years of the reign Godolphin saw his fellow ministers, the religious conservatives, Nottingham and Rochester, frustrate the business of government, and later (1708–9) the war-hungry Junto demand an increasing voice in the ministry. Along the way, he lost faith in his political ally, Harley, ousting him in 1708, and reluctantly surrendered more and more power to the Junto. Despite his difficulties, Godolphin presided over the Union with Scotland, the most important piece of domestic legislation in Anne's reign, and managed to raise funds every year for the war effort.[2] The war itself was going well. Marlborough's mastery of military organization and tactics procured victory after victory (Blenheim, 1704; Ramillies, 1706; Oudenarde, 1709; Bouchain, 1711); but his part in arranging the Methuen Treaty of 1703 helped to alter the war aims of William. The treaty brought Portugal into the alliance, but only on King Peter's terms that English and Dutch armies must be sent to the Peninsula, where the Austrian archduke (proclaimed 'Charles III' by the allies) must fight in person for his inheritance. England was thus committed on two fronts, in Spanish Flanders and in the Peninsula itself. When Louis put out feelers for peace to Holland in 1705, Marlborough convinced the Dutch that Charles must take Philip V's place as King of Spain.[3]

[1] Trevelyan, i. 187.
[2] R. Walcott, *English Politics in the Early Eighteenth Century* (Oxford, 1956), p. 157.
[3] Trevelyan, i. 298–304.

The Spanish venture, because of inept management and the Spaniards' antipathy to 'Charles III', did indeed prove a 'bottomless pit' for the Allies, and Marlborough's campaign in the north, despite its successes, seemed far from coming to a peaceful conclusion. By 1709 France seemed virtually defeated, and reflective men wondered whether Godolphin, in quietly carrying out the business of government (i.e. supplying the war) was not acting more in good faith to his glorious kinsman on the Continent than in the best interests of his country. It appeared then, as it appears now, that Marlborough was not inclined to end hostilities by diplomatic means, and that his prevailing strategy for peace was simply to make more war. In October 1709 he petitioned the Queen to grant him the office of Captain-General for life. Not surprisingly, the Queen denied his request.

3. Dissension in the Church

Although they differed in their views on the aims and strategy of the war, the High Tories in Godolphin's coalition ministry were united and markedly vociferous on certain domestic issues, especially their cherished project of legislation against 'occasional conformity'. Since the Toleration Act of 1689, the growth of 'Dissent' from the Church of England was steady; but the 'Non-conformists' (Baptists, Quakers, Presbyterians, and many other sects) were still hindered by the Corporation Act of 1661 and the Test Act of 1673 which had made the receiving of the Sacrament as administered by the Church of England, at least once a year, the condition of holding offices in corporations and in the government. The Dissenters commonly practised 'occasional conformity' to the Church in order to hold public offices, but otherwise attended their own chapels and meeting-houses.[1] Nottingham and his followers engineered Bills against 'occasional conformity' several times during Anne's reign, and finally succeeded in making such a Bill law in 1711.

Dissension over religious toleration reached its height in 1705 in the arena of the Anglican Convocation with its two houses corresponding to the Lords and the Commons of Parliament, an upper house of bishops, and a lower house of the inferior clergy. William had appointed fifteen 'low Church' bishops who dominated the upper house during the early eighteenth century. Led by Gilbert

---

[1] Everyone knew the story of Sir Humphry Edwin, Lord Mayor of London in 1701, who had ridden to a Presbyterian chapel on Sunday in full mayoral regalia.

Burnet, Bishop of Salisbury, the noted polemicist and historian, they urged the toleration of Nonconformity. Thus the episcopate was virtually the protector and patron of the Dissenters, whose ranks consisted chiefly of the lower commercial classes. The 'low Church-men' in Convocation contended for more 'moderation' in ceremonies of the Church, while the conservative clergy, who predominated in the lower house, advocated stricter observance of ritual. These 'high flyers' thought the Church was in extreme danger because of 'modera-tion'; the latitudinarian bishops, on the other hand, made a formal statement that the Church of England was 'in a most safe and flourish-ing condition'.[1] Arbuthnot would zestfully ridicule these high and low factions by drawing upon his medical expertise and familiarity with the practices of his colleagues in telling the story of John's Mother (the Church of England), a decorous matron troubled by a variety of paralysing distempers.

The 'high flyers' did not confine their lamentations to the halls of Convocation. *The Memorial of the Church of England* by the Reverend James Drake was the most notorious of a spate of tracts which appeared in 1705 attacking Dissenters, moderating clergy, and 'occa-sional conformity'. In addition, this virulent pamphlet denounced Marlborough and Godolphin as hypocritical traitors to the Church, who with the Junto and the Dissenters had conspired to undermine its discipline and unity.[2] The Lord Treasurer was incensed by such attacks, and the resentment he harboured against the High Tory clergy was to take its ill-fated revenge in the Sacheverell trial of 1710.

4. *The Union, 1707*

One of the liveliest allegorical personifications in the satire is John Bull's ill-fed but spirited hyperborean sister, Peg. Scotland in 1700 was a barren land. Primitive methods of cultivation, frequent drought (especially in the 'dear years' of William's reign), and an export trade consisting almost entirely of food and raw materials forced the Scot's standard of living below that of his English counter-part. Despite tremendous economic hardships, the ordinary Scot refused charity with a passion, and sustained a characteristic vitality and independence.

[1] Trevelyan, i. 284–7; ii. 85–90.
[2] James Drake, *The Memorial of the Church of England* (1705), pp. 6–7, 21; **Modera-tion** was the *Word*, the *Passpartout*, that open'd all the *Place* Doors' (p. 7).

James I had united the crowns of Scotland and England in 1603, but each country kept its own Parliament, except for the brief period of Cromwell's dictatorship. In 1701 the English Parliament, with Harley taking a leading part, passed the 'Act of Settlement', which, among other things, provided for a Hanoverian successor to the English throne upon Anne's death. A see-saw of bitter legislative squabbles between the two traditionally hostile peoples in the following years helped impel Arbuthnot himself to promote the Union by preaching a secular sermon to his fellow Scots at Edinburgh in late 1706. In his sermon, which is generally regarded as the best of the numerous Union tracts, he stressed the trade advantages a union with England would bring to Scotland, a victim of the 'three fatal sisters', Pride, Poverty, and Idleness.

In 1707 the terms of the Union were finally settled and Scotland was offered first chance to ratify the treaty. 'If it were first accepted by England, the pride and suspicion of Scotland would take alarm and regard the Treaty as a piece of English goods . . . could Scotland trust her neighbour's good faith? With bitter misgivings she decided to try the experiment.'[1] Scotland was to keep her Presbyterian Church but to lose her Parliament in an incorporating Union. Her system of law was not altered, she was given representation in the Commons, and was granted a large 'Equivalent' for helping to bear the national debt England had contracted before the Union. But Scotland was a long way from enjoying the economic benefits she had been led to expect. The Scots did not yet possess a sufficient economic basis of business organization for trade with the colonies, and their linen manufacture was injured by English underselling. Mortifying in other respects were the prohibition on Scots lords from becoming peers of Great Britain at the time of the Union, and the necessity for Scots Presbyterians to take the Sacramental Test in order to hold office in England.[2]

5. The Barrier Treaty, 1709

All five Junto lords sat on the commission for negotiating the Union and played an active part in devising a treaty acceptable to the Scots. As a condition for their supporting the treaty in the ensuing Parliament, they asked that Sunderland, Marlborough's fiery son-in-law, be made one of the Secretaries of State. The Queen, despite

----

[1] Trevelyan, ii. 270–3.   [2] Ibid., ii. 280–1; cf. also iii. 232–5.

Harley's objection, finally gave Sunderland the seals in the autumn of 1706, but only after Marlborough and Godolphin had threatened to resign from the government. By placing one of their number in the ministry the Junto thought they were 'driving the nail that would go'. Harley, however, was still a thorn in their side. This man, whom they nicknamed 'Robin the Trickster', was for the Junto a far less trustworthy potential ally than Godolphin. In a deliberate attempt to destroy Harley, the Whigs fanned a scandal. William Greg, an employee in Harley's office, was accused of passing state secrets to the French: a committee of Whig lords inquired into the affair and attempted, unsuccessfully, to implicate Harley in Greg's treason. Owing to Whig pressure and to Godolphin's suspicious distrust of his ambitious fellow minister, Harley was dismissed as Secretary of State in February 1708, along with his fellow Tory the mercurial Henry St. John, Secretary at War.[1] As the power of the Tories declined, the Junto pressed forward with their war policy. In the Parliamentary session of 1707–8 Somers and Wharton, going beyond mere support for Marlborough's campaign in the Netherlands, were able to secure approval of the motion 'That no peace can be safe or honourable' which left Spain and the Indies in the possession of the Bourbons. Excluding Philip from the Spanish throne, however, 'proved to be an impossible goal, and for its failure to recognise this fact the Marlborough–Godolphin administration was to pay dearly before two years were out'.[2]

Somers and Wharton themselves joined the ministry in 1708, but Godolphin and Marlborough still held the reins of government. There is no doubt, however, that the 'Moderates', Marlborough, Godolphin, and their court following, the Junto Whigs, and the 'Lord-Treasurer's Whigs' (one of whom, Robert Walpole, was now Secretary of the Navy) shared a common desire to prolong the war.[3] Their motives were mixed. No doubt they believed that keeping up the war meant retaining the benefits of power. They also wished, apparently, to preserve England's trade from the encroachment of a Bourbon; and they knew that a prostrate France could not hinder the Hanoverian Succession. But even in 1709 France had a measure of resilience. As

[1] Cf. A. McInnes, *Robert Harley, Puritan Politician* (1970), chap. v, and Walcott, pp. 143–6.

[2] Walcott, pp. 137–8.

[3] Cf. J. H. Plumb on the whiggish inclinations of Marlborough and Godolphin at this time, in *The Growth of Political Stability in England 1675–1725* (1967: published in the U.S.A. as *The Origins of Political Stability . . .*), pp. 152–3.

Roderick Geikie neatly observes, 'With the Whig leaders the wish was father to the thought.'[1]

There was yet another reason for continuing the war, one which concerned England's relation to its chief ally, Holland, and the vexed question of a Dutch barrier. Marlborough's victory at Ramillies in May 1706 opened the way for the allied conquest of the southern Netherlands, but victory had a way of creating problems for the allies. The Emperor claimed this reconquered territory for himself; the Dutch, in opposition, demanded the return of their 'Barrier' fortress-towns in Spanish territory which they desired to maintain as a defensive bulwark against French invasion. In July of 1706 Godolphin wrote to Marlborough, 'I don't think the Dutch are very reasonable, to be so much in pain about their barrier, as things stand; but it is plain argument to me they think of joining their interest to France, whenever a peace comes, and for that very reason the longer we can keep it off, the better.'[2] That same July, Louis, hoping to draw the Dutch out of the alliance, privately offered them the whole of the southern Netherlands. The States-General agreed, however, to enter into a 'Condominium' over Belgium with the English till the end of the war, at which time the territory would be handed over to Charles III, with the exception of the barrier. The question of which specific towns were to form the barrier was postponed at this time, 'But the help rendered to [the Dutch] by their ally in the critical months of June and July had left them self-supporting. They could afford to wait for payment, and would not on the day of settlement forget to charge full interest.'[3]

By 1709 that day had come. Holland was near exhaustion from her part in supplying the war, and to keep her from faltering in the 'common cause' the Godolphin war ministry sent Charles Townshend, a Junto man, to negotiate a 'Barrier Treaty' with the Dutch. By this treaty, Britain promised to help secure the rest of the Spanish low countries in order that Holland might garrison twenty towns and fortresses there, and guaranteed that the Maritime powers would enjoy equal trading privileges in the Spanish Empire. 'The effect of these Dutch rights of garrison and of the financial and commercial provisions that accompanied them, was to strip Austrian Charles of half the value of his property in the Netherlands and to

[1] Roderick Geikie and Isabel A. Montgomery, *The Dutch Barrier 1705–1719* (Cambridge, 1930), p. 114 n.   [2] Trevelyan, ii. 131.
[3] Geikie and Montgomery, p. 89.

endanger the freedom of British trade.'[1] For its part, the States-General promised to assist and maintain the Hanoverian Succession, and offered to furnish sea and land forces for this purpose. When Tory statesmen eventually came to know the terms of the treaty, they felt that Townshend had not only signed away English trading privileges but had given the Dutch a pretence to interfere at their will in English affairs. Similarly, Arbuthnot was to have his gullible hero make Nic. Frog (the Dutch) the *'Executor of his Last Will and Testament'*, with leave *'to enter his House at any Hour of the Day or Night . . . in order to secure the Peace of* . . . John Bull's *Family'*.[2]

6. *Sacheverell, 1710*

By the summer of 1708, most English taxpayers, especially the Tory squires who shouldered the Land Tax, began to look upon supplying the war less as a patriotic duty than as a severe hardship. As the Government sank deeper in debt to the Bank and to Whig financiers in the City, the Allies seemed to pay less and less of their share in the war. By 1709 Britain's annual expenditure had risen to £13 million from £3 million in 1702.[3] In this atmosphere of growing disenchantment with the war, Godolphin's Whig ministry was the prime target of popular attack. During the autumn of 1709 the Reverend Henry Sacheverell, perhaps the most flamboyant and reckless of High Church polemicists, chose to preach two incendiary sermons on the necessity of 'non-resistance' or 'passive obedience' to King and Church in all circumstances. The second sermon, based upon the text 'In perils among false brethren', was preached at St. Paul's before the High Tory Mayor of London on the fifth of November, a day held sacred by the Whigs as celebrating both the discovery of the Gunpowder Plot and the landing in England of William of Orange. Sacheverell's fulmination was printed and enjoyed unprecedented circulation. In it, besides attacking Whigs, Dissenters, and 'moderate' Tories, he alluded to Godolphin under the thin disguise of his satirical catch-name 'Volpone', and after much political calculation

---

[1] Trevelyan, iii. 30.

[2] Long before the signing of the Barrier Treaty, Tory pamphleteers like Charles Davenant had represented Whig and Dutch financiers working hand in glove to direct English affairs: 'I am told the *Dutch* are deeply concern'd very near in every Fund, which they have bought up here by Commission. . . . That's true enough, but this . . . helps to engage *Holland* in the Measures of our Party', *Tom Double Return'd Out of the Country* (1702), pp. 41–2. Cf. Coombs, pp. 27, 199, 209.

[3] Trevelyan, iii. 45.

(which events were to render misdirected) the thin-skinned Lord Treasurer and his Whig ministers decided to impeach Sacheverell before the House of Peers, 'in order to argue out before the highest tribunal of the land the lawfulness of the existing Constitution and the prospective rights of the Protestant Succession'.[1]

The Sacheverell trial can be considered a touchstone of Whig and Tory sentiment on the question of how England should be governed. The Whig 'managers' of the case against Sacheverell embraced the occasion for publicly restating the foundation of the Revolution Settlement of 1688 in solemn rhetoric which almost deified the principle of revolution itself. Probably the most clever and telling of all the parodies in *John Bull* is the elaborate 'Vindication of the indispensable Duty of Cuckoldom' (or revolution) by John's 'extravagant' first wife. Mrs. Bull rails against the Anglican doctrine of 'passive obedience', echoing not only the Whig managers but also the rhetoric of dissenting preachers and eighteenth-century proponents of women's liberation.

The impeachment raised the passions of the London mob, but against Dissenters instead of Papists. Many meeting-houses were wrecked, and only the Queen's foot and horse guards, who perhaps 'would have been more at ease charging the French lines',[2] were able to quell the riots. On the heels of the riots came the Lords' verdict upon Sacheverell. He was voted guilty by 69 votes to 52 and was forbidden to preach for three years. The slight sentence was tantamount to a Tory victory.

7. *The Return of Harley*

Their ousting by Godolphin and the Whigs in 1708 made Harley and St. John think seriously, perhaps for the first time, about a genuine policy of peace both as a means of regaining power and as a necessary benefit to the British economy. Sensing the first indications of war-weariness, and apprehensive of Marlborough's growing military and political pretensions, they seized upon the one apparent avenue of escape from the 'bottomless pit': peace could only come if Archduke Charles's claim to the Spanish throne was abandoned; by November St. John would exclaim in a letter to Harley, '*For God's sake, let us be once out of Spain!*'

---

[1] Trevelyan, iii. 48. For a detailed account of the man, his trial, and its consequences see Geoffrey Holmes, *The Trial of Doctor Sacheverell* (1973).

[2] Trevelyan, iii. 56.

Harley's immediate strategy for regaining power derived from his influence over Abigail Masham, the Lady of the Bedchamber who had replaced the Duchess of Marlborough in Queen Anne's affections. Sarah was a staunch friend of the Whigs, and Abigail's Tory proclivities meshed perfectly with Harley's intention of overthrowing the Godolphin ministry. The Duchess's tempestuous final interview with Anne on 6 April 1710 'formed a fitting prelude to the removal of Sarah's political allies from power'[1] in that year. The passion for 'High Church and Sacheverell' was now at its height and from April to September 1710 the Queen replaced the war ministry of Godolphin with moderate politicians recommended to her by Harley through his intermediary, Mrs. Masham. After the dismissal of Sunderland in June 'the retreat became a rout, everyone running separately for cover, or secretly intriguing for terms with the victors'.[2] In the words of *John Bull*, 'then happy was the Man that was first at the Door'. Harley was now the new Lord Treasurer, and the country supported him with a landslide Tory election victory in October. He vowed to complete the double task of restoring the financial stability of the country and of bringing Marlborough's war to an end. Edward Harley, for a time auditor of the exchequer, describes the chaos his brother faced in 1711:

When he [Harley] came into the treasury he found the exchequer almost empty; nothing left for the subsistence of the army but some tallies upon the third general mortgage of the customs; the queen's civil list near £700,000 in debt; the funds all exhausted and a debt of £9,500,000 without provision of parliament, which had brought all the credit of the government to a vast discount. In this condition the nation had to pay 255,689 men. . . . Besides these difficulties, the Bank, stock-jobbers, and moneyed men of the city were all engaged to sink the credit of the government.[3]

Harley put into effect several schemes for regaining the financial credit of the nation. In 1711 two lotteries were held raising £1.5 million and £2 million respectively, and the South Sea Company, with a huge monopoly of trade on the east and west coasts of South America, was established. Still England's final debt in the war of the Spanish Succession was £21.5 million.[4]

[1] Trevelyan, iii. 63.   [2] Ibid., iii, 65.
[3] I. S. Leadam, *The History of England from the Accession of Anne to the Death of George II (1702–1760)*, (1912), p. 184.
[4] Trevelyan, i. 291; Trevelyan's general discussion of war taxation and the national debt (pp. 291–5) is especially applicable to *John Bull*.

8. *The Tory Peace*

As early as August of 1710 the Jacobite Earl of Jersey, acting for Harley, had engaged in secret peace negotiations with an agent of the Marquis of Torcy, Louis's chief minister. In the spring of 1711 two accidents altered the course of these preliminary peace talks. In March Harley was stabbed by a would-be assassin, and during the interval of his recovery, St. John, now Secretary of State, stepped into the role of chief English negotiator. A month later the young Habsburg Emperor Joseph I died, and his brother, 'Charles III', was suddenly Emperor Charles VI. At this point it became clear to the ministerial Tories that Charles must be kept from his Spanish inheritance or the 'balance of power' would again go awry. St. John's skilful bargaining throughout the summer and autumn of 1711, under the strict supervision of Harley, helped obtain great trade advantages for England, and the agreement forged that year enabled England and France to dictate terms to the Allies at the general peace conference in Utrecht in 1712 (the 'Salutation Tavern' of *John Bull*). The 'Preliminary Articles of October', signed by the French, acknowledged the Queen's title to the throne and the Protestant Succession after her; specified that the Crowns of France and Spain should never be united; promised a Barrier for Holland in the Netherlands; and stipulated that Louis would dismantle Dunkirk, the notorious French privateering base.

The public denunciation of the 'October Preliminaries' by the Elector of Hanover (the future George I) was applauded by his friends, the Junto lords and Marlborough, and by the Dutch, who saw in the Tory peace programme a revocation of the Barrier Treaty fashioned by Townshend and the Whigs in 1709. 'The Elector's opposition was not due, as the Whigs represented, to fear for the Protestant Succession, but to the dangers anticipated from the cession of the Spanish crown to a Bourbon.'[1] Thus Hanover, Austria, Holland, and the Junto leagued together to prolong the war. Against this formidable alliance, the ministry needed all the skills of the Tory pamphleteers, especially those of Swift, St. John's *chef de propagande*. In *The Conduct of the Allies*, 'probably the most influential single publication of the reign of Queen Anne',[2] Swift argued that Britain should never have entered the war as a principal contender; revealed to the English people for the first time the actual provisions

---

[1] Geikie and Montgomery, p. 234.   [2] See Coombs, pp. 280–1.

of the Barrier Treaty; listed Dutch shortcomings throughout the course of the war; and assailed Marlborough and the Whigs as war profiteers. Both Swift's scathing tract, which appeared on 27 November 1711, and Arbuthnot's more amiable *Law is a Bottomless-Pit*, which was conceived at about the same time, quickly went through six editions.

The great scene of the battle for peace was the Parliamentary session of 7 December 1711, and the Whigs, observing the growing split between Harley (now Earl of Oxford) and St. John (now Viscount Bolingbroke), were confident that they could bring the ministry down. Oxford had rejected political co-operation with the Junto lords, but the Junto was able to convince the High Tory Nottingham, arch-foe of the Dissenters and of 'occasional conformity', that if he would move an amendment in the House of Lords to the Queen's Address, pledging the Lords against any 'Peace without Spain', they would vote for a bill which would subject any Anglican communicant who attended a Nonconformist place of worship to heavy fines.

The Dissenters were gravely discontented at the bargain, but their lordly latitudinarian patrons said the lesser must give way to the greater cause. Only thus, they argued, would the Pope be checkmated and the Hanoverian Succession secured. The Whigs were sacrificing their principles of religious toleration to their factious desire to overthrow the Ministry and the Peace.[1]

Indeed, there is some question whether the Whig's principles of religious toleration were not a thing of the past. (Arbuthnot's version of this unsavoury transaction, the hanging of the Calvinist upstart, Jack, is the most poignant episode in the satire.) Nottingham's motion was supported by Marlborough and the Whigs and carried by 62 to 54. The Captain-General then took the floor of the House, and, in a fulsome speech directed to the Queen, who was present at the session incognito, defended himself against the charge that a peace might have been made after Ramillies, 'if the same had not been put off by some Persons, whose Interest it was *to prolong the War*'.[2] The Whig plot had succeeded, or so it seemed, for unless Oxford could reverse the vote, his ministry would fall. But Oxford still had one card up his sleeve: by means of her royal prerogative, the Queen, on 1 January 1712, at Oxford's insistence, reluctantly 'created'

---

[1] Trevelyan, iii. 195.   [2] *Annals*, x. 286.

twelve additional Tory peers. The peace programme and the ministry were saved.

The Tories now had a chance to complete their demolition of the Whigs and Marlborough. Walpole was quickly expelled from the Commons and lodged in the Tower on a well-prepared charge of misappropriating funds; and Marlborough, the chief Tory target, was accused of taking illicit commissions, particularly a cut of 2.5 per cent (amounting to over £280,000) from the pay of foreign troops in English employ.[1] On 31 December 1711, before the charges against him had even been examined, he was dismissed by the Queen from all his offices. With Marlborough out of the picture, it was easier for the English to come to terms with their timorous foes, the French, than with their suspicious friends, the Dutch. The States-General was appalled at the secret negotiations by which England, disregarding Dutch claims in the Barrier Treaty, had secured from France the monopoly of trade with Spanish America, and had seized control of the Mediterranean trade for England by annexing Gibraltar and Port Mahon as bases for her fleet.[2] At the end of January 1712 the powers in the war, including an extremely reluctant Holland, met at Utrecht for the purpose of making a general peace.

During January and February, Parliament discussed its grievances concerning Dutch deficiencies in the war effort, and the great advantages (detrimental to English trade) which Holland had acquired in the Barrier Treaty of 1709. These discussions were voiced in a Representation, written by Thomas Hanmer with Swift's help, and presented to the Queen by the Commons on 4 March 1712. The Dutch responded first with a conciliating letter to the Queen, but this was followed on 3 April by a strong and able *Memorial* expressing their grievances with the Tory peace programme. England was determined to have its own way, however, and on 3 June 1712 the Queen, through her representative at Utrecht, announced 'herselt disengaged from all alliances and engagements with their high mightinesses',[3] to which the Dutch responded with a last conciliatory plea. The three Dutch apologies were published, and were thus ripe for Arbuthnot's parody. England's other ally was no less indignant than the Dutch with the plan for peace. Imperial and English affairs had become embroiled towards the end of 1711 with the dismissal of Count Gallas, the Austrian ambassador to England, who had consorted with the Whigs and published letters against the peace nego-

---

[1] Trevelyan, iii. 200.   [2] Cf. Trevelyan, iii. 211.   [3] Leadam, p. 199.

tiations. On 30 June, after the Queen's break with the States-General and her demand for a cessation of arms, the Austrian envoy at Utrecht read a *Memorial* to the States outlining five resolutions for the renewal of the Allies' war aims. This *Memorial* was the fruit of Dutch–Imperial talks concerning, in particular, Dutch claims to the fortified towns in the Spanish Netherlands.

While Holland and Austria were attempting to keep up their alliance, the Duke of Ormonde, Marlborough's Tory replacement in the field, received from the Queen the famous 'Restraining Orders' which forbade him to engage in any siege or battle. This policy, originated by Bolingbroke, was kept a secret from the other ministers, including Oxford. On 25 June 1712 Ormonde declared to the States' deputies his orders from the Queen to publish 'a Suspension of Arms, for Two Months, between his Army and the French';[1] two days later the Bishop of Bristol proposed the same suspension of arms at Utrecht. Less than a month later the confederate army, led by Prince Eugene, separated from Ormonde's troops in order to prosecute the campaign. Ormonde now had more to fear from the United Provinces than from France, and, in the course of his march towards Dunkirk, he and his troops were refused entrance by the Dutch at the recently recaptured fortresses of Bouchain and Douai. English resentment of Dutch behaviour gave way to joy when it was learned that a British naval force, cordially welcomed by the French authorities, had taken possession of Dunkirk in the middle of July.

NATIONAL CHARACTERS

The concept of national character can be traced from Aristotle through Renaissance critics into seventeenth-century textbooks of rhetoric;[2] and English fascination with national identity was so ingrained that every facet of John Bull's character (*J.B.* 9: 12–26) can be found established in traditional caricature and contemporary polemic. '*Bull*, in the main, was an honest plain dealing Fellow, Cholerick, Bold, and of a very unconstant Temper, he dreaded not old *Lewis* either at Back-Sword, single Faulcion, or Cudgel-play', wrote Arbuthnot. Even the sceptical Defoe was moved to delight in 'the Superiority of the *English* in Strength of Body, and Genius in

---

[1] *Annals*, xi. 161.
[2] 'Characters of Nations', *Chester Noyes Greenhough Collected Studies*, ed. F. W. C. Hersey (Cambridge (Mass.), 1940), pp. 224–45.

Battle',[1] and Shadwell's audience for *The Volunteers* (1693) readily identified with Major General Blunt, described in the dramatis personae as 'somewhat rough in Speech, but very brave and honest ... of good Understanding and a good Patriot'. Such a generic English-man as John Bull, lured into the bottomless pit of law by 'visionary prospects', might be 'very apt to quarrel with his best Friends, especially if they pretended to govern him; If you flatter'd him, you might lead him like a Child'; for as Defoe put it, 'The Mischief to our People is, when they are *doz'd* with Dreams and Delusions, and go hoodwink'd into the Pit. *English* Men are apter to be wheedled than frighted—When you bully and threaten them, they rouze.'[2] Arbuthnot's suggestion that '*John*'s Temper depended very much upon the Air; his Spirits rose and fell with the Weather-glass' would also have a familiar ring to readers who had been taught that a temperate climate explained both the balanced English character ('Their Manners not too rough, nor too refin'd; / Sincere of Heart, and generous, just and kind')[3] and its tendency to fickleness.[4] In January 1712 Swift advised the October Club to moderate its de-mands for revenge on the fallen ministers 'considering the short Life of Ministrys in our Climate',[5] and a Whig protest against the proposed peace argued that 'if we are as various as our Climate, our Fortune will be so too'.[6] Thus the John Bull who loved 'his Bottle and ... spent his Money' was in essence the same generic Englishman admired by Shakespeare's Iago[7] and attacked by Defoe.[8] The John Bull angered by Frog's suggestion that he should retrench was an appealing personification to readers proud of their freedom to 'Eat

[1] *Review*, 27 July 1706, iii. 358.

[2] Ibid., 22 Dec. 1709, vi. 445. Both Arbuthnot and Swift were rehearsing well-established notions. Cf. Nashe in 1594: 'Englishmen are the plainest dealing soules ... they are greedie of newes, and love to bee fed in their humors, and heare themselves flattred' ('The Unfortunate Traveller', *Works*, ed. R. B. McKerrow (Oxford, 1966), ii. 298).

[3] Preface to Sir Richard Blackmore's *The Nature of Man* (1711) which systematically defined '*the distinct Characters of many* European *Nations, arising from the different Nature of the air and Soil*'. See also, for example, Defoe, 'The True-Born Englishman', ed. A. C. Guthkelch, *Essays and Studies*, iv (1913), 123, and Shaftesbury, 'Advice to an Author', *Characteristics*, ed. J. M. Robertson (1900), i. 142.

[4] Andrew Boorde, like Arbuthnot a successful doctor, also drew a national character of a pugnacious, fickle Englishman to appeal for civil peace in *The First Boke of the Introduction of Knowledge* (c. 1547).

[5] *Some Advice to the October Club*, vi. 73.

[6] *Life and Reign of Henry the Sixth* (1712), p. 3.

[7] *Othello*, III. iii. 71–4.

[8] 'The True-Born Englishman', p. 107.

their own *Beef* and *Pudding*, and Drink their own *October* unmolested'.[1]
And since, 'No Country but Great *Britain* can boast, that . . . its
Natives will . . . go to Foot-ball . . . Cricket . . . Cudgel-playing, or
some such vehement Exercise for their Recreations',[2] John Bull—
even 'in his senses'—'could not help discovering some remains of his
Nature, when he happen'd to meet with a Foot-Ball, or a Match at
Cricket'.

Arbuthnot may have proved himself the man to create an engaging
national character, but the moment was propitious for John Bull's
appearance. English national consciousness, nursed by the Tudors
and brought to maturity in the wars of the seventeenth century,
received a rude shock when the 1688 Revolution established on the
throne a man who 'although King of *England*, was a Native of *Holland*',[3]
with his Dutch guards, Dutch favourites, and Dutch politics. In
1700 John Tutchin gave scope to jingoistic hatred with *The Foreigners*:
Defoe's reply, in his ironic deflation of *The True-Born Englishman*,
bore brave witness to his sense of historical perspective, but it
served only to increase the swell of patriotic fervour occasioned by
the succession of a queen who had the good political sense to declare
her heart 'entirely English'. Anne's reign released animus against
foreigners which the new European war inevitably confirmed.
Parliament debated the wisdom of allowing aliens to hold office, and
was urged to take restrictive measures by hysterical pamphlets.[4]
In 1709, when an influx of refugees from the Palatinate coincided
with the introduction of a General Naturalization Bill, the staunch
Tories—who were already worried about the long term effects of the
Union with Scotland two years previously—raised a howl of protest.[5]
And if every major political issue became a patriotic tug of war
between the parties, many shades of opinion were united by their

[1] *Observator*, 17 Nov. 1705.
[2] James Puckle, *England's Path to Wealth and Honour* (1707), p. 39. See also the
'Character of the English' in *Collection of Poems on State-Affairs* (1712).
[3] Swift, *Conduct of the Allies*, vi. 11.
[4] For example, *The Rights and Liberties of Englishmen Asserted with a Collection of
Statutes . . . against Foreigners* (1701).
[5] Defoe was the almost solitary champion of the Bill against Swift and a chorus
of hostile writers. His campaign in *Brief History of the Poor Palatine Refugees* (1709)
fell on deaf ears, and his confident claim in the *Review* for 15 Mar. that the 'Arguments, *Chimeras I should call them*, of bringing Strangers in upon us, and giving away
our Liberties that our Ancestors fought for to Foreigners—Have had some time to
moulder away into the first Dirt they rose from, I mean, *our National Pride*' (v. 601)
was a desperately optimistic pose. National pride was still a rich source of political
goodwill in 1712 when the Harley ministry demolished the Naturalization Act.

concern for English culture. Swift's *Proposal for Correcting the English Tongue* (1712) found a ready response in readers concerned lest 'The old graceful Bluntness of our Fore-fathers'[1] be lost in the vogue for foreign refinements, and in writers who instinctively used loan-words to increase the impact of their satires:

> Whole floods of Gore distain'd the guilty Years,
> Noses ragou'd, and Fricasies of Ears.[2]

There was, moreover, widespread anxiety over a supposed decline in the quality of life: '*Nothing will go down with the Town now but* French Fashions, French Dancing, French Songs, French Wine, French Kickshaws . . . *All Nations love one another better than the* English . . . *but we are never satisfied with anything of our own growth.*'[3]

Samuel Johnson was later to note that 'In a time of war the nation is always of one mind, eager to hear something good of themselves and ill of the enemy'.[4] Certainly by 1712 the English were growing tired of the seemingly endless military victories against the French which achieved nothing tangible; but these had been successes against the old enemy. Arbuthnot himself trod on dangerous ground by appealing to national consciousness in the name of peace, for he could so easily have stimulated counter-productive hostility towards France. He negotiated the difficulty by confirming traditional prejudices about the enemy, only to demonstrate, by implicit comparison, that England's foreign allies were far less defensible and certainly more dangerous. It was a shrewd polemic ploy. The success of the whole Tory campaign against the war hinged on the destruction of Dutch credibility. The United Provinces provided more money and troops for 'the common cause' than almost all Britain's other allies put together, and the Dutch had assumed a prominence which Defoe recognized when he warned, 'I must be understood, when I mention the *Dutch*, not to mean the *Dutch* only . . . in a strict Literal Sense . . . but the whole Confederacy.'[5] As an extra incentive, the attack was personally satisfying to the many pamphleteers, who—with the notable exception of Defoe—shared the popular and traditional suspicion of all things Dutch.[6] Arbuth-

---

[1] *The Hermit*, 15 Sept. 1711.
[2] 'On the Sentence passed . . . on Dr. Sacheverell', *Whig and Tory* (1712), ii. 20.
[3] *Ladies Catechism* (1703), p. 2.   [4] *Idler*, 11 Nov. 1758.
[5] *Eleven Opinions about Mr. H[arle]y* (1711), p. 79.
[6] Swift was, of course, both intellectually and emotionally hostile to the Dutch: see E. D. Leyburn, 'Swift's View of the Dutch', *PMLA* lxxvi (1951), 734–5, and J. Kent Clark, 'Swift and the Dutch', *HLQ* xvii (1954), 345–56.

CONTEXTS lxi

not's Nicholas Frog, a 'cunning sly Whoreson . . . Covetous, Frugal' who 'minded domestick Affairs; [and] would pine his Belly to save his Pocket'¹ was thus another personification of rooted preconceptions about a people 'rather cunning then wise, crafty then cunning, and close then either; their Commonwealth being managed rather by the subtlety of Tradesmen, then the policy of Statesmen'.² Very properly, this Frog 'did not care much for any sort of Diversions, except Tricks of *High German* Artists, and *Leger de main*; no Man exceded *Nic.* in these', since the United Provinces was supposed to be the breeding-ground for mountebanks and quacks of all descriptions, a point not lost on the pamphleteers who harassed the many Dutch merchants in England: 'in and about the *City*, our *dearly beloved Darling Dutch-men* are continually playing their Dog-tricks . . . a *Jugler* cannot play . . . more nimbly, than these *Whipsters*'.³ Such sleight of hand was the more bitterly resented when employed in the 'artistry' of satirical prints,⁴ and even the whiggish Steele had to admit: 'They are a trading people, and . . . in their very minds mechanics. They express their wit in manufacture, as we do in manuscript.'⁵ This contra-distinction runs through all anti-Dutch satire, as it connects every facet of Frog's character. The Dutch were feared as ruthless and single-minded trading rivals, and Arbuthnot could depend on his readers to appreciate the irony in his concession, 'it must be own'd . . . *Nic.* was a fair Dealer, and in that way had acquir'd immense Riches', even before he revealed Frog as a devious empire-builder in the later pamphlets. Fear of the Dutch was often relieved by scorn, and Arbuthnot's personification was shrewdly calculated to arouse that powerful admixture of apprehension and contempt which characterized so many English responses to an old enemy turned ally.

THE Old *Hollanders* were ormerly despised by their Neighbours, by reason of their *Boorish* Manners, the Meaness of their Habits and Eating. They were called in derision, Milk-sops, Butter-boxes, and Cheese-eaters. But . . . they are now thought to be the most subtle and thriving People of Europe. . . . Those who are sharp and crafty never let these Qualifications lye idle . . .

---

¹ For Arbuthnot's portrait of Frog, see 9: 27–10: 4.
² *Dutch Drawn to the Life* (1664), p. 66.
³ Samuel Grascome, *Appeal to All True English-Men* (1702?), pp. 4–5.
⁴ *Hogan-Moganides* (1674) also conflated comments on Dutch artistry and quackery: 'In Landskip hee'd Lampoon a Saint, / Revil[e] in Words, and worse in Paint: / Hee'd draw Apothecaries Bill, / And give a City for a Pill' (p. 81).
⁵ *Tatler*, iii. 82.

and miss no opportunity to make an Advantage, either of the Ignorance, or Simplicity of those, they deal with.[1]

Thus, before the history of John Bull has properly got under way, all the carefully selected prejudices confirmed in the initial character sketches of the English and Dutch peoples suggest that the relationship between Bull and Frog will be one of honest simplicity pitted against opportunist cunning.

To emphasize the seriousness of this undeclared war Arbuthnot omitted some conventional traits of caricature which might have detracted from the fictional credibility and the political severity of his Dutch character. He employed the easy jibe at drunkenness in reverse: when Frog appears to become drunk during the partition meeting he is at best no more culpable than the often inebriated Bull and at worst plays the sociable friend to make his ally more malleable. Nor does Frog use the pidgin English—so beloved by traditional caricaturists[2]—which would have reduced his stature as a considerable opponent. Yan Ptschirnsooker (the whiggish Bishop Burnet) speaks in conventionally broken English, reminding the reader of the unity of purpose behind Dutch 'quackery' and English whiggery, but Frog himself remains articulate and dangerous. Also pointedly absent from Arbuthnot's first portrait of Frog is the ill-tempered rudeness of the generic Hollander which later emerges as his control over his language, the situation, and Bull begins to slip.[3] In his threatening letter to Lewis he reveals the coarse and brutal side of his nature; and as John comes to his senses so Nic. finds it progressively more difficult to hide his violent irascibility.

With such touches of verisimilitude the conventional skeletons of national types are endowed with the brain and sinew of character in action. Benjamin Boyce has observed that the national character 'is a variety . . . most difficult to keep Character-like . . . the requirement of amplification leads almost irresistibly to picturesque scenes and anecdotes'.[4] He also noted that the most successful examples of such characters in the seventeenth century moved inexorably away from the succinct and consciously rhetorical Theophrastan norm towards

  [1] *History of the Republick of Holland* (1705), ii. 67–8.
  [2] Cf. the clownish Dutchmen in William Haughton's *Englishmen for my Money* (1598), Aphra Behn's *Dutch Lover* (1673), or Thomas D'Urfey's *Wonders in the Sun* (1706).
  [3] Compare Frog's testy bickering with Bull over their accounts (in the last pamphlet) with the angry debate over fishing rights between the Englishman and the Dutchman in James Puckle's *England's Path to Wealth and Honour* (1707).
  [4] *The Polemic Character 1640–1661* (Lincoln (Nebr.), 1955), p. 44.

the parallel tradition of the essay.[1] Arbuthnot took this progression a stage further in *John Bull*, where his characters are first outlined and then gradually developed through idiom, inter-relationships, historical reminiscences, and the like techniques, just as the members of the Spectatorial club are developed in the periodical essays of Addison and Steele. Yet the uneasy alliance between Bull and Frog provides their creator with a rather special polemic weapon. John may be a shopkeeper drunk on ale and law in the first pamphlet, but as he comes to his senses he is also revealed to be a gentleman trader intent on preserving his country manor of Bullock's-Hatch. Thus the contrast between John's early recklessness and Nic.'s concern to be 'both in Court and in his Shop at the proper Hours' is—in one emotive sense—a distinction of social class, and a satiric technique which Swift was later to employ in his *Drapier's Letters*. Richard Cook noted shrewdly that 'As a prosperous, though petty, tradesman, Swift's Drapier is in the advantageous position of being both humble enough to elicit a sense of self-identification from his lower- and middle-class readers, and at the same time imposing enough to give appropriate force to his sneers at Wood as . . . a "diminutive, insignificant Mechanick".'[2] Advance these characters one rung up the social ladder—with a graceless mechanic Frog the 'drapier' remaining consciously inferior to the ally he addresses as 'John Bull, *great Clothier of the World*'—and the same discrimination could be applied to Arbuthnot's pamphlets. Cook also observed, 'In keeping with the Drapier's character . . . Swift writes in a style that is deliberately undistinguished. The Drapier has no hesitation in using the sort of platitudes ("a Word to the Wise is enough") that a purist like Swift normally avoids. Nearly all the Drapier's literary allusions, as might be expected from a man who is largely self-educated, are from the Bible.' Bull's language is full of comparable aphorisms and shows some acquaintance with not only the Bible but the *Apochrypha* and Church Latin. He is in a similar 'advantageous position', while Frog is left in the same cleft stick as the adversary of the drapier, a 'little, impudent . . . Mechanick'.[3]

---

[1] Owen Feltham's *Brief Character of the Low-Countries* (1652) and John Evelyn's *Character of England* (1659) illustrate this tendency.

[2] *Jonathan Swift as a Tory Pamphleteer* (1967), p. 136.

[3] Ibid., p. 137. Cook argues that Swift's political writings show a developing sense of audience with an increasing technical facility in appealing to that audience, culminating in the brilliantly successful *Drapier's Letters*. Perhaps Swift's achievement owed something to Arbuthnot's pioneering work in *John Bull*.

Interaction between characters is crucial to Arbuthnot's satirical method. Frog's attempts to deceive Bull during their settlement of accounts demonstrate that he is not only a lover of 'Tricks . . . and *Leger de main*' but an expert performer, a skill seen again in his melo-dramatic posturings and 'tumblings' at the Salutation. Certainly 'no Man exceeded *Nic.* in these', but a number of quacks challenge his supremacy and in the process create a sinister fictional and political connection between Frog and Cavallo (Somerset), Ptschirnsooker (Burnet), and the trickster Hocus, 'A true State-Jugler'.[1] Whig notables such as Shaftesbury and Burnet had resided in Holland for well-publicized periods, the Whigs had been prime movers in bring-ing William of Orange to the throne, and they had identified the interests of the two countries in the following years. As Defoe complained, 'we cannot send our Honest *Englishmen* Abroad, but they all turn Whigs, grow *Dutchifi'd*, and their Principles quite Debauch'd'.[2] It was difficult for the Whigs to deny the charge in 1712, when they had no polemicist capable of a satire so enjoyably and allusively resonant as *John Bull*.

Failure to take sufficient account of the basic structural conflict between Arbuthnot's two main protagonists perhaps explains the attempts to isolate John Bull from the satire in which he operates and to uncover some precise historical model for his character, such as the seventeenth-century musician of the same name; or George Bull, the sturdy High Church Bishop of St. David's, who died in 1710; or—more plausibly—Henry St. John, Viscount Bolingbroke (Bulling-broke). Lester Beattie dealt very competently with these suggestions, only to follow the same lure of particularity by arguing a case for Sir Richard Bulstrode, whose *Original Letters* to Charles II were published in January 1712.[3] Any or all of these 'Bulls' may have been in Arbuth-not's mind during the formulation of his allegory, but such surmise is both vain and gratuitous. Before he became intrigued by Bulstrode, Beattie had himself recognized the essential and emotive origins of Bull and Frog in two Aesopian fables, 'The Frog and the Ox'[4] and 'The Frogs Fearing the Sun would Marry'. Of course the hoary old joke about Dutch 'Frogs'—partly explained by the geography and the *polders* of the Low Countries—had lost none of its appeal in Tory

---

[1] *Reward of Ambition* (bs. 1712).   [2] *Review*, 4 Dec. 1705, ii. 466.
[3] Beattie, pp. 104–13.
[4] Indeed, a parallel between this fable and Arbuthnot's *John Bull* was noted much earlier, in *NQ* Ser. IX, iii (1899), 242–3.

satire: 'not a Frog in any Ditch in *Holland* but [would] croak' in
harmony with the addressee of the *Letter to a Modern Dissenting Whig*
in 1701, and such men were accused of maintaining a 'perfect Understanding . . . with the *Froglanders*' throughout the war.[1] Here was a
precise polemic relevance in the parallel situations of the importunate
amphibian of 'The Frog and the Ox', who tries to puff himself up to
the size of his great neighbour the bull,[2] and of Nicholas Frog, who
designs to aggrandize himself and ruin John Bull by their lawsuit.
Certainly when John Ogilby moralized 'The Frogs Fearing the Sun
would Marry' with explicit reference to:

> LOw-Country Provinces, United Bogs,
> Once distrest S[t]ates, now *Hogen Mogen* Frogs,

in his *Fables of Aesop Paraphras'd in Verse* (1668), he was reflecting a
common insult of seventeenth-century satire. And if, as Earl Miner
observed, 'images and meanings, plots and morals, beasts and the
men they represent, this and that historical sequence mingle in full
Baroque ease' to an unusual degree in Ogilby's collection,[3] there is
a similar 'mingling' in the *John Bull* pamphlets, where—amid the
restructuring of history in Arbuthnot's burlesque satire of the peace
conferences—the story of 'The Frog and the Ox' is even visually
evoked as John asks, '*Shall I serve* Philip Baboon *with Broad cloth, and
accept of the Composition?* . . . Then *Nic.* roar'd like a Bull, O, o, o, o.'
Such fabular echoes, which range from direct Aesopian allusions to
John's wry picture of himself 'standing in the Market . . . with
Frog's Paws upon his Head' are unobtrusively pervasive in the pamphlets. Even supposing the improbable, that Arbuthnot was oblivious
to previous applications of fable to Anglo-Dutch relations, he could
hardly fail to make the connections anew when they were so obviously implicit in the Tory strategy against the war.

Its plain that they are our Enemies, or else they wou'd not rob the Pilchards
and Heirings out of our Mouths. They have enriched themselves by a
War that every year impoverishes us . . . They design to make a Province of

---

[1] *Letter to a . . . Whig*, p. 21, and *Secret History of Arlus and Odolphus* (1710), p. 22:
see also *Five Extraordinary Letters* (1712), p. 11.
[2] See John Toland's contemporary version in *Fables of Aesop* (1704), p. 123.
[3] Introduction to a special publication of Ogilby's *Fables* by the Augustan Reprint
Society (1965), p. x. This particular fable (which provided a climactic conclusion to
the collection) seems to have caught the public imagination: it was reproduced
in a broadside of 1672 as *The Holland Nightingale, or the Sweet Singers of Amsterdam.*

us, and are already grown too great. . . . They break all their Alliances and shall we keep ours with such Frogs?[1]

Both the contextual implications and the physical associations of Arbuthnot's 'Bull' and 'Frog' are entirely appropriate to the national characters they represent, as are their Christian names. An honest, plain-dealing John, a gentleman trader, has been drawn into dangerous alliance with an ambitious, shopkeeping Frog whose name is redolent of 'Old Nick', 'Nic. Macchiavelli', and 'NICKUM, a Sharper; also a rooking . . . Retailer'.[2]

Lewis Baboon, the third of Arbuthnot's animalized national characters, represents the French people in the person of their king, Louis of Bourbon. Such a deft confirmation of the Sun King's absolutism did not, however, preclude wider allusiveness. As every reader of English literature must be aware, there was nothing startlingly new in Arbuthnot's portrait of the generic Frenchman (*J.B.* 6: 15–28) as inconstant and effeminate but quick-witted and inventive: hence, 'The Proverb, That *all the* French *Fools are dead*'.[3] Nor was Arbuthnot the first satirist to personify these 'apish' characteristics in a Baboon. Thomas D'Urfey tapped a rich vein of chauvinistic scorn in *Wonders in the Sun* (1706), when (after the fearful hero protests 'I am an Ape . . . begot in *France*') the clownish servant admits he is 'a Baboon his Man';[4] and in 1704 a whole pamphlet was devoted to repetition of the clichéd contempt for 'These proud, perfidious, haughty *French*':

> To Friendship, Constancy and Virtue Foes;
> In *English*, Fops and Knaves; in *French*, they're Beaus:
> In short, they are an ill-contriv'd Lampoon;
> And to conclude, A *French*-Man's a BABOON.[5]

[1] *Certain Information of a Certain Discourse* (1712), pp. 8–9.

[2] *Canting Dictionary*: '*the Dutch*' were accused of '*being . . . effascinated with Machiavel's Pollicies*' by *Brandy-Wine in the Hollanders Ingratitude* (1652), and those in the East Indies had become 'Old *Nick* sent o're the Flood' in *Hogan-Moganides* (1674), p. 91. The supporting players in the drama have similarly appropriate names. In particular 'Hocus'—a generic name for mountebanks and jugglers—distinguishes Marlborough as the leader of the attack from within Bull's household in combination with the trickster Frog from without. His whiggish aims and methods are typical of 'a paltry *Hocus*, whose *Jugling Box* is a *Scheme* . . . and his whole Art but a well contriv'd *Faculty* of *Legerdemain* to bubble inquisitive and credulous *Fools* of their Money', *Character of a Quack-Astrologer* (1673), A3ᵛ.

[3] Defoe, *Review*, 26 Feb. 1704, i. 10.   [4] p. 63.

[5] *Baboon A-La-Mode*, p. 22.

Arbuthnot's Baboon is an animated stock satiric type in the early chapters; but, like Bull and Frog, he develops into a character in his own right as the history unfolds. As with Frog, his creator refused to undermine the stature of his Baboon and eschewed the derisive pidgin English found in so much contemporary caricature of 'de Ape, de Antick, de Baboon, dat can cringe and mauk a de Grimace';[1] but unlike Frog, Baboon speaks with the consistent linguistic decorum of a gentleman. This contrast emerges as an important contribution to the political message of the pamphlets.

The Scottish people, in the person of John's sister Peg, is the only national character to speak in a recognizable dialect as opposed to a distinguishing idiom. She is thus differentiated from the other national characters by her sex, her blood-relationship to John, and her language. Having singled out the Scots in this manner, and suggested that north and south Britain were united by more than parliamentary statute, Arbuthnot could afford to draw the sting of traditional caricature by admitting some truth in well-established censures only to give credence to his affirmation of positive virtues. It was an uphill battle against entrenched prejudices.

> The female kind, are a contentious Brood,
> Stubborn, perverse, and not a little proud:
> Addicted to the gossiping infection,
> Rude in discourse and Swarthy in complection . . .
> They're easily provok'd, and out of tune;
> But flatter'd once, are reconcil'd as soon
> Peevish and froward; obstinate, and vain.
> Willing to work,——(they only grudge the pain).[2]

Certainly John is more prone to flattery and more addicted to gossip than Peg, but many of these characteristics can be found in the portrait of his sister (*J.B.* 50: 1–29). As usual, Arbuthnot starts with platitudes and unfolds the character with the history. His burlesque satire on the senseless mutual hostility which brings out the worst in them both, explains and comments upon Peg's comically pugnacious reaction to John's reluctant offer of reconciliation (the Union of 1707): 'I mun never pair my Nails on a Friday, nor begin a Journy on *Childermas day*. . . . Tell him he may e'en gan his get. . . . I'll stay like the poor Country Mouse, in my own Habitation.' Such humane

[1] *British Apollo*, Nov. 1709.
[2] *A Trip Lately to Scotland. With a True Character of the Country and People* (1705), p. 11.

and tolerant objectivity in the work of an exiled Scot during the first
bitter years after the Union reveals as much about Arbuthnot's
character as it does about his literary technique. Amused detachment
was a habit of mind which gave the force of cultured honesty to his
political satire and helps explain its continuing attraction.

INTRODUCTION

I

WE have suggested that Arbuthnot's sense of national character took shape out of a matrix of seventeenth-century xenophobia. But John Bull is, above all, a party figure created in response to the political warfare between Whigs and Tories which had raged in England from the 1680s and was reaching boiling-point in 1712, the year *John Bull* appeared, as the Tories schemed for peace with France and the Whigs for a Hanoverian successor. Since the pamphlets abound in allusions to the political parties and leaders of their time, we should look closely at how those parties were constituted in order to explain how and why Arbuthnot's conception of the party struggle issued forth in a political symbol and weapon like John Bull.

The historiography of the period 1679 to 1725 is almost as strife-ridden as the very politics under discussion. But political—and perhaps historiographical—strife is a concomitant of intense political awareness, and it should come as no surprise that there were more general elections between 1689 and 1715 than at any other period of the same length in modern history.[1] With, for example, an estimated 200,000 voters in William's reign,[2] the battle to control the electorate was furious indeed, employing new methods of political management, especially in the realm of propaganda.[3] The age witnessed an immense outpouring of pamphlets and newspapers which repeatedly assigned the terms 'Whig' and 'Tory', 'Court' and 'Country' to the major political persuasions. Robert Walcott, unable to discern a consistent two-party trend in Augustan politics, saw the situation as 'a pie' with four major pieces, 'Court, Whig, Country, and Tory—forming as it were, the north, east, south, and west quadrants'.[4] J. H. Plumb, however, argued that although the 'Court–Country' frame of reference is vital to an understanding of the period,[5] the modern historian's

[1] Plumb, *The Growth of Political Stability*, p. 71.　　　　[2] Ibid., p. 29.
[3] For a useful discussion of 'the Paper War, 1697–1702', see Frank H. Ellis's introduction to his edition of Swift's *Discourse of the Contests and Dissensions . . . in Athens and Rome* (Oxford, 1967), pp. 1–14, 66–79.
[4] *English Politics in the Early Eighteenth Century* (Oxford, 1956), p. 157.
[5] Plumb, *The Growth of Political Stability*, p. 131; see also Holmes, *British Politics*, chap. 1, and Dennis Rubini, *Court and Country 1688–1702* (1967), 'Introduction' and Appendix A, 'Party Revisited'.

pie was half-baked: contemporaries 'rarely had difficulty, at least after the middle 1690s, in distinguishing Whig from Tory'.[1] These years saw the two parties develop their traditional eighteenth-century characteristics. At the heart of the Tory party was the squirearchy—country gentlemen of moderate estate; controlling the Whigs, from 1694 on, was a small 'Junto' with shared political aims.

When Plumb discusses the country squire, and his town brother, the lesser merchant, stressing their independent strain, he could almost be describing the behaviour of John Bull, clothier and owner of '*the Mannor of* Bullock's Hatch': 'Xenophobic, greedy, unsophisticated, and obstinate, the politically-minded citizens of London could be as suspicious of authority as the squires of Wales.'[2] There was a considerable group of independent squires in the Commons of 1694—neither Whig nor Tory by commitment; and these men were alarmed by the rising cost of elections, the growing number of placemen (i.e. king's ministers) in Parliament and of political appointees in lucrative offices, the spreading influence of the Whig aristocracy in country politics, and the rampant corruption not only in the offices of government but also 'in a tax system that seemed designed for their ruin'.[3] These members were the political heirs of Shaftesbury's 'Country' party (sometimes called 'old Whigs') who had opposed the 'Court' party of Danby (the first Tories) and who demanded the Exclusion of James II. Robert Harley, descended from 'plain country gentry' with Presbyterian sympathies and a distinguished history of legal service in Herefordshire, became the leader of these independent members. First breaking with the Exclusionists and the Junto lords, he 'set out on his own to capture the Country Members who had hesitated to follow the Junto or co-operate with the Court. To the "old Whigs" he offered himself as the new prophet, calling upon them to follow *him* rather than the Junto or Williamites... who were renegade "new Whigs" that had forsaken true Country principles.'[4] Harley also appealed to the 'Church Party' of older Tories, and 'by the close of the century the real task of his life, the fusion of the Church and the "Country" parties, was to be (to all appearances) nearly accomplished'.[5] Harley's coalition of 'old Whigs' and Church Tories was the reconstituted Tory party of 1694. The Whig 'Country' interest had joined with

[1] Plumb, *The Growth of Political Stability*, p. 130.　　　　[2] Ibid., p. 26.
[3] Ibid., pp. 129–32.　　　　[4] Walcott, pp. 86–7.
[5] Keith Feiling, *A History of the Tory Party 1640–1714* (Oxford, 1924), p. 316.

that of the Tories, now more and more the advocates of individual freedom and the separation of executive and legislature.

As the Tories changed, so did the Whigs. From their base of power in the House of Lords, the Junto dominated a coalition consisting of about half the English nobility (many of whom were linked with wealthy City merchants), representatives of the 'new professionalism' (financiers, contractors, estate agents, projectors, attorneys, government officials, 'placemen'), and most of the Dissenters, the clients of the Whig aristocracy.[1] Having shed their 'radical' ties with the country Exclusionists and with those of the middle- and lower-class London citizenry who cried for social change, the 'new Whigs' of 1694 concentrated their efforts on allying themselves with the power of the Court and Treasury:

From this time the Whigs, in constitutional principles, become deeply conservative but not, and this must be stressed, in political practice and management. There, they remained innovators . . . the most powerful groups in the Whig party became preoccupied with the processes rather than the principles of government. They wanted to capture the government machine and run it.[2]

Of course the Tories wanted to run it too; but they were neither so enterprising nor so adept as the Whigs whose minority position both in the Commons and the country forced them to pull together. Trevelyan and Plumb emphasize that while the minority Whigs were united on the major political issues of the day, the majority Tories were a cohesive force only in opposition, where they could indulge their nostalgic ideals of selfless, thrifty, land-based government in a world which was inexorably becoming more and more dependent on the modern commercial system. The Whigs, a 'welldrilled battalion' that acted 'together as one man',[3] paid lip service to 'Revolution Principles' of parliamentary government, but acted to strengthen the power of the executive, and worked their way to single-party rule (under Walpole) through exploitation of all the ways and means of political domination—which they operated far more effectively than the Tories—such as bribery, propaganda,

---

[1] See Trevelyan, i. 189–200, and Plumb, *The Growth of Political Stability*, pp. 8–14, 138–40.

[2] Plumb, op. cit., p. 135. For a further account of the ante-bellum 'country' Whigs, see J. R. Jones, *The First Whigs: the Politics of the Exclusion Crisis 1678–1683* (1961), especially pp. 11–16.

[3] Trevelyan, i. 194.

conspiracy and purge, control of patronage, manipulation of finance, heavy taxation, and the pursuit of full-scale war.

By 1700 the Tories had evolved from Danby's 'Court' contingent into Harley's 'New Country Party'; at the same time the Whigs had become the party not of the small freeholder and artisan but of 'aggressive commercial expansion' managed by aristocratic financiers.[1] The two parties had, in effect, changed roles, as Defoe recognized in his shrewd insistence on Harley's impeccable Whig background and his Tory policy when eulogizing him as the new Tory or '*Old Whig* ... who prefers the Publick Good to all other Considerations. ... That is Zealous against the Mismanagement of the Publick Treasure ... for the Rights, and Privileges of Parliament, and the just Prerogatives of the Crown. ... That is against Favourites of all kinds. ... That is generous, not profuse; Parsimonious of the Nations Wealth, and prudently Liberal of his own.' He summed up the whole tenor of Tory polemic when he demanded 'The *Whig Principles* indeed, and the *Tory Practice* for any Money'.[2]

II

The 'Junto', or 'Modern' Whigs—the new men of their time who managed the government—and their Dutch friends play a large part in the villainy of *John Bull*, whether disturbing John's mother at home or driving on the lawsuit in the neighbourhood at large. Part of the aversion felt by Tory pamphleteers towards this new breed lay in what it meant to be a 'Modern'. For someone like Swift's Tale Teller, modernity is a marked concern for activity in the present, accompanied by weak memory. In fact, '*Memory* being an Employment of the Mind upon things past, is a Faculty, for which the Learned, in our Illustrious Age have no manner of Occasion, who deal entirely with *Invention*, and strike all Things out of themselves.'[3] The Tale Teller's anti-historical bias reinforces his belief that time has meaning only in so far as it affects him in his present moment of existence and in his constant search for innovation. Swift's representation of the Grub Street hack in *A Tale of a Tub* set the philosophical tone for an attack upon 'modern whiggism' eagerly taken up by many minor Tory satirists of Anne's reign. What the Tories seem to have

---

[1] Plumb, *The Growth of Political Stability*, p. xv.
[2] R[ogue]'s on Both Sides (1711), pp. 6–9.   [3] Swift, *Tale*, p. 135.

lacked in political unity they more than made up for in the con-
sistency and cohesiveness of their polemic efforts, an aggressive
platform which gives us an immediate context for understanding the
origins of *John Bull*.

The most effective satiric portrait of the modern Whig politician
during the Godolphin administration (1702–10) was Charles Davenant's 'Tom Double', a rather free caricature of that indefatigable
campaign-manager, Thomas, first Marquis of Wharton. Tom
Double, like the Tale Teller, reiterates his modernity, and shows
that his sense of time is even more cynically concerned with self-
aggrandizement: 'We modern Whigs are for Lying, tho' the Lye will
last but three Hours', because 'we modern Whigs have no aim but
to do our own Business'.[1] That is, all we need to achieve our goals
is a brief moment of public delusion. Time is expedience, and
expedience is politics. In 1711 Joseph Trapp hinted at an even more
basic origin for Tom's remarks than mere selfishness. 'As to [the
Whigs'] *Scheme of Government*, it is of the old *Chaos*-make, *without form
and void, and Darkness is upon the Face of it. A Scheme it is, in which all
Distinctions are lost, all Ranks and Degrees of Men confounded.
For the People are the Sovereign, the Representative, the Magistrate,
and every Body else.*'[2] Here the distinction, however crude, is not so
much one of a moral category as a metaphysical one: the root image
of 'chaos' is the abyss, the void older than creation, and within this
vacuum of their own making the 'Business' of 'modern' Whigs
originates and flourishes.

All the Tory satirists characterize whiggism as a destructive force,
but Swift in particular gives a provocative representation of the
Whigs bent on doing their utmost to limit and nullify the royal
authority of Anne with 'their endless lopping of the Prerogative,
and mincing into nothing her Majesty's Titles to the Crown'.[3]
For Swift as well as the other Tory pamphleteers, the Whigs'
'*Scheme of Government* is of the old *Chaos*-make, *without form and void*':

There was a Picture drawn some Time ago, representing five Persons as
large as the Life, sitting in Council together like a *Pentarchy*. A void Space

---

[1] Charles Davenant, *Tom Double Return'd out of the Country: or, the True Picture of a
Modern Whig* (1702), pp. 12, 93. Cf. Swift's portrait of the 'original' Tom Double:
'The Ends he hath gained by Lying appear to be more owing to the Frequency,
than the Art of them: His Lies being sometimes detected in an Hour, often in a
Day, and always in a Week' (*Short Character of . . . Thomas Earl of Wharton*, iii. 179),
[2] *The Character and Principles of the Present Set of Whigs*, p. 5.
[3] *Examiner*, 3 May 1711, iii. 143.

was left for a Sixth, which was to have been the Queen, to whom [the Whigs] intended that Honour: But her Majesty having since fallen under their Displeasure, they have made a shift to crowd in *two better Friends* in Her Place, which makes it a compleat *Heptarchy*. This Piece is now in the Country, reserved until better times.[1]

As the sons of chaos, the Whigs flourish in a power vacuum. It was no secret that the royal authority of Queen Anne was assailed on all sides, not just by the Whigs, during her reign. The Duchess of Marlborough domineered in Anne's own household until 1710; the high Tories, Nottingham and Rochester, wanted (in 1705) to invite over Anne's legal successor, Sophia, the Dowager Electress of Hanover, and her son George, to set up a rival court in England while Anne still lived; the Scottish Duchess of Gordon presented a medal with the Pretender's head engraved on it to the Faculty of Advocates in Edinburgh in July 1711; and Marlborough (some thought) had wanted to become general for life and displace the Queen. The choice seemed to be either 'No Queen, or No General', as Defoe put it. The character of Anne herself in some ways abetted this nullifying impulse. Even before her accession, Anne's attempts to assert her 'Presence' by withholding it from public view had too often had the opposite effect of diminishing her regal authority. Anne thus became the 'invisible Queen'. She had numerous miscarriages and no progeny who survived childhood; she was often indisposed with a variety of illnesses; and she was not noted for a commanding intellect.[2] Her very authenticity was open to question with her brother, the Prince of Wales ('James III' in French and Jacobite eyes) always in the wings. In the minds of her subjects her image was that of one who lived mainly to be succeeded—but by whom?

The Queen's favourite physician must have been acutely aware of the uncertainty of Anne's role, and he sensed, just as deeply, a similar uncertainty in the hearts of his fellow subjects, for in *John Bull* Arbuthnot represented, allegorically, a nation torn in two; and modern historians agree with him: 'At the height of the struggle [between Whigs and Tories] in the later years of Anne the whole fabric of national life was permeated by the spirit of party, to a

---

[1] *Examiner*, 25 Jan. 1710, iii. 73.

[2] See the description of Anne by the astute German traveller and book-collector, von Uffenbach: 'foreigners have a much higher opinion of her parts than her own subjects', *London in 1710: from the Travels of Zacharias Conrad von Uffenbach*, trans. and ed. W. H. Quarrell and Margaret Mare (1934), p. 116.

degree without precedent. . . . Political history between 1694 and
1716 is the story not just of a divided Parliament, nor even of a
divided electorate, but of a divided society.'¹ If, as Swift thought, the
Whigs' aim was to diminish Anne's authority and fill up her 'void
Space' in the political picture with their own oligarchic numbers, the
Tory pamphleteers must find some means of countering this tendency. They did so, in part, by addressing various audiences within
the 'divided society'. Swift's enterprise of persuasion, aimed chiefly
at a 'country squiredom' which must be roused to action, frequently
invoked the time-worn virtues of Anne's royal nature, her 'Grace',
'Bounty', 'Tolerance', and so on; but he was undeniably more effective in illustrating how well the Whigs were succeeding with their
campaign of diminution than in repairing the damage, and he himself had grave doubts about the Queen's loyalty to the Oxford
ministry. The Lord Treasurer's less public minister of propaganda,
Defoe, sought to placate the whiggish 'commercial middle class'.²

When Arbuthnot felt called upon to do his bit for the Tory peace,
he devised a unique strategy for reasserting the strength of the nation
and at the same time turning the tables on the warmongers. For us
the full significance of *John Bull*'s satiric allegory lies in Arbuthnot's
awareness of the diversity of his audience. Instead of elevating one
party at the expense of the other, he found the means to appeal to
both the town–Whig and the country–Tory persuasions at once. If
the Whigs wanted to replace Anne's image with their own, he would
let them have their way. Perhaps recalling Swift's frequent insistence
that he was 'not sensible of any material Difference . . . between
those who call themselves the *Old Whigs*, and a great Majority of the
present Tories',³ and believing with Swift that if anyone examined
'a reasonable honest Man of either Side, upon those Opinions in
Religion and Government, which both Parties daily buffet each
other about; he should hardly find one material Point of difference
between them',⁴ Arbuthnot fused in the character of John Bull many
of the conventional traits of the 'old Whig' country squires (moderate
wealth, power in the neighbourhood, loyalty to the Church, political
independence, honest business sense, and a taste for violence) with the

¹ *The Divided Society: Parties and Politics in England 1694–1716*, ed. G. S. Holmes and
W. A. Speck (1967), p. 2.
² See R. I. Cook, *Jonathan Swift as a Tory Pamphleteer* (1967), pp. 112–13. For
contrasting estimates of Arbuthnot's intended audience see Beattie, *John Arbuthnot*,
p. 119, and especially Arbuthnot's 'Correspondence', ed. Ross, p. 42.
³ *Examiner*, 22 Mar. 1710, iii. 111.   ⁴ Ibid., 16 Nov. 1710, iii. 15.

role of a similarly obstinate City tradesman—always a dependable Whig adherent—who suddenly falls under the spell of the aristocratic 'new Whigs' and aspires to become a lawyer, the most prominent early eighteenth-century representative of the 'new professionalism' and one of the most frequently satirized. John thinks, 'What immense Estates these Fellows raise by the Law? Besides, it is the Profession of a Gentleman. . . . What a Fool am I to drudge any more in this Woollen Trade?' The 'divided society' could not have found a more immediate and compelling personification. Swift's *'two better Friends'* of the Whigs, intended to occupy Anne's 'void Space', become in Arbuthnot's hands John Bull, the heir of Tom Double, but more complex than Davenant's character because John combines the conflicting personalities of old and new Whig in one body.

Between 1688 and 1712 there was a marked decline in the number of men with enough capital to finance the ever more ambitious governmental schemes, and in consequence a concentration of power and affluence in the hands of the new financiers to the prejudice of the old landed gentry. But the development of large-scale capitalism was equally disadvantageous to the petty artisan and merchant classes: as John Bull remarks, 'The same Man was Butcher and Grasier, Brewer and Butler, Cook and Poulterer', leaving less and less room for the small entrepreneur grappling with his taxes and inflationary prices.[1] Arbuthnot, along with the Whig dramatists of the first decade of the new century, recognized that the booming war-economy discriminated against the little man,[2] and only he among the Tory satirists was able to exploit the polemical possibilities of this development by driving a satiric wedge between the whiggish financiers and the whiggish traders. The thoroughgoing Whigs (represented in the satire by Mrs. Bull, Habbakkuk, the Lawyers, and other villains) could thus be isolated from their more down-to-earth whiggish clients, whose financial embarrassment and growing scepticism about the war are represented by John Bull coming 'to his Senses'. Such tradesmen could thus be shown the urgent necessity of ignoring conventional political associations and taking a stand against the threat posed by a coalition of treacherous foreign allies and City moneyed men. Bolingbroke had indeed 'discovered the source of the

---

[1] See Isaac Kramnick, *Bolingbroke and His Circle: the Politics of Nostalgia in the Age of Walpole* (1968), p. 59; cf. Holmes, p. 155.

[2] See John Loftis *Comedy and Society from Congreve to Fielding* (Stanford, 1959), pp. 3–6, and *Politics of Drama in Augustan England* (Oxford, 1963), pp. 42–3.

conspiracy which depressed aristocracy, gentry, intellectuals, and small traders alike',[1] and he articulated that discovery later in the eighteenth century, but only after Arbuthnot had successfully allegorized and condemned the whiggish attempts to impose their 'Scheme of Government' and finances upon a chaos of their own making.

III

If the *History of John Bull* were merely satirical reportage of events from 1698 to 1712 we should be disturbed by the lack of historical perspective evident in Arbuthnot's devoting the whole fourth pamphlet to the tangled politics of the 1711 Occasional Bill's passage, as if that event were as important, say, as the origins of the war, which are economically dealt with in the first two brief chapters of the first pamphlet. But Swift's praise of the fourth instalment of the history as 'equall to the rest'[2] indicates that he was well aware of Arbuthnot's having written separate but cohesive parts of a moral history in which the deployment of the Occasional Bill warranted careful satiric attention as the apotheosis of Whig villainy. It provided ultimate proof of the immorality and irreligion of a party of men prepared to sacrifice their friends and principles for political ends. At the same time, the outcome of the affair endorsed the very tenets of political honesty they denied: Jack's betrayal was rough poetic justice for years of expedient 'trimming' and proved to be of no benefit to his betrayers. Moreover, it was an eloquent comment on the nature of politics, since the most basic of moral principles became irrelevant when power was at stake, and everyone involved—even Harley on the Tory side—was caught in the growing web of cynical deceit.

It was therefore appropriate that Arbuthnot should choose for his *John Bull* pamphlets the allegorical 'little history' form so popular with Tory satirists during the reign of Anne, for, despite the great disparities between the pamphlets in this very minor genre, most of them made sententious claims for the moral efficacy of their varied representations of Whig villainy.[3] Mrs. Manley, the most celebrated

---

[1] Kramnick, p. 61.

[2] *Journal to Stella*, 10 May 1712, ed. Harold Williams (Oxford, 1948), p. 532.

[3] See, for example, *The Secret History of Arlus and Odolphus* (1710), *The History of Prince Mirabel's Infancy, Rise and Disgrace* (1712), or William King's *Rufinus* (1712).

contemporary theorist and practitioner of this genre,[1] was typically concerned that 'Historical Novels', 'these little pieces which have banished Romances', should be used for moral purposes: 'The chief end of History is to instruct and inspire into men the love of virtue and abhorrence of vice by the examples proposed to them: therefore the conclusion of a story ought to have some tract of morality which may engage virtue.'[2] Of course she proceeded to subvert these noble sentiments by loading her little 'histories' with salacious and vindictive gossip. But Arbuthnot, who must have been very familiar with her contentious fictions (especially *Queen Zarah*, 1705, and *Memoirs of Europe*, 1710), drew upon more than her moralizing tone. In her allegorical representations of Queen Anne either as a woman vulnerable to the usurping power of a ruthless and aggressive 'modern Politician' (*Zarah* = Sarah, Duchess of Marlborough), or as a weak boy (Constantine) duped and manipulated by an overpowering mother (Irene = Sarah, in the *Memoirs of Europe*), Mrs. Manley expressed her version of a monarchy so unstable as to virtually 'uncrown' itself. Despite a total contrast in temperament between the two characters, Arbuthnot's John Bull is a logical extension of Manley's Constantine: both are naïve, put upon, deceived (even twice-married), and each comes into his own with the help of loyal and effectual friends.

Arbuthnot's cryptic compliment to Mrs. Manley (as his 'publisher') on the title-pages of his last three pamphlets was meant perhaps to indicate a debt to her as well as to reflect upon his own gossip prone narrator in *John Bull*. Following Manley's advice that 'every historian ought to be extremely uninterested . . . ought neither to praise nor to blame those he speaks of . . . [and] ought to be contented with exposing the actions' of his characters,[3] Arbuthnot took more than usual pains to preserve the customary anonymity of the Augustan satirist, letting the fools of his satire expose and reveal themselves. If Mrs. Manley is the ostensible publisher of *John Bull*, the work itself was 'printed from a manuscript found in the Cabinet of the famous Sir Humphry Polesworth'. Now this name, as Lester

---

[1] She is best known for her 'New Atalantis' pamphlets: *Secret Memoirs and Manners of Several Persons of Quality, of Both Sexes. From the New Atalantis, an Island in the Mediterranean* (1709), and *Court Intrigues, in a Collection of Original Letters, from the Island of the New Atalantis* (1711).

[2] Preface 'To the Reader', *The Secret History of Queen Zarah and the Zarazians* (1705).

[3] Preface to *Queen Zarah*.

Beattie has suggested, may be a fictional amalgam of several contemporaries, particularly Sir Humphrey Mackworth, a pompous Tory pamphleteer and Member of Parliament; Humfrey Wanley, librarian to the Earl of Oxford; and Sir Robert Molesworth, a Whig politician. The name, whatever its origins, has a history of facetious use by Tories like Prior and the younger Edward Harley.[1] At the very beginning, then, Sir Humphry Polesworth, the narrator of our little history, is an elusive phenomenon, absorbed into the scene of the satire.

This scene is the European 'Neighbourhood', where everyone involved is on the same footing whether he be a tiny nation or a venerable institution, a famous personage or a social malady. The knowing and ubiquitous Polesworth is the voice of the ordinary Englishman, just as the concrete historical matrix of the *John Bull* pamphlets is the news media of the common man—the daily newspapers, broadsides, proclamations, penny-pamphlets, newsletters, travel books, sermons, compilations of trial testimony, all the sub-literary ephemera of Grub Street (lampoons, squibs, lurid romances), the almanacs, the annals, the chronicles. Occasionally Arbuthnot drops his narrator altogether to present his history as a dramatic dialogue between neighbours; various speakers are characterized by dialect (Scottish Peg) or speech pattern (Dr. Radcliffe); one chapter may parody a diplomatic note, another a political treaty. What helps make *John Bull* better than other works of the same kind is the robust language and balanced good humour of its satire, the remarkable density of its historical allusions, and the variety and kind of narrative devices by which Arbuthnot presents his history. These diverse experiments with telling the story of John Bull have, like the diverse productions of the 'news', the uniformity of vivid common speech; and Sir Humphry's story itself is a heightened version, sprinkled with proverbs, Scotticisms, and doggerel, of the common English idiom. The tone of his narrative is that of one Englishman speaking to another, perhaps to a brother in the country who has not heard all the news, or to a small shopkeeper of whiggish inclinations who has begun to question the wisdom of prolonging a ten-year war. Thus Polesworth, like Mackworth, often begins a paragraph with a maxim; and the latter is fond, in characteristic pamphlets such as *A Letter from a Member of Parliament to his Friend in the Country* (1705), of phrases like 'the plain Meaning . . . was no more than this', 'I

[1] Beattie, pp. 168–74.

shall not trouble you at present with the History', 'And here I need not tell you', all echoed in *John Bull*.

Not until the Preface to the final pamphlet, however, do we learn that Sir Humphry Polesworth is John Bull's official historian: '*When I was first call'd to the Office of Historiographer to* John Bull, *he express'd himself to this purpose*: "Sir *Humphry*, I know you are a plain Dealer; it is for that Reason I have chosen you for this important Trust; speak the Truth, and spare not." ' Like Sir Humphrey Mackworth and Abel Boyer (the self-styled Whig annalist of Anne's reign) who are here parodied, or the Gulliver who was to be historiographer of England to the King of Brobdingnag, Sir Humphry professes an unswerving dedication to telling the truth, and his emphasis on the official nature of his function lends an air of certified legality to the narrator in keeping with the legalistic theme of the satire. We should not be surprised at the full revelation of Sir Humphry here. With the third pamphlet the narrator became more than a mere name on a title-page. A 'Publisher's Preface', presumably written by the 'Author of the *New Atalantis*' (an allusion to Mrs Manley), represents Sir Humphry as a retiring fellow who aimed the first two parts of *John Bull* at the 'Meridian of *Grubstreet*'. These were only private memoirs, written in a loose style as 'a help to [his] ordinary Conversation'. By July, apparently, Sir Humphry's authorial reticence has diminished in proportion to the growing fame of his history. He now freely congratulates himself on the beauties of the work and regrets the loss of '*Perfection*' it might have achieved had not an illiterate (Tory) Parliament, '*envying the great Figure I was to make in future Ages*', set out to silence at once the '*whole University of* Grubstreet', Sir Humphry's Alma Mater. Then follows an extravagant mock-panegyric upon the varied productions of this University, the very materials out of which Arbuthnot has fashioned *John Bull*.

Putting himself forward at the moment of popular acclaim (the first pamphlet had by now gone through several 'editions') Sir Humphry appears curiously like the self-serving new Whigs who exist for the expedient moment and for whom '*John's* Cause was a good milch Cow'. In this respect Polesworth recalls the other Humphry of the satire, John's chief lawyer, Hocus. Just as Sir Humphry has been given leave to manage John's historical affairs ('trifling Things' as they are), doling out from his secret strong box just those facts he deems necessary ('he retails it only by Parcels, and won't give us the whole Work'), so on a grander scale Humphry Hocus has brilliantly managed John's legal affairs, achieving victory after victory, but without bringing the suit to a peaceful conclusion. Sir Humphry is as slippery a customer as his namesake of the legal wars. Like Hocus he divides his labours with an assistant, in this case the Publisher, who—late in the fifth pamphlet—ingenuously informs us that another able pen of the University of Grub Street, and not Sir Humphry, is responsible for an important chapter. The Publisher's part in the narration is left deliberately vague. Finally, both Humphrys use John Bull for their own ends, Polesworth to perpetuate his literary fame, Hocus to multiply his wealth. The one parcels out words as the other parcels out victories. Above all, both Humphrys fear the permanent cessation of their activities: Sir Humphry is appalled by the Tory tax which will muzzle his flow of words, Hocus by John Bull's 'Composition' which will put an end to a lucrative war.

After the Queen's death, Arbuthnot, in one of his most moving letters to Swift, expressed a belief that the 'Constitution . . . is in no more danger than a strong man that gott a little surfeit by Drunkenness'.[1] There is a constant tendency in Arbuthnot and Swift to take a humanizing view of their country: England may be a drunken man, a heedless young heir, a sick man, even a dying man, but almost always an individual capable of a new direction. John Bull is the epitome of this humanizing tendency. He is a troubled man, and his troubles are mirrored by those closest to him in his family, by that 'extravagant Bitch' of a first wife, by his mother, and by his sister. These sexual and blood relationships animate the Tory belief in human rather than contractual values; and appropriately enough it is the human concern of his second wife which helps John to reflect upon his past mistakes and to attempt to overcome them. The Bulls' connubial chats dramatize attempts made by the new Harley ministry to untangle England's affairs in mid 1711. John Bull, reflective and confiding under the tactful ministrations of his second wife, here presents us with the larger issues of the proper governance of a nation, and implicitly the related questions of how history should be made and written. Robert Harley was a master at the game of court intrigue, and with the help of his intelligence network and battery of Tory pamphleteers came as close to omniscience about the affairs of Britain as did any Augustan politician. It is significant then that the homely, candid conversations between

[1] 6 Aug. 1715, Arbuthnot, 'Correspondence', ed. Ross, p. 372.

John and his second wife contrast with several more obscure male and female transactions pertinent to the satire (especially the secret correspondence between Hocus and the first Mrs. Bull, and the murky historical collaboration between Sir Humphry and the female 'Author of the New Atalantis') and at this point in the 'history of John Bull' Arbuthnot—despite Harley's known penchant for secrecy —looks with favour upon his good intentions for the country. This passage, in effect, seems to advocate a free and open exchange of ideas between a government and its people, with the government (in this case Mrs. Bull, as she reflects both moderate toryism and Anne's housewifely virtues) responsible to the best interests of the people. The new government will let the people into the truth about their recent past (kept hidden by the self-serving Whigs), and help to guide them out of their difficulties. But the telling of truth is no simple matter.

In the brief space of the *John Bull* pamphlets, Arbuthnot has managed to satirize not only a period of European history but also two of the prevailing modes of Augustan historiography: arrayed on one side with their secret 'little histories' (often anything but little) are Mrs. Manley and her Tory friends, obsessed with the private vices and public crimes of a few famous personages, like the Duchess of Marlborough; on the other side stand the long-winded political 'annalists' of Anne's reign, especially the Whig Boyer whose volumes exemplify the minute, plodding, cumulative approach to the writing of history. Sir Humphrey Mackworth, the jumped-up Tory capitalist with his patronizing assumption of political *savoir-faire* and his pedestrian labouring of the obvious, combines elements of both modes, but he is still essentially an official instructor of the people. And as these public historians often miss the wood in their dogged concern to catalogue all the trees, so the secret historians, wrapped in their cloak of scandal and innuendo, mistake the largest trees for the entire wood. Yet the secret histories (in particular those of Mrs. Manley), despite their vindictive and overriding Tory bias, contain a 'substructure of truth' about the activities of the Whig Junto which is too seldom recognized.[1] As the history of John Bull enters a new narrative dimension with the Bulls' dialogue, Mrs. Manley, the artist of the 'inside story', is again relevant: 'There is . . . a distinction to be made between the character of the Historian and the hero, for

[1] See Gwendolyn B. Needham, 'Mary de la Riviere Manley, Tory Defender', *HLQ* xii (1948–9), 267.

if it be the hero that speaks, then he ought to express himself ingeniously, without affecting any nicety of points or syllogisms,
because he speaks without any preparation.'[1] John Bull, it is true,
speaks with the 'preparation' of his wife's pointed questions, but it
is not too much to say that he now becomes his own historian and
achieves a philosophical perspective on his recent past, naming that
period the 'Age of Lawyers'. 'There was at least two of everything',
a pretender to every estate, and general chaos in the Neighbourhood. Ruefully, 'ingeniously', but with a keen sense of the comic, he
tells how he joined a surveying expedition (the Partition Treaties of
1698–9) with Frog and Lewis in order to divide up the old Lord
Strutt's estate; how he was drawn into the lawsuit much as a heedless
young heir falls into the hands of financiers; how, finally, after five
years of drunkenness and muddle, he discovered that his mother had
been doped with the 'moderating powder' of latitudinarianism.
From then on he began to come to his senses.

What J. Hillis Miller says of Dickens's sympathetic characters is an
apt description of what John Bull learns in recounting his own history:

Like members of a primitive or traditional society, Dickens' characters are
profoundly fearful of self-initiated novelty. They find their most authentic
selves by accepting, after an interval of dissociation, their original place in
the world. Their most real and valid actions are repetitions, reaffirmations.
Dickens' good people take upon themselves the responsibility of making
history.[2]

Though primitive in outline, John Bull's world is built upon complex
moral and political issues, and in his senses John can 'take the responsibility' of making his own history. His personal history of 1698 to
1711 provides a revealing counterpoint to Sir Humphry Polesworth's
more conventional narrative of Neighbourhood affairs in the first
pamphlet. Sir Humphry, who combines both the 'tatling' and the
'official' aspects of the Augustan historian, began his story in the
voice of the common man as an indictment of what the Whigs and
the Dissenters were doing to England during the war, but Sir
Humphry gradually became infatuated with a sense of his own
historical importance. John Bull was infatuated as well, with the
legal profession: but he came to his senses, outwitted the forces of

---

[1] Preface to *Queen Zarah* (1705).
[2] J. Hillis Miller, *Charles Dickens: the World of his Novels* (Cambridge (Mass.),
1958), pp. 325–6.

modern whiggism, and became his own reliable historian and mature politician. In the jargon of eighteenth-century politics, Sir Humphry starts out as an old Whig and becomes a new one; John eventually turns from new Whig to old and reaffirms moderate toryism, for old Whig and new Tory are one.

IV

Early critics of *John Bull* agreed that it did not exhibit the brilliant formal patterning of the best Augustan satires. Lester Beattie contrasted the dovetailed digressiveness of Swift in *A Tale of a Tub* with the 'wandering' digressiveness of Arbuthnot, whose 'mind was keenly alive to the next thing, but not to the unity of all things'; and he concluded that 'an organic development in *John Bull* is not to be sought'.[1] Patricia Carstens, however, found an alternative answer to the teasing structural idiosyncrasy of the pamphlets in the tradition of Menippean satire[2] as outlined by Northrop Frye:

Petronius, Apuleius, Rabelais, Swift, and Voltaire all use a loose-jointed narrative form . . . [which] relies on the free play of intellectual fancy and the kind of humorous observation that produces caricature. . . . The intellectual structure built up from the story makes for violent dislocations in the customary logic of narrative, though the appearance of carelessness that results reflects only the . . . tendency to judge by a novel-centred conception of fiction.[3]

Carstens justly noted that,

Looked upon as a history the piece is disorganized; and as a narrative, digressive. When however we regard it as the story of a nation, told in the manner of Menippean satire, we see that none of the digressions are irrelevant, and that there is no need to present all the historical background material in strictly chronological order. Arbuthnot employs whatever forms lie convenient to his hand, and uses the formal character, the dialogue, and the letter as devices of interest in themselves, and as convenient methods of presenting certain facts and comments upon the facts.[4]

In her analysis of these forms she demonstrates that Arbuthnot may not have commanded the architectonic ability of Swift, but that he animated his 'little history' as a consistent fiction, and that the Menippean strain provides only the most generalized of definitions for Arbuthnot's satiric art.

---

[1] Beattie, p. 64.
[3] *Anatomy of Criticism* (Princeton, 1957), pp. 309–10.
[2] Carstens, pp. 286 ff.
[4] Carstens, p. 289.

At a climactic point in the satire Arbuthnot's master is Horace rather than 'Menippeans' such as Rabelais or Swift.

John receiv'd this with a good deal of *Sang froid; Transeat* (quoth John) *cum caeteris erroribus*: He was now at his Ease; he saw he could now make a very good Bargain for himself, and a very safe one for other Folks. My Shirt (quoth he) is near me, but my Skin is nearer: Whilst I take care of the Welfare of other Folks, no body can blame me, to apply a little Balsam to my own Sores. . . . This is somewhat better, I trow, than for *John Bull* to be standing in the Market, like a great Dray-horse, with *Frog's* Paws upon his Head, *What will ye give me for this Beast?* . . . Though *John Bull* has not read your *Aristotles, Plato's* and *Machiavels*, he can see as far into a Milstone as another.[1]

As James Johnson recognized, 'John Bull's bluff reliance on proverbial wisdom is given an ironic twist by his [evoking] Horace even as he disparages the need of classical learning.'[2] To be precise, Arbuthnot echoes Horace's third satire from the second book on 'The Follies of Mankind',[3] to which both *John Bull* and Swift's *Tale of a Tub* are clearly indebted despite the assertion of Lester Beattie that they represent rhetorical opposites. With the possible exception of Plautus, who is also quoted with unconscious irony by Bull ('My Shirt . . . is near me, but my Skin is nearer'), Horace was the only Roman satirist to use error for 'madness'; and although '*Transeat cum caeteris erroribus*' is not a literal quotation from the third satire, it is an absolutely just reflection of the subject and tenor of this dialogue on madness. Swift borrowed the story of Servius Oppidius (who tried to bind his sons to moderation and sanity with a deathbed will) for his *Tale* itself, and he dramatized the preamble of Damasippus for the central 'Digression on Madness'.[4] Arbuthnot's borrowings are no less structurally important. Horace's interlocutor seeks to prove that the poet's building of a Sabine retreat is a prime example of importunate madness, and he illustrates his argument by reference to Aesop's fable of 'The Frog and the Ox' which we have already

[1] *J.B.* 113: 32–114: 8.
[2] 'The Classics and John Bull', *England in the Restoration and Early Eighteenth Century*, ed. H. T. Swedenberg (1972), p. 26. We are deeply indebted to correspondence with the author of this essay in the following discussion of the influence of Horace on Arbuthnot.
[3] *Horace: Satires, Epistles and Ars Poetica* (Loeb Classical Library), ed. and trans. H. Rushton Fairchild (1966), pp. 149–81.
[4] '*Nunc accipe, quare | desipiant omnes aeque ac tu, qui tibi nomen | insano posuere*': Now learn why all, who have given you the name of madman, are quite as crazy as yourself (*Horace: Satires*, pp. 156–7, ll. 46–8).

discussed as a key allusion behind the fiction of *John Bull*[1] and which is recalled again here by the picture of '*Bull* . . . standing in the Market . . . with *Frog*'s Paws upon his Head'. In addition, aphoristic statements such as '*sanus utrisque | auribus atque oculis: mentem, nisi litigiosus, | exciperet dominus, cum vederet*' (The man was sound in both ears and eyes; but as to his mind, his master, if selling him, would not have vouched for that, unless bent on a lawsuit)[2] prefigure Arbuthnot's pamphlets in their implication that lawsuits symptomize insanity.

Yet the temptation to pin a Menippean or even an Horatian label to *John Bull* (and be done with it) is akin to the temptation to accept Lester Beattie's postulate that the work, however entertaining, is formless. Arbuthnot's deliberate choice of the 'little history' genre provided a dramatic framework for an allegory within which he was free to cross-reference all his social, political, religious, and moral satire in a damning revelation of allied and Whig villainy. Moreover, his format was distinguishable but loose enough to allow scope for his fertile imagination, and for the 'abuse through use' of the myriad themes, images, and conventions beloved by Grub Street.

The first Mrs. Bull's *Vindication of the indispensable Duty of Cuckoldom* which opens the second pamphlet is justly remembered as an ironic *tour de force*, which

conveys mock praise through concession of an opposing opinion—i.e., that a nation may dismiss its king at will—and supports this concession with what at that time seemed an obviously fallacious argument by analogy: as a wife may renounce her husband at will. Then the ironist further complicates his irony by pretending to argue in the opposite direction: i.e., that a wife may renounce her husband just as a nation may dismiss a king.[3]

The argument is also a rich parody of the Whig prosecution speeches at the political show-piece trial of Henry Sacheverell, and as Mrs. Bull propounds a morally sophistical case the reader must conclude that such is the nature of Whig constitutional theory. Thus an apparent digression from the narrative is in fact another illuminating manifestation of the enveloping evil which John is discovering in every facet of his life. Furthermore, as with so many of the local felicities in *John Bull*, the irony carries a secondary but precise allu-

---

[1] *Horace: Satires*, pp. 178–81, ll. 314–23: cf. above, pp. lxiv–lxvi.

[2] Ibid., pp. 176–7, ll. 284–6.

[3] Norman Knox, *The Word Irony and its Context, 1500–1755* (Durham (North Carolina), 1961), p. 124.

sion, in this case to the reputedly bigamous affair between William
Cowper, the Lord Chancellor who presided over the Sacheverell
trial, and Elizabeth Cullen. 'Will Bigamy' compounded his crime,
according to Swift, by writing a defence of polygamy.[1] But Arbuthnot's portrait of the first Mrs. Bull also evoked Shaftesbury's equation of marriage and constitutional monarchy in his *Delenda est
Carthago* speech (reprinted in a 1712 broadside), Whig pamphlet
vindications of the 1688 revolution,[2] and contemporary caricatures
of the generic 'city lady' ('Proud and High-spirited, Self-conceited,
Talkative')[3] who was whiggish in temper and dissenting in conscience. It was commonly held that any 'Female Hypocrite' such as
the first Mrs. Bull would lust after the enthusiasts (like Hocus) and
entertain them on her husband's 'own money'.

She is no less Skill'd in Policies of Government, and is an Earnest Contender
for the *Rights* of Woman-kind, which she claims as her *Due*, and not as a
Benevolence from the good Man's *Prerogative*. She opposes the *Monarchy* of a
Husband, with the *Undeterminable* Privileges of a *Wife*. . . . Doing *what she
Lists*, is her *Liberty*; a separate *Maintenance* is her *Property*, and claims them
by her *Original Contract*. . . . The Man that Closes with her upon these
Principles, of Checking the *Arbitrary* Powers of *Husbands*, tho' a *Meer Rake*,
has Won the Fort of her feigned *Virtue*.[4]

In short, there was nothing new in Arbuthnot's irony except the
application of old ideas, arguments, and images in a densely allusive
narrative. Arbuthnot's fund of ephemera was seemingly inexhaustible: any reader who has followed us through the annotation of the
pamphlets will have noticed that, for example, Jack's 'trial' is a
refinement on previous allegories in the same vein, and any reader of
Augustan literature will be aware of the parallels common in contemporary polemic to minor allegories such as Timothy Trim's
cloak of deceit[5] or John Bull's three daughters.[6] We shall probably

---

[1] *Examiner*, 4 Jan. 1710, iii. 57–8. See also Defoe's satirical defence of Cowper's
adultery in 'Reformation of Manners' (1702), *Poems on Affairs of State*, vol. vi, ed.
Frank Ellis (1970), p. 419, and the extended account in Mrs. Manley's *Secret Memoirs
and Manners . . . from the New Atalantis* (1709), i. 214–44.
[2] For example, *Humble Confession and Petition of a Whig* (1712), pp. 34 ff.
[3] *True-Born English-Woman* (1703), pp. 4–7.
[4] *True Characters* (1708), p. 9; see also *Aesop in Europe* (1706), p. 7.
[5] Cf. the many complaints that such 'crafty, turn-coat Knaves' (*Junto*, 1712,
p. 4) had adopted some remnants of Anglican ceremony as a '*Politick* disguise, / That
Skreen'd their *Tricks* from weaker *Eyes*' (Ned Ward, *Vulgus Britannicus*, 1710, v. 173).
[6] Defoe was particularly fond of genealogical allegory: cf. 'REVOLUTION, the
Eldest Sister, is charg'd with taking up Arms in Conjunction with Foreigners

never know the composition of the 'large parcel of pamphlets' from Arbuthnot's library auctioned in 1779,[1] but it is obvious that he had read them to some effect.

The choice and use of Arbuthnot's 'borrowings' was, however, determined by the conception of national affairs in terms of family relationships, in which the idealistic conservatism of Tory Augustan thought found its most characteristic expression. Of course it was partly a reaction to the Whig theory of contractualism,[2] but it was also a positive assertion of the hallowed (almost metaphysical) ideal of society as an integrated, hierarchical, country estate. Swift protested that the 'new Whig' economics was an alien transplant from the Low Countries, designed to destroy the ancient and virtuous English tradition of self-sufficient, landed, solvency.[3] Nor was the notion of the economy as a family budget exclusive to Tories: even Defoe was worried that Britain might be mortgaged into disaster, and Francis Hare, one of Marlborough's most loyal apologists, did his best to defend an economic situation which he manifestly could not comprehend:

Perhaps it may be objected, that the Case may be the same with a Nation as with a private Gentleman; the Gentleman may exceed in the Splendor of his Living . . . [but] the Decay of the Gentleman in that Case is visible; he runs over Head and Ears in Debt, till he is torn to pieces by his Creditors; whilst *England* goes on with all this Splendor.[4]

If the supporters of the developing credit system could offer only such pious faith and distressingly familiar images, Arbuthnot would be delighted to exploit the widespread bewilderment and the deeply rooted fear that John Bull, 'run so much in Debt', was indeed 'like to be pull'd to Pieces, by Brewer, Butcher, and Baker'.

The immediate cause of Bull's near bankruptcy is his lawsuit, a satirical metaphor which drew upon all the associative force of a long

against her Great Grandfather NATION . . . TOLERATION, the Second Sister . . . with Whoredom . . . UNION, the Youngest . . . with Corruption' (*Review*, 25 Feb. 1710, vi. 555).

[1] *Catalogue of the Capital and Well-Known Library of Books, of the Late Celebrated Dr. Arbuthnot, Deceased* (1779), p. 3.

[2] Isaac Kramnick, *Bolingbroke and His Circle*, pp. 58–60.

[3] See his account of the nation 'household' in *Examiner*, 8 Feb. 1710, iii. 81–2, and P. G. M. Dickson's discussion of his economic views in *Financial Revolution in England* (1967), pp. 17–18.

[4] *Letter to a Member of the October-Club* (1711), pp. 31–2. Defoe voiced concern in *Reasons why this Nation Ought to Put a Speedy End to this Expensive War* (1711), and in *Farther Search* (1712).

tradition in which the law was a symbol of moral depravity. Jack was indeed foolish to hang himself when 'Witnesses might have been brib'd, Juries manag'd, or Prosecution stop'd'. Hocus the attorney stood condemned by his profession, for 'If there was one subject, in a divided and bigoted age, upon which all writers were agreed, it was their opinion of the lower branch of the legal profession. No one had a good word to say for attorneys.'[1] The stream of abuse flowed unchecked throughout the seventeenth into the first decade of the eighteenth century,[2] and the equation of law and whiggery was a common theme of Tory propaganda, shrewdly founded on 'the dependence of the Whigs in the House of Commons on their impressive battery of lawyer-M.P.s'.[3] The 'Deceitful Petty-Fogger, Vulgarly call'd Attorney' followed 'Whig Example, and his Actions . . . [were] guided by . . . what other Men of the same Cut' did:[4] John Bull may possess a small country manor, but he is primarily a man of the trading classes, and therefore doubly vulnerable to such rapacious parasites. 'Out of his Senses' he is, appropriately, yet another of the caricatured merchants who appeared in the polemic of the war. Even the Whig Steele had censured the haberdasher who became so involved with political dispute that he neglected his business and reduced his family to penury,[5] and Bull was, in some respects, a more sympathetic portrait of the generic tradesman who had been the butt of so many Tory jibes, 'Tradesmen . . . as hard to get out of a Tavern . . . till they're Drunk, as . . . to Lug a Dissenter to Church. . . . Sharpers Bubble them, Drawers Cheat them, Coachmen Trick them, and their Wives Cuckold them.'[6] By pushing Steele's mild criticisms of his more humble fellow Whigs to a reductio which comprehended the whole populace, Arbuthnot turned their own commercialism upon the men he believed were destroying trade while they claimed to safeguard it. Even if his satire did not wean all the petty merchants from the Whig cause, it served the purpose of confirming the Tory faithful in their prejudices. It flattered their sense of their own political and literary sophistication by encompassing their scorn for Grub Street productions in parodies which supported all their beliefs.[7]

---

[1] M. Birks, Gentlemen of the Law (1960), p. 113.

[2] In, for example, A New Dialogue Between an Excise-Man and a Bailiff, Proving which of the Two Is the Greatest Cheats (1703), and The Second Part of the Locusts: Or, Chancery Painted to the Life (1704).   [3] Holmes, p. 172.

[4] True Characters (1708), p. 4.   [5] Tatler, 6 Apr. 1710, iii. 218–22.

[6] Daniel de Foe's New Invention (1707), p. 3.

[7] W. T. Laprade believed John Bull 'entertained more than it influenced' its

V

True to the allegory's 'little history' genre, and despite the deft idiomatic touches which distinguish the tumbling rhetoric of Diego from the eloquence of Hocus or the irascible bluntness of Frog, the speech of all the characters is based on simple constructions and a limited vocabulary.[1] Arbuthnot thus maintains the linguistic decorum of his low-life fiction and adds stylistic dimensions to his satire. We find Diego (Nottingham) recanting his opinion of 'the ruinous ways of this Law-suit' only a few pages after Polesworth, the narrator, has praised the efforts of the second Mrs. Bull 'to pay *John*'s clamorous Debts that the unfrugal Methods of his last Wife, and this ruinous Law Suit, had brought him into'. This last wife, says Polesworth, 'was very apt to be Cholerick', which gives an ironic twist to turncoat Diego's questioning of her patient successor, 'For God's sake, Madam, why so Cholerick'? Phrase by phrase such parallels build an appropriate linguistic pattern which develops concurrently with the story of a man beset on all sides. 'Counsel won't tick, Sir; *Hocus* [Marlborough] was urging'; but it is his fault that Sir Roger (Harley) has to implement stringent measures 'that the Maids might not run a-tick at the Market'. John had no sooner put this necessary domestic 'Cause in Sir *Roger*'s Hands' but at 'the News . . . the Lawyers . . . were all in an uproar'; just as when his attempt to reflect, in a tradesman's cautious manner, on his legal 'cause' was hindered by his first wife's so arranging matters that 'when *John Bull* came Home he found all his Family in an uproar'. In his senses at last, John complains to his servants and lawyers, 'it was an unfair thing in you, Gentlemen, to take Advantage of my Weakness, to keep a parcel of roaring Bulleys about me . . . never to let me cool'; and he is distressed to see his delirious mother (the Church) throwing 'away her Money upon roaring swearing Bullies . . . that went about the Streets'. He determines 'to leave off . . . his [own] roaring

readers, which is open to question, and 'reflected a state of mind in St. John's group', which is indisputable (*Public Opinion and Politics in Eighteenth Century England*, New York, 1936, pp. 111–12).

[1] Arbuthnot possessed an astute ear for the idioms and rhythms of low-life prose. Although he was not as sensitive to the nuances of usage as his eminent contemporary William Congreve, there are notable similarities between their colloquialisms. Phrases such as 'ten thousand Devils', 'Heart, Blood and Guts', 'as I hope to be saved', and 'Meat, Drink and Cloth', which vivify the farcical antics of Wittoll and Bluffe in *The Old Bachelor* (all occur within 200 lines of Act II) are given respectively to Frog, Bull, Hocus, and Jack by Arbuthnot.

and bullying about the Streets', and he is impervious to the swelling passions of those who, when told of the composition, 'bawl'd . . . roar'd . . . [and] stamp'd with their Feet'. For 'John was promis'd, That the next and the next [legal action] would be the final Determination' by the lawyers; Hocus insisted 'one Verdict more had quite ruin'd old *Lewis* . . . and put you in the quiet Possession of every thing'; John's servants echoed Hocus in their 'constant Discourse . . . one *Term more, and old* Lewis *goes to Pot*'; and South could only add to the chorus that the advantage would be his, since '*there wants but . . . a Verdict or two more, to put me in the quiet Possession of my Honour and Estate*'. When he compares accounts with Frog ('Why all this Higgling. . . . Does this become the Generosity of the Noble and Rich *John Bull*?') he realizes with a shock of recognition, 'That ever the Rich, the Generous *John Bull* . . . should have his Name in an Advertisement, for a Statute of Bankrupt'; and when his second wife asks 'how is it possible for a Man of Business to keep his Affairs even in the World at this rate? Pray God this *Hocus* be honest', she draws his attention to the dishonesty of his chief attorney's plea that, '*to keep things even in the World*', Frog has bankrupted himself. The linguistic echoes express the disparity between Bull's real and Frog's manifestly pretended problems: they also evoke one of the Tory criticisms of a war which, they argued, was fought by Britain to maintain the balance of power whilst her chief ally built an empire behind the façade of agreement with the same principle. Even partisan editors could not claim on the basis of such examples of fine linguistic propriety that Arbuthnot was as expert a satiric technician as Swift; but no critic should be too eager to accept the old charge that the good doctor was so careless and constitutionally light-hearted as to be unaffected by the rage for order.

The web of stylistic parallels combines with a cyclic scheme of disease, intoxication, and madness to present, in concrete fictional terms, the Tory view of history as an endless circle of triumph and defeat in the struggle against barbarism.[1] The Whig Junto was no Walpolean oligarchy, but it was an ominous warning; and the total madness of society in the last book of the *Dunciad* is already foreshadowed in the madness of *John Bull*. It is no coincidence that the lawyers (the war-party and the military), the financiers (the moneyed

---

[1] See Herbert Davis, 'The Augustan Concept of History', *Reason and the Imagination*, ed. J. A. Mazzeo (1962), pp. 213–29, and J. W. Johnson, *The Formation of English Neo-Classical Thought* (Princeton, 1967), pp. 31–68.

Whigs), and Jack (the Dissenters) are all likened to cormorants and harpies: they represent social forces which prey on everything of value in human life. The seriousness of their challenge is witnessed by John's initial madness (which they encouraged) and their ceaseless, purposeful attacks when he struggles out of their clutches into his senses. It is again no coincidence that every major character in the allegory either falls ill or is in some capacity involved with sickness. John's first wife suffers from both her ulcer and the quackery of Cavallo. Even her sober replacement is thrown into a fit by the mad bargain with Frog (the Barrier Treaty), as is Peg by force-feeding (of episcopacy) and old Lord Strutt by the partition of his estate. Quackery spreads through the pamphlets blighting the neighbourhood: Jack, disguised as Trim, attempts to poison his mistress (the Church), who is already delirious after the dubious ministrations of Ptschirnsooker; Frog combines with the servants to keep John drunkenly insane and allies himself with the raving Esquire South to demand that Baboon, now 'a poor old batter'd Fellow', 'should be purg'd, sweated, vomited, and starv'd'. John drinks and roars his way through years of litigation, and Peg is quite right to dismiss his alliances as 'foolish Bargains in his Cups'. The war is an orgy of drunkenness (Polemia 'us'd to come home in her Cups, and break the *China*'), and even John, when sober, admits he 'was always hotheaded'. His servants were partly to blame, for their design was, 'to take Advantage of my Weakness . . . never to let me cool, and make me set my Hands to Papers, when I could hardly hold my pen'. Like Davenant's new Whig, Tom Double, these rogues knew that 'as soon as our Friends the Rabble come to be cool, and think a little, they will look into this and several other Designs we are forming for our own Advantage'.[1] Although contemporary polemic was full of such metaphors, a comparison demonstrates that, here again, Arbuthnot was true to his genius for transforming the crudely subliterate into considerable art.

No age can have been more obsessed with the metaphors of state sickness and madness than was the English Augustan age.[2] Dryden,

---

[1] *Tom Double Return'd* (1702), p. 23.

[2] In *Grub Street: Studies in a Subculture* (1972), pp. 94–9, Pat Rogers explains this obsession with reference to the conditions of London life and the Augustans' traumatic memories of the Great Plague and the Fire of London, both of which became inextricably associated with the contemporaneous social unrest and revolution. The propriety of the 'metaphor of the body politic' and its 'inevitable decay' was confirmed by its monitory use by revered Roman historians such as Livy,

Defoe, Pope, and the hosts of lesser and justifiably anonymous political commentators used such images almost as a reflex action, while Swift (with his unerring instinct for an emotive formula) 'examined' the whole complex of ideas associated with the concept of national madness. He scorned the fallen Godolphin ministry which was 'so blind, as to imagine some Comfort from this fantastical Opinion, that the People of *England* are at present distracted, but will shortly come to their Senses again' when 'they grow cool and sober enough'; he theorized on 'the Causes and Symptoms of a People's Madness'; and he concluded with a reversal of the Whig notion:

By ... Arts, in Conjunction with a great Depravity of Manners, and a weak or corrupt Administration, the Madness of the People hath risen to such a Height, as to break in Pieces the whole Frame of the best instituted Governments. But however, such great Frenzies being artificially raised ... and under a wise steddy Prince, will certainly decline of themselves ... and then the true Bent and Genius of the People will appear. Ancient and Modern Story are full of Instances to illustrate what I say. In our Island we had a great Example of a long Madness in the People [the Civil War], kept up by a thousand Artifices like intoxicating Medicines, until the Constitution was destroyed; yet the Malignity being spent, and the Humour exhausted that served to foment it ... the People suddenly recovered, and peaceably restored the old Constitution. FROM what I have offered, it will be easy to decide, whether this late Change in the Dispositions of the People were a new Madness, or a Recovery from an old One.[1]

Similarly, John's troubles began before the death of Strutt. Even the lawyers admit as much when they ask 'what is Twenty Two Years towards the finishing a Law-suit?'; Jack 'has been mad these Twenty Years'; and Diego has 'been railing these Twenty Years at Esquire *South*, *Frog* and *Hocus*, calling them Rogues and Pick-Pockets'. Nor is the 1688 Revolution seen as an absolute break in the tradition. There are reminders that new priests are but old presbyters, and that John has a history of mental instability stretching back to the time when he 'turned out' his mother in a 'civil war' which some of his servants remember as their finest hour. Happily recovered, John 'wrought himself up to a great steadiness of Mind, to pursue his own Interest through all Impediments' as his enemies become proportionately phrenetic: '*Frog*, who thought of nothing but carrying *John* to the

Polybius, Diodorus, and Dionysius (Johnson, *Formation of English Neo-Classical Thought*, pp. 56–8), all of whom Polesworth claims, in his preface to the last pamphlet, to have copied 'with incredible Pains'.

[1] *Examiner*, 18 Jan. 1710, iii. 64–5.

Market, and there disposing of him as his own proper Goods, was mad to find that *John* thought himself now of Age to look after his own Affairs'—or, in other words, became mad when he found John sane. Resolved 'to traverse this new Project, and to make him uneasie in his own Family [Nic.] had corrupted or deluded most of [John's] Servants into the extravagantest Conceits in the World, that their Master was run mad.' As they assume John's previous role he begins 'to think that they were all enchanted; he enquires about the Age of the Moon, if *Nic.* had not given them some intoxicating *Potion*', and their reaction to the proposed composition is pointedly similar to that of Esquire South, who came to the Salutation (Utrecht) 'stark staring mad' only to be encouraged by Frog who gave him 'Brandy, and clap'd him on the Back, which made him ten times madder'. Here, in Arbuthnot's fictional pattern, is Swift's theory of cyclical politics. Both Tory satirists propose the same concept of national madness recurrent in history, and have the same belief in the English people when under 'steddy' direction; both connect contemporary upheavals, the madness of the Civil War, and that which possessed the nation under William III; and both employ the same metaphorical conflation of madness, disease, and intoxication encouraged by state quacks. It is hardly surprising that Swift so enjoyed his friend's dramatization of common Tory formulae in an entertaining allegory which reiterated his own exploration of them.

But in one respect Arbuthnot pursued the idea of political madness further than Swift, demonstrating that it was not necessarily an unequivocal state, and that it could be a dangerously shifting mixture of true insanity and a calculatingly antic disposition. If there is an ominous regularity about the mental and physical illness in *John Bull*, there is also a consistently pragmatic quality in the ambiguous madness of the forces hostile to its hero. The Whigs and their allies turn John's little world into a bedlam so that they may dupe and defraud the populace. Other Tory satirists had been sounding the same alarm for some years: Swift asked 'by what Motives, or what Management, we are thus become the *Dupes* and *Bubbles* of *Europe*?';[1] Ned Ward, in *The English Foreigners: Or, the Whigs Turn'd Dutchmen* (1712), berated his countrymen as 'the spendthrift Bubbles of the War';[2] and another polemicist made 'bubbling' his sole concern in

---

[1] *Conduct of the Allies*, vi. 40.
[2] *Poetical Entertainer*, iii (1712), p. 10. See also *Poor England Bob'd at Home and Abroad* (bs. 1712).

The Cheating Age Found Out, when Knaves Was Most in Fashion (also
1712), describing *The Many Frauds, Cheats, Abuses, and Vast Sums of
Money that England Had Been Cheated of in this Long, Bloody and Expensive
War*. Arbuthnot blended this proposition with his scheme of metaphorical madness and wove it into the texture of his narrative, as
when John Bull, fascinated by the lawsuit which was ruining him,
'con'd over such a Catalogue of hard Words [law terms], as were
enough to conjure up the Devil; these he used to bubble indifferently
in all Companies'.[1] The innocent hero of the pamphlets is not even
safe from rapacious enthusiasm in the arms of his first wife. She
condemns the 'pragmatical Parson' (Sacheverell) who reveals her
adultery with Hocus, using her epithet in the sense of 'officious,
meddlesome, interfering . . . opinionated, dogmatic',[2] when her own
defence of cuckoldom (a parody of Whig arguments at his trial) is not
only as 'pragmatical' as the sermon which occasioned it, but also
pragmatic in the sense of 'pertaining to . . . practice' or—as Arbuthnot
puts it—scornful of 'the narrow Maxims . . . *That one must not do
Evil, that Good may come of it*'. John's second wife is 'the reverse of the
other', as Frog reveals when he accuses her of 'pragmatical' behaviour.
Her arguments are indeed pragmatic, but in a third sense, 'business-
like, methodical . . . energetic . . . skilled, shrewd'. She is a woman of
strict principle who can say to her husband, 'I don't blame you,
for vindicating your Honour . . . to curb the Insolent, protect the
Oppress'd, recover ones own, and defend what one has, are good
Effects of the Law'; but implicit in such statements is the wife who
balances moral considerations against everyday necessities: 'I wish
every Man had his own; but I still say, that Lord *Strutt*'s Money . . .
chinks as well as Esquire *South*'s. I don't know any other Hold that
we Tradesmen have of these great Folks, but their Interest; buy
dear, and sell cheap, and I'll warrant ye you will keep your Customer.'

---

[1] Such functional puns are common in *John Bull*. For example, one of Arbuthnot's
most daring techniques was to stud his simple linguistic surface with occasional
reminders of the convergent yet separate levels of political history and allegorical
representation. Thus when Cavallo declares of the dying Mrs. Bull, 'her Constitution mends; if she submits to my Government she will . . . dance a Jig next *October*
in *Westminster-Hall*', the entertaining burlesque is brought firmly down to political
earth without a rupture of the allegorical fiction. Another scheme of puns reminds
us that the lawsuit is in reality a bloody war: 'Sometimes *John*'s House was beset
with a whole Regiment of Attorneys Clerks', Sir Roger is obliged to 'charge thro'
an Army of Lawyers', and the second Mrs. Bull finds 'it is impossible to march up
close to the Frontiers of Frugality, without entering the Territories of Parsimony'.

[2] This and the following definitions of pragmatism are all to be found in *OED*.

The Whig *Protestant Post Boy* for 29 April 1712 was outraged by this presentation of the second Mrs. Bull: 'it's impossible for any good Subject to see Her M[ajesty] introduc'd, saying *We have hardly Money to go to Market, and no Body will take our Words for Six Pence*, and not be astonish'd.' At least one opponent had appreciated Arbuthnot's audacity in identifying the Queen so intimately with her ministry. Mrs. Bull is the moderate ideal; she represents all the old Whig virtues in her new Tory policies.

The contrast between Bull's wives is extended to reflect on all the other personifications of modern whiggery in the pamphlets. That 'pragmatical Coxcomb' Jack is one of the new breed; although he is atypically naïve enough 'to try what his [other] new Acquaintance would do for him' in his distress. These same new Whigs, who condoned the partition of Strutt's estate, are uncertain friends and dangerous enemies: 'it was usual for a parcel of Fellows to meet, and dispose of the whole Estates in the Country: *This lies convenient for me*, Tom; *Thou would do more good with that*, Dick.' During the period in which he was prepared to accept such cynical pragmatism John Bull was one of the

> Senseless . . . Modern Whigish Tools,
> Beneath the dignity of *British* Fools!
> With Beef resolv'd, and Fortify'd with Ale.[1]

In his senses he determines to do his duty, but with one eye on his own interests. Utterly confused, the new Whigs turn on each other, achieving only the death of their pathetic adherent, Jack. The smaller allies are insistent in their demands that John should help them achieve precisely the same kinds of objective which the three chief characters hoped to gain by the partition of Strutt's estate, 'Acres that lay convenient for them'. But John is now convinced 'that Justice is a better Rule than Conveniency, for all some People make so slight on't'. He is in the same grimly resolved mood as Defoe's Tom Flockmaker: 'I'm a poor *Clothier* . . . you used to call me a *Whig* . . . and in the Country I am so still; but you *Whigs* in *London*, are turn'd quite another sort of Folk . . . you had rather we should have no Peace, than that it should be made by the Ministry you do not like.'[2] Lewis Baboon 'turned honest' echoes the rational advice of John's second wife almost to the letter: 'I know of no particular Mark of

---

[1] 'Satyr's Address', *Aesop at Court* (1702), p. 13.
[2] *Worcestershire-Queries About Peace* (1711), pp. 9-10.

Veracity, amongst us Tradesmen, but Interest; and it is manifestly mine not to deceive you at this time.' John Bull 'politician' is now sober enough to recognize the truth when he hears it, and he settles the lawsuit to their mutual advantage. Like Sir Roger, another old Whig or new Tory, he has learned to 'talk to . . . [the modern Whigs] in their own way'. He abandons the 'inchanted Island' dream of success at law for the tangible '*inchanted Islands*' offered by Lewis, but he has an uphill battle against his own worst self and a bewildering array of enemies to achieve this sanity. The very form of the domestic history of *John Bull*, which places it at one remove from topicality, demonstrates that the struggle against evil has its centre everywhere and not least in the national consciousness.

VI

John Bull was Arbuthnot's 'party piece' in both senses of the phrase. His pamphlets work sub-literary forms and images into an effervescent but damning satire on whiggism which contains many elements of the Augustan Tory myth as it has been defined by Bernard Schilling and Ronald Paulson.[1] Like *Absalom and Achitophel*, which 'brought all the elements together in a characteristic fiction',[2] *John Bull* presents a drama in which a few honest people defend the monarch and morality against the madness of a fickle public misled by a cunning villain and his rabble. But Arbuthnot created a variation on the theme by conflating the dupe (Absalom) and the populace in the one figure of John himself, and by placing him in an intimate relationship with his two wives, especially the second who represents both Queen and government. In this respect *John Bull* is more tightly knit than its polemic brethren, and is a deliberate simplification of the myth to suggest that 'the Art of Government . . . requires no more in reality, than Diligence, Honesty, and a moderate Share of plain naturall Sense'.[3] Of course *John Bull* is biased, and what Frank Ellis says of the political satirist—'His art requires him to adopt "some partial narrow" view and to hold up to contempt any deviation from this view'[4]— applies in some measure to Arbuthnot's practice. Herman Teerink should have considered this when he attempted to make sense of the chronological waywardness of the pamphlets by his ingenious but

---

[1] See Schilling, *Dryden and the Conservative Myth: A Reading of Absalom and Achitophel* (1961), and Paulson, *The Fictions of Satire* (Baltimore, 1967), pp. 120-8.
[2] Ibid., p. 120.   [3] Swift, *Enquiry*, viii. 139.   [4] Swift, *Contests*, pp. 11-12.

misguided theory of staggered composition.[1] There can have been few alert contemporary readers of the pamphlets who failed to realize that the settlement of accounts in the fifth pamphlet (which takes place during an impasse at the Salutation, and precedes the conference between Bull and Baboon) was a deliberate confusion of the facts to gloss over a political embarrassment: the examination of domestic abuses and Dutch deficiencies was undertaken by the Commons concurrently with secret negotiations between Britain and France in 1711—negotiations which were expressly forbidden under the terms of the Anglo–Dutch alliance—since these were the twin prongs of a pre-determined campaign to end the war.

Yet for a party work *John Bull* contains some strange admissions. Arbuthnot was clearly unhappy about the wave of Tory hysteria which followed the Sacheverell trial and swept the Harley ministry into power. That ministry is conceded to be parsimonious, and its leader's reaction to the conflict of conscience and political necessity in the Occasional Bill is recorded in a none too flattering manner.

Sir *Roger* (quoth *Habakkuk*) *Jack* has hang'd himself, make haste and cut him down. Sir *Roger* turn'd first one Ear and then t'other, not understanding what he said.

 Hab. I tell you *Jack* has hang'd himself up.
 Sir *Roger.* Who's hang'd?
 Hab. *Jack.* . . .
 Sir *Roger.* Then let him hang. I don't wonder at it, the Fellow has been mad these twenty Years. With this he slunk away.

This is not the mere pose of a satirist concerned to appear objective so that his polemic may carry more force: it is a direct condemnation of the ministry his pamphlets were designed to support. Of course, satire and propaganda can be uneasy associates. Swift seems to have felt satire to be proper and effective in inverse proportion to his own involvement with the business of government; and the ironic gaiety of the *Tale of a Tub* largely disappeared from his work for Harley (when he was the linchpin of the propaganda effort), only to reappear sobered by pessimism in the virtuosity of *Gulliver's Travels*, written in physical and political isolation. Perhaps Arbuthnot was never in such close liaison with Harley and Bolingbroke. He was certainly never so committed to party political propaganda as his friend. Indeed, the broad movement of the allegory suggests that Arbuthnot

[1] Teerink, pp. 18–38.

could never have been an outright party writer, for he shows little confidence in political man as a species. Jack's demise is the ironic consequence of an unprecedented act of trust; Peg's relationship with John reflects little credit on either; and although John may be forgiven his reaction to the death of his first wife, when he 'quickly got the better of his Grief, and being that neither his Constitution, nor the Affairs of his Family could permit him to live in an unmarried state, he resolved to get him another Wife', yet the reader cannot have much confidence that the wheel of his madness will ever cease turning when the changes in political climate that make and break governments are built into his 'Constitution'. Such reservations are implicit in Arbuthnot's manipulation of history to point moral lessons by means of a domestic fiction full of proverb, adage, and fabular echoes, all of which serve the same functions as Dryden's biblical allegory and generalizing language in *Absalom and Achitophel*, to the same end of confirming that the satire is concerned as much with political man as with a particular series of events.

The deceptive urbanity of *John Bull* is enhanced by the sheer *joie de vivre* of Arbuthnot's burlesque satire on events such as the passage of the Occasional Bill, or the Utrecht conferences. Richmond P. Bond has written of the early eighteenth century: 'Burlesque prose was not so prominent as burlesque drama or poetry. Satirical prose . . . abounded . . . but the lack of an outstanding body of burlesque prose may be attributed partly to the inability to distinguish forms so readily as in the case of poetry.'[1] Arbuthnot's deliberate choice of primitive raw materials from Grub Street for his artful allegory provided those distinguishable forms and, as Patricia Carstens has argued,[2] made him a worthy successor to Samuel Butler. His independence of mind did the rest.

Arbuthnot was a man of intellectual aloofness. . . . His opinion of the people of his age was not flattering, and he escaped cynicism only by the kindness of his heart. . . . It is true that his satire dealt with current topics, but he never . . . identified himself with public movements. Thus his Toryism consisted only in a greater readiness to deride the opposite side, but it did not secure the Tories from derision.[3]

Many party writers claimed that 'the distinction' between political

---

[1] *English Burlesque Poetry* (Cambridge (Mass.), 1932), pp. 231–2.
[2] Carstens, pp. 24–33.
[3] F. Turner, *The Element of Irony in English Literature* (Cambridge, 1926), pp. 46, 52.

groups 'was more nominal than real', but few meant it so honestly
and none dramatized the absurdities of political life with such a
consistently mischievous sense of humour. *John Bull* is but a short
step away from the *Poem Address'd to the Quidnunc's* (1724),[1] which
compares political life with the mindless existence of a monkey tribe.
Occasionally one monkey more enterprising than the rest climbs to
the top of the tree until, stepping on a branch too frail to bear his
weight, he falls into the river and is carried away to the momentary
confusion of his fellows:

> Each trembles for the publick Weal,
> And, for a while, forgets to steal.
> A while, all Eyes intent and steddy,
> Pursue him, whirling down the Eddy.
> But out of Mind when out of View,
> Some other mounts the Twig anew;
> And Business, on each Monkey Shore,
> Runs the same Track it went before.

---

[1] *The Quidnuncki's*, as it was reprinted in the 1727 *Miscellanies*, has often been
attributed to Gay, but was almost certainly written by Arbuthnot (see Beattie,
pp. 285–7).

NOTE ON THE TEXT

OUR copy-text is the first edition of the 1712 pamphlets. The verbal changes found in the genuinely new editions among the London 'editions' (i.e. the 'sixth edition' of pamphlet I and the 'second edition, corrected' of pamphlet V) are so few, so isolated, so insignificant, and often so careless that there is insufficient evidence of authorial revision to warrant their inclusion. Indeed, they are characteristic of the normal compositorial differences between contemporary reprints. We have therefore minimized editorial tinkering with the copy-text, according to modern bibliographical practice and on the principle that the reader should be presented with a *John Bull* which retains the physical character of the originals in so far as this does not conflict with clarity and accuracy. Of course it is not the job of editors to produce a facsimile, and we have corrected obvious typographical errors and made changes when sense demanded them. Many of these changes were previously made in editions to which we allow no bibliographical authority, such as the 1712 Edinburgh or the 1712 *Miscellanies* text; but every variation from the copy-text, whether prefigured by an earlier edition or introduced here for the first time, is our responsibility and is detailed in the textual notes, as are all the variants of the 1712 London reimpressions.

So that the reader might have a preliminary guide to the major events and personages of the allegory, and might the more readily reconstruct the 1727 *Miscellanies* text, we have given the annotations of that edition at the foot of each page and listed its substantive variants in the textual notes.

PRINCIPAL CHARACTERS

PAMPHLET I

The late Lord Strutt	Charles II, King of Spain, died 1700.
The Parson	Cardinal Portocarrero of Toledo.
The cunning Attorney	Marshal d'Harcourt, French Ambassador to Spain in 1697 and 1701.
Philip Baboon, Lord Strutt	Philip, Duke of Anjou, King of Spain from 1700.
Esquire South	Charles, Archduke of Austria, pretender to the Spanish crown and (after 1711) Emperor Charles VI.
John Bull	The English people.
Nicholas Frog	The Dutch people.
Lewis Baboon	Louis XIV of France.
Bull's first wife	The Godolphin ministry (1702–10) and its supporters.
The Tradesmen	Smaller states allied to England and Holland.
Ned the Chimney-sweep	Victor Amadeus, Duke of Savoy.
Tom the Dustman	Peter II, King of Portugal.
Humphrey Hocus	John Churchill, First Duke of Marlborough.
Hocus's wife	Sarah Jennings, Duchess of Marlborough.
The Parson of the Parish	Henry Sacheverell.
Signior Cavallo	Charles Seymour, Sixth Duke of Somerset.
Cavallo's wife	Elizabeth Percy, Duchess of Somerset.
Bull's second wife	The Harley ministry (1710–14) and its supporters.
Sir Roger Bold	Robert Harley, from 1711 First Earl of Oxford.
Don Diego Dismallo	Daniel Finch, Second Earl of Nottingham.

PAMPHLET II

Second Guardian (also 'Cuckold of Dover' in III and Dick the Butler, V)	Thomas, First Earl of Wharton.
Third Guardian (also Chum, III)	Charles Spencer, Third Earl of Sunderland.
Signior Benenato (also Hocus's clerk, I)	Prince Eugene of Savoy.

PAMPHLET III

Sir Humphrey Polesworth	Sir Humphrey Mackworth.
Bull's mother (also Martin)	The Church of England.
Bull's sister Peg	The Scots people.
Jack	Protestant Dissenters, particularly Calvinists.
Signiora Bubonia (also Peter)	The Roman Catholic Church.
Bull's bookkeeper, Sir William Crawly	Sidney, First Earl of Godolphin.
Yan Ptschirnsooker (also 'Dragon of Hockley')	Gilbert Burnet, Bishop of Salisbury.
Bull's nephew	The Elector of Hanover, later George I.
Young Necromancer	Edward Harley.

PAMPHLET IV

Timothy Trim	'Jack' in political disguise.
Habbakuk Slyboots (also John the Barber, V)	John, First Lord Somers.

PAMPHLET V

Harry	Henry St. John, from 1711 Viscount Bolingbroke.

L A W

IS A

𝕭𝖔𝖙𝖙𝖔𝖒𝖑𝖊𝖘𝖘-𝕻𝖎𝖙.

Exemplify'd in the C A S E of

The Lord *Strutt*, *John Bull*,

Nicholas Frog, and *Lewis Baboon*.

Who spent all they had in a Law-Suit.

Printed from a Manuscript found in the Cabinet of the famous Sir Humphry Polesworth.

L O N D O N:
Printed for *John Morphew*, near *Stationer's-Hall*, 1712. Price 3*d*.

THE

CONTENTS.

CHAP. I.

Law is a Bottomless-Pit.

CHAP. I.

The Occasion of the Law-Suit.

I Need not tell you of the great Quarrels that have happen'd in our Neighbourhood, since the Death of the late [a] Lord *Strutt*; how the [b] Parson and a cunning Attorney, got him to settle his Estate upon his Cousin *Philip Baboon*, to the great Disappointment of his Cousin Esquire *South*. Some stick not to say, that the Parson and the Attorney forg'd a Will, for which they were well paid by the Family of the *Baboons*: Let that be as it will, it is matter of Fact, that the Honour and Estate have continued ever since in the Person of *Philip Baboon*.

You know that the Lord *Strutts* have for many Years been possess'd of a very great Landed Estate, well condition'd, wooded, water'd, with Coal, Salt, Tin, Copper, Iron, &c. all within themselves; that it has been the Misfortune of that Family, to be the Property of their Stewards, Tradesmen, and inferior Servants, which has brought great Incumbrances upon them; at the same time, not abating of their expensive way of Living, has forc'd them to Mortgage their best Manors: It is credibly reported, that the Butchers and Bakers Bills of a Lord *Strutt* that lived Two hundred Years ago, are not yet paid.

When *Philip Baboon* came first to the Possession of the Lord *Strutt*'s Estate, his [c] Tradesmen, as is usual upon such Occasions, waited upon him to wish him Joy, and bespeak his Custom: The two chief were [d] *John Bull* the Clothier, and [e] *Nic. Frog* the Linnendraper; they told him, that the *Bulls* and *Frogs* had serv'd

[a] *Late* K[ing]. *of* S[pain].　　　　　　　[b] *Card*[inal]. P[orto]c[arrer]o.
[c] *The first Letters of Congratulation from* K[ing]. W[illiam] *and the States of* H[ollan]d, *upon* K[ing]. P[hilip]'s *Accession to the Crown of* Sp[ain].
[d] *The English.*　　　　　　　　　　　　[e] *The Dutch.*

the Lord *Strutts* with Drapery Ware for many Years; that they
were honest and fair Dealers; that their Bills had never been
question'd; that the Lord *Strutts* lived generously, and never used
to dirty their Fingers with Pen, Ink and Counters; that his Lord-
5 ship might depend upon their Honesty, that they would use him
as kindly as they had done his Predecessors. The Young Lord
seem'd to take all in good part, and dismiss'd them with a deal
of seeming Content, assuring them he did not intend to change
any of the honourable Maxims of his Predecessors.

10   CHAP. II.

How Bull *and* Frog *grew jealous that the Lord* Strutt *intended to give
all his Custom* [a] *to his Grandfather* Lewis Baboon.

IT happen'd unfortunately for the Peace of our Neighbourhood,
that this Young Lord had an old cunning Rogue (or as the
15 *Scots* call it) a *false Loon*, of a Grandfather, that one might justly
call a *Jack of all Trades*; sometimes you would see him behind his
Counter selling Broad Cloath, sometimes measuring Linnen, next
Day he would be dealing in Mercery Ware; high Heads, Ribbons,
Gloves, Fans and Lace he understood to a Nicety; *Charles Mather*
20 could not Bubble a young Beau better with a Toy; nay, he would
descend ev'n to the selling of Tape, Garters, and Shooe-Buckles:
When Shop was shut up, he would go about the Neighbourhood
and earn Half a Crown by teaching the young Men and Maids to
Dance. By these Methods he had acquir'd immense Riches, which
25 he used to squander away at Back-Sword, Quarter-Staff, and
Cudgell-Play, in which he took great Pleasure, and challeng'd all
the Country. You will say it is no wonder if *Bull* and *Frog* should be
jealous of this Fellow.

'It is not impossible (says *Frog* to *Bull*) but this old Rogue will
30 'take the Management of the young Lord's Business into his
'Hands; besides, the Rascal has good Ware, and will serve him as

[a] *The Character and Trade of the* French *Nation. The King's Disposition to* War.

'cheap as any Body in that Case: I leave you to judge what must
'become of us and our Families, we must starve or turn Journeymen
'to old *Lewis Baboon*; therefore, Neighbour, I hold it advisable,
'that we write to young Lord *Strutt* to know the Bottom of this
'Matter.   5

CHAP. III.

A Copy of Bull *and* Frog's *Letter to Lord* Strutt.

My LORD,

I *Suppose your Lordship knows that the* Bulls *and the* Frogs *have served
the Lord* Strutts *with all Sorts of Drapery Ware, time out of Mind;*   10
*and whereas we are jealous, not without Reason, that your Lordship intends
henceforth to buy of your Grandsire old* Lewis Baboon; *this is to inform
your Lordship, that this Proceeding does not suit with the Circumstances of
our Families, who have lived and made a good Figure in the World by the
Generosity of the Lord* Strutts: *Therefore we think fit to acquaint your* 15
*Lordship, that you must find sufficient Security to us, our Heirs and Assigns,
that you will not employ* Lewis Baboon, *or else we will take our Remedy
at Law, clap an Action upon you of* 2000l. *for old Debts, seize and distrain your Goods and Chattels, which, considering your Lordships Circumstances, will plunge you into Difficulties, from which it will not be easie* 20
*to extricate your self; therefore we hope, when your Lordship has better
considered on it, you will comply with the Desire of*

Your loving Friends,

John Bull,

Nic. Frog.   25

Some of *Bull*'s Friends advised him to take gentler Methods with
the young Lord; but *John* naturally lov'd rough Play. It is impossible
to express the Surprize of the Lord *Strutt* upon the Receipt of this
Letter; he was not flush in *Ready*, either to go to Law or clear old
Debts, neither could he find good Bail: He offer'd to bring Matters 30
to a friendly Accommodation; and promis'd upon his Word of
Honour, that he would not change his Drapers; but all to no

purpose, for *Bull* and *Frog* saw clearly, that old *Lewis* would have the Cheating of him.

CHAP. IV.

How Bull *and* Frog *went to Law with Lord* Strutt *about the Premises,*
5 *and were joined by the rest of the Tradesmen.*

ALL Endeavours of Accomodation between Lord *Strutt* and his
Drapers prov'd vain, Jealousies encreas'd, and indeed it was
rumour'd abroad that Lord *Strutt* had bespoke his new Liveries of
old *Lewis Baboon.* This coming to Mrs. *Bull*'s Ears, when *John Bull*
10 came Home he found all his Family in an uproar. Mrs. *Bull* you
must know was very apt to be Cholerick. [a] *You Sot,* says she,
*you loyter about Alehouses and Taverns, spend your Time at Billiards,
Nine-pins or Puppet-shows, or flaunt about the Streets in your new gilt
Chariot, never minding me nor your numerous Family; don't you hear how*
15 Lord Strutt *has bespoke his Liveries at* Lewis Baboon's *Shop? don't you
see how that old Fox steals away your Customers, and turns you out of your
Business every day, and you sit like an idle Drone with your hands in your
Pockets? Fie upon't, up Man, rouse thy self; I'll sell to my Shift before
I'll be so used by that Knave.* You must think Mrs. *Bull* had been
20 pretty well tun'd up by *Frog,* who chim'd in with her learn'd
Harangue. No further delay now, but to Counsel learned in the
Law they go, who unanimously assur'd 'em both of the Justice and
infallible Success of their Law-Suit.

I told you before, that old *Lewis Baboon* was a sort of a *Jack of all*
25 *Trades,* which made the rest of the Tradesmen jealous, as well as
Bull and *Frog;* they hearing of the Quarrel, were glad of an Opportunity of joining against old *Lewis Baboon,* provided that *Bull*
and *Frog* would bear the Charges of the Suit; even Lying *Ned* the
Chimney-sweeper and *Tom* the Dustman put in their Claims, and
30 the Cause was put into the Hands of *Humphrey Hocus* the Attorney.
A Declaration was drawn up to shew, 'That *Bull* and *Frog* had

---

[a] *The Sentiments and Addresses of the* P[arliamen]*t at that Time.*

'undoubted Right by Prescription to be Drapers to the Lord *Strutts*;
'that there were several old Contracts to that purpose; that *Lewis*
'*Baboon* had taken up the Trade of Clothier and Draper, without
'serving his Time, or purchasing his Freedom; that he sold Goods
'that were not Marketable, without the Stamp; that he himself was 5
'more fit for a Bully than a Tradesman, and went about through
'all the Country Fairs challenging People to fight Prizes, Wrestling
'and Cudgel-Play: and abundance more to this purpose.

CHAP. V.

The true Characters of John Bull, Nic. Frog, *and* Hocus. [a] 10

FOR the better understanding the following History, the
Reader ought to know, That *Bull*, in the main, was an honest
plain-dealing Fellow, Cholerick, Bold, and of a very unconstant
Temper, he dreaded not Old *Lewis* either at Back-Sword, single
Faulcion, or Cudgel-play; but then he was very apt to quarrel with 15
his best Friends, especially if they pretended to govern him: If
you flatter'd him, you might lead him like a Child. *John*'s Temper
depended very much upon the Air; his Spirits rose and fell with
the Weather-glass. *John* was quick, and understood his business
very well, but no Man alive was more careless, in looking into his 20
Accounts, or more cheated by Partners, Apprentices, and Servants:
This was occasioned by his being a Boon-Companion, loving his
Bottle and his Diversion; for to say Truth, no Man kept a better
House than *John*, nor spent his Money more generously. By plain
and fair dealing, *John* had acquir'd some Plumbs, and might have 25
kept them, had it not been for his unhappy Law-Suit.

Nic. Frog was a cunning sly Whoreson, quite the reverse of
John in many Particulars; Covetous, Frugal; minded domestick
Affairs; would pine his Belly to save his Pocket, never lost a Farth-
ing by careless Servants, or bad Debtors: He did not care much 30

[a] *Characters of the* E[ngli]sh *and* D[utc]h, *and the* G[enera]l, D[uke]. *of* M[arl-
borough].

for any sort of Diversions, except Tricks of *High German* Artists, and *Leger de main*; no Man exceded *Nic.* in these, yet it must be own'd, That *Nic.* was a fair Dealer, and in that way had acquir'd immense Riches.

5   *Hocus* was an old cunning Attorney, what he wanted of Skill in Law, was made up by a Clerk which he kept, that was the prettiest Fellow in the World; he lov'd Money, was smooth-tongu'd, gave good Words, and seldom lost his Temper: He was not worse than an Infidel; for he provided plentifully for his Family, but he lov'd
10 himself better than them all: He had a termagant Wife, and, as the Neighbours said, was plaguy Hen-peck'd; he was seldom observed, as some Attornies will practice, to give his own personal Evidence in Causes; he rather chose to do it *per test. conduct.* in a word, the Man was very well for an Attorney.

---

15   CHAP. VI.

Of the various Success of the [a] *Law-Suit.*

LAW is a Bottomless-Pit, it is a Cormorant, a Harpy, that devours every *thing; John Bull* was flatter'd by his Lawyers that his Suit would not last above a Year or two at most; that before that time he
20 would be in quiet possession of his Business; yet ten long Years did *Hocus* steer his Cause through all the *Meanders* of the Law, and all the Courts; no Skill, no Address, was wanting; and to say Truth, *John* did not starve the Cause; there wanted not *Yellow-boys* to fee Counsel, hire Witnesses, and bribe Juries. Lord *Strutt* was generally
25 Cast, never had one Verdict in his favour; and *John* was promis'd, That the next and the next would be the final Determination; but alas! that final Determination, and happy Conclusion was like an inchanted Island, the nearer *John* came to it, the further it went from him: New Tryals upon new Points still arose; new Doubts,
30 new Matters to be cleared; in short, Lawyers seldom part with so good a Cause till they have got the Oyster, and their Clients the

[a] *The Success of the War*

Shell. *John*'s ready Mony, Book-Debts, Bonds, Mortgages, all went into the Lawyers Pockets; then *John* began to borrow Money upon *Bank-Stock*, *East-India* Bonds, now and then a Farm went to Pot: At last it was thought a good Expedient to set up Esquire *South*'s Title to prove the Will forg'd, and dispossess *Philip* Lord 5 *Strutt* at once; here again was a new Field for the Lawyers, and the Cause grew more intricate than ever. *John* grew madder and madder; where-ever he met any of Lord *Strutt*'s Servants he tore off their Cloaths: Now and then you would see them come home naked, without Shoes, Stockings, and Linnen. As for Old *Lewis* 10 *Baboon*, he was reduc'd to his last Shift, tho' he had as many as any other: His Children were reduced from rich Silks to *Doily* Stuffs, his Servants in Rags and bare-footed, instead of good Victuals, they now lived upon Neck-Beef, and Bullocks-Liver; in short, no Body got much by the Matter, but the Men of Law.   15

CHAP. VII.

How John Bull *was so mightily pleas'd with his Success, that he was going to leave off his Trade, and turn Lawyer.*

IT is wisely observed by a great Philosopher, That Habit is a second Nature: This was verify'd in the Case of *John Bull*, who 20 from an honest and plain Tradesman, had got such a haunt about the Courts of Justice, and such a Jargon of Law-words, That he concluded himself as able a Lawyer, as any that pleaded at the Bar, or sat on the Bench: He was overheard one Day, talking to himself after this manner, "[a] How capriciously does Fate or 25 "Chance dispose of Mankind? How seldom is that Business "allotted to a Man for which he is fitted by Nature? It is plain, I "was intended for a Man of Law: How did my Guardians mistake "my Genius, in placing me, like a mean Slave, behind a Counter? "Bless me! What immense Estates these Fellows raise by the Law? 30 "Besides, it is the Profession of a Gentleman: What a Pleasure it is

[a] *The Manners and Sentiments of the Nation at that Time.*

"to be victorious in a Cause? To swagger at the Bar? What a Fool
"am I to drudge any more in this Woollen Trade? for a Lawyer
"I was born, and a Lawyer I will be; one is never too Old to learn.
All this while *John* had con'd over such a Catalogue of hard Words,
5 as were enough to conjure up the Devil; these he used to bubble
indifferently in all Companies, especially at Coffee-houses; so that
his Neighbour Tradesmen began to shun his Company as a Man
that was crack'd. Instead of the Affairs of *Blackwell-Hall*, and Price
of Broad-cloath, Wool, and Bayses, he talk'd of nothing but *Actions*
10 *upon the Case, Returns, Capias, Alias capias, Demurrers, Venire facias,*
Replevins, Superseda's, Certiorari's, Writs of Error, Actions of Trover and
Conversion, Trespasses, Precipes & Dedimus: This was matter of Jest
to the learned in Law; however *Hocus*, and the rest of the Tribe,
encourag'd *John* in his Fancy, assuring him, That he had a great
15 Genius for Law; That they question'd not but in time, he might
raise Money enough by it to reimburse him of all his Charges;
That if he study'd, he would undoubtedly arrive to the Dignity of
a Lord Chief Justice; as for the Advice of honest Friends and Neighbours, *John* despis'd it; he look'd upon them as Fellows of a low
20 Genius, poor grovelling Mechanicks; *John* reckon'd it more
Honour to have got one favourable Verdict, than to have sold a
Bale of Broad-cloath. As for *Nic. Frog*, to say the Truth, he was more
prudent, for tho' he follow'd his Law-Suit closely, he neglected not
his ordinary Business, but was both in Court and in his Shop at the
25 proper Hours.

CHAP. VIII.

How John *discover'd that* Hocus *had an Intrigue with his Wife*, [a] *and*
what follow'd thereupon.

JOhn had not run on a madding so long, had it not been for an
30 extravagant Bitch of a Wife, whom *Hocus* perceiving *John* to be
fond of, was resolv'd to win over to his side. It is a true saying,

[a] *The Opinion at that time of the* G[enera]*ls tampering with the* P[arliamen]*t.*

That the last Man of the Parish that knows of his Cuckoldom, is himself.
It was observed by all the Neighbourhood, that *Hocus* had Dealings
with *John*'s Wife, that were not so much for his Honour; but this
was perceiv'd by *John* a little too late: She was a luxurious Jade,
lov'd splendid Equipages, Plays, Treats and Balls, differing very   5
much from the sober Manners of her Ancestors, and by no means
fit for a Tradesman's Wife. *Hocus* fed her Extravagancy (what was
still more shameful) with *John*'s own Money. Every body said that
Hocus had a Months mind to her Body; be that as it will, it is matter
of Fact, that upon all occasions she run out extravagantly on the   10
Praise of *Hocus*. When *John* us'd to be finding fault with his Bills,
she us'd to reproach him as ungrateful to his greatest Benefactor;
One that had taken so much pains in his Law-Suit, and retriev'd his
Family from the Oppression of Old *Lewis Baboon*. A good swinging
Sum of *John*'s readiest Cash, went towards building of *Hocus*'s   15
Country-House. This Affair between *Hocus* and Mrs. *Bull* was
now so open, that all the World were scandaliz'd at it; *John* was not
so Clod-pated, but at last he took the Hint. [a] The Parson of the
Parish preaching one Day a little sharply against Adultery, Mrs.
Bull told her Husband, That he was a very uncivil Fellow to use   20
such coarse Language before People of Condition, That *Hocus* was
of the same mind, and that they would join to have him turn'd
out of his Living for using personal Reflections. How do you mean,
says *John*, by personal Reflections? I hope in God, Wife, he did
not reflect upon you. "No, thank God, my Reputation is too well   25
"established in the World to receive any hurt from such a foul-
"mouth'd Scoundrel as he; his Doctrine tends only to make Hus-
"bands Tyrants, and Wives Slaves; must we be shut up, and
"Husbands left to their liberty? Very pretty indeed; a Wife must
"never go abroad with a Platonick to see a Play or a Ball, she must   30
"never stir without her Husband; nor walk in *Spring-Garden* with a
"Cousin. I do say, Husband, and I will stand by it, That without
"the innocent Freedoms of Life, Matrimony would be a most
"intolerable State; and that a Wife's Vertue, ought to be the result
"of her own Reason, and not of her Husband's Government; for   35
"my part, I would scorn a Husband that would be Jealous, if he

[a] *The Story of* Dr. Sacheverel, *and the resentment of the* H[ouse] *of* C[ommon]*s.*

"saw a Fellow a-bed with me". All this while *John*'s Blood boil'd in his Veins, he was now confirm'd in all his Suspicions; Jade, Bitch and Whore were the best Words that *John* gave her. Things went from better to worse, 'till Mrs. *Bull* aim'd a Knife at *John*, tho'
5 *John* threw a Bottle at her Head very brutally indeed: After this there was nothing but Confusion; Bottles, Glasses, Spoons, Plates, Knives, Forks, and Dishes flew about like Dust, the result of which was, [a] That Mrs. *Bull* receiv'd a bruise in her Right-side, of which she dy'd half a Year after: The Bruise imposthumated, and
10 afterwards turn'd to a stinking Ulcer, which made every body shie to come near her she smelt so; yet she wanted not the help of many able Physicians, who attended very diligently, and did what Men of Skill could do, but all to no purpose, for her Condition was now quite desperate, all regular Physicians and her nearest Relations
15 having giv'n her over.

CHAP. IX.

How Signior Cavallo, *an* Italian *Quack, undertook to Cure Mrs.* Bull
of her Ulcer [b].

THere is nothing so impossible in Nature, but Mountebanks
20 will undertake; nothing so incredible, but they will affirm: Mrs. *Bull*'s Condition was look'd upon as desperate by all the Men of Art; then Signior *Cavallo* judged it was high time for him to interpose, he bragg'd that he had an infallible Ointment and Plaister, which being applied to the Sore would Cure it in a few
25 days; at the same time he would give her a Pill that would purge off all her bad Humours, sweeten her Blood, and rectifie her disturb'd Imagination: In spite of all Signior *Cavallo*'s Applications the Patient grew worse, every Day she stank so no Body durst come within a Stone's throw of her, except Signior *Cavallo* and his

[a] *The Opinion of the Tories, about the* H[ouse]. *of* C[ommon]*s*.
[b] *Endeavours and Hopes of some people, to hinder the dissolution of that* P[arliamen]*t*.

Wife, whom he sent every Day to Dress her, she having a very gentle soft Hand. All this while Signior apprehended no Danger. If one ask'd him how Mrs. *Bull* did? Better and better, says Signior *Cavallo*; the Parts heal, and her Constitution mends; if she submits to my Government, she will be abroad in a little time. Nay it is 5 reported, that he wrote to her Friends in the Country, that she should dance a Jig next *October* in *Westminster-Hall*; that her Illness had been chiefly owing to bad Physicians. At last Signior one Day was sent for in great haste, his Patient growing worse and worse; when he came he affirmed, that it was a gross Mistake, that she 10 was never in a fairer way: Bring hither the Salve, says he, and give her a plentiful Draught of my Cordial. As he was applying his Ointments, and administring the Cordial, the Patient gave up the Ghost, to the great Confusion of Signior *Cavallo*, and the great Joy of *Bull* and his Friends. Signior flung away out of the House in 15 great disorder, and swore there was foul Play, for he was sure his Medicines were infallible. Mrs. *Bull* having dy'd without any Signs of Repentance or Devotion, the Clergy would hardly allow her Christian Burial. The Relations had once resolved to sue *John* for the Murder, but considering better of it, and that such a Trial 20 would rip up old Sores, and discover things not so much to the Reputation of the Deceased, they drop'd their Design. She left no Will, only there was found in her strong Box the following Words wrote on a scrip of Paper, *My Curse on* John Bull *and all my Posterity*, *if ever they come to any Composition with my Lord* Strutt. There were 25 many Epitaphs writ upon her, one was as follows;

> *Here lies* John's *Wife,*
> *Plague of his Life;*
> *She spent his Wealth,*
> *She wrong'd his Health,*   30
> *And left him Daughters three*
> *As bad as she.*

The Daughters [a] Names were *Polemia*, *Discordia* and *Usuria*.

[a] *War, Faction, and Usury.*

CHAP. X.

Of John Bull's *second Wife, and the good Advice that she gave him* [a].

JOHN quickly got the better of his Grief, and being that neither his Constitution, nor the Affairs of his Family could permit him to live in an unmarried State, he resolved to get him another Wife; A Cousin of his last Wife's was propos'd, but *John* would have no more of the Breed: In short, he wedded a sober Country Gentlewoman, of a good Family, and a plentiful Fortune; the reverse of the other in her Temper, not but that she lov'd Mony, for she was of a saving Temper, and apply'd her Fortune to pay *John*'s clamorous Debts, that the unfrugal Methods of his last Wife, and this ruinous Law Suit, had brought him into. One day, as she had got her Husband in good Humour, she talk'd to him after the following manner. 'My Dear, since I have been your Wife I have 'observ'd great Abuses and Disorders in your Family; your Ser- 'vants are mutinous and quarrelsome, and cheat you most abomin- 'ably; your Cook-Maid is in a Combination with your Butcher, 'Poulterer and Fishmonger; your Butler purloins your Liquor, and 'your Brewer sells your Hogwash; your Baker cheats both in 'Weight and in Tale; even your Milkwoman and your Nursery- 'Maid have a Fellow-feeling; your Taylor, instead of Shreds, 'cabages whole Yards of Cloath; besides leaving such long Scores, 'and not going to Market with ready Mony, forces us to take bad 'Ware of the Tradesmen, at their own Price. You have not posted 'your Books these Ten Years; how is it possible for a Man of 'Business to keep his Affairs even in the World at this rate? 'Pray 'God this *Hocus* be honest; would to God you would look over his 'Bills, and see how Matters stand between *Frog* and you; prodigious 'Sums are spent in this Law Suit, and more must be borrow'd of 'Scriveners and Usurers at heavy Interest; besides, my Dear, let me 'beg of you to lay aside that wild Project of leaving your Business 'to turn Lawyer, for which, let me tell you, Nature never design'd

[a] *A new* P[arliamen]*t, the aversion of a Tory* H[ouse] *of* C[ommon]*s to War.*

'you. Believe me, these Rogues do but flatter, that they may
'pick your Pocket.' *John* heard her all this while with patience, 'till
she prick'd his Maggot, and touch'd him in the tender point; then
he broke out into a violent Passion, 'What, I not fit for a Lawyer!
'let me tell you, my Clodpated Relations spoil'd the greatest   5
'Genius in the World, when they bred me a Mechanick. Lord
'*Strutt* and his old Rogue of a Grandsire have found to their Cost,
'that I can manage a Law Suit as well as another. I don't deny what
'you say, says Mrs. *Bull*, nor do I call in question your Parts, but I
'say it does not suit with your Circumstances; you and your Pre-   10
'decessors have liv'd in good Reputation among your Neighbours
'by this same Cloathing Trade, and it were madness to leave it off.
'Besides, there are few that know all the Tricks and Cheats of these
'Lawyers; does not your own Experience teach you how they have
'drawn you on from one Term to another, and how you have   15
'danc'd the Round of all the Courts, still flattering you with a
'final Issue, and for ought I can see your Cause is not a bit clearer
'than it was seven Years ago. I will be Damn'd, says *John*, if I
'accept of any Composition from *Strutt* or his Grandfather; I'll
'rather wheel about the Streets an Engine to grind Knives and   20
'Scissors; however I'll take your Advice, and look over my Accounts.

CHAP. XI.

How John *look'd over his Attorney's Bill.* [a]

WHEN *John* first brought out the Bills, the Surprize of all the
Family was unexpressible, at the prodigious Dimensions of   25
them; in short, they would have measur'd with the best Bale of
Cloath in *John*'s Shop. Fees to Judges, puny Judges, Clerks,
Prothonotories, Philizers, Chirographers, Underclerks, Proclama-
tors, Counsel, Witnesses, Jury-men, Marshals, Tipstaffs, Cryers,
Porters; for Enrollings, Exemplifications, Bails, Vouchers, Returns,   30
Caveats, Examinations, Filings of Words, Entries, Declarations,

[a] *Looking over the Accompts.*

Replications, Recordats, *Nolle Prosequi's, Certiorari's, Mittimus,*
Demurrers, Special Verdicts, Informations, *Scire Facias, Supersedeas,*
Habeas Corpus, Coach-hire, Treating of Witnesses *&c. Verily,* says
John, there are a prodigious Number of learned Words in this Law, what
5 *a pretty Science it is! Ay, but Husband, you have paid for every Syllable*
and Letter of these fine Words; bless me, what immense Sums are at the
bottom of the Accompt! John spent several Weeks in looking over his
Bills, and by comparing and stating his Accompts, he discovered
that, besides the Extravagance of every Article, he had been
10 egregiously Cheated; that he had paid for Counsel that were never
fee'd, for Writs that were never drawn, for Dinners that were never
dress'd, and Journeys that were never made: In short, that *Hocus*
and *Frog* had agreed to throw the Burden of the Law-Suit upon
his Shoulders.

---

15   CHAP. XII.

How John *grew Angry, resolved to accept a Composition;* [a] *and what*
Methods were practis'd by the Lawyers for keeping him from it.

WELL might the Learn'd *Daniel Burgess* say, *That a Law-Suit*
is a Suit for Life. He that sows his Grain upon Marble, will
20 have many a hungry Belly before Harvest. This *John* felt by woful
Experience. *John's* Cause was a good milch Cow, and many a
Man subsisted his Family out of it. However *John* began to think it
high time to look about him; he had a Cousin in the Country, one
Sir *Roger Bold,* whose Predecessors had been bred up to the Law,
25 and knew as much of it as any body; but having left off the Profession for some time, they took great pleasure in Compounding
Law-Suits amongst their Neighbours, for which they were the
Aversion of the Gentlemen of the Long Robe, and at perpetual
War with all the Country Attorneys. *John* put his Cause in Sir
30 *Roger's* Hands, desiring him to make the best of it; the News had no
sooner reach'd the Ears of the Lawyers, but they were all in an

[a] *Talk of Peace; and the struggle of the Party against it.*

uproar [a]: They brought all the rest of the Tradesmen upon *John*: 'Squire *South* swore he was betray'd, that he would starve before he compounded; *Frog* said he was highly wrong'd; ev'n lying *Ned* the Chimney-sweeper, and *Tom* the Dust-man complain'd, that their Interest was sacrific'd: [b] As for *Hocus*'s Wife, she took a Hackney-   5 Chair and came to *John*'s House immediately, and fell a scolding at his Wife like the Mother of *Belzebub*, 'You silly, aukward, ill-bred, 'Country Sow you, have you no more Manners than to rail at my 'Husband, that has sav'd that Clod-pated, Numskull'd Ninny-'hammer of yours from Ruin, and all his Family? it is well known   10 'how he has rose early and sate up late to make him easy, when he 'was Sotting at every Ale-house in Town. I knew his last Wife, she 'was a Woman of breeding, good humour, and complaisance, knew 'how to live in the World; as for you, you look like a Puppet mov'd 'by Clock-work; your Cloaths hang upon you, as they were upon   15 'Tenter-hooks, and you come into a Room as you were going to 'steal away a Piss-pot; get you gone into the Country to look after 'your Mothers Poultry, to milk the Cows, churn the Butter, and 'dress up Nosegays for a Holy-day, and meddle not with Matters 'that you know no more of, than the Sign-post before your Door: 20 'It is well known that my Husband has an establish'd Reputation, 'he never swore an Oath, nor told a Lie in all his Life: He is grateful 'to his Benefactors, faithful to his Friends, liberal to his Dependants, 'and dutiful to his Superiours; he values not your Money more than 'the Dust under his Feet, but he hates to be abus'd: Once for all,   25 'Mrs. *Mynx*, leave off talking of my Husband, or I will pull out 'these Saucer-Eyes of yours, and make that red-streak Country-'face look as raw as an Ox-Cheek upon a Butcher's Stall; remember, 'I say, that there are Pillories and Ducking-stools'. With this, away she flung, leaving Mrs. *Bull* no time to reply: No Stone was left   30 unturn'd to fright *John* from this Composition. Sometimes they spread Reports at Coffee-houses, that *John* and his Wife were run mad; that they intended to give up House, and make over all their Estate to old *Lewis Baboon*; That *John* had been often heard talking to himself, and seen in the Streets without Shoes or Stockings;   35

[a] *The endeavours made use of to stop the Treaty of Peace.*
[b] *Reflections upon the* H[ouse] *of* C[ommon]*s, as ignorant, who knew nothing of Business.*

That he did nothing from Morning to Night but beat his Servants, after having been the best Master alive; as for his Wife, she was a meer Natural. Sometimes *John*'s House was beset with a whole Regiment of Attorneys Clerks, Bailiff and Bailiffs-Followers, and 5 other small retainers of the Law, who threw Stones at his Windows, and Dirt at himself, as he went along the Street. When *John* complain'd of want of ready Money to carry on his Suit, they advis'd him to pawn his Plate and Jewels, and that Mrs. *Bull* should sell her Linnen and wearing Cloaths.

10   CHAP. XIII.

How the Lawyers agreed to send Don Diego Dismallo, *the Conjurer,* to John Bull, *to dissuade him from making an end of his Law-Suit; and what pass'd between them.*

Bull. HOW does my good Friend *Don Diego*?
15   *Don.* Never worse. Who can be easie when their Friends are playing the Fool?
   Bull. But then you may be easie, for I am resolv'd to play the Fool no longer: I wish I had hearken'd to your Advice, and compounded this Law-Suit sooner.
20   *Don.* It is true; I was then against the ruinous ways of this Law-Suit, but looking over my Scheme since, I find there is an Error in my Calculation. *Sol* and *Jupiter* were in a wrong House, but I have now discovered their true Places: I tell you I find the Stars are unanimously of Opinion, That you will be successful in this Cause; 25 That *Lewis* will come to an untimely End, and *Strutt* will be turn'd out of Doors by his Wife and Children. Then he went on with a Torrent of Eclypticks, Cycles, Epicycles, Ascendants, Trines, Quadrants, Conjunctions, Bulls, Bears, Goats, and Rams, and abundance of hard Words, which being put together, signify'd nothing. *John* 30 all this while stood gaping and staring, like a Man in a Trance.

FINIS.

JOHN BULL

In His SENSES:

BEING THE

SECOND PART

OF

Law is a Bottomleſs-Pit.

Printed from a Manuſcript found in the Cabinet of the famous Sir Humphry Poleſworth.

******
****
**

LONDON:
Printed for *John Morphew,* near *Stationer's-Hall,* 1712.　Price 3*d.*

x

CONTENTS.

John Bull in his Senses.

CHAP. I.

Mrs. Bull*'s Vindication of the indispensable Duty of Cuckoldom, in-cumbent upon Wives, in case of the Tyranny, Infidelity, or Insufficiency of Husbands: Being a full Answer to the Doctor's Sermon against* Adultery [a].

JOHN found daily fresh Proofs of the Infidelity and bad 5 Designs of his deceas'd Wife; amongst other Things, one Day looking over his Cabinet, he found the following Paper.

IT is evident that Matrimony is founded upon an original Con-tract, whereby the Wife makes over the Right she has by the Law of Nature to the *Concubitus vagus*, in favour of the Husband, 10 by which he acquires the Property of all her Posterity; but then the Obligation is mutual: And where the Contract is broken on one side, it ceases to bind on the other; where there is a Right, there must be a Power to maintain it, and to punish the offending Party. This Power I affirm to be that Original Right, or rather that 15 indispensable Duty of Cuckoldom, lodg'd in all Wives, in the Cases above-mention'd. No Wife is bound by any Law to which she her self has not consented: All Oeconomical Government is lodg'd originally in the Husband and Wife, the executive part being in the Husband, both have their Privileges secur'd to them by Law and 20 Reason; but will any Man infer from the Husband's being invested with the executive Power, that the Wife is depriv'd of her Share, and that which is the principal Branch of it, the original Right of Cuckoldom? and that she has no remedy left but *Preces & Lacrymae*, or an Appeal to a supreme Court of Judicature? No less frivolous 25 are the Arguments that are drawn, from the general Appellations and Terms of Husband and Wife; a Husband denotes several

[a] *The Tories representation of the Speeches at* Sacheverel*'s Trial.*

different sorts of Magistracy, according to the Usages and Customs of different Climates and Countries; in some Eastern Nations it signifies a Tyrant, with the absolute Power of Life and Death. In *Turkey* it denotes an Arbitrary Governor, with power of perpetual
5 Imprisonment; in *Italy* it gives the Husband the power of Poison and Padlocks; in the Countries of *England, France* and *Holland*, it has quite a different Meaning, implying a free and equal Government, securing to the Wife, in certain Cases, the liberty of Cuckoldom, and the property of Pin-money and separate Maintenance; so
10 that the Arguments drawn from the terms of Husband and Wife are fallacious, and by no means fit to support a tyrannical Doctrine, as that of absolute unlimited Chastity, and conjugal Fidelity.

The general Exhortations to Chastity in Wives, are meant only for Rules in ordinary Cases, but they naturally suppose the three
15 Conditions of Ability, Justice and Fidelity, in the Husband; such an unlimited, uncondition'd Fidelity in the Wife could never be supposed by reasonable Men; it seems a reflexion upon the Ch[ur]ch, to charge her with Doctrines that countenance Oppression.

This Doctrine of the original Right of Cuckoldom is congruous
20 to the Law of Nature, which is superior to all human Laws, and for that I dare appeal to all Wives: It is much to the Honour of our *English* Wives, that they have never given up that *fundamental Point*; and that tho' in former Ages they were muffled up in Darkness and Superstition, yet that Notion seem'd engraven on their
25 Minds, and the Impression so strong, that nothing could impair it.

To assert the Illegality of Cuckoldom, upon any Pretence whatsoever, were to cast odious Colours upon the married State, to blacken the necessary Means of perpetuating Families: Such Laws can never be suppos'd to have been design'd to defeat the
30 very end of Matrimony, the Propagation of Mankind. I call them necessary Means, for in many Cases what other Means are left? Such a Doctrine wounds the Honour of Families, unsettles the Titles to Kingdoms, Honours and Estates; for if the Actions from which such Settlements spring were illegal, all that is built upon
35 them must be so too; but the last is absurd, therefore the first must be so likewise. What is the Cause that *Europe* groans, at present, under the heavy Load of a cruel and expensive War, but the

tyrannical Custom of a certain Nation, and the scrupulous Nicety of a silly Queen, in not exercising this indispensable Duty of Cuckoldom, whereby the Kingdom might have had an Heir, and a controverted Succession might have been avoided? These are the Effects of the narrow Maxims of your Clergy, *That one must not do* 5 *Evil, that Good may come of it.*

The Assertors of this indefeasible Right, and *Jus Divinum* of Matrimony, do all in their Hearts favour Gallants, and the Pretenders to married Women; for if the true legal Foundation of the married State be once sap'd, and instead thereof tyrannical Maxims 10 introduc'd, what must follow but Elopements, instead of secret and peaceable Cuckoldom?

From all that has been said, one may clearly perceive the Absurdity of the Doctrine of this seditious, discontented, hot-headed, ungifted, unedifying Preacher, asserting, *That the grand Security* 15 *of the matrimonial State, and the Pillar upon which it stands, is founded upon the Wife's belief of an absolute unconditional Fidelity to the Husband's Bed*: By which bold Assertion he strikes at the Root, digs the Foundation, and removes the Basis upon which the Happiness of a married State is built. As for his personal Reflexions, I would gladly 20 know who are those *Wanton Wives* he speaks of? who are those Ladies of high Stations, that he so boldly traduces in his Sermon? It is pretty plain who these Aspersions are aim'd at, for which he deserves the Pillory, or something worse.

In confirmation of this Doctrine of the indispensable Duty of 25 Cuckoldom, I could deduce the Example of the wisest Wives in all Ages, who by these means have preserv'd their Husband's Families from Ruin and Oblivion, by want of Posterity; but what has been said, is a sufficient Ground for punishing this pragmatical Parson.

CHAP. II.

The two great Parties of Wives, the [a] *Devoto's and the* Hitts.

THE Doctrine of unlimited Chastity and Fidelity in Wives, was universally espous'd by all Husbands, who went about the
5 Country, and made the Wives sign Papers, signifying their utter Detestation and Abhorrence of Mrs. *Bull's* wicked Doctrine of the indispensable Duty of Cuckoldom. Some yielded, others refused to part with their native Liberty; which gave rise to two great Parties amongst the Wives, the *Devoto's* and the *Hitts*. Tho' it must
10 be own'd, the distinction was more nominal than real; for the *Devoto's* would abuse Freedoms sometimes; and those who were distinguish'd by the Name of *Hitts*, were often very honest. At the same time there was an ingenious Treatise came out, with the Title of *Good Advice to Husbands*; in which they are counsell'd not to
15 trust too much to their Wives owning the Doctrine of unlimited conjugal Fidelity, and so to neglect Family Duty, and a due watchfulness over the Manners of their Wives; that the greatest Security to Husbands was a vigorous Constitution, good Usage of their Wives, and keeping them from Temptation; many Husbands
20 having been Sufferers by their trusting too much to general Professions, as was exemplified in the Case of a foolish and negligent Husband, who trusting to the Efficacy of this Principle, was undone by his Wife's Elopement from him.

CHAP. III.

25 *An Account of the Conference between Mrs.* Bull *and* [b] Don Diego Dismallo.

Don Diego. IS it possible, Cousin *Bull*, that you can forget the honourable Maxims of the Family you are come of, and break your word with three of the honestest best meaning

[a] *Those who were for and against the Doctrine of* Nonresistance.
[b] *A Tory Nobleman, who by his influence upon the* H[ouse] *of* C[ommon]*s endeavour'd to stop the Treaty.*

Persons in the World, Esquire *South*, *Frog* and *Hocus*, that have
sacrific'd their Interest to yours? It is base to take Advantage of
their Simplicity and Credulity, and leave them in the lurch at last.

Mrs. Bull. I am sure they have left my Family in a bad Condition, we have hardly Money to go to Market, and no Body will   5
take our Words for Six Pence. [a] A very fine Spark this Esquire
South! My Husband took him in, a dirty, snotty-nos'd Boy, it was
the Business of half the Servants to attend him, the Rogue did
bawl and make such a noise: Sometimes he fell in the Fire and burnt
his Face, sometimes broke his Shins clambering over the Benches,   10
often piss'd a-Bed, and always came in so dirty, as if he had been
dragg'd thro' the Kennel at a Boarding-School. He lost his Money
at Chuck-Farthing, Shuffle-Cap, and All-Fours; sold his Books,
pawn'd his Linnen, which we were always forc'd to redeem. Then
the whole Generation of him are so in love with Bagpipes and   15
Poppet Shows; I wish you knew what my Husband has paid at the
Pastry Cooks and Confectioners for *Naples* Biscuit, Tarts, Custards,
and Sweet-Meats. All this while my Husband consider'd him as a
Gentleman of a good Family that had fallen into Decay, gave him
good Education, and has settled him in a good Credible way of   20
Living, having procur'd him, by his Interest, one of the best Places
of the Country; and what return, think you, does this fine Gentleman make us? he will hardly give me or my Husband a good Word,
or a civil Expression: [b] Instead of plain Sir and Madam (which,
tho' I say it, is our due) he calls us *Goody* and *Gaffer* such a one, that   25
he did us a great deal Honour to Board with us; huffs and dings at
such a rate, because we will not spend the little we have left to get
him the Title and Estate of Lord *Strutt*; and then, forsooth, we shall
have the Honour to be his Woollen-drapers.

D. Diego. And would you lose the Honour of so noble and gener-   30
ous an Undertaking? would you rather accept the scandalous
Composition, and trust that old Rogue, *Lewis Baboon*?

Mrs. Bull. Look you, Friend *Diego*, if we Law it on till *Lewis* turns
honest, I am afraid our Credit will run low at *Blackwell-Hall*; I wish
every Man had his own; but I still say, that Lord *Strutt*'s Money   35

[a] *Something relating to the Manners of a great Prince, Superstition, love of Operas,*
Shows, &c.   [b] *Something relating to Forms and Tithes.*

shines as bright, and chinks as well as Esquire *South*'s. I don't know
any other Hold that we Tradesmen have of these great Folks, but
their Interest; buy dear, and sell cheap, and I'll warrant ye you
will keep your Customer. The worst is, that Lord *Strutt*'s Servants
5 have got such a haunt about that old Rogue's Shop, that it will
cost us many a Firkin of strong Beer to bring them back again, and
the longer they are in a bad Road, the harder it will be to get them
out of it.

D. Diego. But poor *Frog*, what has he done! On my Conscience,
10 if there be an honest, sincere Man in the World, it is that *Frog*.

Mrs. Bull. I think I need not tell you how much *Frog* has been
oblig'd to our [a] Family from his Childhood; he carries his Head
high now, but he had never been the Man he is, without our Help.
Ever since the Commencement of this Law-Suit it has been the
15 Business of *Hocus*, in sharing our Expenses, to plead for *Frog*. *Poor
Frog*, (says he) *is in hard Circumstances, he has a numerous Family, and
lives from Hand to Mouth; his Children don't eat a bit of good Victuals
from one Year's end to the other, but live upon Salt Herring, sowr Crud,
and Bore-cole; he does his utmost, poor Fellow, to keep things even in the
20 World, and has exerted himself beyond his Ability in this Law-Suit, but he
really has not where-withal to go on. What signifies this Hundred Pounds,
place it upon your side of the Account; it is a great deal to poor Frog, and a
Trifle to you.* This has been *Hocus*'s constant Language, and I am sure
he has had Obligations enough to us to have acted another Part.

25 *D. Diego.* No doubt *Hocus* meant all this for the best, but he is a
tender-hearted charitable Man; *Frog* is indeed in hard Circumstances.

Mrs. Bull. Hard Circumstances! I swear this is provoking to the
last degree. [b] All the time of the Law-Suit, as fast as I have
30 Mortgaged, *Frog* has purchas'd: From a plain Tradesman, with a
Shop, Warehouse, and a Country-Hutt, with a dirty Fish-Pond
at the end of it, he is now grown a very rich Country Gentleman,
with a noble-landed Estate, noble Palaces, Manors, Parks, Gardens
and Farms, finer than any we were ever Master of. Is it not strange,
35 when my Husband disburs'd great Sums every Term, *Frog* should

---

[a] *Complaints of the* H[ouse] *of* C[ommon]s *of the unequal burden of the War.*
[b] *The* D[utc]h *acquisitions in* Flanders.

be purchasing some new Farm or Manor? So that if this Law Suit lasts, he will be far the richest Man in his Country. What is worse than all this, he steals away my Customers every Day; I have Twelve of the richest, and the best, that have left my Shop by his Perswasion, and whom, to my certain Knowledge, he has under 5 Bonds never to return again: Judge you if this be neighbourly Dealing.

D. Diego. *Frog* is indeed pretty close in his Dealings, but very honest: You are so touchy, and take things so hotly, I am sure there must be some Mistake in this. 10

Mrs. Bull. A plaguy one indeed! You know, and have often told me of it, how *Hocus* and those Rogues kept my Husband, *John Bull*, drunk for five Years together, with Punch and Strong Waters; I am sure he never went one Night sober to Bed, till they got him to sign the strangest Deed that ever you saw in your Life. The 15 Methods they took to manage him I'll tell you another time, at present I'll only read the Writing.

[a] Articles of Agreement betwixt *John Bull*, Clothier, and *Nicholas Frog*, Linnen-draper.

I. *That for maintaining the ancient good Correspondence and Friendship* 20 *between the said Parties, I* Nicholas Frog *do solemnly engage and promise to keep Peace in* John Bull's *Family; that neither his Wife, Children nor Servants give him any Trouble, Disturbance or Molestation whatsoever, but to oblige them all to do their Duty quietly in their respective Stations: And whereas the said* John Bull, *from the assured Confidence that he has in* 25 *my Friendship, has appointed me Executor of his Last Will and Testament, and Guardian to his Children, I do undertake for me, my Heirs and Assigns, to see the same duly executed and performed, and that it shall be unalterable in all its Parts by* John Bull *or any Body else: For that purpose it shall be lawful and allowable for me to enter his House at any Hour of the Day or* 30 *Night, to break open Bars, Bolts and Doors, Chests of Drawers and strong Boxes, in order to secure the Peace of my Friend* John Bull's *Family, and to see his Will duly executed.*

[a] *The Sentiments of the* H[ouse] *of* C[ommon]*s, and their representation of the* B[arrie]r *Tr*[eat]*y.*

II. *In Consideration of which kind neighbourly Office of* Nicholas Frog, *in that he has been pleas'd to accept of the foresaid Trust, I* John Bull, *having duly consider'd that my Friend* Nicholas Frog *at this time lives in a marshy Soil and unwholesome Air, infested with Fogs and Damps, de-*
5 *structive of the Health of himself, Wife and Children, do bind and oblige me, my Heirs and Assigns, to Purchase for the said* Nicholas Frog, *with the best and readiest of my Cash, Bonds, Mortgages, Goods and Chattels, a landed Estate, with Parks, Gardens, Palaces, Rivers, Fields and Outlets, consisting of as large Extent as the said* Nicholas Frog *shall think fit: And*
10 *whereas the said* Nicholas Frog *is at present hem'd in too close by the* Grounds *of* Lewis Baboon, *Master of the Science of Defence, I the said* John Bull *do oblige my self, with the readiest of my Cash, to Purchase and Enclose the said Grounds, for as many Fields and Acres as the said* Nicholas *shall think fit; to the intent that the said* Nicholas *may have*
15 *free Egress and Regress, without Lett or Molestation, suitable to the Demands of himself and Family.*

III. *Furthermore, the said* John Bull *obliges himself to make the Country-Neighbours of* Nicholas Frog, *allot a certain part of Yearly Rents, to pay for the Repairs of the said landed Estate, to the intent that his good Friend*
20 Nicholas Frog *may be eased of all Charges.*

IV. *And whereas the said* Nicholas Frog *did Contract with the deceased Lord* Strutt *about certain Liberties, Privileges and Immunities, formerly in the Possession of the said* John Bull; *I the said* John Bull *do freely, by these Presents, renounce, quit and make over to the said* Nicholas
25 *the Liberties, Privileges and Immunities contracted for, in as full manner as if they never had belong'd to me.*

V. *The said* John Bull *obliges himself, his Heirs and Assigns, not to sell one Rag of Broad or Coarse Cloath to any Gentleman, within the Neighbourhood of the said* Nicholas, *except in such Quantities and such*
30 *Rates, as the said* Nicholas *shall think fit.*

Sign'd and Seal'd,

John Bull,

Nic. Frog.

The reading of this Paper put Mrs. *Bull* in such a Passion, that she fell downright into a Fit, and they were forc'd to give her a
35 good quantity of the Spirit of Hartshorn before she recover'd. D. *Diego.* Why in such a Passion, Cousin? Considering your

Circumstances at that time, I don't think this such an unreasonable Contract. You see *Frog*, for all this, is religiously true to his Bargain, he scorns to hearken to any Composition without your Privacy.

[a] *Mrs. Bull.* You know the contrary, read that Letter.

[*Reads the Superscription.*] For *Lewis Baboon*, Master of the Noble 5 Science of Defence.

SIR,

I *Understand that you are at this time Treating with my Friend* John Bull, *about restoring the Lord* Strutt's *Custom, and besides allowing him certain Privileges of Parks and Fish-Ponds: I wonder how you, that are a* 10 *Man that knows the World, can talk with that simple Fellow. He has been my Bubble these Twenty Years, and, to my certain knowledge, understands no more of his own Affairs, than a Child in Swadling-Cloaths. I know he has got a sort of a pragmatical silly Jade of a Wife, that pretends to take him out of my Hands, but you and she both will find your selves mistaken,* 15 *I'll find those that shall manage her; and for him, he dares as well be hang'd as make one step in his Affairs, without my consent. If you will give me what you promised him, I will make all things easie, and stop the Deeds of Ejectment against Lord* Strutt; *if you will not, take what follows; I shall have a good Action against you, for pretending to rob me of my* 20 *Bubble. Take this warning from*

Your loving Friend,
Nic. Frog.

I am told, Cousin *Diego*, you are one of those that have undertaken to manage me, and that you have said you will carry a 25 Green Bag your self, rather than we shall make an end of our Law-Suit: I'll teach them and you too to manage.

D. Diego. For God's sake, Madam, why so Cholerick? I say, this Letter is some Forgery, it never enter'd into the Head of that honest Man, *Nic. Frog*, to do any such thing. 30

Mrs. Bull. I can't abide you, you have been railing these Twenty Years at Esquire *South*, *Frog* and *Hocus*, calling them Rogues and Pick-Pockets, and now they are turn'd the honestest Fellows in the World; what is the meaning of all this?

[a] *Secret Negotiations of the* D[utc]h *at that Time.*

C

D. Diego. Pray tell me how you came to employ this Sir *Roger*
in your Affairs, and not think of your old Friend *Diego*?

Mrs. Bull. So, so, there it pinches. To tell you truth, I have employ'd Sir *Roger* in several weighty Affairs, and have found him
5 trusty and honest, and the poor Man always scorn'd to take a
Farthing of me. I have abundance that profess great Zeal, but they
are damnable greedy of the Pence. My husband and I are now in
such Circumstances, that we must be serv'd upon cheaper Terms
than we have been.

10 *D. Diego.* Well, Cousin, I find I can do no good with you, I am
sorry that you will ruin your self by trusting this Sir *Roger*.

CHAP. IV.

How the Guardians of the deceas'd Mrs. Bull's *three Daughters came to*
John, *and what Advice they gave him; wherein is briefly treated the*
15 *Characters of the three Daughters: Also* John Bull's *Answer to the*
three Guardians [a].

I Told you in my first Part, that Mrs. *Bull*, before she departed
this Life, had bless'd *John* with three Daughters; I need not here
repeat their Names, neither would I willingly use any scandalous
20 Reflections upon young Ladies, whose Reputations ought to be
very tenderly handled; but the Characters of these were so well
known in the Neighbourhood, that it is doing them no Injury to
make a short Description of them.

[b] The Eldest was a termagant, imperious, prodigal, lewd,
25 profligate Wench, as ever breath'd; she used to Rantipole about
the House, pinch the Children, kick the Servants, and torture the
Cats and the Dogs; she would rob her Father's strong Box, for
Money to give the young Fellows that she was fond of: She had a
noble Air, and something great in her Mein, but such a noisome
30 infectious Breath, as threw all the Servants that dress'd her into

---

[a] *Concerns of the Party, and Speeches for carrying on the War,* &c. *Sentiments of the*
Tories and H[ouse] *of* C[ommon]*s, against continuing the War, for setting* King Ch[arle]s
upon the Throne of S[pai]n.   [b] *Polemia.*

Consumptions; if she smelt to the freshest Nosegay, it would shrivel and wither as it had been blighted: She us'd to come home in her Cups, and break the *China*, and the Looking-glasses, and was of such an irregular Temper, and so entirely given up to her Passion, that you might argue as well with the Northwind, as with her 5 Ladyship; so Expensive, that the Income of three Dukedoms was not enough to supply her Extravagance. *Hocus* lov'd her best, believing her to be his own, got upon the Body of Mrs. *Bull*.

[a] The second Daughter, born a Year after her Sister, was a peevish, froward, ill-condition'd Creature as ever was born, ugly 10 as the Devil, lean, haggard, pale, with saucer Eyes, a sharp Nose and hunch-back'd, but active, sprightly and diligent about her Affairs. Her Ill-Complexion was occasion'd by her bad Diet, which was Coffee, Morning, Noon and Night. She never rested quietly a Bed, but used to disturb the whole Family with shrieking out in 15 her Dreams, and plague them next Day with interpreting them, for she took them all for Gospel. She would cry out Murder, and disturb the whole Neighbourhood; and when *John* came running down Stairs to enquire what the Matter was, nothing forsooth, only her Maid had stuck a Pin wrong in her Gown. She turn'd 20 away one Servant for putting too much Oil in her Sallad, and another for putting too little Salt in her Water-Gruel. But such as by Flattery had procur'd her Esteem, she would indulge in the greatest Crimes. Her Father had two Coachmen, when one was in the Coach-box, if the Coach swung but the least to one side, she used 25 to shriek so loud, that all the Street concluded she was overturn'd; but tho' the other was eternally Drunk, and had overturn'd the whole Family, she was very angry with her Father for turning him away. Then she used to carry Tales and Stories from one to another, till she had set the whole Neighbourhood together by the Ears; 30 and this was the only Diversion she took pleasure in. She never went abroad, but she brought home such a bundle of monstrous Lyes as would have amaz'd any Mortal, but such as knew her: Of a Whale that had swallow'd a Fleet of Ships; of the Lyons being let out of the *Tower*, to destroy the Protestant Religion; of the Pope's 35 being seen in a Brandy Shop at *Wapping*, and a prodigious strong

[a] *Discordia.*

Man that was going to shove down the *Cupola* of *Paul's*; of Three
millions of Five Pound Pieces that Esquire *South* had found under
an old Wall; of Blazing-Stars, Flying Dragons, and abundance of
such Stuff. All the Servants in the Family made high Court to her,
5 for she Domineer'd there, and turn'd out and in whom she pleas'd;
only there was an old Grudge between her and Sir *Roger*, whom she
mortally hated, and used to hire Fellows to squirt Kennel Water
upon him as he pass'd along the Streets, so that he was forc'd constantly to wear a Surtout of oil'd Cloath, by which means he came
10 home pretty clean, except where the Surtout was a little scanty.

[a] As for the Third, she was a Thief, and a common mercenary
Prostitute, and that without any Solicitation from Nature, for
she own'd she had no Enjoyment. She had no Respect of Persons,
a Prince or a Porter was all one, according as they paid; yea she
15 would leave the finest Gentleman in the World to go to an ugly
pocky Fellow, for Six Pence more. In the practice of her Profession she had amass'd vast Magazines of all sorts of Things; she
had above Five hundred Suits of fine Clothes, and yet went
abroad like a Cynder-Wench: She robb'd and starv'd all the Ser-
20 vants, so that no Body could live near her.

So much for *John*'s three Daughters, which you will say were
Rarities to be fond of. Yet Nature will show it self; no Body could
blame their Relations for taking care of them, and therefore it was
that *Hocus*, with two other of the Guardians, thought it their Duty
25 to take care of the Interest of the three Girls, and give *John* their
best Advice, before he Compounded the Law-Suit.

Hocus. What makes you so shy of late, my good Friend? There's
no Body loves you better than I, nor has taken more pains in your
30 Affairs: As I hop'd to be sav'd I would do any thing to serve you, I
would crawl upon all Four to serve you; I have spent my Health,
and paternal Estate in your Service; I have, indeed, a small Pittance
left, with which I might retire, and with as good a Conscience as any
Man. But the thoughts of this disgraceful Composition so touches
35 me to the Quick, that I cannot sleep: After I had brought the
Cause to the last Stroke, that one Verdict more had quite ruin'd

[a] *Usuria.*

old *Lewis* and Lord *Strutt*, and put you in the quiet Possession of every thing; then to Compound, I cannot bear it. This Cause was my Favourite, I had set my Heart upon it; it is like an only Child, I cannot endure it should miscarry: For God sake consider only to what a dismal Condition old *Lewis* is brought: He is at an end of all $_5$ his Cash, his Attorneys have hardly one Trick left, they are at an end of all their *Chicane*; besides, he has both his Law and his daily Bread now upon Trust: Hold out only one Term longer, and, I'll warrant you, before the next, we shall have him in the *Fleet*. I'll bring him to the Pillory, his Ears shall pay for his Perjuries; for the $_{10}$ Love of God don't Compound, let me be Damn'd if you have a Friend in the World that loves you better than I; there is no Body can say I am Covetous, or that I have any Interest to pursue but yours.

2d Guardian. There is nothing so plain, than that this *Lewis* has a design to Ruin all his neighbouring Tradesmen, and at this time $_{15}$ he has such a prodigious Income, by his Trade of all kinds, that if there is not some stop put to his Exorbitant Riches, he will Monopolize every thing, and no Body will be able to sell a Yard of Drapery or Mercery Ware but himself. I therefore hold it advisable, that you continue the Law-Suit, and burst him at once. My Concern $_{20}$ for the three poor Motherless Children obliges me to give you this Advice, for their Estates, poor Girls, depend upon the Success of this Cause.

3d Guardian. I own this Writ of Ejectment has cost dear, but then consider it is a Jewel well worth the Purchasing, at the Price of all $_{25}$ you have. None but Mr. *Bull*'s declar'd Enemies can say he has any other Security for his Cloathing Trade, but the Ejectment of Lord *Strutt*. The only Question then that remains to be decided, is, Who shall stand the Expences of the Suit? To which the Answer is as plain, Who but he that is to have the Advantage of the Sen- $_{30}$ tence? When Esquire *South* has got Possession of his Title and Honour, is not *John Bull* to be his Clothier? Who then but *John* ought to put him in Possession? Ask but any indifferent Gentleman who ought to bear his Charges at Law? and he will readily answer, his Tradesmen. I do therefore affirm, and I will go to Death with it, $_{35}$ that, being his Clothier, you ought to put him in quiet Possession of his Estate, and with the same generous Spirit you have begun it,

compleat the good Work. If you persist in the bad Measures you
are now in, what must become of the three poor Orphans? My
Heart bleeds for the poor Girls.

John Bull. You are all very eloquent Persons, but give me leave
5 to tell you, that you express a great deal of more Concern for the
three Girls than for me; I think my Interest ought to be consider'd
in the first place. As for you, *Hocus,* I can't but say you have
managed my Law-Suit with great Address, and much to my
Honour; and, tho' I say it, you have been well paid for it; never
10 was Attornies Bill more Extravagant, and, give me leave to say,
there are many Articles which the most griping of your Profession
never demanded. I have trusted you with the disbursing great
Sums of Money, and you have constantly sunk some into your own
Pocket. I tell you I don't like that Sinking. Why must the Burthen
15 be taken off *Frog's* Back, and laid upon my Shoulders? He can drive
about his own Parks and Fields in his gilt Chariot, when I have been
forc'd to Mortgage my Estate! his Note will go farther than my
Bond! Is it not Matter of Fact, that from the richest Tradesman
in all the Country, I am reduced to beg and borrow from Scriveners
20 and Usurers, that suck the Heart, Blood and Guts out of me, and
what was all this for? Did you like *Frog's* Countenance better than
mine? Was not I your old Friend and Relation? Have I not
Presented you nobly? Have I not clad your whole Family? Have
you not had an Hundred Yards at a time, of the finest Cloath in
25 my Shop? Why must the rest of the Tradesmen be not only
indemnified from Charges, but forbid to go on with their own
Business; and what is more their Concern then mine? As to holding
out this Term, I Appeal to your own Conscience, has not that been
your constant Discourse these Six Years, one *Term more, and old*
30 Lewis *goes to Pot*; if thou art so fond of my Cause, be generous for
once, and lend me a brace of Thousands. Ah *Hocus! Hocus!* I know
thee, not a Sous to save me from Goal, I trow. Look ye, Gentlemen,
I have liv'd with Credit in the World, and it grieves my Heart,
never to stir out of my Doors, but to be pull'd by the Sleeve by
35 some Rascally Dun, or another: *Sir, Remember my Bill: There's a*
small Concern of a Thousand Pounds, I hope you think on't, Sir. And to

have these Usurers transact my Debts at Coffee-Houses and Ale-Houses, as if I were going to break-up Shop. Lord! That ever the Rich, the Generous *John Bull*, Clothier, the Envy of all his Neighbours, should be brought to Compound his Debts for Five Shillings in the Pound; and to have his Name in an Advertisement, for a Statute of Bankrupt. The Thoughts of it makes me Mad. I have read some-where in the *Apocrypha*, That one should not *consult with a Woman touching her, of whom she is Jealous; nor with a Merchant, concerning Exchange, nor with a Buyer, of Selling; nor with an unmerciful Man of Kindness*, &c. I could have added one thing more; *Nor with an Attorney, about Compounding a Law-Suit*. This Ejectment of Lord *Strutt* will never do. The Evidence is Crimp; the Witnesses swear backwards and forwards, and Contradict themselves, and his Tenants stick by him. If it were practicable, is it reasonable, that when Esquire *South* is losing his Money to Sharpers and Pick-Pockets, going about the Country with Fidlers and Buffoons, and squandring his Income with Hawks and Dogs, I should lay out the Fruits of my honest Industry in a Law-Suit for him, only upon the hopes of being his Clothier? and when the Cause is over, I shall not have the Benefit of my Project, for want of Money to go to Market. Look ye, Gentlemen, *John Bull* is but a plain Man; but *John Bull* knows when he is ill used. I know the Infirmity of our Family; we are apt to play the Boon-Companion, and throw away our Money in our Cups: But it was an unfair thing in you, Gentlemen, to take Advantage of my Weakness, to keep a parcel of roaring Bulleys about me, Day and Night, with Huzza's, and Hunting-Horns, and Ringing the Changes on Butchers Cleavers; never to let me cool, and make me set my Hands to Papers, when I could hardly hold my Pen. There will come a Day of Reckoning for all that Proceeding. In the mean time, Gentlemen, I beg you will let me into my Affairs a little, and that you would not grudge me very small Remainder of a very great Estate.

CHAP. V.

Esquire South's *Message and Letter to Mrs.* Bull [a].

THE Arguments us'd by *Hocus*, and the rest of the Guardians, had hitherto prov'd insufficient. *John* and his Wife could not be perswaded to bear the Expence of Esquire *South*'s Law-Suit. They thought it reasonable, that since he was to have the Honour and Advantage, he would bear the greatest Share of the Charges; and retrench what he lost to Sharpers, and spent upon Country-Dances, and Puppet-Plays, to apply it to that use. This was not very grateful to the Esquire: Therefore, as the last Experiment, he was resolved to send Signior *Benenato*, Master of his Fox-Hounds, to Mrs. *Bull*, to try what good he could do with her. This Signior *Benenato* had all the Qualities of a fine Gentleman, that were fit to Charm a Lady's Heart; and if any Person in the World could have perswaded her, it was he: But such was her unshaken Fidelity to her Husband, and the constant Purpose of her Mind to pursue his Interest, that the most refined Arts of Gallantry, that were practis'd, could not seduce her Loyal Heart. The Necklaces, Diamond Crosses, and rich Bracelets that were offer'd, she rejected with the utmost Scorn and Disdain. The Musick and Serenades that were given her, sounded more ungratefully in her Ears, than the Noise of a Screech Owl; however she receiv'd Esquire *South*'s Letter, by the Hands of Signior *Benenato*, with that Respect which became his Quality. The Copy of the Letter is as follows; in which you will observe he Changes, a little, his usual Stile.

MADAM,

THE *Writ of Ejectment against* Philip Baboon, *pretended Lord* Strutt, *is just ready to pass; there wants but a few necessary Forms, and a Verdict or two more, to put me in the quiet Possession of my Honour and Estate: I question not, but that, according to your wonted Generosity and Goodness, you will give it the finishing Stroke; an Honour that I would grudge any Body, but your self. In order to ease you of some part of*

---

[a] *Complaints of the deficiencies of the House of* Au[stri]a. *Prince* E[ugene']s *Journey and Message.*

the Charges, I promise to furnish Pen, Ink and Paper, provided you pay for
the Stamps. Besides, I have order'd my Steward to pay, out of the readiest
and best of my Rents, Five Pounds ten Shillings a Year, 'till my Suit is
finished. I wish you Health and Happiness, being, with due Respect,

MADAM,   5
Your assured Friend,
SOUTH.

What Answer Mrs. *Bull* return'd to this Letter, you shall know
in my Third Part, only they were at a pretty good distance in their
Proposals; for as Esquire *South* only offer'd to be at the Charges of 10
Pen, Ink and Paper, Mrs. *Bull* refus'd any more than to lend her
Barge, [a] to carry his Counsel to *Westminster-Hall.*

FINIS.

---

[a] *Sending the* En[glish] *Fl*[eet] *to convey the Forces to* B[ar]c[elon]a.

JOHN BULL
Still
In His SENSES:

BEING THE
THIRD PART
OF
Law is a Bottomlefs-Pit.

Printed from a Manufcript found in the
Cabinet of the famous Sir *Humphry
Polefworth :* And Publifh'd, (as well
as the two former Parts) by the Author of the NEW ATALANTIS.

LONDON:
Printed for *John Morphew,* near *Stationer's-
Hall,* 1712. Price *6d.*

THE

CONTENTS.

CHAP. X.

The Publisher's PREFACE.

THE World is much indebted to the famous Sir *Humphry Polesworth*, for his ingenious and impartial Account of *John Bull*'s Law-suit; yet there is just Cause of complaint against him, in that he retails it only by Parcels, 5 and won't give us the whole Work; This forces me, who am only the Publisher, to bespeak the Assistance of his Friends and Acquaintance, to engage him to lay aside that stingy Humour, and gratify the Curiosity of the Publick, at once. He pleads in excuse, that they are only private Memoirs, wrote for his own Use, in a loose 10 Style, to serve as a help to his ordinary Conversation. I represented to him the good Reception the two first Parts had met, that tho' they had been calculated by him, only for the Meridian of *Grub-street*, yet they were taken notice of by the better sort; that the World was now sufficiently acquainted with *John Bull*, and in- 15 terested it self in his little Concerns. He answer'd with a Smile, that he had indeed some trifling Things to impart that concern'd *John Bull*'s Relations and Domestick Affairs; if these would satisfy me, he gave me free leave to make use of them, because they would serve to make the History of the Law-suit more intelligible. When 20 I had look'd over the Manuscript, I found likewise some further account of the Composition, which perhaps may not be unacceptable to such as have read the two former Parts.

CHAP. I.

The Character of [a] John Bull's Mother. 25

JOHN had a Mother, whom he lov'd and honour'd extremely, a discreet, grave, sober good-condition'd, cleanly old Gentlewoman, as ever liv'd; she was none of your cross-grain'd termagant

[a] *The* C[hurc]*h of* E[*n*glan]d.

scolding Jades, that one had as good be hang'd as live in the House
with, such as are always censuring the Conduct, and telling
scandalous Stories of their Neighbours, extolling their own good
Qualities, and undervaluing those of others. On the contrary,
she was of a meek Spirit, and as she was strictly Virtuous herself,
so she always put the best Construction upon the Words and
Actions of her Neighbours, except where they were irreconcileable
to the Rules of Honesty and Decency. She was neither one of your
precise *Prudes*, nor one of your phantastical old *Belles*, that dress
themselves like Girls of Fifteen; as she neither wore a Ruff, Fore-
head-cloth, nor High-crown'd Hat, so she had laid aside Feathers,
Flowers, and crimpt Ribons in her Head-dress, Furbulow-Scarfs
and Hoop'd-Petticoats. She scorn'd to Patch and Paint, yet she
lov'd to keep her Hands and her Face clean. Tho' she wore no
flaunting lac'd Ruffles, she would not keep her self in a constant
Sweat with greasy Flannel: Tho' her Hair was not stuck with
Jewels, she was not asham'd of a Diamond Cross; she was not like
some Ladies, hung about with Toys and Trinkets, Twiser Cases,
Pocket-Glasses and Essence-Bottles; she us'd only a Gold Watch
and an Almanack, to mark the Hours and the Holy-Days. Her
Furniture was neat and genteel, well fancy'd with *a bon Goust*.
As she affected not the Grandeur of a State with a Canopy, she
thought there was no Offence in an Elbow-Chair; she had laid
aside your Carving, Gilding and Japan Work, as being too apt to
gather Dirt, but she never could be prevail'd upon to part with
plain Wainscot and clean Hangings. There are some Ladies that
affect to smell a stink in every Thing; they are always highly per-
fum'd and continually burning Frankincense in their Rooms; she
was above such Affectation, yet she never would lay aside the Use
of Brooms and scrubbing Brushes, and scrupl'd not to lay her Linnen
in fresh Lavender: She was no less genteel in her Behaviour, well-
bred without Affectation, in the due mean between one of your
affected Cursying pieces of Formality, and your Romps that have
no regard to the common Rules of Civility. There are some Ladies
that affect a mighty regard for their Relations; *We must not eat to
Day, for my Uncle* Tom, *or my Cousin* Betty *dy'd this time ten Years;
Let's have a Ball to Night, it is my Neighbour such a ones Birth-day;*

she look'd upon all this as Grimace; yet she constantly observ'd her Husband's Birth-day, her Wedding-day, and some few more. Tho' she was a truly good Woman, and had a sincere motherly Love for her Son *John*, yet there wanted not those who endeavour'd to create a Misunderstanding between them, and they had so far 5 prevail'd with him once, that he turn'd her out of Doors to his great Sorrow, as he found afterwards, for his Affairs went all at sixes and sevens. She was no less Judicious in the turn of her Conversation and Choice of her Studies, in which she far exceeded all her Sex; your Rakes that hate the Company of all sober, grave 10 Gentlewomen, would bear hers, and she would by her handsome manner of proceeding sooner reclaim than some that were more sower and reserv'd; she was a zealous preacher up of Chastity, and Conjugal Fidelity in Wives, and by no means a Friend to the newfangl'd Doctrine of the *Indispensable Duty of Cuckoldom*: Tho' she 15 advanc'd her Opinions with a becoming Assurance, yet she never usher'd them in, as some positive Creatures will do, with dogmatical Assertions, *This is infallible; I cannot be mistaken; none but a Rogue can deny it*. It has been observ'd, that such People are oftner in the wrong than any Body; tho' she had a thousand good 20 Qualities, she was not without her Faults, amongst which one might perhaps reckon too great Lenity to her Servants, to whom she always gave good Counsel, but often too gentle Correction. I thought I could not say less of *John Bull*'s Mother, because she bears a part in the following Transactions. 25

CHAP. II.

The Character of John Bull's [a] *Sister* Peg, *with the Quarrels that happen'd between Master and Miss, in their Childhood.*

*J*OHN had a Sister, a poor Girl that had been starv'd at Nurse; any Body would have guess'd Miss to have been bred up under 30 the Influence of a cruel Step-Dame, and *John* to be the Fondling of a tender Mother. *John* look'd ruddy and plump, with a pair of

---

[a] *The Nation and Church of* Sc[otlan]d.

Cheeks like a Trumpeter; Miss look'd pale and wan, as if she had
the Green-Sickness; and no wonder, for *John* was the Darling, he
had all the good Bits, was cramm'd with good Pullet, Chicken,
Pig, Goose and Capon, while Miss had only a little Oatmeal and
5 Water, or a dry Crust without Butter. *John* had his golden Pippens,
Peaches and Nectarnes; poor Miss a Crab-Apple, Sloe or a Black-
berry. Master lay in the best Apartment, with his Bed-Chamber
toward the South-Sun. Miss lodg'd in a Garret, expos'd to the
North-Wind, which shrevel'd her Countenance; however, this
10 Usage tho' it stunted the Girl in her Growth, gave her a hardy
Constitution; she had Life and Spirit in abundance, and knew
when she was ill used: Now and then she would seize upon *John*'s
Commons, snatch a Leg of a Pullet, or a bit of good Beef, for which
they were sure to go to Fisticuffs. Master was indeed too strong
15 for her, but Miss would not yield in the least Point, but ev'n
when Master had got her down, she would scratch and bite like a
Tyger; when he gave her a Cuff on the Ear, she would prick him
with her Knitting-Needle. *John* brought a great Chain one Day to
tye her to the Bed-post, for which Affront Miss aim'd a Pen-knife at
20 his Heart: In short, these Quarrels grew up to rooted Aversions,
they gave one another Nick-names, she call'd him *Gundy-guts*, and
he call'd her *Lousy-Peg*: Tho' the Girl was a tight clever Wench as
any was, and thro' her pale Looks, you might discern Spirit and
Vivacity, which made her not indeed a perfect Beauty, but some-
25 thing that was agreeable. It was barbarous in Parents not to take
notice of these early Quarrels, and make them live better together,
such Domestick Fewds proving afterwards the occasion of Misfortunes to them both. [a] *Peg* had indeed some odd Humours and
comical Antipathy, for which *John* would jeer her. "What think
30 "you of my Sister *Peg* (says he) that faints at the Sound of an
"Organ, and yet will dance and frisk at the Noise of a Bagpipe?
"What's that to you, *Gundy-guts*, (quoth *Peg*) every Body's to
"chuse their own Musick." Then *Peg* had taken a Fancy not to say
her *Pater-noster*, which made People imagine strange things of her.
35 Of the three Brothers that have made such a Clutter in the World,
Lord *Peter*, *Martin* and *Jack*; *Jack* had of late been her Inclinations;

[a] *Love of Presbytery.*

Lord *Peter* she detested; nor did *Martin* stand much better in her good Graces, but *Jack* had found the way to her Heart. I have often admir'd what Charms she discover'd in that aukward Booby, till I talk'd with a Person that was acquainted with the Intrigue, who gave me the following Account of it.   5

CHAP. III.

[a] Jack's *Charms, or the Method by which he gain'd* Peg's *Heart.*

IN the first place, *Jack* was a very young Fellow, by much the youngest of the three Brothers, and People indeed wonder'd how such a young upstart Jackanapes shou'd grow so pert and 10 saucy, and take so much upon him. (2.) *Jack* brag'd of greater Abilities than other Men; he was well-gifted, as he pretended; I need not tell you what secret Influence that has upon the Ladies. (3.) *Jack* had a most scandalous Tongue, and persuaded *Peg*, that all Mankind, besides himself, were pox'd by that scarlet-fac'd 15 Whore [b] *Signiora Bubonia.* "As for his Brother Lord *Peter*, the "Tokens were evident in him, Blotches, Scabs, and the Corona: "His Brother *Martin*, though he was not quite so bad, had some "nocturnal Pains, which his Friends pretended were only Scorbu- "tical; but, he was sure, proceeded from a worse Cause." By such 20 malicious Insinuations, he had possess'd the Lady, that he was the only Man in the World, of a sound, pure, and untainted Con- stitution: Tho' there were some that stuck not to say, that *Signiora Bubonia* and *Jack* rail'd at one another, only the better to hide an Intrigue; and, that *Jack* had been found with *Signiora* under his 25 Cloak, carrying her home, in a dark stormy Night. (4.) *Jack* was a prodigious Ogler; he would ogle you the outside of his Eye inward, and the White upward. (5.) *Jack* gave himself out for a Man of a great Estate in the Fortunate Islands, of which the sole Property was vested in his Person: by this Trick he cheated abundance of 30 poor People of small Sums, pretending to make over Plantations in the said Islands; but, when the poor Wretches came there with

[a] *Character of the Presbyterians.*   [b] *The Whore of* Babylon, *or the* Pope.

Jack's Grant, they were beat, mock'd, and turn'd out of doors.
(6.) I told you that *Peg* was whimsical, and lov'd any thing that was
particular: In that way *Jack* was her Man; for he neither thought,
spoke, dress'd, nor acted like other Mortals: He was for your
5 *bold Strokes*; he rail'd at Fops, tho' himself the most affected in the
World; instead of the common Fashion, he would visit his Mistress
in a Mourning-cloak, Band, short Cuffs, and a peaked Beard. He
invented a way of coming into a Room backwards, which he said
shew'd more Humility, and less Affectation; where other People
10 stood, he sat; where they sat, he stood; when he went to Court,
he us'd to kick away the State, and sit down by his Prince, Cheek
by Choul, *Confound these States* (says he) *they are a modern Invention*;
when he spoke to his Prince, he always turn'd his Br[ee]ch upon
him; if he was advis'd to Fast for his Health, he would eat Roast-
15 beef; if he was allow'd a more plentiful Diet, then he would be sure,
that day, to live upon Water-gruel; he would cry at a Wedding,
laugh and make Jests at a Funeral. He was no less singular in his
Opinions; you would have burst your sides to hear him talk
Politicks: [a] "All Government (says he) is founded upon the right
20 "Distribution of Punishments; decent Executions keep the World
"in awe; for that Reason, the majority of Mankind ought to be
"hang'd every Year; for Example, I suppose, the Magistrate ought
"to pass an irreversible Sentence upon all blue-ey'd Children from
"the Cradle; but that there may be some shew of Justice in his
25 "proceeding, these Children ought to be train'd up, by Masters
"appointed for that purpose, to all sorts of Villany, that they may
"deserve their Fate, and the Execution of them may serve as an
"Object of Terror to the rest of Mankind." As to the giving of
Pardons, he had this singular Method, [b] That when these Wretches
30 had the Ropes about their Necks, it should be enquired, who
believ'd they should be hanged, and who not? The first were to be
pardon'd the last hang'd out-right: Such as were once pardon'd,
were never to be hang'd afterwards, for any Crime whatsoever.
He had such skill in Physiognomy, that he would pronounce
35 peremptorily upon a Man's Face, That Fellow (says he) do what

[a] *Absolute Predestination and Reprobation.*
[b] Saving-Faith; *a belief that one shall certainly be sav'd.*

he will, can't avoid Hanging; he has a hanging Look. By the same
Art, he would prognosticate a Principality to a Scoundrel. He was
no less particular in the Choice of his Studies; they were generally
bent towards exploded Chimeras [a], the *perpetuum Mobile*, the
circular Shot, Philosopher's Stone, and silent Gunpowder, making 5
Chains for Fleas, Nets for Flies, and Instruments to unravel Cob-
webs, and split Hairs. Thus, I think, I have given you a distinct
Account of the Methods he practis'd upon *Peg*. Her Brother would
now and then ask her, "What a Devil dost thou see in that prag-
"matical Coxcomb, to make thee so in Love with him? He is a fit 10
"Match for a Tailor or a Shoemaker's Daughter, but not for you
"that are a Gentlewoman. Fancy is free (quoth *Peg*) I'll take my
"awn way, do you take yours: I do no care for your flaunting
"Beaus, that gang with their Breasts open, and their Sarks over
"their Waistcoats, that accost me with set Speeches out of *Sidney*'s 15
"*Arcadia*, or *The Academy of Compliments*. *Jack* is a sober grave
"Youngman; tho' he has none of your study'd Harangues, his
"Meaning is sincere: He has a great Regard to his Father's Will;
"and he that shews himself a good Son, will make a good Husband:
"besides, I know he has the original Deed of Conveyance to the 20
"Fortunate Islands; the others are Counterfeits." There is nothing
so obstinate as young Ladies in their Amours; the more you cross
them, the worse they are.

CHAP. IV.

[b] *How the Relations reconcil'd* John *and his Sister* Peg, *and what* 25
return Peg *made to* John's *Message*.

JOHN BULL, otherwise a good natur'd Man, was very hard-
hearted to his Sister *Peg*, chiefly from an Aversion he had conceived in his Infancy. While he flourish'd, kept a warm House, and
drove a plentiful Trade, poor *Peg* was forc'd to go hawking and 30

[a] *The Learning of the Presbyterians.*
[b] *The Treaty of* Union. *Reason of it, the Succession not being settled in* Sc[otlan]d,
Fears for the Presbyterian Church-Government, and of being burthen'd with the E[ngli]sh
national Debts.

pedling about the Streets, selling Knives, Scissars and Shoe-
buckles; now and then carry'd a Basket of Fish to the Market;
sow'd, spun and knit for a poor Livelihood, till her Fingers-ends
were sore; and when she could not get Bread for her Family, she
5 was forc'd to hire 'em out at Journey-work to her Neighbours:
Yet in these her poor Circumstances, she still preserv'd the Air
and Mien of a Gentlewoman; a certain decent Pride, that extorted
Respect from the haughtiest of her Neighbours; when she came
into any full Assembly, she would not yield the *pas* to the best of
10 them. If one ask'd her, Are not you related to *John Bull*? Yes (says
she) he has the Honour to be my Brother. So *Peg*'s Affairs went,
till all the Relations cry'd out shame upon *John*, for his barbarous
Usage of his own Flesh and Blood; that it was an easie matter for
him to put her in a credible way of living, not only without Hurt,
15 but with Advantage to himself, being she was an industrious
Person, and might be serviceable to him in his way of Business.
Hang her, Jade, (quoth *John*) I can't endure her, as long as she
keeps that Rascal *Jack*'s Company. They told him, the way to
reclaim her was to take her into his House; that by Conversation,
20 the childish Humours of their younger days might be worn out.
These Arguments were enforc'd by a certain Incident. It happen'd
that *John* was at that time about making his [a] Will, and entailing
his Estate, the very same in which *Nic. Frog* is nam'd Executor.
Now his Sister *Peg*'s Name being in the Entail, he could not make a
25 thorough Settlement without her Consent. There was indeed a
malicious Story went about, as if *John*'s last Wife had fall'n in love
with *Jack*, as he was [b] eating Custard a Horseback; that she
perswaded *John* to take his Sister *Peg* into the House, the better
to drive on her Intrigue with *Jack*, concluding he would follow his
30 Mistress *Peg*. All I can infer from this Story, is, that when one has
got a bad Character in the World, People will report and believe
any thing of them, true or false. But to return to my Story; when
Peg receiv'd *John*'s Message, she huff'd and storm'd like the Devil:
'My Brother *John* (quoth she) is grown wondrous kind-hearted
35 'all of a suddain, but I meikle doubt, whether it be not mair for his

[a] *The Act of Succession.*
[b] *A Presbyterian Lord Mayor.*

'awn Conveniency than my good; he draws up his Writs and his
'Deeds, forsooth, and I mun set my Hand to them, unsight unseen.
'I like the young Man he has settled upon well enough, but I
'think I ought to have a valuable Consideration for my Consent:
'He wants my poor little Farm, because it makes a Nook in his 5
'Park-Wall; ye may e'en tell him, he has mair then he makes good
'use of; he gangs up and down drinking, roaring and quarrelling,
'through all the Countrey Merkats, making foolish Bargains in his
'Cups, which he repents when he is sober; like a thriftless Wretch,
'spending the Goods and Gear that his Fore-Fathers won with the 10
'Sweat of their Brows; light come, light go, he cares not a Farthing:
'But why should I stand Surety for his silly Contracts? the little I
'have is free, and I can call it my own; Hame's hame be it never so
'hamely; I ken him well enough, he could never abide me, and
'when he has his ends he'll e'en use me as he did before; I'm sure I 15
'shall be treated like a poor Drudge; I shall be set to tend the
'Bairns, darn the Hose, and mend the Linnen. Then there's no
'living with that auld Carline his Mother, she rails at *Jack*, and
'*Jack*'s an honester Man than any of her Kin: I shall be plagu'd
'with her Spells and her *Pater-nosters*, and silly auld warld Cere- 20
'monies: I mun never pair my Nails on a Friday, nor begin a
'Journy on *Childermas day*, and I mun stand becking and binging as I
'gang out and into the Hall: Tell him he may e'en gan his get, I'll
'have nothing to do with him, I'll stay like the poor Country
'Mouse, in my own Habitation'. So *Peg* talkt; but for all that, by 25
the Interposition of good Friends, and by many a bonny thing that
were sent, and many more that were promis'd *Peg*, the Matter was
concluded, and *Peg* [a] taken into the House upon certain Articles;
one of which was, That she might have the Freedom of *Jack*'s
Conversation, and might take him for Better and for Worse, if she 30
pleas'd; provided always, he did not come into the House at unseasonable Hours, and disturb the Rest of the Old Woman,
John's Mother.

[a] *The Act of Toleration.*

CHAP. V.

[a] *Of some Quarrels that happen'd after* Peg *was taken into the Family.*

IT is an old Observation, that the Quarrels of Relations are harder
to reconcile than any other; Injuries from Friends fret and gall
5 more, and the Memory of them is not so easily obliterated: This is
cunningly represented by one of your old Sages, called *Æsop*, in the
Story of the Bird, that was griev'd extremely, for being Wounded
with an Arrow feather'd with his own Wing; as also of the Oak
that let many a heavy Groan, when he was cleft with a Wedge
10 of his own Timber. There was no Man in the World less subject
to Rancour than *John Bull*, considering how often his good Nature
had been Abus'd; yet I don't know, but he was too apt to hearken
to tatling People, that carried Tales between him and his Sister
Peg, on purpose to sow Jealousies, and set them together by the
15 Ears: They say that there were some Hardships put upon *Peg*, that
had been better let alone; but it was the Business of good People
to restrain the Injuries on one side, and moderate the Resentments
on the other; a good Friend acts both parts, the one without the
other will not do. [b] The Purchase-Money of *Peg*'s Farm was ill
20 paid; then *Peg* lov'd a little good Liquor, and the Servants shut up
the Wine-Cellar [c]; but for that *Peg* found a Trick, for she made a
false Key; *Peg*'s Servants complain'd that they were debar'd from
all manner of Business, and never suffer'd to touch the least thing
within the House; if they offer'd to come into the Warehouse, then
25 strait went the Yard slap over their Noddle; if they ventur'd into
the Counting-Room, a Fellow would throw an Ink-bottle at their
Head; if they came into the best Apartment, to set any thing there
in order, they were saluted with a Broom; if they meddl'd with any
thing in the Kitchen, it was odds but the Cook laid them over the
30 Pate with a Ladle; one that would have got into the Stables, was
met by two Rascals, who fell to work with him with a Brush and a
Curry-comb; some climbing up into the Coach-box, were told, that
one of their Companions had been there before that could not drive,

---

[a] *Quarrels about some of the Articles of Union, particularly the Peerage.*
[b] *The Equivalent not paid.*   [c] Run Wine.

then slap went the long Whip about their Ears: On the other Hand
it was complain'd that *Peg*'s Servants were always asking for [a]
Drink-mony, that they had more than their Share of the *Christmas-box*; to say the truth, *Peg*'s Lads bustl'd pretty hard for that, for
when they were endeavouring to Lock it up, they got in their 5
great Fists, and pull'd out Handfuls of Half-Crowns, some Shillings
and Six-pences, others in the Scramble pick'd up Guineas and
Broad-pieces. But there happen'd a worse thing than all this, it
was complain'd that *Peg*'s Servants had great Stomachs and brought
too many of their Friends and Acquaintance to the Table; that 10
John's Family was like to be Eat out of House and Home. Instead
of regulating this Matter as it ought to be, *Peg*'s young Men were
thrust away from the Table; then there was the Devil and all to do,
Spoons, Plates and Dishes, flew about the Room like mad, and Sir
Roger, who was now *Major Domo*, had enough to do to quiet them. 15
Peg said this was contrary to Agreement, whereby she was in all
things to be treated like a Child of the Family; then she call'd upon
those that had made her such fair Promises, and undertook for her
Brother *John*'s good Behaviour; but alas! to her Cost, she found that
they were the first, and readiest to do her the Injury. *John* at last 20
agreed to this Regulation, that *Peg*'s [b] Footmen might sit with
his Book-keeper, Journey-men and Apprentices; and *Peg*'s better
sort of Servants might sit with his Footmen, if they pleas'd.

Then they began to order Plumb-porridge and Minc'd Pies
for *Peg*'s Dinner: *Peg* told them she had an Aversion to that sort of 25
Food; that upon forcing down a Mess of it some Years ago, it
threw her into a Fit, 'till she brought it up again: Some alledg'd it
was nothing but Humour, that the same Mess should be serv'd
up again for Supper, and Breakfast next Morning; others would
have made use of a Horn, but the Wiser sort bid let her alone, and 30
she might take to it of her own Accord.

[a] *Endeavour'd to get their Share of Places.*
[b] *Articles of Union, whereby they could make a* Scot's *Commoner, but not a Lord, a Peer.*

CHAP. VI.

[a] *The Conversation between* John Bull *and his Wife.*

Mrs. Bull. THO' our Affairs, Honey, are in a bad Condition,
I have a better Opinion of them since you seem
5 to be convinc'd of the ill Course you have been in, and are resolv'd
to submit to proper Remedies. But when I consider your immense
Debts, your foolish Bargains, and the general Disorder of your
Business, I have a Curiosity to know what Fate or Chance has
brought you into this Condition.

10   *J. Bull.* I wish you would talk of some other Subject, the
Thoughts of it make me mad, our Family must have their run.

Mrs. Bull. But such a strange thing as this, never happen'd to
any of your Family before; they have had Law-Suits, but, tho' they
spent the Income, they never Mortgag'd the Stock: Sure you must
15 have some of the *Norman* or the *Norfolk* Blood in you; prithee give
me some Account of these Matters.

J. Bull. Who could help it? There lives not such a Fellow by
Bread, as that Old *Lewis Baboon*, it is the cheatingest, contentious
Rogue, upon the Face of the Earth. You must know, one Day, as
20 *Nic.* Frog and I were over a Bottle making up an old Quarrel, the
old Knave would needs have us drink a Bottle of his *Champagne*, and
so one after another, till my Friend *Nic.* and I, not being used to
such heady Stuff, got bloody Drunk. *Lewis* all the while, either by
the Strength of his Brain, or Flinching his Glass, kept himself
25 sober as a Judge. 'My worthy Friends (quoth *Lewis*) henceforth let
'us live Neighbourly, I am as peaceable and quiet as a Lamb, of
'my own Temper, but it has been my Misfortune to live among
'quarrelsom Neighbours. There is but one thing can make us
'fall out, and that is the Inheritance of Lord *Strutt*'s Estate; I am
30 'content, for Peace sake, to wave my Right, and submit to any
'Expedient to prevent a Law-Suit; I think an [b] equal Division will
'be the fairest way. Well mov'd Old *Lewis* (quoth *Frog*) and I hope
'my Friend *John* here will not be Refractory.' At the same time he

[a] *The History of the* P[a]rt[i]t[io]n *Treaty; Suspicions at that time that the* Fr[ench].
K[ing]. *intended to take the whole, and that he revealed the Secret to the Court of* Sp[ai]n.
    [b] *The* P[a]rt[i]t[io]n *Treaty.*

clap'd me on the Back, and slabber'd me all over from Cheek to
Cheek, with his great Tongue. Do as you please, Gentlemen
(quoth I) 'tis all one to *John Bull*. We agreed to part that Night,
and next Morning to meet at the Corner of Lord *Strutt*'s Park Wall,
with our surveying Instruments, which accordingly we did. Old   5
Lewis carried a Chain and a Semicircle, *Nic.* Paper, Rulers and a
Lead Pencil, and I follow'd at some distance with a long Pole. We
began first with surveying the Meadow-Grounds, afterwards we
measur'd the Corn Fields Close by Close, then we proceeded to the
Wood-Lands, the [a] Copper and Tin Mines. All this while *Nic.* 10
laid down every thing exactly upon Paper, calculated the Acres and
Roods to a great Nicety. When we had finish'd the Land, we were
going to break into the House and Gardens, to take an Inventory
of his Plate, Pictures, and other Furniture.

Mrs. Bull. What said Lord *Strutt* to all this?   15

J. Bull. As we had almost finish'd our Concern, we were accosted by some of Lord *Strutt*'s Servants: 'Hey day, what's here?
'What a Devil's the meaning of all these Trangams and Gim-
'cracks, Gentlemen? What, in the name of Wonder, are you going
'about, jumping over my Master's Hedges, and running your Lines 20
'cross his Grounds? If you are at any Field-Pastime, you might have
'ask'd leave, my Master is a civil well-bred Person as any is.

Mrs. Bull. What could you Answer to this?

J. Bull. Why truly my Neighbour *Frog* and I were still hot-
headed; we told him his Master was an old doating Puppy, that   25
minded nothing of his own Business; that we were Surveying his
Estate, and settling it for him, since he would not do it himself.
Upon this there happen'd a Quarrel, but we being stronger than
they, sent them away with a Flea in their Ear. They went home,
and told their Master, 'My Lord (say they) there are three odd   30
'sort of Fellows going about your Grounds, with the strangest
'Machines that ever we beheld in our Life; I suppose they are going
'to rob your Orchard, fell your Trees, or drive away your Cattle;
'they told us strange things of settling your Estate: One is a lusty
'old Fellow, in a black Wig, with a black Beard, without Teeth;   35
'there's another thick squat Fellow, in Trunk-Hose; the third is a

[a] *The* West-Indies.

'little, long Nos'd, thin Man. (I was then Lean, being just come out
'of a fit of Sickness.) I suppose it is fit to send after them, lest they
'carry something away.

   Mrs. Bull. I fancy this put the Old Fellow in a rare Tweag.

5   *J. Bull.* Weak as he was, he call'd for his long *Toledo*, swore and
bounc'd about the Room, ''Sdeath! what am I come to, to be
'Affronted so by my Tradesmen? I know the Rascals! my Barber,
'Clothier and Linnendraper, dispose of my Estate! bring hither my
'Blunderbuss, I'll warrant ye, you shall see Day-light through
10 'them. Scoundrels! Dogs! the Scum of the Earth! *Frog*, that was
'my Fathers Kitchen-boy, he pretend to meddle with my Estate!
'with my Will! Ah poor *Strutt*, what art thou come to at last, thou
'hast liv'd too long in the World, to see thy Age and Infirmity so
'despis'd? how will the Ghosts of my Noble Ancestors receive these
15 'Tidings? They cannot, they must not sleep quietly in their
'Graves.' In short, the Old Gentleman was carried off in a Fainting
Fit, and after bleeding in both Arms hardly recover'd.

   Mrs. Bull. Really this was a very extraordinary way of Proceeding; I long to hear the rest of it.

20   *J. Bull.* After we had come back to the Tavern, and taken
t'other Bottle of *Champagne*, we quarrell'd a little about the Division
of the Estate; *Lewis* hall'd and pull'd the Map on one side, and
Frog and I on t'other, till we had like to have tore the Parchment to
pieces. At last *Lewis* pull'd out a pair of great Taylor's Shears, and
25 clip'd off a Corner for himself, which he said was a Mannor that lay
convenient for him, and left *Frog* and me the rest to dispose of,
as we pleas'd. We were over-joy'd, to think *Lewis* was contented
with so little, not smelling what was at the bottom of the Plot.
There happen'd, indeed, an Incident, that gave us some Disturb-
30 ance; A Cunning Fellow, one of my Servants, two Days after, peep-
ing through the Key-hole, observ'd that Old *Lewis* had stole away
our part of the Map, and saw him fiddling and turning the Map
from one Corner to the other, trying to join the two pieces together again: He was muttering something to himself, which he did
35 not well hear, only these Words, *'Tis great pity, 'tis great pity!* My
Servant added, that he believ'd this had some ill-meaning; I told
him he was a Coxcomb, always pretending to be wiser than his

Companions: *Lewis* and I are good Friends, he's an honest Fellow, and, I dare say, will stand to his Bargain. The Sequel of the Story prov'd this Fellow's Suspicion to be too well grounded; for *Lewis* reveal'd our whole Secret to the deceas'd Lord *Strutt*, who, in Reward to his Treachery, and Revenge to *Frog* and me, settled his whole Estate upon the present *Philip Baboon*: Then we understood what he meant by piecing the Map together.

Mrs. Bull. And was you surpris'd at this? Had not Lord *Strutt* reason to be Angry? Would you have been contented to have been so us'd your self?

J. Bull. Why, truly Wife, it was not easily reconciled to the common Methods, but then it was the Fashion to do such things: I have read of your Golden Age, your Silver Age, *&c.* one might justly call this the Age of the Lawyers. There was hardly a Man of Substance in all the Country, but had a [a] Counterfeit that pretended to his Estate: As the Philosophers say, that there is a Duplicate of every Terrestrial Animal at Sea, so it was in this Age of the Lawyers, there was at least two of every thing; nay, o'my Conscience, I think there were three [b] Esquire *Hackums* at one time. *Lewis Baboon* entertain'd a Fellow that call'd himself *John Bull*'s Heir; I knew him no more than the Child unborn, yet he brought me into some Trouble and Expence. There was another that pretended to be Esq; *South*; and two Lord *Strutts*, you know. In short, it was usual for a parcel of Fellows to meet, and dispose of the whole Estates in the Country: *This lies convenient for me,* Tom; *Thou would do more good with that,* Dick, *than the Old Fellow that has it.* So to Law they went with the true Owners; the Lawyers got well by it, every Body else was undone. It was a common thing for an honest Man, when he came Home at Night, to find another Fellow domineering in his Family, hectoring his Servants, calling for Supper, and pretending to go to Bed to his Wife. In every House you might observe two *Sosia*'s quarrelling who was Master: For my own part, I am still afraid of the same Treatment, that I should find some Body behind my Counter selling my Broad Cloath.

[a] *Several Pretenders at that Time.*
[b] *Kings of* Po[lan]d.

Mrs. Bull. There are a sort of Fellows that they call Banterers, and Bambouzlers, that play such Tricks; but, it seems, these Fellows were in earnest.

J. Bull. I begin to think that Justice is a better Rule than 5 Conveniency, for all some People make so slight on't.

CHAP. VII.

[a] *Of the hard Shifts Mrs.* Bull *was put to, to preserve the Mannor of* Bullock's Hatch; *with Sir* Roger's *Method to keep off importunate Duns.*

AS *John Bull* and his Wife were talking together, they were 10 surpris'd with a sudden knocking at the Door, *those wicked Scriveners and Lawyers no doubt* (quoth *John*) and so it was; some asking for the Money he ow'd, and others warning to prepare for the approaching Term: *What a cursed Life do I lead* (quoth *John*)? *Debt is like deadly Sin; for God-sake, Sir* Roger, *get me rid of these* 15 *Fellows. I'll warrant you* (quoth Sir *Roger*) *leave them to me.* And indeed it was pleasant enough to observe *Sir Roger*'s Method with these importunate Duns; his sincere Friendship for *John Bull*, made him submit to many things, for his Service, which he would have scorn'd to have done for himself. Sometimes he would stand at the 20 Door with his long Poll to keep off the Duns, 'till *John* got out at the Back-Door. When the Lawyers and Tradesmen brought extravagant Bills, Sir *Roger* us'd to bargain before-hand, for leave to cut off a quarter of a Yard in any part of the Bill he pleased; he wore a pair of Scissars in his Pocket for this purpose, and would 25 snip it off so nicely, as you cannot imagine; like a true Goldsmith he kept all your Holidays; there was not one wanting in his Calender; when ready Money was scarce, he would set them a telling a thousand Pounds in Six-pences, Groats, and Three-penny Pieces: It would have done your Heart good to have seen him charge thro' 30 an Army of Lawyers, Attorneys, Clerks and Tradesmen; some-

[a] *Some attempts to destroy the publick Credit at that Time. Manners of the* E[arl]. *of* O[xford].

times with Sword in Hand, at other times nuzling like an Eel in the
Mud: When a Fellow stuck like a Bur, that there was no shaking
him off, he us'd to be mighty inquistive about the Health of his
Uncles and Aunts in the Country; he could call them all by their
Names, for he knew every Body, and could talk to them in their 5
own way. The extremely Impertinent he would send away to see
some strange Sight, as the Dragon at *Hockley the Hole*; or bid him
call the 30th of next *February*. [a] Now and then you would see him
in the Kitchen, weighing the Beef and Butter, paying ready Money,
that the Maids might not run a-tick at the Market; and the 10
Butchers, by bribing of them, sell Damag'd and Light Meat.
Another time he would slip into the Cellar, and gage the Casks:
In his leisure Minutes he was posting his Books, and gathering in
his Debts; such frugal Methods were necessary where Money was
so scarce, and Duns so numerous. All this while *John* kept his 15
Credit, could show his Head both at *Change* and *Westminster-Hall*;
no Man protested his Bill, nor refus'd his Bond, only the Sharpers
and the Scriveners; the Lawyers and other Clerks pelted Sir *Roger*
as he went along. The Squirters were at it with their Kennel-
Water, for they were mad for the loss of their Bubble, and that they 20
could not get him to Mortgage the Mannor of *Bullocks-Hatch*.
Sir *Roger* shook his Ears, and nuzled along, well-satisfied within
himself that he was doing a charitable Work, in rescuing an
honest Man from the Claws of *Harpies* and *Blood-suckers*. Mrs. *Bull*
did all that an affectionate Wife, and a good Housewife, could do; 25
yet the Boundaries of Virtues are indivisible Lines, it is impossible
to march up close to the Frontiers of Frugality, without entering
the Territories of Parsimony. Your good Housewifes, are apt to
look into the minutest Things [b]: Therefore some blam'd Mrs.
Bull for new heel-piecing of her Shoes, grudging a quarter of a 30
pound of *Soap* and *Sand* to scowre the Rooms, but especially,
[c] that she would not allow her Maids and Apprentices the Benefit
of *John Bunyan*, the *London-Apprentice*, or the *Seven-Champions*, in the
Black Letter.

[a] *Some Regulations as to Purveyance in the* Qu[een']s *Family.*
[b] *Too great savings in the* H[ouse] *of* C[ommon]s.
[c] *Restraining the Liberty of the Press by Act of* P[arliament].

CHAP. VIII.

A Continuation of the Conversation betwixt John Bull *and his Wife.*

Mrs. Bull. IT is a most sad Life we lead, my Dear, to be so teaz'd, paying Interest for old Debts, and still con-
5 tracting new Ones. However, I don't blame you, for vindicating your Honour, and chastizing old *Lewis*; to curb the Insolent, protect the Oppress'd, recover ones own, and defend what one has, are good Effects of the Law: The only thing I want to know, is how you come to make an end of your Mony, before you finish'd
10 your Suit.

John Bull. I was told by the Learned in the Law, that my Suit stood upon three firm Pillars: *More Mony for more Law, more Law for more Mony, and no Composition.* More Mony for more Law, was plain to a Demonstration, for who can go to Law without Mony? and it
15 was as plain, that any Man that has Mony, may have Law for it. The third was as evident as the other two; for what Composition could be made with a Rogue, that never kept a Word he said?

Mrs. Bull. I think you are most likely to get out of this Labyrinth by the second Door, by want of ready Mony to purchase this
20 precious Commodity: But you seem not only to have bought too much of it, but have paid too dear for what you bought; else how was it possible to run so much in Debt, when, at this very time, the yearly Income of what is Mortgag'd to those Usurers would discharge *Hocus*'s Bills, and give you your Belly full of Law, for all
25 your Life, without running one Six Pence in Debt? You have been bred up to Business; I suppose you can Cypher, I wonder you never us'd your Pen and Ink.

J. Bull. Now you urge me too far; prithee, dear Wife, hold thy Tongue. Suppose a young Heir, heedless, raw, and unexperienc'd,
30 full of Spirit and Vigour, with a favourite Passion, in the Hands of Money-Scriveners: Such Fellows are like your Wiredrawing Mills, if they get hold of a Man's Finger, they will pull in his whole Body at last, till they squeeze the Heart, Blood and Guts out of him. [a] When I wanted Money, half a dozen of these Fellows were always

[a] *Methods of preying upon the Necessities of the Government.*

waiting in my Antichamber, with their Securities ready drawn.
I was tempted with the Ready, some Farm or other went to Pot.
I receiv'd with one Hand, and paid it away with the other, to
Lawyers; that, like so many Hell-hounds, were ready to devour
me. Then the Rogues would plead Poverty, and Scarcity of Money, 5
that always ended in receiving Ninety for the Hundred. After they
had got Possession of my best Rents, they were able to supply
me with my own Mony. But what was worse, when I look'd into
the Securities, there was no Clause of Redemption.

Mrs. Bull. No Clause of Redemption, say you; that's hard! 10

John Bull. No great matter, for I cannot pay them. They had
got a worse Trick than that; the same Man bought and sold to
himself, paid the Mony, and gave the Acquittance: The same
Man was Butcher and Grasier, Brewer and Butler, Cook and Poulterer. There is something still worse than all this; there came 15
twenty Bills upon me at once, which I had given Mony to discharge; I was like to be pull'd to Pieces, by Brewer, Butcher, and
Baker, even my Herb-Woman dun'd me as I went along the Streets
(thanks to my Friend Sir *Roger*, else I must have gone to Goal).
When I ask'd the meaning of this, I was told, the Mony went to the 20
Lawyers; Counsel won't tick, Sir; *Hocus* was urging; my Book-
keeper sat Sotting all Day, playing at Putt, and All-fours: In
short, by griping Usurers, devouring Lawyers, and negligent
Servants, I am brought to this pass.

Mrs. Bull. This was hard usage! but methinks, the least re- 25
flection might have retriev'd you.

John Bull. 'Tis true; yet consider my Circumstances, my
Honour was engag'd, and I did not know how to get out; besides,
I was for Five Years often Drunk, always muddl'd, they carried
me from Tavern to Tavern, to Ale-houses and Brandy-shops, 30
brought me acquainted with such strange Dogs: [a] *There goes the
prettiest Fellow in the World* (says one) *for managing a Jury, make him
yours. There's another can pick you up Witnesses. Serjeant such a one has a
Silver Tongue at the Bar.* I believe, in time I should have retain'd
every single Person within the Inns of Court. The Night after a 35
Trial, I treated the Lawyers, their Wives and Daughters, with

[a] *Hiring still more Troops.*

Fiddles, Hautboys, Drums and Trumpets. I was always hot-headed; then they plac'd me in the middle, the Attorneys and their Clerks dancing about me, hooping and hallowing, *Long live* John Bull, *the Glory and Support of the Law*!

5 *Mrs. Bull.* Really, Husband, you went through a very notable Course.

John Bull. One of the things that first alarm'd me was, [a] that they shew'd a Spite against my poor Old Mother; 'Lord (quoth I) 'what makes you so Jealous of a poor, old, innocent Gentlewoman, 10 'that minds only her Prayers, and her Practice of Piety, she never 'meddles in any of your Concerns? Foh (say they) to see a hand- 'some, brisk, genteel, young Fellow, so much govern'd by a doating 'old Woman; why don't you go and suck the Bubby? Do you con- 'sider she keeps you out of a good Jointure? she has the best of your 15 'Estate settled upon her for a Rent-Charge: Hang her, old Thief, 'turn her out of Doors, sieze her Lands, and let her go to Law if she 'dares. Soft and fair, Gentlemen (quoth I) my Mother's my Mother, 'our Family are not of an unnatural Temper. Tho' I don't take 'all her Advice, I won't seize her Jointure; long may she enjoy it, 20 'good Woman, I don't grudge it her: She allows me now and then a 'Brace of Hundreds for my Law-Suit; that's pretty fair.' About this time the old Gentlewoman fell ill of an [b] odd sort of a Distemper; it began with a Coldness and Numbness in her Limbs, which by degrees affected the Nerves (I think the Physicians call them) 25 siez'd the Brain, and at last ended in a Lethargy. It betray'd it self at first in a sort of Indifference and Carelesness in all her Actions, Coldness to her best Friends, and an Aversion to stir or go about the common Offices of Life. She that was the cleanliest Creature in the World, never shrunk now if you set a Close-stool 30 under her Nose. She that would sometimes rattle off her Servants pretty sharply, now if she saw them drink, or heard them talk pro- fanely, never took any notice of it. [c] Instead of her usual Charities to deserving Persons, she threw away her Money upon roaring swearing Bullies, and randy Beggars, that went about the Streets.

[a] *Railing against the Church.*
[b] *Carelesness in Forms and Discipline.*
[c] *Disposing of some Preferments to Libertine and unprincipled Persons.*

What is the matter with the old Gentlewoman (said every Body) *she never us'd to do in this manner?* At [a] last the Distemper grew more violent, and threw her downright into raving Fits; in which she shriek'd out so loud, that she disturb'd the whole Neighbourhood. In her Fits she call'd out upon one Sir *William*; [b] Oh! *Sir* William, *thou hast betray'd me! kill'd me! stabb'd me! sold me to the Cuckold of* Dover! *See, see,* Clum *with his bloody Knife! seize him, seize him, stop him! Behold the Fury, with her hissing Snakes! Where's my Son* John! *is he well! is he well! poor Man, I pity him!* And abundance more of such strange Stuff, that no Body could make any thing of. I knew little of the Matter, for when I enquir'd about her Health, the Answer was, that *she was in a good moderate way*. Physicians were sent for in haste; Sir *Roger*, with great difficulty, brought R[adcli]*ff*; G[ar]*th* came upon the first Message. There were several others call'd in; but, as usual upon such Occasions, they differ'd strangely at the Consultation. At last they divided into two Parties, one sided with G[ar]*th*, and the other with R[adcli]*ff*. [c] *Dr.* G[ar]th. *This Case seems to me to be plainly Hysterical; the Old Woman is Whimsical; it is a common thing for your Old Women to be so: I'll pawn my Life,* Blisters, *with the Steel Diet, will recover her.* Others suggested strong Purging and Letting of Blood, because she was Plethorick. Some went so far as to say the Old Woman was mad, and nothing would do better than a little Corporal Correction. R[adcli]ff. *Gentlemen, you are mistaken in this Case, it is plainly an accute Distemper, and she cannot hold out three Days, without she is supported with strong Cordials.* I came into the Room with a good deal of Concern, and ask'd them what they thought of my Mother? *In no manner of Danger, I vow to God* (quoth G[ar]*th*) *the Old Woman is Hysterical, Fanciful, Sir, I vow to God. I tell you, Sir* (says R[adcli]ff) *she can't live three Days to an end, unless there is some very effectual Course taken with her, she has a Malignant Fever.* Then Fool, Puppy, and Blockhead, was the best Words they gave. I could hardly restrain them from throwing the Ink Bottles at one another's Heads. I forgot to tell you, that one Party of the Physicians desir'd I would take my

[a] *The too violent clamour about the danger of the Church.*
[b] *Sir* William, *a cant Name of Sir* Humphrey's, *for Lord* T[reasure]*r* G[odolphi]n.
[c] G[ar]th *the Low-Church Party.* R[adcli]ff *High-Church Party.*

Sister *Peg* into the House to Nurse her, but the Old Gentlewoman
would not hear of that. At last one Physician ask'd if the Lady had
ever been us'd to take *Laudanum*; her Maid answer'd, not that she
knew; that indeed there was a *High German* Livery-Man of hers,
5 one [a] 𝕯𝖆𝖓 𝕻𝖙𝖘𝖈𝖍𝖎𝖗𝖓𝖘𝖔𝖔𝖐𝖊𝖗, that gave her a sort of a Quack-Powder.
The Physician desir'd to see it; *Nay*, says he, *there is* Opium *in this,
I am sure.*

Mrs. Bull. I hope you examin'd a little into this Matter.

John Bull. I did indeed, and discover'd a great Mystery of
10 Iniquity. The Witnesses made Oath, That they had heard some of
the [b] Livery-men frequently railing at their Mistress. 'They
said, She was a troublesome fiddle faddle old Woman, and so
'ceremonious that there was no bearing of her. They were so
'plagu'd with bowing and cringing as they went in and out of the
15 'Room, that their Backs ach'd; she us'd to scold at one for his dirty
'Shoes, at another for his greasie Hair, and not combing his Head:
'Then she was so passionate and fiery in her Temper, that there was
'no living with her; she wanted something to sweeten her Blood;
'that they never had a quiet Night's rest, for getting up in the
20 'Morning to early Sacraments; that they wish'd they could find some
'way or another to keep the old Woman quiet in her Bed.' Such
Discourses were often overheard among the Livery-men, that the
said 𝕯𝖆𝖓 𝕻𝖙𝖘𝖈𝖍𝖎𝖗𝖓𝖘𝖔𝖔𝖐𝖊𝖗 had undertook this Matter. A Maid made
Affidavit, 'That she had seen the said 𝕯𝖆𝖓 𝕻𝖙𝖘𝖈𝖍𝖎𝖗𝖓𝖘𝖔𝖔𝖐𝖊𝖗, one of the
25 'Livery-Men, frequently making up of Medicines, and administring
'them to all the Neighbours; that she saw him one Morning make
'up the Powder which her Mistress took; that she had the Curiosity
'to ask him whence he had the Ingredients? They come (says he)
'from several Parts of de World; dis I have from *Geneva*, dat from
30 '*Rome*, dis White Powder from *Amsterdam*, and de Red from
'*Edinburgh*; but de chief Ingredient of all comes from *Turkey*.' It was
likewise proved, that the said 𝕯𝖆𝖓 𝕻𝖙𝖘𝖈𝖍𝖎𝖗𝖓𝖘𝖔𝖔𝖐𝖊𝖗 had been frequently seen at the *Rose* with *Jack*, who was known to bear an
inveterate Spite to his Mistress; That he brought a certain Powder
35 to his Mistress, which the Examinant believes to be the same, and

[a] 𝕯𝖆𝖓 𝕻𝖙𝖘𝖈𝖍𝖎𝖗𝖓𝖘𝖔𝖔𝖐𝖊𝖗, *a Bishop at that time a great dealer in Politicks and Physick.*
[b] *The Clergy.*

spoke the following Words; *Madam, here is grand Secret van de Warld; my sweetning Powder, it does temperate de Humour, despel de Windt, and cure de Vapour; it lulleth and quieteth de Animal Spirits, procuring Rest, and pleasant Dreams: It is de infallible Receipt for de Scurvy, all Heats in de Bloodt, and Breaking out upon de Skin; It is de* 5 *true Bloodt Stancher, stopping all Fluxes of de Bloodt. If you do take dis, you will never ail any ding; it will Cure you of all Diseases:* And abundance more to this purpose, which the Examinant does not remember.

John Bull was interrupted in his Story by a Porter, that brought 10 him a Letter from *Nicholas Frog*, which is as follows.

CHAP. IX.

[a] *A Copy of* Nic. Frog's *Letter to* John Bull.

Friend *John*,

[John Bull *W*Hat Schellum *is it that makes thee jealous of thy old* 15
Reads.] *Friend* Nicholas? *Hast thou forgot how some Years ago he took thee out of the* [b] *Spunging-house?* ['Tis true, my Friend *Nic.* did so, and I thank him; but he made me pay a swinging Reck'ning.] *Thou begins now to repent the Bargain that thou wast so fond of; and, if thou durst, would forswear thy own Hand and Seal. Thou sayst, that* 20 *thou hast purchas'd me too great an Estate already; when, at the same time, thou know'st I have only a Mortgage: 'Tis true, I have Possession, and the Tenants own me for Master; but, has not Esquire* South *the Equity of Redemption?* [No doubt, and will redeem it very speedily; poor *Nic.* has only Possession, eleven Points of the Law.] *As for the* [c] *Turn-* 25 *pikes I have set up, they are for other People, not for my Friend* John; *I have order'd my Servant constantly to attend, to let thy Carriages through without paying any thing: only, I hope thou wilt not come too heavy laden, to spoil my Ways. Certainly I have just Cause of Offence against thee, my Friend, for supposing it possible that thou and I should ever quarrel: What Houns-* 30 *foot is it that puts these Whims in thy Head? Ten thousand Last of Devils*

---

[a] *A Letter from the* S[tate]s G[enera]l.   [b] *Alluding to the* Re[volutio]n.
[c] *The* D[ut]ch *prohibition of Trade.*

haul me, if I don't love thee as I love my life. [No question, as the Devil loves Holy-water!] *Does not thy own Hand and Seal oblige thee to purchase for me, till I say it is enough? Are not these Words plain. I say it is not enough. Dost thou think thy Friend* Nicholas Frog *made a Child's*
5   *Bargain? Mark the Words of thy Contract,* tota pecunia, *with all thy Money.* [Very well! I have purchas'd with my own Money, my Childrens, and my Grand-childrens Money, is not that enough? Well, *tota pecunia* let it be, for at present I have none at all: He would not have me purchase with other Peoples Money sure, since *tota*
10 *pecunia* is the Bargain; I think it is plain, no more Money, no more Purchase.] *And whatever the World may say,* Nicholas Frog *is but a poor Man in comparison of the rich, the opulent* John Bull, *great Clothier of the World. I have had many Losses, six of my best Sheep were drown'd, and the Water has come into my Cellar, and spoil'd a Pipe of my best Brandy:*
15 *It would be a more friendly Act in thee, to carry a Brief about the Country to repair the Losses of thy poor Friend. Is it not evident to all the World, that I am still hem'd in by* Lewis Baboon? *is he not just upon my Borders?* [And so he will be if I purchase a thousand Acres more, unless he gets some Body betwixt them.] *I tell thee, Friend* John, *thou hast*
20 *Flatterers, that persuade thee that thou art a Man of Business; do not believe them: If thou would'st still leave thy Affairs in my Hands, thou should'st see how handsomly I would deal by thee. That ever thou should'st be dazzled with the inchanted Islands, and Mountains of Gold, that old* Lewis *promises thee!' Dswounds! why dost thou not lay out thy Money to*
25 *purchase a Place at Court, of honest* Israel? *I tell thee, thou must not so much as think of a Composition.* [Not think of a Composition, that's hard indeed; I can't help thinking of it, if I would.] *Thou complain'st of want of Money, let thy Wife and Daughters burn the Gold-Lace upon their Petticoats; sell thy fat Cattel; retrench but a Sirloin of Beef, and a*
30 *Peck-loaf, in a Week, from thy gormandizing Guts.* [Retrench my Beef, a Dog! Retrench my Beef! then it is plain the Rascal has an ill Design upon me, he would starve me.] *Mortgage thy Manor of* Bullocks-Hatch, *or Pawn thy Crop for Ten Years.* [A Rogue! Part with my Country-Seat, my Patrimony, all that I have left in the World,
35 I'll see him hang'd first.] *Why hast thou chang'd thy Attorney? Can any Man manage thy Cause better for thee?* [Very pleasant! because a Man has a good Attorney, he must never make an End of his Law-

Suit.] *Ah* John, John, *I wish thou knew'st thy own Mind: Thou art as fickle as the Wind. I tell thee, thou had'st better let this Composition alone, or leave it to thy*

Loving Friend,

NIC. FROG.   5

CHAP. X.

Of some extraordinary [a] *Things that pass'd at the* Salutation *Tavern, in the Conference between* Bull, Frog, *Esq;* South, *and* Lewis Baboon.

F*Rog* had given his Word, that he would meet the above-mention'd Company at the *Salutation*, to talk of this Agreement; 10 tho' he durst not directly break his Appointment, he made many a shuffling Excuse; one time he pretended to be seized with the Gout in his right Knee; then he got a great Cold, that had struck him deaf of one Ear; afterwards two of his Coach-Horses fell sick, and he durst not go by Water, for fear of catching an Ague. *John* would 15 take no Excuse, but hurry'd him away: *Come* Nic, (says he) *let's go and hear at least what this old Fellow has to propose; I hope there's no hurt in that. Be it so* (quoth *Nic.*) *but if I catch any harm, woe be to you; my Wife and Children will curse you as long as they live.* When they were come to the *Salutation*, *John* concluded all was sure then, and that 20 he shou'd be troubled no more with Law-Affairs; he thought every body as plain and sincere as he was. *Well Neighbours* (quoth he) *let's now make an end of all Matters, and live peaceably together for the time to come; if every body is as well inclin'd as I, we shall quickly come to the upshot of our Affair: And so pointing to* Frog *to say something, to 25 the great Surprize of all the Company, Frog* was seiz'd with a dead Palsy in the Tongue. *John* began to ask him some plain Questions, and hoop'd and hollow'd in his Ear. *John Bull. Let's come to the Point*, Nic! *Who would'st thou have to be Lord* Strutt? *Would'st thou have* Philip Baboon? *Nic.* shook his Head, and said nothing. *John* 30 *Bull. Wilt thou then have Esquire* South *to be Lord* Strutt? *Nic.* shook his Head a second time. *John Bull. Then who the Devil wilt thou have?*

[a] *The Treaty of* Ut[rec]ht, *the difficulty to get them to meet. When met, the* D[utc]h *would not speak their Sentiments, nor the* F[renc]h *deliver in their Proposals. The House of* Au[stri]a *talk'd very high.*

say something or another. Nic. open'd his Mouth, and pointed to his
Tongue, and cry'd A, a, a, a! which was as much as to say, he
could not speak. *John Bull. Shall I serve* Philip Baboon *with Broad
cloth, and accept of the Composition that he offers, with the liberty of his*
5 *Parks and Fish ponds?* Then *Nic.* roar'd like a Bull, O, o, o, o! *John
Bull. If thou wilt not let me have them, wilt thou take them thy self?* Then
Nic. grin'd, cackled and laugh'd, till he was like to kill himself, and
seem'd to be so pleas'd, that he fell a frisking and dancing about
the Room. *John Bull. Shall I leave all this Matter to thy Management,*
10 Nic, *and go about my Business?* Then *Nic.* got up a Glass, and drank to
John, shaking him by the Hand till he had like to have shook his
Shoulder out of Joint. *John Bull. I understand thee,* Nic; *but I shall
make thee speak before I go.* Then *Nic.* put his Finger in his Cheek, and
made it cry *Buck,* which was as much as to say, I care not a Farthing
15 for thee. *John Bull. I have done,* Nic; *If thou wilt not speak, I'll make my
own Terms with old* Lewis *here.* Then *Nic.* loll'd out his Tongue, and
turn'd up his Bumm to him; which was as much as to say, Kiss——.
John perceiving that *Frog* would not speak, turns to old *Lewis*:
Since we cannot make this obstinate Fellow speak, Lewis, *pray condescend a*
20 *little to his Humour, and set down thy Meaning upon Paper, that he may*
answer it in another Scrap. I am infinitely sorry (quoth *Lewis*) *that it*
happens so unfortunately; for, playing a little at Cudgels t'other day, a
Fellow has given me such a Rap over the Right-arm, that I am quite lame:
I have lost the Use of my Forefinger and my Thumb, so that I cannot hold my
25 *Pen.* John Bull. *That's all one, let me write for you.* Lewis. *But I have a*
Misfortune, that I cannot read any body's hand but my own. John Bull.
Try what you can do with your Left-hand. Lewis. *That's impossible; it will*
make such a Scrawl, that it will not be legible. As they were talking of
this Matter, in came Esquire *South,* all drest up in Feathers and
30 Ribons, stark staring mad, brandishing his Sword, as if he would
have cut off their Heads; crying, Room, room, Boys, for the
grand Esquire of the World! the Flower of Esquires! *What, cover'd*
in my Presence; I'll crush your Souls, and crack you like Lice! With that
he had like to have struck *John Bull*'s Hat into the Fire; but *John,*
35 who was pretty strong-fisted, gave him such a Squeeze, as made his
Eyes water. He went on still in his mad Pranks; *When I am Lord*
of the Universe, the Sun shall prostrate and adore me! Thou, Frog, *shalt*

be my Bailiff; Lewis *my Taylor, and thou,* John Bull, *shalt be my Fool!*
All this while *Frog* laugh'd in his Sleeve, gave the Esquire t'other
Noggan of Brandy, and clap'd him on the Back, which made him
ten times madder. Poor *John* stood in amaze, talking thus to himself: *Well* John, *thou art got into rare Company! One has a dumb Devil,* 5
t'other a mad Devil, and the third a Spirit of Infirmity. An honest Man has a
fine time on't amongst such Rogues. What art thou asking of them, after
all? Some mighty Boon, one would think! Only to sit quietly at thy own
Fire-side. 'Sdeath, what have I to do with such Fellows! John Bull, *after*
all his Losses and Crosses, can live better without them, than they can 10
without him. Would to God I liv'd a thousand Leagues off them: But the
Devil's in't: John Bull *is in, and* John Bull *must get out as well as he can.*
As he was talking to himself, he observ'd *Frog* and *Old Lewis*
edging [a] towards one another to whisper; so that *John* was forced
to sit with his Arms a-kimbo, to keep them asunder. Some People 15
advis'd *John* to blood *Frog* under the Tongue, or take away his
Bread and Butter, which would certainly make him speak; to give
Esquire *South* Hellebore; as for *Lewis,* some were for emollient
Pultas's, others for opening his Arm with an Incision-knife.

I could not obtain from Sir *Humphry,* at this time, a Copy of 20
John's Letter, which he sent to his Nephew by the young *Necro-*
mancer; wherein he advises him not to eat Butter, Ham, and drink
Old Hock in a Morning, with the Esquire and *Frog,* for fear of
giving him a sour Breath.

FINIS.   25

[a] *Some attempts of secret Negotiations between the* Fr[enc]h *and* D[utc]h.

AN
APPENDIX
TO
JOHN BULL
Still
In His SENSES:
OR,
Law is a Bottomless-Pit.

Printed from a Manuscript found in the
Cabinet of the famous Sir *Humphry
Polesworth*: And Publish'd, (as well
as the three former Parts) by the Author of the NEW ATALANTIS.

LONDON,
Printed for *John Morphew,* near· *Stationer's-
Hall,* 1712. **Price 3d.**

APPENDIX

TO

John Bull Still *in his Senses,* &c.

[a] CHAP. I.

The Apprehending, Examination, and Imprisonment of Jack, *for Suspicion of Poisoning.*

THE attentive Reader cannot have forgot, that in my last Part, the Story of 𝔜an 𝔓tschirnsooker's Powder was inter- 5 rupted by a Message from *Frog.* I have a natural Compassion for Curiosity, being much troubled with the Distemper my self; therefore to gratify that uneasy itching Sensation in my Reader, I have procur'd the following Account of that Matter.

𝔜an 𝔓tschirnsooker came off (as Rogues usually do upon such 10 Occasions) by Peaching his Partner, and being extremely forward to bring him to the Gallows; [b] *Jack* was accus'd as the Contriver of all the Roguery. And indeed it happen'd unfortunately for the poor Fellow, that he was known to bear a most inveterate Spight against the old Gentlewoman, and consequently, that never any 15 ill Accident happen'd to her, but he was suspected to be at the bottom of it. If she prick'd her Finger, *Jack,* to be sure, laid the Pin in the way: If some Noise in the Street disturb'd her Rest, who could it be but *Jack* in some of his nocturnal Rambles? If a Servant run away, *Jack* had debauch'd him: every idle Tittle-tattle that 20

---

[a] *The four following Chapters contain the History of passing the Bill against* Occasional Conformity, *and of the* Whigs *agreeing to it.*

[b] *All the Misfortunes of the Church charg'd upon the* P[urit]an *Party.*

went about, *Jack* was always suspected for the Author of it: How-ever, all was nothing to this last Affair of the temperating, modera-ting Powder. The Hue and Cry went after *Jack*, to Apprehend him, dead or alive, wherever he could be found. The Constables look'd
5 out for him in all his usual Haunts; but, to no purpose. Where d'ye think did they find him at last? Ev'n smoaking his Pipe very quietly, at his Brother *Martin*'s; from whence he was carry'd, with a vast Mob at his Heels, before the Worshipful Mr. Justice *Overdo*. Several of his Neighbours made Oath, [a] That of late, the Prisoner
10 had been observ'd to lead a very dissolute Life, renouncing ev'n his usual Hypocrisy, and Pretences to Sobriety: That he frequented Taverns and Eating-Houses, and had been often guilty of Drunken-ness and Gluttony at My Lord-Mayor's Table: That he had been seen in the Company of Lewd Women: That he had transferr'd his
15 usual religious Care of the engross'd Copy of his Father's Will, to Bank Bills, Orders for Tallies, and Debentures [b]: These he now affirm'd, with more literal Truth, to be [c]★ *Meat, Drink, and* ★*Tale of Cloth, the Philosophers Stone, and the Universal Medicine*: That he *the Tub.* was so far from shewing his customary Reverence to the *Will*, that
20 he kept company with those that call'd his Father a cheating Rogue, and his *Will* a Forgery [d]. That he not only sat quietly and heard his Father rail'd at, but often chim'd in with the Discourse, and hugg'd the Authors as his Bosom Friends: [c]★ *That instead* ★*Tale of of asking for Blows, at the Corners of the Streets*, he now bestow'd *the Tub.*
25 them as plentifully as he begg'd them before: In short, That he was grown a meer Rake; and, had nothing left in him of old *Jack*, except his Spight to *John Bull*'s Mother.

Another Witness made Oath, That *Jack* had been overheard bragging of a [e] Trick he had found out to manage the *old formal*
30 *Jade*, as he us'd to call her. 'Damn this numb'd-Skull of mine '(quoth he) that I could not light on it sooner. As long as I go in 'this ragged tatter'd Coat, I am so well known, that I am hunted 'away from the old Woman's Door by every barking Curr about the

[a] *The Manners of the Dissenters chang'd from their former strictness.*
[b] *Dealing much in Stock-Jobbing.*
[c] [*The marginal note, 'Tale of the Tub' transferred to the foot of the page*].
[d] *Herding with Deists and Atheists.*
[e] *Getting into Places and Church Preferments by Occasional Conformity.*

'House, they bid me Defiance; there's no doing Mischief as an
'open Enemy, I must find some way or another of getting within
'Doors, and then I shall have better Opportunities of playing my
'Pranks, besides the Benefit of good keeping.

[a] Two Witnesses Swore, that several Years ago, there came to 5
their Mistriss's Door, a young Fellow in a tatter'd Coat, that went
by the Name of *Timothy Trim*, whom they did in their Conscience
believe to be the very Prisoner, resembling him in Shape, Stature,
and the Features of his Countenance; that the said *Timothy Trim*
being taken into the Family, clap'd their Mistriss's Livery over his 10
own tatter'd Coat; that the said *Timothy* was extremely officious
about their Mistriss's Person, endeavouring by Flattery and Tale-
bearing, to set her against the rest of the Servants; no Body was so
ready to fetch any thing that was wanted, or reach what was drop'd;
that he us'd to shove and elbow his Fellow-Servants to get near his 15
Mistress, especially when Mony was a paying or receiving, then
he was never out of the way; that he was extremely diligent about
every Bodies Business but his own; that the said *Timothy*, while he
was in the Family, us'd to be playing Roguish Tricks; when his
Mistress's back was turn'd he would loll out his Tongue, make 20
Mouths, and laugh at her, walking behind her like a *Harlequin*,
ridiculing her Motions and Gestures; if his Mistress look'd about,
he put on a grave, demure Countenance, as he had been in a fit of
Devotion; that he us'd often to trip up Stairs so smoothly that you
could not hear him tread, and put all things out of Order; that he 25
would pinch the Children and Servants, when he met them in the
dark, so hard, that he left the Print of his Forefingers and his
Thumb in black and blue; and then slink into a corner, as if no
Body had done it: Out of the same malicious Design, he us'd to lay
Chairs and Joint-stools in their way, that they might break their 30
Noses by falling over them. The more young and unexperienc'd,
he us'd to teach to talk Saucily, and call Names: During his stay
in the Family there was much Plate missing; that being catch'd
with a couple of Silver Spoons in his Pocket, with their Handles
wrench'd off, he said, he was only going to carry them to the Gold- 35
smiths to be mended; that the said *Timothy* was hated by all the

[a] *Betraying the Interests of the Church when got into Preferments.*

honest Servants, for his ill-condition'd, splenetick Tricks, but especially for his slanderous Tongue; traducing them to their Mistress, as Drunkards, Thieves and Whore-masters; that the said *Timothy*, by lying Stories, us'd to set all the Family together by the Ears, taking delight to make them Fight and Quarrel; [a] particularly one Day sitting at Table, he spoke Words to this Effect: 'I am of Opinion (*quoth he*) That little short Fellows, such as 'we are, have better Hearts, and could beat the tall Fellows; I wish 'it came to a fair Trial, I believe, these long Fellows, as sightly as 'they are, should find their Jackets well thwack'd.' A parcel of tall Fellows, who thought themselves affronted by this Discourse, took up the Quarrel, and to't they went, the tall Men and the low Men, which continues still a Faction in the Family, to the great Disorder of our Mistress's Affairs: That the said *Timothy* carried this Frolick so far, that he propos'd to his Mistress, that she should entertain no Servant that was above four Foot seven Inches high, and for that Purpose had prepar'd a Gage, by which they were to be mea-sur'd: That the good old Gentlewoman was not so simple as to go into his Projects, she began to smell a Rat. 'This *Trim* (quoth she) 'is an odd sort of a Fellow, methinks he makes a strange Figure with 'that ragged, tatter'd Coat, appearing under his Livery, can't he go 'spruce and clean, like the rest of the Servants? The Fellow has a 'Roguish Leer with him, which I don't like by any means; besides, 'he has such a twang in his Discourse, and an ungraceful way of 'speaking through the Nose, that one can hardly understand him: 'I wish the Fellow be not Tainted with some bad Disease.' The Witnesses farther made Oath, That the said *Timothy* lay out a Nights, and went abroad often at unseasonable Hours; that it was credibly reported, he did Business in another Family; that he pretended to have a squeamish Stomach, and could not eat at Table with the rest of the Servants, tho' this was but a pretence to provide some nice Bit for himself; that he refus'd to Dine upon Salt-fish, only to have an opportunity to eat a Calve's Head (his Favourite Dish) in private; that for all his tender Stomach, when he was got by himself, he would devour Capons, Turkeys and Sirloins of Beef, like a Cormorant.

[a] *The original of the Distinction in the Names of Low-Churchmen and High-Churchmen.*

Two other Witnesses gave the following Evidence, That in his officious Attendance upon his Mistress, he had try'd to slip in a Powder into her Drink, and that once he was catch'd endeavouring to stifle her with a Pillow as she was asleep; that he and 𝕻𝖙𝖘𝖈𝖍𝖎𝖗𝖓-𝖘𝖔𝖔𝖐𝖊𝖗 were often in close Conference, and that they us'd to drink together at the *Rose*, where it seems he was well enough known by the true Name of *Jack*.

The Prisoner had little to say in his Defence; he endeavour'd to prove himself *Alibi*; so that the Trial turn'd upon this single Question, whether the said *Timothy Trim* and *Jack*, were the same Person? which was prov'd by such plain Tokens, and particularly by a Mole under the left Pap, that there was no withstanding the Evidence; therefore the Worshipful Mr. Justice committed him, in order to his Tryal.

CHAP. II.

How Jack's *Friends came to visit him in Prison, and what Advice they gave him.*

JACK hitherto has pass'd in the World for a poor, simple, well-meaning, half-witted, crack'd-brain'd Fellow, People were strangely surpriz'd to find him in such a Roguery; that he should disguise himself under a false Name, hire himself out for a Servant to an old Gentlewoman, only for an opportunity to Poison her. They said, That it was more Generous to profess open Enmity, than, under a profound Dissimulation, to be guilty of such a scandalous Breach of Trust, and of the sacred Rights of Hospitality. In short, the Action was universally Condemn'd by his best Friends; they told him in plain terms, That this was come as a Judgment upon him, for his loose Life, his Gluttony, Drunkenness and Avarice, laying aside his Father's *Will* in an old mouldy Trunk, and turning Stock-jobber, News-monger, and Busie-body, meddling with other Peoples Affairs, shaking off his old serious Friends, and keeping Company with Buffoons and Pick-pockets, his Father's sworn Enemies; That he had best throw himself upon the Mercy of the Court, Repent, and change his Manners. To say truth, *Jack* heard these Discourses with some Compunction; however he 5 resolv'd to try what his new Acquaintance would do for him: They sent [a] *Habakkuk Slyboots*, who deliver'd him the following Message, as the peremptory Commands of his trusty Companions.

Habakkuk. Dear *Jack*, I am sorry for thy Misfortune; Matters have not been carried on with due Secrecy; however, we must 10 make the best of a bad Bargain: Thou art in the utmost Jeopardy, that's certain; Hang, Draw and Quarter, are the gentlest things they talk of. However, thy faithful Friends, ever watchful for thy Security, bid me tell thee, That they have one infallible Expedient left to save thy Life: Thou must know, we have got into some 15 Understanding with the Enemy, by the means of [b] *Don Diego Dismallo*; he assures us there is no Mercy for thee, and that there is only one way left to Escape; it is indeed somewhat out of the common Road, however, be assur'd, it is the result of most mature Deliberation.

20 *Jack.* Prithee tell me quickly, for my Heart is sunk down into the very bottom of my Belly.

Hab. It is the unanimous Opinion of your Friends, that you [c] make as if you hang'd your self; that they will give it out that you are quite dead, and convey your Body out of Prison in a Bier; 25 and that *John Bull*, being busied with his Law-Suit, will not enquire further into the matter.

Jack. How d'ye mean, make as if I had hang'd my self?

Hab. Nay, you must really hang your self up in a true genuine Rope, that there may appear no Trick in it, and leave the rest to 30 your Friends.

Jack. Truly this is a matter of some Concern; and my Friends, I hope, won't take it ill, if I enquire a little into the means by which they intend to deliver me: A Rope, and a Noose, are no jesting Matters!

[a] Habbakuk Slyboots, *a certain Great Man who perswaded the Dissenters to consent to the Bill against* Occasional Conformity, *as being for their Interest.*

[b] *A Noble Tory Lord.*

[c] *Consent to the Bill against* Occasional Conformity.

Hab. Why so mistrustful? hast thou ever found us false to thee? I tell thee, there is one ready to cut thee down.

Jack. May I presume to ask who it is that is entrusted with that important Office?

Hab. Is there no end of thy How's and thy Why's? that's 5 a Secret.

Jack. A Secret, perhaps, that I may be safely trusted with, for I am not like to tell it again. I tell you plainly, it is no strange thing for a Man, before he hangs himself up, to enquire who is to cut him down. 10

Hab. Thou suspicious Creature! if thou must needs know it, I tell thee it is [a] Sir *Roger*; he has been in Tears ever since thy Misfortune. *Don Diego* and we have laid it so, that he is to be in the next Room, and before the Rope is well about thy Neck, rest satisfied, he will break in, and cut thee down: Fear not, old Boy; 15 we'll do't, I'll warrant thee.

Jack. So I must hang my self up, upon hopes that Sir *Roger* will cut me down, and all this upon the Credit of *Don Diego*: A fine Stratagem indeed to save my Life, that depends upon Hanging, *Don Diego*, and Sir *Roger*! 20

Hab. I tell thee there is a Mystery in all this, my Friend, a piece of profound Policy; if thou knew what good this will do to the Common Cause, thy Heart would leap for Joy: I'm sure thou would not delay the Experiment one moment.

Jack. This is to the Tune of *All for the better*. What's your Cause 25 to me, when I am hang'd?

Hab. Refractory Mortal! If thou wilt not trust thy Friends, take what follows; know assuredly, before next full Moon, that thou wilt be hung up in Chains, or thy Quarters perching upon the most conspicuous Places of the Kingdom. Nay, I don't believe 30 they will be contented with Hanging, they talk of Empaling, or breaking on the Wheel; and thou chusest that, before a gentle suspending of thy self, for one Minute. Hanging is not so painful a thing as thou imagines. I have spoke with several that have undergone it, they all agree it is no manner of uneasiness; be sure thou 35

[a] *It was given out that the* E[arl]. *of* O[xfor]d *would oppose the Occasional Bill, and so lose his Credit with the Tories; and the Dissenters did believe he would not suffer it to pass.*

take good notice of the Symptoms, the Relation will be curious; it is but a kick or two with thy Heels, and a wry Mouth or so: Sir *Roger* will be with thee in the twinkling of an Eye.

Jack. But what if Sir *Roger* should not come? will my Friends be there to Succour me?

Hab. Doubt it not; I will provide every thing against to Morrow Morning, do thou keep thy own Secret, say nothing: I tell thee, it is absolutely necessary for the Common Good, that thou shouldst go through this Operation.

CHAP. III.

How Jack *hang'd himself up by the Perswasion of his Friends, who broke their Word, and left his Neck in the Noose.*

JACK was a profess'd Enemy to *Implicit Faith*, and yet I dare say, it was never more strongly exerted, nor more basely abused, than upon this occasion. He was now, with his old Friends, in the state of a poor disbanded Officer after a Peace; or rather a wounded Soldier after a Battle; like an old Favourite of a cunning Minister after the Jobb is over; or a decay'd Beauty to a cloy'd Lover in quest of new Game; or like an hundred such things that one sees every Day. There were new Intrigues, new Views, new Projects on foot; *Jack*'s Life was the Purchase of *Diego*'s Friendship, much good may it do them. The Interest of *Hocus* and Sir *William Crawly*, which was now more at Heart, made this Operation upon poor *Jack* absolutely necessary. You may easily guess that his Rest that Night was but small, and much disturb'd; however the remaining part of his Time he did not employ (as his Custom was formerly) in Prayer, Meditation, or singing a double Verse of a Psalm, but amused himself with disposing of his Bank-Stock; many a Doubt, many a Qualm, overspread his clouded Imagination. 'Must I then '(quoth he) hang up my own personal, natural, individual Self, with 'these two Hands! *Durus Sermo!* What if I should be cut down, 'as my Friends tell me? There is something Infamous in the

'very Attempt; the World will conclude I had a guilty Conscience.
'Is it possible that good Man, Sir *Roger*, can have so much pity upon
'an unfortunate Scoundrel, that has persecuted him so many
'Years? No, it cannot be: I don't love Favours that pass through
'*Don Diego*'s Hands. On the other side, my Blood chills about my 5
'Heart, at the thought of these Rogues, with their bloody Hands
'grabbling in my Guts, and pulling out my very Entrails: Hang it,
'for once I'll trust my Friends.' So *Jack* resolv'd, but he had done
more wisely, to have put himself upon the Tryal of his Country,
made his Defence in Form; many things happen between the Cup 10
and the Lip, Witnesses might have been brib'd, Juries manag'd,
or Prosecution stop'd. But so it was, *Jack* for this time had a sufficient
Stock of Implicit Faith, which led him to his Ruin, as the Sequel
of the Story shews: And now the fatal Day was come, in which he
was to try this hanging Experiment. His Friends did not fail him 15
at the appointed Hour, to see it put in practice. *Habakkuk* brought
him a smooth, strong, tough Rope, made of many a ply of whole-
some *Scandinavian* Hemp, compactly twisted together, with a
Noose that slip'd as glib as a Bird-catcher's Gin. *Jack* shrunk and
grew pale at first sight of it, he handled it, measur'd it, stretch'd it, 20
fix'd it against the Iron-bar of the Window to try its strength, but
no Familiarity could reconcile him to it. He found fault with the
length, the thickness, and the twist, nay, the very colour did not
please him. 'Will nothing less than Hanging serve (quoth *Jack*)?
'Won't my Enemies take Bail for my good Behaviour? Will they 25
'accept of a Fine, or be satisfied with the Pillory and Imprisonment,
'a good round Whipping, or Burning in the Cheek?

Habakkuk. Nothing but your Blood will appease their Rage;
make haste, else we shall be discover'd: There's nothing like surprising the Rogues. How they will be disappointed, when they hear 30
that thou hast prevented their Revenge, and hang'd thine own self?

Jack. That's true; but what if I should do it in Effigies? Is
there never an old Pope, or Pretender, to hang up in my stead?
we are not so unlike, but it may pass.

Hab. That can never be put upon Sir *Roger*. 35

Jack. Are you sure he is in the next Room? Have you provided
a very sharp Knife, in case of the worst?

Hab. Dost take me for a common Lyar? Be satisfy'd, no Damage can happen to your Person, your Friends will take care of that.

Jack. Mayn't I quilt my Rope, it galls my Neck strangely? besides, I don't like this running Knot, it holds too tight, I may be stifled all of a sudden.

Hab. Thou hast so many If's and And's; prithee dispatch; it might have been over before this time.

Jack. But, now I think on't, I would fain settle some Affairs, for fear of the worst: Have a little Patience.

Hab. There's no having Patience, thou art such a faintling, silly Creature.

Jack. O thou most detestable, abominable, *Passive Obedience*! did I ever imagine I should become thy Votary, in so pregnant an Instance; how will my Brother *Martin* laugh at this Story, to see himself out done in his own Calling? He has taken the Doctrine, and left me the Practice. No sooner had he utter'd these Words, but like a Man of true Courage, he ty'd the fatal Cord to the Beam, fitted the Noose, and mounted upon the bottom of a Tub, the inside of which he had often Grac'd in his prosperous Days. This Footstool *Habakkuk* kick'd away, and left poor *Jack* swinging, like the Pendulum of *Paul*'s Clock. The fatal Noose perform'd its Office, and with most strict Ligature, squeez'd the Blood into his Face, 'till it assum'd a purple dye: While the poor Man, heav'd from the very bottom of his Belly for Breath, *Habakkuk* walk'd with great Deliberation into both the upper and lower Room, to acquaint his Friends, who receiv'd the News with great Temper, and with Geers and Scoffs instead of Pity, *Jack* has Hang'd himself (quoth they!) let us go and see how the poor Rogue swings. Then they call'd Sir *Roger*. Sir *Roger* (quoth *Habakkuk*) *Jack* has hang'd himself, make haste and cut him down. Sir *Roger* turn'd first one Ear and then t'other, not understanding what he said.

Hab. I tell you *Jack* has hang'd himself up.

Sir *Roger.* Who's hang'd?

Hab. Jack.

Sir *Roger.* I thought this had not been hanging Day.

Hab. But the poor Fellow has hang'd himself.

Sir Roger. Then let him hang. I don't wonder at it, the Fellow has been mad these twenty Years. With this he slunk away.

Then *Jack*'s Friends began to hunch and push one another, *Why don't you go and cut the poor Fellow down? Why don't you? and why don't you? Not I* (quoth one,) *not I* (quoth another,) *not I* (quoth a third,) *he may hang 'till Doomsday before I relieve him.* Nay it is credibly reported, that they were so far from succouring their poor Friend, in this his dismal Circumstance, that 𝕻𝖙𝖘𝖈𝖍𝖎𝖗𝖓𝖘𝖔𝖔𝖐𝖊𝖗, and several of his Companions, went in and pull'd him by the Legs, and thump'd him on the Breast. Then they began to rail at him for the very thing which they had both advis'd and justify'd before, *viz.* his getting into the old Gentlewoman's Family, and putting on her Livery. The Keeper, who perform'd the last Office, coming up, found *Jack* swinging, with no Life in him; he took down the Body gently and laid it on a Bulk, and brought out the Rope to the Company. *This, Gentlemen, is the Rope that hang'd* Jack; *What must be done with it?* Upon which they order'd it to be laid among the Curiosities of *Gresham* College, and it is call'd *Jack*'s Rope to this very Day. However *Jack* after all, had some small Tokens of Life in him, but lies at this time past hopes of a total Recovery, with his Head hanging on one Shoulder, without Speech or Motion. The Coroners Inquest supposing him Dead, brought him in *Non Compos.*

CHAP. IV.

The Conference between Don Diego Dismallo, *and* John Bull.

During the time of the foregoing Transaction, *Don Diego* was entertaining *John Bull.*

D. Diego. I hope, Sir, this Day's Proceeding will convince you of the Sincerity of your old Friend *Diego*, and the Treachery of Sir *Roger.*

J. Bull. What's the matter now?

D. Diego. You have been endeavouring, for several Years, to have Justice done upon that Rogue *Jack*; but what through the Remissness of Constables, Justices and pack'd Juries, he has always found the Means to escape.

5   *J. Bull.* What then?

D. Diego. Consider then, who is your best Friend, he that would have brought him to condign Punishment, or he that has sav'd him. By my Perswasion, *Jack* had hang'd himself, if Sir *Roger* had not cut him down.

10   *J. Bull.* Who told you that Sir *Roger* has done so?

D. Diego. You seem to receive me coldly; methinks my Services deserve a better Return.

J. Bull. Since you value your self upon Hanging this poor Scoundrel, I tell you, when I have any more Hanging work, I'll 15 send for thee; I have some better Employment for Sir *Roger*: In the mean time, I desire the poor Fellow may be look'd after. When he first came out of the North-Country into my Family, under the pretended Name of *Timothy Trim*, the Fellow seem'd to mind his Loom and his Spinning-wheel, till some body turn'd his Head; 20 then he grew so pragmatical, that he took upon him the Government of my whole Family: I could never order any thing, within or without doors, but he must be always giving his Counsel, forsooth: Nevertheless, tell him, I will forgive what is past; and if he would mind his Business for the future, and not meddle out 25 of his own Sphere, he will find that *John Bull* is not of a cruel Disposition.

D. Diego. Yet all your skilful Physicians say, that nothing can recover your Mother, but a piece of *Jack*'s Liver boil'd in her Soup.

30   *J. Bull.* Those are Quacks: My Mother abhors such Canibal's Food; she is in perfect Health at present: I would have given many a good Pound to have had her so well some time ago. [a] There are, indeed, two or three troublesome old Nurses, that because they believe I am tender-hearted, will never let me have a quiet 35 Nights Rest, with knocking me up: Oh, Sir, your Mother is taken extremely ill! she is fall'n into a fainting Fit! she has a great

[a] *New Clamours about the Danger of the Church.*

Emptiness, and wants Sustenance! This is only to recommend themselves, for their great Care. *John Bull*, as simple as he is, understands a little of a Pulse.

FINIS.

LEWIS BABOON

Turned Honeſt,

AND

JOHN BULL

POLITICIAN.

Being

The FOURTH PART

OF

Law is a Bottomleſs-Pit.

Printed from a Manuſcript found in the Cabinet of the famous Sir *Humphry Poleſworth*: And Publiſh'd, (as well as the Three former Parts and *Appendix*) by the Author of the NEW ATALANTIS.

LONDON: Printed for *John Morphew*, near *Stationers-Hall.* 1712. Price 6 d.

THE

PREFACE

WHEN I *was first call'd to the Office of Historiographer to* John Bull, *he express'd himself to this purpose:* [a] Sir *Humphry,* I know you are a plain Dealer; it is for that Reason I have chosen you for this important Trust; speak the Truth, and spare not. *That I might fulfil those his honourable Intentions, I obtain'd Leave to* repair *to, and attend him in his most secret Retirements; and I put the Journals of all Transactions into a strong Box, to be open'd at a fitting Occasion, after the manner of the Historiographers of some Eastern Monarchs: This I thought was the safest way; tho' I declare I was never afraid to be* [b] chop'd *by my Master for telling of Truth. It is from those Journals that my Memoirs are compil'd: Therefore let not Posterity, a thousand Years hence, look for Truth in the voluminous Annals of Pedants, who are entirely ignorant of the secret Springs of great Actions; if they do, let me tell them, they will be* [c] Nebus'd. *With incredible Pains have I endeavour'd to copy the several Beauties of the ancient and modern Historians; the impartial Temper of* Herodotus, *the Gravity, Austerity, and strict Morals of* Thucidides, *the extensive Knowledge of* Xenophon, *the Sublimity and Grandeur of* Titus Livius, *and to avoid the careless Stile of* Polybius: *I have borrow'd considerable Ornaments from* Dionysius Halicarnasseus *and* Diodorus Siculus: *The specious Gilding of* Tacitus *I endeavour'd to shun.* Mariana, Davila, *and* Fra. Paulo, *are those amongst the Moderns whom I thought most worthy of Imitation; but I cannot be so disingenuous, as not to own the infinite Obligations I have to the* Pilgrim's Progress *of* John Bunyan, *and the* Tenter Belly *of the Reverend* Joseph Hall. *From such Encouragement and Helps, it is easy to guess to what a degree of Perfection I might have brought this great Work, had it not been nip'd*

[a] A Member of Parliament eminent for a certain Cant in his Conversation; of which there is a good deal in this Book.

[b] A Cant Word of Sir *Humphry'*[s].

[c] Another Cant Word signifying *deceiv'd.*

in the Bud by some illiterate People in both Houses of Parliament, who envying the great Figure I was to make in future Ages, under Pretence of raising Money for the War, [a] *have padlock'd all those very Pens that were to celebrate the Actions of their Heroes, by silencing at once the*
5 *whole University of* Grubstreet. *I am perswaded, that nothing but the Prospect of an approaching Peace could have encourag'd them to make so bold a step. But suffer me, in the Name of the rest of the Matriculates of that famous University, to ask them some plain Questions: Do they think that Peace will bring along with it the Golden Age? Will there be never a*
10 *Dying-Speech of a Traitor? Are* Cethegus *and* Cataline *turn'd so tame, that there will be no opportunity to cry about the Streets,* A Dangerous Plot? *Will Peace bring such Plenty, that no Gentleman will have occasion to go upon the Highway, or break into a House? I am sorry that the World should be so much impos'd upon by the Dreams of a* False Prophet, *as to*
15 *imagine the* Millennium *is at hand. O* Grubstreet! *thou fruitful Nursery of tow'ring Genius's! how do I lament thy Downfall? Thy Ruin could never be meditated by any who meant well to* English *Liberty: No modern* Lycaeum *will ever equal thy Glory, whether in soft Pastorals, thou sung the Flames of pamper'd Apprentices and coy Cook-Maids, or mournful*
20 *Ditties of departing Lovers; or if to* Mæonian *Strains thou rais'd thy Voice, to record the Stratagems, the arduous Exploits, and the nocturnal Scalade of needy Heroes, the Terror of your peaceful Citizen, describing the powerful* Betty, *or the artful* Picklock, *or the secret Caverns and Grotto's of* Vulcan *sweating at his Forge, and stamping the Queens Image*
25 *on viler Metals, which he retails for Beef, and Pots of Ale; or if thou wert content in simple Narrative to relate the cruel Acts of implacable Revenge, or the Complaints of ravish'd Virgins, blushing to tell their Adventure before the listening Crowd of City Damsels, whilst in thy faithful History thou intermingles the gravest Counsels and the purest Morals: Nor less*
30 *acute and piercing wert thou in thy Search and pompous Description of the Works of Nature, whether in proper and emphatick Terms thou didst paint the blazing Comets fiery Tale, the stupendous Force of dreadful Thunder and Earthquakes, and the unrelenting Inundations. Sometimes, with* Machiavelian *Sagacity, thou unravellest the Intrigues of State, and the*
35 *traiterous Conspiracies of Rebels giving wise Counsel to Monarchs. How didst thou move our Terror and our Pity with thy passionate Scenes,*

[a] *Act restraining the Liberty of the Press, &c.*

between Jack-catch *and the Heroes of the* Old Baily! *How didst thou describe their intrepid March up* Holborn-Hill! *Nor didst thou shine less in thy theological Capacity, when thou gavest ghostly Counsel to dying Felons, and recorded the guilty Pangs of Sabbath-breakers! How will the noble Arts of* [a] John Overton's *Painting and Sculpture now languish!* 5 *where rich Invention, proper Expression, correct Design, divine Attitudes, and artful Contrast, heighten'd with the Beauties of* Clar-Obscur, *embellish'd thy celebrated Pieces to the Delight and Astonishment of the judicious Multitude! Adieu persuasive Eloquence! the quaint Metaphor, the poinant Irony, the proper Epithet, and the lively Similie, are fled to* 10 ★*Vid.* Bp. of Burleigh on the Hill: *Instead of these, we shall have* I know *St. Asaph's* not what ——[b] ★The Illiterate will tell the rest with Preface Pleasure! *I hope the Reader will excuse this Digression, due by way of Condolance to my worthy Brethren of* Grubstreet, *for the approaching Barbarity that is likely to overspread all its Regions, by this* 15 *oppressive and exorbitant Tax. It has been my good Fortune to receive my Education there; and so long as I preserv'd some Figure and Rank amongst the Learned of that Society, I scorn'd to take my Degree either at* Utrecht *or* Leyden, *though I was offer'd it* gratis *by the Professors there.*

---

[a] The Engraver of the Cuts before the *Grubstreet* Papers.
[b] [*Marginal note*, '*Vid*. . . . *Preface*', *transferred to the foot of the page*.]

THE

CONTENTS.

LEWIS BABOON
Turned Honest,
AND
JOHN BULL
POLITICIAN.

CHAP. I.

The Sequel of the History of the Meeting at the [a] *Salutation,*

WHere, I think, I left *John Bull*, sitting between *Nic.*
Frog and *Lewis Baboon*, with his Arms *a-kimbo*, in great
Concern to keep *Lewis* and *Nic.* asunder. As watchful as 5
he was, *Nic.* found the Means, now and then, to steal a Whisper,
and, by a cleanly Conveyance under the Table, to slip a short Note
into *Lewis*'s hand, which *Lewis* as slyly put into *John*'s Pocket, with
a Pinch or a Jog, to warn him what he was about. *John* had the
Curiosity to retire into a Corner, to peruse these [b] *Billet doux* 10
of *Nic*'s; wherein he found, that *Nic.* had used great Freedom, both
with his Interest and Reputation. One contained these words,
Dear Lewis, *Thou seest clearly that this Blockhead can never bring his*
Matters to bear: Let thee and me talk to night by our selves at the Rose,
and I'll give thee Satisfaction. Another was thus express'd; *Friend* 15
Lewis, *Has thy Sense quite forsaken thee, to make* Bull *such Offers? Hold*
fast, part with nothing, and I will give thee a better Bargain, I'll warrant
thee.

In some of his Billets, he told *Lewis* "that *John Bull* was under his
"Guardianship; that the best part of his Servants were at his 20

[a] *At the Congress of* U[tre]cht.
[b] *Some Offers of the* D[utc]h *at that time, in order to get the Negotiation into their hands.*

"Command; that he could have *John* gagg'd and bound whenever
"he pleased, by the People of his own Family." In all these Epistles,
Blockhead, Dunce, Ass, Coxcomb, were the best Epithets he gave
poor *John*: In others he threatned [a], "that He, Esquire *South*,
5 "and the rest of the Tradesmen, would lay *Lewis* down upon his
"Back, beat out his Teeth, if he did not retire immediately, and
"break up the Meeting.

I fancy I need not tell my Reader, that *John* often chang'd
Colour as he read, and that his Fingers itch'd to give *Nic.* a good
10 Slap on the Chops; but he wisely moderated his cholerick Temper:
[b] "I sav'd this Fellow (quoth he) from the Gallows when he ran
"away from his last Master, because I thought he was harshly
"treated; but the Rogue was no sooner safe under my Protection,
"than he began to lie, pilfer, and steal, like the Devil: When I first
15 "set him up in a warm House, he had hardly put up his Sign, when
"he began to debauch my best Customers from me: [b] Then it was
"his constant Practice to rob my Fish-ponds, not only to feed his
"Family, but to trade with the Fishmongers: I conniv'd at the
"Fellow till he began to tell me, that they were his as much as
20 "mine: In my Manour of [b] *Eastcheap*, because it lay at some dis-
"tance from my constant Inspection, he broke down my Fences,
"robb'd my Orchards, and beat my Servants. When I us'd to
"reprimand him for his Tricks, he would talk saucily, lye, and
"brazen it out, as if he had done nothing amiss. Will nothing cure
25 "thee of thy Pranks *Nic.* (quoth I)? I shall be forced, some time or
"another, to chastise thee: The Rogue got up his Cane and threat-
"ned me, and was well thwack'd for his Pains: But I think his
"Behaviour at this time worst of all; after I have almost drowned
"my self, to keep his Head above Water, he would leave me stick-
30 "ing in the Mud, trusting to his Goodness to help me out. After
"I have beggar'd my self with his troublesome Law-Suit, with
"a Pox to him, he takes it in mighty Dudgeon because I have
"brought him here to end Matters amicably, and because I won't
"let him make me over, by Deed and Indenture, as his lawful

---

[a] *Threatning that the* Allies *would carry on the* War *without the help of the* E[ngli]sh.
[b] *Complaints against the* D[utc]h *for Encroachment in Trade, Fishery,* East-Indies,
&c. *The* War *with the* D[utc]h *on these accounts.*

"Cully; which, to my certain Knowledge, he has attempted several
"times. But, after all, canst thou gather Grapes from Thorns?
"*Nic.* does not pretend to be a Gentleman, he is a Tradesman, a
"self-seeking Wretch, but how camest thou to bear all this, *John*?
"The Reason is plain; Thou conferrest the Benefits, and he receives 5
"them; the first produces Love, and the last Ingratitude: Ah!
"*Nic. Nic.* thou art a damn'd Dog, that's certain; thou knowest
"too well, that I will take care of thee, else thou would'st not use
"me thus: I won't give thee up, it is true; but as true as it is,
"thou shalt not sell me, according to thy laudable Custom. 10
While *John* was deep in this Soliloquy, *Nic.* broke out into the
following Protestation.

Gentlemen,

"I believe every body here present will allow me to be a very
"just and disinterested Person. My Friend *John Bull* here is very 15
"angry with me, forsooth, because I won't agree to his foolish
"Bargains. Now I declare to all Mankind, I should be ready to
"sacrifice my own Concerns to his Quiet; but the care of his
"Interest, and that of the honest [a] Tradesmen that are embark'd
"with us, keeps me from entring into this Composition. What shall 20
"become of those poor Creatures? The Thoughts of their im-
"pending Ruin disturbs my Night's Rest, therefore I desire they
"may speak for themselves. If they are willing to give up this
"Affair, I shan't make two words of it.

John Bull begg'd him to lay aside that immoderate Concern for 25
him; and withal, put him in mind, that the Interest of those
Tradesmen had not sat quite so heavy upon him some Years ago,
on a like Occasion. *Nic.* answer'd little to that, but immediately
pull'd out a Boatswain's Whistle; upon the first Whiff, the Tradesmen came jumping into the Room, and began to surround *Lewis* 30
like so many yelping Curs about a great Boar, or, to use a modester
Similie, like Duns at a great Lord's Levè the Morning he goes into
the Country; one pull'd him by the Sleeve, another by the Skirt, a
third hallow'd in his Ear; they began to ask him for all that had

[a] *The* A[llie]s.

been taken from their Forefathers by Stealth, Fraud, Force, or lawful Purchase; some ask'd for Manours, others for Acres, that lay convenient for them; that he would pull down his Fences, level his Ditches; all agreed in one common Demand, that he should be
5 purg'd, sweated, vomited, and starv'd, till he came to a sizeable Bulk, like that of his Neighbours; one modestly ask'd him Leave to call him Brother; *Nic. Frog* demanded two Things, to be his Porter and his Fishmonger, to keep the Keys of his Gates, and furnish his Kitchen; *John's* Sister *Peg* only desir'd that he would
10 let his Servants sing Psalms a Sundays; some descended even to the asking of old Cloaths, Shoes, and Boots, broken Bottles, Tobacco-pipes, and Ends of Candles.

Monsieur *Bull* (quoth *Lewis*) you seem to be a Man of some Breeding; for God's sake use your Interest with these Messieurs,
15 that they wou'd speak but one at once; for if one had a hundred pair of Hands, and as many Tongues, he cannot satisfy them all at this rate. *John* begg'd they might proceed with some Method; then they stop'd all of a sudden, and would not say a word. If this be your Play (quoth *John*) that we may not be like a Quaker's dumb
20 Meeting, let us begin some Diversion; what d'ye think of Rouly-Pouly, or a Country-Dance? What if we should have a Match at Football! I am sure we shall never end Matters at this rate.

CHAP. II.

How John Bull *and* Nic. Frog *settled their Accompts.*

25 J. Bull. D*Uring this general Cessation of Talk, what if You and I* Nic. *should enquire how Money-matters stand between us?*

Nic. Frog. *With all my Heart, I love exact Dealing; and let* Hocus *Audit; he knows how the Money was disburs'd.*

J. Bull. *I am not much for that at present; we'll settle it between Our-*
30 *selves: Fair and Square* Nic. *keeps Friends together. There have been laid out in this Law-Suit, at one time* 36000 *Pounds and* 40000 *Crowns: In some Cases I, in others you, bear the greatest proportion.*

Nic. Right: *I pay three Fifths of the greatest Number, and you pay two Thirds of the lesser Number: I think this is Fair and Square as you call it.*

John. *Well, go on.*

Nic. *Two Thirds of* 36000 *Pounds are* 24000 *Pounds for your Share, and there remains* 12000 *for mine. Again, Of the* 40000 *Crowns I pay* 24000, *which is three Fifths, and you pay only* 16000, *which is two Fifths;* 24000 *Crowns make* 6000 *Pounds, and* 16000 *Crowns make* 4000 *Pounds:* 12000 *and* 6000 *make* 18000: 24000 *and* 4000 *makes* 28000. *So there are* 18000 *Pounds to my Share of the Expences, and* 28000 *to yours.*

After *Nic.* had bambouzled *John* a while about the 18000 and the 28000, *John* call'd for Counters; but what with Slight of Hand, and taking from his own Score and adding to *John's*, *Nic.* brought the Balance always on his own side.

J. Bull. Nay, good Friend *Nic.* though I am not quite so nimble in the Fingers, I understand Cyphering as well as you: I will produce you my Accompts one by one, fairly writ out of my own Books: And here I begin with the first. You must excuse me if I don't pronounce the Law Terms right.

[*John Reads.*]

	l.	s.	d.
Fees to the Lord Ch. Justice and other Judges, by way of Dividend - - - - - - - - - - - - - - - -	200	10	06
Fees to puny Judges - - - - - - - - - - - - - - - - -	50	00	00
To Esquire *South* for *post Terminums* - - - - - - - - -	100	10	06
To ditto for *Non est Factums* - - - - - - - - - - - - -	200	00	00
To ditto for *Discontinuance, Noli prosequi,* and *Re-traxit* -	80	10	06
To ditto for a *Non Omittas,* and Filing a *post Diem*	50	00	00
To *Hocus* for a *Dedimus potestatem* - - - - - - - - - - -	300	00	00
To ditto for *Casas* and *Fifas* after a *Devastavit* - - -	500	00	00
Carry over - - - - -	1481	11	06
Brought over - - - - -	1481	11	06
To ditto for a *Capias ad computandum* - - - - - - - -	100	10	06
To *Frog's* new Tenants *per* Account to *Hocus,* for *Audita querelas* -	200	00	00
On the said Account for Writs of *Ejectment* and *Destringas* -	300	00	00

	l.	s.	d

To Esquire *South*'s Quota for a Return of a *Non est* }
invent. and *nulla habet bona* - - - - - - - - - - - - - - }   150 10 00

To - - - - for a Pardon *in forma pauperis* - - - - - - -   200 00 00

5 To *Jack* for a *Melius inquirendum* upon a *Felo de se* -   100 00 00

To *Don Diego* for a *Defecit* - - - - - - - - - - - - - -   50 00 00

To Coach-hire -   500 00 00

For Treats to Juries and Witnesses - - - - - - - - -   300 00 00

	Sum	3382	12	00

10 Due by *Nic. Frog*   1691 06 00
Of which paid by *Nic. Frog*   1036 11 00

Remains due by *Nic. Frog*   654 15 00

Then *Nic. Frog* pull'd his Bill out of his Pocket, and began to read.
Nicholas Frog's Account.

15   Remains to be deducted out of the former Account,

	l.	s.	d

To *Hocus* for Entries of a *Rege inconsulto* - - - - - -   200 00 00

To *John Bull*'s Nephew for a *Venire facias*, the }
Money not yet all laid out - - - - - - - - - - - - }   300 00 00

20 The Coach-hire for my Wife and Family, and the }
Carriage of my Goods during the time of this }   200 10 06
Law-Suit - }

For the extraordinary Expences of feeding my }
Family during this Law-Suit - - - - - - - - - - - }   500 00 00

25 To *Major Ab.* -   300 00 00

To *Major Will.* -   200 00 00

	Sum	1700	10	06
	From which deduct	1691	06	00
	There remains due to *Nic. Frog.*	09	04	06

30 Besides, recollecting, I believe I paid for *Diego*'s *Defecit*.

John Bull. As for your *Venire facias*, I have paid you for one
already; in the other, I believe you will be Nonsuited: I'll take care
of my Nephew my self. Your *Coach-hire* and Family Charges are

most unreasonable Deductions; at that rate, I can bring in any Man in the World my Debtor. But who the Devil are those two *Majors* that consume all my Money? I find they always run away with the Ballance in all Accompts.

Nic. Frog. Two very honest Gentlemen, I assure you, that have done me some Service.

To tell you plainly *Major Ab.* denotes thy greater Ability, and Major *Will* thy greater Willingness to carry on this Law-suit. It was but reasonable thou shouldst pay both for thy *Power* and thy *Positiveness.*

J. Bull. I believe I shall have those two honest Majors discount on my side in a little time.

Nic. Frog. Why all this Higgling with thy Friend about such a paltry Sum? Does this become the Generosity of the Noble and Rich *John Bull*? I wonder thou art not asham'd. Oh *Hocus! Hocus!* where art thou, it used to go another-guess manner in thy time, when a poor Man has almost undone himself for thy sake, thou art for fleecing him and fleecing him; is that thy Conscience *John*?

J. Bull. Very pleasant indeed; it is well known thou retains thy Lawyers by the Year, so a fresh Law-suit adds but little to thy Expence, [a] they are thy Customers, I hardly ever sell them a Farthings worth of any thing; nay, thou hast set up an Eating-house, where the whole Tribe of them spend all they can rap or run; if it were well reckon'd, I believe thou gets more of my Money than thou spends of thy own: However, if thou wilt needs plead Poverty, own at least that thy Accompts are false.

Nic. Frog. No marry won't I, I refer my self to these honest Gentlemen, let them judge between us; let Esquire *South* speak his Mind, whither my Accounts are not right, and whither we ought not to go on with our Law-suit.

J. Bull. Consult the Butchers about keeping of *Lent.* I tell you once for all, *John Bull* knows where his Shoe pinches, none of your Esquires shall give him the Law, as long as he wears this trusty Weapon by his side, or has an inch of broad Cloath in his Shop.

Nic. Frog. Why there it is, you will be both Judge and Party; I am sorry thou discoverest so much of thy head-strong Humour

[a] *The Money spent in* H[ollan]d *and* Fl[ander]s.

before these strange Gentlemen, I have often told you that it would prove thy Ruin some time or another.

John saw clearly he should have nothing but wrangling, and that he should have as little Success in settling his Accounts as
5 ending the Composition: Since they will needs overload my Shoulders (quoth John) I shall throw down the Burden with a squash amongst them, take it up who dares; a Man has a fine time of it, amongst a combination of Sharpers, that Vouch for one anothers Honesty. John look to thy self, Old Lewis makes reasonable Offers,
10 when thou hast spent the small Pittance that is left, thou wilt make a glorious Figure when thou art brought to live upon Nic. Frog and Esquire South's Generosity and Gratitude, if they use thee thus, when they want thee, what will they do when thou wants them? I say again, John look to thy self.
15 John wisely stiffled his Resentments, and told the Company that in a little time he should give them Law, or something better.

All. [a] Law! Law! Sir, by all means, what is Twenty Two poor Years towards the finishing a Law-suit? For the Love of God more Law, Sir!
20 J. Bull. Prepare your Demands, how many Years more of Law you want, that I may order my Affairs accordingly. In the mean while farewel.

CHAP. III.

[b] *How* John Bull *found all his Family in an Uproar at Home.*

25 Nic. Frog, who thought of nothing but carrying John to the Market, and there disposing of him as his own proper Goods, was mad to find that John thought himself now of Age to look after his own Affairs: He resolv'd to traverse this new Project, and to make him uneasie in his own Family. He had corrupted or deluded
30 most of his Servants into the extravagantest Conceits in the World, that their Master was run mad, and wore a Dagger in one Pocket,

[a] *Clamours for continuing the War.*
[b] *Clamours about the danger of the Succession.*

and Poison in the other; that he had sold his Wife and Children to *Lewis*, disinherited his Heir, and was going to settle his Estate upon a Parish Boy; that if they did not look after their Master, he would do some very mischievous Thing. When *John* came home he found a more surprising Scene than any he had yet met with, and that you will say was somewhat extraordinary.

He call'd his Cook-maid *Betty* to bespeak his Dinner, *Betty* told him, *That she beg'd his Pardon, she could not dress Dinner till she knew what he intended to do with his Will.* Why *Betty*, Forsooth (quoth *John*) thou art not run mad art thou? My Will at present is to have Dinner: That may be (quoth *Betty*) but my Conscience won't allow me to dress it, till I know whither you intend to do righteous Things by your Heir? I am sorry for that *Betty* (quoth *John*) I must find some body else then. Then he call'd *John* the Barber. Before I begin (quoth *John*) I hope your Honour won't be offended, if I ask you whither you intend to alter your Will? If you won't give me a positive Answer, your Beard may grow down to your Middle, for me. I gad and so it shall (quoth *Bull*) for I will never trust my Throat in such a mad Fellows Hands. Where's *Dick* the Butler? Look ye (quoth *Dick*) I am very willing to serve you in my Calling, d'ye see, but there are strange Reports, and plain-dealing is best, d'ye see. I must be satisfied if you intend to leave all to your Nephew, and if *Nic. Frog* is still your Executor, d'ye see; if you will not satis-fie me as to these Points, d'ye see, you may drink with the Ducks: And so I will (quoth *John*) rather than keep a Butler that loves my Heir better than my self. *Hob* the Shoemaker, and *Pricket* the Taylor told him, they would most willingly serve him in their several Stations, if he would promise them never to talk with *Lewis Baboon*, and let *Nicholas Frog*, Linnen-draper, manage his Concerns; that they could neither make Shoes nor Cloaths to any that were not in good Correspondence with their worthy Friend *Nicholas*.

J. Bull. Call *Andrew* my Journey-Man: How goes Affairs, *Andrew*? I hope the Devil has not taken Possession of thy Body too.

Andrew. No, Sir, I only desire to know what you would do if you were dead?

J. Bull. Just as other dead Folks do, *Andrew*.
This is Amazing [*Aside.*

Andrew. I mean if your Nephew shall inherit your Estate?

J. Bull. That depends upon himself. I shall do nothing to hinder him.

Andrew. But will you make it sure?

5   *J. Bull.* Thou mean'st, that I should put him in Possession, for I can make it no surer without that, he has all the Law can give him.

Andrew. Indeed Possession, as you say, would make it much surer; they say, it is eleven points of the Law.

John began now to think that they were all enchanted; he
10 enquires about the Age of the Moon, if *Nic.* had not given them some intoxicating *Potion*, or if old Mother *Jenisa* was not still alive. No, o'my faith (quoth *Harry*) I believe there is no *Potion* in the Case, but a little *Aurum Potabile*. You will have more of this by and by. He had scarce spoke the Word, when of a sudden *Don*
15 *Diego*, follow'd by a great Multitude of his Tenants and Work-men, came rushing into the Room.

D. Diego. Since those worthy Persons, who are as much concern'd for your Safety as I am, have employ'd me as their Orator, I desire to know whither you will have it by way of *Syllogism*,
20 *Enthymem*, *Dilemma* or *Sorites*.

John now began to be diverted with their Extravagance.

J. Bull. Let's have a *Sorites* by all means, tho' they are all new to me.

D. Diego. It is evident to all that are versed in History, that there
25 were two *Sisters* that play'd the Whore, two thousand Years ago: Therefore it plainly follows, that it is not lawful for *John Bull* to have any manner of Entercourse with *Lewis Baboon*. If it is not lawful for *John Bull* to have any manner of Entercourse (Correspondence, if you will, that is much the same thing) then *a Fortiori*, it is much
30 more unlawful for the said *John* to make over his Wife and Children to the said *Lewis*; if his Wife and Children are not to be made over, he is not to wear a Dagger and Ratsbane in his *Pockets*; if he wears a Dagger and Ratsbane, it must be to do Mischief to himself or some body else; if he intends to do Mischief, he ought to be under
35 Guardians, and there is none so fit as my self and some other worthy Persons, who have a Commission for that purpose from *Nic. Frog*, the Executor of his Will and Testament.

J. Bull. And this is your *Sorites*, you say; with that he snatch'd
a good tough Oaken Cudgel, and began to brandish it; then happy
was the Man that was first at the Door; crouding to get out, they
tumbled down Stairs, and it is credibly reported some of them
drop'd very valuable Things in the hurry, which were pick'd up 5
by others of the Family.

That any of these Rogues (quoth *John*) should imagine I am not
as much concern'd as they about having my Affairs in a settled
Condition, or that I would wrong my Heir for I know not what.
Well *Nic.* I really cannot but applaud thy Diligence, I must own 10
this is really a pretty sort of a Trick, but it shan't do thy Business
for all that.

CHAP. IV.

[a] *How* Lewis Baboon *came to visit* John Bull, *and what pass'd
between them.*   15

I Think it is but ingenuous to acquaint the Reader, that this
Chapter was not wrote by Sir *Humphry* himself, but by another
very able *Pen* of the University of *Grubstreet*.

John had (by some good Instructions that was given him by Sir
Roger) got the better of his Cholerick Temper, and wrought him- 20
self up to a great steadiness of Mind, to pursue his own Interest
through all Impediments that were thrown in the way; he began to
leave off some of his old Acquaintance, his roaring and bullying
about the Streets; he put on a serious Air, knit his Brows, and for
the time had made a very considerable progress in Politicks, 25
considering that he had been kept a stranger to his own Affairs.
However, he could not help discovering some remains of his Nature,
when he happen'd to meet with a Foot-Ball, or a Match at Cricket;
for which Sir *Roger* was sure to take him to task. *John* was walking
about his Room with folded Arms, and a most thoughtful Counten- 30
ance, his Servant brought him Word that one *Lewis Baboon* below

[a] *Private Negotiations about* Dunkirk.

wanted to speak with him. *John* had got an Impression that *Lewis* was so deadly a cunning Man, that he was afraid to venture himself alone with him: At last he took heart of Grace. *Let him come up* (quoth he) *it is but sticking to my Point, and he can never over-reach me.*

5   *Lewis Baboon.* Monsieur *Bull* I will frankly acknowledge, that my Behaviour to my Neighbours has been somewhat uncivil, and I believe you will readily grant me, that I have met with Usage accordingly. I was fond of Back-sword and Cudgel play from my Youth, and I now bear in my Body many a black and blue Gash
10 and Scars, God knows. I had as good a Ware-house, and as fair Possessions as any of my Neighbours, tho' I say it; but a contentious Temper, flattering Servants, and unfortunate Stars, have brought me into Circumstances that are not unknown to you. These my Misfortunes are heighten'd by domestick Calamities,
15 that I need not relate. I am a poor old batter'd Fellow, and I would willingly end my Days in Peace: But alas, I see but small hopes of that, for every new Circumstance affords an Argument to my Enemies to pursue their Revenge; formerly I was to be bang'd because I was too Strong, and now because I am too Weak to
20 resist, I am to be brought down when too Rich, and oppressed when too Poor. *Nic. Frog* has used me like a *Scoundrel*; You are a Gentleman, and I freely put my self in your Hands, to dispose of me as you think fit.

J. Bull. Look you, Master *Baboon*, as to your Usage of your
25 Neighbours, you had best not dwell too much upon that Chapter; let it suffice at present that you have been met with, you have been rolling a great Stone uphill all your Life, and at last it has come tumbling down till it is like to crush you to pieces: Plain-dealing is best. If you have any particular Mark, Mr. *Baboon*, whereby one
30 may know when you Fib, and when you speak Truth, you had best tell it me, that one may proceed accordingly; but since at present I know of none such, it is better that you should trust me, than that I should trust you.

L. Baboon. I know of no particular Mark of Veracity, amongst
35 us Tradesmen, but Interest; and it is manifestly mine not to deceive you at this time; you may safely trust me, I can assure you.

J. Bull. The Trust I give is in short this, I must have something in hand before I make the Bargain, and the rest before it is concluded.

L. Baboon. To shew you I deal fairly, name your Something.

J. Bull. I need not tell thee, old Boy; thou canst guess.   5

L. Baboon. [a] *Ecclesdown Castle*, I'll warrant you, because it has been formerly in your Family! Say no more, you shall have it.

J. Bull. I shall have it to m'own self?

L. Baboon. To thy n'own self.

J. Bull. Every Wall, Gate, Room, and Inch of *Ecclesdown Castle*, 10 you say?

L. Baboon. Just so.

J. Bull. Every single Stone of *Ecclesdown Castle*, to m'own self, speedily!

L. Baboon. When you please, what needs more Words?   15

J. Bull. But tell me, old Boy, hast thou laid aside all thy *Equivocals* and *Mentals* in this case?

L. Baboon. There is nothing like Matter of Fact; Seeing is Believing.

J. Bull. Now thou talk'st to the purpose; let us shake Hands, 20 old Boy. Let me ask thee one Question more, What hast thou to do to meddle with the Affairs of my Family? To dispose of my Estate, old Boy?

L. Baboon. Just as much as you have to do with the Affairs of Lord *Strutt*.   25

J. Bull. Ay, but my Trade, my very Being, was concern'd in that.

L. Baboon. And my Interest was concern'd in the other: but let us drop both our Pretences; for I believe it is a moot point, whether I am more likely to make a Master *Bull*, or you a Lord 30 *Strutt*.

J. Bull. Agreed, old Boy; but then I must have Security that I shall carry my Broad-cloth to Market, old Boy.

L. Baboon. That you shall: *Ecclesdown Castle! Ecclesdown!* Remember that: Why would'st thou not take it when it was offer'd 35 thee some Years ago?

[a] Dunkirk.

J. Bull. I would not take it, because they told me thou would'st not give it me.

L. Baboon. How could Monsieur *Bull* be so grosly abused by downright Nonsense? They that advised you to refuse, must have believed I intended to give, else why would they not make the Experiment? But I can tell you more of that Matter than perhaps you know at present.

J. Bull. But what say'st thou as to the Esquire, *Nic. Frog*, and the rest of the Tradesmen? I must take care of them.

L. Baboon. Thou hast but small Obligations to *Nic*, to my certain Knowledge: He has not us'd me like a Gentleman.

J. Bull. *Nic*, indeed, is not very nice in your Punctilio's of Ceremony; he is Clownish, as a Man may say; Belching and Calling of Names have been allow'd him time out of mind, by Prescription: but however, we are engag'd in one Common Cause, and I must look after him.

L. Baboon. All Matters that relate to him, and the rest of the Plantiffs in this Law-Suit, I will refer to your Justice.

CHAP. V.

Nic Frog's *Letter to* John Bull; *wherein he endeavours to vindicate all his Conduct, with relation to* John Bull *and the Law-Suit.*

NIC. perceiv'd now that his Cully had elop'd, that *John* intended henceforth to deal without a Broker; but he was resolv'd to leave no Stone unturn'd to recover his Bubble: Amongst other Artifices, he wrote a most obliging Letter, which he sent him Printed in a fair Character.

[a] *Dear Friend,*

"When I consider the late ill Usage I have met with from you, I "was reflecting what it was that could provoke you to it; but upon "a narrow Inspection into my Conduct, I can find nothing to "reproach my self with, but too partial a Concern for your Interest.

[a] *Substance of the States Letter.*

"You no sooner set this Composition a-foot, but I was ready to
"comply, and prevented your very Wishes; and the Affair might
"have been ended before now, had it not been for the greater
"Concerns of Esq; *South*, and the other poor Creatures, embark'd
"in the same Common Cause, whose Safety touches me to the 5
"Quick. You seem'd a little jealous that I had dealt unfairly with
"you in Money-matters, till it appear'd by your own Accounts,
"that there was something due to me upon the Ballance. Having
"nothing to answer to so plain a Demonstration, you began to
"complain as if I had been familiar with your Reputation; when it is 10
"well known, not only I, but the meanest Servant in my Family,
"talk of you with the utmost Respect. I have always, as far as in
"me lies, exhorted your Servants and Tenants to be dutiful; not
"that I any ways meddle in your domestick Affairs, which were
"very unbecoming for me to do. If some of your Servants express 15
"their great Concern for you in a manner that is not so very polite,
"you ought to impute it to their extraordinary Zeal, which
"deserves a Reward rather than a Reproof. You cannot reproach
"me for want of Success at the *Salutation*, since I am not Master of
"the Passions and Interests of other Folks. I have beggar'd my self 20
"with this Law-Suit, undertaken merely in Complaisance to you;
"and if you would have had but a little Patience, I had still greater
"things in Reserve that I intended to have done for you. I hope what
"I have said will prevail with you to lay aside your unreasonable
"Jealousies, and that we may have no more Meetings at the *Saluta-* 25
"*tion*, spending our Time and Money to no Purpose. My Concern
"for your Welfare and Prosperity, almost makes me mad. You
"may be assur'd I will continue to be

Your Affectionate
Friend and Servant, 30
NIC. FROG.

John receiv'd this with a good deal of *Sang froid; Transeat* (quoth
John) *cum caeteris erroribus*: He was now at his Ease; he saw he could
now make a very good Bargain for himself, and a very safe one for
other Folks. My Shirt (quoth he) is near me, but my Skin is nearer: 35
Whilst I take care of the Welfare of other Folks, no body can blame

me, to apply a little Balsam to my own Sores. It's a pretty thing, after all, for a Man to do his own Business; a Man has such a tender Concern for himself, there's nothing like it. This is somewhat better, I trow, than for *John Bull* to be standing in the Market,
5 like a great Dray-horse, with *Frog*'s Paws upon his Head, *What will ye give me for this Beast? Serviteur* Nic. Frog, *you may kiss my Backside if you please.* Though *John Bull* has not read your *Aristotles, Plato*'s and *Machiavels*, he can see as far into a Milstone as another: With that *John* began to chuckle and laugh, till he was like to
10 burst his Sides.

CHAP. VI.

[a] *The Discourse that pass'd between* Nic. Frog *and Esquire* South, *which* John Bull *overheard.*

J*Ohn* thought every Minute a Year till he got into *Ecclesdown*
15   *Castle*; he repairs to the *Salutation*, with a Design to break the Matter gently to his Partners: Before he enter'd, he overheard *Nic.* and the Esquire in a very pleasant Conference.

Esq; South. Oh the Ingratitude and Injustice of Mankind! That *John Bull*, whom I have honour'd with my Friendship and Protec-
20 tion so long, should flinch at last, and pretend that he can disburse no more Money for me; that the Family of the *Souths*, by his sneaking Temper, should be kept out of their own.

Nic. Frog. An't like your Worship, I am in amaze at it; I think the Rogue should be compell'd to do his Duty.

25 *Esq; South.* That he should prefer his scandalous Pelf, the Dust and Dregs of the Earth, to the Prosperity and Grandeur of my Family!

Nic. Frog. Nay, he is mistaken there too; for, he would quickly lick himself whole again by his Vails. It's strange he should prefer
30 *Philip Baboon*'s Custom to *Esq; South*'s.

Esq; South. As you say, that my Clothier, that is to get so much by the Purchase, should refuse to put me in Possession; did you ever know any Man's Tradesman serve him so before?

[a] *Negotiation between the* E[mpero]r *and the* D[utc]h *for continuing War, and getting the property of* Fl[ande]rs.

Nic. Frog. No, indeed, an't please your Worship, it is a very unusual Proceeding; and I would not have been guilty of it for the World. If your Honour had not a great Stock of Moderation and Patience, you would not bear it so well as you do.

Esq; South. It is most intolerable, that's certain *Nic.* and I will 5 be reveng'd.

Nic. Frog. Methinks it is strange, that *Philip Baboon*'s Tenants do not all take your Honour's part, considering how good and gentle a Master you are.

Esq; South. True, *Nic.* but few are sensible of Merit in this 10 World: It is a great Comfort, to have so faithful a Friend as thy self in so critical a Juncture.

Nic. Frog. If all the World should forsake you, be assur'd *Nic. Frog* never will; let us stick to our Point, and we'll manage *Bull*, I'll warrant ye. 15

Esq; South. Let me kiss thee, dear *Nic.* I have found one honest Man amongst a thousand at last.

Nic. Frog. If it were possible, your Honour has it in your Power to wed me still closer to your Interest.

Esq; South. Tell me quickly, dear *Nic.* 20

Nic. Frog. You know I am your Tenant; the Difference between my Lease and an Inheritance is such a Trifle, as I am sure you will not grudge your poor Friend; that will be an Encouragement to go on; besides, it will make *Bull* as mad as the Devil: You and I shall be able to manage him then to some purpose. 25

Esq; South. Say no more, it shall be done *Nic.* to thy Heart's Content.

John, all this while, was listening to this comical Dialogue, and laugh'd heartily in his Sleeve, at the Pride and Simplicity of the *Esquire*, and the sly Roguery of his Friend *Nic.* Then of a sudden 30 bolting into the Room, he began to tell them, that he believ'd he had brought *Lewis* to reasonable Terms, if they would please to hear them.

Then they all bawl'd out aloud, *No Composition, Long live Esquire South and the Law!* As *John* was going to proceed, some roar'd, 35 some stamp'd with their Feet, others stop'd their Ears with their Fingers.

Nay, Gentlemen (quoth *John*) if you will but stop proceeding for a while, you shall judge your selves whether [a] *Lewis*'s Proposals are reasonable.

All. Very fine indeed, stop proceeding, and so lose a Term.

5   *J. Bull.* Not so neither, we have something by way of Advance, he will put us in Possession of his Mannor and Castle of *Ecclesdown*.

Nic. Frog. What dost talk of us, thou mean'st thy self?

J. Bull. When *Frog* took Possession of any thing, it was always said to be for *Us*, and why may not *John Bull* be *Us*, as well as

10   *Nic. Frog* was *Us*? I hope *John Bull* is no more confin'd to Singularity than *Nic. Frog*; or take it so, the constant Doctrine that thou has preach'd up for many Years, was that Thou and I are One; and why must we be supposed Two in this Case, that were always One before? It's impossible that Thou and I can fall out *Nic.* we

15   must trust one another: I have trusted thee with a great many things, prithee trust me with this one Trifle.

Nic. Frog. That Principle is true in the main; but there is some Speciality in this Case, that makes it highly inconvenient for us both.

20   *J. Bull.* Those are your Jealousies, that the common Enemies sow between us; how often hast thou warn'd me of those Rogues, *Nic.* that would make us mistrustful of one another?

Nic. Frog. This *Ecclesdown*-Castle is only a Bone of Contention.

J. Bull. It depends upon you to make it so, for my part I am as

25   peaceable as a Lamb.

Nic. Frog. But do you consider the unwholesomness of the Air and Soil, the Expences of Reparations and Servants, I would scorn to accept of such a Quag-mire.

J. Bull. You are a great Man, *Nic.* but in my Circumstances,

30   I must be e'en content to take it as it is.

Nic. Frog. And you are really so silly, as to believe the old cheating Rogue will give it you.

J. Bull. I believe nothing but Matter of Fact, I stand and fall by that, I am resolv'd to put him to it.

35   *Nic. Frog.* And so relinquish the hopefulest Cause in the World, a Claim that will certainly in the End, make thy Fortune for ever.

[a] *Proposals for a Cessation of Arms, and deilvery of* Dunkirk.

J. Bull. Wilt thou purchase it *Nic*? thou shalt have a lumping
Pennyworth; nay, rather than we should differ, I'll give thee something to take it off my Hands.

Nic. Frog. If thou would'st but moderate that hasty impatient
Temper of thine, thou should'st quickly see a better thing than all 5
that: What should'st thou think to find old *Lewis* turn'd out of his
paternal Estates and Mansion-house of [a] *Clay-Pool*? Would not
that do thy Heart good to see thy old Friend *Nic. Frog* Lord of
Clay-Pool? Then thou and thy Wife and Children shall walk in my
Gardens, buy Toys, drink Lemonade, and now and then we should 10
have a Country-dance.

J. Bull. I love to be plain, I'd as lieve see my self in *Ecclesdown-*
Castle, as thee in *Clay-Pool*. I tell you again, *Lewis* gives this as a
Pledge of his Sincerity, if you won't stop proceeding to hear him,
I will. 15

CHAP. VII.

[b] *The rest of* Nic's *Fetches to keep* John *out of* Ecclesdown-*Castle*.

WHEN *Nic.* could not diswade *John* by Argument, he try'd
to move his Pity, he pretended to be sick and like to dye,
that he should leave his Wife and Children in a starving Condition, 20
if *John* did abandon him; that he was hardly able to craul about the
Room, far less capable to look after such a troublesome Business
as this Law-Suit, and therefore begg'd that his good Friend would
not leave him. When he saw that *John* was still inexorable, he
pull'd out a Case-Knife, with which he used to Sneaker-snee, and 25
threaten'd to cut his own Throat. Thrice he aim'd the Knife to his
Wind-pipe with a most determin'd threatning Air. "What sig-
"nifies Life (quoth he) in this languishing Condition, it will be
"some Pleasure that my Friends will revenge my Death upon this
"barbarous Man, that has been the Cause of it?" All this while 30

[a] Clay-Pool, P[ar]*is. Lutetia.*
[b] *Attempts to hinder the Cessation, and taking Possession of* Dunkirk.

John look'd Sedate and Calm, neither offering in the least to snatch
the Knife, nor stop his Blow, trusting to the Tenderness *Nic.* had
for his own Person: When he perceiv'd that *John* was immoveable
in his Purpose, he apply'd himself to *Lewis*.

5   Art thou (quoth he) turn'd Bubble in thy Old Age, from being a
Sharper in thy Youth? what occasion hast thou to give up *Ecclesdown*-
Castle to *John Bull*? his Friendship is not worth a Rush, give it me
and I'll make it worth the while. If thou dislikest that Proposition,
keep it thy self, I'd rather thou shouldest have it than he. If thou
10   hearkens not to my Advice, take what follows; Esquire *South* and
I will go on with our Law-suit in spite of *John Bull*'s Teeth.

     L. Baboon. Monsieur *Bull* has used me like a Gentleman, and
I am resolv'd to make good my Promise, and trust him for the
Consequences.

15   *Nic. Frog.* Then I tell thee thou art an old doating Fool. With
that *Nic.* bounc'd up with a Spring equal to that of one of your
nimblest Tumblers or Rope dancers, falls foul upon *John Bull* to
snatch the [a] Cudgel he had in his Hand, that he might Thwack
Lewis with it. *John* held it fast, so that there was no wrenching it
20   from him. At last *Esquire South* buckl'd to, to assist his Friend *Nic.*
John hall'd on one side, and they two on the other; sometimes they
were like to pull *John* over; then it went, all of a sudden again, on
John's side, so they went see-sawing up and down, from one End
of the Room to the other: Down tumbl'd the Tables, Bottles,
25   Glasses, and Tobacco Pipes: The Wine and the Tobacco were all
spilt about the Room, and the little Fellows were almost trod
under Foot, 'till more of the Tradesmen joyning with *Nic.* and the
Esquire, *John* was hardly able to pull against them all, yet he never
quit hold of his trusty Cudgel; which by the contranitent Force of
30   two so great Powers, [b] broke short in his Hands. *Nic.* seiz'd the
longer end, and with it began to Bastinado Old *Lewis*, who had
slunk into a Corner, waiting the Event of this Squabble. *Nic.*
came up to him with an insolent menacing Air, so that the old
Fellow was forc'd to skuttle out of the Room, and retire behind
35   a Dung-cart: He call'd to *Nic*, thou insolent Jackanapes, time,
was when thou durst not have used me so, thou now takest me

[a] *The Army.*   [b] *The Separation of the Army.*

unprovided, but old and infirm as I am, I shall find a Weapon by and by to chastise thy Impudence.

When *John Bull* had recover'd his Breath, he began to parly with *Nic*. *Friend* Nic, *I am glad to find thee so strong after thy great Complaints; really thy Motions* Nic. *are pretty Vigorous for a consumptive Man.* 5 As for thy worldly Affairs *Nic*, if it can do thee any Service, I freely make over to thee this profitable Law-suit; and I desire all these Gentlemen to bear witness to this my Act and Deed, yours be all the Gain, as mine has been the Charges, I have brought it to bear finely: However, all I have laid out upon it goes for nothing, thou 10 shalt have it with all its Appurtenances, I ask nothing but leave to go home.

Nic. Frog. The Counsel are fee'd, and all Things prepared for a Tryal, thou shalt be forced to stand the Issue: It shall be pleaded in thy Name as well as mine: Go home if thou can'st, the Gates are 15 shut, [a] the Turnpikes locked, and the Roads barracado'd.

J. Bull. Even these very ways *Nic*. that thou toldest me, were as open to me as thy self? If I can't pass with my own Equipage, what can I expect for my Goods and Waggons? I am deny'd Passage through those very Grounds that I have purchased with my own 20 Money; however, I am glad I have made the Experiment, it may serve me in some stead.

John Bull was so over-joy'd that he was going to take Possession of *Ecclesdown*, that nothing could vex him. *Nic*. (quoth he) *I am just a going to leave thee, cast a kind look upon me at parting.* 25

Nic. look'd sower and grum, and would not open his Mouth.

J. Bull. I wish thee all the Success that thy Heart can desire, and that these honest Gentlemen of the long Robe may have their Belly full of Law. *Nic*. could stand it no longer, but flung out of the Room with disdain, and beckon'd the Lawyers to follow him. 30

J. Bull. Buy, buy Nic, *not one poor Smile at parting, won't you shake your day-day,* Nic? *Buy* Nic: With that *John* march'd out of the common Road cross the Country, to take Possession of *Ecclesdown*.

---

[a] *Difficulty of the March of part of the Army to* Dunkirk.

CHAP. VIII.

Of the great Joy that John *express'd when he got Possession of* [a] Ecclesdown.

WHEN *John* had got into his Castle, he seem'd like *Ulysses* upon his Plank after he had been well sous'd in Salt-water; who (as *Homer* says) was as glad as a Judge going to sit down to Dinner, after hearing a long Cause upon the Bench. I dare say *John Bull*'s Joy was equal to that of either of the two; he skip'd from Room to Room; ran up Stairs and down Stairs, from the Kitchen to the Garrets, and from the Garrets to the Kitchen; he peep'd into every Crany; sometimes he admired the Beauty of the Architecture, and the vast Solidity of the Masons Work; at other times he commended the Symetry and Proportion of the Rooms. He walk'd about the Gardens; he Bath'd himself in the Canal, swimming, diving, and beating the liquid Element, like a milkwhite Swan. The Hall resounded with the sprightly Violin and the martial Hautboy. The Family trip'd it about and Caper'd like *Hail-stones bounding from a Marble Floor*: Wine, Ale and October flew about as plentifully as Kennel-Water; then a Frolick took *John* in the Head to call up some of *Nic. Frog*'s Pensioners that had been so mutinous in his Family.

J. Bull. Are you glad to see your Master in *Ecclesdown*-Castle?

All. Yes indeed, Sir.

J. Bull. Extremely glad?

All. Extremely glad, Sir.

J. Bull. Swear to me that you are so.

Then they began to damn and sink their Souls to the lowest Pit of Hell, if any Person in the World rejoyc'd more than they did.

J. Bull. Now hang me if I don't believe you are a parcel of perjur'd Rascals; however take this Bumper of October to your Master's Health.

Then *John* got upon the Battlements, and looking over he call'd to *Nic. Frog*.

How d'ye do *Nic*? D'ye see where I am *Nic*? I hope the Cause

[a] Dunkirk.

goes on swimmingly *Nic*; when dost thou intend to go to *Clay-Pool, Nic*? Wilt thou buy there some High-Heads of the newest Cut for my Daughters? How comest thou to go with thy Arm ty'd up? Has old *Lewis* given thee a rap over the Finger-ends? Thy Weapon was a good one when I weilded it, but the Butt-end remains in my Hands. I am so busy in packing up my Goods, that I have no time to talk with thee any longer: It would do thy Heart good to see what Waggon Loads I am preparing for Market; if thou wantest any good Office of mine, for all that has happen'd, I will use thee well *Nic*; buy *Nic*.

*⁎*John Bull's *Thanks to Sir* Roger, *and* Nic. Frog's *Malediction upon all Shrews, the Original Cause of his Misfortunes, are reserv'd for the next Volume.*

FINIS.

NOTES

... although the present Age may understand well enough the little Hints we give, the Parallels we draw, the Characters we describe; yet this will all be lost to the next. However, if these Papers, *reduced into a more durable Form*, should happen to live until our Grand-children be Men; I hope they may have Curiosity enough to consult Annals, and compare Dates, in order to find out what *Names* were then intrusted with the Conduct of Affairs, in the Consequence whereof, themselves will so deeply share.

Swift, *Examiner*, 7 December 1710

To annotate *John Bull* adequately would be the labour of a lifetime.

Colvile, *A Miscellany of the Wits*, 1920

NOTES TO PAMPHLET I

5: 2 *The Occasion of the Law-Suit* : the diplomatic prelude to the War of the Spanish Succession. See 'Background 1698–1712', pp. xlii–xliv, above.

5: 4–5 **the late Lord** *Strutt* : Charles II, King of Spain from 1665 to 1700. He is the 'old Lord *Strutt*' of the satire. The name reflects proverbial Spanish pride ('strut', to swell or protrude [*OED*]) and possibly alludes to English stage representations of arrogant foreign kings: cf. Sir Roger de Coverley at a performance of *The Distrest Mother:* 'Upon the entring of *Pyrrhus*, the Knight told me, that he did not believe the King of *France* himself had a better Strut' (*Spectator*, 25 Mar. 1712, iii. 241).

5: 5 **the Parson** : Luis Manuel F. de Portocarrero, Cardinal Archbishop of Toledo, and the adviser most responsible for effecting Charles II's last will and testament. Cf. 'the Cardinal de Porto Carero, when the King was at the point of Death, and not *compos mentis*, came into the Room with a Crucifix in his Hand, threatning him with Damnation, if he did not sign the Will in favour of the Duke of Anjou' (*FP*, 24 May 1701).

5: 5 **a cunning Attorney** : Henri Duc d'Harcourt, Marshal of France and Ambassador to Spain in 1697 and 1701, who also worked to secure the success of the French claimant to the Spanish crown (see *PM*, 4 Jan. 1701). The third and subsequent editions of the *Key* identified this 'Attorney' as the 'D[uke] of *Medina Celi*' who was in disgrace during the latter years of the reign of Charles II—albeit for his over-enthusiastic support of the Bourbons—and was not directly involved in the Succession crisis.

5: 6 *Philip Baboon* : Philip of Bourbon, Duke of Anjou, who (in 1700) succeeded Charles II as Philip V, King of Spain, and reigned until 1746. He is the 'young Lord *Strutt*' of the satire. 'Upon the Death of *Charles* II. King of *Spain*, the *French* by the Treachery of the *Spanish* Council and Governors, and their own Native Perfidiousness, took Possession of that Monarchy and all its Dependencies, under the Coverture of the *Dauphin's* and his Son's Title to that large Succession' (*Compleat . . . Memoirs for the Curious*, 1710, i. 306).

5: 7 **Esquire** *South* : Charles, Archduke of Austria, and (after 1711) Emperor Charles VI. His father, Emperor Leopold, had endowed the Austrian claim to the Spanish crown on Charles, his youngest son, whom he believed to be the only true claimant, particularly since the French claim (which devolved upon the Duke of Anjou) had twice been renounced. It was on this basis that the allies of the Empire—chiefly

England, Holland, and the German states—proclaimed Charles the true
King of Spain as 'Charles III' after their declaration of war on France
and Spain. Charles had previously appeared as 'Squire *South*' in *Examiner*,
16 Jan. 1711, vi. 167.

5: 8 **the Parson and the Attorney forg'd a Will.** 'This Memorable
Will being the subtle Work of *Portocarrero*, and the result of the Marquis
D'*Harcourt's* Intriegues, was Sign'd the 2d. of Octob. [1700] N.S. in
a Month after which his Catholick Majesty [Charles II] expir'd' (Abel
Boyer, *History of King William the Third*, 1702, iii. 465). Portocarrero
and Harcourt were often coupled as the intriguers who obtained the Will:
'Q. Who made the King of *Spain*'s Will? A. Old *Porticarrero*, at my
proper cost and charge, and chiefly at my direction' (*King of France his
Catechism*, 1703, p. 4); cf. 'it is universally believed, that *Will* was a
Writing Forged by the Cardinal *Portocarrero*, and some other *French*
Pensioners' (*Some Conjectures*, 1705, p. 7).

5: 13 **a very great Landed Estate.** The Spanish empire at this time
included 'the Spanish Indies' (Florida, Mexico, the isthmus of Panama,
Cuba, and other islands in the Caribbean); all of South America except
the Guianas and Portuguese Brazil; the Philippines; the Canaries; Milan,
Sicily, Naples, Sardinia, and the Balearics; and 'the Spanish Netherlands'
(Belgium and Luxembourg). Cf. 'This Monarchy is beyond dispute the
largest in extent and if we consider the infinite Wealth of the West *Indes*,
perhaps the Richest in the World' (Stevens, *Brief History of Spain*,
1701, p. 269). It was considered to be 'the Fountain from whence all
the Riches of Europe do now proceed' (*Observator Reformed*, 4 Jan. 1705).

5: 16 **Property of their . . . inferior Servants.** The incompetence
and corruption of the Spanish civil service, the efficiency of foreign
merchants, and the negligence of the native aristocracy were all considerable factors in the economic decline of Spain (see R. Trevor Davies,
Spain in Decline, 1957). The Spaniards surrendered the conduct of their
own trade to English and Dutch merchants 'thinly disguised under
Spanish names' operating through the port of Cadiz (Trevelyan, i. 123).
'It is the Custom of the great Lords never to visit their Estates, but trust
all to their Stewards, who turns all to his own private Interest, and makes
them believe what he pleases; and to enquire into his Management of
their Affairs would be below them. . . . It is reported that Kings Revenues
are at least Thirty Five Millions of Crowns *per Annum*; yet the Roguery
of his Officers is such, that not one fourth of it comes into his Coffers.
And at *Cadiz* there are followers which are called *Metadores*, which
Publickly profess to Cheat the King of his Plate; which, for Money,
they put on Board the Ships of all Nations' (*Trip to Spain*, 1704/5, pp. 7–
12). Canaro, the Venetian Ambassador to Spain from 1678 to 1681,
wrote that the Spanish empire was, 'like a skeleton out of the relics of
which, France, England and Holland have built up their own profit and
advantage' (Trevor Davies, p. 146). 'Property' can mean 'a mere means
to an end . . . a cat's paw' (*OED*).

5: 20–1 **Butchers and Bakers Bills . . . not yet paid**: Emperor Charles V, and Charles I of Spain (1516–58), whose 'fantastically expensive foreign policies and . . . dependence on credit to finance them . . . had disastrous consequences. . . . The country's resources were mortgaged for an indefinite number of years ahead' (Elliott, *Imperial Spain*, 1963, pp. 199, 191).

5: 24 **to wish him Joy, and bespeak his Custom.** William of England and the States-General of Holland sent formal letters of congratulation to King Philip upon his accession to the Spanish crown. In 1711 these letters were reprinted in several pamphlets. The following is an extract from William's letter: 'Indeed We have willingly imbraced this Occasion, both to Congratulate your Majesty's happy Exaltation to the *Spanish* Throne, and to shew you how much Esteem We have for your Majesty, and how much We desire to make it appear to You, that our Inclination doth most readily prompt us to endeavour what We can, that the mutual Conjunction of Friendship and Alliance between Us, may be confirmed and knit faster; and the Common Good of the two Nations may daily more and more flourish. . . .' '*Madrid*, March 24. The Heer Van Schonenberg, Envoy Extraordinary of the States-General, had Yesterday Audience of the King [Philip V], and delivered a Letter, in which their High and Mightinesses Acknowledge his Majesty. . .' (*PB*, 5 Apr. 1701). See also Oldmixon, *History of England*, 1735, p. 225.

5: 25–6 *John Bull* **the Clothier and** *Nic. Frog* **the Linnendraper**: respectively the English and Dutch nations. The significance of their names is discussed above, pp. lvii–lxvi. Frog is a retail trader who deals in linens and calicoes, the trading rival of the 'clothier', who sells cloth. 'Both these nations endeavoured to obtain from Spain commercial advantages, as a composition for their not insisting on the treaty of partition' (Scott). The commercial advantages England sought to gain were chiefly those connected with the cloth trade, 'the typical industry of the time. Two fifths of English exports consisted of cloth woven in England' (Trevelyan, i. 96). 'The *Spanish* Wool is necessary to the working up of our fine Cloth . . . and considering that our Woollen Manufactory is one of the chief Fountains of our intrinsick Wealth, it would be a very dangerous Blow to that Manufacture, if the *French* should hinder the Importation of *Spanish* Wool into *England*' (*Duke of Anjou's Succession*, 1701, p. 6). To the commercial interests the wool trade was an emotive symbol of England's power and prosperity. Defoe calls attention to 'Our Wool, the Treasure of *Britain*', 'the *English Bull-Dog*', and 'our *Black-Cattle*' as English originals (*Review*, 2 and 5 June 1711, viii. 123–7). Arbuthnot brings these native elements together in his own 'true-born Englishman', John Bull.

6: 5–6 **use him as kindly**: i.e. treat him with kindness, but also use him after the same fashion as they had used his predecessors.

6: 7–9 **The young Lord . . . seeming Content . . . his Predecessors.** Both England and the United Provinces received protestations of friendly intent from Philip. One optimistic contemporary wrote, 'The Duke of *Anjou*, is of a Sweet, Affable, Judicious Nature, and promises a great deal' (*Characters of the Royal Family*, 1705 [1st edn., 1702], p. 4). Perhaps he was encouraged by the fact that Philip received the States' Letter 'very graciously, and seemed much pleased' (*PB*, 5 Apr. 1701), and in his replies to both Maritime powers assured them that since he 'continu'd in the Resolution of maintaining the Publick Tranquillity, he would consent to every Expedient that might conduce towards securing the Common Good and Repose of *Christendom*' (Oldmixon, *History of England*, 1735, p. 225).

6: 11 *jealous* : suspicious.

6: 12 *his Grandfather* Lewis Baboon. Louis Bourbon, Louis XIV of France, who reigned from 1643 to 1715, was the grandfather of Philip of Anjou.

6: 15 *false Loon* : colloquial Scots for rogue or scamp (*OED*). After the Union in 1707 one pamphleteer wrote, 'For *Scotch* and *English*, as United *Loons*, / Do now defie the Dev'l and all his Sons' (*Pulpit-Fool*, p. 9).

6: 16 a *Jack of all Trades*. Louis XIV was respected for his grasp of commercial matters: 'The King has . . . mightily encourag'd and improv'd Trade, as well the Manufactures as Foreign Commerce' (Veryard, *Account of Divers Choice Remarks*, 1701, p. 108). Louis's versatility is also stressed in another tract: 'By his daily Conversation with the best Masters and Professors, he has got the knowledge of the most useful Parts of all Arts and Sciences. His Occupations are never at an end, giving himself up as entirely to Trifles, as to Affairs of Moment . . .' (*Characters of the Royal Family*, 1705, p. 1).

6: 17–19 *selling* Broad Cloath . . . to a Nicety : perhaps alluding to the French trade in 'druggets', a cheap stuff often made from a mixture of wool and linen, used for clothing. Cf. Defoe, who complains of 'the Invasion of our Capital Trade of Woollen Cloth, by our running upon light, thin, and Novel Wearing of Stuffs, Druggets, and Toys, in the room of our Broad-Cloth, the Ancient Standard Commodity, and Staple Trade of this Nation' (*Review*, 10 Mar. 1705, ii. 14). A little later, also in the *Review*, he asserts that the French 'cannot so well make Broadcloth . . . Because their Country being generally hotter than ours, and the Temper of their People Nimble and Easie, they are best suited and pleas'd with a thin light Stuff' (20 Mar. 1705, ii. 25).

6: 19–20 *Charles Mather* . . . Bubble . . . with a Toy : a famous toy maker of Fleet Street. Steele pictured him as Charles Bubbleboy, 'a person of a particular genius, the first that brought toys in fashion, and baubles to perfection . . . a perfect master of words, which, uttered with a smooth voluble tongue, flow into a most persuasive eloquence' (*Tatler*, 7 Mar. 1710, iii. 152; see also 11 June 1709, i. 228, and 29 Dec. 1709, ii. 418). He appeared in *Spectator*, 17 Mar. 1712, iii. 206 and 21 July 1714, iv. 546; and in Swift's 'Virtues Of Sid Hamet', *Poems*, i. 135.

6: 20–1 **would descend . . . Shooe-Buckles.** This comment reflects the mixture of envy and scorn found in many contemporary comments on French manufactures: 'Their Ribands, Lace, Perfumes, Paints, and Womens Dresses, with an infinity of other Trifles (of which the greatest part goes out of the Kingdom) turn to their incredible Benefit' (Veryard, *Divers Choice Remarks*, p. 109).

6: 22–4 **would go about the Neighbourhood . . . to Dance.** French dancing-masters had, of course, been the targets of much chauvinistic ridicule during the seventeenth and early eighteenth centuries. Swift characterized the French as 'a People, whose Genius seems wholly turned to singing, and dancing, and prating' (*Examiner*, 15 Mar. 1710, iii. 107), and Arbuthnot was by no means the only satirist to use love of French fashions *apropos* of the contemporary political situation. For example, in D'Urfey's *Wonders in the Sun*, 1706, the Dutchman 'Industry' was pictured saying pointedly to the Frenchman 'Profuseness': '*Whilst we are all busick and mind de main Chance, / Laet ve and oldt* England *gae on met your Dance: / Laet on's Fish in haer Water and chouse you of Wine, / Dance spiel and Zewp on, 'tis no business of mine*' (p. 37). There is also a suggestion here that 'multitudes of [the French] seek their Fortunes abroad; and, indeed, *Italy, Spain, Germany*, and *Holland*, are full of them. . . .' (Veryard, *Divers Choice Remarks*, p. 108).

6: 25–7 **to squander away . . . Back-Sword . . . all the Country:** French expansionist ambitions. After eleven years of unprecedented success in the field, English polemicists could indulge themselves in the luxury of deriding French military power through such analogues: cf. 'The *Old Bully* seems, in his declining Age, to have fallen into the same Romantick Notions of his *Prowess*, and *Chivalry*, as the Famous and Renown'd *Knight* of *Mancha*' (*PPB*, 26 Feb. 1712). A Back-Sword had only one cutting edge (*OED*), and like the other arms mentioned was a lower-class weapon commonly used by the bear-garden duellists of the period. Steele quotes from James Miller's 'Challenge' to Timothy Buck to meet him '*and exercise at the several Weapons following*, viz. *Back-Sword, Sword and Dagger, Sword and Buckler, Single Falchon, Case of Falchons, Quarter-Staff*' (*Spectator*, 21 July 1712, iv. 31). Cf. also *Spectator*, 26 Sept. 1711, ii. 208–12, on Louis's wars of aggression; and 9: 6–7 n.

6: 31–7: 1 **the Rascal has good Ware . . . as cheap as any Body.** 'It's well enough known that the *French* have been endeavouring to set up a Woollen Manufactory of their own, and to have all the Materials for Dying, &c. of their native Product, in order to rival our Trade . . . they will be able to carry cheaper than we can do; and that they can sail and victual cheaper, there's no body will offer to controvert' (*Duke of Anjou's Succession*, 1701, pp. 6–7).

7: 7 **Bull *and* Frog's *Letter to Lord* Strutt.** In March of 1701 'Mr [Alexander] Stanhope [English envoy to The Hague] and the Ministers of the States-General demanded from those of France and Spain, as security for the peace of Europe, that Ostend and Nieuport should be delivered up to the English, and that the British subjects should not only enjoy all their former privileges in Spain, but be admitted to a participation of all such as might be either actually possessed by those of France, or hereafter extended to them. It was farther proposed, that no part of the dominions of Spain should ever be united to France' (Scott, paraphrasing Burnet, *History*, iv. 466). Stanhope's *Memorial* is printed in *FP*, 25 Mar. 1701. 'We are now Impatient, whether a War or a Peace will be the Result of this Incident' (*LP*, 31 Mar. 1701). These negotiations preceded the Treaty of Grand Alliance.

7: 27–8 **It is impossible to express the Surprize of the Lord** *Strutt*. '*Don Quiros*, Ambassador of *Spain* [at The Hague] bounces and frets at an unusual rate, and gives out, that the *Spaniards* will rather lose their Crown, than submit to the conditions desired of 'em [in Stanhope's *Memorial*]. As the Ministers of *Spain* are now but the Organs of the *French* Court, the Complaints of *Don Quiros* are looked upon, as the sentiments of the *French*, for the *Spaniards* who are here do own, that what we [the Dutch and the English] have demanded is reasonable, and will be accepted by *Spain*, if the *Spanish* Council intend to preserve their Monarchy from being Independent of the Crown of *France*' (*PM*, 27 Mar. 1701; see also *LP*, 5 May 1701).

7: 29 **he was not flush in** *Ready*. '*Paris*, May 14. Our last advices from *Madrid* say, that all the Projects that were on foot for augmenting their Troops are at a stand for want of Money, and they tell us, that the new King has been oblig'd to write to his Grandfather, and desire a supply from hence' (*PM*, 8 May 1701).

7: 30 **neither could he find good Bail**: political and commercial securities. Scott noted that the only concrete offer Philip and Louis made was to renew the Treaty of Ryswick (1697).

7: 30–2 **He offer'd ... his Drapers.** The French Ambassador D'Avaux was frequently quoted as protesting that the Bourbon Kings earnestly desired a peaceful resolution of all problems: 'Here Monsieur *d'Avaux* was enjoin'd to take on him the Character of an *Actor*, and play the Part his Master impos'd upon him, without any Regard to Sincerity or Honour' (Oldmixon, *History of England*, 1735, p. 225).

8: 7–9 **it was rumour'd ... new Liveries of old** *Lewis Baboon*. Scott was the first editor to gloss this allusion to the economic measures taken by Louis XIV and Philip V to cement their alliance. The lucrative *Asiento* contract for the supply of slaves to Spanish colonies was made over to France, a Company was established in Paris to control trade with Mexico and Peru, and the Spanish woollen market was restricted to French merchants (see *FP*, 29 Apr. 1701 and *PM*, 12 July 1701).

8: 9–10 **This coming to Mrs.** *Bull*'s **Ears ... in an uproar.** Mrs. Bull here represents the Godolphin ministry, which became increasingly whiggish in temper, and which, in the later years of its existence (1708–10) had the almost unanimous support of the evenly divided Parliament (returned in 1702) in its determination to pursue a vigorous war against the Bourbons.

8: 11–17 *You Sot . . . loyter . . . an idle Drone.* The tone of this entire passage vividly recalls a similar outburst in Mrs. Manley's *Memoirs of Europe*, 1710. When 'Irene' (the Duchess of Marlborough) learned of the arts practised upon her 'obliging' son, 'Constantine' (Queen Anne) by 'Theodecta' (Mrs. Masham), 'she took upon her to correct the Emperor, shut him up in his Chamber, and box'd him with her own Hands, calling him ungrateful to her Cares, her Toil, sensless Fool! Drone! unfit for Government, and the Reins of Empire! which he had never held a Month but by her wise Conduct and Advice . . . . What had he to do with Politicks? Cou'd not he eat, and sleep, and loll, and yawn, and fool away the Day unmolested, or had he a Mind to have his Weaknesses discover'd.' The 'good Emperor' was 'mortify'd by the Termagancy of his Mother' (i. 216–17). Cf. Mrs. Hocus's similar treatment of the second Mrs. Bull (19: 5–7 n.).

8: 13 *Nine-pins or Puppet-shows.* William's dying efforts to forestall Bourbon hegemony had met with widespread euphoria or hostility among the people, and only in 1702 did the Whigs succeed in communicating a sense of urgency to them. These lower-class recreations convey well the mood of 1701–2, deriding the diversions indulged in by an optimistic populace.

8: 13–14 *flaunt about . . . new gilt Chariot.* Here Arbuthnot ironically allegorizes the Whig ministry scolding the English for their dereliction of duty, in terms commonly used by the Tories to attack the 'new' unprincipled Whigs who dominated the ministry and were supported by the commercial *nouveau riche*. One Tory writer protested, 'What a miserable, what a contemptible scandalous prospect is it, to see at Court an Upstart distinguish'd from his *quondam* Brethren the Mob, rattling in his Coach and six' (*Letter to a Modern Dissenting Whig*, 1701, p. 16), and another complained that 'Publick Wealth has been pillag'd by Scoundrel Fellows; whereof a vast number may be found, who at the Revolution were not worth a Groat, and now ride in their Coach and Six' (*Modest Defence of the Government*, 1702, p. 7); see also Holmes, p. 157.

8: 16 *that old Fox.* The 'cunning' Louis XIV was commonly allegorized as the fox; e.g. in *Where's your Peace now*, 1712, he appeared as the fox caught stealing the allied geese. Other comparable 'fables' such as 'The Superannuated Fox' (*Aesop in Europe*, 1706, pp. 20–2) made satiric capital of Louis's age.

8: 16–19 *turns you out . . . that Knave.* See 'Background 1698–1712', p. xliii, above.

8: 19–20 *You must think . . . tun'd up by Frog.* The first of many allusions to the common Tory charge of collusion between England's chief ally and 'The *Dutch*-hearted 𝔚𝔥𝔦𝔤𝔰' (*Peace and Dunkirk*, bs. 1712).

Here Arbuthnot reverses the direction of the attack, which usually affirmed that Dutch interference in English domestic affairs (see, e.g., 18: 12–14 n., 19: 2–5 n., and 33: 16 n.) was 'prompted by Agents from the Discontented Party here' (*Natural Reflections*, 1712, p. 37); see also *Essay Towards the History of the Last Ministry*, 1710, pp. 21–2.

8: 26–8 they hearing . . . joining against old *Lewis* . . . Charges of the Suit. During the winter of 1701–2 the Triple Alliance between England, the United Provinces, and the Empire was augmented by treaties with a number of smaller states such as Prussia, Munster, and Hanover. These contracted to send specified numbers of troops to the allied army in return for subsidies. 'Already the Maritime Powers were the paymasters of the Alliance' (Trevelyan, i. 158).

8: 28–9 Lying *Ned* the Chimney-sweeper: Victor Amadeus, the Machiavellian Duke of Savoy, who joined the Alliance in October 1703. English contempt for Savoy was a reflection of the chauvinistic suspicion with which they regarded all foreigners, and it was confirmed by the politics of Victor Amadeus who, in order to maintain his precarious independence during the bitter struggles of the late seventeenth and early eighteenth centuries, had '"trimmed" not towards the victor . . . but against him to hold the balance even' (Trevelyan i. 304); see also *Secret Intrigues of the Duke of Savoy*, 1705. Swift's analogous joke that, 'beyond Sea, all the Chimney-Sweepers come from Savoy' (*Hue and Cry after Dismal*, 1712, vi. 140) was based on a popular insult: 'Foreigners are welcome in this Country . . . some of them . . . carry away the Soot from Chimneys, which is the priviledge of the *Savoyards*, who are seen in the Streets blacker than *Ethiopians*, and more stinking than *a Synagogue*' (*Present State of the Court of France*, 1712, p. 4).

8: 29 *Tom* the Dustman: King Peter II of Portugal, who was enticed away from alliance with France and Spain by the Methuen Treaty of 1703. He was an even more unreliable ally than Savoy, and in 1711 was discovered to be making clandestine overtures to his former Bourbon friends for a peace which would—it was rumoured—be the signal for the massacre of all British troops in the Iberian peninsula (see *History of Utrecht*, pp. 190–4). Defoe summarized the consensus when he wrote: 'The *Portuguese* are Mercenary, Impatient, and make their Advantage of our Circumstances' (*Defence of the Allies*, 1712, p. 29). The Portuguese troops were ill fed, badly paid, hostile to their Protestant comrades-in-arms, and totally unreliable (see *Fable of the Cods-Heads*, bs. 1712; Defoe, *British Visions*, 1711, p. 9, and *Review*, 10 July 1707, iv. 255–6). Here Arbuthnot appears to be using the common physical conception of the Portuguese: 'The Mens Habit is like their Persons, very grave, a Black Coat and Band is worn from the King to the Cobler . . . it is to be feared a third part of the Country are concealed Jews, and truly by their Countenances you would believe most of them so, they retaining very much of the Swarthy Moorish Complexion' (Bromley, *Several Years Travels*, 1702, pp. 5–6). But he may also be employing the associations of

'Dustman' with indolence or sleepiness (*OED*) to deride a people whose 'Natural Laziness . . . draws them Abroad in hopes of being more at Ease' (Stevens, *Ancient and Present State of Portugal*, 1705, p. 9). Arbuthnot clearly singled out Portugal and Savoy from the other small allies because the Whigs argued that they were 'two Allies of the greatest Consequence to us, who have no Strength to resist the Force that will be poured in upon them' (*Bishop of Salisbury's Speech*, 1704, p. 4).

8: 30 *Humphrey Hocus* the Attorney : John Churchill, First Duke of Marlborough, and Commander-in-chief of the allied armies in the Low Countries during the most successful years of the war. Cf. 'HOCUS-*Pocus*, a Jugler that shews Tricks by Slight of Hand' (*Canting Dictionary*). The name 'Hocus' for the General doubtless owes something of its origin to Mrs. Manley's extended description of how 'Stauracius' (Marlborough) learned magic secrets from the witch 'Damerata' (Mrs. Jennings) which rendered him 'invincible': 'encompass'd as he is by *Damerata*'s Magick . . . he concludes himself invulnerable; and that he need never put an End to a War, that is so fruitful of golden Laurels, and so barren of Dangers' (*Memoirs of Europe*, 1710, ii. 48, 51; cf. also i. 19).

8: 31–9: 8 A Declaration . . . and Cudgel-Play. The Treaty of Grand Alliance was signed on 7 Sept. 1701, and 'The allies published manifestoes charging Louis XIV with breach of the Treaty of Ryswick . . . and with various arbitrary encroachments upon the liberties of Europe' (Scott). War was declared on 4 May 1702.

9: 2 old Contracts : i.e. treaties of trade.

9: 4–5 that he sold Goods . . . without the Stamp. The *OED* quotes this phrase to illustrate the meaning of 'stamp' as an official mark certifying the quality of cloth goods.

9: 6–7 a Bully . . . challenging People : Lewis as the prize-fighting exhibitionist again. 'That Nation [France] . . . has *Bullyed Europe* for 30 Years past' (Defoe, *Review*, 24 June 1704, i. 143); ''Tis for *France* only to Bully *Europe*' (22 Aug. 1704, i. 209).

9: 10 *The true Characters of* John Bull, Nic. Frog. For Arbuthnot's treatment of the English and Dutch 'characters', see above, pp. lvii–lxvi.

9: 14–15 single Faulcion. A falchion was a slightly curved broad sword with the edge on the convex side: *OED* cites this usage to define single falchion as a species of sword-play.

9: 22 a Boon-Companion : 'A merry Drinking Fellow' (*Canting Crew*).

10: 1 *High German Artists.* 'High German' referred to one who spoke the High German language of southern Germany (*OED*). The Dutchman (also known as the 'Hogen') was thought to be so fond of paintings that 'he that hath not Bread to eat hath a Picture' (*Dutch Drawn to the Life*, p. 68). 'Hogen Mogen' was a popular corruption of the Dutch 'Hoogmo-gendheiden', 'High Mightinesses', the title of the States-General (*OED*).

Addison gives an interesting sketch of a Dutch painter in his 'Morning's Dream', *Spectator*, 5 June 1711, i. 355.

10: 5 *Hocus* **was an old cunning Attorney.** 'Hocus' represents the traits most often associated with Marlborough in the popular mind of the time: a wily self-interest, which permitted him to vow fidelity to King James II while he corresponded secretly with the Prince of Orange; a love of money, which was gratified by immense material benefits from the war; a remarkable coolness in moments of crisis; and great skill in diplomacy. According to Trevelyan, 'the weak spot in his character was his proneness to double-dealing learnt in the dynastic intrigues of English politics' (ii. 135). Cf. Arbuthnot's 'character' with the following account of Marlborough's bad points written by the Dutch Deputy, Sicco van Goslinga, in 1707: 'The Duke is a profound dissembler, all the more dangerous that his manner and his Words give the impression of frankness itself. His ambition knows no bounds, and an avarice which I can only call sordid, guides his entire conduct. If he has courage—and of this there is no question . . . — he certainly wants that firmness of soul which makes the true Hero. Sometimes, on the eve of an action, he is irresolute, or worse . . . he lacks the precise knowledge of military detail which a Commander-in Chief should possess' (Churchill, i. 478–9). Churchill calls this account 'on the whole the best word-picture of [Marlborough]' (i. 478).

10: 6–7 **a Clerk which he kept . . . the prettiest Fellow.** The 'Clerk' is probably Prince Eugene, the Emperor's general and Marlborough's military partner in most of the major battles of the war. Eugene was known for great bravery and exemplary skill as a tactician; as to his appearance, reports varied. Swift's opinion changed perceptibly from 13 Jan. 1712 ('I saw prince Eugene to-day at Court: I don't think him an ugly faced fellow, but well enough, and a good shape') to 10 Feb. 1712 ('I saw Pr Eugene at Court today very plain; he is plaguy yellow, and tolerably ugly besides', *Journal*, pp. 463, 485). Descriptions of 'the misshapen little abbé' (Frischauer, *Prince Eugène*, 1934, p. 164) by political writers tended to be as contradictory as their party convictions (cf. Steele, *Spectator*, 31 Mar. 1712, iii. 263–4). The 6th edn. of the *Key* glossed this Clerk as Major General Cadogan, Quartermaster General and the modern equivalent of both Chief of Staff and Director of Intelligence. Churchill (i. 465–6) paid generous tribute to the military significance of Cadogan in the campaigns of his superior, and the contemporary Tories used his reputation as a lever to discredit the great General as a man whose 'conduct . . . is all owing to Cadogan's advice' (see Trevelyan, ii. 120). Yet they used the reputation of Eugene in a similar way (ibid. iii. 202), and Defoe ironically 'disputed' 'Another Scandal . . . that he [Marlborough] may thank the Prince of *Savoy* . . . more than his own Skill in War, for his great Reputation' (*Short Narrative*, 1711, p. 26). Cf. the 'Deceitful Pettifogger' in the *True Characters*, 1708, who '. . . by Employing an Able *Entring Clerk*, commences an *Attorney* at large, without being able to Read a *Writ*, or distinguish a *Common Process* from an *Execution*. . . .

He has neither the Theory, nor Practice of the Law; but, his own Vil-
lanous Arts excepted, is wholly steer'd by the Compass of his *Entring
Clerk*' (pp. 3–4). Although the balance of the evidence would indicate
that Eugene is the intended reference, the two identifications need not
be mutually exclusive.

10: 7 **he lov'd Money.** 'This love of money in Marlborough as in a few
years it became generally known was the topic of numerous taunts from
his opponents' (Earl Stanhope, *History of England*, 1872, i. 83). The
catholicity of this accusation is demonstrated by a performance of the
Recruiting Officer in 1710 at which 'the actors represented a . . . satirical
Interscenium . . . a troop of soldiers came on, singing at the top of their
voices an English song which had been made by the army in Flanders
about the Duke of Marlborough. In it Prince Eugène is praised for his
open-handedness, while Marlborough . . . is blamed for his avarice, so
that every verse ended: "but Marlborough not a penny". The people, who
are very bitter against the whole family, even the Duke himself, laughed
prodigiously and bandied about monstrous insults, although Marlborough's daughter, the Duchess of Montaigu, was herself at the play
and was so greatly shamed that she was covered with blushes' (von
Uffenbach, *London in 1710*, pp. 138–9).

10: 7–8 **was smooth-tongu'd . . . seldom lost his Temper.** Many
contemporaries, e.g. King (*Rufinus*, 1712, pp. 4–5) and Swift (*Four Last
Years*, vii. 7), made satiric capital out of the Duke's sophisticated eloquence. But even Defoe had to admit, 'My Lord has always been esteem'd
a nice Courtier, well guarded in his Words' (*Short Character*, 1711, p. 12),
and van Goslinga (10: 5 n.) wrote, 'He expresses himself well and
pleasantly . . . his intonation is warm and melodious; he is deemed one of
the most attractive of speakers in his own language. He has a very gracious
manner, and if his handsome and prepossessing countenance disposes
everyone in his favour, his manners and gentleness captivate all those
who are biased against him or displeased with him' (quoted by Barnett,
Marlborough, 1974, p. 172). Marlborough's self-control was as celebrated
as his wife's quick temper was infamous (10: 10–11 n., below).

10: 8–9 **not worse than an Infidel.** Teerink noted a parallel with
Swift's comment: '*He who doth not provide for his own house*, St. Paul
sayeth [Timothy 5: 8], *is worse than an Infidel.* And I think, he who pro-
videth *only* for his own House, is just equal with an Infidel' (*Thoughts*,
iv. 251–2).

10: 9 **he provided . . . for his Family.** Before the war (in which he
amassed a private fortune), the Duke had arranged shrewd matches for
his daughters. Henrietta married Francis, eldest son of Godolphin, in
1698, and Anne married Charles Spencer, son of the Earl of Sunderland,
in 1701; so that 'when Queen Anne came to the throne, Marlborough and
Godolphin had already forged domestic links with one another and with
one of the great Whig Houses' (Trevelyan, i. 185): 'THE FAMILY, *as they*

call'd them' (Defoe, *Review*, 14 Sept. 1712, i[xi]. 25), was charged with vicious nepotism by the Tory writers.

10: 9–10 **he lov'd himself better than them all.** 'His ambition knows no bounds', said van Goslinga (10: 5 n.) Cf. Swift's ironic distinction: 'We are not to take the Height of his Ambition from his soliciting to be General for Life: I am persuaded, his chief Motive was the Pay and Perquisites by continuing the War' (*Four Last Years*, vii. 7).

10: 10–11 **a termagant Wife . . . was plaguy Hen-peck'd.** The violent temper of Sarah Jennings, Duchess of Marlborough, became a popular satiric weapon in Tory hands after her notorious final interview with Queen Anne (19: 5–7 n.). They persistently suggested that she was the dominant partner in her marriage: 'not all his Valour can withstand / The Witchcraft of *Sempronia's* Golden Hand' (Shippen, *Moderation Display'd*, 1705, pp. 20–1); 'Alas what ease those Furies of thy life / Ambition, Av'rice and th'imperious Wife' (Pope, 'Character', ii. 15–16, *Poems*, p. 821). Even modern historians allow some basis in fact to the legend of the woman of great passions and the wife of 'masculine' will-power in relation to a conciliatory and more malleable husband (see Green, *Sarah Duchess of Marlborough*, 1967, pp. 96, 144–5, 173–4).

10: 11–13 **was seldom . . . *per test. conduct.*** : presumably *'per testimonium conductorum'*, a manufactured 'legal' term to suggest the gross charges of cowardice made by many Tory polemicists: 'he got a Reputation afterwards for a Man of Courage, but upon no other Grounds, than by setting the Country Fellows to Cudgelling or Boxing, and being a Spectator of a broken Head and a bloody Nose' (*Story of the St. Alb[a]n's Ghost*, 1712, p. 9). Another crude allegory pictured him being shamed by the valorous Eugene, who 'gallop'd out to fight, leaving the Horseman with his Teeth all shattering in his Head for fear' (*Account of a Dream*, 1708, p. 8). Swift, like Arbuthnot here, was shrewd enough to realize that such ill-founded abuse might be a double-edged weapon, and was content to imply cowardice indirectly in *Examiner*, 15 Feb. 1710, iii. 87, and *Four Last Years*, vii. 7.

10: 17 *LAW is a Bottomless-Pit* : an image apparently coined by Arbuthnot (see *Oxford Dictionary of Quotations*). One contemporary saw 'Charles III' as the Spanish 'Phaeton in a Coach-Box Driving Post to the Bottomless Pit' (*Pacquet from Parnassus*, 1702, p. 5 [6]).

10: 17 *a Cormorant, a Harpy.* Such metaphors had long been popular in anti-law satires: 'The Lawyers are . . . Harpies . . . who suck the Blood . . . of the Nation' said Defoe (*Review*, 23 Sept. 1704, i. 245); and many years before, a solicitor had been characterized as 'a kind of *Cormorant*, that fishes for others' (*Character of a Solicitor*, 1675, p. 3). Similarly Whig financiers were supposed to be 'rav'nous *Harpies*' (*Monster*, 1705, p. 7) and 'greedy *Cormorants*' (*Answer to an Infamous Libel*, 1701, p. 24). Above all, 'there are none but raptious Cormorants . . . that are so forward for pushing [the war] on' (*Miserable Case*, 'Amsterdam' [London],

1712, p. 1); and Whigs prosecuted for financial abuses in military supply were 'Harpies, Beasts of Prey, Vultures feeding upon the Bowels of their Country (*Re-Representation*, 1711, p. 10). John Hopkins, Member for St. Ives 1710–14, and a successful stockbroker, was commonly known as 'Vulture Hopkins' (Holmes, p. 156).

10: 22 **Courts**: fields of battle.

10: 23 ***Yellow-boys***: slang for gold coins, guineas, or sovereigns (*OED*).

10: 25 **Cast**: i.e. defeated (in an action at law—*OED*).

10: 26–8 **the next and the next . . . final Determination . . . inchanted Island.** Cf. the complaint of Defoe's Tom Flockmaker: 'every Spring When I came to Town they would be saying, they hoped this would be the last Year of the War, and this would be the last Year of the War' (*Worcestershire-Queries*, 1711, p. 5); or 'One Year's Tax more—And one more—This will be the last—Every one has been the last since the War began' (*Natural Reflections*, 1712, p. 27). Swift claimed, 'our Victories only served to lead us on to further visionary Prospects; Advantage was taken of the Sanguin Temper, which so many Successes had wrought the Nation up to; new Romantick Views were proposed, and the old, reasonable, sober Design, was forgot' (*Conduct*, vi. 48). Arbuthnot's image was particularly appropriate since it reflected the old suspicion that '*these Gentlemen* [lawyers] *have . . . a kinde of lip-learning, or artifice, especially of words and tearms, beyond men of other Trades and Callings, wherewith their Customers are either enchaunted, or led into by-paths, beyond their owne knowledge, and there left and lost both they and their Estates*' (Robinson, *Certaine Proposals*, 1653, Preface, p. 6).

10: 30–11: 1 **Lawyers seldom part with . . . the Shell.** As Beattie noted, this is an allusion to the fable of the lawyer who settles a dispute between two farmers over an oyster by eating it and giving half the shell to each 'client'. It appeared on a number of occasions in contemporary writings, such as *Aesop at Tunbridge*, 1698, p. 21, Mandeville's *Aesop Dress'd*, 1704, p. 48, and Arbuthnot's own *Annus Mirabilis*, 1722.

11: 1–3 ***John*'s ready Mony . . . all went . . . *Bank-Stock*, *East-India* Bonds**: the cost of the wars against Louis XIV. The War of the League of Augsburg or King William's War, which had cost England an average of £3 million for the nine years of its duration, was largely financed by the newly created National Debt and Bank of England. In 1708 and 1709 Godolphin, to supplement sums borrowed from the public, took out loans from the East-India Company and the Bank to help finance the War of the Spanish Succession (see Dickson, p. 62). This is the first of many allusions connecting two frames of reference which are satirically effective if 'inconsistent' in narrative terms, i.e. the financial burdens of the 'lawsuit' and the physical cost of John's 'cudgel-fights' (or the monetary and military aspects of 'new Whig' war policy). Cf. Tom Double's account of the Whigs' creation of 'an Army of Men with their pockets full of Bank-bills, Bank-stock, Malt and Lottery Tickets, Exchequer-Bills, *East-India* Stock, and who bore in their Hands Tallies instead of Staves and Truncheons' (Davenant, *True Picture of a Modern Whig*, 1701, p. 11).

11: 3–4 **a Farm went to Pot**: an allusion to the sale of crown lands (cf. 65: 1–2 n.) and to the increasingly severe land tax (see Holmes, pp. 160–2).

11: 5–6 **dispossess . . . Lord *Strutt* at once**: the Allies' determination, resulting from the Methuen Treaty negotiations of 1703, to substitute Charles of Austria for Philip V as King of Spain (see Trevelyan, i. 302–3).

11: 9–10 **Now and then . . . without Shoes, Stockings, and Linnen**. Until April 1707 and the battle of Almanza, the war in the Peninsula had been an almost unrelieved series of disasters for Philip and the Bourbon interest. Although the Allies continued to control large areas of Spain and were to enjoy future tactical successes, their defeat at Almanza was a strategic and political turning-point.

11: 12 **from rich Silks to *Doily* Stuffs**. Doily was a French draper, 'who raised a Fortune by finding out Materials for such Stuffs as might at once be cheap and genteel, I have heard it affirmed, that had not he discovered this frugal Method of gratifying our Pride, we should hardly have been able to carry on the last War' (*Spectator*, 24 Jan. 1712, iii. 4). See Trevelyan, ii. 103, for the effects of the war on the French economy.

11: 13–14 **his Servants in Rags . . . Bullocks-Liver**. 'I heard divers of 'em [the French people] say, that they had nothing left to make a little Broth in for their Children; Others, that they had not a Bed to lie on, nor a Blanket to cover 'em' (*Memoirs of the Present Condition of France*, 1711, p. 12). Cf. the English version of the typical Frenchman's war-weariness in a dialogue between Lewis and a spokesman for his people: '*Lewis*: 'Tis enough for me to take care of the War, and defend you from your Enemies. *Quest. Ay, but your Majesty has defended us so long till we have no occasion to be defended any longer: we have nothing left now to lose*' (*French King's Catechism*, 1709, p. 3).

11: 19–20 **Habit is a second Nature**: an Aristotelian proposition which had passed into proverbial English: *Dictionary of Proverbs* (C. 932) cites seventeen examples of usage between 1547 and 1721. Cf. Sir Humphrey Mackworth (47: 2–3 n.) on 'Custom, (which is a second Nature)' in the 'Preface' to *Peace at Home* (1703).

11: 23–4 **as able a Lawyer . . . on the Bench**. 'The manners and sentiments of all the nation became extravagant and chimerical' (Hawkesworth). Scott elaborated on this: 'and began, from the successes of the Duke of Marlborough, to assume a military character, rather inconsistent with the commercial interests of England'. The war was at this time (1704–7) enthusiastically supported by the populace.

11: 29–12: 2 **a mean Slave . . . a Fool . . . to drudge.** This recalls the 'admirable lesson of Government' which Mrs. Manley's 'Irene' (the Duchess of Marlborough) imparts to 'Constantine' (Queen Anne): 'shou'd a Monarch load himself with dirty Business?' The 'Empire' is 'his Creature! his Slave! Let *Them* born with drudging Souls, Wretches! fed and cloath'd, for such abject Uses, charge themselves with Business' (*Memoirs of Europe*, 1710, i. 187).

11: 30 **What immense Estates . . . by the Law?** The principal allusion is clearly to the 'immense estate' of Woodstock given to Marlborough by his grateful Queen (13: 14–16 n.); but there is also a reflection of the profiteering among lesser ranks, from James Brydges the Paymaster of the army down to the most junior subalterns, who were 'notoriously Guilty of *Plundering the Nation*, by the fraudulent and corrupt Practises, which they have been found Guilty of, in false Musters, and other evil Methods of getting from the Publick' (*Re-Representation*, 1711, p. 18); see also G. Davies, 'The Seamy Side of Marlborough's War', *HLQ* xv (1952), 21–4.

11: 31–12: 1 **What a Pleasure . . . To swagger at the Bar?** At this point John is very like Addison's 'political upholsterer' (*Tatler*, 6 Apr. 1710), a 'character' designed 'for the particular benefit of those worthy citizens who live more in a coffee-house than in their shops, and whose thoughts are so taken up with the affairs of the Allies, that they forget their customers' (iii. 222). Defoe struck a more direct cautionary note in warning that 'When the Officers, coming from *Flanders*, after the Campaign, appear in the newest Fashions, which they bring over with them, with a good Ayre and genteel Mien, which is almost common to them, the People, who never saw the Hardships which they undergo, think them only design'd for Pleasure and Ease, and their Profession to be desir'd above any thing in the World besides' (*Short Narrative*, 1711, p. 40).

12: 8 *Blackwell-Hall.* Blackwell or Bakewell Hall, London's cloth exchange, was on the West side of Basinghall Street (see *London Past and Present*).

12: 9 **Bayses:** a coarse woollen material, from 'baise' (*OED*).

12: 9–12 *Actions upon the Case . . . Dedimus.* Definitions of the elements in this legal torrent may all be found in *OED*; for the precise application of legal terms in the allegory see 103: 19 n. to 104: 32–3 n.

12: 13 **the Tribe:** a common and derisory collective noun. Over half a century before, Henry Robinson had written, 'The Lawyers, the men of Law; the whole Tribe, from the Judges to the Prison door-keepers . . . seem to have but one chief shop at *Westminster*' (*Certaine Proposals*, 1653, pp. 1–2).

12: 17–18 **arrive to . . . Justice:** 'Hold the balance of power' (Hawkesworth).

12: 20 **poor grovelling Mechanicks**: tradesmen, belonging to the 'lower orders'; vulgar, low (*OED*); 'also a mean, inconsiderable contemptible Fellow' (*Canting Crew*).

12: 21-2 **A Bale of Broad-cloath.** Cf. Defoe's fears for the loss of trade in 'Broad-Cloath, the Ancient Standard Commodity, and Staple Trade of this Nation' (*Review*, 10 Mar. 1705, ii. 14).

12: 22-4 **Frog . . . neglected not his ordinary Business.** The Maritime powers argued bitterly over the moral and economic rights and wrongs of continuing trade with the enemy. The English, in general, accepted that a boycott was necessary, but many Dutch merchants acted on the principle that trade (with the enemy if necessary) provided their only means of existence, and thus their only means of continuing the war (see Clark, *Dutch Alliance*, 1923, pp. 63-85, and Trevelyan, i. 295-6). During the later years of the conflict, and under a Tory ministry, polemicists made much of the continuation of commerce between France and the States. In three successive *Reviews* (24 and 27 Feb., 1 Mar. 1711, viii. 573-84), Defoe elaborated on the benefit reaped by the Dutch from this trade; see also Swift, *Examiner*, 31 May 1711, iii. 165, and Coombs, pp. 41-8, 87-9, 98, 272-3.

12: 27 **Hocus** *had an Intrigue with his Wife.* Marlborough and Godolphin worked in effective political harmony to ensure the success of the pro-war lobby in Parliament. See 'Background, 1698-1712', pp. xliv-xlv, above. Mrs. Manley lost no time in pointing out 'the wonderful good Understanding between the Marquis [Marlborough] and the Count [Godolphin]. . . . So perfect was their Intelligence, that the General did nothing in the *Army*, without the Advice of the *Minister*; nor the *Minister* anything in the *Cabinet*, without the Approbation of the General' (*Secret Memoirs*, 1709, ii. 144). This is Arbuthnot's first direct reference to collusion on the part of the Whigs in order to control Parliament. Mrs. Manley overloads her case in order to make the point: '*Irene* [the Duchess of Marlborough] and *Stauratius* [the Duke] with five or six of their Creatures . . . manage Affairs, to the Exclusion of all those who are either capable of the Cabinet, Army, or lov'd the ancient Glory of the Empire' (*Memoirs of Europe*, 1710, i. 173).

13: 1 **the last Man . . . is himself.** *Dictionary of Proverbs* (C. 877) cites four examples of usage between 1636 and 1693.

13: 5 **lov'd . . . Plays.** 'With a virtual monopoly of talent and powerful backing, Whig writers did not hesitate to project their political opinions' into drama of all kinds (Holmes, p. 24).

13: 9 **a Months mind:** an inclination, a liking (*OED*).

13: 10-11 **upon all occasions . . . Praise of** *Hocus.* One or both Houses of Parliament addressed praise and gratitude to Marlborough on eight occasions (see Boyer, *History of . . . Anne*, 1722, pp. 36, 167, 169, 220, 272, 273, 367, 376). Another proposed address was abandoned in the face of growing hostility during 1709.

13: 11–12 **When *John* . . . his greatest Benefactor.** The reputation of Marlborough was the single greatest obstacle to the Tories' policy of convincing the populace that final victory was impossible; but the persistent sniping of Tory writers, which escalated into a campaign of abuse after the fall of the Godolphin ministry in 1710, brought immediate and often justified accusations of gross ingratitude from his Whig supporters: 'Oh Gratitude! whether art thou fled? Shall we see that Man, to whom, next under God, we owe all that we now Enjoy . . . used like a Traytor, by Men that deserve Pillorys' (*History of Ingratitude*, 1712, p. 33); see also *English Gratitude*, 1713, p. 2, and *Duke of M*[arlborough]'s *Vindication*, 1712, p. 5.

13: 14–16 **A good swinging Sum . . . *Hocus*'s Country-House:** Blenheim Palace, Woodstock, Oxfordshire. In December 1704 the Queen gave the Royal Manor of Woodstock with all its offices and perquisites to the Churchill family in perpetuity, and Vanbrugh was commissioned to build the Palace. Swift claimed that the building cost £200,000 (*Examiner*, 23 Nov. 1710, iii. 21), and later commented in ironic innocence: 'in *England*, as I was informed, the Wealth of the Kingdom was so divided among the People, that little or nothing was left to their Sovereign; and that . . . some Subjects had Palaces more Magnificent than Queen *Anne* her self' (*New Journey*, iii. 213); see also *Gulliver's Travels*, xi, 115, and *Annals*, v. 426–9.

13: 18–19 **The Parson of the Parish . . . against Adultery:** Sacheverell's sermons in 1709 on the necessity of 'non-resistance'. See 'Background 1698–1712', pp. li–lii, above. None of the Tories seems to have respected Sacheverell's intelligence. Swift tells Stella, 'Trap is a coxcomb, and tother [Sacheverell] is not very deep, and their Judgmt in things of Witt or Sense is miraculous'(*Journal*, 17 Mar. 1712, p. 516). This remark is followed by a reference to Pamphlet II of *John Bull*. See also Holmes, *The Trial of Doctor Sacheverell* (1973), p. 218.

13: 22–3 **they would join . . . for using personal Reflections.** Cf. 'the famous tryal of Dr. Sacheverell . . . arose from a foolish passionate pique of the Earl of Godolphin, whom this divine was supposed, in a sermon, to have reflected on under the the the name of *Volpone* [see *Tryal*, p. 44] . . . Lord Sommers . . . confessed . . . that he had earnestly, and in vain endeavoured, to dissuade the Earl from that attempt' (Swift, *Memoirs*, viii. 115). Godolphin was, for his time, remarkably sensitive to personal attack, particularly when his loyalty to the Queen and Church was impugned (see Holmes, pp. 189–90). Arbuthnot used the joke again in *Brief Account of Mr. John Ginglicutt's Treatise*, 1731, p. 9.

13: 27–8 **his Doctrine . . . Wives Slaves.** For Arbuthnot's detailed allegory of the trial and his parodies of the prosecution speeches, see 25: 2–4 n. to 27: 24 n.

13: 31 ***Spring-Garden*:** either the 'Old Spring Garden', a public park at Charing Cross (*London Past and Present*, iii. 295), the scene of midnight masquerades, which were the cause of much scandal (*Spectator*, 9 Mar. 1711, i. 36 n.), or 'Spring Gardens' at Vauxhall, described in 1710 as consisting 'entirely of avenues and covered walks where people stroll up and down.... Generally vast crowds are to be seen here, especially females of doubtful morals, who are dressed as finely as ladies of quality' (von Uffenbach, *London in 1710*, p. 131). Mrs. Bull, like the typical merchant's wife, 'commends the Play-houses, *Spring-Garden*, and the Park, and never desists till she has got the Cully to coach her to one of them' (*Ape-Gentle-Woman*, 1675, p. 5); see also *Parliament of Ladies. Or Divers Remarkable Passages of Ladies in Spring-Garden*, 1647.

14: 4–6 **aim'd a Knife . . . threw a Bottle . . . nothing but Confusion.** A bitter pamphlet war raged over the Sacheverell trial. Few of the hundreds of polemics which poured from the London presses managed to rise above the level of conflict at Westminster where 'The house complained of being *aspersed* and *vilified*; opprobrious terms were used by both parties' (Hawkesworth). Indeed, the conflict went much further during the riots occasioned by the trial, when George Purchase, the most notorious ringleader of the mob, 'run resolutely with his Sword in his Hand, and made a full Pass at . . . Captain *Hansberg*' (*Annals*, ix. 199-202).

14: 8 **a bruise in her Right-side:** the 'defeat' of the ministry at the trial. Perhaps the 'Right-side' alludes to the practice by which Government and Opposition supporters sit on the right and left hand of the Speaker of the House. Although this tradition was not fully established until later in the century, 'right' was consistently associated with the dominant Whig party during these early years. The 'Right-side' also recalls Addison's well-known *Spectator* on 'Party-patches' (2 June 1711, i. 346–9): the 'Body of *Amazons*' on his right hand at the theatre are Whigs, 'being Spotted on the Right Side of the Forehead'; the Tory contingent is spotted on the left side. Addison is struck by the ladies' 'way of declaring War upon one another' and urges English women 'to distinguish themselves as tender Mothers and faithful Wives, rather than as furious Partizans'. Swift referred to his Tory tracts as chains and padlocks on his left leg in *Gulliver's Travels*, xi. 11–12. Carstens postulated a verbal echo of Sacheverell's condemnation of hostile personal criticism, 'thus *Wounding* the *Ministry*, thro' the *Sides* of the *Minister*' (*Tryal*, p. 34).

14: 14 **all regular Physicians:** a popular collocation used to distinguish the true doctor from the quack. 'A Regular Physician, that has travell'd and seen as much of the Venereal Practice . . . as perhaps any one . . . has discover'd one Medicine (a Panacea) that never yet fail'd' (advertisement in *British Mercury*, 30 July 1712).

14: 17–18 *Signior* **Cavallo . . .** *of her Ulcer***:** Charles Seymour, sixth Duke of Somerset, and Master of the Horse. The first edition of the *Key* identified Cavallo ambiguously as the 'D— of S—', the second specifically as the 'D[uke] of S[hrewsbur]y', and all later editions as the

'D[uke] of S[omerse]t'. Scott also identified Cavallo as Somerset, and argued that the allusion was 'suppressed [1727–33], probably because disrespectful to the Queen'; Aitken agreed with this identification in his edition of the *Works* of Arbuthnot (1892), but did not dispute the point a few years later (in 1903) when he supervised a new edition of Arber's *Later Stuart Tracts*, in which Cavallo was glossed as Shrewsbury. Both Shrewsbury and Somerset were noted Whigs, and were, in their different ways, instrumental in helping Harley to destroy the Godolphin ministry. Shrewsbury spent much of Anne's reign in Italy being nursed by his Italian wife, and was a most surprising and effective political ally of Harley in 1710 (see *Wentworth Papers*, ed. Cartwright, 1883, p. 133, and Nicholson and Turberville, *Charles Talbot*, 1930, p. 181). Yet as Swift was at some pains to show (*Four Last Years*, vii. 12–14), Somerset was the key figue in the changes as an important Whig Lord who openly supported them. His 'intelligence was limited, but he was independent, ambitious, bold, and could upon occasion be both violent and forcible' (Churchill, ii. 655). Harley played on these characteristics, persuading him to co-operate in the changes by deluding him that he was to become the leader of a new moderate ministry. The quack's name also points to Somerset, not only since 'Cavallo', Italian for horse, alludes to his position at Court, but also as 'Cavallero' was a common term for the obsessively proud Spanish gentry (see *Trip to Spain*, 1704/5, pp. 5, 10, 15), and thus a neat suggestion of the arrogance of this 'Stamm'ring, Hot, Conceited, Laughing L[ord], / Who prov'd his want of Sense in ev'ry word' (Shippen, *Faction Display'd*, 1705, p. 5). In the face of such evidence we must discount identifications of Cavallo as 'Hannover' (MS. note on a copy of this pamphlet, BM. 12314 aa. 16), 'Prince Eugene' (MS. note, National Library of Scotland, H. 34, f. 2/197), or the horse which threw King William and was thus 'responsible' for his death (*PPB*, 29 Apr. 1712).

14: 23–5 **an infallible Ointment . . . a few Days.** Somerset 'affected to appear the Head of . . . [the Whig] Party, to which his Talents were no way proportioned' (Swift, *Four Last Years*, vii. 13). Indeed 'he fancy'd the World turn'd round with him, and that the REVOLUTION was just about doing the . . . *Somerset*' (*True . . . Account of the Last Distemper*, 1710, i. 2).

15: 1–2 **Wife . . . to Dress her . . . a very gentle soft Hand.** Somerset's wife, who brought him his wealth and enhanced his importance at Court, was Elizabeth Percy, sole heiress of the last Earl of Northumberland, confidante of Queen Anne, and Groom of the Stole in 1711. She is the 'Carrots' of Swift's 'Windsor Prophecy' ('*They* Assassine *when young, and* Poison *when old*'). The word 'Dress' in the allusion has its medical sense, and also recalls the Groom of the Stole 'having the office and honour to present and put on His Majesties first Garment . . . every morning' (*OED*). It seems likely that 'gentle soft hand' suggests the character given her by the Tories, 'insinuating, and a Woman of Intrigue' (Swift, *Corres.* i. 248) noted for 'a most obsequious Behaviour' (*Enquiry*,

viii. 146); but it is possible that her gentleness reflects the Queen's emotional dependence on the Duchess. When Somerset threatened to remove his wife from Court the Queen sent one of her physicians, Sir David Hamilton, to argue that her health 'would be greatly Impar'd, if it happen'd that the Duke would not let her stay in' (quoted by P. Roberts, 'Swift, Queen Anne, and "The Windsor Prophecy"', *PQ* xlix [1970], 255–6).

15: 4–5 **her Constitution ... Government ... a little time.** These puns seem to confirm the reference to Somerset, and 'The brilliant prospect he had seen for himself at the Head of a Ministry of both Parties, the prime favourite of the Queen, and revered as the honest man whom the nation trusted' (Churchill, ii. 761).

15: 7 **dance a Jig next** *October* **in** *Westminster-Hall*: that is, the Whigs would again have a parliamentary majority after the general election of October 1710. The Tories, however, swept to victory (see Trevelyan, iii. 59–60).

15: 13–17 **the Patient gave up the Ghost ... Medicines were infallible.** Cf. 'When the dissolution [of Parliament] was announced', Somerset 'flew off in a greater Rage than ever' (Swift, *Four Last Years*, vii. 14), and 'Without resigning his office of Master of the Horse he gathered the Whig ex-ministers at his house and announced his intention of fighting the election hand in glove with them ... Somerset went off "in a pet to Petworth" and flung himself into the election fight against Harley, while his Duchess wrestled vigorously with Abigail [Masham] for the Queen's favour' (Churchill, ii. 761). Cf. also the generic quack doctor who, 'after a thousand promises of Health ... most perfidiously leaves a man Gasping, and ... when persons are Kill'd by his improper Applications, he Chides their Friends for not sending for him sooner; Rails at the Nurses for not observing directions, or alledges the Sick would not be rul'd' (*Character of a Quack-Doctor*, 1676, p. 6).

15: 18–19 **the Clergy would hardly allow her Christian Burial.** By February 1711, 146 back-bench members of High Tory persuasions had formed a powerful pressure group—known as the October Club— to demand that Harley abandon his moderate policies, and in particular that the government institute rigorous investigations into and punishment of the mismanagements and corruptions of the fallen Godolphin ministry (see H. T. Dickinson, 'The October Club', *HLQ* xxxiii [1969–70], 155–73).

15: 22–3 **She left no Will:** a possible allusion to 'Sir William Crawley', i.e. Godolphin (67: 5–6 n. and 84: 22 n.). Arbuthnot plays on the word 'Will' more than once in the satire.

15: 24 *My Curse.* The 'Curse', as noted in the *Key* (4th edn.), refers to the Whigs' repeated demand (which became something of a watchword) for 'No Peace without Spain'.

15: 33 *Polemia, Discordia,* and *Usuria* : see 34: 24 n. to 35: 8 n.; 35: 9 n. to 36: 9–11 n.; 36: 11–13 n. to 36: 17–20 n.

16: 7–8 **he wedded a sober Country Gentlewoman** : the Harley ministry and its supporters in the new Parliament which met on 25 Nov. 1710. One contemporary judged that it contained '178 Tories, 61 Whigs & 14 doubtfull' from the reported returns (quoted by Holmes, p. 19). Many of the newly elected Tories were staunchly conservative country gentlemen. Cf. 'the best type of country member [of Parliament] . . . had . . . a genuine concern for "good husbandry" in government, and felt an obligation to his constituents to see to it that the Queen's administration was as frugal and incorrupt as Parliament could make it' (ibid., p. 121).

16: 15 **great Abuses and Disorders in your Family** : the financial abuses practised and indulged by the fallen ministry. (Walpole was one scapegoat.) The satire directed against 'the Tyranny and Insolence of those ungrateful Servants, who as they *wexed the Fatter*, did but *kick the more*' (Swift, *Conduct*, vi. 43) which follows, and indeed which runs throughout these pamphlets, drew on the traditional associations of lower-class tradesmen with the Civil War rebels to demonstrate the parallel between Commonwealth Parliamentarianism and contemporary whiggery. Cromwell had long been the apocryphal 'Brewer' and in 1690(?) one Jacobite ballad compared the Coronation of William with the execution of Charles II as a time 'When Brewers and Bakers / And such undertakers / Did settle the church and the state / A fine reformation / Was made in our nation / And little things then became great' (BM. Add. MSS. 22640).

16: 18–19 **your Butler purloins . . . your Brewer sells your Hogwash.** In a 'Report from the Committee appointed to enquire into the Abuses of the Victualling [15 Feb. 1711] . . . it was *unanimously resolv'd,* . . . "That in the Management of Her Majesty's Brew-house, as well as in the Contracts for furnishing the Navy with Beer, there have been many notorious Embezlements, and scandalous Abuses, to the defrauding the Publick of great Sums of Money . . ."' (*Annals*, ix. 313). The brewers seem to have been the most flagrant offenders (see also *Annals*, ix. 319–22; Boyer describes the 'collusory Contracts' between Agent-Victuallers and Clerks of Brewhouses on p. 321; cf. William Pittis, *History of the Present Parliament and Convocation*, 1711, pp. 67 ff.). Cf. also Swift's attack on the abuses of the Godolphin ministry, especially the debt run up in the Office of the Navy, in *Examiner*, 7 Dec. 1710, iii. 32–4. Brewers and Vintners were unpopular anyway for adulterating their wares and off-setting their taxes by raising prices (see *Cheating Age*, 1712, p. 11). The allegory also includes a palpable jibe at Marlborough as 'butler' in collusion with Whig suppliers, as in *The Very Case, or the Story of John the Butler*, bs. 1712 (which associated the Duke with the butler to one 'J. B. of *Ramsbury*', who embezzled 'the *Chippings and Parings of the Bread*' see following note) or the praise of his successor as commander-in-chief, 'Brave ORMOND disdains to make Sale of Commissions, / To be brib'd by Contractors on Terms and Conditions; / He's a *Butler* that ne'er will be censur'd for Tripping' (*Queen's* . . . *New Toast*, bs. 1712).

16: 19–20 **your Baker cheats . . . in Tale:** an unequivocal allusion to Marlborough's peculation. Sir Soloman Medina informed the Commission established to investigate accounts that he had paid £63,000 to the Duke between 1702 and 1711 in 'commissions' on bread contracts (see Trevelyan, iii. 200). Tory polemicists were quick to seize this weapon against the General (see Swift, *Four Last Years*, vii. 65; *Perquisite-Monger*, 1712; and Defoe, *Short Narrative*, 1711), but few use it as inventively as does Arbuthnot here. On the level of personal allusion, Marlborough acts as both butler (see previous note) and baker to his master, which is entirely appropriate since—as Bull is later to discover to his horror—'The same Man was Butcher and Grasier, Brewer and Butler' (65: 13–15 n.). Yet the allegory again provides a wider frame of reference, for the bakers too were generally unpopular; 'Price of Bread, and Weight of Bread was all in their own Breasts' (*Review*, 4 May 1710, vii. 66).

16: 22 **cabages:** i.e. pilfers surreptitiously. This is the first usage recorded in *OED*. The *Canting Dictionary* affirmed: 'CABBAGE; Taylors are so called, because of their general and immoderate Love of that Vegetable . . . . The Cloth they steal and purloin from the Raiment they make up, is also called *Cabbage*'.

16: 22–3 **long Scores . . . to Market with ready Mony:** one of several allusions to government long-term borrowing, perhaps the most revolutionary financial innovation in Augustan economics. 'The first measures taken to create a system of government long-term borrowing were . . . marked by haste, carelessness, and episodic failure' (Dickson, p. 57); cf. also Holmes, p. 152. Mrs. Bull believes in more old-fashioned theories of national economy.

16: 24–5 **You have not posted . . . Ten Years.** To post the books was to transfer to the ledger all the items in the auxiliary books to provide a complete record of all transactions (*OED*); an allusion to '*The Public Accounts not regularly past*' (*Key*, 4th edn.). The new ministry declaimed against 'the scandalous Negligence that hath been shewn in *inspecting* and stating the publick Accounts' (*Annals*, ix. 235), and resurrected the Commission of Accounts which had last been used to scourge the 'moneyed men' in 1702–3 by the previous Tory-dominated ministry (see Holmes, pp. 138–40). Swift commented with some satisfaction: 'THE Earl of *Godolphin* . . . knew that his long Neglect of compelling the Accountants . . . might be punished as a Breach of Trust: He had run the Kingdom into immense Debts' (*Four Last Years*, vii. 22).

16: 30 **Scriveners and Usurers.** Mrs. Bull consistently uses the older and more derogatory terms for the new-fangled 'stock-broker' and 'jobber'.

16: 32–17: 1 **Nature never design'd you.** The tone of Mrs. Bull's speech recalls that of Mrs. Manley's 'Irene' (the Duchess of Marlborough) who makes the following appeal to her son 'Constantine' (Queen Anne): 'What Enjoyment do you want? Cannot you pray and play, and do any thing but puzzle your self with State-Affairs? which, credit me, your Genius was never born for' (*Memoirs of Europe*, 1710, ii. 258).

17: 3 **Maggot:** a whimsical or perverse fancy (*OED*).

17: 3 **touch'd him in the tender point.** Cf. 'You touch me in the tend'rest part, / Both of my Int'rest, and my Heart' (*Fox Set to Watch the Geese*, 1705, p. 16).

17: 21 **I'll . . . look over my Accounts.** On 20 Dec. 1711 the Commons resolved to address Anne for an account 'of the Quotas and Proportions of Her Majesty and Her Allies by Sea and Land, during the present War, including Subsidies . . . and also how the same had been observ'd' (Coombs, p. 286).

17: 23 *his Attorney's Bill.* The 'Attorney's Bill' does not refer specifically to Marlborough's military expenditures, but to Whig financing of the war from 1702 to 1710.

17: 27–9 **Fees to Judges . . . Witnesses &c.** For Arbuthnot's more precise use of such legal processes and offices see 103: 22 n. to 104: 32–3 n.

18: 7–10 *John . . . looking over his Bills . . . Cheated.* 'On February 4th [1712], the Committee of the Whole House compared the details of allied promises with those of allied fulfillment. Their conclusions they embodied in eleven resolutions, all of them damning' (Coombs, p. 291). These resolutions were overwhelmingly approved the next day.

18: 10–12 **he had paid for Counsel . . . never fee'd . . . Journeys . . . never made:** the deficiencies of the Allies in terms of common military abuses. Arbuthnot conflates the examinations into 'the conduct of the Allies' and those into domestic corruptions, the latter by the Commission of Accounts in January and February 1712 (see Holmes, pp. 140–2). Unscrupulous officers drew pay for men killed in action or never recruited ('*Paying Troops in Roll, not in Field*', *Key*, 4th edn.), falsified reports on equipment, and collaborated with fraudulent suppliers.

18: 12–14 *Hocus* and *Frog* . . . **Burden . . . upon his Shoulders:** a common metaphor in Tory polemic. Defoe commented: '*we . . . carry'd our Burthen so true*; / *The* Dutch *tho't we had been so beat to the* Road, / *We should be their* Pack-Horse *quite thro''* (*Reasons against Fighting*, 1712, p. 22); and he defended the 'Resolutions' on the grounds that 'the *British* Court entering into a more narrow Inspection of Things, have not thought fit so calmly to suffer the Weight of the War to lye heavier upon one Shoulder than another' (*Farther Search*, 1712, p. 5).

18: 18–19 **Daniel Burgess . . .** *a Law-Suit is a Suit for Life.* Daniel Burgess was the celebrated Presbyterian minister who once addressed his

congregation on the subject of Job's 'robe of righteousness': 'if . . . any
of you would have a *suit* for a twelvemonth, let him repair to Monmouth-
Street; if for his lifetime, let him apply to the Court of Chancery; and,
if for all eternity, let him *put on* righteousness' (Scott). Arbuthnot turns
the witticism against its creator with this allusion to the physical danger
in which Burgess found himself during the riots occasioned by the 'law-
suit' against Sacheverell: his meeting-house in New Court, between
Little Sheer Lane and Carey Street, was wrecked and partially burned by
the pro-Sacheverell mob on the night of 1 Mar. 1710 (see Holmes, *Trial
of Doctor Sacheverell*, 1973, pp. 161–76). It was with a measure of
malicious satisfaction that Tory writers used his misfortunes to spice
their polemics (see *Collection of Poems*, 1710, ii. 6–7).

18: 21–2 *John*'s Cause . . . milch Cow . . . out of it. Cf. 'From the
very beginning, we [the Whigs] resolv'd to make a great Milch-Cow of
the Common-wealth; and that she might yield the more Milk, 'twas
determined to throw her into a Field of Clover [the war], where she might
have rank Feeding' (Davenant, *Sir Thomas Double at Court*, 1710, p. 95).

18: 23–4 a Cousin . . . Sir *Roger Bold*: Robert Harley, from 1711
First Earl of Oxford and Mortimer. Roger was a generic name for countrymen: cf. the 'honest *Roger Bold*' of the *British Apollo*; the 'Trusty Roger'
who was the articulate countryman of the *Observator*; and similar 'Rogers'
in *Heraclitus Ridens Redivivus*, 1688, *Tackers Toss'd in a Blanket*, 1705,
and Ned Ward's *London Spy*. The surname Bold suggests the Tory view
of his administration, but also alludes, with affectionate irony, to his
disposition: the Tory Brothers called their singularly reserved and mild-
mannered leader 'the Dragon'. McInnes commented that 'Harley was
a very ordinary man' and despite his 'spectacular political success . . . he
remained a shy, fumbling figure' (*Robert Harley*, 1970, pp. 175–8).

18: 24–7 Predecessors . . . bred up to the Law . . . amongst their
Neighbours. Harley's ancestors were landowning gentry of the Herefordshire and Welsh Border area. They had been 'lawyers' in both the
literal and allegorical senses. Oxford's father, Sir Edward Harley, had
led a regiment of foot in the Parliamentary army in 1643 and had signed
a 'Remonstrance' against 'the Protector's lawless intentions'. 'He avoided
party connections and obtained the act for abolishing the arbitrary court
of the marches of Wales' (*DNB*). Oxford's grandfather, Sir Robert Harley,
acted as magistrate and deputy lieutenant of Herefordshire; his great-
grandfather, Thomas Harley, was sheriff of that county, as was Oxford
himself for a time in 1689.

18: 28 Gentlemen of the Long Robe: a common euphemism for Judges
and Magistrates. Cf. the *Examination, Tryal, and Condemnation of
Rebellion*, 1703, before 'the Gentlemen of the Long Robe' (p. 5), and
the description of the great Whig lawyer Somers as 'the best *Pen* the
Long Robe can boast of' (*Thoughts of a Country Gentleman*, 1710, p. 9).

18: 29–30 *John* put his Cause in Sir *Roger*'s Hands, desiring him
to make the best of it. Harley took over the new ministry in 1710 with

the avowed intention of bringing the war to an end, and was made Lord Treasurer in June 1711, when he was finally accepted as the prime minister of the government.

19: 2–5 **'Squire *South* swore . . . *Frog* . . . was sacrific'd.** The allies protested violently against the ministerial changes, the decision to seek a peace, and Marlborough's projected dismissal. The Emperor was prominent among the protesters (see *Annals*, x. 232–3, 247–8, 253–9, 263), but the Dutch complaints, delivered by their Envoy Vryberg, were taken more to heart by Tory polemicists: 'The *D*[utc]*h-m*[a]*n* too must Frown and pout, / The ill-bred Cur, / Did make a stir, / And dar'd to say, 'twas wrong that they shou'd be turn'd out' (*Changes*, 1711, p. 11). When the 'Preliminary Articles' (p. liv, above) were revealed to 'Count *Gallas*, King *Charles's* Envoy . . . and to the Ministers of *Portugal*, *Savoy*, *&c* . . . [these] Gentlemen were variously affected' (*Annals*, x. 253–8, 263): see also Coombs, pp. 224–6, 231, 240, 305.

19: 5–7 *Hocus's* **Wife . . . fell a scolding . . . like the Mother of** *Belzebub*: the stormy final interview between Anne and her former friend, the Duchess of Marlborough, in April 1710: cf. the picture of the Duchess as 'an oldish Woman . . . her Eyes glaring like Lightning . . . Out of her Nostrils came a sulphurous Smoke, and out of her Mouth Flames of Fire' (*Account of a Dream*, 1708, p. 12), and Bolingbroke's rhetorical satisfaction that the 'Fury, who broke Loose to execute the Vengeance of Heaven on a Sinful People is restrain'd, and the Royal Hand . . . reach'd out to Chain up the Plague' (see Swift, *Letter to the Examiner*, iii. 225). Mrs. Bull may here represent not only the Queen but also the Harleys, particularly Harley's second wife, Sarah Middleton, 'an incurable domestic mouse. The ladies of Queen Anne's Court never tired of poking fun at her unfashionable ways. To them she was ' "an old housekeeper". . . . The contrast with the pushing, politically conscious Sarah Churchill is almost total' (McInnes, *Robert Harley*, 1970, p. 179). Besides recalling Irene's excoriation of Constantine in Mrs. Manley's *Memoirs of Europe*, 1710, i. 216–17 (8: 11–17 n.), this passage also echoes Irene's reproach of 'Leonidas' (Mrs. Masham, ii. 261).

19: 9–10 **Ninny-hammer:** simpleton (*OED*); 'A silly Senseless Fellow' (*Canting Crew*).

19: 16 **Tenter-hooks:** hooks or bent nails set in a close row along the upper and lower bar of a tenter, by which the edges of cloth are firmly held (*OED*).

19: 21–2 **my Husband . . . never swore an Oath, nor told a Lie . . . He is grateful.** Marlborough's self control was legendary in his own time. Cf. '*you are said to excel in the Art of bridling and subduing your Anger, and stifling or concealing your Resentments*' (Swift, *Examiner*, 8 Feb. 1710, iii. 83). See the 1710 panegyric, *Reasons why the Duke of Marlborough Cannot Lay Down his Commands, Deduced from the Principles of Loyalty, Gratitude, Honour, Interest, &c.*, p. 3. The General's 'Gratitude' is discussed on the same page. For a panegyric on Marlborough's

Ability, Dexterity, Wisdom, Humanity, Sweetness, Zeal, Affection, Quiet, Unity, Credit, Vigour, and Harmony, see Hare, *The Conduct of the Duke of Marlborough*, 1712.

19: 23 **liberal.** Cf. 'That Liberality which Nature hath denied him with respect to Money, he makes up by a great Profusion of Promises' (Swift, *Four Last Years*, vii. 7).

19: 24 **dutiful to his Superiours.** Cf. '*Loyalty, as I take it, consists in an Implicit Obedience to the Lawful Commands of whatsoever Prince you are subject to* . . . he [Marlborough] . . . was never found Tardy in the minutest Breach of one of Her [Anne's] Orders' (*Reasons why . . . Marlborough Cannot Lay Down his Commands*, 1710, p. 2).

19: 25 **Dust:** possibly a pun on dust as slang for money (*OED*; see also *Canting Crew*).

19: 26 **Mrs. Mynx:** a lewd or wanton woman (*OED*); '*Minks, a proud Flirt' (*Canting Crew*).

19: 27-8 **red-streak Country-face . . . Ox-Cheek.** A 'red-streak' is an apple, hence 'a girl with red cheeks' (*OED*). Mrs. Hocus may be hinting at Oxford's florid complexion.

19: 29-30 **away she flung . . . no time to reply.** This points the conflation of the Harley ministry and the Queen in the person of Mrs. Bull. Clearly the outpouring at once reflects Whig censures of Harley's government 'as totally ignorant of business' (Hawkesworth), and also alludes to the interview with Anne for which the Duchess had petitioned and at which, having promised to require no reply, 'After pouring out the vials of her bountiful wrath upon . . . Harley, the Duchess waited for an answer. The Queen only repeated again and again, "You desired no answer, and you shall have none"' (Morgan, *English Political Parties*, 1920, p. 369).

19: 32-3 **Reports at Coffeehouses, that *John* and his Wife were run mad.** Cf. Swift's derision of Whig hopes 'That this great Turn of Affairs was only occasioned by a short Madness of the People, from which they will recover in a little Time' (*Examiner*, 18 Jan. 1710, iii. 64). Cf. also the activities of whiggish 'Faction' (35: 9-14 n. to 36: 1-2 n.) and the marauding Mohocks and Hawkubites (39: 24-6 n.). The coffee-house was not only 'the real hub of social life for most upper- and middle-class Londoners' but also a centre for news, and even for stock-jobbing (at Jonathan's and Garroway's); Holmes, p. 22.

19: 33-4 **that they intended to give up House . . . old *Lewis Baboon*:** '*Stories spread by the Emissaries of the* Old *against the* New Ministry' (*Key*, 4th edn.). The skeleton of Tory Jacobitism was vigorously rattled, and when D'Aumont arrived in England with a shipment of luxury goods after the cessation of hostilities, one Whig wrote, 'O *Lewis* at last, thou has played the best Card, / Lay Hero's aside, and Tricksters reward, / Thou has got by *D'Aumont* what thou lost by *Tallard* [a French Marshal]' (*Merchant a-la-Mode*, bs. 1712).

20:1 he . . . beat his Servants: the dismissal of the Whigs from the government.

20: 3–6 a whole Regiment . . . who threw Stones . . . and Dirt. As Teerink observed, the pun on 'Regiment' points the allusion to the group of officers who were dismissed in 1710 after ostentatiously drinking 'Damnation and Confusion to the new Ministry' (see Leadam, *History of England*, 1912, p. 178). To Tory polemicists this was merely one facet of a Whig campaign which followed 'the old Maxim of our Party, *Throw dirt enough, some of it will Stick*' (Davenant, *True Picture of a Modern Whig*, 1701, p. 62); see also *An Examination*, 1711, p. 28, *Thoughts of an Honest Whig*, 1710, p. 11, and Bissett, *Modern Fanatick*, 1710, ii. 14.

20: 8 pawn his Plate and Jewels. On 8 Dec. 1711 the Commons resolved 'That the Officers of the Mint, should lay before the House an Account of the Deficiency of the Money produc'd by the Coinage of the Plate brought in upon the *Lottery Act* of 1711' (*Annals*, x. 293). 'Pawn' refers to Harley's first lottery (see p. liii, above).

20: 8–9 Mrs. *Bull* should sell her Linnen. On 26 Mar. 1712 the Commons resolved '*That an additional Duty be laid upon the Importation of all Chequer'd or Strip'd Linnens*' (*Annals*, xi. 2).

20: 10 Don Diego . . . *the Conjurer*: Daniel Finch, Second Earl of Nottingham, who was first nicknamed 'Dismal' by either Steele or Swift (see *Tatler*, 31 May 1703, i. 184), on account of his sallow countenance and solemn bearing. His conjuring masterpiece was his volte-face in agreeing to support the war during the critical debates of December 1711 in return for the withdrawal of Whig opposition to the Occasional Bill. (For Nottingham's opposition to Marlborough's strategy in the Netherlands and Germany see Horwitz, *Revolution Politicks, the Career of Daniel Finch Second Earl of Nottingham*, 1968, pp. 167 ff.) After his breach with the ministry the following advertisement was printed in *PB*, 6 Dec. 1711: 'Whereas a very tall, thin, swarthy Complexion'd Man, between 60 and 70 Years of Age, wearing a brown Coat, with little Sleeves and long Pockets, has lately withdrawn himself from his Friends, being seduc'd by wicked Persons to follow ill Courses. These are to give Notice, That whoever shall Discover him, shall have 10s. Reward; or if he will voluntarily return, he shall be kindly receiv'd by his Friends, who will not Reproach him for past Follies, provided he gives good Assurances, that, for the future, he will firmly adhere to the Church of England, in which he was so carefully educated by his honest Parents' (reprinted in *Annals*, x. 281 n.). The name Don Diego had, by this time, become evocative of two preconceptions about the Spanish national character, both of which were relevant to Arbuthnot's caricature of Nottingham. In the first place, 'Diego' (Spanish for sword), had long been a correlative for Spanish pride—hence 'Don Diego' the generic Spaniard (e.g. in Middleton's *Spanish Gypsy*, 1623; Ogilby's *Fables of Aesop*, 1668; and Wycherley's *Gentleman Dancing Master*, 1672, where Sir James Formal is 'renamed' Don Diego to ridicule his arrogant posturing). Moreover, the

name was redolent of hypocritical untrustworthiness: cf. the Don Diego
in Beaumont and Fletcher, *The Spanish Curate*, 1622, who made extravagant gifts in his will to ruin his friend and executor. The personal satire
against Nottingham is neatly integrated with the political in this name
for a Tory who bargained with the Whigs to assert that peace could only
be contemplated if Spain was removed from Bourbon control. The fourth
John Bull pamphlet presents the religio-political aspect of affairs during
the critical days of late 1711 and early 1712 in much greater detail.

20:11–29 **Don Diego . . . *to dissuade him* . . . a Torrent of Eclypticks
. . . and abundance of hard Words.** Diego's long-winded torrent of
jargon parodies Nottingham's opening speech in the House of Lords,
7 Dec. 1711: 'The Earl of *Nottingham* made a long elaborate Speech,
wherein he set forth the Insufficiency and Captiousness of the late
Preliminaries [of peace]; made a lively Representation of the Danger of
Treating upon so precarious a Foundation; urged the express Engagements, *Great-Britain* had enter'd into with the High Allies, to restore the
entire Monarchy of *Spain* to the house of *Austria*; and the Necessity of
carrying on the war with Vigour, till those Engagements were made
good' (*Annals*, x. 284).

20:22 *Sol* and *Jupiter* were in a wrong House: i.e. 'Sol' (Louis XIV,
the 'Sun' King), currently in the Spanish 'House' through his grandson
Philip, was usurping the 'true Place' of 'Jupiter' (the Emperor).

20:25–6 *Lewis* . . . **untimely End, and *Strutt* will be turn'd out
of Doors.** It was no prophetic revelation that Louis XIV had suffered
decisive defeats in France, and Diego echoes the by then discredited
English belief that Philip would not be popular with the government and
people of Spain. (On Nottingham's consistent opposition to Philip, see
Trevelyan, iii. 195.) It is possible this whole chapter was stimulated by
a curious epigram which appeared in Swift's *Miscellanies in Prose and
Verse*, 1711: 'I never heard a finer Piece of Satyr against *Lawyers*, than
that of *Astrologers*, when they pretend by Rules of Art to tell when a Suit
will end, and whither to the Advantage of the Plantif or Defendant: thus
making the Matter depend entirely upon the Influence of the Stars,
without the least Regard to the Merits of the Cause' (Scolar Press facsimile
edn. 1972, p. 242). As the *Various Thoughts Moral and Diverting* among
which this appears are 'certainly Swift's own and spring from his experience' (ibid., introductory note by C. P. Daw) Arbuthnot may here
employ a private Scriblerian joke to more public advantage (cf. 93: 7, 11,
16 n.). The *Miscellanies* of 1711 was of course Swift's first collection of
pieces to be given an overt Tory bias.

20:28 **Bulls, Bears, Goats, and Rams.** The pun on both astrological
and stock-market 'Bulls' and 'Bears' underlines Nottingham's new 'Conjunction' with the moneyed men.

25: 2–4 **Mrs.** Bull's *Vindication . . . against* **Adultery**: the case for the prosecution against Sacheverell; see 'Background 1698–1712', pp. li–lii, above. P. J. Köster (*née* Carstens), in 'Arbuthnot's Use of Quotation and Parody in his Account of the Sacheverell Affair', *PQ* xlviii (1969), 201–11, was the first commentator to pursue the suggestions of the 1727 note and the *Key* (4th edn.) to '*See the Parallel . . . Way of Arguing in* Walpole's *Speech at* Sacheverell's *Tryal*', and to show that Mrs. Bull's 'Vindication' parodies the arguments of the chief Whig prosecutors at the impeachment in February and March 1710, particularly 'The Speeches of the Managers . . . *Stanhope, Lechmere, King, Parker,* and some other' (Swift, *Publick Spirit*, viii. 40). 'Matrimony' in Mrs. Bull's apologia means the relationship between a government (herself) and the monarch (John Bull, who here represents both Queen and people). This is entirely appropriate as the real issue of the trial was a long and acrimonious debate between the Tory defenders of Sacheverell, who supported the theory of passive obedience (here allegorized as marital fidelity) and the Whig prosecutors, who argued the contractual concept of government (cuckoldom) which Sacheverell had attacked. In 1712 Charles Hornby reminded Arbuthnot's audience that it should not be so ingenuous as to 'think that all the Parade at *Westminster-Hall*, was only to crush one single Person . . . the Scaffolding there, was built for a Theatre, whereon to fight a pitch'd Battle of Opinions' (*Fourth . . . Part of the Caveat*, p. 123). Sir Humphrey Mackworth (47: 2–3 n.) was fond of the term 'Vindication' which appeared in the grandiose titles of three of his tracts. Arbuthnot divides his representation of parliamentary matters between, on the one hand, John's two wives, and on the other, Sir Roger Bold (Harley) and Sir Humphry Polesworth (i.e. Mackworth, who posed as the voice of the 'common man' in the 'Commons'). Of course the image of constitutional monarchy as 'state matrimony' was not unknown to Arbuthnot's readers: cf. Defoe, 'the Queen is *Married* to the *Nation* . . . They cannot be separated, but on the express Crimes stipulated in the Contract, *viz.* ADULTERY . . . . TYRRANY, is *a State Adultery* . . . Nations may Sue out a Divorce against their Prince . . . The like in Sovereigns to their People; Rebellion in Subjects, is a Popular Tyranny, and is State Adultery in the other Part' (*Review*, 19 Dec. 1710, vii. 457); see also lxxxvi-ii, above.

20: 2 *the indispensable Duty of Cuckoldom.* Cf. the opening speech of Nicholas Lechmere, Q.C., 'the Subjects of this Realm had not only a Power and a Right in themselves to make that Resistance [the 1688 Revolution], but lay under an indispensable Obligation to do it. . . . it becomes an indispensable Duty upon us . . . to demand your Lordships Justice . . . [and the Commons] will account it their Indispensable Duty to Her Majesty and their Country to assert the Justice and Wisdom of Her Administration' (*Tryal*, pp. 22, 27). Tory polemicists were quick to exploit these emotive collocations: one wrote '*Whenever*, say the 𝕸𝖔𝖉𝖊𝖗𝖓 𝖂𝖍𝖎𝖌𝖘, *the Original Contract is Broken . . . it becomes the Indispensible Duty of Subjects to* RESIST' (*True . . . Modern Whigg-Address*, 1710, p. 3), and another recounted a dream in which he met the ghost of a Cromwellian regicide who 'seem'd to brandish the *Original Contract* in his Hand, and in his Mouth had a Label with the *Indispensable Duty of Resistance*' (*Thoughts of a Country Gentleman*, 1710, p. 7).

20: 7 **he found the following Paper.** The Godolphin ministry ordered the publication of a transcript, the *Tryal of Dr. Henry Sacheverell, Before the House of Peers*, 1710. The detailed parodies which follow suggest that Arbuthnot took the advice of a fellow Tory who exhorted his contemporaries to read Sacheverell's 'famous bills / Printed in folio, and dispers'd of late / by Jacob Tonson', the Whig bookseller (*Mad-Mans Hospital*, 1710, BM. Add. MSS. 23904).

25: 8–10 **Matrimony is founded . . . original Contract . . . in favour of the Husband.** Cf. 'The Nature of our Constitution is that of a limited Monarchy, wherein the Supreme Power is communicated and divided between Queen, Lords and Commons. . . . The Terms of such a Constitution do not only suppose, but express an Original Contract, between the Crown and the People, by which the Supreme Power was (by mutual Consent, and not by Accident) limited and lodg'd in more Hands than one' (Lechmere, in *Tryal*, p. 22). Cf. also Locke's 'original compact' in *Two Treatises of Civil Government*.

25: 10 **the law of Nature to the *Concubitus vagus*.** Here the natural law of Hobbes and Locke is reduced to indiscriminate copulation. Cf. Horace, *Ars Poetica*, l. 398.

25: 11–17 **he acquires . . . Cases above-mention'd.** Cf. 'if the Executive Part endeavours the Subversion, and total Destruction of the Government, the Original Contract is thereby broke, and the Right of Allegiance ceases, that Part of the Government, thus fundamentally injur'd hath a right to Save or Recover that Constitution, in which it had an Original Interest. Nay, the Nature of such an Original Contract of Government proves, that there is not only a Power in the People, who have inherited its Freedom, to Assert their own Title to it, but they are bound in Duty to transmit the same Constitution to their Posterity also' (Lechmere, in *Tryal*, pp. 22–3).

25: 24 **Preces & Lachrymae.** Cf. the complaint of Sir Thomas Parker, M.P., Lord Chief Justice of the Queen's Bench, that the sermon was couched 'Not . . . in a Language that might become one that thought the only *Arms* of the Church to be *Prayers* and *Tears*; but with all Malice' (*Tryal*, p. 106).

25: 25 **a supreme Court of Judicature.** Cf. Sir John Hawles, yet another Whig lawyer: 'The Commons of *Great Britain* own your Lordships to be the Supream Court of Judicature in this Government' (*Tryal*, p. 64). Perhaps there is a shrewd pun on the temporal supreme court to which Sacheverell 'appealed' in his defence, and the divine 'supreme court' to which he appealed as champion of *Jure Divino*.

26: 3–9 **In *Turkey* . . . *Italy* . . . *England, France* and *Holland* . . . liberty of Cuckoldom.** Cf. 'I hope and believe that there is a real distinction of Governments, and that the Subjects of all Governments are not in the same wretched Condition that those of *France* and *Turkey* are in' (*Bishop* . . . *of Oxford's Speech*, 1710, p. 10). Arbuthnot extends the comparison to draw upon the common preconceptions about the nature and status of women in different countries. Turkish husbands were reported to 'boast a sort of unconfin'd Authority, which makes their *Wives* submissively Obedient' (*Full* . . . *Account* . . . *of the Ottoman Empire*, 1709, p. 97). Italian husbands, 'in their malice unappeaseable', were by tradition insanely jealous of wives who were 'Goats in the Garden . . . and Syrens at the Window' (*Character of Italy*, 1660, p. 52). By contrast, French ladies were supposed to 'have . . . the privilege of commanding their Husbands' (*Present State of the Court*, 1712, p. 14); as were Dutch wives since, 'Both within doores, and without, they govern all . . . which . . . maketh them too imperious and burdensome' (Heylyn, *Microcosmus*, 1625, p. 277); see also *Dutch Drawn*, 1664, p. 8. The English woman, '*born where Women reign*', in Mary Pix's *Spanish Wives* (1696) might have agreed with the caricatured whiggish City lady who hated 'every thing our dull Country brings forth, but the tameness of an *English* husband, and the liberty of an *English* Wife' (*Ladies Catechism*, 1703, p. 5).

26: 9 **Pin-money and separate Maintenance.** A subtle confirmation of the Tory charge that the 'new Whig' Godolphin was guilty of mal-practices. Mrs. Bull (here the Godolphin ministry) assumes the right to parliamentary supply for 'pin money' which Addison had recently deprecated as a dangerous innovation, 'furnishing [a Man's Wife] with Arms against himself, and in a manner becoming accessory to his own Dishonour' (*Spectator*, 7 Feb. 1712, iii. 52). Perhaps Arbuthnot also intended a shrewd comment on the Duchess of Marlborough. One Tory polemic reported 'That her Husband, since his being turn'd out of Place, had shrunk her *Pin-Money*' (*Petticoat Plotters*, bs. 1712); and she was unjustly rumoured to have indulged 'the indispensable duty of cuckoldom' with Treasurer Godolphin. Mrs. Manley in particular elaborated on their supposed adultery in her *New Atalantis* allegories.

26: 10–12 **the Arguments . . . conjugal Fidelity.** Lechmere argued that Sacheverell had compounded his political crimes by asserting 'so pernicious a Tenet, as that of absolute unlimited Non-Resistance, to be a Fundamental Part of our Government, and by asserting this as the Doctrine of the Church of *England*' (*Tryal*, p. 24).

26: 13–14 **The general Exhortations . . . in ordinary Cases.** Cf. 'is it not most evident, that the General Exhortations to be met in the

Homilies of the Church of *England* . . . are meant only as Rules for the Civil Obedience of the Subject to the Legal Administration of the Supreme Power in ordinary Cases' (Lechmere, in *Tryal*, p. 24).

26: 14–17 **they naturally suppose . . . reasonable Men.** Cf. 'The Doctrine of unlimitted, unconditional Passive Obedience, was first invented to support Arbitrary and Despotick Power' (Robert Walpole, in *Tryal*, p. 62).

26: 17–18 **a reflexion upon the Ch[ur]ch . . . Oppression.** Cf. The Commons 'esteem it an high Reflection on Religion it self, and the Church of *England*, to charge its purest Doctrine with such Constructions, by which all Irreligion and Oppression would be Authoriz'd' (Lechmere, in *Tryal*, p. 24).

26: 19–21 **This Doctrine . . . to all Wives.** Cf. 'As to the Doctrine it self of absolute Non-Resistance . . . it is inconsistent with the Law of Reason, with the Law of Nature, and with the Practice of all Ages and Countries. . . . And indeed one may appeal to the Practice of all Churches, of all States, and of all Nations in the World, how they behaved themselves when they found their Civil and Religious Constitutions Invaded and Oppressed by Tyranny' (Major-General James Stanhope, in *Tryal*, pp. 71–2).

26: 21–5 **It is much to the Honour . . . impair it.** Cf. 'the Subjects have an Inheritance in their ancient fundamental Constitutions . . . 'Tis the Tenor of all Antiquity, Our Histories and Records afford innumerable Proofs of it. . . . "Such was the Genius of a People, whose Government was built on that noble Foundation, *not to be bound by Laws to which they did not Consent*; that, muffled up in Darkness and Superstition, as our Ancestors were, yet that Notion seem'd engraven on their Minds, and the Impressions so strong, that nothing could impair them"' (Lechmere, in *Tryal*, p. 23).

26: 27–8 **to cast odious Colours . . . blacken the necessary Means.** Sacheverell had preached that to claim the Revolution of 1688 had involved 'resistance' was 'to cast . . . *Black* and *Odious* Colours' upon both it and King William ('In Perils among False Brethren', *Tryal*, p. 38); and the Commons sought to prove that he had thus argued '*That the necessary Means us'd to bring about the . . . Happy Revolution, were Odious and Unjustifiable*' (*Tryal*, p. 3). The phrases 'black and odious colours' and 'necessary means' were brought together and explicated by Solicitor General Sir Robert Eyre (pp. 52–6), and alluded to *ad nauseam* in the speeches of Robert Walpole, Sir Joseph Jekyll, and Sir John Holland, among many others (pp. 50–1, 60).

26: 33–6 **if the Actions . . . were illegal . . . so likewise.** Cf. 'if the Justice of the Revolution, which is our Foundation, be questioned, every thing that is built on it is in some Degree shaken' (Jekyll, in *Tryal*, p. 47).

26: 36–27: 4 **the Cause that *Europe* groans . . . a silly Queen . . . avoided**: Anna of Neuberg, the German Queen of Charles II of Spain.

Cf. ''Twou'd have been happy for *Europe* if the Queen had had less Vertue or more Wisdom, if she had been Vain and Amorous enough to have taken the Cardinal [Portocarrero] to her Arms, or wise enough to discover the trick he was going to play. The former wou'd have embroil'd the Affairs of *Spain*, and kept the Duke of *Anjou* in the Colledge of decay'd Kings and Princes at *Paris*' (*History . . . of Cardinal Portocarrero,* 1704, p. 225); for Portocarrero see 5 : 5 n.

27 : 4–6 **These are the Effects . . .** *Good may come of it.* High Church writers never forgave Gilbert Burnet, Bishop of Salisbury (63 : 7 n. and 68 : 4–5 n.) for justifying occasional violations of the temporal law after St. Paul: 'Let us do evil, that good may come' (Romans 3 : 8). In 1705 he had been condemned as a hypocrite, who 'justifies all People may, / Serve God, or Him, in their own way; / And prove it plain from Scripture sence, / That Subjects may Depose their Prince, / And that 'tis lawful *to do Evil / That Good may come,* That's like the D[evi]l' (*Picture of the First Occasional Conformist,* 1705, p. 2); and in 1712 Charles Leslie repeated the accusation: '𝕰𝖛𝖎𝖑 Be thou my GOOD. THESE words were Pronounced, with a Prophetick Fury, by a Scotch Presbyterian *Sibyl . . .* over the Head of a hapless Son of hers Born in an *Eclips* 1641' (*Salt for the Leach,* p. 3). The same rationalization had been turned against the Whigs in a wider political context (which is also implicit here): 'We have liv'd too long in those very wrong and absurd Notions of doing *Evil, that Good may come thereby*; to boggle at nothing that will serve the *Ends* of our Party' (*Thoughts of an Honest Whig,* 1710, p. 10).

27 : 7–11 **The Assertors . . . favour . . . Pretenders. . . . if the . . . Foundation . . . be once sap'd . . . Elopements.** Stanhope accused the Tories of disguised Jacobitism, claiming that 'the true and real Object of their darling Doctrines, such as *Jus Divinum, Non-Resistance, the Undefeasible, Unalienable Hereditary Right . . .* is a Prince on the other side the Water' (*Tryal,* p. 71), and that these were calculated to 'sap the Foundation of the . . . Revolution' (p. 74). The same image was used by Walpole (27 : 18–20 n.) and by Parker, who accused Sacheverell of '*labouring* to *sap* the Establishment' (p. 118).

27 : 14–15 **this seditious, discontented . . . unedifying Preacher.** Sacheverell had predicted that he would be abused in the same manner as had been St. Paul (2 Corinthians 10 : 10) 'as a Little, *Unedifying, Ungifted Preacher, of a weak Bodily Presence, and Contemptible Speech*' (*Tryal,* p. 34). Walpole turned the prophecy back on him with heavy irony, 'borrowing [this] String of Epithets from him, and . . . using a little of his own Language' (*Tryal,* p. 62).

27 : 15–18 *the grand Security of . . . the Husband's Bed.* Sacheverell had proclaimed in his sermon that 'The *grand Security* of our *Government,* and the very *Pillar* upon which it *stands,* is founded upon the *steady Belief* of the *Subject's Obligation* to an *Absolute,* and *Unconditional Obedience* to the *Supreme Power,* in *all* things *lawful,* and the utter *Illegality* of *Resistance* upon any *Pretence* whatsoever' (*Tryal,* p. 38).

27: 18–20 he strikes at the Root, digs the Foundation . . . upon which . . . a married State is built. Again Walpole turned Sacheverell's rhetoric back upon him: 'to Assert Non-Resistance in that boundless and unlimited Sense . . . is to Sap and Undermine the very Foundations of our Government, to remove the natural Basis and Fundamental Strength of our Constitution, and to leave it underset with imaginary Props and Buttresses. . . . And 'tis a most surprising Assurance in the Enemies of our Government, that whilst they are striking at the Root, and digging up the Foundations, upon which our present and future Settlement is built, that they should hope to pass upon the World as Friends to either' (*Tryal*, p. 61). Lechmere also opposed 'Principles . . . delivered from the Pulpit, that strike at the Root of the present Government' (p. 123), and Walpole's mixed metaphor rang through Whig polemic such as the *Medley* for 15 Jan. 1711 which claimed that Sacheverell's propositions would 'shake all the Foundations of Trade and Credit'. Both factions in the constitutional debate were thus echoing Locke who, referring to the arbitrary exercise of royal power, had asked, 'what is it but to cut up the government by the roots, and poison the very fountain of public security?' (*Two Treatises of Civil Government*, Everyman edn., p. 229).

27: 23 It is pretty plain who these Aspersions are aim'd at. On 17 Mar. 1710, Burnet attacked Sacheverell for having 'so well mark'd out a noble Peer there present, by an ugly and scurrilous Epithet, (which he would not repeat) that 'twas not possible to mistake him. This set the whole House a-laughing; and several Lords cry'd, *name him, name him*' (*Annals*, viii. 320). This indirect and tactless allusion to Godolphin as 'Volpone', 'tho' most People believe was the chief Motive of the *Impeachment* [13: 22–23 n.], was, to our Surprize, never made any use of in the *Tryal*' (*Thoughts of a Country Gentleman*, 1710, p. 33).

27: 24 the Pillory, or something worse. Lechmere asked that the Lords, 'in a Parliamentary way . . . fasten a Brand of indelible Infamy' on Sacheverell (*Tryal*, p. 24); and one Tory allegory described the doctor after Lechmere's prosecution 'in a Tatter'd Habit . . . indeed he look'd as if he had been lately Pillory'd' (*Limehouse Dream*, 1710, p. 6).

27: 29 pragmatical: used here in the sense of unduly or improperly busy or forward; officious, meddlesome; opinionated, dogmatic; crotchety (*OED*).

28: 2 the Devoto's and the Hitts. Despite the constant inversion of these two parties in the six editions of the *Key*, they clearly represent those who supported and attacked Sacheverell, or (with very substantial reservations) the Tory and Whig parties respectively.

28: 4–7 Husbands, who went about . . . Cuckoldom. Cf. 'the *Tories* boasted that none of the Managers against Doctor *Sacheverel*, shou'd be Elected; for that End they used their utmost Endeavours' (*Faction Display'd*, 1739, p. 10). 'Loyal Addresses' were made to the Queen from all corners of the realm as Tory politicians sought to turn the swelling pro-Sacheverell enthusiasm of the electorate to advantage and to persuade the Queen that the dissolution of Parliament was an urgent necessity (see Holmes, *The Trial of Doctor Sacheverell*, 1973, pp. 238–55).

28: 10 **the distinction was more nominal than real.** Cf. 'let . . . one examine a reasonable honest Man on either Side, upon those Opinions in Religion and Government, which both Parties daily buffet each other about; he shall hardly find one material Point in difference between them' (Swift, *Examiner*, 16 Nov. 1710, iii. 15).

28: 13–19 **an ingenious Treatise . . .** *Good Advice to Husbands . . .* **Temptation.** Teerink thought this was an allusion to an ingenuous pamphlet of 1703, *The Late King James his Advice to his Son. Written with his own Hand, and Found in his Cabinet after his Death* (extracts from which were reprinted in an appendix to Petrie, *The Jacobite Movement*, 1958, pp. 459–64), in which the king counselled, 'Use all your Endeavours to Establish Liberty of Conscience by Act of Parliament in your Dominions', and warned against 'Idleness [which] lays you open to all sorts of Temptations', enjoining 'Continual Watchfulness' against the unlawful love of women (Teerink, pp. 8–11). The verbal parallels are impressive: yet considering the wider political context of a constitutional battle fought out in pamphlets and addresses it is possible that Arbuthnot also intended to glance at Whig polemics such as Benjamin Hoadly's *Serious Advice to the Good People of England*, 1710 (addressed to the readers of Sacheverell's *Tryal*) or Arthur Maynwaring's influential pamphlets. One of these, possibly written in collaboration with the Duchess of Marlborough, *Advice to the Electors of Great Britain; Occasioned by the Intended Invasion from France*, 1708, was an aggressively pro-war, anti-Tory tract which applauded anti-Jacobite addresses and asserted whiggish constitutional principles as 'to have a just Concern for the common Good and Welfare of their Fellow-Subjects. To keep the Monarchy within its just Bounds, and secure it with Laws from Tyranny at home' (p. 2). This *Advice* provided the 1708 election with its most famous tract which Arbuthnot may here have wished to associate with Maynwaring's second celebrated polemic, *Four Letters to a Friend in North Britain, upon the Publishing the Tryall of Dr. Sacheverell*, 1710, a bitter attack on the high Tory champion and the many 'absurd' addresses on his behalf.

28: 21–2 **a foolish and negligent Husband.** 'The author alludes to the Revolution, when James lost his kingdom, by miscalculating the degree of reliance which ought in reason to be placed upon the non-resisting doctrines of the Church of England' (Scott). Cf. the tract *Serious Advice* (see previous note) on the 'miscalculations' of James (p. 1).

28: 25–6 **Don Diego Dismallo:** see 20: 10 n., above. We can find no evidence of Nottingham making a special plea for the Dutch. Diego's conference with Mrs. Bull continues the satire of Nottingham's reversal to the Whig cause and of the supposed alliance between the Whigs, the Dutch, and Marlborough for continuing the war.

29: 1 Esquire *South*. Since Portugal would not enter the war in 1703 unless the Archduke Charles of Austria came in person to the Peninsula, England insisted that the young man stop first at Windsor where in late December 1703, he was given royal treatment as 'Charles III of Spain'.

29: 7 My husband took him in, a dirty, snotty-nos'd Boy. When 'Charles III' wrote in 1707 to thank Queen Anne for her help, he provided useful material for hostile polemicists. Five years later Defoe cited this letter with an outraged comment: 'Well may King *Charles*, and the Emperor, his Father, call Her Majesty Mother. . . . *England* has acted upon . . . meer Care and Concern, truly Maternal, seeking no Reward, articling for no Return' (*Imperial Gratitude*, 1712, p. 36).

29: 8–12 the Business of half the Servants . . . at a Boarding-School. This is primarily an allusion to the vast amounts of men and money expended in the vain attempt to put Charles on the Spanish throne: 'The war in the Peninsula came to cost England almost as much per year as the war in Flanders' (Trevelyan, ii. 159). But the 'bawling' demands for attention recall the entertainment of the Archduke in Windsor: 'When he calls [for wine] . . . his Taster, who is also one of the Lords of his Bed-Chamber brings the Liquor in a little Bottle . . . . I believe he has an Aversion for Dogs, because I observ'd one of his Noblemen take up a Dog while the King Supt, and with great Caution and Secrecy carry it out of the Room' ('Account of the King of Spain's Reception', *Annals*, ii, appendix iii. 13).

29: 12–14 He lost his Money . . . forc'd to redeem: the war in terms of low gambling games. Chuck-Farthing was a form of pitch, Shuffle-Cap a play involving money being shaken in a hat, and All-Fours a card game (*OED*): 'The "King and Court without a farthing" looked to England to pay everything, and were furious when cash was not forthcoming' (Trevelyan, ii. 76).

29: 15–16 the whole Generation . . . so in love with Bagpipes and Poppet Shows. Charles 'liked under-dogs, elaborate deference and punctilio' (Henderson, *Prince Eugen*, 1964, p. 235) and was frequently pilloried by Tory writers for his extravagant frivolities. In one satiric allegory he appeared as Prince Widgeon conquering the Province of Grapes (Spain): 'but Fortune . . . finding [him] Tame and Spiritless . . . left him to change the Glorious Diversion of obtaining a Diadem, for the diminitive and mechanick Pastime of a Country *Bull-baiting*' (*History of the Royal-Oak*, 1712, p. 4). The 'whole Generation' embraces Charles's servants, of whom Peterborough reported, 'Never . . . was prince accompanied by such wretches for ministers. They have neither money, sense nor honour' (Trevelyan, ii. 76), and possibly expands the satire to comprehend the elaborate Popish ceremonial of all 'Austrian' courts, ceremonial which Swift had previously allegorized as '*Puppets* and *Raree Shows*' (*Tale*, p. 109).

29: 16–18 I wish you knew . . . *Naples* Biscuit . . . and Sweet-Meats. The 'Naples Biscuit', a sweet cake or loaf (*OED*), points the specific allusion to the early and successful years of the war when Emperor Leopold steadfastly refused to consider a French proposal for a negotiated peace under which Charles would take the bulk of the Spanish inheritance if he would concede Naples, Sicily, and Sardinia to Philip of Anjou. Cf. 'all *Europe* fought up to the Knees in Blood, to preserve to an *Austrian* TYRANNICAL *Popish* Race, the paltry Kingdoms of *Naples* and *Sicily*' (Defoe, *Review*, 15 July 1712, vii. 823). The whole tenor of Arbuthnot's burlesque history of the Imperial posture in Spain reflects a widespread English response. Cf. Defoe's extended treatment of Austrian affairs, which 'if it was not too Melancholy a Tale to jest with . . . would make a very good Comedy' (*Review*, 29 July 1707, iv. 285); he was not alone in his revulsion against the 'supine Negligence' (p. 283) of Austrian conduct and in his scorn for 'the pretty way of the Imperialist making War' (p. 286): 'In Italy, he is invading the Kingdom of *Naples*, in *Spain* losing his brother [i.e. 'Charles III']; here Conquering a Kingdom, there losing an Empire; here gaining a Feather, there losing the Hat' (p. 285).

29: 19 Gentleman . . . that had fallen into Decay. Under Emperor Leopold 'Such was the financial chaos that, in the words of the Venetian envoy, "the officials live without salary, the troops without bread, the workmen without pay"' (Leadam, *History of England*, 1912, pp. 6–7); and, as Defoe reported in 1707, the Empire 'sets down Impoverish'd, Maim'd, and Dislocated, and has . . . miserably declin'd in Force, and dwindled away into all manner of Deficiencies and Impotence, both in Arms and Politicks, till they are become the Contempt of the World' (*Review*, 7 Aug. 1707, iv. 303).

29: 20 Credible: creditable (*OED*).

29: 21–2 procur'd him, by his Interest . . . the best Places of the Country. 'Charles III' held Court in Barcelona after it capitulated to Peterborough in October 1705. 'Interest', a 'magical word in the language of the day' (Holmes, p. 25), here denotes the cost to England of the ventures of the Archduke whom 'the Tories . . . by Way of Banter call *Le petit Roy de Barcellone*' (Defoe, *Review*, 16 Dec. 1707, vi. 526).

29: 24–5 Instead of . . . Sir and Madam . . . calls us *Goody* and *Gaffer*: rural colloquialisms for old woman and man implying humble status (Eric Partridge, *A Dictionary of Slang and Unconventional Usage*, 3rd edn., Routledge & Kegan Paul, London, 1949). After the death of Leopold and the succession of Joseph to the Empire (on 5 May 1705) the Viennese Chancery made a gross diplomatic blunder in changing its form of address to Queen Anne from 'Majesty' to 'Serenity'. This implicit questioning of her title was particularly ill-received from a penurious Emperor at a time when Anne was being made increasingly aware that one of his minor princes, the Elector of Hanover, would succeed her. Cf. Defoe on the addresses of the Emperor to 'his Nursing Mother, *for* *so once he thought fit to Term her Majesty, and no less indeed was the Queen to him at that time, tho'* he talks *in another Stile now'* (*Review*, 13 Dec. 1711, viii. 455).

29: 26–8 huffs and dings . . . Lord *Strutt*: '*To Huff and Ding*, to Bounce and Swagger' (*Canting Crew*). For Arbuthnot's more extensive satire on Charles's imperious and provocative posture towards Britain see 72: 28–9 n. to 72: 36–7 n.

29: 34 *Blackwell-Hall*: see 12: 8 n.

29: 35–30: 4 I still say . . . keep your Customer. Mrs. Bull (the Tory ministry) presents the arguments of Dutch economic theory, which was espoused by Whig admirers of the United Provinces (see *Coombs*, pp. 7–11). Ironically she is even more modern and whiggish in outlook than the *Spectator's* Sir Andrew Freeport who proclaimed, 'It is the very Life of Merchandise to buy cheap and sell dear' (26 Nov. 1711, ii. 403).

30: 11–13 I need not tell you . . . without our Help. For Arbuthnot's more extensive and detailed version of the common Tory argument that the Dutch owed their initial existence and continuing prosperity to England see 100: 11–13 n. to 101: 9–10 n.

30: 14–15 the Business of *Hocus* . . . to plead for *Frog*. A recurring charge in Tory polemic (e.g. Swift's *Conduct*) was that Marlborough protracted the war for the benefit of the Dutch and of his personal fortune. Cf. 'I shall say nothing . . . of the grand Perquisites in a long successful War, which are so amicably adjusted between Him and the *States*' (vi. 41–2).

30: 17–19 *his Children . . . live upon Salt Herring, sowr Crud, and Bore-cole*. Whig and Tory were united in amazement and varying degrees of contempt for Dutch diet (Coombs, pp. 14–15). It had long been a joke that 'They eat much . . . . Roots and stock-fish are staple commodities' (*Dutch Drawn to the Life*, 1664, p. 74); and in 1695 Robert Ferguson drew a bitter comparison between the standard of living of William's Dutch Guards in England and their native condition, 'feeding commonly upon *Herbs*' (*Brief Account of . . . Late Incroachments*, p. 31). 'Sowr crud' is an early English form of the word sauerkraut, and 'Bore-cole' (from the Dutch *boerenkool*, 'peasant's cabbage') a loose and open-ended variety of cabbage (*OED*).

30: 19–23 *he does his utmost . . . a Trifle to you*. This speech does not seem to parody any particular declaration by Marlborough but rather to serve as a general reflection of the Dutch plea (used on many occasions by both the States and their English apologists) that their involvement in the war was greater while their resources were inferior. In April 1712 Lord Berkeley of Stratton wrote, 'I know it hath been all along their excuse that they did what they could . . . but it was impossible for them to doe more. Wriberg [Vryberg, the Dutch Ambassador] . . . made use of the same argument, saying they were undone and beggars; and he was told that tho' one would give what could be spar'd, one would not suffer one self to be cheated by beggars' (*Wentworth Papers*, ed. Cartwright, 1883, p. 286).

30: 30–4 **From a plain Tradesman . . . ever Master of.** As territory was conquered in the Low Countries it was garrisoned by Dutch troops. The Tories saw this arrangement as a blatant example of the 'old Dutch trick', using the military exertions of other nations to reap economic and territorial advantage. Cf. the epigraph to the *Key*: 'WAR *is a Trade, a Gain, or what else | Makes Cunning* Nick *in Love with Battles? | He thrives apace,* John, *Bankrupt, breaks; | For tho'* Bull *wins,* Frog *sweeps the Stakes.*' See also Swift, *Conduct*, vi. 20–1.

31: 4–6 **Twelve of the richest . . . never to return again.** Under the terms of the Barrier Treaty (31: 18 n.) twelve strategic towns and fortresses were to be garrisoned by the Dutch and never returned to any Bourbon king: 'The effect of these Dutch rights of garrison and of the financial and commercial provisions that accompanied them, was to strip Austrian Charles of half the value of his property in the Netherlands and to endanger the freedom of British trade' (Trevelyan, iii. 30).

31: 12–13 *Hocus . . . kept . . . John Bull,* **drunk for five Years together.** An allusion to the rejoicing and war fever generated by Marlborough's great victories. 'Five years (together)' was a popular collocation: it occurs again at 65: 29, and in Burnet's account of Rochester, who was, 'as he told me, for five years together . . . continually drunk' (*Some Passages*, 1680, p. 12). Cf. the accusation that Marlborough had cheated his country 'for Twenty Years together' (*The D*[uke] *of M*[arlborough']*s Confession*, 1711, p. 7), which is as much a part of the allegorical framework here as the suggestion of a typical 'pettifogger's' tactics: 'at Night he makes 'em *Drunk*, and sets 'em a Fighting to Create Actions of *Battery*, and so gets double Fees' (*True Characters*, 1708, p. 5).

31: 15–16 **The Methods . . . I'll tell you another time.** Mrs. Bull does not fulfil her promise; but cf. John Bull's own account of the lawyers in Pamphlet III, pp. 64–6.

31: 18 **Articles of Agreement:** the Barrier Treaty (see 'Background, 1698–1712', pp. xlviii–li above). Swift had revealed the first full version of the text of the bargain between the Godolphin ministry and the Dutch in 1709 in his *Remarks on the Barrier Treaty* (21 Feb. 1712) which, with his *Conduct of the Allies* (27 Nov. 1711) formed the spearhead of the Tory propaganda campaign against the war.

31: 20 **I.** *That for maintaining the ancient good Correspondence and Friendship.* The first article of the Barrier Treaty reaffirmed the 'Treaties of Peace, Friendship, Alliance and Confederacy' between Britain and Holland, including of course the Treaty of Grand Alliance (1701) which had professed 'There shall be and remain for ever a constant perpetual and inviolable friendship and correspondence' between the signatories (quoted by C. Bruneteau, 'John Arbuthnot . . . et les Idées au Début du Dix–huitième Siècle' 1974, i. 461 n.).

31: 22–33 *keep Peace in* John Bull's *Family . . . see his Will duly executed.* By the second article 'The Dutch engaged to guarantee the succession of the British crown, as settled by Parliament on the House of Hanover, against any person who should attempt to oppose the same, whether by open war, or by fomenting sedition and domestic conspiracy. And as the States engaged to furnish forces, by sea and land, for this purpose, it was contended by the Tories that the stipulation gave them a pretence to interfere in the affairs of England at their pleasure' (Scott). This was the article which stuck most firmly in Tory throats: see Swift, *Remarks,* vi. 99–100, and Defoe, *Farther Search,* 1712, pp. 6–7.

32: 1–16 II. *In Consideration . . . himself and Family.* Articles 3 to 10 stipulated towns to be garrisoned by the Dutch (31: 4–6 n.) as a barrier against France: see Swift, *Remarks,* vi. 100–2.

32: 11 **Master of the Science of Defence.** The title assumed by professional duellists who performed at such places as the bear garden at Hockley-in-the-Hole (63: 7 n.): 'Here stood the valiant Masters of Defence, / Who fight with equal Rage for Fame and Pence' (*Aesop at the Bear-Garden,* 1715, p. 10). Arbuthnot uses such metaphors (cf. 6: 25–7 n.) to denigrate French military ambitions and to suggest their ultimate fate, as disastrous reversals forced Louis XIV to abandon his dreams of conquest and to fight a series of desperate defensive campaigns. Cf. the dialogue between the French king and a war-weary spokesman for his people: '*Lewis*: 'Tis enough for me to take care of the War, and defend you from your enemies. *Quest. Ay, but your Majesty has defended us so long till we have no occasion to be defended any longer: we have nothing left now to lose*' (*French King's Catechism,* 1709, p. 3).

32: 17–20 III. *Furthermore . . . Frog may be eased of all Charges.* Under article eleven a million Livres was 'settled for the Payment of One hundred thousand Crowns every three Months, out of the clearest Revenues of the *Spanish Low-Countries . . .* for maintaining the Garrisons of the *States*', and article fourteen added, 'the Queen shall assist their High Mightinesses to maintain them in the Enjoyment of the Revenues, and to find the Million of Livres a Year above-mentioned' (Swift, *Remarks,* vi. 102–3).

32: 21–6 IV. *And whereas . . . never had belong'd to me.* Article 15 gave the States the right to close off the River Schelde and associated waterways, to impose export and import duties in Flanders, and to share in the Hanse trade (ibid. 104).

32: 27–30 V. *The said* John Bull *. . . shall think fit.* Article 15 also stipulated that 'THE Queen of *Great Britain* promises and engages, That their High Mightinesses shall never be disturbed in their Right and Possession, in that respect [of commercial control], neither directly nor indirectly' (ibid. 104).

32: 33–5 **The reading . . . Hartshorn before she recover'd:** ammonia used for smelling salts (*OED*). On 16 Feb. 1712 the treaty was condemned by the Commons as 'destructive to the Trade and Interest of Great-Britain', and Townshend, with the other Whigs who ratified it, were labelled 'enemies of the queen and of the kingdom' (Coombs, p. 299).

33: 2 *Frog . . . is religiously true to his bargain.* Perhaps an ironic reflection on 'High Church' Nottingham's own bargain with the Whigs to push through the Bill against Occasional Conformity by advocating the prolongation of the war (see 'Background 1698–1712', p. lv, above).

33: 3 **Privacy:** intimate or confidential knowledge (*OED*).

33: 8–12 *I Understand . . . my Bubble these Twenty Years.* This does not seem to parody any specific document but to dramatize the Tory charge that since 1688 the Dutch had cheated and deluded England in every respect, not least in clandestine overtures to Louis XIV (33: 17–19 n. and 99: 6–9 n.), The same complaint and the same metaphor had been used by Robert Ferguson in his vitriolic attack on the 'Dutch' King William and his countrymen in 1695: 'IT may justly astonish . . . those who give themselves liberty to think, that a Nation pretending to so much Wit and good Sense (and that very rightfully) as the *English* do, should suffer themselves . . . to be Tricked, Cheated, and Bubbled to the degree they are by the *Dutch* . . . so well known for Treachery and Fraud, as the peculiar qualities they excell in' (*Brief Account . . . of the Late Incroachments*, p. 1).

33: 16 *I'll find those that shall manage her.* Another allusion to the connivance of the Dutch with the Whigs whose Commons 'Managers' prosecuted Sacheverell before the Lords. By 1712 the term manager had become synonymous with any prominent Whig since, at Sacheverell's trial, there was 'Not a *Confiding* Man, who had any Character for speaking . . . but was appointed a *Manager*' (*Thoughts of a Country Gentleman*, 1710, p. 2): see also *The Managers Pro and Con*, 1710. Swift used the noun in this wider and more derogatory sense throughout his *Four Last Years*, as did Ned Ward when he greeted the Tory Peace at Utrecht as a severe blow against 'those impious Managers' of the 'Whiggish Race' ('English Foreigners', *Poetical Entertainer*, iii, 1712, p. 19).

33: 17–19 *If you will give me . . . take what follows.* This letter is suggestive of the clandestine negotiations between the French and Dutch which were discovered or were rumoured to be taking place at various times during the war (see Coombs, pp. 35, 95, 192–3, 310–11). In particular it alludes to the intelligence that Britain was not the only allied state treating with Louis XIV in 1712 when Anne heard 'from *Utrecht* that the *Dutch* were again attempting a separate Correspondence' (Swift, *Four Last Years*, vii. 124).

33: 25–6 **you will carry a Green Bag your self:** a bag formerly used by barristers and lawyers for documents and papers (*OED*). Cf. '*Green-bag*, a Lawyer' (*Canting Crew*). Nottingham, the first speaker in the celebrated session of the Lords on 7 Dec. 1711, declared 'That tho' he had a numerous Family, he would readily contribute Half his Income towards it [the war], rather than acquiesce in a Peace which he thought unsafe and dishonourable' (*Annals*, x. 284).

33: 31–3 you have been railing . . . Rogues and Pick-Pockets. Nottingham had been the leader of the extreme High Tories for two reigns, and as recently as 1708 had been bitterly criticized by Defoe for his intransigent opposition to the war (see *Review*, 6 Mar. 1708, iv. 666).

34: 1–2 Pray tell me . . . Sir *Roger* . . . Friend *Diego*. The Tories held that Nottingham's desertion was motivated by political frustration and hatred of Harley. He had resigned from the Godolphin ministry in 1704 when, in Tory conscience, he could no longer remain in place, and he expected to be rewarded with both the Privy Seal and the leadership of the ministry formed after the election of 1710. When disappointed on both counts, 'he was . . . reported among his former colleagues to be "as sour and fiercely wild as you can imagine anything to be that has lived long in the desert"' (Trevelyan, iii. 194). See also Horwitz, *Revolution Politicks* (1968), pp. 233–4.

34: 5–7 the poor Man always scorn'd . . . greedy of the Pence. Harley, like Walpole, began his career in public service as a man of comfortable means and ended it a millionaire. Although the details of both transformations are unclear, it is hardly likely that Harley's was achieved by the kind of selfless probity suggested here. Arbuthnot's pun on 'poor' is thus a more subtle reflection of a common propagandist ploy, for ministry writers persistently hailed the integrity of the government in comparison with the corruption which (they claimed) emanated from Godolphin's leadership. Certainly Harley was conscious of the public standards demanded by his office and Holmes cites a noteworthy example of his incorruptibility (p. 267). The French diplomat, Mesnager, was more objective but sensitive to the political images cultivated by the two Lord Treasurers: 'As to Money, [Harley] strove even to a Fault, to merit that Character given . . . to his Predecessor . . . [being] *frugal of the Queen's Money, and lavish of his own*' (Defoe, *Minutes of the Negotiations*, 1717, p. 53).

34: 17 in my first Part. Mrs. Bull's three daughters were first mentioned above, 15: 31–33.

34: 24 The Eldest was a termagant: Polemia, or War. Cf. Swift on the English army: 'no Troops abroad are so ill disciplined as the *English*; which cannot well be otherwise, while the common Soldiers have perpetually before their Eyes the vicious Example of their Leaders' (*Project for . . . Religion*, ii. 51).

34: 25 Rantipole: to behave in a romping, rude, or noisy fashion (*OED*).

34: 27 rob her Father's strong Box. Alluding to the charges of peculation brought against Marlborough in 1711 (see p. lvi, above), and to the notoriously lucrative office of Paymaster-General.

35: 6–7 **so Expensive . . . three Dukedoms . . . her Extravagance.**
The war was, of course, contested between the claims of the Duke of
Anjou and the Archduke of Austria; but Arbuthnot also includes Marlborough in the ironic pun on 'Dukedoms' representing the three Kingdoms of England, Scotland, and Ireland. To the Tories the Duke of
Marlborough was chief among the Whigs who had 'enjoy'd the *Plunder*
of Three Kingdoms' (Davenant, *Sir Thomas Double at Court*, 1710,
p. 7).

35: 8 **got upon the Body of Mrs. *Bull*.** Cf. 12: 27 n.

35: 9 **The second . . . born a Year after her Sister.** The birth of
Faction coincides with the assumption of power by the Godolphin
ministry in 1702, a few months after the declaration of war.

35: 9–14 **a peevish, froward . . . Creature . . . Coffee, Morning,
Noon and Night.** Teerink was the first editor to cite the parallel here
with Swift's genealogy in *Examiner*, 8 Mar. 1710: 'LIBERTY . . . *was at
last delivered of her youngest Daughter, called* FACTION; *whom* Juno [the
Junto?], *doing the Office of Midwife, distorted in its Birth . . . from whence
it derived its* Peevishness *and* Sickly Constitution. . . . *Her great Employment was to breed* Discord *among Friends and Relations. . . . She intruded
into all Companies at the most unseasonable Times . . . haunted every
Coffee-house and Bookseller's Shop; and by her perpetual Talking filled all
Places with Disturbance and Confusion*' (iii. 102–3).

35: 15–16 **shrieking out in her Dreams . . . next day . . . interpreting them.** Cf. 'I confess, we are a Nation willing to be deluded, willing
to be imposed upon, and nothing is so absurd, but we are pleased with it,
rather than not have some News; and this encourages the Wretches that
do it to the last Degree' (Defoe, *Review*, 18 Dec. 1707, iv. 531).

35: 17–20 **cry out Murder . . . a Pin wrong in her Gown.** Cf. the
account of the Mohocks, 39: 24–6 n.

35: 20–2 **She turn'd away . . . Salt in her Water-Gruel.** This
clearly alludes to the periodic reshuffling of government officials, but we
can suggest no particular relevance for 'Oil' and 'Salt' other than their
disparity, or as references to the excise; certainly the salt excise was
notoriously unpopular.

35: 24–9 **Her Father had two Coachmen . . . turning him away.**
Two of Anne's chief ministers, Harley and Marlborough. Again it was
Teerink who first noted the parallel with Swift's *Examiner*, 30 Nov.
1710: 'Suppose I should complain, that last Week my Coach was within
an Inch of overturning, in a smooth, even Way, and drawn by very
gentle Horses; to be sure, all my Friends would immediately lay the fault
upon *John* [Duke of Marlborough, or Lord Somers], because they knew, he
then *Presided* in my Coach-Box' (iii. 25). Conversely, a Whig fable
showed a treacherous servant (Harley) engineering the downfall of all
the honest servants in the employ of his mistress and ultimately 'At

Harvest turns off Carter *John*' (Marlborough again: *PPB*, 5 Feb. 1712). Such allegories were extensions of the more common Phaethon metaphor. Cf. one Whig description of the Harley ministry: 'Like *Phaethon*, they desire to get into the Box, tho' they have no Skill in driving; and so must of Necessity overturn the Chariot, and in the end ruin both themselves and others' (*Medley*, 28 July 1712), and the obverse Tory eulogy of Harley as 'a new *Phaeton* guiding the triumphal Chariot and Horses' (*Oxford Almanack*, 1711, p. 8).

35: 33–4 **a Whale that had swallow'd a Fleet of Ships.** Early in 1707, '40,000 gallons of brandy were landed in the Firth of Forth' by a Dutch merchant fleet (Coombs, p. 274), whose arrival coincided with the appearance of 32 'small Whales and *Grampus*'s, which for Want of good Pilots run all on Shoar in *Kircaldy Bay*' (Defoe, *Review*, 17 May 1707, iv. 166). Wine and spirit merchants in London protested violently that the Scots were planning a financial killing through the cumbersome tariff agreements worked out for the union of the two kingdoms (56: 20–2 n.) and it was rumoured that the 'whale' carcasses contained smuggled liquor. Scots anti-Unionists were equally vociferous: 'you would wonder at the mighty Prognostications, the learned Sooth-sayers of the *North* fill our Heads with about it; One *that wishes the Union* at the *D*[evi]*l*, crys . . . the Union will not last above 32 days' (ibid., p. 166). This strange absurdity of faction would probably have had particular interest for Arbuthnot who was born on the east coast of Scotland; but the allusion has more general relevance of unequivocal concern to him. In another of his pamphlets, *Proposals for Printing . . . Political Lying*, published on 16 Oct. 1712, he commented ironically: 'As to the . . . *Prodigious* [lies], he has little to advise, but that their Comets, Whales and Dragons should be sizable' (p. 15). This points the identification of Faction's rumour with, 'the Politick Whigs, that Fright the foolish World with Incredible Fears, and Invisible Dangers' (*True Characters*, 1708, p. 6).

35: 34–5 **the Lyons being let out of the *Tower*, to destroy the Protestant Religion.** The Tower lions had long been one of the sights of London (see von Uffenbach, *London in 1710*, 1934, pp. 38–9), and early in 1712 there were 'Great Endeavours to make the sudden Death of the Lions . . . a certain Presage of Peace, or the dreadful Sign of a Whig Plot' (Kennet, *Wisdom of Looking Backward*, 1715, p. 162). Faction is, appropriately, more certain of the political interpretation of events than her human contemporaries, and the association of 'Peace' with the destruction of Protestantism places her securely among the Whigs. She is also clearly related to the Political Rumourmonger who appeared in the *Story of the St. Alb[a]n's Ghost* (which was possibly the work of William Wagstaffe with contributions by Arbuthnot, and was published in February 1712): 'he often cloaths his whole Family *by* . . . *a Whale seen at* Greenwich, *or thereabouts*; and I am credibly inform'd, that his Wife has made a Visit with a Brand new Sable Tippet on, since the Death of the *Tower Lions*' (p. 4).

35: 35–6 **the Pope's being seen in a Brandy Shop at *Wapping*.** An ironic 'confirmation' of Whig rumours that Tory ministers were disguised Jacobites. Cf. Swift on the Catholic subversives, 'who personating *Tradesmen* and *Mechanicks* . . . mix with the People, and under the Pretence of a further and purer *Reformation*, endeavour to divide us into as many Sects as possible' (*Examiner*, 3 May 1711, iii. 143). As brandy was imported from Catholic France, and Wapping was a sleazy dockside area noted for its sectarianism, the connections are neatly made. One Tory satire described the typical Whig as a 'young Lump of *Wapping* Zeal' (*Character of a Whig*, 1700, p. 65), and a witness nominated to attest the supremacy of the Low Church Bishop Burnet as a religious quack (68: 29–31 n.) was 'Hannah Hearts-ease at the Brandy-shop at Wapping' (*True Spirit . . . of Cant*, bs. 1684). Perhaps Arbuthnot also intended to revive more specific memories of the 1689 'Brandy Bottle' plot, in which Jacobite papers were discovered in the false bottoms of two large imported bottles (see *Pepys Ballads*, ed. Rollins, 1929–32, v. 61).

35: 36–36: 1 **a prodigious strong Man . . . the *Cupola* of *Paul's*.** This refers back to the Whig claim that Sacheverell intended to subvert the Church and Government (27: 18–20 n.); but it turns the accusation back on its propagators by evoking memories of the 'Pins' or 'Screws' plot of November 1710. Shortly after Sacheverell's incendiary sermon, a structural weakness in the roof of St. Paul's (eventually traced to careless workmanship) was rumoured to be the scheming of dissenting tradesmen who had removed rivets so that the cupola would collapse on the royal party on Thanksgiving day. Bolingbroke twice offered rewards for information on the 'plotters' (see Kennet, *Wisdom of Looking Backward*, 1715, pp. 83–4). Another Tory satirist had used this affair to invert the charges against Sacheverell in a dream allegory describing a crowd of Whigs, tradesmen, and devils 'imploy'd . . . in Pulling down the Church to Enlarge the Meeting-House' (*Limehouse Dream*, 1710, p. 7): the frontispiece to this pamphlet portrayed Sacheverell supporting the central pillars of St. Paul's as his enemies attempted to pull down the cupola with ropes.

36: 1–2 **Three millions . . . Esquire *South* had found.** The ultimate absurdity of factious rumour is that the Austrians truly intended to keep their promise and to bear a greater share of the cost of the war (41: 1–3 n.). Cf. 'I am not going (Chimist like) to teach my Readers the tedious Art of *Labour in vain* to find out *The Philosopher's Stone*, back'd with Strange and Miraculous Stories of turning Cart Loads of *German Hob Nails* into *French Pistoles*, only by the Vertue of *Hocus Pocus*' (*Daniel de Foe's New Invention*, 1707, p. 1).

36: 3–4 **Blazing-Stars . . . and abundance of such Stuff.** The verbal echoes in the accounts of Nottingham's oratory (20: 23–9) and Grub Street productions (94: 32–3) further confirm the identification of Faction with the Whig cause.

36: 7–8 **hire Fellows to squirt Kennel Water upon him.** Cf. Defoe:
'How do our News-Writers carry on the Wicked War, and throw Lyes
at one another every Post, just as our Boys throw Dirt at one another in
the Street' (*Review*, 19 July 1712, viii. 830): see also 20: 3–6 n.

36: 9–10 **a Surtout of oil'd Cloath . . . a little scanty:** From the
French *sur tout*, a man's greatcoat or overcoat (*OED*). Carstens commented, 'in this image Arbuthnot simultaneously twits Harley and Swift
and slaps at the lesser ministerial writers. These cannot defend Harley
because of their own literary deficiencies, and also because the material
is scanty' (p. 176). Harley was notoriously secretive and imperturbable
(see Swift, *Four Last Years*, vii. 74). Cf. Swift's allegory of 'Political
Lying' whose, 'Wings . . . are of no Use but while they are moist; she
therefore dips them in *Mud*, and soaring aloft scatters it in the Eyes of
the Multitude . . . but at every Turn is forced to stoop in *dirty Ways* for
new Supplies' (*Examiner*, 9 Nov. 1710, iii. 10).

36: 11–13 **the Third . . . a common mercenary Prostitute . . . had
no Enjoyment.** Usury represents the 'new Whig' financiers, for under
Godolphin's administration, '*Soldiers* turn'd *Usurers* in their *Tents*, and
Sailors in their *Cabbins*; the *Merchant* went no more Abroad for Gain,
but Traded safer with the Government' (Manley, *Secret History of Queen
Zarah*, 1705, p. 104), Cf. Defoe's 'Wagering and Stockjobbing': 'this
native Pick-Pocket was born a Thief, bred up a Cheat, and will die a
Prostitute; she goes dress'd up all in Bear-skins, her great Bawdy-House
is *Exchange-Alley*, her Pimps are the Brokers, her Cullies the Merchants
and Tradesmen' (*Review*, 2 Dec. 1708, v. 428). Teerink pointed to a comparable allegory in Swift's *Examiner*, 19 Apr. 1711.

36: 17–20 **vast Magazines . . . Five hundred Suits . . . starv'd all
the Servants:** 'Credit' is pointedly identified not only with the war party
in general but Marlborough in particular. The 'Magazines' she stores and
the 'Servants' she cheats allude again to the General's peculation on
military supply. The 'five hundred' seems to be a thinly veiled reference
to the £5,000 per annum settled on the Duke by Anne in December 1704
(see Trevelyan, i. 274). Like Usuria, Marlborough continued the habits
formed in a frugal youth, and 'the English made it a crime in the man
who had given them victory, that he blew out unnecessary candles, and
walked home when other rich men would call a coach' (ibid. 182). John
Bull is later to refer to his clothing Marlborough's family (38: 23–5).

36: 22 **Nature will show it self.** *Dictionary of Proverbs* (N. 48) quotes
six usages of 'Nature will have her course' between 1578 and 1660.

36: 24–6 *Hocus*, **with two other . . . give *John* their best Advice.**
The speeches of Marlborough, Wharton, and Sunderland on 7 Dec. 1711,
when the Queen opened Parliament and announced her government's
intention to seek a peace despite '*the arts of those who delighted in war*
[which] seemed to be levelled at the Duke' (Burnet, *History*, vi. 78).
Nottingham promptly kept his bargain with the Whigs and moved that

there should be 'no peace without Spain' (20: 11–29 n.). He was supported by Wharton and Sunderland. Ormonde retorted with further unsubtle disparagement of Marlborough, and the Duke replied directly to the Queen (who had remained in the Lords incognito).

36: 27–30 There's no Body . . . crawl upon all Four to serve you. Cf. 'he thought himself obliged to such an Acknowledgement to Her Majesty, and his Country, that he should always be ready to serve them, if he could but crawl along, to obtain an Honourable and Lasting Peace' (*Annals*, x. 286–7).

36: 29 As I hop'd to be sav'd. This calling of divine witness parodies Marlborough's rhetorical protest that 'in the Presence of her Majesty, of that Illustrious Assembly, and of that Supream Being . . . before whom, according to the Ordinary Course of Nature, he must soon appear, to give an Account of his Actions' (Annals, x. 286), he could, in good conscience, claim never to have frustrated peace negotiations.

36: 30–3 I have spent my Health, and paternal Estate . . . a Conscience as any Man. Cf. 'his advanc'd Age, and the many Fatigues of War, made him ardently wish for Retirement and Repose the Remainder of his Days, in order for him to think of Eternity: The rather because he had not the least Motive, on any Account whatsoever, to desire the Continuance of the War; having been so generously rewarded, and had Honours and Riches heap'd upon him, far beyond his Desert and Expectation, both by Her Majesty and Her Parliaments' (ibid. 286). Swift estimated Marlborough's 'small pittance' at £540,000 (*Examiner*, 23 Nov. 1710, iii. 23).

36: 33–4 the thoughts of this disgraceful Composition . . . I cannot sleep. Cf. 'he must take the Liberty to declare, that he could, by no means, give into the Measures . . . lately . . . taken to enter into a Negotiation of Peace with *France*' (*Annals*, x. 287) Cf. the construction of these lines with that of 39: 6 and 58: 10–11, below.

36: 37–1 the last Stroke, that one Verdict more had quite ruin'd old *Lewis* and Lord *Strutt*. After the capture of Bouchain in August 1711 only one minor fortress lay between Marlborough and Paris. Cf. the outraged Whig protestation: 'They dare not face our Armies in the Field, and nothing but the *Indes* can recruit their Treasury, and shall we therefore give them Possession of that Country? And that too when our Armies are upon the Frontiers of their own? When one Blow more would make them uneasy even at *Paris*?' (*PPB*, 28 June 1712).

37: 3–4 like an only Child, I cannot endure it should miscarry. A reminder that Polemia is the child of the affair between Hocus and the deceased Mrs. Bull, and possibly a sly suggestion of the cruel Tory jibe that the war had become a substitute for the General's second (and only surviving) son who had died of smallpox in 1703. Cf. 'the many Battles and Seiges, fought and won by our great *Marlborough* . . . shall be far excelling the most numerous Progeny to eternize his Name' (Defoe, *Short Narrative*, 1711, p. 31).

37: 7–8 **has both his Law and his daily Bread now upon Trust.**
The French people suffered terrible privations as the result of many
military and natural disasters; and French troops were reduced to
plundering 'the Towns they were quarter'd in, for Want of Bread . . .
and Want of Money' (Defoe, *Review*, 10 May 1709, vi. 62–3): this
'surprizing Extremity of the French Affairs [was] nothing else than . . . a
Rupture of their publick Credit' (ibid., 21 April, p. 30)

37: 9 **in the** *Fleet* **:** i.e. hopelessly in debt; the 'Fleet' was a debtors'
prison.

37: 12–13 **no Body can say I am Covetous.** Cf. 'he was always very
far from any Design of Prolonging the War for his own private Advantage,
as his Enemies had most falsly insinuated in several Libels' (*Annals*, x.
286). Defoe ironically refuted the 'Scandal that is put abroad upon his
Grace . . . That he has avoided several Opportunities of Fighting . . .
because the War should be continued longer, whereby he may increase
his Riches and keep up his Power' (*Short Narrative*, 1711, p. 21).

37: 14 *2d Guardian* **:** probably Thomas, first Earl of Wharton. Colvile
identified this 'guardian' as the Duke of Somerset (for no explicit or
discernible reason), and most commentators have followed the *Key* gloss
of Godolphin. Yet although there is no idiomatic parody in the following
speech, it does support the apologia of Marlborough, as did Wharton's
speech when he successfully challenged Harley's counter motion that it
would be improper to debate the Queen's speech. The obvious political
prominence of the guardian also suggests Wharton, who with Sunderland ('Clum', 67: 7 n.) and Somers ('Slyboots', 82: 6–7 n.), formed the
inner circle of the Whig Junto, and had been singled out as Dammy-
blood, Clumzy, and Splitcause in the *Story of the St. Alb[a]n's Ghost*,
1712.

37: 14–23 **There is nothing so plain . . . the Success of this Cause.**
Wharton 'spoke with notable Vehemence against the Preliminary Articles
offer'd by *France*; and insisted on the Necessity of inserting in the Address [of thanks to the Queen] the Clause offer'd by the Earl of *Nottingham*' (*Annals*, x. 285).

37: 24 *3d Guardian* **:** probably Charles Spencer, third Earl of Sunderland, and the junior member of the Junto since his father's death in 1702.
The *Keys* identified this guardian as Cowper. Again Colvile disagreed,
suggesting Nottingham, '*alias* Don Diego', and again he made no attempt
to explain or justify his gloss. It seems reasonable to suppose that this
speech is a continuation of the Whig protests in the debate when Wharton
'was back'd by the Earl of *S*[underlan]*d*, who smartly answer'd the Objection rais'd by some Peers on the opposite Side. *viz*. That they were not
prepar'd to speak to that Motion' (*Annals*, x. 285).

37: 25–6 **it is a Jewel well worth . . . the Price of all you have:**
perhaps an ironic pun on the Whig panegyric to the imprisoned Walpole,
On the Jewel in the Tower, 1712. The 'discovery' and punishment of his

malpractices (p. lvi, above) were propagandist measures to show that the ambitious policies and financial abuses of the Whigs would have led to national bankruptcy.

37: 26–8 **None but Mr.** *Bull's* **declar'd Enemies . . . Ejectment of Lord** *Strutt*. Cf. the periphrastic attack on Harley in Sunderland's speech: '*even that Lord who sits on the Wool Packs* (meaning the Lord T[reasure]r) *may well remember, That in the late Reign, Four Lords were impeach'd [in* 1701] *for having made a Partition Treaty*' (*Annals*, x. 285).

37: 29–38: 2 **Who shall stand . . . three poor Orphans?** Cf. the string of rhetorical questions in Sunderland's appeal for solidarity: '*What! My Lords . . . Do not We sit in the same House? And are not We the same Peers, who have ever been of Opinion . . . That no Safe and Honourable Peace can be made, unless* Spain *and the* West-Indes *be recover'd from the House of* Bourbon?' (ibid. 285).

38: 4–6 **all very eloquent Persons . . . more Concern for the three Girls.** Cf. '[Marlborough's] Speech, deliver'd with a most affectionate and hearty Concern, had the greater Weight, in that it was back'd by the Eloquent Lord *Cowper*, late Lord Chancellor; the Bishop of *Sarum*, the Lord *Hallifax*, and some other Peers of the Moderate Party' (ibid. 287).

38: 7–8 **you have managed my Law-Suit with great Address.** Marlborough never suffered a significant military defeat throughout the war.

38: 11 **griping**: grasping (*OED*).

38: 13–14 **you have constantly sunk some into your own Pocket**: the charges of peculation brought against Marlborough in 1711.

38: 17 **Mortgage my Estate.** Cf. Steele's *Spectator*, 4 June 1711, on the dangers of falling in debt and on the practice of the gentry mortgaging their estates on succeeding generations. See also 58: 13–14 n.

38: 19–20 **Scriveners and Usurers, that suck the Heart, Blood and Guts.** Cf. the 'Wheedling Cheating Scrivener' in *Character of a Whig*, 1700, pp. 117–20, and the opinion of an unidentified correspondent who wrote to Harley in 1702 (when he was a member of the pro-war ministry): 'upon the foot you now are, you certainly ruin those that have only land to depend on, to enrich Dutch, Jews, French, and other foreigners, scoundrel stock-jobbers and tally-jobbers, who have been sucking our vitals for many years' (Coombs, p. 24). Arbuthnot had previously used the same image in his *Sermon . . . at the Mercat Cross*, 1706, when he challenged anti-Union sentiment in Scotland: '*Pride* eats out the Heart, Blood, and Gutts of Poverty' (p. 5).

38: 29–30 **one** *Term more, and old* **Lewis goes to Pot.** Cf. 10:26–8 n.

38: 34–5 **pull'd by the Sleeve by some Rascally Dun.** 'The creditors of the Navy and Ordnance Boards, including London finance Houses who had discounted bills for contractors, were owed over £4m. and applied increasing pressure on the Treasury for payment in the winter of 1711' (Dickson, p. 64).

39: 2–6 Lord !. . . Bankrupt. The Thoughts of it makes me Mad.
Arbuthnot here draws upon a deep fund of emotion among tradesmen
in the Age of Anne, the dread of bankruptcy. Steele wrote eloquently of
'that most dreadful of Humane Conditions' in the *Spectator* for 11 July
1712, and Defoe spent several *Reviews* attacking the severe laws against
bankrupts as, 'Barbarous and Inhumane, in Practice Unjust, and Unequal in its Nature; Ruinous to Trade, and tending to make Men Desperate' (12 Feb. 1706, iii. 74). John Bull will eventually exclaim, 'Debt is
like deady Sin'; and the hell of 'Perpetual Imprisonment' for debt against
which the *Review* campaigned is certainly one version of his 'bottomless
pit'. In another *Review*, which coincided with the publication of *John
Bull*, Defoe wrote: 'Well may our Parliament make Laws for the Relief
of Bankrupts and Insolvent Debtors; even Trade itself seems to be turning Bankrupt, and sinks under the insupportable Weight of innumerable
Taxes' (22 May 1712, viii. 731).

39: 4–5 to Compound his Debts for Five Shillings in the Pound.
Before Harley's financial measures in 1711 (see p. liii, above), 'A weight
of debt lay heavy on the nation' (Trevelyan, iii. 123). Indeed, 'Six per
cent Navy Bills, a principal item in the floating debt, were already at
12% discount at the end of 1708. The discount increased to between
13% and 20% in 1709, to 26%–30% in 1710, and to 33% in the following
year. Victualling bills, also at 6%, had gone to 45% discount by March
1711' (Dickson, p. 362).

**39: 7–10 the *Apocrypha . . . an unmerciful Man of Kindness.* Cf.
'Do not consult with a woman about her rival, or with a coward about
war, with a merchant about barter or with a lawyer about selling, with a
grudging man about gratitude or with a merciless man about kindness'
(Ecclesiasticus 37: 11, *Oxford Annotated Apocrypha*).

**39: 12–13 The Evidence is Crimp; the Witnesses . . . Contradict
themselves:** the evidence is not consistent. According to *OED* 'Crimp'
is found only in this passage and may be a misprint for 'scrimp', scant,
or limited. However, Dr. Johnson's gloss, 'Not consistent; not forcible'
is very relevant to the campaigns in the Peninsula, where, 'Still, as in the
days of Peterborough and his rivals, the movements of the army were
determined not by any one General, but by a confusion of discordant
advice' (Trevelyan, iii. 78).

39: 13–14 his Tenants stick by him. Cf. 'The enthusiasm of the
Catalans for Charles was indeed stubborn enough, but Catalonia was
only a single province. To the majority of the Spaniards the English
and Dutch armies were unpopular as heretics, and the Portuguese as
ancient enemies and former subjects. It is true that they hated the
French, but they hated the Dutch, English and Portuguese even more. . . .
By 1707, if not before, the great mass of the nation identified Philip with
Spanish nationality, and Charles with alien conquest' (ibid. ii. 78).

**39: 25–7 a parcel of roaring Bulleys . . . Ringing the Changes on
Butchers Cleavers:** the Whig 'device' of keeping the nation in a

ferment of military celebration, personified in the Mohocks. Arbuthnot maintains the 'low life' texture of *John Bull* in this allusion to Whig agitation in terms of a traditional form of merry-making among trades-men. 'The performance of butchers with marrow bones and cleavers was particularly associated with Clare Market and known as an "English concert"' (A. D. McKillop, 'Bonnell Thornton's Burlesque Ode', *NQ*, cxciv [1949], 321–4: we are indebted to Dr. R. Lonsdale for this reference). Tory writers persistently poured cold water over the people's intoxication with successive victories and their celebration; and they did so with an increasing sense of urgency on the arrival of Prince Eugene (next note), when 'there were ringing of bells, bonfires, illuminations, and all other demonstrations of joy' (Henderson, *Prince Eugen*, 1964, p. 95). As one commented: 'We've beat the *French*, rang Bells like mad, / And fought away our Senses, / And yet the cunning tough old Dad / Finds ev'ry Year new Fences' (*Bob for the Court*, bs. 1712). One group of enthusiasts who carried their fervour to extremes was the 'Mohocks' or 'Hawkubites', gangs of young men who roamed the London streets by night during Eugene's stay and committed various atrocities. That Arbuthnot was using the Mohocks as a personification of Whig hysteria is indicated by the verbal parallels between his allegory, Gay's comment that 'they all had swords as broad as butchers clevers' ('The Mohocks', 1712, *Plays*, 1923, i. 12), and Swift's derision for the same, '*Pack of roaring Bullies, when they scower the Streets*' (*Tale*, p. 193). Swift was prominent among the Tory writers who claimed that Mohock activities were part of a Whig plot, 'proposed [as] an Expedient' by Eugene himself, to discredit Harley and the peace party, 'by encouraging some proper People to committ small Riots in the Night, and . . . [act] inhumane Outrages, on many Persons' (*Four Last Years*, vii. 26–7).

40: 2–11 *Esquire* **South's** *Message* **. . . Signior** *Benenato*, **Master of his Fox-Hounds.** Prince Eugene of Savoy was sent to England by Charles (now Emperor) in a last attempt to block the peace negotiations with France. He arrived on 16 Jan. 1712 and departed, honoured but unsuccessful, on 17 March. As Marlborough's second-in-command he had 'hounded' the 'old Fox', Louis XIV (cf. 8: 16 n.) to the verge of total defeat. Arbuthnot's allegory was picked up in *Prince Eugene not the Man you Took him for*, 1712, where Eugene was satirized as Prince Bonenetto.

40: 10 **grateful:** acceptable, welcome. *OED* cites a 1670 example as its last usage in this sense of acceptable with respect to persons.

40: 13–18 **all the Qualities of a fine Gentleman . . . her Loyal Heart.** Again the Harley ministry is identified with the Queen who, in her first speech from the throne on 11 Mar. 1702, had declared, 'I know my own Heart to be intirely *English*' (*Collection of all Her Majesty's Speeches*, 1712, p. 4); and ten years later Defoe was still complaining about the Tory misapplication of 'these *By-words* . . . *a Heart entirely English* . . . implying, that King *William* was not a Native, and that the Honour of the Nation had suffer'd in his Hands' (*Present State of the*

Parties, 1712, p. 17). The allusion is neatly integrated with the fiction, for Eugene was notably charming and sophisticated.

40: 18–20 **Diamond Crosses . . . she rejected with . . . Disdain.** An ironic conflation of the icily polite reception and the only tangible reward received by Eugene when, 'having waited upon Her Majesty, [he] was by her presented with a fine Sword enrich'd with Diamonds' (*Annals,* x. 344).

40: 20–2 **The Musick and Serenades . . . Noise of a Screech Owl.** Eugene is shrewdly identified with the calculated magnificence of Whig celebrations in his honour. Cf. 'Yesterday being Her Majesty's Birth-Day, there was a very great Appearance at Court, where Prince *Eugene* was present in a very splendid Dress. In the Evening there was an Opera . . . And it is said, That the Court has not appear'd so Gay and Splendid for many Years' (*PPB,* 7 Feb. 1712). The Whigs intended to stimulate the enthusiasm of the populace, which joined the celebrations but remained as divided as before on the question of the Tory peace.

40: 22–4 **she receiv'd . . . Respect which became his Quality.** Cf. 'After a short Complement, which Her Majesty very graciously return'd, his Highness deliver'd to Her a Letter from the Emperor, which he desired Her Majesty to peruse, because it contain'd the substance of his Errand' (*Annals,* x. 336).

40: 25 **he Changes, a little, his usual Stile.** Defoe also quoted this letter—among the other pleas for renewed hostilities from Charles to the Queen—and contrasted it with Charles's wonted arrogant posture: 'we cannot content ourselves to omit them,' he wrote, 'because of the different Stile from what we have read and quoted before' (*Imperial Gratitude,* 1712, p. 54).

40: 27–31 *THE Writ . . . wants but . . . the finishing Stroke.* The Emperor's letter promised that the Austrian Chancery would increase its effort at 'no small Ease to England . . . [and to the extent of] the greatest that his Imperial Majesty is able to make; and if the Two Maritime Powers make the like Efforts now, as in the preceding Years, we may hope to put a speedy and happy End to this War' (*P[rince] Eugene's Memorial,* bs. 1712). Cf. the parody in *Prince Eugene not the Man,* 1712: '*What if the Emperour, my Master, gets the Advantage of your Conquests, your Majesty gains Honour, which of itself is a sufficient Reward to any but those mean-spirited Wretches, who regard nothing but Self-Interest*' (p. 34).

41: 1–3 *I promise to furnish . . . ten Shillings a Year.* The Emperor offered to increase the number of his troops in Spain to thirty thousand, and to pay one million crowns to the war effort, respectively 75 and 25 per cent of the amounts he calculated necessary for victory (*Annals,* x. 362).

41: 11–12 **Mrs.** *Bull* **refus'd . . . to** *Westminster-Hall.* 'This proportion was however thought to be so inconsiderable, that the letter produced no other effect, than the [offer to] convoy . . . forces by the *English* fleet to Barcelona' (Hawkesworth).

47: 2–3 **Sir *Humphry Polesworth*.** As a model for Sir Humphry Polesworth, Arbuthnot seems to have in mind that famous 'Church Tory'
pamphleteer, 'Mine-Adventurer', and Member of Parliament, Sir
Humphrey Mackworth (1657–1727). The career of Sir Humphrey in
some ways recalls the intermixture of Whig and Tory elements found in
John Bull himself. He was called to the bar in 1682, developed a string of
collieries in Wales (called 'The Company of Mine-Adventurers'), was
accused by his enemies of peculation, and on 31 Mar. 1710 was unanimously voted guilty of frauds by the House of Commons. In his business
dealings he acted like an enterprising 'new Whig'; but the Whigs hated
him. He helped to found the Society for Promoting Christian Knowledge, and in his later years wrote religious tracts (*DNB*). In his major
political pamphlets (all dating from 1701–5), Sir Humphrey takes upon
himself the office of explaining the laws of England (especially as they
relate to Parliament). Hence he makes an ideal subject for parody in
Sir Humphry Polesworth, who is also well-versed in the 'law'.

47: 13–14 **calculated . . . for the Meridian of *Grubstreet* . . . better
sort.** The *Protestant Post Boy* picked up this phrase in its dismissal of
this third *John Bull* pamphlet: 'this Celebrated Pamphlet, that is Calculated for the Meridian of such as are for *Peace* without *Spain*' (29 Apr.
1712). Cf. Mackworth's insistence in the 'Epistle Dedicatory' to *A
Vindication of the Rights of the Commons of England*, 1701, on 'Demonstrating to all sorts of Capacities' that happiness and prosperity depended
upon preserving the Constitution.

47: 17 **some trifling things.** Mackworth's political tracts appeared in
impressive folio editions (and with imposing titles) signed 'Sir Humphry
Mackworth'. Despite their verbosity, he was fond of referring to the
tract at hand as 'this little Treatise' in his prefatory remarks.

47: 25–8 **John Bull*'s Mother* . . . cleanly old Gentlewoman:** the
Church of England. This personification of the Anglican *via media*
has much in common with Martin in Swift's *Tale* (1704). Beattie (pp. 114–
34) traced a number of other possible antecedents, all of which centred on
the basic Tory belief in 'Ceremonys and forms of Worship . . . being no
way repugnant to or disagreeing with the word of God, but only for
decency and Order, as is thereby requir'd; And being also Established
and confirmed by Law' (*Trimmer Catechised*, bs. 1683).

47: 28–48: 4 **she was none of your . . . scolding Jades . . . of others.**
Cf. 'The Evils we must fence against are, on one side Fanaticism and
Infidelity in Religion; and Anarchy . . . On the other Side, Popery,
Slavery, and the Pretender . . . misled by both Sides, on mad, ridiculous

Extreams, at a wide Distance on each Side from the Truth' (Swift, *Examiner*, 16 Nov. 1710, iii. 13–14).

48: 9–13 **precise *Prudes* . . . Fore-head-cloth, nor High-crown'd Hat . . . Furbulow-Scarfs and Hoop'd-Petticoats.** Cf. Prior's description of 'Jinny the Just': 'With a just trim of virtue her soul was endued / Not affectedly pious nor Secretly Lewd / She cutt even between the Coquette, and the Prude' (*Literary Works*, ed. Wright and Spears, 1971, i. 302). Arbuthnot again commends Anglican moderation and condemns Catholic and Dissenting extremism, here represented by the traditionally antagonistic prudes and belles or coquettes (see Schneider, *Ethos of Restoration Comedy*, 1971, pp. 151–2). The 'Hat' is clearly a reference to the papal crown; and the 'Head-dress of a Prude' (Pope, *Rape of the Lock*, iv. 74) is identified with the headgear of Puritan ladies who 'brought in the *Fore-head* Cloth and *formal-band*' (Breval, *The Art of Dress*, 1717, p. 13). Cf. Arbuthnot's 'precise *Prudes*' with the 'Precise She-Sinner' or 'Female Hypocrite' of *True Characters*, 1708: 'She rails at the Women of the World as *Damn'd*, for Wearing Fringes on their Petticoats. . . . High Heads and Lac'd Shoes puts her into horrible Exclamations' (p. 9). *OED* cites Arbuthnot's usage of 'Furbulow' here in the adjectival formulation to mean having furbelows, pleated: it is, of course, a satiric correlative for Catholic formal 'excesses'.

48: 16 **greasy Flannel:** Church Tory opinion of the uniform flannel cloth worn by radical sectarians. Dissent was personified as 'Jack Greasy' in a *Plain Dealer* allegory (12 and 21 June 1712), and the Low Church Bishop Burnet had been described as a 'Greasy . . . Brawny Folio' in the Tory *New Dialogue Between Monsieur Shacoo*, 1701, p. 3.

48: 17–19 **she was not . . . hung about with . . . Essence-Bottles.** Arbuthnot's satire on Catholic ceremonies and forms is singularly appropriate within the context of the war against 'popish' Bourbons: 'The looking-Glasses, Essences, Perfumes, / Patches, Paints, Washes, Ornaments for Rooms, / With all those Trinkets that the Ladies prize: / If not from *France*, as trifles they despise' (*Baboon a-la-Mode*, 1704, pp. 4–5). Cf. Pope, *Rape of the Lock*, v. 115–16, and a passage on a young courtier from *Memoirs of Martinus Scriblerus*, ed. Kerby-Miller, p. 135: 'Has this amorous gentleman presented himself with any Love-toys; such as gold Snuff-boxes, repeating Watches, or Tweeser-cases?'.

48: 19–20 **a Gold Watch and an Almanack.** The Low Church frequently attacked the 'popery' of the more splendid editions of the *Book of Common Prayer* in which the Calendar, order of service, and table of Psalms and Lessons were printed in coloured bold type, often gold. One High Church tract ridiculed the solemnity of criticisms directed against the minister who observed all the Anglican forms and which, 'declaim against *Antichrist* in his nose; the *Roman Rubrick*, or our *Church Calendar* must be seen in his *Holy-day face*' (*Short Treatise*, [1701?], pp. 14–15).

48: 21 **with *a bon Goust*:** i.e. with a fine, discriminating taste.

48: 22–3 she affected not . . . a Canopy . . . no Offence in an Elbow-Chair. *OED* cites this as its last recorded example of 'Canopy' to mean a throne, or chair with a canopy. The Pope used such a throne when in official state or during Mass. Anglican bishops, on the other hand, used a simpler chair with struts to support the arms.

48: 23–6 she had laid aside . . . Japan Work . . . clean Hangings. An allusion to the eschewal of Catholic decoration and statuary by the Anglican Church, which, however, revered 'decent linen' and used appropriate sets of altar decoration and hangings for different periods of the Calendar. Again Arbuthnot tars Catholic and Dissenting extremists with the same brush, for there is also an echo of Tory scorn for whiggish city ladies: cf. the description of one such lady entertaining her enthusiast lover in 'her *Chinese* Gown and Petticoat' (*Character of a Whig*, 1700, p. 11), or the *London Ladies Dressing-Room* (1705) with its, 'Tea Tables, Skreens, *new* Trunks *and* Stand, / Large Looking-Glass, *and well Japan'd*, / . . . *China Plate Guilt*, and *Emboss'd*, / With many other things of Cost' (p. 4).

48: 27–31 a stink in every Thing . . . fresh Lavender. Perhaps this is not only an allusion to Catholic practice but an ironic reflection on the neo-Catholicism of the High Church which still used incense. In 1711 Henry Dodwell had written a passionate attack on this 'popish' practice in his *Discourse concerning the Use of Incense in Divine Offices*.

48: 33 Cursying: curtseying.

48: 33–4 your Romps that have no regard . . . of Civility. Cf. Kitty Termagant's 'Club of She-Romps' in Budgell's *Spectator*, 8 Nov. 1711: 'We are no sooner come together than we throw off all that Modesty and Reservedness with which our Sex are obliged to disguise themselves in publick Places. . . . As our Play runs high the Room is immediately filled with broken Fans, torn Petticoats, Lappets of Head-dresses, Flounces, Furbelows . . . once a month we *Demolish a Prude*' (ii. 345–6).

48: 35–49: 2 mighty regard for their Relations. . . and some few more. 'The observation of Christmas, Easter, and other solemn festivals, distinguished from the numerous holidays of the Catholics' (Scott).

49: 1 Grimace: affectation, pretence, sham (*OED*).

49: 6–8 once . . . turn'd her out of Doors . . . at sixes and sevens: a conflated allusion to the fate of the Church during the Civil War and the impeachment of Sacheverell. Hawkesworth noted justly that the Church was 'turn'd out' in the 1640s: cf. the accusation that the sectarians joined with the Catholics against Charles I, 'And betwixt them Both . . . Set *Fire* to the *House* . . . Stript my *Mother* stark *Naked*, and turn'd her out of Doors' (Leslie, *Rehearsal*, 16 Dec. 1704). But there is also a precise allusion to the six bishops who voted Sacheverell not guilty (Chester, Bath and Wells, Rochester, Durham, London, and York) and the seven who condemned him (St. Asaph, Norwich, Lincoln, Oxford, Peterborough, Ely, and Salisbury). It soon became a popular joke that 'Their votes so divided, as plainly does shew, / At Sixes and Sevens Religion does go' (*Collection of Poems*, 1710, i. 16).

49: 8–13 Judicious in . . . her Conversation . . . sower and reserv'd : a pointed contrast between the 'reasonableness' of Anglican theology and the severe fundamentalism of the Dissenters (53: 4–5 n.).

49: 13–19 a zealous preacher up of Chastity . . . *a Rogue can deny it.* 'The Church is averse to anti-monarchical government . . . but makes no pretence to infallibility' (Scott).

49: 22 too great Lenity to her Servants. Defoe mounted a sustained attack in the *Review* on the corruptions of the Anglican clergy: his argument was not that the lesser clergy were more corrupt than Dissenting ministers, but that they went unpunished (66: 31–2 n.).

49: 27–50: 2 *Sister Peg* . . . had been starv'd . . . had the Green-Sickness : the Scots nation. Both the *Keys*, which identified her as '*The Kirk of* Scotland', and the 1727 note, '*The Nation and Church*', are somewhat misleading. In the following satire Peg clearly represents the Scots people while her lover Jack symbolizes Scottish Presbyterianism (among other shades of Dissent). Teerink noted a parallel with Swift's allegorical treatment of Scotland in his *Story of the Injured Lady* (which was probably written before 1707, although not published until 1746): 'she is tall and lean, and very ill-shaped; she hath bad Features, and a worse Complexion; she hath a stinking Breath, and twenty ill Smells about her besides; which are yet more unsufferable by her natural Sluttishness' (ix. 3). What similarities there are between the two national portraits merely underline the fact that Arbuthnot's character of his native Scotland reads like a good humoured 'answer' to his friend's manuscript.

50: 2–3 *John* . . . was cramn'd with good Pullet : See the quotation from Pennecuik's attack on English luxury, 50: 21–2 n.

50: 4 Miss had only a little Oatmeal. Cf. the description of Scots diet, 'Onions *and* Oatcakes *like* a *Parcel of* Beats', in the crude satire *Caledonia*, 1700, p. 6; and Swift's contempt for, 'their universally feeding upon oats, (which grain . . . is the only natural luxury of that hardy people)' (*On the Bill for the Clergy's Residing*, xii. 184–5).

50: 5 golden Pippens. Cf. Swift's use of 'Pippens' to symbolize English plenty in the *Fable of the Widow and her Cat*, 1712, when the Cat [Marlborough] complains to the Widow [Anne], 'Your Golden Pippins, and your Pies, / How oft have I defended' (*Poems*, i. 154). John is here the generic country gentleman who, like Sir Roger de Coverley, dines on 'Good *Cheshire* Cheese, best Mustard, [and] a Golden Pippin' (*Spectator*, 2 Jan. 1712, ii. 530).

50: 8–9 Miss lodg'd in a Garret, expos'd to the North-Wind. In a famous speech to the Scots Parliament on 2 Nov. 1705, Lord Bellhaven contrasted the wealth and prosperity of the English with the condition of the Scots: 'we are an obscure poor people, tho' formerly of better account, removed to a remote corner of the world, without name

. . . our Posts mean and precarious' (Defoe, *History of the Union*, ed. Chambers, 1786, p. 323).

50: 9–11 this Usage . . . stunted the Girl . . . gave her . . . Life and Spirit. According to Defoe, the Scots 'are poor at Home . . . [but] their Figure . . . is meaner than their Merit' (*Review*, 19 Apr. 1705, ii. 78).

50: 12–18 she would seize upon *John's* Commons . . . her Knitting-Needle. 'Commons' conflates the meanings of rations, daily fare (*OED*) and common land. Defoe constantly invoked memories of bitter conflict in his almost single-handed campaign for the Union: 'look into the Histories of both Kingdoms, and see there the black Description of the Wars between these two Nations, the Blood, the Fury, the Animosities of the respective Inroads of Armies on either side, the Burnings, Plunderings, and Desolation' (*Review*, 1 May 1707, iv. 138). Cf. Swift's *Injur'd Lady*: 'As for the Gentleman [England] who is now so fond of her [Scotland], she still beareth him an invincible Hatred. . . . Her House is frequented by a Company of Rogues and Thieves, and Pickpockets, whom she encourageth to rob his Hen-Roosts, steal his Corn and Cattle . . . . Once attended with a Crew of Ragamuffins, she broke into his House, turned all Things topsy-turvy, and then set it on Fire' (ix. 4).

50: 18–20 *John* brought a great Chain . . . a Pen-knife at his Heart. Hawkesworth identified this altercation as the war which ensued when James V refused the hand of Mary, daughter of Henry VIII; while Scott believed it was a reference to the troubles occasioned by the attempt of Charles II to force the Anglican liturgy on a rebellious Kirk. Neither suggestion can be discounted, but the 'Chain' and 'Pen-knife' seem to indicate another and more contemporary pre-Union squabble. In 1704 William Atwood outraged the Scots with his *Superiority and Direct Dominion of the Imperial Crown of England, over the Crown and Kingdom of Scotland . . . Asserted*. War was threatened from the North, and Alexander Pennecuik, a Burgess of Edinburgh, replied to Atwood in a vitriolic pamphlet, *A Pil for Pork-Eaters: or, a Scots Lancet for an English Swelling*, in 1705. Its opening advertisement seems to be echoed in Arbuthnot's allegory: 'England *is now turn'd* Bully; *and Commands you . . . with a swinging long Chain of* Musty Spurious Records' (p. 3). The polemic, which continued in doggerel, 'Mungrel *Atwood* says, / That by a Chain of long Dependencies, / We are born Vassals to the *English* Crown' (p. 9), was a 'pen' knife equal in malevolent sharpness to the 'knife' which the first Mrs. Bull aimed at John (14: 4–6 n.).

50: 21–2 Nick-names . . . *Gundy-Guts,* and . . . *Lousy-Peg*: the gross national characters bestowed on each by the other. A 'Gundy Guts' was 'a fat pursy fellow' (*Canting Dictionary*); and '*Louse-Land*' was a common synonym for Scotland (*Canting Crew*). Such outbursts as; 'MAY *England* for its Luxury be damnd, / Base *Epicures* with *Pork* and *Pudding* cramm'd :/ Let *Surfeits* in thy Families prevail, / Till each disgorge a Soul at every Meal; / And Gormandizing be thy chiefest Trade, / Till all thy Sons of

Luxury be dead' (*Pil for Pork-Eaters*, p. 7), were countered by traditional
English abuse: 'their flesh naturally abhors cleanliness; their breath
commonly stinks of Pottage, their linnen of Piss, their hands of Pigs
turds' (Howell, *Perfect Description*, 1659, p. 19). Defoe had also called
attention to these insults in his campaign for moderation and Union, 'for
the Admonition of those People, who think *Scotland* a Desert . . . a Place
of wild Folks that . . . feed upon they know not what . . . in *Scotland* they
want nothing that you enjoy, except . . . your Overplus, your Excess,
your Luxury and abused Plenty' (*Review*, 30 Sept. 1708, v. 318).

50: 22 **tight**: neat in appearence, competent (*OED*).

50: 30–31 *Peg* . . . **faints at the Sound of an Organ and yet will
dance . . . at the Noise of a Bagpipe**: an allusion to Presbyterian
hatred of Church music, with a secondary reference to Scots national
pride in their own instrument. Cf. 'who can blame that Country Man
(though all the Church laught at him . . .) when the Pipes begun to Play,
he fell a Dancing, having never heard the like before, except the Bagpipes in an Ale-house, where he did always use to Trip it' (Hickeringill,
Ceremony-Monger, 1689, pp. 34–5). The bagpipes had long been a symbol
of religious polarities, since 'The *Bag-pipers of Sedition* . . . tune their
Pipes in opposition to *Authority*' (*Short Treatise of the Epidemical
Diseases*, [1701 ?], p. 12). Such were the antecedents of the Jack in Swift's
Tale, who 'would run Dog-mad, at the Noise of *Musick*, especially a *Pair
of Bag-Pipes*' (p. 196).

50: 33–4 **to say her** *Pater-noster* . . . **strange things of her.** Cf.
'while the Affair of the Union with *Scotland* was the Subject of Conversation . . . a Reverend Clergy-man of the Church of *England* . . . inveighing
. . . against the *Scots Presbyterians*, told his Auditory . . . [they] *left out the
fifth Petition of the Lords Prayer, because they would not forgive their Episcopal
Brethren*' (Defoe, *Review*, 26 June 1707, iv. 229–30). This was eagerly
expanded upon by polemicists; 'Ye Covenanters, Cruds and Cream; /
E're one a *Pater Noster* utter, / Some will turn Cheese, and others Butter'
(Colvile, *Mock Poem*, 1711, p. 31), since the whole affair recalled bitter
memories of the conflicts under Charles II who 'was *over-perswaded*,
that the People of *Scotland* were such *fierce Presbyterians*, and had so
great an *Aversion* to the Book of *Common Prayer*' (*Honesty the Best
Policy*, 1711, p. 12).

50: 35–6 **the three Brothers** . . . *Peter, Martin* **and** *Jack.* A compli-
mentary reference to Swift's *Tale of a Tub* which had run through five
editions between 1704 and 1710. Arbuthnot's Jack is obviously based on
the character of the same name in his friend's allegory, but he owes a
good deal more to personal experience of Scots Presbyterianism.

51: 8–9 *Jack* **was** . . . **the youngest of the three Brothers.** Arbuthnot
refines on Swift's allegory by using the relatively recent development of
Protestant sectarianism to underline the 'presumption' of young Jack.
Cf. 'Once upon a Time, there was a Man who had Three Sons by one

Wife, and all at a Birth, neither could the Mid-Wife tell certainly which was the Eldest' (*Tale*, p. 73).

51: 11–13 *Jack* **brag'd of . . . Influence . . . upon the Ladies.** Radical sectarianism and sexual immorality had been associated in hostile polemic throughout the seventeenth century: see C. M. Webster's articles on the background to the attack on the Puritans in Swift's *Tale*, *PMLA* xlvii (1932), 171–8, and l (1935), 210–23. Cf. *Tale*, pp. 280–1, 287–9.

51: 15–16 **all Mankind . . . pox'd by . . .** *Signiora Bubonia*: the scarlet whore of Rome, the Catholic Church. 'Bubonia' is from 'Bubo', an inflamed swelling or abscess in the glandular parts of the body (*OED*): cf. '*Bube* . . . the Pox' (*Canting Crew*).

51: 17 **the Corona**: a term for syphylitic blotches on the forehead which often extended around it like a crown (*OED*). Perhaps this is another sly allusion to the papal crown (48: 9–13 n.) or, as Arber postulated ingeniously in *Later Stuart Tracts*, to 'the tonsure'.

51: 19 **pretended**: claimed.

51: 19–20 **Scorbutical**: caused by scurvy (*OED*).

51: 23–6 *Signiora Bubonia* **and** *Jack* **rail'd . . . to hide an Intrigue . . . in a dark stormy Night.** Cf. the allegory of the *Tale* in which Peter (Catholicism) and Jack (Dissent) plot to waylay Martin (Anglicanism) on a rainy night, under the protection of the Court of King's Bench, which (as the 1720 note explained) 'alludes to K[ing]' *James*'s dispensing with the penal Laws against Papists and Protestant Dissenters, & granting full liberty to both; which made the Church of England turn against him' (*Tale*, p. 204). In both allegories there is a more general reference to the common charge that the religious extremes were morally and even physically united in enmity to the established Church: see *Glorious Life . . . of St. Whig*, 1708, p. 3, and Robertson, *Dissenters Self-Condemn'd*, 1710, pp. 117–36.

51: 26–8 *Jack* **was a prodigious Ogler . . . the White upward.** Cf. the parallel correlation of ogling (sexual promiscuity) and canting in the *Tale*, pp. 287–8.

51: 28–30 *Jack* **gave himself out . . . Fortunate Islands . . . in his Person.** A conflated allusion to '*the* Scots *Settlement at* Darien' (*Key*, 3rd edn.), and to '*The Imposition of the* Kirk, *who deny Salvation to all without their unwarranted Communion*' (4th edn.). The Company for Trading with Africa and the Indies, set up in 1695 to colonize the Darien isthmus, a part of the Spanish West Indies (long known as the 'fortunate isles'), was apparently granted 'sole right'; 'His Majesty [William III] . . . giving and granting . . . all Powers, Rights and Priviledges . . . that by Laws are given to Companies. . . . And His Majesty for their greater Encouragement, did promise to give . . . His Letters patent under the Great Seal, confirming to them the whole foresaid Powers and Priviledges' (*Full . . . Collection of . . . Publick Papers*, 1700, pp. iii–iv). Hostile polemicists pilloried the Scots colonists as pretentious Calvinists, using the same

pun on predestination as Arbuthnot: 'their Title to Rule was as *firm*
and *clear* / As the *Scots* were *ordain'd for Salvation*; / Nor could the poor
sorrowful place where they were / Be design'd for a *Sanctify'd* Nation'
(*Caledonia*, 1700, p. 6).

**51: 30–52: 1 by this Trick he cheated abundance of poor People . . .
turn'd out of doors.** Hundreds of Scots families sank their savings into
the Darien enterprise and a large number colonized the isthmus. It was
a brave and desperate venture by a people whom the English mercantile
interests had frustrated in their every attempt to expand trade in safer
and less disputed areas. Spain inevitably protested against this 'incursion', and William III—anxious to pacify his ally against France—not
only abandoned the settlers to the hostile environment and Spanish
attack but also instructed other English colonies in America and the West-
Indies to give them no aid: 'Two Thirds being *dead*, and another made
Slaves / By the Spaniard for fear of his Oar, / They left *felling Trees* and
ceas'd *digging Graves*; / And *crawl'd* to their Ships from the Shore' (ibid.,
p. 30). The Scots accused England of gross treachery (see *Enquiry into
the Causes*, 1700, p. 5), and Darien remained a bitter memory for generations to come (see Prebble, *The Darien Disaster*, 1968).

52: 3 particular: peculiar (*OED*). Another allusion to the Calvinist
doctrine of 'particular redemption' or 'election'. The following account
of Jack's contrariness certainly draws on the satire of the *Tale* (p. 195)
although it does not follow it exactly.

52: 4–5 He was for your *bold Strokes*: a pejorative collocation: cf.
Defoe's condemnation of Whig measures during Harley's administra-
tion, 'which oblig'd him to make what the other Party call'd BOLD
STROKES' (*Secret History of the White Staff*, iii, 1715, p. 4).

52: 5–7 he rail'd at Fops . . . a peaked Beard. The 'Band' (a starched
white collar with twin hanging strips), the matching 'Cuffs', and the
'Mourning cloak' (a cloak worn by people following a funeral and usually
hired from the undertaker: *OED*) formed the traditional dress of the
Presbyterian 'Crop Ear'd Brethren of *Bands* and *Bugle-Cuffs*' (*True
Characters*, 1708, p. 4). Arbuthnot's addition of a goatee beard might
again suggest the disguised fellow feeling between Catholic 'Fops' and
'affected' Dissenters, since the caricatured Puritan was clean-shaven.

52: 9–10 where other People . . . sat, he stood. Numerous polemics
condemned 'The Deformity of Holiness among the Presbyterians'
(Leslie, *Rehearsal*, 25 Aug. 1708), and particularly the fact that they,
'rather than to Bended knees submit, / In disrespectful Postures, Lolling
sit' (Ned Ward, *Ecclesia & Facto*, 1698, p. 9) in the belief that 'To *Bow
a Head*, or *Bend a Knee*, / I' th' Church was rank Idolatrie' (*Heaven-
Drivers*, 1701, p. 5).

52: 10–12 when he went to Court . . . *a modern Invention*. A pun on
what Churchmen regarded as the religious and political indecorum of the
Dissenters. In one respect Jack's 'Prince' is God, and the allusion is to

the rejection of the raised altar by sectarians. Charles Leslie ridiculed the supposed concern of the Whig *Observator* to compel the Austrian arch-duke to use an altar at his Spanish 'court', '*Barn-wise*, with a long *Table* . . . in the Middle', and he sneered at the historical genesis of such conceptions of worship which 'the *Presbyterians* us'd in the Days of *Purity*' (*Rehearsal*, 25 Aug. 1708). This suggests the second level of allusion, relating once more to the charge that the sectarians had 'kicked away' the political 'State' once before, during the Civil War (49: 6–8 n.), and would do so again. In the claim that the 'State' of the Church is 'a modern invention', Arbuthnot follows Swift's play in the *Tale* (p. 135) on the modern Dissenters' desire for ancient purity.

52: 13–14 when he spoke to his Prince . . . his Br[ee]ch upon him. An allusion to extempore prayer and preaching which clearly recalls Jack's imitation of the flatulent Aeolists in the *Tale* (pp. 150–61): 'it was purely in Opposition to our [Anglican] *Liturgy*, and to Prejudice Men against it (for they were Resolv'd to *Quarrel*) that they Set up the *Extempore* Way. And instead of the *Form* of *Sound Words*, and the *Majesty* of our *Offices*, they Introduc'd the most *Nasty* and *Slovenly* Method of *Worship* . . . treating the *Almighty* with *Beastly* and *Kitchen* Language' (Leslie, *Rehearsal*, 25 Aug. 1708).

52: 14–17 if he was advis'd . . . make Jests at a Funeral. 'The Scottish Kirk reversed the fasts and holidays of the English Church' (Scott). Cf. William Robertson, 'lately a Dissenting Preacher': 'The *Non-Conformists* are for *Negative Arguments*, as their own way of Arguing proves . . . for *Negative Ceremonies* . . . and for *Negative Superstition*' (*Dissenters Self-Condemn'd*, 1710, p. 9).

52: 19–22 All Government . . . hang'd every Year. Cf. Swift: 'In all Revolutions of Government, he [Jack] would make his Court for the Office of *Hangman* General' ('*They are severe Persecutors, and all in a Form of Cant and Devotion*' [Wotton's note], *Tale*, p. 195). In the fourth pamphlet, Jack is himself hanged.

52: 23 an irreversible Sentence : absolute predestination.

52: 26–7 that they may deserve their Fate : reprobation, or rejection by God and condemnation to eternal misery.

52: 30–3 who believ'd . . . any Crime whatsoever. Calvinist doctrine held that the Elect could be distinguished by their personal conviction of their predestined salvation by Grace.

53: 1 a hanging Look. Cf. 'a good favour you have, but that you have a hanging look' (*Measure for Measure*, IV. ii. 30–2).

53: 2 he would prognosticate a Principality to a Scoundrel : perhaps another conflated allusion to the 'Darien Calvinists' (51: 28–30 n.). It was a Calvinist notion that the Elect bore witness to their salvation in marks of worldly success, indications of divine favour; and William Paterson, the inventor of the whole Darien scheme, was reputedly trained for the Kirk but poured all his energies (and his savings) into the ill-fated 'noble undertaking': 'The Prospect of *Gain* made him off with his *Band*, / And away with his *Bible-Geneve*' (*Caledonia*, 1700, p. 4). Paterson was one of Arbuthnot's large acquaintance (see *Works*, p. 29) but that does not preclude the possibility of his inclusion in the satire at this point: cf. Garth, ibid., p. 30 and 67: 14 n.

53: 3–4 **his Studies . . . bent towards exploded Chimeras**: 'The learning of the presbyterians chiefly exercised upon the most useless and obscure disquisitions of school divinity' (Scott).

53: 4–5 **the *perpetuum Mobile*, the circular Shot, Philosopher's Stone**: another echo of the *Tale*, in which, as Wotton noted, Swift used the still popular alchemical projects to satirize the Dissenters' love of '*using Scripture Phrase on all Occasions*' (p. 190). Cf. also the passage from Arbuthnot's *Examination of Dr. Woodward's Account of the Deluge*, 1697: 'If any man besides the Doctor should have pretended to such a secret, it would have found the same credit as the philosopher's stone, circular shot, perpetuum mobile—or some such chimera' (quoted by Beattie, p. 40). The 'circular shot' was the dream of inventing a gun with an angled trajectory of fire, allowing the marksman, for example, to shoot around corners.

53: 5–7 **silent Gunpowder . . . and split Hairs.** Here Arbuthnot expands the satire on whiggish Jack to comprehend all 'modern' scholarship: cf. the modern doctors and their propagandists, who 'shot Bullets of a most malignant Nature, and used *white Powder* which infallibly killed without *Report*' (*Tale*, p. 236), or the fashionable projects such as 'Cages for Gnats, and Chains to yoak a Flea; / Dry'd Butterflies, and Tomes of Casuistry' (Pope, 'Rape of the Lock', v. 121–2).

53: 14–15 **their Sarks over their Waistcoats.** As Scott was the first editor to note, Sark, colloquial Scots for shirt or chemise (*OED*), alludes to the bitter theological disputes over the surplice which had divided the Church for decades (see Gwatkin, *Church and State*, 1917, pp. 252, 272, 288, 350, 359). One virulent contemporary manuscript poem pictured the Presbyterian praying for 'the downfall of Episcopacy, Toleration without End, No Surplice but a Cloak Everlasting' (*Fanatick's Creed*, Bodleian MS. Rawl. D. 383/97).

53: 15–16 **set Speeches out of *Sidney's Arcadia,* or *The Academy of Compliments***: *The Book of Common Prayer.* In 1709 Defoe had judged, 'the Aversion of the Generality of the People in *Scotland* to the Common-Prayer is such, and so known, that no Attempt to introduce [it] . . . there can prosper, *but by Force*' (*Review*, 4 Oct. 1709, vi. 310). Beattie realized that 'Peg's sentiment is definitely anti-Jacobite. The prayer of Pamela (Sidney's *Arcadia*, Book III) is supposed to have been used by Charles I in prison' (p. 124 n.). Scots hatred of formal prayers and ceremonies is neatly expressed in Peg's dismissal of the *Academy of Complements. Wherein Ladyes, Gentlewomen, Schollers, and Strangers may accomodate their Courtly Practice with most Curious Ceremonies, Complementall,*

Amorous, High Expressions, and Formes of Speaking or Writing, (1640?), which was very popular throughout the later half of the seventeenth century.

53: 18 **a great Regard to his Father's Will**: another allusion to the allegory of the *Tale* in which the 'Will' is the New Testament: cf. 'his [Jack's] common Talk and Conversation ran wholly in the Phrase of his Will' (p. 191).

53: 20–1 **the original Deed of Conveyance . . . others are Counterfeits.** See 51: 28–30 n.

53: 30–54: 2 **poor *Peg* was forc'd . . . pedling . . . to the Market.** The Scottish economy was pitifully weak before the Union. The herring fishery 'was a chief source of the nation's wealth, but even so the Dutch fishermen took many more herrings off the Scottish coast than did the Scots themselves' (Trevelyan, ii. 196), and many Scots *émigrés*—less gifted than Arbuthnot—became pedlars: hence, '*Pedlars,* Scotch Merchants' (*Canting Crew*). The English were generally content with this status quo, and *Caledonia* (1700) mocked the importunity of the Darien venture: 'why should not she who had *Guts in her brains* / From a *Pedlar* turn likewise a *Merchant*' (p. 2). See also T. C. Smout, *Scottish Trade on the Eve of the Union* (1963), and *A History of the Scottish People 1560–1830* (1969), chaps. v, vii, x.

54: 3 **sow'd, spun and knit . . . Journey-work to her Neighbours.** Scots cloth was crudely and locally produced. Cf. Defoe, 'the poor People make their own C[l]othes, card, spin, and weave their own Wool in every Village' (*Review,* 9 July 1709, vi. 167): he contrasts England's flourishing trade, which involves many countries, with Scotland's lack of 'Circulation'. Arbuthnot himself was, of course, one of the many Scots at 'Journey-work' in neighbouring England.

54: 7–13 **a Gentlewoman . . . decent Pride . . . barbarous Usage.** Cf. Defoe, 'compare People and People, and . . . I entreat of you *True-Born-English-Men,* One Thing, in Regard to your own exalted Character . . . that you would never bring your MORALS into the Comparison, no nor much of your good Manners . . . such as relate to Civility to Strangers, Gratitude to Friends, and the like' (*Review,* 24 May 1709, vi. 87). He was swimming against the jingoistic tide: 'Pride is a thing bred in their bones', wrote Howell in his *Perfect Description,* 1659 (p. 19); and even Arbuthnot admits some truth in the traditional charge in this ironic treatment of 'decent Pride' illustrated by haughty arrogance: cf. his appeal in the *Sermon . . . at the Mercat Cross,* 1706, against the 'three dismal Companions, *Pride, Poverty,* and *Idleness*' (p. 5).

54: 13–16 **an easie matter . . . an industrious Person . . . his way of Business.** Defoe in particular campaigned vigorously for recognition of the fact that 'were you [the English] in your trading Senses . . . you might bring all . . . to a Regularity——Do but encourage *Scotland* in their own Manufactures . . . they will grow rich with you, and you will grow rich by them' (*Review,* 19 July 1709, vi. 184).

54: 22–5 *John* was . . . making his Will . . . without her Consent.
See 'Background 1698–1712', pp. xlvii–xlviii, above.

54: 25–30 a malicious Story . . . Custard a Horseback . . . his Mistress *Peg.* Anglicans and Scots Episcopalians feared the Union was an attempt to unite the Presbyterian forces of both nations in offensive action (see Drake, *Memorial*, 1705, pp. 5, 30), and Defoe was at great pains in the *Review* to lay this particularly dangerous ghost. The malicious story itself is another echo of Swift's *Tale*, in which Jack '*got upon a great Horse, and eat Custard*', and which Wotton realized was an allusion to '*Sir* Humphrey Edwyn, a *Presbyterian* . . . *Lord Mayor of* London [in 1697, who] . . . *had the Insolence to go in his Formalities to a Conventicle, with the Ensigns of his Office*' (pp. 204–5). 'Orthodox Custard' (*Whigs Feast*, 1712, p. 7) or 'enlightning Custard' (*Collection of Poems*, 1710, ii. 17) was symbolic of the City / Whig / Dissent nexus, since custard was a traditional dish at city feasts.

54: 30–2 All I can infer . . . true or false: an ironically patient comment on those who, despite various safeguards for Scots Episcopalians (see Trevelyan, ii. 280–1), were still claiming in 1712 that, 'the Union of *Scotland* and *England*, was brought about by . . . Low-Church Men, Whigs, and Presbyterian Dissenters . . . to make them a Majority in both Houses, that . . . they might the easier bring about the ruine of the Church and the State at one Blow' (*Sauce for an English Gander*, p. 4).

54: 33 she huff'd and storm'd like the Devil. The Union was bitterly opposed in both Parliaments—in Scotland most eloquently by Lord Bellhaven, whose speech of 2 Nov. 1705 is parodied in the opening sentences of Peg's outburst.

55: 1–4 he draws up his Writs . . . for my Consent. Cf. Lord Bellhaven: 'England having declared their succession and extended their intail without ever taking notice of us. . . . Now . . . whether the desire they had to have us engaged in the same succession with them . . . or whether they were afraid of our Act of Security . . . I leave it to themselves; this I must say only, they have made a good bargain' (*History of the Union . . . by Daniel De Foe*, ed. G. Chalmers, 1786, pp. 324–5). The 'young Man' is the Elector of Hanover and future George I.

55: 7–12 he gangs up and down . . . his silly Contracts. Bellhaven continued acidly: 'we have the honour to pay their old debts, and to have some few persons present [at Westminster] for witnesses to the validity of the deed, when they are pleased to contract more' (ibid., p. 327). The 'foolish Bargains' refer to the diplomatic arrangements made to support the war, including the Partition and Barrier treaties. Scotland had already suffered from England's conduct of the war. In 1702 certain trading privileges with France were witheld, French privateers began to prey on Scottish vessels, and 'throughout [Anne's] reign, Scotland paid the penalty of a war which the majority of her people regarded with indifference and even with disapproval' (Hume Brown, *Legislative Union*, Oxford, 1914, pp. 141–3).

55: 13–14 **Hame's hame be it never so hamely.** The *Oxford Dictionary of Quotations* incorrectly ascribes this proverb to Arbuthnot. 'Hame is hamely, though never so seemly' was listed in a *Collection of Scotch Proverbs by Puppity Stampoy*, 1663, p. 26, a collection which was based on work done by David Ferguson (1525–98) and which provided the basic material for other volumes printed in the later seventeenth century (such as *Adagia Scotica*, first published in 1668) which included variants on the proverb.

55: 18 **Carline :** colloquial Scots for old woman, implying contempt or disparagement on the part of the speaker (*OED*).

55: 19–21 **plagu'd with her Spells and . . . auld warld Ceremonies :** formal Anglican Chants, Responses, Prayers, and forms of service.

55: 21 **I mun never pair my Nails on a Friday :** Scots fears on behalf of the Presbyterian establishment. We are indebted to Mr. J. Y. Mather and the Linguistic Survey of Scotland for the information that this example of strict Sabbatarianism occurred in the Highlands and certain Lowland districts for a Sunday, but still survives in the north of England and the Border areas for a Friday.

55: 21–2 **begin a Journy on *Childermas day*.** The Festival of the Holy Innocents (28 December), and by extension the same day of the week throughout the year (*OED*) 'used to be reckoned the most unlucky . . . and . . . no one who could possibly avoid it, began any work, or entered on any undertaking' (Chambers's *Book of Days*, quoted by Donald Bond in *Spectator*, i. 32 n.). In these comments Peg turns back on the Anglicans their charges of superstition.

55: 22–3 **becking and binging as I gang out and into the Hall :** becking, making an obeisance or bow, and binging, the initial sound of bow plus the closing sound of cringe (*OED*), allude to the Anglican custom of bowing towards the altar on entering or leaving church.

55: 23 **gan his get :** 'Gang his gait', or 'go his way' (*OED*).

55: 24–5 **I'll stay like the poor Country Mouse :** as in Aesop's fable *The Town Mouse and the Country Mouse*. For one contemporary version, see Toland, *Fables of Aesop*, 1704, p. 32.

55: 25–33 **by the Interposition . . . *John*'s Mother.** The union proposals were signed by the great majority of the negotiating commissioners on 22 July 1706, and, after stormy debates in both Parliaments, Great Britain came into statutory being on 1 May 1707. Among the terms were an 'Equivalent' of £358,085 (to offset the burden of the English national debt and to compensate the Darien stockholders), and guarantees for both equal trading rights and the Scots Presbyterian establishment.

56: 3–4 **the Quarrels of Relations are harder to reconcile.** 'The quarrels of those nearest akin are the sharpest' (*ut ferme accerima proximorum odia sunt*). Tacitus, *Histories*, Bk. iv, sec. 70.

56: 6–10 *Æsop*, in the Story . . . his own Timber. These two popular
fables had been reworked on many occasions during the seventeenth
century, and again for Arbuthnot's audience by L'Estrange in his *Fables
of Aesop*, 1704, pp. 48–50.

56: 14 Jealousies: suspicions (*OED*).

56: 19–20 The Purchase-Money of *Peg*'s Farm was ill paid.
Through gross original miscalculation and subsequent maladministration,
the Equivalent (55: 25–33 n.) proved totally inadequate. Numerous
minor creditors were placated with dubious debentures with no fixed
date for the payment of interest; the transportation of the money (three-
quarters of which was in the form of 'new-fangled' Exchequer bills) was
long delayed; and there were bitter quarrels among those appointed to
distribute it (see Munro, *History of the Royal Bank of Scotland 1727–1927*,
Edinburgh, 1928). Davenant's 'new Whig' prided himself on misusing
the money (*Sir Thomas Double at Court*, 1710, pp. 27–8), and it is a
measure of the controversy that as late as 1712 there appeared a seventy-
two page pamphlet itemizing the unsatisfied demands of the most famous
colonist in the Darien venture in *A State of Mr. Paterson's Claim upon
the Equivalent* (see 53: 2 n.).

56: 20–2 *Peg* lov'd a little good Liquor . . . made a false Key. This
alludes to what Trevelyan called 'the game that could be played only
once,' an attempt by Scots (and some English) merchants to take advantage of the fact that after the Union on 1 May 1707, goods originally
landed in Scotland, which had a lower import tax, could be shipped to
England without paying further duty. A cargo of French wine and brandy
was seized on the Thames by Customs officials and held as smuggled goods
(35: 33–4 n.). With Scottish and English dealers at each other's throats,
Godolphin suggested two alternative temporary arrangements: 'the Scots
traders should either give bail for the arrested goods, or allow them to be
deposited in cellars, of which both they and Customs officials should have
the keys' (Hume Brown, *Legislative Union*, 1914, p. 138). The Scots
refused and the embargo was eventually lifted; but there seems to be no
justification in this context for the *Keys* gloss of 'false Key' as 'Occasional
Conformity', since the obvious allusion concerns the widespread smug-
gling (particularly of French goods) which had long been a respectable
and now became a patriotic activity (see Hume Brown, pp. 132–3,
362–3).

56: 22–4 *Peg*'s Servants complain'd . . . within the House. Scott
followed Hawkesworth in identifying this as an allusion to the Test Act
by which Presbyterians were 'excluded from places and appointments'.
This may be implicit, but the economic context seems to direct the reader
more obviously to the series of acts which were manœuvred through
Parliament by the English commercial lobby to deprive their Scots
counterparts of guaranteed equality.

56: 24–5 if they offer'd . . . over their Noddle. The Scots protested
violently when the new British Parliament imposed a tax on the exported

linen which was one of their chief sources of foreign exchange (see Mackinnon, *The Union*, 1907, p. 420).

56: 25–8 **if they ventur'd . . . saluted with a Broom.** For Arbuthnot's more detailed treatment of discrimination against Scots in executive and administrative areas see 57: 9–10 n. to 57: 20–3 n.

56: 28–30 **if they meddl'd . . . in the Kitchen . . . with a Ladle.** Cf. 'Prohibition of victual of all kinds from Ireland had been a standing policy of Scotland for over half a century. . . . Since the Union, however, Irish victual had been surreptitiously imported in such quantities that an address, signed by the most influential men in the country, was sent to the queen to represent the culpable neglect of the authorities' (Hume Brown, pp. 140–1).

56: 32–57: 1 **some climbing up into the Coach-box . . . about their Ears.** 'Alluding to the misconduct of the Stuarts' (Scott). Again Arbuthnot uses the image of the coach of state (cf. 35: 24–9 n.), on this occasion to suggest discrimination against Scots in Parliament itself (cf. 57: 20–3 n.).

57: 2–8 *Peg*'s **Servants . . . pick'd up Guineas and Broad-pieces.** Another allusion to the maladministration of the Equivalent in terms of the earthenware box in which apprentices collected their Christmas gratuities (*OED*). It is pointed by the reference to 'Broad-pieces', coins of £1 value minted during the reign of James I of England and VI of Scotland (the first monarch to rule both kingdoms), and nicknamed 'Unites' (*OED*). Despite the general delays in payment, a number of Scots who had been prominent in the Union negotiations received arrears of salary and expenses ranging in value from Marchmont's £1,104. 15s. 7d. to Banff's £11. 2s. 0d. Disgruntled creditors talked of bribery (see Riley, *English Ministers and Scotland 1707–1727*, 1964, pp. 210–11), and so did Tory writers such as Davenant: 'I proportion'd my Rewards . . . giving the largest Share to those, whose Endeavours in the Union had been least Meritorious; and leaving the rest to scramble for the small remainder' (*Sir Thomas Double at Court*, 1710, p. 28).

57: 9–10 *Peg*'s **Servants had great Stomachs . . . to the Table:** 'Fanaticks getting into Places of Trust' (*Key*). The allusion seems more specific than this: 'In 1711 the Queen made the Duke of Hamilton a Peer of Great Britain, with the title of Duke of Brandon. As such he proposed to sit in his own right, and not as one of the sixteen elected Scottish Peers. To his astonishment, and to the universal indignation of all Scots, the House of Lords challenged his right to sit, on the ground that under the Union Treaty Scotland was to be represented by no more than sixteen Peers. The application made was a legal misreading of the words of the Treaty' (Trevelyan, iii. 234). Queensberry, as Duke of Dover, was also declared ineligible.

57: 11–14 **Instead of regulating . . . about the Room like mad:** 'Fanaticks Excluded by passing the Conformity Bill [of 1711]' (*Key*).

Again the allusion is more specifically to a controversy (similar to the above) over the right of elected sons of Scots peers to sit in the Commons in 1709 (see Mackinnon, *The Union*, pp. 366–7). When the application against Hamilton was upheld it 'was taken as a national disaster' in Scotland (Riley, *English Ministers and Scotland*, p. 231) and there was rioting in both Glasgow and Edinburgh (see *Annals*, v. 345–6, 401).

57: 14–15 **Sir *Roger*, who was now *Major Domo* . . . to quiet them.** Harley was raised to the peerage and the vacant Treasurership in May 1711, and he opposed the Whig challenge against Hamilton as strongly as he had supported the Whig policy of Union.

57: 16–17 ***Peg* said this was contrary . . . Child of the Family.** 'The most disgraceful circumstance in the affair was that the prime movers of this injustice to Scotland were the Whig Lords who had most keenly promoted the policy of the Union that was to reconcile the two peoples. Their motive was fear lest the Crown should swamp the Upper House with Tory creations' (Trevelyan, iii. 235). The point was not lost on polemicists: 'With the *Scotch* they unite, / When they think to get by't, / But when the Noose pinches they strive to unty't (*Excellent New Song*, bs. 1711/12); and Defoe protested in terms very close to Arbuthnot's allegory: 'We assur'd them of all Faithful . . . keeping the Treaty when made . . . and Kind, Friendly, and Brotherly Treatment from the English, when United' (*Review*, 3 May 1711, viii. 66).

57: 20–3 ***John* at last agreed . . . if they pleas 'd.** 'Articles of Union, whereby, as they were then understood, a Scots commoner, but not a Lord, might be made a peer; a regulation admirably parodied by the domestic arrangement in the text' (Scott). Moreover, extreme Tory Scots peers were not given places in the moderate Harley ministry, and Defoe was later to comment on such representational disappointments, again in similar terms: 'Some *Scotch* Gentlemen . . . said, they were not treated like Gentlemen, but rather like Footmen, *and such like*' (*Secret History of the White Staff*, iii, 1715, p. 70).

57: 24–5 **Plumb-porridge and Minc'd Pies for *Peg*'s Dinner:** dishes symbolic of Anglican and Episcopalian dominance. They had, of course, been among the trappings of celebration forbidden by Parliament after the Civil War, and were therefore, 'as hateful . . . as . . . Christmas porridge to an English Puritan' (*London Spy*, p. 188); see also *Spectator*, 8 Jan. 1712, ii. 550–1.

57: 25–7 ***Peg* told them . . . she brought it up again.** The revolt of 1637 when Charles I attempted to introduce Episcopacy and the Common Prayer into the Scottish Kirk.

57: 27–31 **Some alledg'd . . . others . . . of her own Accord.** The Toleration and Patronage Acts of March and May 1711, both of which were opposed by the 'wiser sort' such as Harley, who remained 'more loyal to the maintenance of the Union than the Whig Lords whom he had helped to pass it' (Trevelyan, iii, 240).

58: 13–14 **tho' they spent the Income, they never Mortgag'd the Stock.** Cf. 'National Debts secured upon Parliamentary Funds of Interest, were things unknown in *England* before the last Revolution under the Prince of *Orange*' (Swift, *Four Last Years*, vii. 68). Tory writers persistently lamented, 'Our Riches are gone, / Our Trade is undone, / The Nation is mortgag'd, for Money at Loan' (*Excellent New Song*, bs. 1711/12), pointing accusingly at 'a prodigious Land Tax, and a Mortgage laid upon their Grand Children' (*Plain Dealer*, 9 May 1712). Dickson credits Gilbert Burnet with introducing the 'new style of finance' from Holland (p. 17).

58: 15 **the *Norman* or the *Norfolk* Blood.** Both these peoples were reputed to be exceedingly litigious. Cf. 'the Laws of England . . . are full of pleadings, ambiguities, and contrarieties in themselves: for, they were invented and established by the Normans, then whom no Nation is more litigous' (*Looking-Glasse for All Proud . . . and Corrupt Lawyers*, 1646, p. 5). Similarly, '*Norfolk*, where they say, there are 1500. Petty Attorneys; and where the people frequently spend 5s. in Law, to recover a Debt of Two Groats' (Defoe, *Review*, 23 Sept. 1704, i. 428) had long been notorious (see *NQ*, ix [1866], 539–40). Carstens noted that 'Townshend, who had signed the ill-famed Barrier Treaty, and Walpole, who had recently been expelled from the House of Commons . . . both came from Norfolk' (p. 274).

58: 19–20 **You must know . . . making up an old Quarrel:** an ironic allusion to the notoriously secret diplomacy of William III. The War of the League of Augsburg was concluded by an agreement reached by the Dutch William Bentinck, Earl of Portland, and Marshal Boufflers, unknown even to William's most trusted ministers (see Lodge, *History of England*, 1905, pp. 415–17).

58: 28–33 **but one thing . . . equal Division . . . will not be Refractory.** Tory reservations about the Partition Treaties (see 'Background, 1698–1712', pp. xlii–xliv, above) are neatly expressed by the suspicious ingenuousness of Lewis and the equally ominous enthusiasm of Frog for 'the . . . *Partition* of a Country, where they had neither Title nor Pretence, and wherein they had involv'd us' ('Word in Season', 1701, *Collection of State Tracts*, iii, 1707, p. 193).

59: 1–2 **slabber'd me all over . . . with his great Tongue:** another facet of traditional Dutch caricature. 'Slobbering talk . . . To wet in a dirty and disagreeable manner' (*Dictionary of the Low-Dutch Element in the English Vocabulary*, ed. Bense, 1926–39) had long been associated with the country of its origin. Cf. the triumph of Vendice whose poison is eating away the Duke's tongue: 'Your tongue? 'twill teach you to kiss closer, / Not like a slobbering Dutchman' (Tourneur, *Revenger's Tragedy*, III, v. 164–5).

59: 2–3 **Do as you please . . . all one to *John Bull*.** By the first Partition Treaty of October 1698 'most of the Spanish Empire went to the young Bavarian [Joseph Ferdinand], but important consolation prizes were assigned to France and to Austria' (Trevelyan, i. 126).

59: 6 **a Chain and a Semicircle**: a measuring line and a protractor for the calculation of angles (*OED*).

59: 16–17 **accosted by some of Lord *Strutt*'s Servants.** The powers involved in the Partition attempted to keep their deliberations secret, but Don Quiros, Spanish Ambassador at The Hague, 'followed the trial with such skill and perseverance that he discovered . . . enough to furnish materials for a despatch which produced much irritation and alarm at Madrid' (Macaulay, *History of England*, 1913–15, vi. 2857).

59: 18–19 **Trangams and Gimcracks**: Trangam, an intricate toy, seems to have originated from a fictitious legal term, and Gimcrack, defined by the *Canting Dictionary* as a 'Bauble or Toy' could also mean a fanciful notion, dodge, or mechanical contrivance (*OED*).

59: 25 **an old doating Puppy**: a reflection of the Partitioners' attitude to the dying Charles II (see Macaulay, vi. 2846–50). Puppy and 'puppet' (perhaps the political suggestion here) were often used interchangeably as terms of contempt (*OED*).

59: 28–9 **Upon this . . . a Quarrel . . . a Flea in their Ear.** The Marquis de Canales complained of this gross interference by William III in his master's affairs and 'delivered . . . a note abusive and impertinent beyond endurance' (Macaulay, v. 2906); then, 'for calling it by its true Name, a detestable Machination, he was commanded to go out of the Kingdom' ('Account of the Debate', 1701, *Collection of State Tracts*, iii, 1707, p. 96).

59: 34–5 **a lusty old Fellow . . . without Teeth**: Louis XIV.

59: 36 **another thick squat Fellow, in Trunk-Hose**: the Dutch. The generic Hollander was supposed to be squat and fat (owing to his predilection for cheese and butter) and to dress in trunk-hose, full bag-like breeches covering the hips and upper thighs, sometimes stuffed with wool (*OED*): cf. 'With Cord of Pack for Vest and Breeches, / Cut round, and bagging *a-la-mode* / . . . Shapt like *Bragmardoes* with a Spunge-hole, / And spacious Draw-bridge at the Bung-hole' (*Hogan-Moganides*, 1674, p. 10).

60: 1–2 **little, long Nos'd, thin man . . . a fit of Sickness.** A portrait of John Bull which conflates the physical characteristics of William III and the financial state of the nation after his wars against Louis XIV. By 1698 a debt of some £5 million had been incurred by a King who was always in a 'weak Condition . . . from his Childhood, by Flux or Rheum, and an Asthma' (Pittis, *Some Memoirs*, 1715, pp. 22–3), and to whom Steele was alluding when he observed that '*Roman* Noses . . . reviv'd again in Eighty eight' (*Spectator*, 6 Apr. 1711, i. 135).

60: 4 **in a rare Tweag**: in a state of excitement or agitation (*OED*). The partition of 1698 was made without the knowledge of the King of Spain.

60: 5–6 **he call'd for his long** *Toledo* **. . . bounc'd about the Room.**
Another allusion which conflates references to both monarch and people.
When the news of the first partition reached Madrid 'Charles II . . . "flew
into an extraordinary passion, and the Queen in her rage smashed to
pieces everything in the room"' (*Cambridge Modern History*, v. 391),
and the populace reacted with equal passion: 'The Spaniards, noble and
simple, were indifferent to the question who should succeed to the
Empire . . . provided the whole inheritance in Europe and America passed
unimpaired. How the safety and interests of the rest of Europe were
affected . . . was of no account to Castilian pride' (Trevelyan, i. 127).
Toledo, the chief city of Castile, was synonymous with the fine swords
made there which had long been the symbol of its pride.

60: 10–11 *Frog,* **that was my Fathers Kitchen-boy.** For Arbuthnot's
more detailed treatment of the history of the United Provinces from an
insignificant part of the Spanish Empire to a powerful independent state
see 100: 11–13 n. to 101: 5–6 n.

60: 11–12 **he pretend to meddle . . . with my Will.** Charles II left
his sickbed to declare his will under which the Empire was to descend
to the Bavarian Joseph Ferdinand, whose death shortly thereafter in
February 1699 necessitated fresh negotiations among the partitioners and,
in reply, a second will in favour of the Duke of Anjou.

60: 13 **thy Age and Infirmity.** The debility of the Habsburgs is satirized
here and in the similar behaviour of Esquire South, below 72: 29–32 n.

60: 14–16 **how will the Ghosts of my Noble Ancestors . . . in their
Graves.** Cf. the account of the King's necrophiliac ravings in Macaulay,
vi. 2904–5, and his declaration in the second will that '*he would never
consent, that a Monarchy founded by his Ancestors with so much Glory,
should be dismember'd or diminish'd in any manner*' ('Account of the
Debate', 1701, *Collection of State Tracts*, iii, 1707, p. 96).

60: 22–6 *Lewis* **hall'd . . . clip'd off a Corner . . . convenient for
him.** After prolonged bargaining the second Partition Treaty was
approved by Louis XIV and William III. France was to receive 'Naples
and Sicily, as in the former treaty, and in addition . . . Milan; but she
was to give Milan to the Duke of Lorraine in exchange for his province,
already practically a French possession' (Trevelyan, i. 128).

60: 30–6 **A Cunning Fellow . . . believ'd this had some ill-meaning.** This 'Cunning Fellow' may be Lord Somers or, more probably,
John Howe, though the two possible identifications need not be mutually
exclusive. When Somers finally received a draft of the first partition, he
expressed his disapproval in a carefully worded letter to William on
28 Aug. 1698. However, the importunity of the servant might suggest
Howe, who on 15 Feb. 1701 'attacked the King in . . . violent terms . . .
and called the treaty of partition a felonious treaty of three thieves'
(Swift, *Contests*, p. 42). The incident became such a political touchstone
that the Whig *Character of a Sneaker*, 1705, defined a Tory as one who,

'is for saying *K[ing]*. *W[illiam]*. made a *Felonious Treaty* in the last Reign' (p. 1). See also below.

60:36–61:2 I told him he was a Coxcomb . . . stand to his Bargain. Again the figure of John Bull is used to represent both the people, who were enthusiastic about the partition, and the King, who 'so highly resented [Howe's attack], that he dropt an Expression, signifying, that if the disparity of their Condition had not restrain'd him, he wou'd have had the Satisfaction of him, which all Gentlemen have a Right to demand of one that gives the Lye' (Oldmixon, *History of England*, 1735, p. 209).

61:3–4 *Lewis* reveal'd our whole Secret. Hostile politicians and their polemicists argued that Louis XIV revealed the second partition to Charles II as one of his manœuvres to win Charles over to the Bourbon interest and to persuade him to declare his second will in favour of the Duke of Anjou. Scott quoted a long section of the 'Account of the Debate', 1701, to illustrate this.

61:17 Duplicate of every Terrestrial Animal at Sea. This notion goes back to Pliny. Sir Thomas Browne discussed it in *Pseudodoxia Epidemica* (*Works*, ed. Keynes, 1964, ii. 242–4), and Marvell had previously used it in a comparably ironic way in 'The Garden': 'The Mind, that Ocean, where each kind / Does streight its own resemblance find' (*Poems*, ed. Margoliouth, 1952, p. 49).

61:19–20 three Esquire *Hackums* at one time: the three chief pretenders to the Polish throne in 1696. The chaotic political situation in Poland at the close of the seventeenth century provided a confusing subplot to the drama of the Spanish Succession. At the death in 1696 of John Sobieski, elective King of Poland, twelve candidates were proposed for his throne: 'There being so many Pretenders, the Kingdom fell into Faction, and he that had the most Money seemed to have the best Interest' (*Ancient and Present State of Poland*, 1697, p. 16). The three most considerable claimants were Prince James (son of the dead King), the Prince of Condé (who was supported by the Abbott of Polignac and French money), and the Elector of Saxony. (For an account of the affair see *New Cambridge Modern History*, vi, chap. xx [2].) English pamphleteers followed their machinations with relish. Defoe asserted that the English remained 'the most Divided, Quarrelsome Nation under the Sun', but was prepared to admit that, '*Poland* is the only Nation of *Europe* which can pretend to Match us in this Ill-natur'd Quality' (*Free-Holders Plea*, 1701, pp. 1–2). The troubled Polish Succession was used as a condemnatory metaphor in the *Picture of a Low Flyer* (1704 ?), by which time Poland had become synonymous with political faction: see the allegories of the Popish Plot in the *Last Will and Testament of Anthony King of Poland*, 1682, of contemporary English politics in Defoe's *Dyet of Poland*, 1705, and of Sacheverell's trial in the 'Tryal and Sentence in Poland' (*Whig and Tory*, 1712, iii. 10–11). 'Hackum' may recall the peculiar emphasis in the *Ancient and Present State* (pp. 17–18) on 'cutting to pieces' various individuals and factions, or may simply refer to the divisive state of the kingdom. Cf. Defoe on the 'mock kings' of Poland (*Review*, 6 Mar. 1711, iv. 41).

61: 20–2 *Lewis* . . . entertain'd . . . *John Bull*'s heir . . . the Child unborn . . . brought . . . some . . . Expence. As the *Keys* recognized, this alludes to 'the Imposter [the Old Pretender] on the other side of the Water, which the *French* King vamp'd up with the Title of King of *England*' (Defoe, *Present Negotiations*, 1712, p. 34). 'Child unborn' puns on the enthusiastic questioning of his legitimacy during Anne's reign: he appeared as 'a Slip, as some believe of the late Abdicated Monarch, tho' others negatively declare him Spurious' in the *History of the Royal-Oak*, 1712, pp. 4–5. The most direct source of 'Trouble and Expence' which he occasioned was the abortive invasion attempt of 1708; but there may be another ironic allusion to the Barrier Treaty, which was designed, in part, to obviate the possibility of a second Stuart Restoration (31: 22–33 n.).

61: 32 two *Sosia*'s quarrelling who was Master. Cf. Dryden's play *Amphitryon; or the Two Sosias* (1690) which was based on the *Amphitruo* of Plautus, and which recounted the myth of Jupiter and Mercury assuming the forms of Amphitryon and his Servant Sosia so that the amorous deity might enjoy Alcmena, the human's wife. It was performed on at least a dozen occasions between 16 May 1705 and 18 Mar. 1712, i.e. a month before the publication of this third *John Bull* pamphlet (see *London Stage*, 1960), and Tonson had produced a 'Third Edition' of the play in 1706. Much of its broadest humour centred on the confrontation of the twin Sosias, the human and the divine, and a Tory satirist had, in 1710, used the farcical associations of this scene to satirize the Whigs in the *True . . . Account of the Last Distemper*, ii. 32.

62: 1–2 Banterers and Bambouzlers: tricksters or hoaxters (*OED*). Swift and Steele complained that 'certain words invented by some pretty fellows, such as banter, bamboozle . . . are now struggling for the vogue' (*Tatler*, 28 Sept. 1710, iv. 179). Frog is one such 'Bambouzler' (103: 8).

62: 4–5 Justice is a better rule than Conveniency . . . slight on't. Cf. 'waylaying another Prince [Charles II of Spain] is said to be convenient for *Europe* . . . But what Law, or what Right had the three contracting Powers, to assume this Authority' (*Fable of the Lions Share*, 1701, pp. 16–17). Arbuthnot also echoes the many other Tory polemicists who saw the policy of King William as the model for the political theory of their 'new Whig' opponents after the succession of Anne: ''Tis true, we talk of owing great Duty to the Queen, but we never pay it . . . longer than it suits with our *Conveniencies*' (*Thoughts of an Honest Whig*, 1710, p. 6). See also Charles Hornby on 'the New-fashion'd popular Notions of Government' exhibited by Whigs from the Partition Treaties to the Utrecht conferences in *Third Part of the Caveat*, 1712, pp. 99–100.

62: 7–8 *the Mannor of* Bullock's Hatch. Queen Anne and her people are identified in this use of the Crown lands to equate with the national

finances. The *Keys* failed to make sense of this allusion, but Hawkesworth recognized its wide implications when he paraphrased Boyer
(*Annals*, ix. 231) and wrote: 'After the dissolution of the parliament [in
1710], the sinking ministry endeavoured to support themselves, by
propagating a notion, that the publick credit would suffer, if the Lord
Treasurer *Godolphin* was removed . . . the alarm became general, and all
the publick funds gradually sunk. Perhaps by *Bullocks-Hatch* the author
meant the crown lands', to which Scott added 'or the public revenue in
general'. For contemporary expression of the Whig 'notion' see *Moderator*,
28 July 1710, and for typical Tory replies see Davenant, *Sir Thomas
Double at Court*, 1710, p. 85, and Defoe, *Eleven Opinions*, 1711, p. 31.

**62: 11–13 *Scriveners and Lawyers* . . . asking for the Money . . . for
the approaching Term.** Arbuthnot again suggests the unity of purpose
which connects the 'new Whig' profiteers, both military and financial,
in their support for the war policy (see also 65: 4 n.). Cf. Defoe on the
stock-jobbers, who 'declare a new sort of Civil War among us. . . . the
war they manage is carried on with worse Weapons than Swords and
Musquets . . . these People . . . can wheedle Men to ruin . . . by the
strange and unheard of Engines, of *Interests, Discounts, Transfers, Tallies,
Debentures*. . . . They can draw up their Armies and levy troops, set
Stock against *Stock* . . . and the poor Passive Trades-men, like the
Peasant in *Flanders*, are plunder'd by both sides' (*Villany of Stock-
Jobbers Detected*, 1701, p. 13).

62: 14–15 *Sir Roger, get me rid of these Fellows*. See 'Background,
1698–1712', p. liii, above, for a contemporary account of the task Harley
faced in 1711 and the measures he took to stabilize the economy; cf. also
Swift, *Examiner*, 7 June 1711, and *Four Last Years*, vii. 64–78.

**62: 15–24 *I'll warrant you* . . . a pair of Scissars . . . for this
purpose.** Cf. Swift, 'They say, my lord treasurer [Harley] has a dead
warrant in his pocket, they mean, a list of those who are to be turned out
of employment, and we every day now expect those changes' (*Journal*,
5 May 1711, p. 285).

62: 20 his long Poll: the Treasurer's staff of office.

62: 22–5 *Sir Roger* us'd to bargain . . . and would snip it off:
Harley's vigorous measures to 'stop the Depradations of those who
dealt in Remittances' (Swift, *Four Last Years*, vii. 76).

62: 25–6 like a true Goldsmith he kept all your Holidays. Gold-
smiths observed the same holidays as the Bank of England. Their credit
notes, which had been the original credit system, were still in use, and,
like Treasury Bills, were payable on the date following any bank holiday
on which they became due.

62: 27–8 he would set them a telling . . . Three-penny Pieces.
In May 1711 the Treasurer launched two lotteries to fund the unprovided national debts. They realized £3,500,000, and Defoe commented
with malicious enthusiasm: 'all the Resolution of the Whigs to damn

Credit . . . and not lend a Penny to the Government, fell flat to the Ground at the . . . Act of Parliament for 9 *per Cent.* upon a Lottery. Then we found Whigs . . . running and treading on the Heels of one another, to share the General Plunder . . . and ever since railing and quarrelling' (*Eleven Opinions*, 1711, p. 24).

63: 1 **Sword in Hand . . . nuzling like an Eel.** Cf. 'Mr' Harley is generally allowed as cunning a man as any in England' (*Wentworth Papers*, ed. Cartwright, 1883, p. 132). Harley showed himself capable of decisive and unorthodox action in counselling the Queen to create twelve new Tory peers to save his ministry (see 'Background, 1698–1712', pp. lv–lvi, above), but was better known for his ability to procrastinate and delay. A Whig described him as 'one day a Saint, the t'other Fiend / now true, & then a knave; / Boistrous sometimes, at others kind, / But all ye Game to save' (*Choice New Song Call'd She-Land*, bs. 1712). *OED* cites this usage of 'nuzling' to exemplify 'to burrow or dig with the nose'; but another sense it records, 'to nestle, to lie snug' would seem equally appropriate.

63: 5–6 **he knew every Body, and could talk to them in their own way.** Cf. 'Harley had an astonishing number of relations in the Commons' and 'an astonishing range of contacts' in all strata of society (Holmes, pp. 265–7). Perhaps Arbuthnot alludes to his use of veiled threats of dismissal from place or of withdrawl of lucrative supply contracts: these were indeed means of talking 'in their own way' to the commercial interests. It certainly suggests the efficiency of Harley's network of intelligence agents, with Defoe chief among them.

63: 7 **the Dragon at *Hockley the Hole*:** Gilbert Burnet, the Low Church 'B[isho]p of S[alisbur]y' (*Key*, 3rd edn.). This is the only specific reference we have found to Burnet as the 'dragon' of 'Hockley in the Hole', a bear garden in Clerkenwell celebrated for its animal baitings, trials of skill, and 'monsters, too terrible for the encounter of any heroes' (*Tatler*, 14 June 1709, i. 234). Hockley was associated with the grotesque entertainments of Bartholomew Fair (held in neighbouring Smithfield) where, in 1707, the sadly declined Elkanah Settle 'made his last appearance, hissing in a green leather dragon of his own invention' (*London Past and Present*, p. 34); but the most tangible connection between Burnet and the bear garden is the fact that he was resident in Clerkenwell from 1709, when he inherited his third wife's property in St. John's Court. From a map in Stow's *Survey of the Cities of London and Westminster* (1720, II. iv. 62) it would appear that Burnet's house was a mere 300 yards from the bear garden; hence the attack on the Bishop, in 1710, as 'A Prelate *Adroit*, at Text and Debate, / [who] Sent to eight trusty Brethren in Council to meet; / They whip on their Cloaks, and to *Hockley* they go, / To know what his *Kirkship* had for 'em to do' ('Salisbury Steeple revers'd', *Collection of Poems*, i. 4). *A Supplement to the History of the Crown-Inn* (1717), the Whig 'reply' to *John Bull*, in which the violently rhetorical Henry Sacheverell became 'the Curate of *Hockley*', turned back on Arbuthnot another level of allusion buried in this old joke against Burnet, who was wont to deliver celebrated fire and brimstone expositions at his home in Clerkenwell, before such Whig leaders as the Marlboroughs, Godolphin, and Somers. The style of these 'sermons' was anathema to the Tories, who often attacked Low Church pulpit histrionics as 'Bear-garden Language' (Defoe, *Dissenters Answer*, 1704, p. 4); and homilies on the millenium by 'the most celebrated *extempore* preacher of his day' may have suggested another 'Dragon' of Revelation to Tory wits (cf. W. F. Mitchell, *English Pulpit Oratory*, 1937, pp. 341–2, and the *Whitson-Fair: Rary-Show*, bs. [1703?]).

63: 7–8 **bid him call the 30th of next *February*.** Even Swift was compelled to admit that Harley 'often gave no Answer at all, and very seldom a direct one . . . he was likewise heavily charged with the common Court vice of promising very liberally and seldom performing' (*Enquiry*, viii. 137).

63: 9–11 **in the Kitchen, weighing . . . Light Meat:** allusions to the regulation of finance in both the Queen's household and national military supply. 'He took care by the utmost Parcimony or by suspending Payments where they seemed least to press, that all Stores for the Navy should be bought with ready Money' (Swift, *Four Last Years*, vii. 77), and at the same time he directed the campaign against Marlborough and his Duchess; the latter had lately been the Queen's chief 'maid' as Groom of the Stole, and was rumoured to have embezzled huge sums.

63: 10 **a-tick:** buy on credit; run into debt (*OED*).

63: 12 **slip into the Cellar, and gage the Casks.** Dissatisfied with Godolphin's plans for long-term reform in the Customs, Harley decided to bypass the commissioners and instituted a temporary system under his personal supervision to effect immediate economies.

63: 16 ***Change.*** Exchange or Change Alley was the centre of stock-jobbing activity and hence a physical manifestation of all that the Tories and conservative Whig economists hated in the new financial system, and where 'all the old Subtilties of Trick, Cheat, Fore-saying and Back-saying are laudable receiv'd Practices' (Defoe, *Review*, 7 June 1709, vi. 111).

63: 19–20 **The Squirters were at it . . . for the Loss of their Bubble.** Cf. 'The Libels and Pamphlets published against him . . . [Harley] frequently read by way of Amusement with a most unaffected Indifference' (Swift, *Enquiry*, viii. 136).

63: 22 **shook his Ears.** 'He may go shake his Ears', a proverb which seems to have originated from the ass shaking its ears when relieved of a burden: *Dictionary of Proverbs* (E. 16) cites nine examples between 1560 and 1639. *OED* tentatively suggests made 'the best of a bad bargain (?)': cf. 'make the best of it', 18: 30 above.

63: 24–8 **Mrs. *Bull* did all . . . Territories of Parsimony.** Arbuthnot allows some truth in the Whig claims that there was 'a great Suspicion of Avarice and Narrowness of Spirit' in the prolonged financial witch-hunting demanded of the ministry by extreme Tories in Parliament (*Reasons for Restoring the Whigs*, 1711, p. 6).

63: 29–31 **blam'd Mrs.** *Bull* **for . . .** *Soap* **and** *Sand* **to scowre the Rooms.** Unpopular duties were imposed on hides, skins, all soap (whether imported or home-produced) and building materials (see *Annals*, x. 374 and xi. 2, 35–6).

63: 32–4 **she would not allow . . . the** *Seven-Champions,* **in the Black Letter:** the '*Act* for *Restraining the Press against Seditious Pamphlets*' (*Key*), which was devised by Bolingbroke to silence the opposition press by a heavy duty on paper. It passed on 10 June and came into force on 1 August 1712. Arbuthnot suggests that the violent protests it occasioned were from Grub Street hacks who feared for their livelihood. *London's Glory: or, the History of the Famous and Valiant London 'Prentice* narrated the romantic adventures of its humble hero, and was not only frequently reprinted throughout the late seventeenth century but was also the inspiration for a particularly banal genre. There seems to be significance in the specification of 'Black Letter' type, although it was indeed commonly used for the works of Bunyan and Richard Johnson's *Most Famous History of the Seaven Champions of Christendome*, both perennially popular with dissenting audiences: Arbuthnot was rarely so specific for no purpose, and his choice of 'whiggish' books here points the equation of Grub Street entertainments with opposition polemic as surely as does the preface to the fifth pamphlet (94: 1–7 n.). This equation may well be quite precise if it is a sly allusion to the 'Black-List' controversy of 1702–3, sparked by the anonymous *List of One Unanimous Club*, 1701 [2], which picked out in black letter the Tories whose loyalty to the Hanoverian succession was suspect (see Holmes, pp. 90–1). A bitter pamphlet war ensued, and as late as 1708 a Tory pamphlet recalled the dispute in a complaint which Bolingbroke might have taken as his text in 1712: 'three Cunning men will do more hurt by their Pamphlets . . . then a Hundred Honest Men can do good, and if the Commons take more pains then ordinary to serve their Country . . . then out comes . . . the *Black-List*, and sets the Mob upon them' (*New Dialogue . . . upon the Present Juncture*, p. 7). These 'uncommon pains' of 'black listed' Tories were, in part, proceedings against Whig ministers on charges of corruption very similar to those laid against the Godolphin ministry nine years later in 1711.

64: 6–8 **to curb the Insolent . . . good Effects of the Law.** Cf. the opening thesis of Swift's *Conduct of the Allies*: 'THE Motives that may engage a wise Prince or State in a War, I take to be one or more of these: Either to check the overgrown Power of some ambitious Neighbour; to recover what hath been unjustly taken from Them; to revenge some Injury They have received . . . to assist some Ally in a just Quarrel; or lastly, to defend Themselves when They are invaded' (vi. 7).

64: 17 **a Rogue, that never kept a Word he said.** Another allusion which identifies a monarch with his people. In this case, the perfidy of

Louis XIV ('I still resolve . . . to keep no Word or Oath further than my own Interest' [*King of France his Catechism*, 1703, p. 8]) epitomizes the French 'way of dealing, . . . they are seldome deceived, for they trust no body, and if any body trust them, they had as good burn the bill of their particulars, if they are not under lock and key, or can but find out any evasion to shift themselves' (*Character of France*, 1659, p. 36).

64: 18 this Labyrinth. Defoe refers to the 'Labyrinth' or 'Maze' of the tradesman sinking into bankruptcy in *Review*, 19 Feb. 1706, iii. 85–6, as does Ned Ward in his portrait of the '*Climbing Lawyer*' who, 'By a close Application to that Labyrinth, the Law . . . has made himself a Master of all those little Turnings and Windings in that intricate Maze, by which some Men are led out of the World, and others out of their Estates' (*Modern World Disrob'd*, 1708, pp. 148–9). There are other relevant parallels in Mrs. Manley's comment on 'the *intricacies* of . . . the *Labyrinth*' of Godolphin's mind (*Secret Memoirs*, 1709, ii. 114), and in Ned Ward's character of Harley: 'He knows the Lab'rinth, and has gain'd the Clue. / What Mazes has he trod . . . / what Good for *Britain* done' ('English Foreigners', *Poetical Entertainer*, iii, 1712, p. 21).

64: 23–5 the yearly Income . . . is Mortgag'd . . . in Debt. The annual income of the government from all tax sources would have almost equalled military expenditure had it not been eaten up by interest repayments on earlier loans (see the financial statements in Dickson, p. 63, and Trevelyan, iii. 324–5). The income of John's estate is thus mortgaged to the usurers.

64: 29–31 a young Heir . . . in the Hands of Money-Scriveners. Cf. '*Power*, which, according to the old Maxim, was used to follow *Land*, is now gone over to *Money*; and the Country Gentleman is in the Condition of a young Heir, out of whose Estate a Scrivener receives half the Rents for Interest, and hath a Mortgage on the Whole; and is therefore always ready to feed his Vices and Extravagancies while there is any Thing left' (Swift, *Examiner*, 2 Nov. 1710, iii. 5). Arbuthnot here alludes to an emotive satiric type: cf. 'Trapland the Scrivener' in Congreve's *Love for Love*, 1695.

64: 31 Such Fellows are like your Wiredrawing Mills. A wiredrawing mill is a machine for making wire by drawing a piece of ductile metal through a series of holes, successively decreasing in diameter (*OED*). Cf. 'What one Whim could not do, new Tricks supply'd, / B[an]k, Lott'ries, Loans, and fifty Cheats beside, / The Kingdom's Well-fare every Year annoy'd. / Good Workmen always diff'rent Tools require, / Thro' sundry Holes the Artist draws his Wyre' (*Fair Shell*, 1705, p. 58). The same metaphor was also traditional in anti-law satire, as in the description of Attornies determined 'to invent and wyre-draw Suits and controversies' (*Looking Glasse for . . . Lawyers*, 1646, p. 5).

64: 33 they squeeze the Heart, Blood and Guts out of him. Cf. 'the Lawyers are degenerated by Practice, are Harpies, Monsters and Devils, who suck the Blood and Wealth of the Nation, and that ruin, as far as in them lies, those that fall into their hands, whether for Life or Estate' (Defoe, *Review*, 23 Sept. 1704, i. 247).

65: 1–2 Securities ready drawn . . . the Ready . . . went to Pot. Securities here are simply shares in the funds (cf. 62: 7–8 n.): 'ready drawn' again suggests the analogue between stocks and weapons (cf. Tom Double's 'Tallies insted of Staves and Truncheons', etc. (11: 1–3 n.). In order to get 'Ready' cash, John, like monarchs down to the seventeenth century, sells part of his landed holdings: i.e. England is attempting, with ill success, to combine both old and new methods of raising money for the war.

65: 4 Lawyers . . . like so many Hell-hounds. 'A Lawyer's purse is the mouth of hell' *Dictionary of Proverbs* (L. 127). It is obvious from this passage that 'Lawyers' in the satire represent both military men and stock-jobbers.

65: 5–6 the Rogues would plead Poverty . . . Ninety for the Hundred. Cf. 'the needy Trades-men, who sold their Goods at common rates, were fain to Discount more than their profit to get their Money... the Exchequer Notes design'd for a currency in Payments were Jobb'd about the Town; and by the Policy of these Gentlemen put upon the Trades-men, in order to be brought again at high Discounts, and then Engross'd again by the Money'd Men, who obtain'd the Discount as a *Premio* added to the Interest upon the Originals' (Defoe, *Villany of Stock-Jobbers Detected*, 1701, p. 3).

65: 7–8 my best Rents . . . with my own Mony. The 'Rents' here are the major taxes, such as those on land, malt, or coals (i.e. the 'Funds'), upon which loans were raised in anticipation of collection (see Holmes, p. 157, and Dickson, pp. 59 ff.).

65: 9 no Clause of Redemption. A conflated allusion to the permanent national debt and to the expedient of the 'issue of short-dated paper beyond the capacity to redeem it regularly' (Dickson, p. 341).

65: 12–13 a worse Trick . . . gave the Acquittance: the practice, inaugurated in the 1690s and later refined, of raising money on tallies of fictitious loan: 'When Parliament authorised a loan of £x in anticipation of a specific tax, the Exchequer would make out tallies of receipt for, say, one third of this sum, together with the corresponding Orders of Pay-ment. The Orders would be in the name of a departmental paymaster, such as the Treasurer of the Navy. Though the latter had not himself lent a penny, the tallies and Orders he held were valuable claims on future revenue, and could be used for payment, or as security for private advances' (ibid., p. 351). After 1708, the cumulative floating departmental debt grew so large as to imperil the credit of the nation.

65: 13–15 The same Man was Butcher . . . Cook and Poulterer. Cf. in 'the system of naval contracting . . . many small suppliers financed their contracts with the Navy Board by borrowing, making a contract with the lender to assign to him the Navy bills which would later be made out . . . and the extent to which Navy bills, often of large dimensions, found their way into the hands of London financiers . . . in 1709–11 . . . suggests that transfer facilities were also useful to the large contractors' (ibid., p. 402). Cf. 16: 19–20 n.

65: 15–17 **there came twenty Bills . . . I had given Mony to discharge.** Cf. 'the Navy creditors, in particular, [were] relentless in their pressure on the Treasury' (ibid., p. 363).

65: 19 **Goal.** 'It is difficult to say whether the form *goal(e)*, common alike in official and general use, from the 16th to the 18th c., was merely an erroneous spelling of gaol, after this had become an archaism, or was phonetic' (*OED*).

65: 21–2 **my Bookkeeper sat Sotting all Day, playing at Putt, and All-Fours.** Godolphin was 'addicted to gambling and horse-racing' (Scott). A number of Tory satirists such as Swift, Pope, and Mrs. Manley accused him of squandering the nation's money 'to spark it, / 'Mong the Racers at *New-Market*' (*Fox Set to Watch the Geese*, 1705, p. 9). Another anonymous allegorist used the same metaphor of lowly card games in an earlier description of the Treasurer as 'An old swarthy Man . . . a Stick [the Staff of office] in his Right Hand, in his Left a Pack of Cards; before him was a Table, one end of which was fill'd with Dice, and all sorts of Coin; and the other with Heaps of Papers and Accounts' (*Account of a Dream*, 1708, p. 8).

65: 31–4 **There goes the prettiest Fellow . . . at the Bar**: another ironic joke at the expense of Prince Eugene 'that was the prettiest Fellow in the World' (10: 6–7 n.) and noted for his eloquence (40: 13–18 n.) The pun on 'Silver Tongue' thus confirms him as the leader of the foreign troops and mercenaries in British pay, whose corruption and inefficiency was the subject of Swift's anger (see *Conduct*, vi. 38–9).

65: 35–66: 3 **The Night after a Trial . . . hooping and hallowing**: the celebration of Marlborough's victories, 'the many Rejoicings and Triumphs, Processions to St. *Paul*'s, Bonfires and Holidays, on Account of his repeated Successes' (Defoe, *No Queen: or no General*, 1712, p. 7).

66: 10 **Practice of Piety**: another allusion to the 'ordered decency' of the Anglican Church in a pun on the title of a devotional guide, *The Practise of Pietie, Directing a Christian how to Walke, that he May Please God*, written by Lewis Bayly, Bishop of Bangor, early in the seventeenth century. It had been so popular (on a wide denominational basis) that a 'fifty ninth' edition appeared in 1735. The guide, divided into sections which elaborated devotions appropriate for various parts of the day and for contingencies such as sickness or bereavement, had therefore become a useful symbol for Anglican ceremonies and liturgy by the turn of the century. One Churchman had previously employed it in his *New Practice of Piety*, 1704, to attack the very Dissenters who used it to laud personal piety: cf. a Whig comment on Daniel Burgess (18: 18–19 n.) whose 'Conversation . . . is a daily *Practise of Piety*' (*Post Angel*, Nov. 1701, ii. 315).

66: 16 turn her out of Doors, sieze her Lands. The verbal echo of John's earlier account of the Church's fate during the Civil War period (49: 6–8 n.) again connects the Low Church Whigs and Dissenters of Anne's reign with their Cromwellian 'antecedents'.

66: 17 Soft and fair. '*Soft and Fair goes far*; or not more Haste than good Speed' (*Canting Crew*). *Dictionary of Proverbs* (S. 601), cites eighteen examples between 1542 and 1721.

66: 19–21 I won't seize her Jointure . . . that's pretty fair. The Queen waived her right to her 'Rent Charge', Tithes and First Fruits, but, as Arber noted, the Church did contribute in small measure to the war by 'taxation of the Clergy' (*Later Stuart Tracts*). Indeed, one pamphleteer was moved to ask, 'Are not . . . the great deficiency in Tythes sufficient, but that Four Shillings in the Pound [land tax] must be added' (*Taxes not Grievous*, 1712, pp. 13–14).

66: 22–5 the old Gentlewoman . . . ended in a Lethargy: the '*Discouragement shewn by the Late* [Godolphin] *Ministry to the Church of England*' (*Key*, 6th edn.). In the following allegorical treatment of High Church alarms, Arbuthnot dramatizes a metaphor popular with the polemicists for the previous seven years: cf. 'there is a *Hecktick Feavour* lurking in the very *Bowels* . . . which, if not timely *Cur'd*, will Infect all the *Humours*, and at length *Destroy* the very *Being* of it' (Drake, *Memorial of the Church of England*, 1705, p. 3); the Church, 'being sick and Weak in Body, but of Sound and Orthodox Judgment' (*Last Will and Testament of the C[hurc]h*, 1710, p. 7).

66: 25–8 It betray'd it self . . . common Offices of Life. The power of the Low Church had so increased under the direction of William III that during the next reign there was always a clear majority of 'moderate' Whig Bishops in the Upper House of Convocation who were prepared to relax Anglican formalities much more readily than the largely Tory and fiercely conservative Lower House.

66: 28–30 She that was the cleanliest . . . a Close-stool under her Nose. The Low Church clergy are here damningly equated with the 'atheist' Whigs in the person of Wharton who had defiled a Church in the Diocese of Gloucester (see Swift, *Examiner*, 4 and 25 Jan. 1710, iii. 57, 68–9). Cf. also von Uffenbach's account of an election contested by 'Pulpitshisser' Stanhope, Wharton's fellow Whig (*London in 1710*, pp. 146–7).

66: 31–2 if she . . . heard them talk profanely . . . any notice. Cf. Defoe's account of a blasphemous prebenary in *Review*, 15 Jan. 1709, v. 503, one case illustrative of his repeated argument that the disciplinary failings of the Church were responsible for much dissent: 'Could we but see the Sacred Vestments taken from the Drunken, the Swearing, the Blaspheming, the W[hor]ing, the Heretical, and the scandalously Ignorant among the Clergy' (ibid., 9 Aug. 1709, vi. 219).

66: 33–4 roaring swearing Bullies, and randy Beggars: The Low

Church clergy epitomized in Gilbert Burnet, Bishop of Salisbury. 'Randy', Scots for rude, aggressive, and coarse spoken, was commonly used of beggars (*OED*). Cf. the descriptions of Burnet as a 'Greasy, Butcherly, Brawny Folio' (*New Dialogue between Monsieur Shacoo*, 1701, p. 3), and as 'the *Stentor* of *Sarum* [who] has deafen'd his Audience from the Pulpit' (Bolingbroke, *Letter to the Examiner*, iii. 223).

67: 1–4 **What is the matter . . . disturb'd the whole Neighbourhood.** The first five editions of the *Key* suggested the '*Complaint against Moderation*' and the sixth added, more accurately and precisely, '*in her Celebrated Memorial*'. James Drake's violent alarm, the *Memorial of the Church of England*, 1705, ignited a long-smouldering controversy which reached its climax in December when Rochester moved that the Church was in danger (see Trevelyan, ii. 88–9). 'Books were writ and dispersed over the nation with great industry, to possess all people with the apprehensions that the church was to be given up, that the bishops were betraying it, and that the court would sell it to the dissenters . . . there was an evil spirit and a virulent temper spread among the clergy' (Burnet, *History*, v. 223–44).

67: 5–6 **Sir *William* . . . thou hast . . . stabb'd me!** Another allusion to Godolphin. There appears to be no justification for the identification of Sir William as Sunderland ('Clum', 67: 7 n.) in the third and subsequent editions of the *Key*. (It is significant that, apart from Sir William, the only other knight in the story is Harley [as Sir Roger], Godolphin's successor as Lord Treasurer and Prime Minister.) This is confirmed when the surname 'Crawly' is added in the fourth pamphlet (84: 22 n.), alluding again to the horse-racing activities of the fallen Whig at 'Newmarket . . . his spiritual home' (Trevelyan, i. 194). In *Later Stuart Tracts* Arber postulated that the intended reference was William III, and Carstens agreed on the reasonable grounds that the King had favoured the Low Church. Perhaps the allusion was deliberately ambiguous, but in the context of the *Memorial* 'raving fit' it would have been appropriate for Arbuthnot to accord Godolphin the same irreligious eminence given him by Drake in the crudely ironic observation, ''tis whispered among us (as so great a Secret ought to be) *That the L*[ord] *T*[reasurer] *does not in his Heart care a Farthing for the* F[anati]cks *and* Wh[i]gs' (p. 18).

67: 6–7 **sold me to the Cuckold of Dover:** Thomas, Earl of Wharton. As Carstens first observed, the expansion of Dover to Dover Street in the 1727 note confirms the allusion to Wharton who lived in an impressive mansion there. His cuckoldom was a standing joke: 'HE bears the Gallantries of his Lady with the Indifference of a Stoic, and thinks them well recompenced by a Return of Children . . . without the Fatigues of being a Father' (Swift, *Short Character*, iii. 180). Again there is a parallel in Drake's *Memorial* (p. 15) and in Manley's reference to Wharton as '*Cataline*' . . . A voluntary Cuckold, who for the envied name of Parent, willingly Fathers the Children of his Wive's *junto*' (*Memoirs of Europe*, 1710, ii. 249).

67: 7 **Clum** *with his bloody Knife* : Charles Spencer, Third Earl of
Sunderland; although Scott's note, 'Cromwell, perhaps', points a second
level of suggestion which runs through the pamphlets whenever the
Whigs' attitude to the Church and sovereign is under examination
(cf. 49: 6–8 n. and 52: 10–12 n.). In the *Story of the St. Alb[a]n's Ghost*
(which had run through at least five 'editions' by the end of July 1712),
Sunderland had appeared as 'Clumzy' and had been identified as such in
the *Key* which was appended to the *Key* to these *John Bull* pamphlets.
The name alludes to Sunderland's 'rough way of treating his sovereign'
(Swift, *Four Last Years*, vii. 9) and thus, in Arbuthnot's usage, neatly
associates Anne with the Church she so loved.

67: 8 *the Fury, with her hissing Snakes* : another allusion to the
Duchess of Marlborough. Cf. Trevelyan's comments on the Tory
'clamour against the "fury," the "plague," "the worst of women"' (iii.
116); see also Swift, *Four Last Years*, vii. 8, and Pope, *Poems*, p. 821. In
this context it is also interesting that Low Church 'Moderation' (see
following note) should have appeared as a fury in Shippen's *Moderation
Display'd*, 1705.

67: 12 *she was in a good moderate way.* 'Moderation' was the rally-
ing cry of the Low Church. In the *Memorial* Drake poured vituperation
on these descendants of the Cromwellian regicides who were working to
destroy the Church under cover of 'the Specious, Deceitful *Name* of
Mo[deratio]*n*' (p. 27), and he was supported by pamphlets such as *The
Mask of Moderation Pull'd off the Foul Face of Occasional Conformity*,
1704, *Moderation in Fashion*, 1705, and *The New Association of those
Called Moderate-Church-Men, with the Modern-Whigs and Fanaticks to
Under-mine and Blow-up the Present Church and Government*, 1705 (first
published in 1702). Indeed, the word and concept, which had been a
source of contention since the 1680s, continued to be a religious and
political touchstone throughout the reign of Anne, as 'mightily in Use
and Vogue, among those very fashionable People, the Republican
Whiggish Dissenters and Occasional Conformists' (*Sauce for an English
Gander*, 1712, p. 3).

67: 13 **with great difficulty, brought** *R*[adcli]*ff* : the 'famous Dr.
[John] RADCLIFF, *who amass'd so vast an Estate by his Practice, that future
Ages will hardly credit it*' (*Pharmacœpia Radcliffeana*, 1716, A2). In 1714
Arbuthnot was to write to Swift of a Scriblerian project which was to
centre on a map of diseases with 'R[adcli]ff . . . painted at the corner . . .
contending for the universal empire of the world, & the rest of his
physicians opposing his ambitious designs, with a project of a Treaty of
partition [cf. 60: 22–6] to settle peace' (Swift, *Correspondence*, ii. 42).
Radcliffe's fame fed the arrogance which his colleague Arbuthnot
satirizes here by alluding to the most notorious Radcliffean anecdote:
'her Royal Highness [Princess Anne] being indispos'd, caus'd him to be
sent for; in Answer to which, he made a Promise of coming to St. *James*'s
soon after. But he not appearing, that Message was back'd by another. . . .
At which the Doctor swore by his Maker *That her Highness's Distemper*

was nothing but the Vapours' (Pittis, *Some Memoirs*, 1715, pp. 38–9). In a satire on Burnet, *Notes and Memorandums*, 1715 (a pamphlet sometimes attributed to Arbuthnot) the Whig Bishop muses, 'Wish *Radcliffe* was alive: Hang him, he would not come to me' (p. 3). Perhaps Arbuthnot intended a sly personal joke at the expense of a rival whose pride backfired on him, for after Anne became Queen she 'was so prepossessed in favour of Dr. *Arbuthnot* . . . that she would by no means consent to [Radcliffe's] coming to Court' (Pittis, p. 45).

67: 14 G[ar]*th* came upon the first Message. The celerity of Dr. Samuel Garth suggests his political leaning towards the 'moderate' Whigs. The satire is, however, muted, as Garth was friendly with Arbuthnot; and perhaps there is even an intended compliment to Garth who was as jovial and accommodating as Radcliffe was brusque and arrogant (see Cushing, *Dr. Garth, the Kit-Kat Poet*, 1906, pp. 27–30). Certainly there was no love lost between Garth and Radcliffe: when Garth heard that Radcliffe had endowed the Oxford library which bears his name, he declared it 'as inappropriate as for an eunuch to found a seraglio' (ibid., p. 29).

67: 16–17 they divided into two Parties . . . with R[adcli]ff: respectively the Low and High Church factions in Parliament, Convocation, and the nation. Radcliffe was a fierce Tory, first advanced by James II. He refused a baronetcy from William III, contributed to the legal defence of Drake's *Memorial* (see Pittis, pp. 58–60), and was unfairly declared by Burnet 'a professed Jacobite'. On the other hand, Garth was 'for the members of the Whig party . . . the fashionable and honored medical consultant' (Cushing, p. 28). In the age of Anne, 'A fashionable doctor could lose a lot of patients if he espoused a party cause too warmly' (Holmes, p. 23), and the political affiliations of these two doctors were eagerly exploited by polemicists.

67: 18–20 *This Case seems . . . Hysterical . . . Blisters, with the Steel Diet*. Cf. 'Chast Hallifax and Pious Wharton cry, / The Church has Vapours, there's no Danger nigh' (*On the Church's Being in Danger*, 1705, BM. Add. MSS. 23904). Arbuthnot uses his medical expertise to concentrate satire on both extremes of opinion represented in the following dispute over the Church. Together they have made of her one of those 'Women, in whom, besides the frequency of Fits and disorders of the Nerves [66: 24, above] to which they are subject without any visible Cause, we may discover many Symptoms of Indigestion' (Mandeville, *Treatise of the Hypochondriack and Hysterical Passions*, 1711, pp. 175–6). Garth, noted for his severe treatments (see *Notes and Memorandums*, 1715, p. 18), not only makes an optimistic diagnosis but a confused prescription. The Steel Diet, internally administered iron or steel filings (*OED*), was normally prescribed in case of fever, which is the diagnosis of Radcliffe (67: 31, below); and a certain Dr. R. Pitt pronounced categorically that only a quack would blister the wakeful and raving patient (*Crafts and Frauds of Physic Expos'd*, 1703, p. 11). This allegorical illness provides an interestingly inverse parallel with that of another Tory satire, the *True and Faithful Account of the Last Distemper and Death of Tom. Whigg*, 1710, on the fall of the Godolphin ministry: 'His Distemper, according to the Opinion of his first Physician, and second best Poet [Garth], was only an Emptiness in his Veins, but it appear'd to be a malignant Fever [cf. 67: 29–31 n.] upon his Spirits, which chang'd in a few Days to a Delirium or Decay in his Understanding' (i. 1–2).

67: 20–1 **Others suggested . . . Letting of Blood, because she was Plethorick:** the disguised enmity of the Low Church. 'Plethorick' constitutions, according to Arbuthnot, had an overplus of animal fluids due to good diet, little exercise, too much sleep, and the suppression of 'usual evacuations' such as perspiration: thus, 'Blood-letting . . . often increaseth the Force of the Organs of Digestion, and increaseth the Distemper' (*Essay . . . of Aliments*, 1732, pp. 285–6).

67: 22–3 **the Old Woman was mad . . . Corporal Correction.** 'Many of the Whigs advised severe measures against the high church' (Scott). Drake was prosecuted for the *Memorial*: 'Investigations and proceedings dragged on for a year, in the course of which Dr. Drake, though not positively convicted, was worried into a fever that killed him; and poor Ned Ward . . . expiated his *Hudibras Redivivus* in the pillory' (Trevelyan, ii. 85).

67: 24–6 *you are mistaken . . . with strong Cordials.* Radcliffe, an Oxford graduate, championed the use of rich cordials contrary to the blood-letting in vogue at Cambridge, Garth's Alma Mater (see *Pharmacœpia Radcliffeana*, 1716, i. 108). Yet although his Tory diagnosis is more accurate, his prescription is equally dubious, since, 'distill'd Compound Waters are Pernicious and Destructive in Fevers' (Pitt, *Crafts and Frauds of Physic*, 1703, p. 153 [149]). There is also a strong element of personal satire against Radcliffe, who, quite typically, scorns the opinions of his fellow doctors (even when they accord with his diagnosis) to the extent of denying the validity of his 'favourite remedy—a "blistering plaister"—in case of delirium or convulsions' (Hone, *Life of . . . Radcliffe*, 1950, p. 63).

67: 27–8 *In no manner of Danger . . . I vow to God.* Rochester's motion (67: 1–4 n.) was defeated, and the Whigs replied by voting that 'whoever goes about to suggest and insinuate that the Church is in danger . . . is an enemy to the Queen, the Church and the Kingdom' (Trevelyan, ii. 88). Here again the allegory also works on a personal level: 'This pointed, airy way of speaking was characteristic of Garth. Arbuthnot with a few touches depicts his manner' (Moore, *Physician in English History*, 1913, p. 43). Cf. Garth's conversation with Burnet in *Notes and Memorandums*, 1715: 'Sir, I am sorry to see you so ill; but *Egad* I think you deserve it. . . . Not Robert [Boyle], *Egad*! . . . he . . . for Physick, is as great a Dunce as the late R[adcli]*ffe*' (pp. 16–17).

67: 29–31 *I tell you, Sir . . . three Days to an end . . . a Malignant Fever.* Cf. Ned Ward's Tory opinion that the Church, 'Inflam'd by too much Toleration, / Was grown . . . / So mad with a Malignant Fever, / That no Man's Care could yield Protection / Against the prevalent Infection' (*Hudibras Redivivus*, 1705, i. 1–2). Radcliffe 'incurred great odium by his plain speaking' (Hone, *Life of Radcliffe*, 1950, p. 57) and was given to making specific and peremptory estimates of how much longer a patient had to live. When called in to examine Queen Mary he declared her a dead woman; and he pronounced that Prince George, when suffering from a 'malignant feaver' (ibid., pp. 52–3), '*had been so tamper'd with, that nothing in the Art of Physick, could keep* [him] *alive more than six Days*' (Pittis, *Some Memoirs*, 1715, p. 65).

67: 31–3 **Fool, Puppy, and Blockhead . . . Ink Bottles at one another's Heads.** In March 1705 it was reported that 'lampoons fly thick as hail in order to influence the approaching elections' (Richards, *Party Propaganda Under Queen Anne*, 1972, p. 58 n.) Cf. the same image for the polemic war of 1710, 14: 4–6 n.

67: 34–68: 2 **one Party . . . Sister *Peg* . . . would not hear of that.** The policy of union was, of course, promoted by the Low Church Whigs. The Queen, who intervened in the squabbles of Convocation to declare her support for the status quo, is here again identified with the Anglican Church although she did not oppose the Union.

68: 4–5 **a *High German* Livery-Man . . . one 𝔓an 𝔓tſchirnſooker:** Gilbert Burnet, Bishop of Salisbury, who was the energetic and voluble leader of the Low Church (see also 63: 7 n.). This identification is confirmed, as Teerink noted, by a name which shows the influence of Swift's little language: '*P-t-schirn-sooker* = *Bitte schön Zucker*, an allusion to Burnet's weakness for more sugar in his tea' (p. 90). He was the supreme 'Mountebank of State' (*Junto*, bs. 1712) to Tory writers, who had long since realized the satiric potential in his own accounts of apostolic visits to dying rakes such as Rochester (1680), and to condemned men such as Stafford (also 1680) and Horneck (1682). He was 'The Reverend *Scot* . . . Remarkable for disturbing the Sick' (*Last Words and Sayings*, bs. 1682) in the 'groaning board' series of broadsides (also, *Notes conferr'd*, and *Sober Vindication*, 1682). Indeed, the joke became almost ritualistic in polemics directed against Burnet: 'a *Physician* . . . so Famous among all St. *Whigg*'s *Kindred* that . . . no Body of *Quality* durst venture to depart this World without . . . his *Pass-port*' (*Glorious Life . . . of St. Whig*, 1708, p. 20). Moreover, he was one of the '*High German* Artists' so beloved of Frog (p. lxi, above) since he abandoned his Scots nationality and became a Dutch citizen, resident in Amsterdam, to escape the wrath of James II (see Clarke and Foxcroft, *Life of Gilbert Burnet*, Cambridge, 1907, pp. 232–3). As a Scots / Dutch Low Churchman, promoted to his bishopric for sterling service to William III (ibid., pp. 265–7), he could hardly have been more distasteful to Church Tories, who released their hatred in appropriate satires at a time when 'Scarce a County in *England* but . . . [was] invested with a High-*German* Quack-Salver, and his Vagabond Retinue' (Ned Ward, *World Bewitch'd*, 1699, p. 21), and a famous '*Hogen-Dutchman* got Money, being carried about from *Fair* to *Fair*, amongst the Fops that admir'd his Brawny-Bulk' (Hickeringill, *Cere-mony Monger*, 1689, p. 10; cf. 66: 33–4 n. and 69: 1–7 n.). Burnet is thus condemned as the ultimate monitory example in that contemporary satiric tradition which lumped together astrologers, palmists, sleight of hand tricksters, quacks, and magicians as brothers under the skin. Carstens noted that Arbuthnot might have been using the confusion over High German (German proper) and Low (Dutch) to play on the fact that Burnet was 'high' for the Dutch, whereas he ought to have been 'high' for the Church-party, being a bishop, or that he supported the Whig alliance with the truly 'High German' Elector of Hanover (p. 224). The Hanoverian connection was certainly observed by one contemporary who wrote 'Jan-Hanover' on the flyleaf of a copy of this pamphlet now in the National Library of Scotland (H. 34 f. 2/197).

68: 5–6 gave her a sort of a Quack-Powder . . . Opium *in this*. Scott realized the allusion was to the 'Pastoral Letters of the celebrated Dr. Burnet . . . designed to operate as a sedative upon the violent irritation of the high churchmen'. They were intended to 'quiet all Mens Minds' (*Pastoral Letter . . . Concerning the Oaths of Allegiance*, 1689, p. 23), and were persistently attacked as whiggish ministrations of the kind combated by the measures of the Harley government which, according to Defoe, 'should have awaken'd every Honest *Briton* that had not taken too strong an Opiate' (*Present Negotiations*, 1712, p. 35).

68: 9–10 a great Mystery of Iniquity: a pun on the title of Burnet's tract, *The Mystery of Iniquity Unvailed: in a Discourse, wherein is Held Forth the Opposition of the Doctrine, Worship, and Practices of the Roman Church, to the Nature, Designs, and Characters of the Christian Faith*, 1673. Burnet was evoking memories of *A Mysterye of Iniquyte*, 1545, a seminal Protestant work by Johan Bale, which in turn echoed St. Paul's warning that 'the mystery of iniquity doth already work' (2 Thessalonians 2: 7). It was inevitable that such an evocative phrase, which had been used in many religious tracts such as *Westminster Projects: or, the Mystery of Iniquity of Darby-House Discovered* (the scene of a Catholic plot), 1648, and *Mystery of Iniquity somewhat Laid Open*, 1692, should also be employed in political contexts. Thus Whig financial corruptions were described as 'a *Mystery of Iniquity* that has darken'd the understandings of some' (*Dialogue Between a Modern Courtier*, 1696, p. 13); Swift condemned the new age of stock-jobbers as 'a Mystery of Iniquity, and . . . unintelligible *Jargon*' (*Examiner*, 2 Nov. 1710, iii. 7); and the Whigs replied by warning that the peace preliminaries were a '*Mistery of French Iniquity*' (*PPB*, 21 Feb. 1712).

68: 12–21 a troublesome fiddle faddle . . . bowing and cringing . . . quiet in her Bed. The complaints of Low Church clergy are significantly akin to those of Presbyterian Peg, 55: 17–23, above.

68: 25–6 making up of Medicines, and administring them. We can find no evidence that Burnet pursued medical studies; in 1682, however, he 'built a laboratory' in his house where he 'ran through some courses of chemistry' (Clarke and Foxcroft, *Life*, p. 177), and Arbuthnot was here employing another minor polemic tradition: e.g. an undated poem instructed the reader to 'Take of ye herbs of Hypocrisy, & Ambition of each one handfull . . . of ye Roots of . . . Covetiousness, & Rebellion of each one Quarter of a Pound . . . then pound them altogether, in the Mortar of vain Glory' to make up a *New Reciept, of ye Fanaticks, Diascordium* (Bodleian, MS. Rawl. D. 383/94).

68: 29–31 **dis I have from** *Geneva* **. . . from** *Turkey:* an allusion to Burnet's celebrated account of his travels through Europe and his vaunted communion with many different Churches between 1684 and 1686. It was first published in Amsterdam in January or February 1687 and 'created an enormous sensation. . . . As this "succès de scandale" was entirely due to the lurid picture of countries blessed in double measure with Popery and arbitary Government' (Clarke and Foxcroft, *Life*, p. 229). Although its sale was prohibited, it was almost immediately reprinted as *Some Letters, Containing, an Account of what Seemed most Remarkable in Switzerland, Italy*, etc., 1686 [1687], and his opponents seized on the work as a prime example of Low Church hypocrisy: 'He walked from *Dort*, to *Switzerland*; / Did *Calvin*, at *Geneve* profess, / And when at *Rome*, did say the Mass' (*Whitson-Fair*, bs. [1703?]). As in the prescriptions of the true doctors above, Arbuthnot maintains the fictional vraisemblance of his satire in a quack pronouncement typical of a generic 'Doctor *Panacea*, whose generous Nostrum cures every Thing. . . . He, in an unintelligible Jargon, between Dutch and English, would . . . ascribe to his Pill what he had deny'd to the Pope' (Ned Ward, *Secret History of Clubs*, 1709, p. 156). 'Yan' is here advocating a mixture of Calvinism (Geneva, where he communed with the Church), Catholicism (Rome, where he had an audience with Innocent XI), Dutch Protestantism (Amsterdam, where he resided in 1664), and Scots Presbyterianism (Edinburgh, where he was born). Although, as Carstens noted, 'Arbuthnot does not seriously charge Burnet with trying to introduce Islam; "Turkey" is on the allegorical level a climactic but ludicrous exaggeration [connoting tyranny], though literally a source of opium' (p. 225).

68: 32–3 **Yan . . . seen at the** *Rose* **with** *Jack***:** the correspondence between Low Church Whigs and Dissenters. Cf. Swift's *Tale* in which Jack and his brothers are refused admission to the fashionable Rose Tavern in Russell Street (p. 82). In the 1680s the Rose had become famous for both gambling and whiggish politics. The Junto had used it for meetings with their backbenchers during the reign of William (see Macaulay, *History of England*, 1913–15, vi. 2658); hence the cryptic gloss on this passage in the *Key* (4th edn.): '*The* Cabal *of Seven*, i.e. *the* Junto'.

69: 1–7 *here is grand Secret . . . it will Cure you of all Diseases.* Cf. 'Dr. *Sal Volatile Oliosium*, would be Jabbering, in broken *English*, such Hyperbolical Encomiums on his Chimical Infallibility, as if his all-Curing Secret was the very Quintessence of the Philosopher's Stone'

(Ned Ward, *Secret History of Clubs*, 1709, p. 155). Again Arbuthnot echoes the allegory of the *Tale* (and Jack's 'infallible Remedies', pp. 190–1) which was picked up by Leslie in his definition of 'moderation' (67: 12 n.): 'It's a *Catholicon*, and Cures all *Diseases*! Take but a *Dose* of this, and thou may'st . . . Break all the *Ten Commandments*, without any *Offence*' (*Rehearsal*, 15 Jan. 1705). Such metaphors were singularly appropriate for Arbuthnot's purpose of ridiculing the extravagant sermon style of Burnet, 'a Big bon'd Northern Priest, / With pliant Body, and Brawny Fist; / Whose weighty Blows the dusty Curtains thrash, / And make the trembling Pulpit's Wainscot crash' (*Histrio Theologicus*, 1715, p. 13). See also Addison's comment on *'the great Secret'* of the Rosicrucian philosopher (Spectator, 30 July 1714, iv. 561): there is an interesting anecdote about Burnet's visit, in disguise, to a meeting of Rosicrucians in London in Clarke and Foxcroft's *Life*, pp. 172–3.

69: 2–3 **it does . . . cure de Vapour.** Yan's pronouncement implicitly denies that 'the Church is in danger': cf. the uncompromising title of Mandeville's *Treatise of the Hypochondriack . . . Passions, Vulgarly Call'd the . . . Vapours in Women*, 1711.

69: 5–6 **It is de true Bloodt Stancher, stopping all Fluxes of de Bloodt.** Carstens's note (p. 226) that this 'is perhaps an allusion to the High Church veneration for "Charles the Martyr", a cult mocked by the Whiggish Calves-Head Club' (80: 32–4 n.), is supported by the frequent attacks on Burnet as 'A *Scotch*, Seditious, Unbelieving Priest, / The Brawny Chaplain of the *Calves-Head-Feast*' (Shippen, *Faction Display'd*, 1705, p. 6).

69: 13 **Nic. Frog's Letter to John Bull.** The States-General anticipated the Commons verdict on the Barrier Treaty (32: 33–5 n.), and on 19 February 1712 sent a letter to Anne 'affirming their right to enjoy all the provisions of the Treaty but at the same time expressing willingness to rectify anything in it that might be prejudicial to British trade' (Coombs, p. 299): 'This letter . . . was soon after made Publick' (*Annals*, x. 351). A few weeks later the Dutch sought to justify their conduct during the war in a *Memorial* which was also published (in two special issues of the *Daily Courant*, on 7 and 8 Apr.). Arbuthnot had apparently not finished this third *John Bull* pamphlet (published on 17 Apr.) at that time, since some of the *Memorial*'s major arguments are treated in the following parody of the earlier letter, although its more detailed 'balancing of accounts' was reserved for the fifth pamphlet (102–6).

69: 15 **Schellum**: from the German 'shelme' (Dutch, 'schelm'), 'A rascal (a term of abuse or contempt, attributed to German speakers)' (*OED*).

69: 17 **Spunging-house**: 'A house to which debtors are taken before commitment to prison, where the bailiffs sponge upon them, or riot at their cost' (Johnson, *Dictionary*).

69: 18 **he made me pay a swinging Reck'ning.** Lord Macaulay cited John's complaint here (see also 104: 31–2 n.) to exemplify the lasting

Tory anger over the immediate aftermath of the 1688 Revolution, when 'The Commons granted, with little dispute, and without a division, six hundred thousand pounds for the purpose of repaying to the United Provinces the charges of the expedition which had delivered England' (*History of England*, 1913–15, iii. 1346). The 'Act . . . *for Paying the States-General*' was one of those cited by the Whig 'managers' at the prosecution of Sacheverell (*Tryal*, pp. 140–1).

69: 20 *forswear thy own Hand and Seal.* Perhaps this allusion to the Barrier Treaty (to which the States agreed only reluctantly) links it with the partitions as a piece of Dutch and Whig perfidy, since Lord Somers had been unsuccessfully impeached in 1701 for misuse of the Great Seal in acquiescing to the King's schemes of partition.

69: 21–4 *thou hast purchas'd . . . a Mortgage . . . the Equity of Redemption* : The right which a mortgagor who has in law forfeited his estate has of redeeming it within a reasonable time by payment of the principal and interest (*OED*). The States' letter denied the 'ill-grounded and erroneous Opinion, that the States might design to take Advantage by [the Barrier Treaty] . . . to make themselves Masters of the said *Spanish* Netherlands' (*Annals*, x. 350). Arbuthnot puns on the Dutch demand for not only the continuation of trading and garrison privileges after 1711 (in compensation for maintaining conquered territory for 'Charles III') but also 'the mortgaging to them of the revenues of the posts of the Spanish Netherlands for another ten years' (Coombs, p. 243). On 6 April 1711 Bolingbroke wrote to Drummond complaining bitterly of 'how by Barrier, by Mortgage, or by Enclosure they contrive to reduce them absolutely to their Obedience' (ibid., p. 244).

69: 25 **Possession, eleven Points of the Law** : *Dictionary of Proverbs* (P. 487) cites eleven examples of 'Possession is eleven (nine) points of the law' between 1596 and 1697—'eleven Points' and 'nine' seem to have been interchangeable.

69: 25–8 *As for the Turn-pikes . . . without paying any thing* : the tariffs imposed in territories under Dutch control: 'all English goods imported into the Spanish Netherlands by way of Ostend, and sold to merchants of that country for resale in the "New Conquests", had to bear both a duty of entry at Ostend and a duty of entry into the "New Conquest" . . . If, on the other hand, English merchants sent their goods to the "New Conquests" without first selling them they had to pay, in addition, a transit duty of two and a half *per cent*. . . . These "double duties" soon became a favourite topic of Tory propagandists [see *History of the Dutch Usurpations*, 1712, pp. 36–7], and were specifically complained of in the Commons "Representation"' (Coombs, p. 301 n.). In its letter the States-General promised to remove these inequalities (see *Annals*, x. 350), but the Dutch were later to close two barrier towns against the English (119: 15–16 n.).

69: 30–1–70: 1 *Hounsfoot . . . as I love my life* : 'Houndsfoot', scoundrel (*OED*). Frog's protestations reflect the fact that 'the States' professions would indeed have been more convincing had they been accompanied by any steps to implement them' (Coombs, p. 301 n.).

70: 2–6 *to purchase for me . . . enough . . . with all thy Money.* In their *Memorial* the Dutch argued that all treaties between the maritime powers since the reign of Charles II had confirmed the same basic agreement that '*Great Britain* and this *States* are obliged each to employ all their Force . . . against the Common Enemy' (*Annals*, xi, appendix, p. 9). In particular, the Treaty of Grand Alliance had stipulated mutual support, '*with their whole Strength*' (Swift, *Conduct*, vi. 18), and the Barrier Treaty that they should 'employ all their Force to recover the rest of the *Spanish Low-Countries*' (*Remarks*, vi. 100). Bolingbroke voiced the Tory answer when he complained that Dutch interpretation of these agreements meant that '*Great Britain* will never contribute Enough, nor the *United Provinces* too Little' (*Annals*, xi. 11).

70: 11–13 **Frog** *is but a poor Man in comparison of . . .* **John Bull,** *great Clothier of the World.* The *Memorial* asserted, "'tis evident, that the Strength of *Great Britain* is incomparably greater than that of this *State*. To be convinced of this, one need only consider the Extent of the Countries, Possessions and Commerce of *Great Britain*, with the Number and Wealth of its Inhabitan[t]s, and in a word, every thing which can contribute to make a *State* Powerfull' (ibid., appendix, pp. 9–10). 'Complement is an idleness, those busie people were never skilled in' (*Dutch Drawn to the Life*, 1664, p. 71). But cf. Defoe: '*England, Scotland* and *Ireland*, have Wooll enough to Work, and People enough to Work it, to Cloath all the World' (*Review*, 12 July 1711, viii. 191).

70: 13–14 *my best Sheep were drown'd . . . the Water . . . spoil'd . . . my best Brandy*: a mocking allusion to the ironic situation in which the Dutch were compelled to flood their land against the French, a people with whom they were openly trading. Cf. the complaint of the *Memorial* that 'the Dominions of the *State*, being the Seat of the War, suffer'd very much by it; one Part of their Country was overflow'd by breaking in of the Sea, another part was laid under Water to defend it against the Enemy' (*Annals*, xi, appendix, pp. 10–11). Defoe also ridiculed this complaint in his *Highland Visions*, 1712, predicting 'A great Storm this Month [March] may do great Damage . . . but it seems the *Dutch* will be the principal Sufferers' (p. 5). Frog's spoiled 'Pipe' (a large cask used for wine) reflects on the Tory belief in 'the Folly of our *Prohibition* of Trade [with France] . . . whilst the *Dutch* and others carry it on. . . . We are only the Bubbles, whilst the rest of the World see and pursue their Interest' (*Observator Reformed*, 11 Jan. 1704).

70: 18–19 **so he will . . . unless he gets some Body betwixt them.** Tories argued that 'The Dutch and their advocates . . . had found a way of extending the barrier endlessly by claiming that the barrier proper needed *its* barrier, which in turn needed *its* barrier . . . and so on *ad infinitum*' (Coombs, p. 305). Charles Leslie was one of many polemicists who questioned whether Anne 'Ought . . . to be so Lavish of the Lives of her Subjects, as to Conquer one Country as a Barrier to another, till there be no Country left' (*Salt for the Leach*, 1712, p. 5).

70: 23–4 *dazzled with the inchanted Islands* . . . Lewis *promises thee*. In separate negotiations Britain relinquished her claims for territorial securities against Bourbon power in the West Indies in return for a thirty-year extension of the coveted *Asiento* monopoly (for supplying slaves to the Spanish colonies) which was to be made over to the South Sea Company (see Trevelyan, iii. 184).

70: 25 *purchase a Place at Court, of honest* Israel. Carstens noted that this is 'on the narrative level meant to imply a Jew, presumably a money-lender, and certainly a cheat. There is in addition an allusion to an actual person, Israel Fielding, who for some time sold court "places" over which he had no influence' (p. 267): see also *The Cheating Age*, 1712, pp. 4–5, and Swift, *Journal*, 23 Mar. 1712, p. 522.

70: 28 *let thy Wife and Daughters burn the Gold-Lace*. On 4 Apr. 1712 the Commons resolved 'to lay a Duty on all Wrought Silks . . . and upon all manner of Fringes, Tapes, and Wrought Incle [linen tape], which shall be imported' (*Annals*, xi. 5).

70: 29–32 *sell thy fat Cattel* . . . he would starve me. Cf. Defoe: 'let our *Black-Cattle* bear Witness to the Soil of England . . . what vast Dimensions of Fat do they feed to' (*Review*, 5 June 1711, viii. 127). As for the English people, '*English* Beef their Courage does uphold: / No Danger can their Daring Spirit pall, / *Always provided* that their Belly's full' (*True-Born Englishman*, ed. Guthkelch (1913), p. 123).

70: 32–3 *Mortgage thy Manor . . . or Pawn thy Crop*. Frog here advises John to practise the 'new finance' (65: 5–6 n. to 65: 13–15 n.) which has already resulted in his near bankruptcy.

70: 35 *Why hast thou chang'd thy Attorney*. 'The recal of the Duke of Marlborough, and substitution of [James Butler, Duke of] Ormond in his command, was complained of by the States' (Scott).

71: 1–2 *Thou art as fickle as the Wind*. The Dutch complained bitterly that 'since Queen *Elizabeth*'s Time there had been nothing but perpetual Fluctuation in our Conduct; so that they could not rely on our Measures for two Years together' (*Duke of Anjou's Succession*, 1701, p. 35). The Whigs agreed and claimed that Dutch resolution was in marked contrast 'to the Unsteddiness' of Britain (*Annals*, xi. 173; Boyer here quotes a letter from Amsterdam dated 12 July 1712). One commented: 'This Inconstancy of our Temper has more than once reduc'd us from a Condition that made us the Envy of our Neighbours to a state of Contempt . . . and has render'd our Friendship as dangerous as our Enmity' (*Life and Reign of Henry the Sixth*, 1712, pp. 1–2).

71: 7 *the* Salutation *Tavern*. The principal powers concerned in the war met at Utrecht in January 1712 to discuss the 'preliminaries' agreed between Britain and France. The Salutation tavern, Newgate street, 'in the reign of Anne was much resorted to for social gatherings' (*London Past and Present*); it therefore had a name and a character appropriate for the venue of a peace congress, but it provided an ironic contrast with the bitterness of the conferences.

71: 11–15 **he durst not . . . for fear of catching an Ague.** Cf. Defoe's comment on the Dutch, who 'were brought to Consent to a Congress with the greatest Difficulty imaginable . . . and . . . if the *D*[ut]*ch* are, as they have been Cordially Represented a-late, a Covetous, Rapacious, Selfish People, it's no wonder they were for playing their Old Game at . . . Grasping at all in the Dark, and not standing to the Decision of an Open Congress' (*Present Negotiations*, 1712, p. 15). Buys was sent to London to fight a diplomatic delaying action while his masters gave their wholehearted support to Eugene's visit (40: 2–11 n.) and attempted their own secret negotiations with France. We can find no specific relevance in the excuses listed here.

71: 21–2 **he thought every body as plain and sincere as he was.** 'The Congress was opened by a speech from the Bishop of Bristol, Lord Privy Seal, recommending a frank communication on the subject of debate' (Scott): 'Messieurs . . . We bring sincere Intentions . . . We hope you have the same Disposition, and . . . will . . . answer the Expectations of the High Allies, by explaining yourselves clearly and roundly' (Swift, *Four Last Years*, vii. 117). The Queen's envoys at the Congress were John Robinson, Bishop of Bristol, and Thomas Wentworth, third Earl of Strafford. The text of Bristol's opening speech was printed in several English newspapers.

71: 26–7 *Frog* **was seiz'd with a dead Palsy in the Tongue.** The first conferences foundered on Dutch prevarication over 'a frivolous Nicety, (viz.) whether they should Treat by Conference, and Word of Mouth, or by delivering in Answers in Writing' (Defoe, *Justice and Necessity*, 1712, p. 29).

71: 27–72: 17 *John* **began to ask . . . as much as to say, Kiss ——.** Arbuthnot satirizes the political manœuvrings at Utrecht in this grotesque burlesque of the procedural quibbles which were 'in every Mouth, and by every Ear, even to Weariness, heard among the Commons' (Defoe, *Reasons Why a Party*, 1711[12], pp. 3–4). Frog's climactic (and obscenely proverbial) insult is a dramatization of the Tory view of the Dutch, who 'began to discover their Ill-humour upon every Occasion: They raised endless Difficulties . . . And in One of the first general Conferences they would not suffer the *British* Secretary to take the Minutes, but nominated some *Dutch* Professor . . . which the Queen refused, and resented . . . as an useless Cavil, intended only to shew their want of Respect' (Swift, *Four Last Years*, vii. 118).

72: 3–9 *Shall I serve* **Philip Baboon . . . dancing about the Room.** The English wished to have sole monopoly of trade with Spanish America; the Dutch wanted an equal share in the trade.

72: 14 **cry Buck:** an insulting gesture with obscene overtones made by popping the cheek: cf. '*Buck*. Copulation of Conies' (*Canting Crew*).

72: 19–21 *Since we cannot . . . in another Scrap.* The Dutch insisted that the French answer allied demands in writing (see Defoe, *Justice and Necessity*, 1712, p. 29).

72: 22–5 *playing a little at Cudgels . . . cannot hold my Pen.* In his last campaign, during the summer of 1711, Marlborough turned the 'impregnable' French lines of *Ne plus Ultra* and captured Bouchain (see Trevelyan, iii. 129–34).

72: 25–8 *let me write for you . . . will not be legible.* In rejecting the demand for written replies as pointlessly time-consuming (see *Annals*, xi. 85–9), the French laid themselves open to the old charge of opportunism: ''tis agreeable to the Character of the *French* and . . . 'tis no strange thing in a *French* Minister to shuffle and prevaricate' (*Vindication of the Present M[inistry]*, 1711 [12], p. 5).

72: 28–9 **As they were talking . . . in came Esquire *South*:** the late and dramatic arrival of the Imperial Plenipotentiaries in March 1712. Defoe commented with malicious satisfaction: 'The Emperor, who stood out longest . . . tho' he had profest himself UNALTERABLY resolved not to send his Ministers to *Utrecht*, yet came afterwards' (*Justice and Necessity*, 1712, p. 7). Even then, 'The Count de *Zinzendorf*, first Plenipotentiary of the Emperor, did not arrive till an Hour after the rest' (*PPB*, 4 Mar. 1712).

72: 29–32 **all drest up in Feathers . . . room, Boys, for the grand Esquire of the World.** Hawkesworth noted, 'The Archduke was now become Emperor', and Scott paraphrased Boyer to add, 'His ministers stood high upon points of form, and particularly objected to the term "Ambassadors of the House of Austria", as derogatory to His Imperial Majesty'. Even before succession to the Empire, his titles as 'Charles III' had shown him 'to be as vain as his Subjects. He calls himself . . . King of *Castile, Leon, Navarre, Arragon* . . . *Jerusalem, Naples, Sicily* . . . the *East* and *West-Indes* . . . Arch Duke of *Austria* . . . Marquis of the Holy Empire . . . and Grand Seignior of *Asia* and *Africa*' (*Trip to Spain*, 1704/5, pp. 4–5). The 'Grand Seignior' was properly the Turkish Sultan, and other hostile writers had mocked Charles for assuming the title: cf. his appearance as the '*Grand Seignior*' in *Cobler of Gloucester* (1710?), p. 3, and in Trapp's *Character and Principles*, 1711, p. 45, and as 'Seignior *Philip*' in *Account of a Second Dream*, 1711, p. 5. Cf. also von Uffenbach's account of 'the most foolish and ludicrous' of the Bedlam inmates who 'wore a wooden sword at his side and had several cock's feathers stuck into his hat' (*London in 1710*, p. 51).

72: 34–6 *John* . . . **gave him such a Squeeze, as made his Eyes water.** Cf. 'The Imperial Plenipotentiaries were of Opinion, that as the Proposals of the *French* had been deliver'd to all the Allies in General, so their Answer ought to be return'd in General. The *British* Ministers said, that the *French* having distinctly set down what they Offered to, or Demanded of the Chief Members of the Grand Alliance, every one of them ought to Answer in particular' (*History of Utrecht*, p. 252). The Austrians had to concede the point, thus paving the way for Britain's separate peace with France.

72: 36–7 ***When I am Lord of the Universe, the Sun shall . . . adore me.*** Tories now saw the danger of Austrian hegemony replacing the threat from united Bourbon power. A theme important in Swift's *Conduct* appears also in lesser polemics such as *Peace-Haters* (1711): 'The Exorbitance of *Lewis* of *France*, / Has been the Pretence of the War, Sir, / If we raise it again, at *Vienna* or *Spain*, / Pray what have we fought *Twenty Year* for' (p. 4). To underline the danger, Arbuthnot puns again on Louis XIV as the 'Sun King' (cf. 20: 22 n.). In Utrecht the British representatives were well aware that Austrian pressure for a general reply to the French 'was to engage all the . . . Allies to support their Demand of *Spain* and the *Indes*' (*History of Utrecht*, p. 252).

73: 2 ***Frog*** laugh'd in his Sleeve. *Dictionary of Proverbs* (S. 535) cites eleven examples between 1546 and 1700.

73: 2–4 **gave the Esquire t'other Noggan . . . made him ten times madder.** Cf. 'The *Dutch* Ministers did also apply themselves with Industry to cultivate the Imperial Plenipotentiaries in order to secure all Advantages of Commerce with *Spain* and the *West-Indes*, in case those Dominions could be procured for the Emperour' (Swift, *Four Last Years*, vii. 118).

73: 5–6 ***rare Company . . . a Spirit of Infirmity.*** Defoe saw the Congress of Utrecht as 'a STAGE-PLAY . . . [where] all Sides *play the F*[oo]*l* in their Turns' (*Review*, 5 Apr. 1712, viii. 649).

73: 13–14 **As he was talking . . . towards one another to whisper.** Arbuthnot skirts the problem of the secret 'Preliminaries' between Britain and France by making John's decision to find his own salvation contingent upon an open and chaotic meeting of friends and by concentrating attention upon the intrigues of the Dutch: 'this was the Cause which made them so litigious and slow in all their Steps, in hopes to break the Congress, and find better Terms' (Swift, *Four Last Years*, vii. 118).

73: 15 **Arms a-kimbo :** with hands on hips and elbows turned outward (*OED*).

73: 15–17 **Some People advis'd *John* to blood *Frog* . . . make him speak :** i.e. to 'let blood' (*OED*). Cf. 'Though Defoe was the only ministerial writer actually to talk of a Dutch war [in *Justice and Necessity*, 1712], the *Examiner* and several pamphleteers did their best to make such a suggestion acceptable. . . . Now that the Dutch were openly "defying" the queen they abandoned what shreds of restraint they had retained' (Coombs, p. 340). See, for example, the *Enquiry into the Danger and Consequences of a War with the Dutch*, 1712.

73: 17–18 **give Esquire** *South* **Hellebore**: the ancient classification of plants with poisonous medicinal properties, and especially reputed as specifics for mental diseases (*OED*): cf. Defoe, 'If ever *Hellebore* was necessary . . . this is the Critical Minute for giving it' (*Present Negotiations of Peace Vindicated*, 1712, p. 3).

73: 19 **Pultas**'s: poultices.

73: 19 **others for opening his Arm with an Incision-knife.** Whig polemicists demanded that the war be vigorously renewed since France had wrecked the peace conferences: see Oldmixon, *Dutch Barrier Our's*, 1712.

73: 21–2 *John*'s **Letter . . . sent to his Nephew by the young** *Necromancer*. 'E[dward] H[arle]y' (*Key*, 3rd edn.), the younger brother of Robert, was sent to the court of Hanover in an attempt 'to perswade the Elector to come into the *British* Measures' (*Annals*, xi. 263–4). His older brother was frequently ridiculed in Whig polemic as a political conjurer: cf. the 'Juggler . . . reduced to very low Circumstances' (*Medley*, 13 June, 1712), and Steele, *Tatler*, 4 July 1710, iii. 408–9.

73: 22–4 **he advises him not to eat Butter . . . drink Old Hock . . . a sour Breath.** 'Sour Breath' refers to the Elector's support for the Allies and his vociferous protests against the peace which rendered the prospect of his succession to the English crown alarming to the Tories. Harley's mission was a complete failure; but Arbuthnot's culinary joke was well chosen, since 'When Englishmen contemplated the diet . . . on which, so it was said, these Dutch "butter-boxes" lived, all political differences were forgotten as Whig and Tory alike were overcome by a mixture of amazement and distaste' (Coombs, p. 14). '*Brunswick* Mum' was reputed the favourite drink of Dutch dignitaries (see *True . . . Account of the Last Distemper*, 1710, p. 16).

77: 2 *The Apprehending . . . of* Jack. This short pamphlet satirizes the Dissenters and the Whigs for their part in passing the Occasional Conformity Bill of 1711. See 'Background 1698–1712', p. lv, above.

77: 5 **the Story of Yan Ptschirnsooker's Powder.** See 68: 23–69: 10, above.

77: 11 **Peaching:** to give incriminating evidence against, inform against (an accomplice or associate); to 'round upon'; to betray (*OED*).

77: 11–12 **being extremely forward to bring him to the Gallows.** Gilbert Burnet did not in fact support the new Bill against Occasional Conformity; but he did not oppose it, as he had done whenever it had been previously introduced. He described its virtually unopposed passage in his *History* (vi. 85) in an uncomfortably objective tone. Dartmouth, in a note on this passage, said that Burnet assented to the Bill 'because he loved faction better than he did the dissenters'. Arbuthnot exaggerates the sin into one of commission to emphasize the betrayal of the Dissenters by their most distinguished Low Church champion, whose speech in opposition to the 1704 Bill had been immediately printed and had provoked accusations that he himself was a mere '*Occasional Conformist*' (see Leslie, *Lay-Man's Letter*, p. 4).

77: 19 *Jack* **in . . . his nocturnal Rambles.** The *Keys* believed that this ultimate suggestion of Jack's involvement with the Mohocks (39: 24–6 n.) '*shews the entire Agreement of the* Whigs *and* Fanaticks' (3rd edn.). There is, certainly, an intended allusion to the connections between the mob, whiggery, and Dissent, but the neutral tone in which these all-embracing charges is reported also reflects upon the blind violence of High Church enmity to the occasional conformists.

78: 6–7 **smoaking his Pipe . . . at . . . *Martin*'s.** This allusion to Martin, the Church of England in Swift's *Tale*, neatly dramatizes the accusation that Dissenters had infiltrated the Establishment under the protection of the Low Church clergy.

78: 8 **Mr. Justice *Overdo*.** Arbuthnot's attitude to the Bill is clearly reflected in this personification of the House of Lords, which is identified with the conscientious but ingenuous Justice Overdo of Ben Jonson's *Bartholomew Fair*, or the less praiseworthy magistrate of the same name in Ned Ward's *London Spy* (p. 108). The 'trial' allegory was a popular satiric convention: cf. the *Tryal, Examination and Condemnation of Occasional Conformity. At a Sessions of Oyer and Terminar . . . Before Mr. Justice Upright, and Baron Integrity*, 1703, in which the 'lady' (occasional conformity) was indicted on the charge that she had planned '*to Kill and Destroy*' the Established Church (p. 2); or the *Examination, Tryal, and*

Condemnation of Rebellion Ob[servato]*r*. . . . *Before Mr. Justice Orthodox, and Mr. Baron Cathedral,* 1703, which attacked the Whig newspaper's campaign against the second Occasional Bill of the reign and the 'Endeavour by the Assistance of Pen, Ink, and Paper, three Poysonous Weapons, to Stab the Church Establish'd and the Present Constitution' (pp. 3–4). Mob support for Parliamentary 'overdoing' makes the whole affair deliberately difficult to distinguish from the Sacheverell trial (15: 18–19 n.). Perhaps there is also a hint at Thomas Parker, who was Lord Chief Justice in 1711, and was noted for his severity.

78: 9–10 **the Prisoner . . . a very dissolute Life.** The decline of the 'Nonconformist ideal' of strict independence in religious belief is discussed in H. W. Clark's *History of English Non-conformity,* 1911–13, ii. 137–50. Arbuthnot emphasizes the link between the Presbyterians and the Whigs, or the Puritan religious spirit fusing with commercial enterprise, especially in Pamphlet II.

78: 12–13 **guilty of Drunkenness . . . at My Lord-Mayor's Table.** Another allusion to the strength of Dissent in the City. In a note on Burnet's *History* (v. 49), Dartmouth suggested that the indiscretion of Sir Humphrey Edwyn in attending a Presbyterian service in full mayoral state (54: 25–30 n.) was the immediate occasion of the 1702 Occasional Bill.

78: 14–22 **in the company of Lewd Women . . . heard his Father rail'd at.** 'Lewd Women' would refer to 'Signiora Bubonia', Roman Catholicism (51: 15–16 n.); these phrases glance at Wharton and those Whigs who were 'Presbyterians grafted with Atheists'; cf. Swift: 'He [Wharton] is a Presbyterian in Politics, and an Atheist in Religion; but he chuseth at present to whore with a Papist' (*Character of Wharton,* iii. 179). For salacious pamphlet attacks on the sexual morality of the Dissenters, see 51: 11–13 n.

78: 14–16 **transferr'd . . . his Father's Will, to . . . Debentures.** Cf. Swift's *Tale,* p. 190: the 'Will' is of course the New Testament. Cf. also: 'This *Treacherous Saint,* I vow 'tis very odd, / Must represent in Truth the Cause of God; / Yet represents such strange inhumane Wills, / The Cause of *Tallies,* and of *Chequer Bills;* / Mindful of Gain, not to his Nature strange, / He makes the *Senate-House* a meer *Exchange*' (*Suffragium,* 1702, p. 5).

78: 17–18 *Meat, Drink, and Cloth, the Philosophers Stone, and the Universal Medicine.* Cf. Swift's Jack: '*Gentlemen,* said he, *I will prove this very Skin of Parchment* [a fair copy of the Will] *to be Meat, Drink, and Cloth, to be the Philosopher's Stone, and the Universal Medicine*' (*Tale,* p. 190).

78: 20–1 **he kept company . . . his *Will* a forgery.** Cf. 'the Dissenters address'd themselves to the Deists, those profess'd Enemies of all Reveal'd Religion, (*and who abound too much in most great* Posts *and* Places) to abett and countenance them' (Baron, *Dutch Way of Toleration,* 1699, A 2).

78: 21–3 **he . . . often chim'd in . . . Bosom Friends.** 'The *Atheists, Deists* and *Scepticks* . . . under the Patronage of the Low-Church, attack'd the Church' (*Word to the Wise*, 1712, p. 8): see also *Character of a Church-Trimmer*, bs. 1683.

78: 23–4 *That instead of asking for Blows, at the Corners of the Streets,* **he now bestow'd them.** Cf. 'HE would stand in the Turning of a Street, and calling to those who passed by, would cry to One; *Worthy Sir, do me the Honour of a good Slap in the Chaps*: To another, *Honest Friend, pray, favour me with a handsom Kick on the Arse*' (*Tale*, p. 197). Wotton glossed this episode as, '*The Fanaticks . . . affecting to run into Persecution*'. Jack's transformation from masochist to bully glances, as Scott noted, at 'The mobbing and persecuting the episcopal clergy in Scotland by the more violent presbyterians', and also at the increased militancy of their English brethren: cf. 'Dick Hotspur', 'stripped to the very Skin, at Charing-Cross, and Challenging every one he met, to fight, or box' (*Plain Dealer*, 21 June 1712).

78: 32 **this ragged tatter'd Coat.** Cf. the Jack of Swift's *Tale*, who became so enraged at the 'Popish' magnificence of his coat, that 'being Clumsy by Nature, and of Temper, Impatient . . . he tore off the whole Piece, Cloth and all, and flung it into the Kennel' (pp. 138–9).

79: 5 **Two Witnesses Swore.** Perhaps James Drake and Henry Sacheverell, whose High Church alarms had 'witnessed' the 'disguised antipathy' of Low Church and Dissent.

79: 7 *Timothy Trim.* This is Arbuthnot's 'Character of a Trimmer,' differing considerably from Halifax's *Character* of 1688. 'Trimmers' was a name given by the High Church to a group of men who adopted a pragmatic view of Parliamentary 'balance' on controversial issues, and who emerged as a political force towards the end of the reign of Charles II. The 'Trimmers' were abused as unprincipled, and gradually came to be associated, in hostile Tory polemic, with the Low Church and Dissenters. Cf. 'Mr. Amphibious Trimmer' in the *Tryal . . . of Occasional Conformity*, 1703. According to the *Key* (3rd edn.), '*Jack* and *Timothy Trim,* [are] *the same in all Respects, which shews the entire Agreement of the* Whigs *and* Fanaticks.' One of the *True Characters* (1708) is 'A Trimmer, or, Jack of All Sides'.

79: 10–11 **clap'd their Mistriss's Livery over his own tatter'd Coat:** the '*Occasional Conformity*' (*Key*, 6th edn.) of Dissenters. Here Arbuthnot expands the clothing imagery of Swift's *Tale*, which reflected a long tradition of satiric convention. Cf. another Tory view of 'Trimmers': '*Q. Are you for Occasional Conformity? A.* Yes by all means and the sooner the better, for to tell you truely I am not so squemish Stomach'd nor so tender Conscienc'd, but I could turn my Religion as soon as my Coate if there was any thing to be got by't' (*The Dissenters Catechism*, 1703, p. 5). Hence Tory abuse of the 'Trimmer' with his 'New way of Politick *Masquerading*, under a Coat that fits all *Factions* and *Opinions*'

(*True Characters*, 1708, p. 14). See also Leslie, *Wolf Stript of his Shepherd's Cloathing*, 1704, and *Presbyterian Loyalty*, 1705, p. 5.

79: 12–13 **Flattery and Tale-bearing . . . the rest of the Servants.** 'He insinuated into the great Ministers of *Church* and *State*, and presumed to make lists . . . of *Worthy men* . . . to blacken and defame all *Loyal* Clericks, and recommend those of his own *stamp* as the only men of *Merit*; to cry down the *one* as men of hot heads, and *Popishly* inclined, and magnifie the *other* as great *Masters* of *Prudence*, *Conduct* and *Moderation*' (*Character of a Church-Trimmer*, bs. 1683).

79: 15–16 **he us'd to shove and elbow . . . paying or receiving.** Cf. 'Occasional Conformity' attempting to get into St. Paul's 'to keep out the Members of the Church establish'd and Elbow 'em out of Places of Trust' (*Tryal . . . of Occasional Conformity*, 1703, p. 18). The same energetic business was supposed typical of Dissenters and the Low Church who 'had no sooner rigled themselves into most of the Posts, Places and Preferments . . . and had as it were justled out all the Church Members from their Offices, but they cast about and contrive how to perpetuate themselves' (*Sauce for an English Gander*, 1712, p. 3). Cf. also Sacheverell on the occasional Conformists' plan 'to *Justle* the Church out of *Her Establishment*' (*Tryal*, p. 42).

79: 19–20 **when his Mistress's back was turn'd.** 'A Presbyter is he, who doth defame / Those Reverend Ancestors from whence he came, / And like a Graceless Child, above all other, / Denies Respect unto the Church, his Mother' (from John Denham's *True Presbyterian Without Disguise: or, A Character of a Presbyterian's Ways and Actions*, bs. 1680).

79: 20–4 **loll out his Tongue . . . a fit of Devotion:** allusions on the literal level to the behaviour of Dissenting preachers: cf. 'let him Wink, with his Eyes, & make wry Faces' (*New Receipt*, Bod. MS. Rawl. D. 383/99), and on the metaphorical level to the thinly disguised antipathy of the Trimmer to the Church, under a conformity which 'was only a Copy of his Countenance . . . to make a greater *Figure* in the Church, that he might be the more able to serve *Her* a Dog-trick' (*Character of a Church Trimmer*, bs. 1683).

79: 24–5 **to trip up Stairs . . . and put all things out of Order.** The Upper House of Convocation (the stronghold of the Low Church faction) and the House of Lords, where the Low Church 'Trimmers' were able to block the early Occasional Bills sent up by the Commons whose 'whole Management' in drafting them was, according to one Tory, 'all of a Piece; there's no Trimming in it' (*New Practice of Piety*, 1704, p. 60 [74]): cf. Bolingbroke's description of 'the spirit . . . both above and below stairs', when he reported the mood of Parliament to Ormonde (27 May 1712, *Letters*, ed. Parke, 1798, ii. 515).

79: 26–8 **would pinch the Children . . . Print . . . in black and blue:** trimming and Low Church polemic. The Covenanters had adopted 'blue' as their colour in opposition to the royal red, and 'blue', or especially 'true-blue', was associated in the seventeenth century with the Scottish Presbyterian and Whig party (*OED*). Cf. Dryden's contempt for the 'True-Blew-Protestant Poet', Thomas Shadwell. In 1710 the author of a whiggish tract was 'said to have retain'd the Blue of the Plumb in his Frontispiece, since his Looks are consonant to that Colour' (*The Character of a Modern Addresser*, 1710, p. 5), and Burnet is referred to as the 'black white Monster cloath'd in blue' in *The Whitson-Fair: Rary Show* (1703?); 'black Print' may allude again to the 'Black List' controversy (see 63: 32–4 n.).

79: 29–31 **us'd to lay Chairs . . . break their Noses . . . over them.** Another allusion to the increased militancy of those hostile to the Established Church, through an ironic inversion of Jack's comments on Predestination in Swift's *Tale*: "*Tis true, I have broke my Nose against this Post . . . But, let not this encourage either the present Age or Posterity, to trust their Noses into the keeping of their Eyes*' (p. 193).

79: 33–6 **much Plate missing . . . to be mended:** the wealth amassed by the Low Church clergy. The third and subsequent editions of the *Key* glossed this as an allusion to the '*Field-Plate, which was given to the* D[uke] *of* M[arlboroug]h, *tho' it properly belonged to the Crown*'; but this seems to be a forced reading since a large number of tracts used comparable images in comparable contexts to accuse Low Churchmen and Dissenters of petty larceny: 'Some challeng'd for dreadful Things, / As Stealing Silver-Spoons, and Rings' (Colville, *Mock Poem*, 1711, p. 24). Cf. the description of the 'house' of 'Moderation' with its 'very spacious fair Room, hung with the richest *Arras*, and . . . a *Sideboard* of *Plate*' (*Glorious Life . . . of St. Whig*, 1708, p. 33). It makes more sense to read this as a joke against the 'occasional conformists' among the Low Church clergy, who 'stole' from the Church, particularly as Church silver could be a symbol of the Sacrament of Communion to which they took exception.

80: 2–4 **slanderous Tongue . . . lying Stories.** The 'Trimmer' 'talks of *Dangers*, and fills Peoples Heads with *Frightful* Stories of them', in *True Characters*, 1708, pp. 13–14. It was commonly held that such men used 'false and Groundless Calumnies, [to] bespatter and slander out of all Employments . . . the true Sons of the Church' (*Short Abstract of the Behaviour of the Occasional Communicants*, 1702, p. 4).

80: 6–8 **one Day . . . little short Fellows . . . beat the tall Fellows.** The transference of 'High' and 'Low' Church into physical images was common in contemporary polemic: cf. the 'Upstart, Little, Whiggish Fellows' of *Modest Defence*, 1702, pp. 3–4, and Swift's allegory of Lilliputian politics in terms of 'two struggling Parties . . . *Tramecksan*, and *Slamecksan*, from the high and low Heels on their Shoes' (*Gulliver's Travels*, xi. 32). High and Low Churchmen even argued over the point in time at which their disagreements commenced. Burnet affirmed that the Church split into the two factions after the bitter debates in the Convocation of 1702 (*History*, v. 70). This is the occasion of the split suggested by Arbuthnot's allegory and by some other Tory satires (see, for example, *History of the Mohocks* [1712?], p. 3). Yet the narration of the quarrel is deliberately vague enough to allow for Swift's assertion that it grew from the encouragement of the Low Church by William III: 'SOME Time after the Revolution, the Distinction of *High* and *Low-*Church came in; which was raised by the Dissenters, in order to break the Church Party, by dividing the Members . . . and the Opinion raised, That the *High* joined with the Papists' (*Examiner*, 31 May 1711, iii. 163). For an analysis of the 'Church divided' see Holmes, *The Trial of Doctor Sacheverell*, 1973, pp. 29–41.

80: 16–18 **no Servant . . . above four Foot seven . . . a Gage . . . to be measur'd.** The general import of the allusion is clearly that of an earlier allegory in which the 'new Whig' Tom Double admitted, 'I have a Scale . . . whereby I measure what Lengths every Man will go, what desperate Councils he will engage in, and what bold Motions he is willing first to open; by which Scale, I proportion Rewards of Merit' (Davenant, *Sir Thomas Double at Court*, 1710, p. 26). The only specific relevance we can find for 'four Foot seven' (i.e. 55 inches) is that within a few weeks of the 'final judgement' of the Lords on Sacheverell (20 Mar. 1710, see pp. li–lii, above) a division list was circulating with the names of 55 Whig peers who had voted him guilty (Holmes, pp. 421–35).

80: 22–6 **a Roguish Leer . . . speaking through the Nose . . . bad Disease.** Swift's analogous play on the nasality of Dissenting preaching and the symptoms of venereal disease in the *Tale* (pp. 279–82) was an old joke: cf. 'As I was *Preaching* on the *secret point* / of *Venery*, I did but slip a *joint* / Too far, when straight old *Bishop pox*, cry'd cease, / You do encroach upon my *Diocess*, / Since when I have so rattled in the *Nose*, / That all the *disaffected* do suppose / It, as a *scandal* to the *Brethren*, and say / The *Presbyterian Tone* first came that way' (*Answer to Wild*, bs. 1663), or the crude jibe that the Dissenters 'translated what they called *Antichristian* in the *Organ*, into their more sanctified *Noses*' (*Short Treatise*, [1701?], p. 6).

80: 29 **he did Business in another Family.** Again the suggestion of venereal disease naturally leads to the association of Jack with the 'Whore of Babylon' (51: 15–16 n.). The Trimmers were, of course, hated as much by extreme Whigs as extreme Tories, and in one Whig polemic the 'Tory Trimmer' was described as 'a *Crab-Protestant*, that *crawls backwards* as fast as he can to *Rome*' (*Character of a Tory*, bs. 1681).

80: 29–31 **he pretended to have a squeamish Stomach . . . the Servants.** 'The high-churchmen objected to their antagonists a dislike of the church ritual and form of communion; a neglect of her fasts and festivals, and an inclination to republicanism' (Scott). Again Arbuthnot was employing a popular satiric metaphor: cf. the Dissenting, whiggish City Lady who, 'When she has almost *Dined* . . . Complains of a *Tender Conscience*, the Weakness of her Stomach, and her want of Appetite; and immediately a Piece of *Tart*, that, by Accident was bottom'd with a Leaf of the *Apocripha*, made her *Puke*' (*True Characters*, 1708, p. 8).

80: 32–4 **he refus'd . . . Salt-fish, only to . . . eat a Calve's Head . . . in private.** The Whig Calves-Head Club was supposed to celebrate the execution of Charles I on 30 January each year at a feast during which the members drank from a calf's head. The fact that there is little evidence (of any kind) to suggest that the tradition actually existed did not deter Tory satirists: cf. *The Secret History of the Calves-Head Club. . . . Or, The Republican Unmask'd. Wherein is fully Shewn, the Religion of the Calves-Head Heroes, in their Anniversary Thanksgiving Songs on the Thirtieth of January. . . . Now Published to Demonstrate the Restless, Implacable Spirit of a Certain Party among us, who are never to be Satisfied 'till the Present Establishment in Church and State is Subverted*, 5th edn., 1705. That Jack, for the occasion, is willing to forsake even salt-fish (the staple diet of Frog, 30: 17–19 n.) again neatly draws all John Bull's enemies together in one unobtrusive image.

81: 4–7 **he and Ptschirnsooker . . . together at the *Rose* . . . true Name of *Jack*:** for the Whig associations of the Rose tavern, see 68: 32–3 n. There is an interesting parallel at this point between Arbuthnot's allegory and an exchange shared by 'Mr. Amphibious Trimmer' and the prosecuting Council in the *Tryal . . . of Occasional Conformity*, 1703, when the former admits to conversing with the prisoner 'at *Dick*'s Coffee-House, and at *Manwaring*'s, and at the *Rose-Tavern* without the Bar. . . . We laid our Heads together how to prevent a certain Bill [the Occasional Bill] that had Pass'd the H[ouse] of C[ommons] from taking effect' (p. 11; see also p. 23). It is entirely appropriate that Trim/Jack should dabble in the political quackery of which 'Yan' (Burnet) is such a master, since the 'Trimmer' was often pilloried as 'a Church-Politico, a Conforming Non-Conformist, a Spiritual Jugler, a Mountebank Divine' (*Character of a Church-Trimmer*, bs. 1683); see also *Trimming Court-Divine*, 1690, p. 1.

81: 12 **a Mole under the left Pap.** Arbuthnot may have intended the inadequacy of this 'external proof' of guilt to be a dramatically ironic jibe against the Dissenters who were '*eternally cavelling against some few little things . . . such as relate only to the* Externals [of Worship] *. . . a* Mole *or a* Wart, *which the comliest* Bodies *are seldom without*' (Baron, *Historical Account of Comprehension*, 1705, A 2). Cf. *Cymbeline*, II. ii. 37–8.

81: 30 **Stock-jobber:** 'A low wretch who gets money by buying and selling shares in the funds' (Johnson, *Dictionary*, 1755). Cf. '*Stock-jobbing*, a sharp, cunning, cheating Trade of Buying and Selling Shares of Stock in *East-India, Guinea* and other Companies; also in the Bank, Exchequer, &c.' (*Canting Crew*).

82: 6–7 *Habakkuk Slyboots* **. . . his trusty Companions:** John, 'Lord S[ome]rs' (*Key*, 3rd edn.), a brilliant lawyer and sometime Solicitor General, 'that great Genius, who is the Life and Soul, the Head and Heart of our Party' (Swift, *A Letter of Thanks from My Lord Wharton*, vi. 152). Although Sunderland, whom Mrs. Manley had characterized as

'*Cethegus!* the Executioner of the *Junto*' (*Memoirs of Europe*, 1710, i. 218—see 94: 10–12 n.), was a key intriguer in the alliance between Whigs and High Tories and actually moved the introduction of the Occasional Conformity Bill, it was Somers who was credited with engineering the agreement. The Whig *Medley*, 2 May 1712, celebrated the coalition 'between *D*[aniel] *E*[arl] of *N*[ottingham], *Plenipo*' of the *March Club*, of the one part; and *J*[ohn] *L*[ord] *S*[omers] *Plenipo*' *of the* Hanover *Club*'. Habakkuk, eighth of the minor prophets of the Old Testament, had secret knowledge of the 'enemy'. In the legend of *Bel and the Dragon*, Daniel, incarcerated for the second time, was fed by Habakkuk, brought miraculously from Judaea. Here, of course, 'Habakkuk' offers 'miraculous' relief to Jack only to betray him, hence the surname 'Slyboots', 'a seeming Silly, but subtil Fellow' (*Canting Crew*): cf. Swift's opinion of Somers: 'his Detractors . . . reckon Dissimulation among his chief Perfections' (*Four Last Years*, vii. 6).

82: 8–9 **Matters have not been carried on with due Secrecy.** Cf. '[Wine] Makes even Somers to disclose his art, / By racking every secret from his heart, / As he flings off the statesman's sly disguise', from the imitation of *Horace, Book I Ep. V.*, falsely attributed to Swift, *The Poetical Works of Jonathan Swift*, Aldine edn. of the British Poets, 1833, iii. 70. Because of his prominence and reputation for 'mature Deliberation', Somers is chosen as the Whigs' spokesman.

82: 14–15 **some Understanding with the Enemy . . . Don Diego:** for Nottingham and his part in all this, see 'Background 1698–1712', p. lv, above. As Defoe pointed out, the Whigs were depending on 'a Man, whose Character, *even in their own Mouths*, was not long before too mean for a Satyr'. The Whigs' declared enemy is specifically the ministry and not France, another point which Defoe was quick to make: 'Must the *Dissenters* be Sacrifiz'd to Purchase Hands against a Peace' (*Review*, 22 Dec. 1711, viii. 475).

83: 6 **a Secret.** Defoe was outraged at the Whigs' betrayal of the Dissenters: 'Is this Defending the Cause of the Protestant Interest? Oh, but there is some SECRET in it which we do not Understand, says an easie Christian that is willing to hope still — *Enter not into their Secret, O my Soul.* . . . What Secret can this be? Of what Value must this Secret be, that such an Evil must be yielded to, to bring to pass this mighty *Good*?' (ibid., p. 475).

83: 12 **Sir *Roger* . . . has been in Tears.** The Whigs were engaged in an ingenious scheme to undermine Oxford's position. He had rejected their earlier offer of voting for a bill against occasional conformity if he would revise his peace plans. Since Oxford's Puritan background, moderate politics, and former opposition to the bill were well known, the Whigs, hoping to discredit him with his Tory adherents, reported that he would oppose the Bill. And if the Lords voted Nottingham's amendment to carry on the war, Oxford's ministry would fall unless he could reverse the vote (see Defoe, *Eleven Opinions*, 1711, p. 18). Oxford's view of the situation is given in a letter to John Shower, the minister of a Presbyterian congregation in London, dated 21 Dec. 1711 (see also 85: 2–8 n. and 86: 30–87: 2 n.): 'as to myself, the engineers of this bill thought they had obtained a great advantage against me: finding I had stopped it in the House of Commons, they thought to bring me to a fatal dilemma, whether it did, or did not pass. This would have no influence with me: for I will act what I think to be right, let there be the worst enemies in the world of one side or other' (Swift, *Correspondence*, v, appendix viii. 228).

83: 21 **a Mystery.** The passing of the Occasional Bill 'seems the Greatest Mystery of Politicks that this Age has been acquainted with' (Defoe, *Review*, 25 Dec. 1711, viii. 474).

83: 22–3 **if thou knew . . . Common Cause . . . leap for Joy.** 'Common Cause' was a popular euphemism for the War. The extreme Whigs made no bones of their true reason for supporting the Occasional Bill, and one was later to pronounce, 'I do not believe there was a *Dissenter* in *England*, but would have been glad to have voted for the Bill, if he could by that means have hinder'd the *French Peace*' (*Memoirs of . . . Wharton*, 1715, p. 94).

83: 24 **the Experiment.** Possibly an allusion to Defoe's *THE EXPERIMENT: Or, the Shortest Way with the Dissenters Exemplified,* 1705 (a reworking of his notorious irony published in 1702), acknowledged by at least one contemporary as his 'well Penn'd *Experiment*' (*Thoughts of an Honest Whig*, 1710, p. 8). Defoe's ironic 'final solution' to the problem of Dissent in the first *Shortest Way* is neatly inverted, since Habakkuk here propounds a similar resolution with quite literal intent. Of course this double irony is the more effective as Defoe himself suffered in the pillory for his ingenious attempt to defend the Dissenters.

83: 25 **All for the better.** This seems to be the title of a tune which we cannot identify.

83: 27–34 **Refractory Mortal! . . . Hanging is not so painful a thing.** Cf. Swift on Somers's repressed temper: 'no man is more apt to take fire upon the least appearance of Provocation; which Temper he strives to subdue with the utmost violence upon himself; so that his Breast hath been seen to heave, and his Eyes to sparkle with Rage, in those very moments when his Words and the Cadence of his Voice were in the humblest and softest manner' (*Four Last Years*, vii. 6).

83: 29–30 **Quarters perching . . . conspicuous.** This recalls that at the Restoration Cromwell's severed head was pitched atop a pole on Westminster Hall, just as the remains of executed traitors had been displayed for centuries.

83: 31–2 **Empaling, or breaking on the Wheel.** 'Undoubtedly the principal motive which induced the Dissenters to give way to the proposed bill, was the reasonable apprehension that the Tory power, then in its zenith, was strong enough to introduce yet harsher provisions against them' (Scott).

84: 1 take good notice of the Symptoms, the Relation will be curious. This seems to be a gibe at Somers's scientific interests and the powers of 'objective description' he shared with fellow members of the Royal Society, which included Burnet and Arbuthnot himself.

84: 13 *JACK* was a profess'd Enemy to *Implicit Faith*. 'Implicit Faith' is faith in spiritual matters, not independently arrived at by the individual, but involved in or subordinate to the general belief of the Church (*OED*). Edmund Hickeringill was speaking for many Dissenters when he devoted the second chapter of his *Ceremony-Monger*, 1689, to a rhetorical condemnation of the 'popish' Implicit Faith of the High Church in its Bishops (pp. 12–15).

84: 16–20 a poor disbanded Officer . . . one sees every Day: further allusions to the profiteering of the fallen Whig administration and, of course, to Marlborough, who had been dismissed on 31 Dec. 1711: cf. Swift's description of Jack in his tattered coat, 'like a drunken *Beau*, half rifled by *Bullies*; Or like a fresh Tenant of *Newgate* . . . Or like a *Bawd* in her old Velvet-Petticoat' (*Tale*, p. 140).

84: 20 new Intrigues, new Views, new Projects: specifically, the new Whigs' innovations in governmental administration and finance. Cf. Mrs. Manley's satire upon 'Cicero' (Somers) in *Memoirs of Europe*, 1710: 'the Church was defil'd, new Articles, new Manners, new Forms crept among the People' (ii. 62).

84: 22 The Interest of *Hocus* and Sir *William Crawly*: Marlborough and Godolphin. Although the later editions of the *Key* suggested '*Lord* S[underlan]d' (3rd edn.), Sir William Crawley 'was a kind of code name for Godolphin' (*Poems on Affairs of State*, vol. vii, ed. Ellis, 1975, p. 57 n.); see also 67: 5–6 n. The identity of interest and the power of Marlborough and Godolphin was a recurrent theme in Tory polemic. Cf. 'Poor deluded Dissenters, / You are sold like Debentures, / By the *Junto* made over by Deed and Indentures' (*Excellent New Song*, bs. 1711).

84: 27 singing a double Verse of a Psalm: Dissenters and the Low Church disliked the practice of antiphonal singing and chanting. In the *Ceremony-Monger*, 1689, Hickeringill devoted his fourth chapter to '*Of Reading the Psalms*, Te Deum . . . &c. *Alternately, every other Verse*, by the People' and declared it to be '*another* Nonsensical Ceremony, that is *point-blank* against Holy Scripture, as well *against Reason* and Edification' (pp. 19–21).

84: 31–2 *Durus Sermo* ! . . . my Friends. 'None but a Friend could have given this Wound! None but the Men we Trusted! . . . Hard Fate!' (*Review*, 25 Dec. 1711, viii. 474). For 'durus sermo', a traditional collocation, see Burton, *Anatomy of Melancholy*, ed. H. Jackson, 1948, iii. 471 n.

85: 2–8 Is it possible . . . Sir *Roger*, can . . . pity . . . persecuted him . . . I'll trust my Friends. Cf. 'it is worth Observing with what

Resignation the *Junta* Lords . . . are submitted to . . . For it is well known that the Chief among the Dissenting Teachers in Town were consulted upon this Affair; and such Arguments used as had power to convince them, that nothing could be of greater Advantage to their Cause' (Swift, *Four Last Years*, vii. 21). In his letter to Shower on 21 Dec. 1711—the day after the Bill had been given the royal assent—Harley justified his 'neglect' of the Dissenters on similar grounds and declared himself 'ready to do every thing that is practicable, to save people who are bargained for by their leaders, and given up by their ministers' (Swift, *Correspondence*, v, appendix viii, p. 228). Sir Roger's treatment of Jack in this pamphlet could be taken as a betrayal by Harley of his family heritage (cf. McInnes, *Robert Harley*, 1970, p. 22). For Harley's relations with dissenting ministers like Daniel Burgess (18: 18–19 n.) and Daniel Williams, especially his unsuccessful attempts to gain their support, see McInnes, p. 181.

85: 9–10 **more wisely . . . put himself upon the Tryal . . . in Form.** An ironic allusion to the rumour that Harley had contacted the Dissenters when the Bill was mooted, promising to forward a petition against it to the Queen, 'But that . . . they had made a wise Answer, that it was a Matter of too high a Nature for them to meddle in; they must even trust themselves with the Queen and the Parliament' (Kennett, *Wisdom of Looking Backward*, 1715, p. 157).

85: 12–13 **sufficient Stock:** a pun on bank stock.

85: 14 **the fatal Day:** 7 Dec. 1711.

85: 17–18 **tough Rope . . . *Scandinavian* Hemp, compactly twisted together:** a comment on the complexity of the Bill, which became law under the misleadingly contrived title of *An Act for Preserving the Protestant Religion, by better securing the Church of England as by Law Established; and for Confirming the Toleration Granted to Protestant Dissenters*, etc. (*Annals*, x, appendix iv. 67). A large proportion of Britain's naval supplies, including hemp, were of course imported from the Baltic area (see Trevelyan, i. 9). In his lament at the passing of the Occasional Bill, Defoe asks, 'What *Norway* Witch has rais'd this Storm' (*Review*, 25 Dec. 1711, viii. 474). Since this is followed by a reference to 'a Groaning-Board', Defoe's allusion may be to Burnet (cf. 77: 11–12 n.), whose multitude of interests included studies in the 'occult' (see the note to p. 298 of Clarke and Foxcroft's *Life of Burnet*). Addison's *Spectator*, 14 July 1711 (i. 480), discusses Norway and Lapland witches; cf. also Bond's excellent note.

85: 22 **no Familiarity could reconcile him to it.** 'It may be supposed that it was very difficult to couch the bill against occasional conformity in such terms as would satisfy the Dissenters. That which finally passed was . . . more moderate than those which had been rejected on former occasions' (Scott). For the severe monetary penalties provided by the bill, see H. W. Clark, *History of English Non-conformity*, 1911–13, ii. 147–51.

85: 27 **Burning in the Cheek.** Cf. von Uffenbach's account of a brand-
ing session at the Old Bailey (*London in 1710*, pp. 125–6).

85: 32 **what if I should do it in Effigies?** An ironic allusion to the
Whig attempt to revive the lapsed custom of parading the Pope in
effigy, which was planned for 17 Nov. 1711, to coincide with the return
of Marlborough from Flanders, and was intended to whip up enthusiasm
for the war. Tory writers claimed that among effigies of such dangerous
personages as the Pope and the Pretender were more seditious models:
'One was designed to represent the L[ord] T[reasure]r . . . and the rest
the other Great Officers of the Court' (Manley, *True Relation of the
Several Facts*, 1711, p. 7). These were all seized on 16 November (see
Annals, x. 278–9, and Swift, *Four Last Years*, vii. 212). The whole affair
became a political touchstone for some time following (see *Thanksgiving*,
bs. 1711, *Story of the St. Alb[a]n's Ghost*, 1712, p. 12, *Plain Dealer*,
12 July 1712, and Goldgar, *Curse of Party*, 1961, pp. 91–4).

86: 21–2 **like the Pendulum of** *Paul's* **Clock.** St. Paul's, Covent
Garden, possessed 'the first long pendulum clock in Europe . . . invented
and made . . . in 1641' (*London Past and Present*).

86: 25–6 **walk'd . . . into both the upper and lower Room.** The
Bill passed swiftly and almost unopposed through both the Lords and
the Commons.

86: 27 **Temper:** composure.

86: 30–87: 2 **Sir** *Roger* **. . . not . . . hanging Day . . . he slunk away.**
Scott was the first editor to note a verbal allusion to Harley's justification
of his conduct. In a letter to Oxford, the Revd. John Shower described
the Dissenters as having been 'shamefully abandoned, sold, and sacri-
ficed by their professed friends', and went on to say 'the fatal consequences
of that [Occasional Conformity] bill cannot be expressed: I dread to
think of . . . them' (Swift *Correspondence*, v, appendix viii. 227). Oxford
replied, in a letter probably written by Swift, that he disclaimed all
responsibility for the Act, and added: 'I pity poor deluded creatures,
that have for seventeen years been acting against all their principles, and
the liberty of this nation' (ibid. 227). In addition, there seems also to be
an echo of the uncomfortable reply which Arbuthnot himself elicted
from Harley when he inquired about the Bill; 'Arbuthnott asked, How
he came not to secure a majority? He could answer nothing, but that he
could not help it, if people would lie and forswear' (Swift, *Journal*,
8 Dec. 1711, p. 434).

87: 8 **his dismal Circumstance:** i.e. circumstances of Dismal's
(Nottingham's) contriving.

87: 8–9 **Ptschirnsooker . . . pull'd him by the Legs.** Ptschirnsooker's
treatment of Trimming Jack may be a sly hint at Burnet's account of the
sickness and death of 'Jack' Wilmot in his celebrated *Some Passages of
the Life and Death of the Right Honourable John Earl of Rochester, who*

Died the 26th of July, 1680. Written by his own Direction on his Death-Bed, by Gilbert Burnet, D.D.: 'I thought it better to leave him without any Formality. Some hours after he asked for me, and when it was told him, I was gone, he seem'd to be troubled, and said, *Has my Friend left me, then I shall die shortly*' (p. 157).

87: 13 **The Keeper:** Sir Simon Harcourt, Lord Keeper of the Privy Seal in 1711.

87: 15 **Bulk:** a stall in front of a shop (*OED*).

87: 17–18 **the Curiosities of** *Gresham* **College.** Until 1710 the Royal Society met in the former house of its founder, Sir Thomas Gresham, in Bishopsgate Street, which housed a museum notorious for its un-seemliness. Among its curious specimens were 'An *Egyptian* mummy', 'the entire *Skin of a Moor*', 'A Tooth taken out of the Testicle of a Woman $\frac{1}{2}$ an Inch long, painted like the Eye-tooth of a Man; given by Dr. *Tyson*', 'a *Brasilian* fighting Club', 'A Pot of *Macassar Poison* where-with to poison Arrows', and to top it off, 'A *Chusan* Chair of natural growth as well as shape, a very extraordinary Curiosity, given by my Lord *Somers*', 'Habbakuk Slyboots' himself (see Hatton, *A New View of London; or, an Ample Account of that City*, 1708, ii. 664–85). It is par-ticularly appropriate that 'Jack's Rope' should be preserved there among 'the . . . abortives put up in pickle, and abundance of other memorandums of mortality' (Ned Ward, *London Spy*, p. 46) which were the special concern of John Woodward, Professor of Physic at the College from 1693, and the butt of several Scriblerian pieces to which Arbuthnot made significant contributions (see Beattie, p. 130). See also von Uffenbach on the filthy disorder of the museum (*London in 1710* p. 98).

87: 18 *Jack's* **Rope.** Arbuthnot picked up this joke again in *Three Hours After Marriage*, 1717, the burlesque play which he wrote in collaboration with Gay and Pope. Fossile (Woodward, see previous note) suspects his wife of infidelity and exclaims, 'poor Fossile? couldst thou not still divert thyself with the spoils of quarries and coal-pits, thy ser-pents and thy salamanders . . . is there no rope among my curiosities' (*Augustan Reprint Society*, 91–2, 1961, p. 144).

87: 25 **Don Diego Dismallo.** This chapter is a continuation of the satire on Nottingham's ambition and his spite against Harley for keeping him out of the ministry of 1710.

88: 1 **endeavouring, for several Years.** Bills had been introduced (but not enacted) against occasional conformity in 1702, 1703, and 1704.

88: 22 **without doors.** 'Without doors' here suggests 'outside Parlia-ment' (*OED*); cf. Defoe's *A Speech Without Doors*, 1710.

88: 33–89: 2 **troublesome old Nurses . . . their great Care.** '*Those that continue to say the Church is in Danger during the Queen's Administra-tion*' (*Key*, 6th edn.). Arbuthnot clearly had little sympathy with the opinions of extreme Tories.

89: 2–3 *John Bull* . . . **understands a little of a Pulse:** alluding to 'the Pulse of the Nation, about the several *Schemes* that were made for a Peace' (*Annals*, x. 235). Cf. the allusion to the World's pulse at the end of Swift's *Tale*.

NOTES TO PAMPHLET V

93: 4 Sir *Humphry*. See above, 47: 2–3 n., for Sir Humphrey Mackworth, the loquacious Member of Parliament who may be a model for the narrator.

93: 5–6 a plain Dealer . . . for this important Trust; speak the Truth: a conflated allusion to Mackworth and the Huguenot historian, Abel Boyer. Teerink noted that this preface bears comparison with Swift's parody in the *Tale* of the elaborate prefatory material which characterized Grub Street productions. Mackworth, perhaps facetiously, refers to the 'plain and homely . . . Dress' of his sumptuous folio pamphlet *Peace at Home . . .* (1703), a 'Vindication' of the Commons' proceedings against occasional conformity, and 'since the Case appears to him to be very plain, when fully and fairly stated, he thought plain *English* must be sufficient for it'. He also asserts that he publishes his remarks only 'for the sake of Truth' (the 'Preface'). In the preface to his 1704 tract, *Free Parliaments*, a 'Vindication' of the Commons' right to judge electoral issues, he stresses that 'since he has the Honour to be one of those, who are intrusted with the Rights and Liberties of their Country, and since it is the Duty of all Persons, in that Station, to act with Sincerity and Courage, according to the best of their Understanding, in discharge of the great Trust reposed in them', he humbly offers some reasons for the Commons' recent decisions. Boyer protests in the *Dedication* (to Wharton) and *Introduction* in the tenth volume of his *Annals* that 'the following Sheets . . . contain a *Plain, disinterested*, and *Impartial* Narrative' (p. v).

93: 7, 11, 16 *Leave to* repair *to* . . . chop'd . . . Nebus'd. Cant phrases in the preface pick up one of the unexplained and apparently inexplicable private jokes of which the Tory wits were so fond. Cf. two letters written by Prior, one, 'To Sr: Humphry Polesworth', dated 13 May 1712: 'Look You Sr: Humphry, as to the Promissory circumstances of our repairing, I cannot be upon the Categorical . . . I am no specious Gilder . . . I shou'd deserve to be Chop't most damnably by You if from any omission . . . of mine you shou'd happen to be Nebust', and another letter addressed to Edward Harley in June 1720: 'I hope—to use Sir Humphrey Polesworth's style—you will shortly be repairing' (quoted by Beattie, pp. 166–8).

93: 8–10 *I put the Journals . . . some Eastern Monarchs*: an ironic allusion to the Whig oriental allegory, the *History of Prince Mirabel's Infancy, Rise and Disgrace*, Part I, which was advertised in *PPB*, 23 Feb. 1712. This crude narrative panegyric to Marlborough and attack on Harley (as Mirabel and Novicius respectively) claimed to be taken from a long hidden manuscript.

93: 11 chop'd: a pun on 'executed' and 'defeated in argument'.

93: 9–16 *Transactions . . . I was never afraid . . . let not Posterity, a thousand Years hence, look for Truth . . . secret Springs . . . With incredible Pains.* Cf. Boyer's introduction to the tenth volume of his *Annals*: 'The first Consideration of the Difficulties that obstruct the Discovery of the secret Springs which have occasion'd those new Motions [the peace Preliminaries of 1711]; and the Danger that may attend the Touching upon nice, ambiguous Steps of Men in Power, went near to deter the Writer of these Papers from pursuing this Annual History: But upon second Thoughts, he resolv'd neither to refuse any Pains, nor to fear any Danger in the Prosecution of an Undertaking honestly design'd for the Information of the present Age and Posterity: Confidently hoping, that the Candor and perfect Disinterestedness with which he relates Truth, will bear him out . . . because he shall . . . presume . . . only to record such Councils and Transactions for which he has undeniable Vouchers' (pp. 1–2). Teerink also noted a parallel with Swift's assertion that history 'ought to be recorded in Words more durable than Brass, and such as our Posterity may read a thousand Years hence, with Pleasure as well as Admiration' (*Proposal for Correcting . . . the English Tongue*, iv. 17). Cf. also Mrs. Manley's ironic dedication 'To Isaac Bickerstaff, Esq;' (i.e. Steele) in vol. i of her *Memoirs of Europe*, 1710: 'I am ravish'd at the Thoughts of *living a thousand Years hence* in your indelible Lines, tho' *to give Offence*'.

93: 16 **Nebus'd**: deceived. This is the only occurrence cited by *OED*.

93: 16–17 *I endeavour'd to copy . . . the ancient and modern Historians.* Teerink noted that 'Polesworth' was 'in this respect surpassing his rival, who, in his *To the Reader*, of vol. 1, 1703, had humbly said that his *Annals* were "destitute of the Ornaments of a Good and Regular History" . . . [and] in the *Introduction* to vol. 5, 1707, p. 2: "what shall be wanting in Ornament, he hopes to make up in Exactness, Truth, and Impartiality"' (p. 72).

93: 19–20 *the Sublimity . . . of* Titus Livius. Cf. the more modest Boyer: 'As for Me, My *Lord*, who never could reach such *Sublime Notions*, I content my self with *relating Matters* of Fact' (*Annals*, x. vi).

93: 21 *considerable Ornaments from* Dionysius Halicarnasseus. Cf. Swift: 'What I have hitherto said of *Rome*, hath been chiefly Collected out of that exact and diligent Writer *Dionysius Halicarnasseus*' (from *Contests*, p. 104). Gulliver refers to this Dionysius in Part II, chap. vii, of the *Travels*.

93: 22 **Diodorus Siculus**: referred to as 'that great Author' in *Contests*, p. 198, and quoted in *A Tale of a Tub* and *The Mechanical Operation of the Spirit*.

93: 22 *The* specious Gilding *of* Tacitus. Cf. Swift on the decline of Roman letters, 'when they began to quit their Simplicity of Style for affected Refinements; such as we meet in *Tacitus*' (*Proposal for Correcting the English Tongue*, iv. 14).

93: 23 **Mariana, Davila,** *and* **Fra. Paulo.** Three historians from whose work Swift took some of his source material for the ancients versus moderns controversy in the *Tale* (see pp. 236–7).

93: 26 *the* **Tenter Belly** *of the Reverend* **Joseph Hall.** Beattie was the first scholar to gloss this as a 'reference to Hall's merry picture of the commonwealth of gluttons in *Mundus Alter et Idem* (about 1605)' (p. 166), the first chapter of which was a 'Description of Tenter Belly' in John Healey's translation (1608). A 'tenterbelly' is one who 'tenters', or distends, his belly; hence, a glutton (*OED*).

94: 1–7 *illiterate People . . . silencing . . . University of* **Grubstreet** *. . . an approaching Peace . . . so bold a step*: another allusion to the Stamp Act of 1712 (63: 32–4 n.), which seriously curtailed the number of polemics, largely whiggish in temper, which emanated from Grub Street; hence the satisfaction of Tory writers: 'The Vict'ry's won, while Tories mount on high, / And the gagg'd Whigs below in Silence lie' (*Press Restrain'd*, 1712, p. 16). Cf. Swift on the death of Grub Street (*Journal*, 7 Aug. 1712, p. 553) and Addison in *Spectator*, 31 July 1712: 'This is the Day on which many eminent Authors will probably Publish their Last Words. I am afraid that few of our Weekly Historians, who are Men that above all others delight in War, will be able to subsist under the Weight of a Stamp, and an approaching Peace' (iv. 62–3). There may also be a cruel personal glance here at Mackworth's condemnation for fraud by the Commons in 1710. The following lament for Grub Street has a persistent secondary level of reference to the collapse of Mackworth's financial empire. See also Rogers, *Grub Street: Studies in a Subculture*, 1972, pp. 59–60.

94: 10 *Dying-Speech of a Traitor.* Polesworth's elegy for popular subliterary genres is very comparable with a letter of protest printed by *PPB*, 24 Apr. 1712. Its complaint, that the tax would 'discourage many an excellent Exhortation in *Paul Lorrain's* last Dying Speeches; be of killing Consequences to Murthers, and Hues and Cries; let Ghosts sleep quietly in their Graves; keep Blazing Stars in their own proper Element, and stifle very useful Madrigals and Ballads', introduced an attack on Tory pamphlets such as the '*dull* Tom Double, *or* John Bull'.

94: 10–12 *Are* **Cethegus** *and* **Cataline . . . A Dangerous Plot.** Plots, real and imaginary, provided the Grub Street hacks with lucrative material: 'Nay any Plot in the World, tho' it were but a Plot of the Apprentices, or of the Butchers to burn the *Pope*, there would be Money got by it . . . let it be true or false' (*Hawkers Lamentation*, bs. 1682). One ironic Tory broadside, *Summons from a True-Protestant Conjurer*, 1682, mourned the passing of the Commonwealth as the heyday of plotting, and was addressed to the ghost of Cethegus whose 'Voice of old in *Rome* was deem'd Divine/Surpassing, our *Grand Patron's*, *Cataline*'. Mrs. Manley attacked Sunderland and Wharton, respectively, under the names 'Cethegus' and 'Cataline' in her *Memoirs of Europe*, 1710, i. 206–7, 218; ii. 249–51, 259.

94: 14–15 *the Dreams of a* False Prophet . . . *the* Millennium *is at hand* : John Lacy, the English leader of a group of Cevennois Dissenters who fled to England in 1706 from the persecution of Louis XIV, and whose histrionic prophecies of doom fascinated the London public: 'some *French* Sparks living in and near *Hog-Lane* in *Soho,* being addicted to Enthusiasms, pretended to have the *Spirit* of *Prophecy,* and . . . impudently attempted to Prophesie, *That the World should be at an End in Three Months time*' (*Full . . . Account of the Apprehending,* bs. 1707); see also Sutherland, *Background for Queen Anne,* 1939, pp. 58–9.

94: 19 *the Flames of pamper'd Apprentices and coy Cook-Maids.* H. E. Rollins's comment that 'The spacious times of William III . . . are . . . cluttered up with the heart-affairs of cooks and scullions' (*Pepys Ballads,* 1929–32, vii. 294) could be applied to the reign of Anne with equal validity.

94: 20 Maeonian : a poetical designation of Homer.

94: 21–2 *the Stratagems . . . the nocturnal Scalade of needy Heroes* : another ironic allusion to the 'needy' hero Marlborough, whose exploits were energetically celebrated by the hacks. Wagstaffe assumed the mask of a member of '*the Fraternity of* Grub-street' in an open letter to the Duke, which claimed, ''Tis to Us You owe Your Character in a great Measure, We have Established it in such a Manner, by Congratulating Your Victories . . . and . . . by the Immortality of our Rhimes' (*Plain Dealer,* 17 May 1712). Again the association of war with menial (and in this case criminal) pursuits is satirically effective, as is the use of 'Scalade', scaling the walls of a fortified place by the use of ladders (*OED*): cf. Addison's wry comment, 'the *French* [are] obliged to lend us a part of their Tongue before we can know how they are Conquer'd' (*Spectator,* 8 Sept. 1711, ii. 150).

94: 23 *the powerful* Betty . . . *the artful* Picklock. A 'Betty' is 'a small Engin to force open the Doors of Houses' (*Canting Crew*), and 'Picklock' may designate a thief or one of the tools of his trade (*OED*).

94: 23–5 *the secret Caverns . . . of* Vulcan . . . Forge . . . *viler Metals . . . Pots of Ale.* Cf. ballads such as *Mr. Moor the Tripe-Man's Sorrowful Lamentation for Clipping and Coyning; with an Account of his Contrivance at his Country-House at Tripe-Hall near Hounsloe; where, in his Garden, he had Made a Trap-door, whereon Grew both Goosberry-Trees and Currant-Trees to Prevent the Discovery thereof . . .,* 1695 (*Pepys Ballads,* ed. Rollins, 1929–32, vii. 79–82). Besides referring to the labours of the Grub Street hack, this alludes possibly to Mackworth's coal mines and his putative shady dealings.

94: 30–2 *thy Search . . . of Nature . . . Comets fiery Tale.* Tory writers frequently mocked Grub Street's fascination with natural disturbances and their significations. Davenant assumed the mask of a hack to triumph over the discomfiture of Whiggish writers after the Sacheverell trial: 'My Astrological Observations made it appear, that a *Comet* with a long Tail, should be visible from the 14th of *December,* to the 23d of *March* [the date on which the trial ended] . . . threatning this our *Hemisphere* with *Famine*——among Knaves that now wallow in Wealth' (*Sir Thomas Double at Court*, 1710, pp. 68–9). Yet perhaps Arbuthnot intended a more specific allusion to the '*great Star, at the end of which was a long Tail or Streak of Fire*' which was 'cry'd about the Streets' just prior to the arrival of Prince Eugene (40: 2–11 n.), as signifying 'a Prince or Leader . . . [and] . . . a Prosperous Voyage' (*Collection of Severall Visions*, 1712, pp. 12–13). Such a Whig banality must have provided a tempting target for ridicule.

95: 1 **Jack-catch.** Jack Catch (or Ketch) was hangman from 1663 to 1686, and notorious for his bungling sadistic executions. Among the many contemporary references to him is Dryden's ironic allusion in the *Discourse . . . of Satire* (*Essays*, ed. Ker, 1900, ii. 93). The name of Ketch became so synonymous with his office that when, in January 1685, his successor Pascha Rose was punished for uttering 'scandalous words', a ballad written on the occasion was entitled *A Pleasant Discourse . . . Between the Old and New Jack Catch.*

95: 3 *thy theological Capacity . . . ghostly Counsel*: referring of course to the spiritual advice in 'last dying speeches' of convicted felons, and possibly also to Mackworth's religious tracts. Moreover, broadsides and pamphlets which recounted ghostly visitations in the literal sense—such as the works on the supposed appearance of the ghost of Stephen College to William Hone as he awaited execution for his part in the Rye House plot, *Protestant Joyners Ghost to Hone*, *Strange News from Newgate*, and *Strange and Wonderful Apparition*, all published in 1683—provided the background for Tory satires such as the *Story of the St. Alb[a]n's Ghost*, 1712, and *Grandsire Hambden's Ghost*, also 1712.

95: 4–5 *the noble Arts of* John Overton*'s Painting and Sculpture.* John Overton, 1640–1708(?), was a famous retailer of mezzotinto. His political affiliations, and hence his association here with Grub Street, are made clear by the title of a pamphlet advertised in *PPB*, 10 May 1712: 'Good Advice to the Whigs, by an Old Dying Whigg: Or, Mr. Overton's last Letter to his Friends'. His son Henry, who had inherited both his father's business and politics, did his best to support the flagging Whig cause. In the *Supplement*, 7 May 1712, he advertised 'The Effigies of His Highness Prince Eugene of Savoy, curiously done in Metsotinto'.

95: 6–9 *rich Invention . . .* Clar-Obscur *. . . judicious Multitude* ! 'The *Claro Obscuro* [chiaroscuro] is the art of distributing lights and shadows advantageously' (*Art of Painting*, 1706, quoted by *OED*). Tory writers were antipathetic to popular illustrations: in 1710, when the Sacheverell case occasioned a remarkable activity of satirical talent, both native and foreign, the Tories declared that caricatures had only recently been introduced from Holland, and were used as a political instrument by the Whig party. ' "The Print", says one writer, "is originally a Dutch talisman" ' (Paston, *Social Caricature in The Eighteenth Century*, 1905, p. 2).

95: 9–11 *Adieu persuasive Eloquence . . . to* Burleigh on the Hill. Carstens recognized that this was another allusion to the 'nauseous Rhetorick' of Nottingham (*Dialogue betwixt Whig and Tory*, 1710, p. 5), whose country house was 'Burley-On-The-Hill' near Oakham in Rutland (see Swift, *Four Last Years*, vii. 16, and H. J. Habakkuk, 'Daniel Finch . . . His House and Estate', *Studies in Social History*, ed. Plumb, 1955, pp. 139–78).

95: 11–13 I know not what——the Illiterate will tell the rest with Pleasure ! The closing lines of the 'Preface' to an edition of *Four Sermons* by William Fleetwood, the Whig Bishop of St. Asaph, published in May 1712, had warned darkly that national harmony had been destroyed by the pernicious peace negotiations, with 'in its Stead, I know not what——our Enemies will tell the rest with Pleasure' (see Swift, appendix C, vi. 195). The Preface was condemned by the Commons as 'malicious and factious', and was burnt by the hangman on 12 June (*Annals*, xi. 132). Swift also parodied Fleetwood's prophecy (in *Examiner*, 17 July, vi. 161), as did many other Tory satirists.

95: 18–19 *either at* Utrecht *or* Leyden . . . *the Professors there.* The two ancient and prestigious Dutch universities are equated with the Whig 'University' of Grub Street, since the Tories held that prominent Whigs often precluded the 'danger' of an English education by sending their children 'to *Leyden, Utrecht,* or *Geneva* . . . there to be impregnated with Presbyterian and Republican Doctrines' (Trapp, *Character and Principles*, 1711, p. 36). The political radicalism of the Dutch universities prompted one Tory to attack Bishop Burnet as a state '*Physician,* who . . . took his *Degrees* at *Leyden*' (*Glorious Life . . . of St. Whig*, 1708, p. 20). Utrecht of course was the site of the peace conference.

99: 2 *The Sequel.* For the first meeting at the Salutation, see pp. 71–3 above.

99: 3 WHere, I think, I left *John Bull.* Cf. Swift: 'WE left the Plenipotentiaries of the Allies, and those of the Enemy preparing to Assemble at *Utrecht* . . .' (opening words of 'Lib. 4' of *Four Last Years*, vii. 108).

99: 6–9 *Nic.* found the Means . . . to slip a short Note . . . what he was about. Scott was the first editor to point out that this alludes to an incident reported by Swift when 'the Maréchal *d'Huxelles* one of the *French* Plenipotentiaries at *Utrecht* . . . assured the Lord Privy Seal that the *Dutch* were then pressing to enter into separate Measures with his Master. And His Lordship in a Visit to the Abbé *de Polignac* observing a Person to withdraw, as he entred the Abbot's Chamber, was told by this Minister, that the Person He saw was one *Moleau* of *Amsterdam* . . . but that he had refused to treat with *Moleau* without the Privity of *England*' (*Four Last Years*, vii. 143).

99: 11–12 *Nic.* had used great Freedom . . . Reputation. Tory writers had long complained that the Dutch were wont to 'triumph over and Insult us . . . Representing us a Poor, Feeble and Dastardly People' (Ferguson, *Brief Account of . . . the Late Incroachments*, 1695, p. 12), and it was with some satisfaction that Bolingbroke reported to Lord Raby on 23 Mar. 1711 that the States had begun to realize that 'there is on our side some latent resentments at the air of superiority which in many instances they have assumed, and at the gross impositions which they have passed upon us' (*Letters*, ed. Parke, 1798, i. 78).

99: 14 *at the* Rose: the Rose Tavern, see 68: 32–3 n.

99: 19–100: 2 *John Bull* was under his Guardianship . . . bound . . . by . . . his own Family: further allusions to the Dutch guarantee of the Protestant Succession in the Barrier Treaty (31: 22–33 n.), and to the collusion between the States and the fallen Whig leaders. Swift reported that the Dutch plenipotentiaries, 'who held constant Correspondence with their old ejected Friends in *England* were daily fed with the vain Hopes of the Queen's Death, or the Party's Restoration' (*Four Last Years*, vii. 124).

100: 4–7 he threatned . . . beat out his Teeth . . . break up the Meeting: a parody of Dutch indignation at the French proposals of ceding the Spanish Netherlands to the Elector of Bavaria and of repossessing a large number of barrier fortresses. The Allies resolved 'to spend their last Penny to carry on the War' (*Annals*, xi. 55). This determination is denigrated by association with a sordid fight which took place between the retainers of the chief French and Austrian representatives at Utrecht. This incident necessitated 'Regulations' prescribing that 'The Pages, Footmen, and generally all such as are in Liveries, shall neither carry Sticks, nor Arms; as Swords, Knives, Pocket-Pistols. . . . All the Plenipotentiaries shall very strictly forbid their Domesticks, as well Gentlemen as others, having any Quarrels or Janglings among themselves . . . January 23, 1712' (*Annals*, xi. 43–5); and Defoe treated the affair as indicative of the ill will among negotiators in his *Enquiry into the Real Interest of Princes*, 1712. Cf. 102: 17–18 n. for 'break up the meeting'.

100: 11–13 I sav'd this Fellow . . . when he ran away . . . he was harshly treated. Tory writers constantly harped upon the theme that the Dutch Republic was only saved from defeat in its revolt against the Spain of Philip II by the intervention of Elizabeth I: 'Did not [E]ngland in Queen *Elizabeth*'s time preserve the poor and distressed States of *Holland* from their utter ruin? Was not *England* a nursing Mother to their State in its Infancy' (*Dutch Won't Let Us Have Dunkirk*, 1712, p. 5); see also *Account of the Obligations*, 1711, pp. 10–15.

100: 13–14 the Rogue was no sooner safe . . . then he began to lie, pilfer, and steal. After winning independence in 1609, 'From Poor Distress'd States, being now become High and Mighty, their next business was to get the . . . Cautionary Towns [given as security for English trading interests in Brabant] out of our Hands' (*Account of the Obligations*, pp. 15–16). The States after 'having secured themselves against Spain, and trick'd the *English* out of all the strong places *they were* possess'd of, sends them home with *fair promises*, and a *seeming respect*; but afterwards laugh'd at their Credulity and despised them' (*Search after Dutch Honesty*, 1712, p. 8).

100: 14–16 **When I first set him up . . . he began to debauch my best Customers from me.** 'In proportion as we and the Spaniard grew Weak and Poor, Holland became Rich and Insolent, making a perfect trade of War in those early days as they have done of late' (*Account of the Obligations*, 1711, p. 12).

100: 17–18 **to rob my Fish-ponds . . . trade with the Fishmongers.** The Dutch fishery was regarded by many Englishmen as a sort of state-organized poaching concern. In 1664 *The Dutch Drawn to the Life* devoted almost a whole chapter to 'The Inestimable benefit the *Dutch* make of the *British* Seas' (pp. 82–123). See also the pamphlets of James Puckle, especially *England's Path to Wealth and Honour, in a Dialogue Between an Englishman and a Dutchman*, 1702 (1st edn., 1699; pp. 10–15). In this context 'Fish-ponds' is a variant of the more common metaphor 'herring-pond' for the North Sea: cf. the accusation that the Whigs had long been intriguing with 'a certain ungrateful Gang over the Herring-Pond' (*We Are Bravely Serv'd at Last*, 1712, p. 3).

100: 18–20 **I conniv'd at the Fellow . . . his as much as mine.** 'Connived at', took no notice of (*OED*). Cf. 'The forced Connivance . . . relates to our Fishery, which, tho' Heaven has put it into our Hands, and entail'd upon us as a peculiar inheritance, yet the *Dutch* have run away with the greatest part of it for above a Hundred Years. . . . were they only to take what was absolutely necessary for their subsistence, Motives of Charity might induce us to give them leave: But so many Millions every year is a little too much, and a great deal more than we owe them' (*Account of the Obligations*, 1711, pp. 18–25). When Hugo Grotius challenged the assumption that the English had a divinely confirmed right to the seas in his *Mare Liberum* (1609), English polemicists hastened to refute him. This 'impertinent' Dutch claim was still being rejected by writers in the reign of Anne (for example in Justice, *General Treatise of the Dominion and Laws of the Sea*, 1705, pp. 104–94), and it provided one of the key emotional appeals in the propagandists' case against the States and their Whig friends: cf. the *Whigs Feast*, 1712, in which one of the dishes was '*Four Cods-Heads . . . caught by the* Dutch *in the* English *Seas*' (p. 6).

100: 20–2 **In My Manour of** *Eastcheap* **. . . beat my Servants:** the English colonies in the East Indies seized by the Dutch. The specific allusion here is to the infamous 'Amboyna', a spice island in the Moluccas, Indonesia, where in 1623 the Dutch massacred a rival English trading settlement. 'Scarce had our *English* Blood done reeking in *Amboyna*, but by Force and Treachery they seize upon our other Islands. . . . In this manner we lost at one stroke most of the Noble Settlements we had in the *East-Indes*' (*Account of the Obligations*, 1711, pp. 36–7); see also *History of the Dutch Usurpations*, 1712, and *Search after Dutch Honesty*, 1712, pp. 10–11. Bull's ruminations run through all the 'well worn subjects' of polemic hostile to the Dutch, 'as Amboyna, the British fishery, English help to the Republic in its early years and the returns that it made' (Coombs, p. 329).

100: 23–4 he would talk saucily . . . nothing amiss. Cf. 'How Cringing, how Supple, how Humble were they to Queen *Elizabeth*, and how Daring, how Rude, how Arrogant to her Successors' (*Account of the Obligations*, 1711, p. 14).

100: 26–7 The Rogue . . . was well thwack'd for his Pains. Arbuthnot follows the jingoistic pattern of Tory polemic, and says nothing of the reversals suffered during the Anglo-Dutch wars of the seventeenth century but alludes to the 'defeat' of Van Tromp by Blake in 1653.

100: 28–30 after I have almost drowned my self . . . in the Mud. Cf. 'we held up their Heads, when they could not swim; we *raised* them to a *State*, or else they had *sunk* in *their Bogs*: And yet as soon as they were able, they flew in our Faces' (Grascome, *Appeal to All True English-Men*, 1702, p. 5). As Arbuthnot was a keen numismatist, he may also have remembered that 'No sooner had [Elizabeth I] . . . concluded upon an *open amity* with them, but the *Zelanders* triumphing with joy (and to *honour Her*) did stamp money with the Arms of *Zeland* . . . and this inscription, *Luctor & emergo*, that is, *I struggle and get above the water*' (Vine, *Justification of the Present War*, 1672, pp. 25–6).

101: 1 Cully: 'A rogue, a Fool or silly Creature drawn in and Cheated by Whores or Rogues' (*Canting Crew*).

101: 2 canst thou gather Grapes from Thorns? 'Ye shall know them by their fruits. Do men gather grapes of thorns, or figs of thistles?' (Matthew 7: 16).

101: 5–6 Thou conferrest the Benefits . . . the last Ingratitude. Bull's concluding remark reflects the whole tenor of the anti-Dutch polemics, which, 'to confirm' the deficiencies of the Dutch during the war 'as a Piece of Ingratitude . . . run whole Ages back . . . and . . . fly as far as the *East-Indes* to bring Home Dirt to throw in their Faces' (Defoe, *Justification of the Dutch*, 1712, pp. 13–14).

101: 9–10 I won't give thee up . . . laudable Custom. Embarrassed by the secrecy of the negotiations with France, Tory writers stressed the efforts made by the Queen to accommodate the Dutch. Swift considered the States as an ungrateful 'Ally upon whom she had conferred so many signal Obligations, whom She had used with so much Indulgence and Sincerity during the whole Course of the Negociation' (*Four Last Years*, vii. 124).

101: 12 following Protestation. This does not seem to allude to any specific document. It is a general reflection of Dutch protestations, such as those in the letter to the Queen which is treated in more detail later (112: 24–5 n.).

101: 26–8 the Interest of those Tradesmen . . . on a like Occasion: at The Hague and Gertruydenbergh in 1709–10, where peace negotiations foundered on the exorbitance of Dutch demands.

101: 29–34 **upon the first Whiff . . . hallow'd in his Ear.** Each of the Allies presented their 'Specific Demands' to the French on 4 Mar. 1712. The confusion which Arbuthnot presents as a Dutch ploy was, in fact, the result of the British refusal to accept that the allies should submit a single general statement which would include not only the formulaic expression of solidarity (102: 4–6 n.) but also all the separate concessions demanded by each allied state (72: 34–6 n.).

101: 34–102: 2 **they began to ask . . . Fraud, Force, or lawful Purchase.** Britain's chief Allies demanded concessions which they calculated would be rejected by the French: the Emperor demanded that France should 'restore entirely to the Empire . . . all that has been yielded up to *France* by the Treaties of *Munster*, *Nimeghen*, and *Ryswick*, or otherwise detain'd by that Crown', and Portugal that '*France* renounce all Pretence or Claim to the *North Cape*, notwithstanding any former Treaty provisional or decisive' (*History of Utrecht*, pp. 254–8).

102: 2–3 **some ask'd for Manours . . . convenient for them.** Prussia demanded 'that . . . *Neufchattel* and *Valengin* shall be acknowledg'd a Part of the Helvetick Body' (ibid., p. 258); Savoy asked for lands adjacent to its frontiers; and the other smaller Allies demanded similar concessions.

102: 4–6 **all agreed in one common Demand . . . till he came to a sizeable Bulk.** Before they offered their individual claims, the Allies agreed on a '*general Claim . . . That a just and reasonable Satisfaction should be given to all the Allies, according to Treaties, Engagements, and other Conventions*' (*Annals*, xi. 57). Cf. Swift's Weaver: '*A Plague confound you . . . for an over-grown Sloven . . . Bring your own Guts to a reasonable Compass . . . and then I'll engage we shall have room enough for us all*' (*Tale*, p. 46). If all the demands had been conceded, France would have lost the acquisitions of decades, and would have left herself susceptible to attack from Flanders to the Alps.

102: 6–7 **one modestly ask'd him Leave to call him Brother.** Frederick I, King of Prussia and Elector of Brandenburg, demanded recognition of his title, i.e. he asked leave to call Louis a brother-king (Carstens). Arbuthnot singles this out for attention because of the farcical potential in the diplomatic agreement 'that in the Visits between the Ministers of *Prussia* and *France*, they should both use sometimes the word Master, and sometimes that of King, without the Addition of *France* or *Prussia*' (*History of Utrecht*, p. 230).

102: 7–8 *Frog* **demanded . . . to be his Porter and his Fishmonger . . . keys of his Gates.** The Dutch demanded that France withdraw from the Spanish Netherlands, that she honour previous trade agreements and tariffs (Articles I and V; *Annals*, xi. 69 and 71–2), and that a barrier between the two powers should be assured by the concession of twenty-five towns and fortresses, to 'remain to the Lords the States-General with their whole Extent, without any Exception', which should on no condition 'devolve to any of the House of *France*' (*History of Utrecht*, p. 257).

102: 9–10 *Peg* only desir'd . . . sing Psalms a Sundays. Britain specified 'That the Demands in Favour of the *French* Protestants, be discuss'd in this Negociation' (*Annals*, xi. 256). It was, in fact, the Huguenot exiles in London rather than the Scots Presbyterians who were largely responsible for the prominence of this demand, since they persistently lobbied Queen Anne on behalf of their oppressed brethren (ibid., pp. 263–6).

102: 11–12 old Cloaths . . . and Ends of Candles: demands for minor towns and fortresses.

102: 15–17 if one had a hundred pair of Hands . . . at this rate. 'Like bold Briareus, with a hundred hands' (Pope, *Dunciad*, Bk. iv, l. 66). 'The *French* Plenipotentiaries took all Occasions to express their Dislike of the Demands of the Allies, saying always they were unreasonable and exorbitant' (*History of Utrecht*, pp. 268).

102: 17–18 *John* begg'd they might proceed . . . would not say a word. The British representatives had to concede to allied pressure for written replies to the demands. When the French refused, 'one of the Plenipotentiaries of the States said with some Warmth, *That then the Congress was broke up*' (ibid., p. 270).

102: 20–1 Rouly-Pouly: a game in which the rolling of a ball is the chief feature (*OED*).

102: 21–2 What if we should have a Match at Football ! John's ironic comment on the antics of the negotiations recalls Defoe's characterization of the first Utrecht conferences: '*Spain* is the case, the Foot-ball is thrown down amongst the Gamesters, *France* gave it a hand kick . . . and *Philip* catch'd it; *Charles* the III. pushes at him and bids him give him the Ball' (*Felonious Treaty*, 1711, p. 21).

102: 24 *How* . . . Bull . . . and . . . Frog *settled their Accompts.* A continuation of the satire on Holland's response to the *Representation* of the House of Commons (4 Mar. 1712) in the *Memorial* of 7 Apr. 1712 (see 'Background 1698–1712', p. lvi, above), which was published by the sympathetic *Daily Courant* on 7 and 8 April. For a similar tabular comparison of English and allied contributions to the war, see *An Explanation of the Eleven Resolves of the 5th of February last, 1711. In which the Nation may see, at One View, the Mighty Loss to E[ngla]nd; and the Great Advantages and Savings, both in Men and Money, that the A[llie]s and the D[ut]ch have Made, by Not Being on an Equality with the E[ngli]sh and by their Deficiencies in their Quota's According to their Conventions and Agreement Made with Her M[ajest]y of E[ngla]nd, 1712.* The following chapter is concerned primarily with the *Memorial*.

102: 25 *general Cessation of Talk*: alluding to the 'general cessation' of hostilities.

102: 27–8 *let* Hocus *Audit . . . I am not much for that at present.* 'Audit' here has the obsolete meaning, 'to draw up or render an account'

(*OED*). Marlborough had been dismissed on 31 Dec. 1711, but the Dutch unwisely continued to champion his cause. Consequently, 'the Ministry were full of Resentments against the *Dutch*; not only for their offering to interpose with the Queen in the Case of the late Changes at Court . . . But for their . . . entring into Confidences, and keeping Correspondences with the old Ministers, after they were displaced; supporting their Intrigues, and making Engagements with them . . . *particularly* their prevailing with the Duke of *M*[arlborough] not to demit the Command of the Army' (Defoe, *Minutes of the Negotiations*, 1717, p. 146). Claude Bruneteau noted that, ironically enough, Marlborough had himself written to Oxford in Oct. 1711, 'I am perfectly convinced that besides the draining our nation both of men and money, almost to the last extremity, our allies do by degrees so shift the burthen of the war upon us [cf. 18: 12–14 n.] that, at the rate they go on, the whole charge must at last fall on England' (quoted in *John Arbuthnot . . . et les Idées au Début du Dix-huitième Siècle*, 1974, ii. 662).

102: 33–4 *I pay three Fifths . . . lesser Number.* The *Memorial* argued that 'the Quota of the *States* in Naval Armaments . . . is three to five' and in respect of military expenses, 'the . . . Proportion of Three to Two, which they agreed with the late King *William*' (*Annals*, xi, appendix, pp. 13, 16). Arbuthnot skirts the fact that the Dutch admitted paper deficiencies in respect of the expenditure taken into account by Parliament, and concentrates attention on their attempt to 'evade the Force of the Charge by Disputing the Proportions, and explaining what they understood by the Two Fifths to Three Fifths' (Defoe, *Farther Search into the Conduct*, 1712, p. 55). The point in *John Bull* is not that Frog cheats at his sums but that John is 'bambouzled' if he agrees at the start to Frog's paying three-fifths of 'the greater number', 40,000 crowns (i.e. £10,000) and also agrees to pay as his own share two-thirds of 'the lesser number', £36,000.

103: 2–7 *Two Thirds of 36000 . . . 28000 to yours.* A parody of the bewildering computations in the *Memorial*: cf. 'if they would follow the Proportion of two thirds . . . *Great Britain* should have brought to the Field 120000 Men against the said 60000 . . . if instead of seeking for the Proportion in the Augmentation of the Troops of *Great Britain*, with relation to those of this State, they had rather chose to seek it in the Reduction of the Troops of the State with relation to those of *Great Britain*, it will be found that the *States-General* were not obliged to furnish on the Foot of three to five, any more than 24000 Men, and on the Foot of one to two, only 20000, which would have fully answered their Proportion to the 40000 Men of *Great Britain*' (*Annals*, xi, appendix, p. 19).

103: 9–11 *John call'd for Counters . . . always on his own side.* A satirically effective confusion of chronology in an allusion to the Commissioners for the public accounts, whose report led to the parliamentary Representation which in turn precipitated the Dutch *Memorial*.

'There is an old and a new Way of telling Twenty, and the D[ut]*ch* are as far behind in their Notions of Number, as they run before us in their *Calendar* . . . the Commissioners of A[ccount]s ought to have been set right in this Matter, before they determined upon the D[ut]*ch Quota*. It is plain, according to their Sentiments, and the Practice of their Friends in the last P[arliamen]t, that Two are more than Five, and according to those Rules, they have maintained their *Quota*' (*Plain Dealer*, 28 June 1712).

103: 19 **the Lord Ch. Justice**: presumably Marlborough.

103: 21 **puny Judges.** 'Nay, even Serjeants, and the Corp'rals too, Will have a Snack, and take what's not their Due' (*The Cheating Age*, 1712, p. 2).

103: 22 **To Esquire South for** *post Terminums*: a writ returned 'not merely after the day assigned . . . but after the end of the term in which that day fell' when a fine, also known as a *post terminum*, was imposed (Jowitt and Walsh, *Dictionary of English Law*, 1959). This is another allusion to the delays and lost opportunities which characterized the war in Spain.

103: 23 **To ditto for** *Non est Factums*. A *non est factum* 'denied that the deed mentioned in the declaration was the defendant's deed; under this, the defendant might contend at the trial that the deed was never executed in point of fact, but he could not deny its validity in point of law' (*Dictionary of English Law*). The Allies sought to deny the will of Charles II of Spain in favour of the Duke of Anjou, but it had 'in point of fact' been 'executed' by most Spaniards, who accepted Anjou as their rightful King.

103: 24–5 **To ditto for** *Discontinuance, Noli prosequi,* **and** *Retraxit*: Further allusions to the Austrian claim on the Spanish inheritance. A *discontinuance* 'was where a man wrongfully alienated certain lands or tenements and died, whereby the person entitled to them was deprived of his right of entry and was compelled to bring an action to recover them'; a *nolle prosequi* was 'a proceeding in the nature of an undertaking by the plaintiff when he had misconceived the nature of the action, or the party to be sued, to forbear to proceed in a suit altogether'; and a *retraxit* was 'a proceeding similar to *nolle prosequi*, except that a *retraxit* was a bar to any future action for the same cause' (*Dictionary of English Law*). The use of such legal terms in political polemic was not new; cf. the description of the intervention of the Dutch against James II: 'They like a *Noli prosequi* came in, / And spoil'd the Farce just going to begin' ('Satyr Against the Dutch', *Occasional Poems*, 1712, p. 23).

103: 26 **To ditto for a** *Non Omittas*. As a *non omittas* was 'a clause usually inserted in writs of execution, directing the sheriff not to omit to execute the writ by reason of any liberty, because there were many liberties or districts in which the sheriff had no power to execute process unless he had special authority' (*Dictionary of English Law*): this suggests that the English 'sheriff' was attempting to execute an Austrian 'writ' against a King who had not only been nominated by his predecessor but had won the support of his people.

103: 26 **Filing a *post Diem*.** Tory writers derided the Austrian contribution to the war and the lateness of the offer to increase it (41: 1–3 n., 36: 1–2 n.). A *post diem* was filed 'Where a writ was returned after the day assigned, [when] the *custos brevium* received a fee of fourpence' *Dictionary of English Law*).

103:27 **To *Hocus* for a *Dedimus potestatem*.** This 'was required when a person wished to appoint an attorney to represent him in court', and was most commonly granted in the case of illness (*Dictionary of English Law*). It could allude to the accusation that Marlborough delegated responsibility for battles to avoid personal danger (10: 11–13 n.), or equally to the fact that 'Charles III' himself only set out for Spain at the insistence of Portugal in 1703: 'the Emperor Leopold was most unwilling to send his dearly loved younger son to the other end of Europe' (Trevelyan, i. 301).

103: 28 **To ditto for *Casas* and *Fifas* after a *Devastavit*.** An allusion to Marlborough's many victories, which had not yet resulted in possession by 'Charles III' of the Spanish throne, and to the allied determination to impose upon France unconditional surrender. A *devastavit* is the 'devastation or waste of the property of a deceased person by an executor or administrator by extravagance or misapplication of the assets, which makes him personally liable to persons having claim on the assets' (*Dictionary of English Law*). Louis XIV was in this sense the culpable executor of the property of the deceased Charles II of Spain. *Ca. sa.* was the usual abbreviation for *capias ad satisfaciendum*, a writ to imprison the defendant after judgement when the plaintiff's claim remained unsatisfied, and would seem to be an allusion to the later campaigns of the war, which were planned to force the wary French and Spanish armies to commit themselves to decisive battle by laying siege to strategic Bourbon strongholds in the Low Countries. Here the sum of £500 is significant, since (like the 'Five hundred Suits of fine Clothes' owned by Usuria, 36: 17–20 n.) it associates the cost of the war with the private fortune endowed on Marlborough by a grateful Queen and Parliament. We cannot find any meaning for *fifa* in contemporary law.

103: 31 **To ditto for a *Capias ad computandum*.** *Capias* was 'the generic name of several writs directing the sheriff to arrest the person therein named'. As there does not seem to have been a *capias ad computandum*, this is probably a manufactured term, suggestive of Marlborough's peculation and the investigation of accounts undertaken by the Harley Ministry.

103: 32–3 **To *Frog*'s new Tenants . . . for *Audita querelas*.** '*Frog*'s new Tenants' would be the inhabitants of the fortress towns besieged and conquered by Marlborough in the Netherlands. An *audita querela* 'in the old common law practice, was a writ given in order to afford a remedy to the defendant in an action where matter of defence (such as release) had arisen since judgment' (*Dictionary of English Law*). This suggests again that the Dutch had no intention of releasing the barrier fortresses—garrisoned by their troops—to the Austrian Charles (see also 69: 21–4 n.).

103: 34–5 **On the said Account for writs of** *Ejectment* **and** *Destringas*: further allusions to the war and also to the Utrecht negotiations. *Ejectment* was 'the mixed action at common law to recover the possession of land . . . and damages and costs for the wrongful withholding of the land', and *distringas* was the generic title of various types of writ 'commanding the sheriff to distrain on a person for a particular purpose' (*Dictionary of English Law*), both of which are clearly applicable to the defeat of Bourbon ambitions and to the allied demands at Utrecht.

104: 2–3 **Esquire** *South***'s Quota . . .** *Non est invent. Non est inventus* ('he was not found') was 'the return . . . made by the sheriff upon a writ commanding him to arrest a person who was not within his bailiwick' (*Dictionary of English Law*). Marlborough's 'bailiwick' was the Low Countries and Germany, and Philip, the 'defendant' throughout this account, was of course in Spain. The Tories disagreed with his strategic intention of crushing France in the north in order that Louis XIV must concede Spain to 'Charles III'.

104: 3 *nulla habet bona*: a further allusion to the indecisive and abortive campaigns in the Peninsula, 'nulla bona' (no goods) being 'the name given to the return made by a sheriff . . . to a writ or warrant authorizing him to seize the chattels of a person, when he had been unable to find any to seize' (*Dictionary of English Law*).

104: 4 **To——for a Pardon** *in forma pauperis.* The Tories held that Britain's Allies were 'pardoned' contribution to the cost of the war, and therefore acted '*in forma pauperis*', under which 'every poor person desirous of bringing an action who could swear that he had not property worth £5, was to be allowed to bring an action without payment of the court fees, and was to have assigned to him an attorney and counsel who acted for him without payment' (*Dictionary of English Law*). Cf. Bolingbroke to Drummond, 7 Aug. 1711: 'We look on the House of Austria, whatever you do in Holland, as a party who sues for a great estate in *formâ pauperis*; and since they have been at no part of the expence of the law-suit, it would be very impertinent if they should cavil with us on the terms of a composition' (*Letters*, ed. Parke, 1798, i. 183–4). Bolingbroke's remark suggests that the legal metaphor for the war was in circulation among court wits months before the first pamphlet of *John Bull* appeared, and one Tory satirist had applied the same analogue to England as early as 1702: 'Who first wants Money, first must sheath their Swords, / For War no *Forma Pauperis* affords' (*Miseries of England*, p. 14).

104: 5 **To Jack for a** *Melius inquirendum* **upon a** *Felo de se. Ad melius inquirendum* was a writ 'by which the holding of a second inquest by a coroner was directed' (*Dictionary of English Law*). Jack was not technically a *felo de se*, since his 'suicide' was occasioned by political betrayal and not unsoundness of mind.

104: 6 **To Don *Diego* for a *Defecit***: a manufactured' 'legal' term to remind the reader of '*The* E[arl] *of* N[ottingham's] *Desertion of the Tory Party*' (*Key*, 6th edn.) in the Parliamentary session of 7 Dec. 1711.

104: 7–8 **To Coach-hire . . . Treats to Juries and Witnesses**: further allusions to the widespread corrupton of the military. Cf. the account of legal expenses—submitted to the King by Edward Whittaker in 1699 and used by Davenant to exemplify Whig abuses—which concluded with items set out as in Bull's account: 'Expences in Summoning and Entertaining Witnesses . . . Horse-hire, Coach-hire, and other Expences on Travelling' (*True Picture of a Modern Whig*, 1701, pp. 47–8).

104: 17 **To *Hocus* for . . . a *Rege inconsulto***: 'A writ which issued from the king to the judges commanding them, in order to prevent prejudice to him, not to proceed with a cause until he had been consulted' (*Dictionary of English Law*). Another reference to the collusion between Marlborough and the Dutch to direct and control English affairs.

104: 18–19 **To *John Bull*'s Nephew for a *Venire facias* . . . not yet all laid out**: '*The Guaranty of the Protestant Succession*' (*Key*, 6th edn.). That the money is 'not yet all laid out' implies that the Dutch intended to take full advantage of the terms of the Barrier Treaty to impose the Hanoverian Succession; hence the relevance of *venire facias*, 'A writ in the nature of a summons to appear' (*Dictionary of English Law*), which, as Scott noted, seems also to carry another level of allusion to 'the writ by which the Elector of Hanover demanded to be called to the House of Peers as Duke of Cambridge, which with every proposal to bring him to Britain, the Queen obstinately refused'.

104: 30 **I paid for *Diego's Defecit***: another hit at Nottingham's supposed alliance with the Whig–Dutch interests.

104: 31–2 **As for your *Venire facias*, I have paid you for one already**: after the Revolution of 1688 (69: 18 n.). Charles Hornby picked up this idea in the *Fourth . . . Part of a Caveat*, published in October 1712, when he warned that had the Godolphin ministry not fallen, 'our dear Neighbours had, long e're now, embark'd a second Time in Defence of the British Laws and Liberties, and we had paid another Bill of Costs for being still deeper engaged in their Service' (p. 105).

104: 32–3 **in the other . . . Nonsuited . . . I'll take care of my Nephew my self**: another suggestion of the Dutch and Whig interest in the Hanoverians. A judge orders 'a nonsuit when the plaintiff fails to make out a legal cause of action or fails to support his pleadings by any evidence' (*Dictionary of English Law*). John is here identified with the Queen and the Tory ministry against the Whigs, some of whom combined attacks on the peace with exhortations to the Elector: '*Over, over,* Hanover, *over,* / Haste and assist our Queen and our State, / *Haste over,*

Hanover, *fast as you can over*; / Put in your Claim before 'tis too late' (*New Song*, bs. 1711).

105: 2–8 **who . . . are those two** *Majors* **. . . greater Ability . . . Willingness.** The *Memorial* pleaded the old Dutch justification that the States were poorer than Britain and that their contribution was justifiably smaller, since, 'according to the Alliances, *Great Britain* and this *States* are obliged each to employ all their Force in the present War . . . it follows necessarily . . . that no other proportion . . . ought to be inquired into, or alledged than that of their Ability' (*Annals*, xi, appendix, p. 9). Arbuthnot also echoes polemicists such as Defoe, who complained that in supplying allied deficiencies, '*Britain* has all along shown, by a Zeal Fatal to herself, her Willingness to push on the War with all imaginable vigour' (*Farther Search into the Conduct*, 1712, p. 14). The contraction of Willingness to 'Will' is a pun on the fact that the war was the original policy of William III, and was carried on by Godolphin ('Sir William', 67: 5–6 n.).

105: 15–16 *Hocus*! *Hocus*! **where art thou.** Frog's *cri de coeur* recalls his earlier allusion to John's 'Attorney' (102: 27–8 n.).

105: 16 **another-guess:** of another fashion or sort (*OED*).

105: 19–23 **thou retains thy Lawyers by the Year . . . thou hast set up an Eating-house.** The *Memorial* pointed out that Britain 'in time of Peace . . . keeps very few Troops on Foot; and . . . after the Peace of *Ryswick* . . . disbanded most of those at that Time in her Pay, which was a very great Ease to her: Whereas this *State* was obliged to maintain above 40000 Men' (*Annals*, xi, appendix, p. 10). It was an undiplomatic complaint, since the Tories had long resented what they imagined were the profits made by the Dutch on supply to allied troops in Flanders: cf. Defoe's ironic defence of the States from the accusation 'that they have no other View in the War than bringing a Trade into their Countrey' (*Justification of the Dutch*, 1712, p. 13). Of the great armies involved in the war, the Dutch in particular relied on the use of mercenary troops whom they regarded with 'the attitude of a careful trader to the stock in which he has invested his money' (Trevelyan, i. 231). The 'Eating-house' may refer specifically to the States-General furnishing bread at a profit to the foreign troops in English pay in 1712 (see Count Zinzendorf's *Memorial* to the States, in *Annals*, xi. 166).

105: 23–4 **rap or run:** from 'rap and rend'; snatch, seize (*OED*).

105: 33–4 **this trusty Weapon:** the trusty 'Cudgel' (the British army) referred to later, 118: 16–30 n. and 121: 4–6 n.

106: 9–14 **Old** *Lewis* **makes reasonable Offers . . . look to thy self.** The intransigence of the Allies provided a convenient excuse for concluding a separate peace. On 2 June 1712 the Bishop of Bristol announced to the Dutch representatives at Utrecht that '*Her Majesty did now think Her self at Liberty to enter into Separate Measures, in order to obtain a Peace for Her own Conveniency*' (*Annals*, xi. 100).

106: 13–14 **what will they do when thou wants them?** 'They love none but those that do for them, and when they leave off they neglect them' (*Dutch Drawn to the Life*, 1664, p. 72).

106: 17–18 **Twenty-Two poor Years towards the finishing a Law-suit**: including the War of the League of Augsburg, 1689–97. Cf. 'We have Warr'd twenty Years . . . The *Dutch* for good Towns. We for Whimsies and Fears' (*Excellent New Song*, bs. 1712).

106: 24–30 *an Uproar at Home* . . . [Nic.] **had corrupted or deluded most of** [John's] **Servants**. Fears about the Protestant Succession, which were to become more intense during the next two years, caused some Whig politicians to move 'That [Her Majesty] will be pleased to give particular Instructions to Her Plenipotentiaries, That in the Conclusion of the . . . Treaty, the several Powers in Alliance with Her Majesty may be Guarantees for the Protestant Succession' (17 June, 1712; *Annals*, xi. 134–5). Public dissension concerning the Queen's attitude towards the Succession is reflected in several addresses to the Queen from Westminster, the Isle of Wight, the county of Chester, and the High Sheriff of Durham, printed in *Annals*, xi. 148–52. Swift derided the Whigs as 'Malecontents' ever ready 'to bawl out *Popery, Persecution, Arbitrary Power*, and *the Pretender*' (*Examiner*, 7 Dec. 1710, iii. 34). This chapter telescopes events from early 1710 to the time of its composition in the summer of 1712. There are allusions to abuses in the former administration and to the Whigs being turned out of office, as well as to concern about the Pretender. On 9 Dec. 1711 Baron de Bothmar, the Elector's envoy to Great Britain, read a *Memorial* condemning the present scheme of peace. The Tories, according to Boyer, reflected 'that this Memorial had more the Air of an Original written in *English*, than a Translation from the *French*; and so concluded, that it was framed in *London*, in concert with the leading Men of the *Whig-Party*' (*Annals*, x. 277).

107: 2–3 **settle his Estate upon a Parish Boy.** An alarm was raised that the Queen would call in the Pretender (Hawkesworth). In late 1710, a paper in favour of 'JACOBUS TERTIUS' was dispersed at the doors of several Whigs (*Political State of Great Britain*, i. 24). 'About the middle of *June* [1711], upon a Report that the *Pretender* was either embark'd, or ready to go on Board a Ship at *Brest*, the Stocks of Publick Funds fell two or three *per Cent*.' (*Annals*, x. 215). A month later *PB* reported that Charles Leslie, the Tory journalist and pamphleteer, had gone to Switzerland to convert 'a certain YOUNG GENTLEMAN . . . from *Popery* to *Protestantism*' (ibid. 213).

107: 7–9 **He call'd his Cook-maid** *Betty* . . . *his Will*. Whig alarms concerning the Succession are satirized in the following exchanges by the old Tory device of associating them with the complaints of inferior servants (16: 15 n.). There seems to be no evidence for Colvile's identification of Betty as the Duchess of Somerset. Arbuthnot satirizes the whiggish fervour of the populace by employing the generic name for maids of all kinds.

107: 11–12 **my Conscience won't allow me.** It was feared, of course, that the Pretender would introduce Roman Catholicism.

107: 14–19 **he call'd *John* the Barber . . . *Dick* the Butler?** Possibly, as Colvile thought, Somers and Wharton. Only the barber's Christian name might suggest John, Lord Somers, but the butler seems quite clearly an allusion to Wharton, who had been prosecuted for corruption in military supply (p. lvi, above), and had previously appeared as 'Dick Hotspur' in two issues of the *Plain Dealer* on 21 June and 12 July 1712. The second of these crude allegories is a letter from Dick to his friends urging them 'to Publish and spread any Story concerning my *Mother* [the Queen] or *Harry* [Bolingbroke, cf. 108: 12 n.], though never so impossible. . . *Dated from my House, in* Dover Street' (cf. 67: 6–7 n.).

107: 24 **Drink with the Ducks:** a children's proverb. Harold Williams noted this occurrence as analogous to, 'when the ducks have eaten up all the dirt' (Swift, *Journal*, 23 Dec. 1710, p. 137).

107: 25–6 **And so I will . . . better than my self.** The Tories countered a Whig motion to address the Queen on the Succession with a resolution, 'That this House has such an Entire Confidence in the repeated Declarations her Majesty has been pleased to make, of her Securing to these Kingdoms the Protestant Succession . . . And that this House will support her Majesty against Faction at Home, and her Enemies abroad' (*History of Utrecht*, p. 340).

107: 26–32 **Hob . . . Pricket . . . Andrew.** We can find no evidence to support Colvile's identification of Halifax, Cowper, and Queensberry, respectively. The names represent Whigs (like Wharton) who in 1712 were eager to ensure the Hanoverian succession by setting up Sophia and her son in England while Anne lived. 'Hob' signifies 'a plain Country Fellow; or Clown' (*Canting Crew*); 'Pricket' is a common generic name for a tailor; 'Andrew' signifies a valet, or gentleman's servant.

107: 34–5 **I only desire to know what you would do if you were dead?** This logical contradiction affirms the conflation of the English Queen and people in the figure of Bull: cf. Defoe's ironic pamphlet, *Answer to a Question that No Body Thinks of, Viz. But what if the Queen should Die*, 1713.

108: 7–8 **Possession . . . is eleven points of the Law:** for the Regency Act of 1705 and the proposals for inviting over the Electress and her son, see Trevelyan, ii. 90–7. Cf. 69: 25 n.

108: 9–12 **he enquires . . . if old Mother *Jenisa* was not still alive.** The Dutch are unflatteringly associated with the accusation of witchcraft which had been frequently levelled against Francis Jenyns (the mother of the Duchess of Marlborough), although 'based on nothing more sinister than, as one contemporary put it, "knowing more than the common race of mortals"' (Green, *Sarah Duchess of Marlborough*, 1967, p. 24). Mrs. Manley was apparently the first Tory satirist to designate Mrs. Jenyns as 'Jenisa'. See her *Secret History of Queen Zarah*, 1705.

108: 12 **Harry.** This is the only overt allusion in the satire to Henry St.
John, Viscount Bolingbroke.

108: 12–13 **there is no *Potion* . . . but a little *Aurum Potabile*.**
Bolingbroke was one of the prime movers behind the investigations into
the corruptions of the fallen Ministry. *Aurum potabile*, 'gold held in a
state of minute subdivision in some volatile oil, formerly in repute as
a cordial' (*OED*) was a well-tried political metaphor: cf. 'the Court of all
sorts of Physick, ever hated Purges. They will take Gold Cordials . . .
but Purging they mortally hate' (*Dialogue between a Modern Courtier*,
1696, p. 16).

108: 14–18 **Don Diego . . . their Orator :** Nottingham's '*Presentment
of the* L[ords] *Address against Peace without* Spain' (*Key*, 6th edn.).
This passage recalls the Tory view of the bargain arranged between the
Whigs and Nottingham (20: 10 n.).

108: 19–20 **I desire to know . . . *Syllogism, Enthymen, Dilemma
or Sorites*.** Cf. 'Leave hunting after Bribes, forget your Tropes' (Swift,
'T[o]l[a]nd's Invitation to Dismal', *Poems*, i. 162). The trick *syllogism*,
the *enthymeme* which suppresses a premise of the argument, the *dilemma*
which presents two equally unfavourable alternatives, and particularly
the *sorites* (which, in Don Diego's usage, is a series of illogically progres-
sive propositions), are all ironically appropriate rhetorical devices to
introduce the nonsense which follows.

108: 24–6 **It is evident . . . it plainly follows.** Cf. Defoe's ridicule of
Nottingham's sophistical logic which 'we find fill'd up with the Phrases
necessary to such Way of Arguing, *viz. It may be concluded, it may be
supposed, it is Reasonable to believe . . . it is probable*, and the like Figures
of Speech' (*Not*[tingh]*am Politicks Examin'd*, 1713, p. 6).

109: 2–6 **a good tough Oaken Cudgel . . . valuable Things . . .
pick'd up by others of the Family.** Here John is identified with the
Harley ministry, his 'cudgel' referring not to the army (as in 118: 16–30 n.)
but to the powers used by Harley to displace ministerial and lesser officers,
and more particularly to his personal triumph in persuading the Queen to
create twelve new Tory peers. Marlborough's dismissal 'was attended
with other Removes; and consequently made way for several Promotions'
(*Annals*, x. 313). Somerset lost his position as Master of the Horse on
17 January, and a number of less important Whigs were turned out of
place shortly afterwards (see *Annals*, x. 315, 333–6, 396–7). There is
perhaps a suggestion of distaste in Arbuthnot's treatment of these
changes, which finds an echo in Whig attacks on the new Tory placemen:
cf. 'we all hoped to be Sharers, and every one to get in the Scramble as
much as he could for himself' (*Dialogue Between a New Courtier*, 1712,
p. 4).

109: 14 **How Lewis Baboon *came to visit* John Bull :** the secret
negotiations between Torcy and Bolingbroke in 1711. Arbuthnot deliberately confuses chronology and venue (Bolingbroke visited France)

to avoid the embarrassment of admitting that the ministry had instituted private discussions before the public Congress at Utrecht.

109: 19–24 **John had ... good Instructions ... steadiness ... he began to leave off ... roaring and bullying about the Streets.** The progress of the 1711 negotiations is anticipated by this allusion to the mood of the government in May 1712. When it appeared that the Dutch intended to sabotage the Congress, the Queen 'resolved ... to exert Herself with Vigour, Steadiness and Dispatch' in her people's interest (Swift, *Four Last Years*, vii. 124). John not only assumes the character of the Queen but also the qualities which Swift argued were characteristic of her prime minister, Harley: 'Firm and Steady in his Resolutions, not easily diverted from them, after he hath once possessed himself of an Opinion that they are right' (ibid. 73). This identification separates populace, Queen, and ministry from John's 'old Aquaintance', the fallen Whigs, who are again associated with the Mohock rowdies (cf. 39: 24–6 n.). Sir Roger's 'good Instructions' for John may refer specifically to Harley's blueprint for peace, which guided St. John in his negotiations (see McInnes, *Robert Harley*, 1970, pp. 130 ff.).

110: 3 **he took heart of Grace.** *Dictionary of Proverbs* (H. 332) cites eleven examples of usage between 1530 and 1687.

110: 14–15 **domestick Calamities, that I need not relate.** ''Tis very surprising this News to day of the Dauphin and Dauphiness both dying within 6 days. They say the old King is almost heart-broke. He has had prodigious mortifications in his Family. The Dauphin has left 2 little Sons of 4 and 2 years old, the eldest is sick' (Swift, *Journal*, 15 Feb. 1712, p. 489).

110: 15–16 **I am a poor old batter'd Fellow ... I would willingly end my Days in Peace.** Cf. 'The present King of *France* has but few Years to live, by the Course of Nature, and, doubtless, would desire to end his Days in Peace' (Swift, *Conduct*, vi. 58). Louis XIV was seventy-three years of age and sickly.

110: 18–21 **formerly I was to be bang'd ... when too Poor.** Cf. Defoe's appraisal of the situation: 'the War was begun upon no other Account whatsoever but the keeping a Ballance of Power in *Europe* ... it has reduc'd *France* to the last Extremity, impoverish'd *England*, and enrich'd the *Dutch*' (*Justification of the Dutch*, 1712, pp. 11–12): see also *Plain Dealer*, 19 July 1712.

110: 21–3 **Nic. Frog has used me like a Scoundrel ... as you think fit.** Cf. 'at the *Hague* ... [and] *Gertruydenbergh*; in the Years 1709–10 ... the *French* conceived themselves to be too haughtily and arrogantly treated by the *D[utc]h* ... this the *French* King, after another Campaign, laid hold of as a Pretence to apply himself to *Great Britain*, to see what Effect his Offers might have on that Side' (*Management of the Four Last Years*, 1714, p. 16).

110: 26–8 **you have been rolling a great Stone uphill all your Life
. . . crush you to pieces.** Sisyphus, the legendary King of Corinth
(famous for his cunning) was condemned in Hades to eternal punishment,
by having to roll a large stone to the top of a hill, whereupon it for ever
rolled back down again. He makes an apt correlative to the crafty and
ageing Lewis. Lewis's and John's respective problems with stones and
pits are neatly stated in Ecclesiasticus, Arbuthnot's favourite book of the
Apocrypha: 'Whoso casteth a stone on high, casteth it on his own head . . .
Whoso diggeth a pit, shall fall therein' (Ecclesiasticus 27: 25–6).

111: 6–7 *Ecclesdown Castle* . . . **has been formerly in your Family:**
'Ecclesia-Dun, *i.e.* Dunkirk; which had been garrisoned by the English
in Cromwell's time, and is therefore said to have been formerly in John
Bull's family' (Scott). Cf. Mrs. Manley's '*Dunecclesia*' for Dunkirk in *The
Secret History of Queen Zarah*, 1705. In June 1712 Louis wrote to Anne,
'That altho' Her *Britannick* Majesty had not yet been able to procure
a general Suspension of Arms [at Utrecht], yet the King of *France*, to
shew his sincere Intentions for Peace, and the Confidence he repos'd in
Her Majesty, was willing to deliver *Dunkirk* into Her Hands' (*Annals*,
xi. 177–8). This was a shrewdly timed offer, since Dunkirk housed
pirates who had for years made serious inroads into British shipping, and
the destruction of its defences was one of the conditions for peace demanded at Utrecht. Scott was quite justified in noting the long history of
Dunkirk as an English outpost, but he failed to mention the more precise
allusion which identifies Bull with Harley whose family history was—as
Tory polemicists were eager to point out—closely connected with Dunkirk. Francis Hoffman in his *Impartial Character of the Noble Family of
the Most Honourable the Earl of Oxford*, bs. 1712, eulogized Sir Robert, his
grandfather, Governor of Dunkirk, and Sir Edward, his father, who had
refused a French bribe to acquiesce in the sale of Dunkirk to the French:
'Thus what the Father Strove to save / And Would not Quit for Gallick
Gold, / The Son do's without Bloodshed have / Restor'd more strong a
Hundred-fold' (see also Swift, *It's Out at Last*, vi. 189–90). The Harleys
thus stand in marked contrast to the Duke of Marlborough who was im-
plicated in devious and possibly treasonous machinations over the sale
of Dunkirk. Defoe commented ironically: 'that business . . . is trump'd up
against my Lord to this very Day. . . . The Loss of Dunkirk is not to be
forgotten, and 'tis fresh in the Minds of the common People, both in
Town and Country' (*Short Narrative*, 1711, p. 9): see also *D*[uke] *of
M*[arlborough']*s Confession*, 1711, p. 4.

111: 16–17 **But tell me . . . thy *Equivocals* and *Mentals* in this case?**
'Equivocals', equivocal words or terms, and 'Mentals', mental reservations (*OED*). John's excitement and disbelief reflect the Tory attitude to
Louis's offer: 'NOw *Dunkirk's* surrendered no Room's left for fear, /
But subtle Old *Lewis* at length's grown sincere' (*French Sincerity Exemplified*, bs. 1712). The Whig-biased author of the *History of Utrecht*
commented sardonically, 'The Surrender of *Dunkirk* was so evident

a Proof of the *French* King's Sincerity, that it was afterwards esteem'd
a Sort of Stupidity or Sedition to suspect it' (p. 355).

111: 32 **I must have Security.** See Trevelyan on the French concessions in the Preliminaries which were 'of immense advantage to the security and the trade of England' (iii. 186 n.).

111: 34–6 *Ecclesdown Castle! Ecclesdown!* . . . **offer'd thee some
Years ago?** Louis's rhetoric reflects ironically on the fact that Dunkirk
had been supposed one of the chief stumbling-blocks in the 1709 negotiations: one Whig polemic pictured Louis raving, '*Dunkirk! Dunkirk!*
Do but look into the Addresses of the *British* Parliament, and there you'll
see it. For speak of it I can't without a Fit of Cholick at least . . . the very
Thoughts on't make my Fistula shoot with new Anguish' (*French King's
Catechism*, 1709, p. 8). In fact Louis had been willing to concede the
point. Swift was careful to set the record straight in his ironic praise of
the fallen Godolphin ministry, which had 'scorn'd to accept of *Dunkirk*
and a dozen more strong Towns of the *French* King, when they were
offer'd; a plain and convincing Proof that they had no secret Dealings
with *France*' (*It's Out at Last*, vi. 190).

112: 10 **Thou hast but small Obligations to *Nic.*** Cf. Wagstaffe's
comment that the war had so far only benefited the Allies, 'But the
taking *Dunkirk* is our own Advantage; and howsoever a certain *King*
may have formerly been branded for his Breach of Faith and Promise,
Her Majesty has received a better Treatment from him, than from those
who are more obliged to pay Her their Acknowledgements' (*Plain Dealer*,
19 July 1712).

112: 11 **He has not us'd me like a Gentleman.** Cf. 'they gaze at,
and envy, but never reverence a Gentleman' (*Dutch Drawn to the Life*,
1664, p. 69).

112: 12–13 **Nic, indeed, is not very nice in your Punctilio's of
Ceremony:** an ironic reversal of the situation at Utrecht where, in 1712,
Dutch delaying tactics 'run, for the most part, upon meer *Punctilio* about
the Ceremonials' (*FP*, 19 Jan. 1712). Wagstaff intended the same inference
when he wrote that those pursuing peace 'know better than to insist on
Trifles and Punctilio's for other People' (*Plain Dealer*, 14 June 1712).

112: 13–14 **Clownish . . . Calling of Names . . . time out of mind.**
Another allusion to the tactless letters and the *Memorial* sent by the
States to Anne. The Dutch had long been dismissed as boors, 'Clownish
and blunt to men . . .' (*Dutch Drawn to the Life*, 1664, p. 69) and there is
an interesting parallel with Arbuthnot's satire in the indignant complaint
of Charles Vine against the States' communications with Charles II:
'the expressions they use against . . . the present King . . . are so *rude*
and *barbarous*; the suggestions so palpably false, that in a Controversie
between *private persons*, such a procedure were intolerable' (*Justification
of the Present War*, 1672, p. 1).

112: 15–16 **however, we are engag'd . . . I must look after him.**
As late as October 1711 the Queen wrote to Strafford at Utrecht affirming

that she was 'determin'd to accept of no advantages to our Selves repugnant to [the States'] interests, nor of any Peace which may not be to their reasonable Satisfaction' (Swift, *Four Last Years*, vii. 200).

112: 17–18 **All matters that relate to him . . . to your Justice.** The Dutch complained bitterly when France agreed that Britain should act as mediator in the Utrecht conferences.

112: 24–5 **Amongst other Artifices, he wrote a most obliging Letter.** Scott was the first editor to recognize that the following missive was a parody of a letter sent by the States to the Queen on 5 June 1712. Unlike some of their previous efforts, it was 'a very submissive, pathetick' attempt to justify their conduct (Oldmixon, *History of England*, 1735, p. 490).

112: 26 **Printed in a fair Character.** The States jeopardized their cause by (yet again) allowing the text of their official correspondence to be printed for propagandist effect. The Queen replied, 'we cannot pass over in Silence our Great Surprize, to see that your Letter of the 5th Instant *N.S.* was printed and publish'd almost as soon as we received it from the Hands of your Minister [Van Borsele]; a Proceeding which is equally contrary to Good Politicks and Decency. 'Tis a Remonstrance instead of a Representation, and an Appeal to the People, instead of an Address to the Sovereign . . . our Honour will engage us to give no Answer to any Letters or Memorials which shall be publish'd in that Manner' (*Annals*, xi, appendix ii. 57).

112: 29–31 **upon a narrow Inspection into my Conduct . . . nothing to reproach my self with.** The States' letter was immediately occasioned by the Queen's declaration that she intended to settle matters with France separately (106: 9–14 n.), and it expressed puzzlement in, 'not being able to conceive, how such a *sudden Change* could happen, with Respect to us, we are not only surpriz'd, but afflicted at it. We have carefully examin'd our Conduct, and find nothing in it that can have given Ground to that Dissatisfaction which Your Majesty expresses with us by this Declaration' (ibid. 51). Perhaps Arbuthnot's close parody was intended to stir recent memories of Swift's enormously influential *Conduct of the Allies*, of which the States must also have been conscious when composing the letter.

113: 1–6. **I was ready to comply . . . Safety touches me to the Quick.** Cf. 'we were never backward to communicate and consult . . . upon the Affairs of the Peace. . . . We declare, that we have always been inclinable and ready to do it, and are so still, as far as we can, *without Prejudice to the other Allies* . . . Had that Plan *related only to Your Majesty's Interest and Ours, we should perhaps have been in the Wrong not to have forthwith come into it* . . . But as the *Plan in Question concerned the Interest of all the Allies, and almost all* Europe, we had very strong Apprehensions' (ibid. 53–4).

113: 2 **prevented:** a pun on the modern 'forestalled', and the archaic meaning 'anticipated' (*OED*).

113:5 **the same Common Cause.** In the six pages of the States' letter, 'Common Cause' and associated usages such as 'common Interests' and 'common Enemy' occurred nine times. Wagstaffe may have been thinking of these emotive appeals and the many echoes in Whig polemic when he wrote, '*The pursuing the Common Cause,* is an Expression some People have made use of in order to act the contrary, and is nothing else, when it comes to be construed, than taking Care of the different Interests of the several Princes of the Alliance' (*Plain Dealer,* 2 Aug. 1712).

113: 6–8 **You seem'd a little jealous . . . upon the Ballance.** There was in fact no mention of the financial disputes of the Resolutions and *Memorial* in the States' letter.

113: 14 **meddle in your domestick Affairs.** The Letter offered to renegotiate the article of 'Mutual Guaranty' for the Protestant Succession in England in the Barrier Treaty of 1709 (*Annals,* xi, appendix ii. 52).

113: 20–1 **I have beggar'd my self with this Law-Suit.** Cf. *'we have done more in this present War, than could in Justice and Equity have been expected from Us'* (ibid. 55).

113: 22–6 **I had still greater things . . . to no Purpose.** Cf. 'we are sorry to see *one of the finest Opportunities lost,* being uncertain whether we shall have another so favourable . . . to the inestimable Prejudice of the common Cause' (ibid., 50).

113: 26–31 **My Concern for your Welfare . . . NIC. FROG.** This elaborate conclusion parodies the diplomatic respect which characterized the whole letter, and was epitomized in its final appeal: 'We again renew to Your Majesty the Assurances of Our high and perfect Esteem for Your Person and Friendship, as also of our Intentions and sincere Desires to entertain with Your Majesty the same good Correspondence, Harmony and Union, as before' (ibid. 56).

113: 32 *John* **receiv'd this with a good deal of** *Sang froid*: the Queen's reply (112: 26 n.); '*With a great deal of Coolness and Indifference*' (*Key,* 6th edn.). John's 'sang froid' is perhaps a wry comment on his new found confidence in the French.

113: 32–3 *Transeat* **(quoth John)** *cum caeteris erroribus*: 'Let it pass with all the other madnesses'. This seems to be an evocation rather than a direct quotation of Horace (see Introduction, p. lxxxv, above). In 'The Classics and John Bull, 1660–1714' (*England in the Restoration and Early Eighteenth Century,* ed. H. T. Swedenberg, 1972, p. 26), James W. Johnson suggested that this solitary scrap of Latin is explicable in cultural terms and is a phrase Bull might have been expected to pick up from a sermon. In subsequent correspondence Professor Johnson elaborated on this possibility: 'If I can judge by its absence from all modern anthologies of classical quotations, the maxim . . . is not genuinely ancient but some post-classical summation of the "lesson" of a classical work. Although John's experiences with the Law and Latin terms might equip him thus to speak, I doubt that the phrase is in fact legalese. Its tone and crypto-philosophical phrasing resound of lawn-and-linen . . . maybe one of those 17th. century anthologies of quotations: Suidas, Photius, Constantine, or John Stobaeus.' We are unable to trace the precise source of this phrase, but we agree with Professor Johnson that it is Horatian in essence.

113: 35 **My Shirt (quoth he) is near me, but my Skin is nearer**: 'tunica propior palliost' (Plautus, *Trinummus*, l. 1154), an aphorism which had passed into proverbial English. *Dictionary of Proverbs* cites nine examples between 1596 and 1721.

114: 2-3 **a Man has such a tender Concern for himself.** This echo of the standard form of address from Parliament to the monarch, which solicited or expressed thanks for her 'tender concern' or 'tender regard', points the identification of the interests of people and Queen in concluding peace.

114: 3-6 **This is somewhat better . . . Dray-horse . . . *this Beast*?** Beattie (p. 88 n.) first noted this parallel with Defoe's allegory of Utrecht as a horse fair in two issues of the *Review*. The first, which appeared on 14 Feb. 1712, pictured the allied 'traders' eager to consolidate their alliance, 'lest . . . the *French* Jockey . . . bubble them out of the Horse' (vii. 563). The second, published on 1 March, was hostile to Britain's Allies: '*Rough John,* an Old Horse-Scourser' is plagued by the inflated demands of '*Chap Vloormane,* a *High German*' (the Emperor) who wants the head (Spain) and the rest of the horse (its Empire), while the '*Low-Dutch* Jockey demands the Legs [the Barrier, so] that he might be able to stand by himself', leaving John with nothing but the guts (viii. 589–91).

114: 8 **see as far into a Milstone as another.** *Dictionary of Proverbs* (M. 965) cites fifteen examples of usage between 1540 and 1721, and comments, 'A claim to acuteness, often used ironically'.

114: 12-13 **The Discourse . . . which John Bull overheard**: '*A Separate Conference between the* Imperial *and* Dutch *Ministers at* Utrecht' (*Key*, 6th edn.), which resulted in an agreement read to the Congress by Count Zinzendorf, the chief Austrian representative, on 30 June. The Queen had proposed an armistice, but 'Count *Zinzendorf* . . . did not give the States Leisure to think. . . . He was prodigal of his Offers in his Master's Name . . . and . . . presented a Memorial to the States-General, which he call'd, *His Sentiments upon the Affairs of the present Conjuncture*' (*History of Utrecht*, p. 359). Something of the kind had been expected since *PB*, 15 March, had reported a private meeting between the Dutch and the Imperial representatives.

114: 24 **the Rogue should be compell'd to do his Duty.** It was, in fact, Zinzendorf who suggested that the two Allies should jointly '*make Representation to the* QUEEN *of* Great Britain, *requesting Her Majesty to perform Her Engagements*' (*History of Utrecht*, pp. 360–1), chiefly 'the Recovery of the *Spanish* Monarchy to the House of *Austria*; the Security of this State [Holland], by a Barrier, in the *Netherlands*; the securing their Commerce in *Spain*, and the *West-Indies*' (*Annals*, xi. 167) in a renewal of the alliance among the three countries.

114: 25–7 That he should prefer . . . Pelf . . . to the . . . Grandeur of my Family ! The associations of pelf, 'trash, rubbish, property pilfered or stolen' (*OED*) ironically reflect on the Tory complaint that 'we have not much besides immortal Honour to boast' (*Natural Reflections,* 1712, p. 28), and that the French concessions would provide the only tangible rewards from a long, costly, and 'successful' war. Cf. 'hitherto we seem to have been fighting like *Knights-Errants*, for *Honour's sake,* and to redress Publick Grievances, without any Regard to our private Interest' (Defoe, *True Account of the Design,* 1711, p. 5).

114: 29 by his Vails : advantages, perquisites, from its early application to the remnants of material left over by a tailor after making a garment or suit (*OED*).

115: 7–8 *Philip Baboon*'s Tenants do not all take your Honour's part. By now it was common knowledge that Philip V did, and Charles of Austria did not, have the support of the Spanish people.

115: 12 so critical a Juncture : a pun on the title of Zinzendorf's *Sentiments upon the Affairs of the present Conjuncture*; see 114: 12–13 n.

115: 16–17 one honest Man amongst a thousand : a rather archaic adage; *Dictionary of Proverbs* cites only five examples of usage and all between 1508 and 1666. Cf. 'to be honest, as this world goes, is to be one man picked out of ten thousand' (*Hamlet*, II. ii. 177–8).

115: 21–4 I am your Tenant . . . Lease and an Inheritance . . . make *Bull* . . . mad. These *Sentiments* called upon all the allies to win the whole barrier demanded by the Dutch, and agreed to allow the troops of the States to continue in occupation for an unspecified length of time (see *History of Utrecht*, p. 360).

115: 30–5 Then of a sudden . . . *Long live Esquire* South *and the Law!* The Dutch and Austrians were, of course, replying to the announcement of the agreement between France and Britain, in demanding that the war continue. Arbuthnot transposes the events, and thus strengthens John's moral case in making his separate agreement with Lewis.

116: 1–4 but stop proceeding for a while . . . and so lose a Term : alluding to Ormonde's declaration of suspension of arms in June 1712. The envoys of the Allies 'exclaimed that they would lose thereby the fairest prospect of a successful campaign, which the war had yet offered' (Scott). Cf. Swift, *Four Last Years*, vii. 136.

116: 6 put us in Possession . . . of *Ecclesdown*. Joined to the proposal of a cessation of arms was the news of Louis's offer of Dunkirk. Cf. a broadside, possibly by Swift: '*Old* Lewis *thus the Terms of Peace to Burnish,* | *Has lately let out* Dunkirk *Ready Furnish'd*; | *But whether 'tis* *by* Lease, *or* Coppy-hold, / *Or* Tenure in Capite, *we've not been told* : / *But this we hope, if yet he pulls his Horns in,* / *He'll be oblig'd to give his Tenants warning'* ('Dunkirk to Be Let', 1712, *Poems*, iii. 1097).

116: 8–14 **When** *Frog* **took Possession . . . constant Doctrine . . . always One before?** The sanctity of the 'Common Cause' had indeed been the constant doctrine of the Dutch (113: 5 n.) and it had been the constant complaint of Tory polemic that the States had used it to excuse self-aggrandizement. Cf. Swift on the implications of the Barrier Treaty in relation to the Utrecht conferences: 'This I humbly conceive to be perfect Boys Play, *Cross I win,* and *Pile you lose*; or *What's yours is mine,* and *What's mine is my own.* Now if it should happen that in a Treaty of Peace, some Ports or Towns should be yielded to us for the Security of our Trade . . . I suppose the *Dutch* would go on with their Boys Play, and *challenge Half'* (*Remarks*, vi. 92); see also Defoe, *Justification of the Dutch*, 1712, p. 30.

116: 14–15 **we must trust one another.** 'They may always deceive, for you must trust them . . . you must pay what they ask as sure as if it were the assessement of a Subsidy' (*Dutch Drawn to the Life*, 1664, p. 71).

116: 31–2 **And you are really so silly . . . will give it you.** Even the whiggish *History of Utrecht* had to admit that 'the *Dutch* were at this Time very much out of Humour with us, for threatening to leave them . . . Their Discourse was soure, and so were their Writings. . . . They gave the worst Turn to all our Transactions, and from every Thing we did, rais'd Matter of Jealousie and Apprehension' (p. 363).

117: 6–7 **old Lewis turn'd out . . . of** *Clay-Pool?* 'Clay-pool, Paris' (*Key*, 6th edn.). Paris, in prehistoric times, was on an island standing in the marshes of the Seine. The Roman town which grew up in the first century A.D. was called 'Lutetia' (after 'lutum', mud, clay). The States' Letter urges a continuation of the war because the Allies have never had a better advantage over the enemy (*Annals*, xi, appendix ii. 50).

117: 25 **Sneaker-snee :** to use a knife as a weapon (*OED*). From 'snick or snee' (Bense, *Dictionary of the Low-Dutch Element in the English Vocabulary*).

117: 27–30 **What signifies Life . . . has been the Cause of it?** In this burlesque Arbuthnot ridicules a famous speech made at a meeting of Amsterdam Burgomasters on 1 July 1712, three days after Strafford (at Utrecht) had officially announced the British decision to suspend hostilities: 'Monsieur *Corver* their Senior . . . made a memorable Speech . . . *That he was an old Man . . . and had seen far more difficult Times, even the* French *at the very Gates,* but that he feared for the Common Cause'. He concluded, '*if at last we are over-power'd, then let us lay our Cities under Water, betake our selves to our Ships, and sail to the* East Indies, *and let those who see our Country laid wast, say*; There liv'd a People who chose to lose their Country rather than their Liberty' (*History of Utrecht*, pp. 352–3).

118: 10–11 **Esquire *South* and I will go on with our Law-suit.**
After the British declaration of a suspension of arms, the Dutch ministers
and Prince Eugene concerted methods to engage the general of the
auxiliary troops in British pay (*Annals*, xi. 160).

118: 16–30 *Nic* **bounc'd up . . . the Cudgel . . . broke short in his
Hands.** This complicated tussle represents the separation of the Confederate armies on 16 July 1712. Prince Eugene broke camp near Brussels
and marched off with the '*Confederate Troops, in Her Majesties Pay*'
(*Key*, 6th edn.) in order to prosecute the campaign. Ormonde immediately
ordered a cessation of arms for two months, and decamped the same day
(*Annals*, xi. 180).

118: 29 **contranitent:** striving in opposite directions (*OED*).

118: 30–1 *Nic.* . . . **began to Bastinado Old *Lewis*.** Before the separation of the army, 'Major General *Grovestein*, Governor of *Bouchain*,
who had been detach'd by Prince *Eugene* with about 1500 Horse, Dra-
goons, and *Hussars*, made a successful Incursion into *France*; and having
ravag'd, plunder'd, and burnt several open Towns and Villages in
Champagne, and the Country of *Metz*, and struck Terror and Consterna-
tion as far as *Paris* . . . march'd to *Brussels* in order to rejoin the Confederate Army' (*Annals*, xi. 168).

118: 33–5 **the old Fellow was forc'd . . . behind a Dung-cart.**
This raid forced the French to '*retreat within their Lines*' (*Key*, 6th edn.).
The King himself 'was not judged safe at Versailles, with his usual
guards, and all the troops about Paris were summoned to defend his
person' (Scott).

119: 15–16 **the Gates are shut, the Turnpikes locked.** 'Before the
Separation of the Confederate Forces, the Deputies of the States said
openly, that they hoped the Duke of Ormonde did not intend to march
through any of their Towns' (*London Gazette*, 'Published by Authority',
15 July 1712). On his march to take possession of Dunkirk by the land
side, Ormonde encountered some obstacles. Part of his army was 'refused
Entrance at the Gates' of Bouchain (the recently recaptured fortress in
Flanders), and the main army itself was not allowed into Douai. See also
History of Utrecht, p. 374.

119: 19–21 **I am deny'd Passage through those very Grounds that
I have purchased with my own Money.** Ormonde's troops were also
'refus'd Passage' through Petteghem, near Oudenarde, 'which occasion'd
here bitter Reflections against the *Dutch*. It appear'd indeed at first very
strange, *that the* British *Officers should be refused Entrance into those
Towns which Her Majesty's Forces in Conjunction with those of Her Allies,
had conquer'd this War*' (*Annals*, xi. 184).

119: 23–6 *John Bull* **was so over-joy'd . . . *Nic.* . . . look'd sower
and grum:** i.e. morose, gloomy, surly (*OED*). Cf. Defoe's description
of the appearance of the pacifically inclined: 'their Faces are covered with

Smiles, a sort of Calm and Smoothness of Temper sits on their Brow; they look pleased and serene, like the Spirit that possesses them. The Men that are for War seem in a Ferment, their Eyes sparkle, something Boisterous appears in their Faces, they look as uneasie as they talk' (*Essay at a Plain Exposition*, 1711, p. 8).

119: 31-2 *shake your day-day*: a childish expression for 'good-bye'; cf. 'ta-ta' (*OED*).

119: 32-3 *John* march'd out . . . to take Possession of *Ecclesdown*. Ormonde changed the direction of his march, occupying Ghent and Bruges on his way through Flanders, and thus avoided the necessity of passing through any of the 'common' garrisoned towns. Eugene protested vigorously, and the Dutch States apologized hastily for the 'impetuous' behaviour of the commanders who closed their gates against Ormonde (see *History of Utrecht*, pp. 374-5). 'The *Dutch* therein to see our Banners / Display'd, begin to mend their Manners, / To eat their words and stink for fear' (*Description of Dunkirk*, bs. 1712).

120: 2-3 *when he got Possession of* Ecclesdown. On 19 July 1712 'a small force of troops from England under the redoubtable Jack Hill [the brother of Abigail Masham], landed from Admiral Leake's squadron and were welcomed into Dunkirk by the French authorities as guests and friends' (Trevelyan, iii. 221).

120: 4-7 he seem'd like *Ulysses* . . . upon the Bench. Ulysses, in danger of being sucked into Charybdis, 'clung grimly, thinking my mast and keel / would come back to the surface when she spouted. / And oh! how long, with what desire, I waited! / till, at the twilight hour, when one who hears / and judges pleas in the market-place all day / between contentious men, goes home for supper, / the long poles reared from the sea' (*Homer's Odyssey*, tr. R. Fitzgerald, 1962, Bk. xii, ll. 432-41, p. 202). Cf. Pope, 'Rape of the Lock', iii. 20-2. If Lewis Baboon's classical counterpart is Sisyphus (110: 26-8 n), that of John Bull is Odysseus, wandering over the unresting sea while others devour his substance. But John, like Odysseus in this passage, is compared to a judge when the war of legal jargon ceases. Like a judge too, John has mastered and brought to an end a lawsuit. Finally, as John is often associated with Harley in these pamphlets, it is interesting that at least one contemporary believed the Treasurer's character to be 'much the same with that of the famous *Ulysses* in *Homer*' (*History of Ingratitude*, 1712, p. 35).

120: 8 *John Bull's* Joy was equal to that of either. When a special *Postscript to the Post Boy*, 10 July, announced the occupation of Dunkirk two days previously, 'an universal Joy spread over the Kingdom, this Event being looked on as the certain Forerunner of a Peace' (Swift, *Four Last Years*, vii. 142-3).

120: 12-14 the vast solidity of the Mason's work . . . the Canal. The expansive style of this passage provides a wry comment on the fascination of the public with Britain's new acquisition: '"Tis incredible to relate the strength of the outworks [of the town], which with the addition of Canal Rivulets, and other work renders it the wonder of all that sees it . . . the walls [of the town] are wide enough for 4 or 5 coaches to go a breast . . . the walls are prodigious high built with brick, all surrounded with 4 prodigious wide Ditches at small distances one from the other' (*A Particular Description of the Famous Town and Citadel of Dunkirk with all its Fortifications*, 1712, p. 13).

120: 18 *Hail-stones bounding from a Marble Floor.* We cannot identify this quotation, if indeed, it is a quotation and not a case of misplaced italics.

120: 20 *Nic. Frog*'s **Pensioners** : '*The* Whigs' (*Key*, 6th edn.).

120: 30 **take this Bumper of October :** a pun on the name of the High Tory October Club (15: 18–19 n.).

121: 4–6 **Has old *Lewis* given thee a rap . . . the Butt-end remains in my Hands.** 'Hardly had the Two Confederate Armies been separated a Week, when [on 24 July] the *French* . . . fell with 30000 Men on the Earl of *Albermarle*'s Body of Troops of about 10000, Posted in the Lines of *Denain* . . . to the unspeakable Detriment of the *Common Cause.* There was nothing so shocking to Reasonable Men on this fatal Event, as to see some *English* Papers insult the *Dutch* and Prince *Eugene* upon it' (*History of Utrecht*, p. 376); see also Coombs, pp. 343–4.

121: 8 **what Waggon Loads I am preparing for Market.** Trade with France, particularly in French luxury goods for English manufactured ware, began almost immediately after the cessation of arms: 'ATtend and prepare for a Cargo from *Dover*, / Wine, Silk, Turnips, Onions, with the Peace are come over' (*Merchant a-la-Mode*, bs. 1713).

121: 11 **John Bull'*s* Thanks to Sir Roger.** Harley was elevated to the Peerage as Baron Harley of Wigmore, Herefordshire, Earl of Oxford, and Earl of Mortimer, on 23 May 1711.

121: 11–12 **Nic. Frog'*s* Malediction . . . Shrews, the Original Cause of his Misfortunes.** The play on 'original' again suggests the connection between the Dutch and the Godolphin ministry (the 'shrewish' first wife of John). The trial of Sacheverell and the question of 'original right' (25: 8–10 n.) was one of the 'original causes' of John's return to his senses and hence of Nic.'s misfortunes.

TEXTUAL NOTES

The following list includes all editorial changes to the copy-text and all variants of the 1712 London editions. Although they have no bibliographical authority, we have also included the substantive variants of the 1727, 1731, and 1733 *Miscellanies* texts (i.e. those *Miscellanies* published during Arbuthnot's lifetime signified as 1727–33) and those of the 1712 Edinburgh 'reprints', so that the reader might test for himself our conclusions in the textual introduction on the relative merits of the Edinburgh and *Miscellanies* texts. The sigla used for the 1712 London editions correspond to those of the Bibliographical Appendix below. 1712 E denotes the Edinburgh 'reprints' of each separate pamphlet. Variants cited without sigla are those shared by the *Miscellanies* editions.

11 : 3	*East-India*] and *East-India*
11 : 4	a good Expedient] expedient
11 : 8	Lord] *Om.* 1712E
11 : 12	reduced] reduc'd 1712i
11 : 14	upon] on 1712E
12 : 2	for] For 1712i, E
12 : 5	bubble] babble
12 : 7	Tradesmen] -Tradesmen 1712i, 1727–33
12 : 9	talk'd] talks 1731–33
12 : 11	*Superseda's*] *Supersedeas's*
12 : 12	matter] Matter 1712i, E
13 : 13	Suit] suit 1712i
13 : 19	a little sharply] with more Zeal than Sense
13 : 21	coarse] 1727–33 course 1712a–E
13 : 34	Vertue,] Vertue 1712g–i Virtue 1712E, 1727–33
14 : 5	After this] 1712E And this 1712e–g And then 1712h, i And after this 1727–33
14 : 11	her she smelt so; yet] her: Yet
14 : 15	giv'n] given 1712i
14 : 17	*Signior . . . Quack,*] *some Quacks*
14 : 22–3	then . . . that he] but there were those that bragg'd they
14 : 25	he] they
14 : 27	Signior *Cavallo*'s] *Om.*
14 : 28	stank] stunk 1731–33
14 : 29–15 : 2	Signior . . . Signior] those Quacks, who attended her close, and
15 : 3	him] them
15 : 3–4	says Signior *Cavallo*] said they
15 : 5	my] our
15 : 6	he] they
15 : 7	should] would 1712E
7	that] and that
15 : 8	Signior one Day] one of them
15 : 14	Signior *Cavallo*] the Quack
15 : 15	Signior] The Quack
15 : 24	scrip] Script 1712E
15 : 25	*my*] *the*
15 : 25–32	There . . . *she*] *Om.*
15 : 33	The Daughters] SHE left him three Daughters, whose
16 : 3	being] seeing
16 : 4	nor] or
16 : 10	of . . . Temper, and] saving and
16 : 28	between] betwixt 1712E
17 : 2	Pocket.] Pocket; (*Add.*) observe what a parcel of hungry ragged Fellows live by your Cause, to be sure they will never make an end on't; I foresee this haunt you have got about the Courts will one day or another, bring your Family to Beggary. Consider, my Dear, how indecent it is to abandon your Shop,

and follow Pettifoggers; the habit is so strong upon you, that
there is hardly a Plea between two Country Esquires about
a barren Acre upon a Common, but you draw yourself in as
Bail, Surety or Solicitor.

17: 6   Genius in the World] 1712i, 1727–33   Genins in World
         1712a–h   Genius in World 1712E

6   Lord] Ld. 1712i

17: 9   you say, says] 1712E   you, says 1712a–i   you say, reply'd
         1727–33

17: 11   Reputation] Reputaiton 1712i

17: 26   in short] *Om.*

18: 12   *Hocus*] The Tradesmen, Lawyers

18: 16   *resolved*] *and resolved*

19: 5   sacrific'd:] sacrific'd. 1712i

19: 5–7 sacrific'd . . . *Belzebub*] sacrific'd; The Lawyers, Solicitors,
         Hocus and his Clerks were all up in Arms, at the News of the
         Composition, they abus'd him and his Wife most shamefully

19: 8   Sow you,] Sow, (quoth one)

19: 8–9, 21, 26 my Husband] *Hocus*

19: 30   she] they

20: 10–30 CHAP. XIII] *This whole chapter om.*

20: 31 / FINIS /] *Om.*

25: *Title*] *Om.*

25: 1   I] XIII

25: 17   she *Om.*

27: 2   Queen] Quean 1712a–i, 1727

27: 26   deduce] 1712a: 1, 2   bring 1712a: 3–E, 1727–33

28: 1   II] XIV

28: 7   yielded] 1712a: 2–E, 1727–33   yeilded 1712a: 1

28: 24   III] II 1712a–i   XV 1727–33

28: 26   Dismallo] *Om.*

28: 27   *Don Diego*] *Preceding add.* THE Lawyers, as their last effort
         to put off the Composition, sent *Don Diego* to *John*. *Don
         Diego* was a very worthy Gentleman, a Friend to *John*, his
         Mother, and present Wife; and therefore suppos'd to have
         some Influence over her: He had been ill us'd himself, by
         John's Lawyers, but because of some animosity to Sir *Roger*,
         was against the Composition: The Conference between him
         and Mrs. *Bull* was Word for Word, as follows.

29: 24   plain] *Om.*

29: 25   one, that] one; says 1727   one; says, 1731–33

29: 26   deal] deal of

29: 29   Woollen-drapers.] *Add.* Besides Esquire *South* will be Esquire
         South still; fickle, proud, and ungrateful. If he behaves himself
         so when he depends on us for his daily Bread, can any Man
         say what he will do, when he is got above the World?

30: 26   Man] 1712E, 1727–33   Men 1712 a–i

31: 3   I have] *Om.*

31: 4   that] *Om.*
32: 28   *Coarse*] 1731–33   *Course* 1712a–E, 1727
33: 3   Composition] 1727–33   Competition 1712a–E
33: 5   ] *Square brackets in the copy-text*
33: 27   too] *Om.* 1712E
33: 30   thing] 1712E, 1727–33   think 1712a–i
34: 7   damnable] damnably 1733
34: 12   IV] XVI
34: 17   my first Part] a former Chapter
35: 10   born] *Om.*
35: 22   Gruel] 1727–33   Cruel 1712a–E
36: 1   *Paul's*] St. *Paul's*
36: 29   hop'd] hope
37: 4   God] God's
37: 12   Friend] better Friend 1712E
37: 14   than] as
37: 18   thing, and no] thing; no
37: 19   therefore] then
38: 5   that] *Om.*
     5   of] *Om.*
38: 9–14   ; never . . . Sinking] *Om.*
38: 21   was] *Om.* 1727–31   is 1733
38: 35   another] other
39: 6   Thoughts] Thought
39: 14   him.] *Add.* One tells me that I must carry on my Suit, because
           Lewis is poor; another, because he is still too rich: whom
           shall I believe? I am sure of one thing, that a Penny in the
           Purse is the best Friend *John* can have at last, and who can
           say that this will be the last Suit I shall be engag'd in.
     14   If it] Besides, if this Ejectment
39: 32   very small] the small
40: 1   V] XVII
40: 7   would] should
40: 18   Loyal] *Om.*
40: 28   *wants*] *want*
41: 9   Third] Second
41: 11   Mrs.] 1712E, 1727–33   Mrs 1712a–i
41: 12   Counsel] Council
41: *FINIS. |*] *Om.*
47: *Title*] *Preceding, a new title-page: Law is a Bottomless Pit. || OR,
           THE | HISTORY | OF | JOHN BULL. || THE | SECOND
           PART. || MDCCXIII.*
47: 5   retails] retales 1731–33
47: 12   two first Parts had met,] first Part had met with;
47: 14   yet they were] it was yet
47: 16   little] *Om.*
47: 23   two former Parts] former Part
49: 21   her] the 1712b: 2–f

51: 11   (2.) *Jack*] *n.p.* [*Jack*
51: 14   (3.) *Jack*] *n.p.* [*Jack*
51: 17   in] on
51: 26   (4.) *Jack*] *n.p.* [*Jack*
51: 28   (5.) *Jack*] *n.p.* [*Jack*
51: 29   sole] sold 1712E
52: 2   (6.) I] *n.p.* [I
52: 5   tho'] tho' he was
52: 12   Choul,] Jole;
52: 15   was] mus 1712e–f
52: 18   talk] talk of
53: 4   Chimeras] Chimera's 1712a–E, 1727–33
53: 5   and] *Om.*
53: 6   Fleas] 1712E, 1727–33   Flea's 1712a–f
53: 7   you] *Om.*
53: 13   no] not
53: 22   young Ladies in their] a young Lady in her
53: 23   them, the worse they are] her, the worse she is
54: 3   poor] *Om.*
54: 23   *Nic.*] 1712E, 1727–33   *Nic* 1712a–f
55: 1   than] than for
     1   Writs] 1712E, 1727–33   Weits 1712a–f
55: 12   silly] *Om.*
55: 14   enough] 1712E, 1727–33   enongh 1712a–f
55: 18   auld] old
55: 20   auld warld] old-world
55: 27   were] was
56: 7   extremely, for] extremely at
56: 13   carried] carry 1731–33
56: 15   , that] , which
57: 6   some] *Om.*
57: 10   too] se 1727   so 1731–33
58: 18   *Baboon, it is the cheatingest*] *Baboon*: He is the most cheat-
             ing,
58: 20   *Nic.*] 1712E, 1727–33   *Nic* 1712a–f
58: 22   *Nic.*] 1727–33   *Nic* 1712a–E
58: 21   Knave] Fellow
59: 4   *Strutt's*] 1727–33   *Strut's* 1712a–E
59: 6   *Nic.*] 1712E, 1727–33   *Nic* 1712a–f
60: 14   how] how how 1712a: 1, 3
61: 19   Esquire] Esq; 1712a: 3, 4, E
61: 20–3   *Lewis . . . know.*] *Om.*
61: 20   that] *Om.* 1712a: 1, 2
62: 1   that] *Om.*
62: 14   *God-sake*] *God's sake* 1731–33
62: 20   Poll] Staff
63: 16   Credit] Credits
63: 17–18   Bond, only . . . Scriveners;] Bond. Only . . . Scriveners,

63: 31   especially,] especially 1712e: 2, f, 1727–33
65: 6   that] which
65: 31   brought] and brought
66: 3   hooping] whooping 1731–33
66: 34   randy] *Om.*
67: 5   out] *Om.*
67: 7   Dover] Dover-*street* 1727   Dover street 1731–33
67: 17   and] *Om.*
67: 25   *without*] *unless*
67: 32   was] were
68: 4   that] but
68: 20   that] *Om.*
68: 22   that] while
68: 30   dis] 1712E   this 1712a–f, 1727–33
68: 30, 31 de] 1712E   the 1712a–f, 1727–33
69: 15–16] *Square brackets here and throughout this letter in the copy-text*
69: 19   begins] begin'st 1727   beginn'st 1731–33
70: 2   *thy*] *thine* 1712E
70: 19   gets] get
71: 28, 30–1, 32 *John Bull*] *Om.*
72: 3, 6, 9, 12, 15 *Bull.*] *Bull.*]
72: 10, 13, 16 *Nic.*] 1712E, 1727–33   *Nic* 1712a–f
73: 20–5   I could . . . *FINIS.*] *Om.*
77: *Title*] *Om.*
77: 1   I] XI
77: 4–5   in my last Part,] *Om.*
78: 6   did they find] they found
78: 15   religious] *Om.*
79: 2   another] other
79: 22   if] but if
79: 23   as] as if
79: 28   blue;] blue 1712d–f   blue, 1712E
    28   into] inta 1712d–f
79: 33   that] *Om.*
80: 8   Hearts,] 1727–33   Hearts. 1712a–E
80: 14, 18 That the] The
80: 28   that] and
81: 2   in] *Om.*
81: 3   once he was] he was once
81: 4   asleep] 1727–33   a sleep 1712a–E
81: 7   the] his
81: 15   II] XII
81: 29   laying] for laying
82: 16   *Dismallo*] *Om.*
82: 23   that they] they
82: 24   Bier] 1727–33   Beir 1712a–E
82: 25   that] *Om.*
82: 27   had] *Om.*

83: 3–4   that important] so important an
83: 13   *Don*] Don. 1712d–f
    13   it] *Om.* 1712d–f
83: 23   would] wouldst
83: 34   imagines] imaginest
84: 10   III] XIII
85: 2   Is it possible] It is impossible 1712E
85: 10   made] and made
85: 20   measur'd] he measur'd
85: 31   hast] 1712E, 1727–33   hast hast 1712a–f
86: 25   *Habakkuk*] 1712E, 1727–33   *Habakuk* 1712a–f
87: 11   both] *Om.*
87: 18   is] was 1712E
87: 22   Dead] to be dead
87: 24   IV] XIV
87: 25   Dismallo] *Om.*
88: 30   Canibal's] 1712a: 1, 1727–33   Cannibal's 1712a: 2–f
           Cabinal's 1712E
89: 1   and] *Om.*
89: 4   *FINIS*] *Om.*
93: THE PREFACE] *Used as the general preface to the bi-partite*
           'History of John Bull': *roman and italic inverted throughout in*
           1712b
93: 4   *Humphry*] *Humphry Polesworth*
93: 22   *endeavour'd*] *have endeavour'd*
93: 24   *Imitation; but*] Imitation. But 1712b
94: 3   *Money*] Mony 1712b
94: 15   Grubstreet] *Grub-street* 1712b
94: 16   *Downfall*] Downfal 1712b   Downfal 1727–33
94: 18   *sung*] *didst sing*
94: 24   *Queens*] Queen's 1712b
94: 25   *retails*] *retales*
94: 28   *Damsels,*] -Damsels, 1712b   *Damsels*; 1727–33
94: 29   *intermingles*] *interminglest*
94: 32   *Tale*] *Tail* 1712E, 1727–33
94: 34   *the Intrigues*] *Intrigues*
95: 4   *recorded*] *didst record*
95: 6   *Attitudes*] 1727–33   *Altitudes* 1712a, E   Attitudes 1712b
95: 9   *Adieu*] Adieu, 1712b
95: 10–11 *to* Burleigh on the Hill:] *for ever!*
95: 13   *this*] *the* 1712E
95: 19   there.] *in those Universities.* (*Add.*) AND *now, that Posterity*
           may not be ignorant in what Age so excellent a History was
           written (*which would otherwise, no doubt, be the subject of its*
           enquiries) *I think it proper to inform the Learned of future times,*
           that it was compiled when Lewis *the* XIV*th was King of* France,
           and Philip *his Grandson of* Spain, *when* England *and* Holland,
           in conjunction with the Emperor *and the* Allies, *enter'd into a*

War against these two Princes, which lasted Ten Years, under the Management *of the Duke of* Marlborough, *and was put to a Conclusion by the Treaty of* Utrecht, *under the Ministry of the Earl of* Oxford, *in the Year* 1713.

MANY *at that time did imagine the History of* John Bull, *and the Personages mention'd in it, to be* Allegorical, *which the Author would never own. Notwithstanding, to indulge the Readers Fancy and Curiosity, I have printed at the bottom of the Page the* suppos'd *Allusions of the most obscure Parts of the Story.*

99: Title]	*Om.*
99: 1	I] XV
99: 2	*the History of*] *Om.*
99: 10	*doux*] 1727–33 *deux* 1712a–E
99: 15	*thee*] *the* 1712E
100: 6	Back,] Back and
100: 25	*Nic.* (quoth I)?] *Nic.* (quoth I?) 1712a–E *Nic.?* (quoth I) 1727–33
101: 11–12	While ... Protestation] *Within the preceding quotation marks,* 1712a–E
102: 7	Brother;] Brother. 1712b
102: 9	Kitchen;] Kitchen. 1712
102: 23	II] XVI
103: 18–35	] *Columns of figures om.*
103: 19–21	Fees ... puny Judges] For the *Expences ordinary* of the Suits, Fees to Judges, puny Judges, Lawyers innumerable of all sorts ------------------------------- Of *Extraordinaries,* as follows *per* Accompt ---------------------
103: 22	*South*] *South's* Accompt
103: 24	for ... *prosequi*] for *Noli Prosequi's, Discontinuance*
103: 26	To ... *Diem*] For Writs of Error --------------------- Suits of *Conditions unperform'd* ------------
103: 27	a] *Om.*
103: 28	To ... *Devastavit*] *Om.*
103: 29–30	Carry ... Brought over -----] *Om.*
103: 33	*querelas*] *querela's* 1712b, 1727–33
103: 35	*Destringas*] *Distringas* 1712b
104: 1–29	] *Columns of figures om.*
104: 6	To ... *Defecit*] *Om.*
104: 9–12	Sum ... *Frog*] *John* having read over his Articles, with the respective Summs, brought in *Frog* Debtor to him upon the Ballance ----- / 3382 – 12 – 00
104: 15	Account,] Account. (*Add.*) Paid by *Nic. Frog* for his Share of the *ordinary Expences* of the Suit
104: 27–9	Sum ... 06] And summing all up, found due upon the Ballance by / *John Bull* to *Nic. Frog* ----- 09 – 04 – 06.
104: 33	Family] Family- 1712b

105: 6–7   Service. / To] Service. To 1712b
105: 16   thou, it] thou? It 1712b, 1727
105: 16–17   time, when] time; when 1712b   Time. When 1727–33
105: 19   retains] retainst 1712b   retain'st 1727   retainest 1727–33
105: 21   Expence,] Expences;
105: 24–5   gets . . . spends] getst . . . spends 1712b   get'st . . . spendest
             1727–33
105: 29   whither] whether 1712E, 1727–33
     29   are] art
105: 31   *Lent.*] *Add.* Dost think that *John Bull* will be try'd by
             Pypowders?
106: 1   you] thee
     1   that] *Om.*
106: 2   another.] another: (*Add.*) Let it never be said that that the
             famous *John Bull* has departed in despite of Court.
                  J. Bull. And will it not reflect as much on thy Character,
             Nic. to turn Barreter in thy old Days; a stirrer up of Quarrels
             amongst thy Neighbours? I tell thee *Nic.* some time or other
             thou wilt repent this.
106: 3   *John*] BUT *John*
106: 11   Figure] Figure, 1712b, 1727–33
106: 12   Gratitude, if] Gratitude; if 1712b   Gratitude: If 1727–33
106: 13   wants] wantest
106: 14   *John*] *John,* 1712b
     14   self.] 1712b, 1727–33   self? 1712a
106: 23   III] XVII
106: 30   extravagantest] most extravagant
107: 3   Parish Boy] *Parish Boy* 1712b   *Parish-Boy* 1727–33
107: 7   Dinner,] Dinner. 1712b   Dinner; 1727–33
107: 9   Forsooth] forsooth 1712b   *Om.* 1727–33
107: 10   mad] mad, 1712b, 1727–33
107: 11   Dinner:] Dinner. 1712b
107: 12   whither] whether 1712E, 1727–33
107: 13   Heir?] Heir. 1712b
107: 16   whither] whether 1712E, 1727–33
107: 24   d'ye see,] *Om.*
     24   Ducks:] Ducks. 1712b   *Ducks.* 1727–33
107: 29, 31 *Nicholas*] 1727–33   *Nicolas* 1712a–E
107: 37   Amazing] Amazing. 1712b, 1727–33
108: 5   Possession,] Possession; 1712b
108: 10   enquires] enquired
     10   *Nic.*] 1712E, 1727–33   *Nic* 1712a–b
108: 11   not] *Om.*
108: 14–16   of . . . Room] another Friend of *John*'s accosted him after the
             following manner
108: 17   *D. Diego.* Since] SINCE
108: 19   whither] whether 1712E, 1727–33
108: 22   means,] means; 1712b

108: 22–3   they . . . me] I understand them all alike 1712b
108: 24   *D. Diego.*] *Friend.*
     24   that are] who are 1712b
109: 1   And . . . say] *Use of roman and italic inverted,* 1712b
     1   say; with] *say?* With 1712b   say. / With 1727–33
109: 13   IV] XVIII
109: 16–18   Think . . . *Grubstreet*] *Use of roman and italic inverted,* 1712b
109: 19   that was] *Om.*
109: 29   *John*] As *John* 1712b
110: 2   a cunning] cunning a
110: 6   uncivil,] uncivil; 1712b
110: 10   Scars] Scar 1712b, 1727–33
110: 20   resist,] resist. 1712b   resist; 1727–33
111: 31   *Strutt*] 1712E, 1727–33   *Strut* 1712a–b
112: 18   Plantiffs] Plaintiffs
112: 19   V] XIX
113: 11   Servant] *Servants*
113: 35   My Shirt . . . nearer] *Italic,* 1712b, 1727
114: 11   VI] XX
114: 14 ⎫
116: 6 ⎭   *Ecclesdown*] 1727–33   *Ecclesdoun* 1712a–b   *Ecclesdun* 1712E
116: 9   for *Us,*] for *Us;* 1712b
116: 15   another:] another. 1712b
116: 23   *Ecclesdown*] 1727–33   *Ecclesdoun* 1712a–b   *Ecclesdun* 1712E
116: 33   Fact,] Fact; 1712b
117: 9   shall] should
117: 12   *Ecclesdown*] 1727–33   *Ecclesdoun* 1712a–b   *Ecclesdun* 1712E
117: 16   VII] XXI
117: 17   Ecclesdown]   1727–33   Ecclesdoun   1712a–b   Ecclesdun
             1712E
117: 25   Sneaker-snee] *Sneaker-snee* 1712b   Snicker-snee 1727–33
117: 26–7   Thrice . . . Air] 1727–33: *within the following quotation marks,*
             1712a–E
118: 5–11   Art . . . Teeth] *Use of roman and italic inverted,* 1712b:
             within quotation marks, 1727–33
118: 6   *Ecclesdown*] 1727–33   *Ecclesdoun* 1712a   Ecclesdoun 1712b
             Ecclesdun 1712E
118: 8   the] thy
118: 9   I'd] I'd had 1712E
     9   than] *then* 1712b
118: 9–10   thou hearkens] thy hearkenst 1727   thou hearkenest 1731–33
118: 16   *Nic.*] 1712E, 1727–33   *Nic* 1712a–b
118: 17   falls] and fell
118: 18   Cudgel] *Cudgel* 1712b
     18   Cudgel . . . Hand] *Italic,* 1727–33
     18   Thwack] thwack 1712b
118: 23   side,] side; 1712b, 1727–33
     23   see-sawing] *see-sawing* 1712b

118: 28   yet] yet would
118: 29   contranitent] contrary
118: 32, 119: 17, 24, 26 *Nic.*] 1712E, 1727–33   *Nic* 1712a–b
119: 29   *Nic.*] 1727–33   *Nic* 1712a–E
119: 24, 33 *Ecclesdown*] 1727–33   *Ecclesdoun* 1712a–b   *Ecclesdun* 1712E
119: 31–2   *Buy, buy . . . Buy*] *B'y, b'y . . . B'y* 1712a–b   *B'uy, b'uy . . . B'uy* 1727–33
120: 1   VIII] XXII
120: 2–3   Ecclesdown] 1727–33   Ecclesdoun 1712a–b   Ecclesdun 1712E
120: 6–7   was . . . Bench] *Italic,* 1712b
120: 20   *Nic.*] 1712E, 1727–33   *Nic* 1712a–b
120: 22   *Ecclesdown*] 1727–33   *Ecclesdoun* 1712a–b   *Ecclesdun* 1712E
120: 33   *Nic.*] 1727–33   *Nic* 1712a–E
120: 34   d'ye do] do's ye do, 1712b
121: 4   Finger-ends] Knuckles 1712b
121: 10   buy] b'y 1712b   B'uy 1727–33
121: 11–13 *Om.*
121: 11   Nic.] 1712E   Nic 1712a–b
121: 14   / *FINIS.*] *Om.*

The following postscript was appended to the text, 1727–33 (text of the 1727 *Miscellanies* edition).

POSTSCRIPT.

It has been disputed amongst the *Literati* of *Grubstreet*, whether Sir *Humphrey* proceeded any farther in the History of *John Bull*. By diligent Inquiry we have found the Titles of some Chapters, which appear to be a Continuation of it; and are as follow:

Chap. I. *How John was made Angry with the* Articles of Agreement. *How he kick'd the Parchment through the House, up Stairs and down Stairs, and put himself in a great Heat thereby.*

Ch. II. *How in his Passion he was going to cut off Sir* Roger's *Head with a* Cleaver. *Of the strange manner of Sir* Roger's *Escaping the Blow, by* laying his Head upon the Dresser.

Ch. III. *How some of* John's *Servants attempted to scale his House with Rope-Ladders; and how many unfortunately dangled in the same.*

Ch. IV. *Of the Methods by which* John *endeavour'd to preserve the Peace amongst his Neighbours: How he kept a pair of* Stillyards *to weigh them; and by Diet, Purging, Vomiting, and Bleeding, try'd to bring them to* equal Bulk *and* Strength.

Ch. V. *Of false Accounts of the* Weights *given in by some of the* Journeymen; *and of the* New-market *Tricks, that were practic'd at the Stillyards.*

Ch. VI. *How* John's *new Journeymen brought him other-guess Accounts of the Stillyards.*

Ch. VII. *How Sir* * Swain Northy *was by Bleeding, Purging, and a Steel-Diet brought into a* Consumption; *and how* John *was forc'd afterwards to give him the* Gold Cordial.

Ch. VIII. *How* † Peter Bear *was over-fed, and afterwards refus'd to submit to the Course of Physick.*

Ch. IX. *How* John *pamper'd Esquire* South *with Tit-bits, till he grew wanton; how he got drunk with Calabrian Wine, and long'd for* Sicilian *Beef, and how* John *carried him thither in his Barge.*

Ch. X. *How the Esq; from a foul-feeder grew dainty: Now he long'd for* Mangos, Spices, *and* Indian Birds-Nests, *&c. and could not sleep but in a* Chince Bed.

Ch. XI. *The Esq; turn'd Tradesman; how he set up a* ‡ China-Shop *over-against* Nic. Frog.

Ch. XII. *How he procur'd* Spanish Flies *to blister his Neighbours, and as a Provocative to himself. As likewise how he Ravish'd* Nic. Frog's *favourite* Daughter.

Ch. XIII. *How* Nic. Frog *hearing the Girl squeak, went to call* John Bull *as a* Constable: *Calling a Constable no preventive of a Rape.*

Ch. XIV. *How* John *rose out of his Bed in a cold Morning to prevent a Dual between Esq;* South *and Lord* Strutt; *how, to his great surprise, he found the Combatants drinking* Genever *in a* Brandy-Shop, *with* Nic's *favourite Daughter between them. How they both fell upon* John, *so that he was forced to fight his way out.*

Ch. XV. *How* John *came with his Constable's Staff to rescue* Nic's *Daughter, and break the Esquires* China-Ware.

Ch. XVI. *Commentary upon the* Spanish *Proverb,* Time and I against any two; *or Advice to dogmatical Politicians, exemplify'd in some new Affairs between* John Bull *and* Lewis Baboon.

Ch. XVII. *A Discourse of the delightful Game of* Quadrille. *How* Lewis Baboon *attempted to play a Game* Solo *in Clubs, and was beasted: How* John *call'd* Lewis *for his King, and was afraid that his own Partner should have too many Tricks: And how the success and skill of Quadrille depends upon calling a right King.*

FINIS.

This postscript was followed by 'The Contents', in two parts, Chapters I–XVII and I–XXII (plus postscript), composed of the chapter headings listed in succession.

* K[ing]. of *Sw*[ed]*en.* † *Cz*[ar]. of *M*[uscov]*y.*
‡ The *O*[ste]*nd* Company.

BIBLIOGRAPHICAL APPENDIX

COLLATION of the 1712 London editions of the pamphlets from notes but without recourse to the Hinman collator was sufficient to establish the copy-text and to reveal the relatively few variants. An exhaustive collation of the widely scattered holdings in the major British and American libraries would have presented considerable difficulties and was not immediately relevant to our concerns. In consequence our printing history has no claim to final bibliographical authority and does not include reference to any but the most obvious distinguishing features of editions and reimpressions. We offer it as an incomplete record of the way in which *John Bull* went through the press.

LOCATION SIGLA

Bower	Personal copies
CT	Rothschild Library, Trinity College, Cambridge
E	National Library of Scotland
EU	University of Edinburgh
L	British Museum
LL	London Library
LUC	University College, London
LVA–F	Victoria and Albert Museum, Forster Collection
O	Bodleian Library
UL	University of Leeds, Brotherton Collection
CLU-C	Clark Library, Los Angeles
CSmH	Huntington Library, San Marino
CtY	Yale University
Lewis	Wilmarth S. Lewis Walpole Collection, Farmington
MB	Boston Public Library
MH	Harvard University
NN	New York Public Library
PR	Rosenbach Foundation, Philadelphia
PU	University of Pennsylvania

We have noted press marks whenever they were necessary (and available) to distinguish the reimpressions within any 'edition' among the copies owned by the same library.

PAMPHLET I

1712 a [Within a double rule] LAW / IS A / Bottomless-Pit. / Exemplify'd in the CASE of / The Lord *Strutt, John Bull,* / *Nicholas Frog,* and *Lewis Baboon.* / Who spent all they had in a Law-Suit. // *Printed from a Manuscript found in the Cabinet* / *of the famous Sir* Humphry Polesworth. // *LONDON*: / Printed for *John Morphew*, near *Stationer's-* / *Hall*, 1712. Price 3*d*.

8° (in half sheets): [A] B–C⁴, 12 leaves; pp. [1–4], 5–24; $2 signed.

Contents; p. [1] title (verso blank); [3–4] THE CONTENTS; 5–24 text.

Publication date: Advertised In *PB* for 4 March. Copyright was entered in the Stationers' Register to John Darby on 20 March.

Copies: L LUC O CLU–C CtY (2 copies) MB MH PU Bower

1712 b [as preceding except] Polesworth. // 𝕿𝖍𝖊 𝕾𝖊𝖈𝖔𝖓𝖉 𝕰𝖉𝖎𝖙𝖎𝖔𝖓. // . . .

Page numbers are as preceding except 19 as 91. A reimpression in which the rule above 'FINIS' on page 24 is removed and that word and its rule moved upwards to make space for an advertisement: 'On *Tuesday* next [i.e. 18 March] will be Publish'd, *JOHN BULL* in his Senses'.

Publication date: From the preceding, in the week beginning 10 March

Copies: E (2 copies) EU L (2 copies) O CtY NN PU

1712 c [as preceding except] Polesworth. // 𝕿𝖍𝖊 𝕿𝖍𝖎𝖗𝖉 𝕰𝖉𝖎𝖙𝖎𝖔𝖓. // . . .

Page 19 correctly numbered. A reimpression with pages 5 and 6 reset (the last line of the latter page transferred to the head of page 7) and a new advertisement for several works on page 24. One MH copy (* EC 7 Ar 197 712lc) is paginated sequentially but its gatherings are incorrectly ordered.

Publication date: Before 26 April (*Plain Dealer*).

Copies: EU LVA–F O MH (2 copies) Lewis

1712 d [as preceding except] Polesworth. // 𝕿𝖍𝖊 𝕱𝖔𝖚𝖗𝖙𝖍 𝕰𝖉𝖎𝖙𝖎𝖔𝖓. // . . .

Pagination (5)[6](7)[8](9)–(24). A reimpression with reset rules on page [3] and the order of advertisements on page 24 altered.

Copy: O (Rad. f. 154)

1712 e [as preceding]

A hidden reimpression with some resetting on page 15 line 29 (where 'And then' replaces the 'After this' of preceding impressions) and in a catch word correction on page 16.

Copies: NN PU (* 50–42)

1712 f [as preceding]

Pagination [5][6](7)[8][9](10)[11][12](13)(14)[15](16)–(23)(42)[for 24]. Another hidden reimpression with, on page 19, a change in the positional relationship of signature to text which also characterizes the following impression.

Copies: CSmH CtY (Ik W125 712) PU

1712 g [as preceding except] *LONDON*, . . . [as opposed to *LONDON*: . . . in preceding impressions].

Page 24 correctly numbered: [5](6)–(8)[9](10)[11][12](13)(14) [15](16)–(24). Another hidden reimpression with a single replacing the double rule of preceding impressions on page 5. Page 15 and the last lines of pages 16 and 18 are reset as are the advertisements on page 24.

Copies: E L (3 copies) O (GP. 1145) UL CtY (By 50 A3) MH

1712 h [as preceding]

This is the missing 'fifth edition'. Pagination (5)–(8)[9]–[13](14) [15][16](17)–(24). The advertisements on page 24 are again reset, and there are distinctive correspondences between this further hidden reimpression within the 'fourth edition' and the 'sixth edition' below in the accidental omission of a colon on page 6 line 2 and in the correction of 'And this' (*1712 e–g*) to 'And then' on page 15 line 29.

Copies: L (104 a. 77) LL CtY (C.P. v. 1461) MB (2 copies)

1712 i [as preceding except] Polesworth. // 𝕿𝖍𝖊 𝕾𝖎𝖝𝖙𝖍 𝕰𝖉𝖎𝖙𝖎𝖔𝖓. // . . .

A new edition with wholesale resetting and a number of textual changes.

Copies: E LVA–F O MB PR PU

PAMPHLET II

1712 a [Within a double rule] JOHN BULL / In His SENSES: / BEING THE / SECOND PART / OF / *Law is a Bottomless-Pit.* // *Printed from a Manuscript found in the Cabinet* / *of the famous Sir* Humphry Polesworth. // [ornament] // *LONDON*: / Printed for *John Morphew*, near *Stationer's-* / *Hall*, 1712. Price 3*d*.

8° (in half sheets): [A]B–C⁴, 12 leaves; pp. [1–4], 5–24; $ 2 signed.

Contents: p. [1] title (verso blank); [3–4] THE CONTENTS; 5–24 (upper half) text, (lower half) advertisement.

Pages 8 and 24 exist in variant states. In the PU copy the lower half of 24 is blank, but all other copies have an advertisement for several works, including the 'second edition' of pamphlet I. The page 8 variants are:

1. deduce (line 9)   yeilded (line 21)
2. deduce   yielded
3. bring   yielded

None of these variant pages shows any further evidence of resetting and none is a cancel. The first state was probably 1, corrected to 2 and finally 3 during the course of printing.

Publication date: On 17 March Swift wrote that it was 'just now printed' (*Journal*, p. 516). See also *PB* 18 March. Copyright was entered to John Barber on 20 March.

Copies: 1. L
   2. O MH
   3. CT EU MB PU

1712 b [as preceding except] Polesworth. // 𝕿𝖍𝖊 𝕾𝖊𝖈𝖔𝖓𝖉 𝕰𝖉𝖎𝖙𝖎𝖔𝖓. // . . .
A reimpression of state 3 of the preceding.
Copies: E (2 copies) EU L (2 copies) CLU–C CtY MH NN PU Bower

1712 c [as preceding except] Polesworth. // 𝕿𝖍𝖊 𝕿𝖍𝖎𝖗𝖉 𝕰𝖉𝖎𝖙𝖎𝖔𝖓. // . . .
A reimpression with a reset advertisement on page 24 (e.g. for the seventh as opposed to the sixth edition of *The Conduct of the Allies* advertised in preceding impressions). The most distinguishing feature of this impression is a sequence of pagination (5)–(19)[20 and 21 omitted](22)–(26).
Copies: LVA–F O (3 copies) Lewis MH (* EC 7 Ar 197 712 jc)

1712 d [as preceding]
Sequence of pagination corrected: (5)–(16)[17]–[23](24).
A hidden reimpression within the 'third edition'.
Copies: E (H. 34 f. 1) L (C. 108 bbb. 37) CSmh NN PU

1712 e [as preceding]
Pagination (5)[6](7)[8](9)–(16)[17]–[23](24). Another hidden reimpression in which the damaged numeral in the pagination of page 6 is replaced.
Copies: E (2. 87) L (G. 2233) CtY (Ik W125 712) MH (*EC 7 197 712 jca)

1712 f [as preceding except] LONDON, . . . [as opposed to LONDON: . . . in preceding impressions].
Pagination (5)–(12)[13](14)–(24). A further hidden reimpression in which 'THE CONTENTS' of page [3] is misprinted as 'THE COTNENTS'.
Copies: L (104 a. 78) LL CtY (C.P. v. 1461) MB

1712 g [as preceding except] Polesworth. // 𝕿𝖍𝖊 𝕱𝖔𝖚𝖗𝖙𝖍 𝕰𝖉𝖎𝖙𝖎𝖔𝖓 = // . . .
Pagination as preceding. A reimpression in which there is some disturbance of the type on pages 4, 9 (where the positional

relationship of signature to text changes), and 16. The rules on pages 5 and 24 are also changed, and the misprint on page [3] is corrected.

Copies: LVA–F PR PU (EC 7 Ar 195 7121 f)

1712 h [as preceding except] 𝕱𝖔𝖚𝖗𝖙𝖍 𝕰𝖉𝖎𝖙𝖎𝖔𝖓. . . . [as opposed to 𝕱𝖔𝖚𝖗𝖙𝖍 𝕰𝖉𝖎𝖙𝖎𝖔𝖓 = . . . of the preceding impression].

Pagination [5][6](7)[8](9)–(16)[17]–[23](24). A hidden reimpression within the 'fourth edition'.

Copies: L O (2 copies) UL CSmH CtY (3 copies) MB MH PU (EC 7 Ar 195 712jd)

PAMPHLET III

1712 a [Within a double rule] JOHN BULL / Still / In His SENSES: / BEING THE / THIRD PART / OF / *Law is a Bottomless-Pit*. // Printed from a Manuscript found in the / Cabinet of the famous Sir *Humphry* / *Polesworth*: And Publish'd, (as well / as the two former Parts) by the Au- / thor of the NEW ATALANTIS. /// *LONDON*: / Printed for *John Morphew*, near *Stationer's-* / *Hall*, 1712. Price 6*d*.

8° (in half sheets): [A] B–F⁴, 24 leaves; pp. [1]–[4], 5–47, [48]; $ 2 signed.

Contents: p. [1] title (verso blank); [3]–[4] THE CONTENTS; 5–6 (top quarter) The Publisher's PREFACE; 6 (bottom three-quarters)–47 text; [48] advertisement for several works.

Pages 25 and 27 exist in variant states:

(*a*) In the uncorrected state of 25 the last word of the last line 'how' (and the catchword 'will') are repeated on page 26: in the corrected state 'how' is removed from the text to become the correct catchword.

(*b*) In the uncorrected state of 27 the catchword 'that' is not carried over to 28: in the corrected state 'that' is accommodated in the last line of 27 by the resetting of the last two lines (particularly the contraction of 'Esquire' to 'Esq;') and 'call'd' becomes the correct catchword.

Among the 20 copies consulted were 4 permutations on these:

    1. (*a*) and (*b*) uncorrected
    2. (*a*) corrected (*b*) uncorrected
    3. (*a*) uncorrected (*b*) corrected
    4. (*a*) and (*b*) corrected.

As these seem to be the only variants (of any kind) it would appear that the compositor or compositors made erratic correcttions during the course of impression.

Publication date: Advertised in both *PB* and *PM* for 16 April and entered in the Stationers' Register twice, once on the date

of publication to John Barber, and again on 13 May by Barber
to John Morphew.

Copies: 1. L (T. 2074) MB (* Defoe A8J2)
      2. CT E (2 copies) EU (2 copies) L (T. 1107)
         LVA–F O (3 copies) CLU–C CtY MH Bower
      3. PU (* 50–42) Lewis
      4. CSmH MB (* Defoe A8J2a) PU (EC 7 Ar 195 712j2)

1712 b [as preceding except] ATALANTIS. // 𝕿𝖍𝖊 𝕾𝖊𝖈𝖔𝖓𝖉 𝕰𝖉𝖎𝖙𝖎𝖔𝖓. // . . .

The pagination of *1712 a*, [5]–[15](16)–(24)[25](26)–(40)[41]–
[47], is regularized in this reimpression of state 4 of the preceding
to the sequence (5)–(24)[25](26)–(47). The type shows some
disturbance on page [3] where the signature A2 is introduced,
and there is a second state of page 9 in the CtY copy where the
last word of the first line is changed from 'her' to 'the' (the reading followed by subsequent impressions).

Publication date: Advertised in both *PB* and *EP* for 24 April.

Copies: L CtY MH

1712 c [as preceding except] ATALANTIS. // 𝕿𝖍𝖊 𝕿𝖍𝖎𝖗𝖉 𝕰𝖉𝖎𝖙𝖎𝖔𝖓. // . . .

Pagination as preceding. A reimpression with new rules substituted on pages [3] and 5 (on which page they are distinctively
broken). There is also evidence of some resetting at the head of
page [3] where the definite article of 'THE CONTENTS' is
in smaller caps.

Copies: E L O CtY (3 copies) MH NN (C 1 pv. 114) PU

1712 d [as preceding]

Pagination (5)–(8)[9]–[15](16)–(24)[25](26)–(47). A hidden reimpression within the 'third edition'.

Copy: NN (* C pv. 662)

1712 e [as preceding except] *LONDON*, . . . [as opposed to *LONDON*:
. . . in preceding impressions].

Pagination (5)–(16)[17]–[21](22)[23][24](25)–(47). Another hidden reimpression in which new rules are again substituted on
page [3] (where they are now broken) and on page 5 (where
the damaged rules of *1712 c* and *d* are replaced). On page
13 line 16 'was' is printed as 'mus'. The word occurs at the
beginning of the line and was therefore vulnerable in any minor
accident to the type pages. Perhaps it was pulled out during inking
or lost from the loosely tied-up page and replaced carelessly.

    Page 31 exists in two variant states, the first of which retains
the comma after 'especially' on line 26 and a second in which
the line is reset and the comma omitted.

Copies: 1. E L LL LVA–F PR
      2. CSmH MB PU

1712 f [as preceding except] ATALANTIS. // 𝕿𝖍𝖊 𝖋𝖔𝖚𝖗𝖙𝖍 𝕰𝖉𝖎𝖙𝖎𝖔𝖓. // ...

Pagination (5)–(16)[17]–[21](22)[23]–[25](26)–(47). A reimpression with new rules again substituted on pages [1], [3], and 5, but with 'mus' for 'was' again on page 13 and the comma again omitted on page 31.

Publication date: Probably before 26 April when *PPB* attacked this pamphlet, 'usher'd into the World by four Impressions'.

Copies: L CSmH NN

PAMPHLET IV

1712 a [Within a double rule] AN / APPENDIX / TO / JOHN BULL / Still / In His SENSES: / OR, / *Law is a Bottomless-Pit.* // Printed from a Manuscript found in the / Cabinet of the famous Sir *Humphry / Polesworth*: And Publish'd, (as well / as the three former Parts) by the Au- / thor of the NEW ATALANTIS. // *LONDON*, / Printed for *John Morphew*, near *Stationer's-* / *Hall*, 1712. Price 3*d*.

8° (in half sheets): [A]B–C⁴, 12 leaves; pp. [1–2], 3–22, [23–24]; $ 2 signed.

Contents: p. [1] title (verso blank); 3–22 text; [23–24] advertisement for several works.

Page 22 exists in two variant states: line 22

1. 'Canibal's'
2. 'Cannibal's'.

The page was not otherwise reset: indeed, both states are characterized by the same damaged initial capital in the relevant word. The fact that 2 predominates among the copies consulted (and was followed by all subsequent impressions) suggests that 1 was the first state and 2 introduced during the course of impression.

Publication date: On 10 May Swift wrote 'The Appendix to the 3d Part of John Bull was published yesterday' (*Journal*, p. 533): see also *PB* for 8 and 10 May and *Examiner* 8 May. Copyright was entered by Barber to Morphew on 13 May.

Copies: 1. L (8132 aa. 40) O (P. 304; Rad. f. 154; GP. 1891)
CLU–C CtY (By 52. 48)
2. CT E (2 copies) EU (2 copies) L (T. 2074; E. 1984)
LL LVA–F O (P. 306; GP. 1145) UL CLU–C CSmH
CtY (Medical Historical Lib.) MB MH NN PU
Lewis Bower

1712 b [as preceding except] ATALANTIS. // 𝕿𝖍𝖊 𝕾𝖊𝖈𝖔𝖓𝖉 𝕰𝖉𝖎𝖙𝖎𝖔𝖓. // ...

Pagination (3)(4)[5][6](7)[8](9)–(22). A reimpression of state 2 of the preceding. The MH copy is identical in all respects save for 'Price 2*d.*' on the title-page as opposed to 'Price 3*d.*' in all other impressions.

Copies: L (2 copies) CtY (2 copies) MH NN (2 copies)

1712 c [as preceding except] the two former . . . ATALANTIS. // 𝕿𝖍𝖊 𝕿𝖍𝖎𝖗𝖉 𝕰𝖉𝖎𝖙𝖎𝖔𝖓. // . . .

Pagination (3)–(16)[17]–[21](22). A reimpression in which the positions of the signature on page 3 and of the pagination on pages 4, 5, 7, and 9 change in relation to the text. On page 9 the damaged numeral of preceding impressions is replaced and on page [23] the advertisement is reset in small type to accommodate a new item for this *Appendix* and the three previous pamphlets, despite the fact that the advertisement for the first three pamphlets alone still appears on page 24 as it does in preceding impressions. Moreover, a clear gap now appears between the first four and the last five letters of the word 'Operation' on page 14 line 15. As this word is the only one on the line (concluding a chapter) the gap is probably the result of a slight type movement within a page tied up between impressions.

The CtY copy is corrupt: it contains the correct A and C gatherings but the B gathering of Pamphlet III (in fact from *1712 e-f* as it has 'mus' for 'was' on page 13).

Copies: L LVA–F O (2 copies) CtY MB PR

1712 d [as preceding except] ATALANTIS. // 𝕿𝖍𝖊 𝕱𝖔𝖚𝖗𝖙𝖍 𝕰𝖉𝖎𝖙𝖎𝖔𝖓. // . . .

Sequence of pagination incorrect (3)–(17)(19) [? upper half cut off] (18)(20)(22)(21). A reimpression in which the gap between the letters of 'Operation' is closed and in which there are indications of type movement and careless resetting on pages 3, 4, 6, 7, and 12: on page 6 line 12 the '*Timothy*' of previous impressions is printed as '*Timothy*' and on page 7 line 13 'into' as 'inta'.

Copy: E

1712 e [as preceding]

Another incorrect sequence of pagination (3)–(16)(16)(18) [? upper half cut off] (19)(19)(20)(21). A hidden reimpression in which '*Timothy*' is correctly printed.

Copy: PU

1712 f [as preceding]

Sequence of pagination partially corrected (3)–(20)(22)(21). Another hidden reimpression within the 'fourth edition'.

Copy: MB

PAMPHLET V

1712 a [Within a double rule] *LEWIS BABOON* / Turned Honest, / AND / JOHN BULL / POLITICIAN. / Being / The FOURTH PART / OF / *Law is a Bottomless-Pit.* // Printed from a Manuscript found in the / Cabinet of the famous Sir *Humphry* / *Polesworth*: And Publish'd, (as well / as the Three former Parts and *Appen-* / *dix*) by the Author of the NEW / ATALANTIS. // *LONDON*: Printed for *John Morphew*, near / *Stationers-Hall.* 1712. Price 6 d.

8° (in half sheets): A–F⁴, 24 leaves; pp. [1–8], 1–37 [9–45], [46–8]; $ 2 signed.

Contents: p. [1] title (verso blank); [3–7] THE PREFACE; [8] THE CONTENTS; 1–37 [9–45] text; [46–7] advertisement for several works; [48 blank].

Publication date: Advertised in both *PB* and *Examiner* for 31 July: see also *Daily Courant* 29 and 30 July. Barber entered copyright to Morphew on 1 August.

Copies: E (2 copies) EU (2 copies) L (3 copies) LVA–F O (3 copies) CLU–C CtY (3 copies) MH MB (2 copies) NN (2 copies)

1712 b [as preceding except] ATALANTIS. // 𝕿𝖍𝖊 𝕾𝖊𝖈𝖔𝖓𝖉 𝕰𝖉𝖎𝖙𝖎𝖔𝖓, 𝕮𝖔𝖗𝖗𝖊𝖈𝖙𝖊𝖉. // . . .

Contents: p. [1] title (verso blank); [3] THE CONTENTS (verso blank); 5–9 (top half) The PREFACE; 9 (bottom half)–45 text; [46–47] advertisement for several works; [48 blank].

Copies: E L LL LVA–F O MB MH PR PU

In 1712 there were also pirated editions of all the five pamphlets printed in Edinburgh by James Watson and in Dublin by Edward Waters. Watson in fact printed editions of each individual pamphlet (E. RR. 7 / 1–4 and 2. 348 / 14) and a separate collected edition of *Law is a Bottomless-Pit . . . In Three Parts. With the Appendix, and a Compleat Key* (E. 2. 197 / 1) all in 1712. Copies of these Edinburgh 'reprints' may also be found in various other British and American libraries. See John Freehafer, 'Arbuthnot and the Dublin Pirates', *The Scriblerian*, II. ii (1970), 65–7, for a bibliographical account and details of some American locations of the five pamphlets and Key published in Dublin: in Britain, Durham University Library has copies of them all.

BIBLIOGRAPHY

All works cited were published in London unless otherwise stated.

1. *Principal editions of 'The History of John Bull'*

POPE, Alexander, and SWIFT, Jonathan, *Miscellanies in prose and verse . . . the second volume* (printed for Benjamin Motte, 1727).

—— *Miscellanies. the second volume* (printed for Benjamin Motte . . . and sold by Weaver Bickerton . . . and Lawton Gilliver, 1731).

—— *Miscellanies. the second volume. the second edition* (printed for Benjamin Motte, 1733).

—— *Miscellanies. the second volume* (printed for Benjamin Motte, and Charles Bathurst, 1736).

—— *Miscellanies. the third volume. by Dr. Arbuthnot, Mr. Pope, and Mr. Gay* (printed for Charles Bathurst . . . and L. Gilliver, 1742).

SWIFT, Jonathan, *The works of Dr. Jonathan Swift, dean of St. Patrick's, Dublin. vol. vi. consisting of miscellanies in prose. by Dr. Swift, Dr. Arbuthnot, Mr. Pope, and Mr. Gay* (printed for C. Bathurst, 1751).

—— *The works of Dr. Jonathan Swift, D.D., dean of St. Patrick's, Dublin, accurately revised in twelve volumes, adorned with copper-plates; with some account of the author's life, and notes historical and explanatory, by John Hawkesworth, volume v.* (printed for C. Bathurst, C. Hitch, and C. Hawes, 1754).

—— *The works of the Rev. Dr. Jonathan Swift, dean of St. Patrick's, Dublin. arranged, revised, and corrected, with notes, by Thomas Sheridan, A.M. a new edition, in seventeen volumes. vol. xvii.* (printed for C. Bathurst, W. Strahan, B. Collins, J. F. & C. Rivington, L. Davis, W. Owen, J. Dodsley, T. Longman, R. Baldwin, T. Cadell, J. Nichols, T. Egerton, and W. Bent, 1784).

—— *The works of the Rev. Jonathan Swift, D.D., dean of St. Patrick's, Dublin. arranged by Thomas Sheridan, A.M. with notes, historical and critical. a new edition, in nineteen volumes; corrected and revised by John Nichols, F.S.A. . . . volume xvii.* (printed for J. Johnson, J. Nichols, R. Baldwin, Otridge & Son, J. Sewell, F. & C. Rivington, T. Payne, R. Faulder, G. & J. Robinson, R. Lea, J. Nunn, W. Cuthell, T. Egerton, Clarke & Son, Vernor & Hood, J. Scatcherd, T. Kay, Lackington Allen & Co., Carpenter & Co., Murray & Highley, Longman & Rees, Cadell Jun. & Davies, T. Bagster, J. Harding, and J. Mawman, 1801).

—— *The works of Jonathan Swift, D.D. dean of St. Patrick's, Dublin; containing additional letters, tracts, and poems, not hitherto published; with notes, and a life of the author, by Walter Scott, esq. volume vi.*

(Edinburgh, printed for Archibald Constable & Co., Edinburgh; White, Cochrane & Co., & Gale, Curtis, & Fenner, London; and John Cumming, Dublin, 1814).

—— *The works of Jonathan Swift, D.D., and dean of St. Patrick's, Dublin; containing interesting and valuable papers not hitherto published. in two volumes. with a memoir of the author, by Thomas Roscoe . . . volume ii.* (Henry Washbourne, 1841).

ARBUTHNOT, John, *An English garner: later Stuart tracts*, ed. Edward Arber (1883; reprinted under supervision of George A. Aitken, Constable & Co., 1903).

—— *The history of John Bull by John Arbuthnot, M.D.*, ed. Henry Morley (Cassell & Co., 1889).

—— *The life and works of John Arbuthnot, M.D., Fellow of the Royal College of Physicians*, ed. George A. Aitken (Clarendon Press, Oxford, 1892).

—— *A miscellany of the wits: being select pieces by William King, D.C.L., John Arbuthnot, M.D., and other hands*, ed. Kenneth N. Colvile (Philip Allan & Co., 1920).

—— *The History of John Bull for the first time faithfully re-issued from the original pamphlets, 1712, together with an investigation into its composition, publication and authorship*, ed. Herman Teerink (H. J. Paris, Amsterdam, 1925).

2. *Contemporary sources*

The following list includes books, pamphlets, and broadsides from the early seventeenth to the late eighteenth centuries, though the great majority to which we refer were more truly 'contemporary' and were published between 1690 and 1712. As many items were anonymous publications we have listed them alphabetically under title for ease of reference, e.g. from the cue-titles used in our annotation; but we have given the author when known or generally accepted, and have bracketed attributions which are doubtful. We have also shortened excessively long titles while providing enough information for the reader to recognize catalogue entries for the same works. The dates quoted are those which appear in the imprints of the copies consulted. When relevant to our concerns in the editorial matter we have also repeated information as to the 'edition', again taken from the imprint of the copy consulted, despite the bibliographical unreliability of such pronouncements.

The academy of complements. wherein ladyes, gentlewomen, schollers, and strangers may accomodate their courtly practice with most curious ceremonies, complementall, amorous, high expressions, and formes of speaking, or writing, 1640.

An account of a dream at Harwich. in a letter to a member of parliament about the Camisars, 1708.

An account of a second dream at Harwich, supplying all the omissions and defects in the first dream. in a letter to the same member of parliament, about the Camisars, 1711.

Ellis Veryard, *An account of divers choice remarks, as well geographical as historical, political, mathematical, physical, and moral; taken in a journey through the Low-Countries, France, Italy, and part of Spain etc.,* 1701.

'An account of the debate in town concerning peace and war. in letters to a gentleman in the country', 1701. *A collection of state tracts publish'd during the reign of king William III,* 1707.

(Robert Ferguson), *An account of the obligations the states of Holland have to Great-Britain, and the return they have made both in Europe and the Indes. with reflections upon the peace,* 1711.

'R. B.', *Adagia Scotica or a collection of Scotch proverbs and proverbial phrases,* 1668.

Arthur Maynwaring (with Sarah Jennings, Duchess of Marlborough), *Advice to the electors of Great Britain; occasion'd by the intended invasion from France,* 1708.

Aesop at court. or, state fables, 1702.

Aesop at the bear-garden: a vision, 1715.

Aesop at Tunbridge. or, a few select fables in verse. by no person of quality, 1698.

Bernard Mandeville, *Aesop dress'd. or a collection of fables writ in familiar verse,* 1704.

Aesop in Europe, or a general survey, of the present posture of affairs in, England, Scotland, France, Holland, Germany, Hungary, Spain, Portugal, Savoy, Italy. by way of fable and moral adapted suitably, to the circumstances of each kingdom, 1706.

Aesop in Scotland, exposed in ten select fables relating to the times, 1704.

Aesop in Spain. or, a few select fables in verse. translated from the Spanish, 1701.

The age of mad-folks, 1710.

All men mad: or, England a great Bedlam. a poem, 1704.

Anatomyes of the true physitian, and counterfeit mounte-bank, 1602.

The ancient and present state of Poland. giving a short, but exact, account of the situation of that country. the manners and customs of the inhabitants. the several successions of their kings. their religion &c., 1697.

John Stevens, *The ancient and present state of Portugal. containing the description of that kingdom, its former and present division, the manner of the cortes or parliament, its several names, forts, rivers, lakes, baths, minerals, plants, and other products etc.,* 1705.

John Arbuthnot, *Annus mirabilis: or, the wonderful effects of the approaching conjunction of the planets Jupiter, Mars, and Saturn. by Abraham Gunter, philomath,* 1722.

An answer to an infamous libel entituled, a list of one unanimous club of members of the late parliament, Nov. 11 1701. that met at the Vine tavern in Long Acre. wherein all those gentlemen, mention'd in the said scandalous pamphlet, are vindicated, from its malicious and false suggestions and insinuations, 1701.

Daniel Defoe, *An answer to a question that no body thinks of, viz. but what if the queen should die?,* 1713.

An answer to Wild. or, a poem, upon the imprisonment of Robert Wild D.D. in Cripplegate. by a brother in the same congregation, bs. 1663.

The ape-gentle-woman, or the character of an Exchange-wench, 1675.

Samuel Grascome, *An appeal to all true English-men, (if there be any such left,) or, a cry for bread,* 1702.

An appendix to the history of the Crown-inn: with a key to the whole, 1714.

John Breval, *The art of dress, a poem,* 1717.

Daniel Defoe, *Atalantis Major. printed in Olreeky, the chief city of the north part of Atalantis Major. anno mundi 1711,* Edinburgh, 1711.

An auction of state pictures; containing a most curious collection of original low-church faces: drawn exactly to the life by a high-church limner, 1710.

The baboon a-la-mode, a satyr against the French, 1704.

Gilbert Burnet, *The bishop of Salisbury's and the bishop of Oxford's speeches in the house of lords on the first article of impeachment of Dr. Henry Sacheverell,* 1710.

—— *The bishop of Salisbury's speech in the house of lords, upon the bill against occasional conformity,* 1704.

A bob for the court; or, prince Eugene's welcome, bs. 1712.

Brandy-wine in the Hollanders ingratitude, being a serious expostulation of an English souldier with the Dutch: wherein he debateth with them of former kindnesse received from England, and the cause of their base requittal now etc., 1652.

John Arbuthnot, *A brief account of Mr. John Ginglicutt's treatise concerning the altercation or scolding of the ancients,* 1731.

Robert Ferguson, *A brief account of some of the late incroachments and depradations of the Dutch upon the English; and a few of those many advantages which by fraud and violence they have made of the British nations since the revolution, and of the means enabling them thereunto,* 1695.

Owen Feltham, *A brief character of the Low-Countries under the states. being three weeks observation of the vices and vertues of the inhabitants,* 1652.

John Stevens, *A brief history of Spain. containing the race of its kings from the first peopling of that country etc.,* 1701.

Daniel Defoe, *A brief history of the poor Palatine refugees, lately arriv'd in England etc.,* 1709.

—— *The British visions: or, Isaac Bickerstaff's twelve prophecies for the year 1711,* 1711.

Walter Herries), *Caledonia; or, the pedlar turn'd merchant, a tragi-*

comedy, as it was acted by his majesty's subjects of Scotland, in the king of Spain's province of Darien, 1700.

Charles Leslie, Cassandra. (but I hope not) telling what will come of it. num. 1. in answer to the occasional letter num. 1, 1705.

A catalogue of the capital and well-known library of books, of the late celebrated Dr. Arbuthnot deceased; which will be sold by auction, by Mess. Christie and Ansell etc., 1779.

Edmund Hickeringill, The ceremony-monger, his character. in six chapters etc., 1689.

Henry Robinson, Certaine proposals in order to a modelling of the lawes and law-proceedings, for a more speedy, cheap, and equall distribution of justice throughout the common-wealth, 1653.

Thomas Burnet, A certain information of a certain discourse. that happen'd at a certain gentlemans house, in a certain county. written by a certain person then present, to a certain friend now at London, 1712.

The changes: or, faction vanquish'd. a poem, most humbly inscrib'd to those noble patriots, defenders of their country, and supporters of the crown, the not guilty lords, 1711.

Joseph Trapp, The character and principles of the present set of whigs, 1711.

The character of a church-trimmer, bs. 1683.

The character of a modern addresser, 1710.

Character of a quack-astrologer: or, the spurious prognosticator anatomiz'd, 1673.

The character of a quack-doctor, or the abusive practices of impudent illiterate pretenders to physick exposed, 1676.

The character of a sneaker, 1705.

The character of a solicitor. or the tricks and quillets of a pettyfogger. with his manifold knaveries, cheats, extortions, and other villanies, 1675.

The character of a tory, bs. 1681.

George Savile, Marquess of Halifax, The character of a trimmer etc., 1688.

The character of a whig, under several denominations. to which is added, the reverse, or the character of a true English-man, in opposition to the former, 1700.

John Evelyn, A character of England, as it was lately presented in a letter, to a noble man of France, 1659.

A character of France. to which is added gallus castratus. or an answer to a late slanderous pamphlet, called the character of England, 1659.

The character of the most honourable Robert Harley, earl of Oxford and Mortimer, lord high-treasurer of Great-Britain, bs. 1712.

Characters of the royal family, ministers of state, and of all the principal persons in the French court. with an exact account of the French king's revenue, 1705.

The cheating age found out, when knaves was most in fashion. wherein are describ'd the many frauds, cheats, abuses, and vast sums of money that England had been cheated of in this long, bloody and expensive war, 1712.

A choice new song call'd she-land and robinocracy, bs. 1712.

The cobler of Gloucester reviv'd, in a letter to the Observator's country-man (1710?).

A collection of all her majesty's speeches, messages, &c. from her happy accession to the throne, to the twenty first of June 1712, 1712.

A collection of poems, for and against Dr. Sacheverell (parts I and II) 1710.

A collection of Scotch proverbs by Puppity Stampoy, 1663.

A collection of severell visions; one relating to the Irish nation, the rest concerning the royal family of England. with an account of three prodigies which were seen in the element by several people, with their signification and interpretation, as they were made known to Richard Bury, 1712.

A compleat volume of the memoirs for the curious, 1710.

William Wagstaffe, *A complete key to the three parts of law is a bottomless-pit, and the story of the St. Alban's ghost*, 1712.

—— *The second edition corrected*, 1712.

—— *to the four parts of law is a bottomless-pit, and the story of the St. Alban's ghost. the third edition corrected*, 1712.

—— *The fourth edition corrected*, 1712.

—— *The fifth edition corrected*, 1712.

—— *to law is a bottomless-pit, the story of the St. Alban's ghost, and prince Mirabel, &c. the sixth edition enlarged*, 1713.

Francis Hare, *The conduct of the duke of Marlborough during the present war. with original papers*, 1712.

A continuation of the history of the Crown-inn: with characters of some of the late servants; and the proceedings of the trustees to the coming of the new landlord, part II, 1714.

The country-gentlewoman's catechism: or, a true answer to the town-ladies catechism, 1703.

Mary de la Riviere Manley, *Court intrigues, in a collection of original letters, from the island of the New Atalantis*, 1711.

Robert Pitt, *The crafts and frauds of physic expos'd. the very low prices of the best medicines discover'd. the costly medicins . . . censur'd. and the too frequent use of physic prov'd destructive to health. with instructions to prevent being cheated . . . by the prevailing practice*, 1703 (1st edn., 1702).

(William Wagstaffe), *Crispin the cobler's confutation of Ben H[oa]dly, in an epistle to him*, 1712.

The dancing-school. with the adventures of the Easter holy-days, 1700.

The danger of moderation (1704?).

Daniel de Foe's new invention to get money, 1707.

Daniel Defoe, *A defence of the allies and the late ministry: or, remarks on*

*the tories new idol. being a detectation of the manifest frauds and falsities'
in a late pamphlet entituled, the Conduct of the allies and of the late
ministry, in beginning and carrying on the war,* 1712.

Jonathan Swift, *The description of Dunkirk with Squash's and Dismal's
opinion. how easily prince Eugene may retake it, and many other matters
of the last importance,* bs. 1712.

*The devill of a whigg: or, Zarazian subtilty detected. done from the original,
by a fellow of the academy of insensati, or the society of the unthankful
club at Bologna in Italy,* 1708.

A dialogue between a modern courtier, and an honest English gentleman,
1696.

A dialogue between a new courtier and a country gentleman, 1712.

*A dialogue betwixt whig and tory. wherein the principles and practices of
each party are fairly and impartially stated; that thereby mistakes and
prejudices may be remov'd from amongst us,* 1710.

Henry Dodwell, *A discourse concerning the use of incense in divine offices.
wherein it is proved, that that practice, taken up in the middle ages, is,
notwithstanding, an innovation from the doctrine of the first and purest
churches, and the traditions derived from the apostles,* 1711.

R. H[awkins], *A discourse of the nationall excellencies of England,* 1658.

Daniel Defoe, *The dissenters answer to the high-church challenge,* 1704.

The dissenters catechism, 1703.

William Robertson, *Dissenters self-condemn'd: being a full answer to Mr. de
Laune's plea for the non-conformists, lately recommended by Mr. Daniel
Foe, author of the review,* 1710.

*The duke of Anjou's succession further consider'd, as to the danger that may
arise from it to Europe in general; but more particularly to England, and
the several branches of our trade,* 1701.

The duke of M[arlborough's] catechism, 1709.

*The d[uke] of M[arlborough]'s confession to a jacobite priest, February the
6th, 1711,* 1711.

*The duke of M[arlboroug]h's vindication. in answer to a pamphlet falsely so
called,* 1712.

(John Oldmixon), *The Dutch barrier our's: or, the interest of England and
Holland inseperable. with reflections on the insolent treatment the emperor
and states-general have met with from the author of the conduct, and his
brethren* etc., 1712.

*The Dutch drawn to the life. In I. an exact description and character of the
several provinces of the Netherlands. II. an account of their trade and
industry. III. a well-weigh'd re-search into their policy, government, and
strength* etc., 1664.

*The Dutch-mens pedigree, or a relation, shewing how they were first bred,
and descended from a horse-turd, which was enclosed in a butter-box,*
bs. 1653.

(William Baron), *The Dutch way of toleration, most proper for our English dissenters*, 1699.

The Dutch won't let us have Dunkirk, and high treason happily discover'd. or the D[u]tch und[erstoo]'d. with the shortest way to understand aright, and confute any Dutch memorial whatsoever. and the reasons why those that massacred the English at Amboyna . . . thwart the general peace of Europe etc., 1712.

Duty of a Wife, 1707.

Daniel Defoe (or William Pittis), *The dyet of Poland, a satyr*, Dantzick [London], 1705.

Edward Ward, *Ecclesia & facto. a dialogue between Bow-steeple dragon, and the Exchange grasshopper*, 1698.

Daniel Defoe, *Eleven Opinions about Mr. H[arle]y; with observations*, 1711.

James Puckle, *England's path to wealth and honour, in a dialogue between an Englishman and a Dutchman* etc., 1702 (1st edn., 1699).

Edward Ward, 'The English foreigners: or, the whigs turn'd Dutchmen. a satyr', *The poetical entertainer: or, tales, satyrs, dialogues, &c. Numb. III*, 1712.

English gratitude: or, the whig miscellany, consisting of the following poems. I. On the duke of Marlborough's going into Germany. II. The Oak and the briar. a tale. III. An inscription upon a triumphal arch erected by the French king in memory of his victories, for which the author had a thousand pound etc., 1713.

An enquiry into the causes of the miscarriage of the Scots colony at Darien. or an answer to a libel entituled a defence of the Scots abdicating Darien. submitted to the consideration of the good people of England, Glasgow, 1700.

Daniel Defoe, *An enquiry into the danger and consequences of a war with the Dutch*, 1712.

—— *An enquiry into the real interest of princes in the persons of their ambassadors, and how far the petty quarrels of ambassadors, or the servants and dependents of ambassadors one among another, ought to be resented by their principals . . . impartially applied to the affair of monsieur Mesnager, and the count de Rechteren, plenipotentiaries at Utrecht*, 1712.

—— *An essay at a plain exposition of that difficult phrase a good peace. by the author of the review*, 1711.

John Arbuthnot, *An essay concerning the nature of aliments, and the choice of them, according to the different constitutions of human bodies. in which the different effects, advantages, and disadvantages of animal and vegetable diet, are explain'd. the second edition. to which are added practical rules of diet in the various constitutions and diseases of human bodies*, 1732.

Charles Davenant, *Essays upon peace at home and war abroad. in two parts*, Part 1, 1704.

An essay towards the history of the last ministry and parliament: containing seasonable reflections on I. favourites II. ministers of state III. parties IV. parliaments and V. publick credit, 1710.

An examination of the third and fourth letters to a tory member. relating to the negociations for a treaty of peace in 1709. in a second letter to my lord **, 1711.

The examination, tryal, and condemnation of rebellion Ob[servato]r. at a sessions of oyer and terminer, held at Justice-hall, (in what town or county the reader pleases) on the 24th of August 1703. being St. Bartholomew's day, before Mr. justice Orthodox, and Mr. baron Cathedral, 1703.

An excellent new song, call'd the trusty and true Englishman, bs. 1711/12.

An exhortation to the love of our country: with some reflections on a late protest, 1712.

Daniel Defoe, *The experiment: or, the shortest way with the dissenters exemplified* etc., 1705.

An explanation of the eleven resolves of the 5th of February last, 1711. in which the nation may see, at one view, the mighty loss to E[ngla]nd; and the great advantages and savings, both in men and money, that the A[llie]s and the D[ut]ch have made, by not being on an equality with the E[ngli]sh, and by their deficiencies in their quota's according to their conventions and agreement made with her m[ajest]y of E[ngla]nd, 1712.

The fable of the cods-heads: or, a reply to the Dutch-men's answer to the resolutions of the house of commons, 1712.

The fable of the lions share, versified in the pretended partition of the Spanish monarchy, 1701.

Roger L'Estrange, *Fables, or Aesop and other eminent mythologists: with morals and reflections*, 1704.

James Ogilby, *The Fables of Aesop paraphras'd in verse: adorn'd with sculpture and illustrated with annotations*, 1668.

John Toland, *The fables of Aesop. with the moral reflections of Monsieur Baudoin. translated from the French*, 1704.

William Shippen (or Bertram Stote), *Faction display'd. a poem*, 1705.

Faction display'd: or, a short history of the second parliament of Great Britain called in the year 1710 upon the change of the ministry, 1739.

(Edward Ward), *A fair shell, but a rotten kernel: or, a bitter nut for a factious monkey*, 1705.

A farther continuation of the history of the Crown-inn. part III. containing the present state of the inn, and other particulars, 1714.

Daniel Defoe, *A farther search into the conduct of the allies and the late ministry, as to peace and war. containing also a reply to the several letters and memorials of the states-general* etc., 1712.

(Robert Harley and Simon Clement), *Faults on both sides: or, an essay upon the original cause, progress, and mischievous consequences of the factions in this nation* etc., 1710.

Daniel Defoe, *The felonious treaty: or an enquiry into the reasons which moved his late majesty king William of glorious memory, to enter into a treaty at two several times with the king of France for the partition of the Spanish monarchy. With an essay proving that . . . the Spanish monarchy should never be united in the person of the emperor,* 1711.

Five extraordinary letters suppos'd to be writ to Dr. B[entle]y, upon his edition of Horace, and some other matters of a great importance, 1712.

John Tutchin, *The Foreigners. a poem,* 1700.

Arthur Maynwaring, *Four letters to a friend in North Britain, upon the publishing the tryall of Dr. Sacheverell,* 1710.

William Fleetwood, *Four sermons: I. On the death of queen Mary, 1694. II. On the death of the duke of Gloucester, 1700. III. On the death of king William, 1701. IV. On the queen's accession to the throne, in 1703. by William lord bishop of St. Asaph,* 1712.

Charles Hornby, *The fourth and last part of a caveat against the whiggs, &c. in a short historical account of their behaviour in the reign of her majesty queen Anne,* 1712.

The fourth and last part of the history of the Crown-inn: with the character of John Bull, and other novels. part IV, 1714.

(William Pittis), *The fox set to watch the geese: a state-paradox. being a welcome from Newmarket, by way of fable,* 1705.

Daniel Defoe, *The free-holders plea against stock-jobbing elections of parliament-men,* 1701.

Humphrey Mackworth, *Free parliaments; or a vindication of the fundamental right of the commons of England in parliament assembled, to be sole judges of the privileges of the electors and elected; being a vindication of the proceedings of the house of commons in the case of Ashby against White,* 1704.

The French king's catechism. or madam Maintenon's last advice, 1709.

The French king vindicated; being a full answer to all the reflections cast upon him, during the course of his long and glorious reign, 1712.

A full and exact collection of all the considerable addresses, memorials, petitions, answers, proclamations, declarations, letters and other publick papers, relating to the company of Scotland trading to Africa and the Indes, since the passing of the act of parliament, by which the said company was established in June 1695, till November 1700, 1700.

Aaron Hill, *A full and just account of the present state of the Ottoman empire in all its branches: with the government, and policy, religion, customs, and way of living of the Turks, in general. faithfully related from a serious observation, taken in many years travels thro' those countries,* 1709.

A full and true account of the apprehending and taking six French prophets, near Hog-lane in Soho etc., bs. 1707 .

Alexander Justice, *A general treatise of the dominion and laws of the sea. containing what is most valuable upon that subject, in ancient and modern authors etc.,* 1705.

The glorious life and actions of St. Whig: wherein is contain'd an account of his country, parentage, birth, kindred, education, marriage, children, &c. with the lives of his principal friends and enemies etc., 1708.

Charles Gildon, *The golden spy: or, a political journal of the British nights entertainments of war and peace, and love and politics: wherein are laid open, the secret miraculous power and progress of gold, in the courts of Europe,* 1709.

Grandsire Hambden's ghost. and peace, or, no peace. two poems. together with a prefatory answer, to some late whiggish scurrility, especially, a certain dedication, 1712.

The hawkers lamentation in a dialogue between Nick and Humphrey, bs. 1682.

The heaven-drivers. a poem, 1701.

Heraclitus ridens redivivus: or, a dialogue between Harry and Roger, concerning the times, 1688.

Daniel Defoe, *The highland visions, or the Scots new prophecy: declaring in twelve visions what strange things shall come to pass in the year 1712,* 1712.

(William Baron), *An historical account of comprehension and toleration. from a general retrospect of the severall reformations at first, with the pernicious principles and practices of that which the dissenters among us have always followed, and so factiously oppos'd, to our much more orthodox establishment,* 1705.

John Oldmixon, *The history of England, during the reigns of king William and queen Mary, queen Anne, king George I* etc., 1735.

The history of ingratitude: or, a second part of antient precedents for modern facts. in answer to a letter from a noble lord, 1712.

Abel Boyer, *The history of king William III,* 1702.

The history of prince Mirabel's infancy, rise and disgrace: with the sudden promotion of Novicius. in which are intermix'd all the intrigues, both amorous and political relating to those memorable adventures: as also the characters of both sexes in the court of Britomartia, 1712.

The history of the Dutch usurpations. their maxims and politicks in point of government, and their remarkable ingratitude to England. particularly their unheard of cruelties at Amboyna, and the debates thereon in the English council in the reign of king James I. with their usual method of managing treaties, 1712.

Abel Boyer, *The history of the life and reign of queen Anne. illustrated with all the medals struck in this reign, with their explanations; and other useful and ornamental cuts* etc., 1722.

The history of the Mohocks from queen Elizabeih to this present time (1712?).

(William Pittis), *The history of the present parliament and convocation,* 1711.

Abel Boyer, *The history of the reign of queen Anne, digested into annals,* 11 vols., 1703–13.

The history of the republick of Holland, from its first foundation to the death of king William. as also, a particular description of the United Provinces . . . in two volumes, 1705.

The history of the royal-oak, and her three branches, 1712.

The history of the treaty of Utrecht. in which is contain'd, a full account of all the steps taken by France, to bring the allies to a treaty during the war, and by that means to divide them, 1712.

Daniel Defoe, *The history of the union between England and Scotland, with a collection of original papers relating thereto by Daniel De Foe*, ed. George Chalmers, London, 1786.

The history political and gallant of the famous card[inal] Portocarrero archbishop of Toledo. done out of the French, 1704.

Histrio Theologicus: or, an historical-political-theological account of the most remarkable passages and transactions in the life of the late b[isho]p of S[aru]m found among his l[ords]hip's papers, and inscrib'd to his old friend and admonitor, Mr. L[esle]y, 1715.

Hogan-Moganides: or, the Dutch Hudibras, 1674.

John Ogilby, *The Holland nightingale, or the sweet singers of Amsterdam: being a paraphrase upon the fable of the frogs fearing the sun would marry*, 1672.

Honesty the best policy: or the mischiefs of faction shewed in the character of an high, and a low-church clergy-man, 1711.

Edward Ward, *Hudibras redivivus: or, a burlesque poem on the times*, 1705.

The humble confession and petition of a whig with his eyes open; deserving to be heard in the behalf of himself, and all such as shall think fit to rank themselves under his class. whereunto some fresh thoughts are added to unlimited obedience. dedicated to the d[uke]. of M[arlborou]gh, 1712.

(Francis Hoffman), *An impartial character of the noble family of the most honourable the earl of Oxford and Mortimer, lord high treasurer of Great Britain etc.*, bs. 1712.

The impartial secret history of Arlus, Fortunatus, and Odolphus, ministers of state to the empress of Grand-Insula . . . humbly offer'd to those good people of Grand-Insula who love their country, are not bigoted by party, and blinded by the fulsom flatteries bestow'd on Arlus by a gang of mercenaries, 1710.

Daniel Defoe, *Imperial gratitude, drawn from a modest view of the conduct of the emperor Ch[arl]es VI, and the king of Spain Ch[arl]es III: with observations on the difference, &c. being a farther view of the deficiencies of our confederates*, 1712.

The infallible mountebank, or quack doctor, 1707.

'C. D.', *Iter boreale: or, a voyage to the north. a poem*, 1708.

The junto, bs. 1712.

The junto. a poem, 1712.

Daniel Defoe, *The justice and necessity of a war with Holland, in case the Dutch do not come into her majesty's measures, stated and examined*, 1712.

—— *A justification of the Dutch from several late scandalous reflections: in which is shewn the absolute necessity of preserving a strict and inviolable friendship betwixt Great-Britain and the States-General: with the fatal consequences that must attend a war with Holland*, 1712.

Charles Vine, *A justification of the present war against the United Netherlands. wherein the declaration of his majesty is vindicated, and the war proved to be just, honourable, and necessary; the dominion of the sea explained, and his majesties rights thereunto asserted; the obligations of the Dutch to England, and their continual ingratitude* etc., 1672.

The king of France his catechism, 1703.

The ladies catechism, 1703.

The last will and testament of Anthony king of Poland, 1682.

The last will and testament of the c[hurc]h of E[nglan]d. with a preface shewing the reason of its publication, in spite of enemies, &c., 1710.

The last words and sayings of the true-protestant elm-board, which lately suffer'd martyrdom in Smithfield, and now in Southwark: together with a true relation of a conference between Dr. B[urnet], and the said board, bs. 1682.

Charles Leslie, *The lay-man's letter to the b[isho]p of S[alisbur]y in answer to his speech for occasional conformity*, 1704.

Humphrey Mackworth, *A letter from a member of parliament to his friend in the country; giving an account of the proceedings of the tackers, upon the occasional and self-denying bills*, 2nd edn., 1705.

Francis Hare, *A letter to a member of the October-club: shewing, that to yield Spain to the duke of Anjou by a peace, wou'd be the ruin of Great Britain*, 1711.

A letter to a modern dissenting whig concerning the present juncture of affairs; with a comparison between the former principles and the present practises of that party, 1701.

The life and reign of Henry the sixth. giving a full account of the English glory abroad. their factions at home. the fatal treaty of Tours. the loss of France, and, the civil wars in England. about the hereditary and parliamentary right, between the two houses of York and Lancaster, 1712.

The Limehouse dream; or, the churches prop, 1710.

A list of one unanimous club of members of the late parliament, Nov. 11. 1701 that met at the Vine-tavern in Long Acre, 1701.

The London ladies dressing-room: or, the shop-keepers wives inventory. a satyr, 1705.

London's glory: or, the history of the famous and valiant London 'prentice: being an account of his parentage, birth and breeding, together with many brave and heroick exploits perform'd by him throughout the course of his life; to the honour of London, and the whole English nation, n.d.

A looking-glasse for all proud, ambitious, covetous and corrupt lawyers. wherein they may see their fore-fathers love and humility, 1646.

The mad-mans hospital: or, a cure for the presbyterian itch, by an eminent doctor that has lately cur'd many a thousand blind people in this nation, bs. 1710.

The management of the four last years vindicated: in which her late majesty, and her ministry, are fully cleared from the false aspersions cast on them in a late pamphlet, 1714.

The managers pro and con: or, an account of what is said at Child's and Tom's coffee-houses for and against Dr. Sacheverell, 1710.

(Samuel Grascome), *The mask of moderation pull'd off the foul face of occasional conformity: being an answer to a late poisonous pamphlet, entitul'd moderation still a vertue* etc., 1704.

Mary de la Riviere Manley, *Memoirs of Europe, towards the close of the eighth century, written by Eginardus and done into English by the translator of the New Atalantis,* 1710.

(John Oldmixon), *Memoirs of the life of the most noble Thomas, late marquess of Wharton; with his speeches in parliament, both in England and Ireland. to which is added his lordship's character by Sir Richard Steel,* 1715.

Memoirs of the present condition of France, and the strength of its fortifications; particularly, such as lye exposed to the arms of the allies . . . in a letter from the honourable Ja. Preston, esq; an English student in Doway, to his friend in London, 1711.

John Macky, *Memoirs of the secret services of John Macky esq; during the reign of king William, queen Anne, and king George I. including, also, the true secret history of the rise, promotion, &c. of the English and Scots nobility,* 1733.

James Drake, *The memorial of the church of England, humbly offer'd to the consideration of all true lovers of our church and constitution,* 1705.

The merchant a-la-mode. to the tune of which no body can deny, bs. 1713.

Peter Heylyn, *Microcosmus. a little description of the great world. augmented and revised,* 1625.

Daniel Defoe, *Minutes of the negotiations of m[onsieu]r Mesnager at the court of England, towards the close of the late reign. wherein some of the most secret transactions of that time, relating to the interest of the Pretender, and a clandestine separate peace, are detected and laid open,* 1717.

John Arbuthnot, *The miscellaneous works of the late Dr. Arbuthnot . . . the second edition, with additions, Glasgow: printed for James Carlisle,* 1751 (1st edn., 1750).

—— *Miscellaneous works of the late Dr. Arbuthnot. with an account of the author's life. in two volumes. London: printed for W. Richardson and L. Urquart . . . and J. Knox,* 1770.

The miserable case of poor old England fairly stated, in a letter to a member of the honourable house of commons, 'Amsterdam' [London], 1712.

The miseries of England, from the growing power of her domestick enemies. a poem, 1702.

'Mercurius Melancholius', *Mistris parliament brought to bed of a monstrous childe of reformation. with her 7 years teeming, bitter pangs, and hard travaile, that she hath undergone in bringing forth her first-borne* etc., 1648.

—— *Mistris parliament her gossiping. full of mirth, merry tales, chat, and other pleasant discourse, between Mrs. statute. justice. truth. and Mrs. parliament* etc., 1648.

—— *Mistris parliament presented in her bed, after the sore travaile and hard labour which she endured last weeke, in the birth of her monstrous off-spring, the childe of reformation* etc., 1648.

(Samuel Colville), *Mock poem: or, whiggs supplication,* 1711.

Moderate reflections on the approaching surrender of Dunkirk, as a pledge of the sincere disposition of the French king, to yeild us a safe speedy and lasting peace, bs. 1712.

William Shippen (or Bertram Stote), *Moderation display'd. a poem,* 1705.

(Samuel Grascome), *Moderation in fashion: or, an answer to a treatise, written by Mr. Francis Tallents, entituled, a short history of schism* etc., 1705.

James Owen, *Moderation still a vertue: in answer to several bitter pamphlets: especially two, entituled, occasional conformity a most unjustifiable practice. and the wolf stripp'd of his shepherd's cloathing. which contain the substance of the rest* etc., 1704.

The moderator: or a view of the state of the controversie betwixt whigg and tory. short animadversions on the picture of a modern whigg. with a defence of the treaty of partition, and the impeach'd lords. a vindication of his majesty in dissolving the late parliament. by a true English man of no party, 1702.

William Bissett, *The modern fanatick. part II. containing what is necessary to clear all the matters of fact in the first part; and to confute what has been printed in the pretended vindication of Dr. Sacheverell,* 1710.

Edward Ward, *The modern world disrob'd: or, both sexes stript of their pretended virtue. in two parts. first, of the ladies. secondly, of the gentlemen. with familiar descant upon every character,* 1708.

A modest defence of the government. in a dialogue between Kinglove, an old cavalier, and Meanwell, a modern tory, 1702.

The monster: or, the world turn'd topsy turvy. a satyr, 1705.

Richard Johnson, *The most famous history of the seaven champions of christendome: Saint George of England, Saint Dennis of France, Saint James of Spaine, Saint Anthonie of Italie, Saint Andrew of Scotland, Saint Pattrick of Ireland, and Saint David of Wales,* 1596.

Mris Rump brought to bed of a monster, with her terrible pangs, bitter teeming, hard labour . . . and the great misery she hath endured by this ugly, deformed, ill-begotten babe or monster of new reformation, bs. 1660.

Mrs. parliament, her invitation of Mrs. London, to a thanksgiving dinner.

for the great and mighty victorie, which Mr. Horton obtained over Major Powell in Wales, 1648.

The Muses mercury: or the monthly miscellany. consisting of poems, prologues, songs, sonnets, translations, and other curious pieces, never before printed, 1707.

Johan Bale, *A mysterye of iniquyte,* Geneva, 1545.

The mystery of iniquity somewhat laid open: in a letter to the present governour; wherein is also contained an history and recital and proposal of sundry things to be made known and remembred, and to be done accordingly, 1692.

Gilbert Burnet, *The mystery of iniquity unvailed: in a discourse, wherein is held forth the opposition of the doctrine, worship, and practices of the Roman church, to the nature, designs, and characters of the Christian faith,* 1673.

Natural reflections upon the present debates about peace and war. in two letters to a member of parliament from his steward in the country, 1712.

Richard Blackmore, *The nature of man. a poem,* 1711.

Charles Leslie (or Henry Sacheverell), *The new association of those called, moderate-church-men, with the modern-whigs and fanaticks, to undermine and blow-up the present church and government,* 1702.

A new canting dictionary: comprehending all the terms, antient and modern, used in the severall tribes of gypsies, beggars, shoplifters, highwaymen, foot-pads, and all other clans of cheats and villains etc., 1725.

A new dialogue between a member of parliament, a divine, a lawyer, a freeholder, a shopkeeper, and a country farmer, upon the present juncture of affairs (1708?).

A new dialogue between an excise-man and a bailiff, proving which of the two is the greatest cheats, 1703.

A new dialogue between Monsieur Shacoo, and the Poussin doctor, 1701.

'B. E.', *A new dictionary of the terms ancient and modern of the canting crew, in its several tribes of gypsies, beggars, thieves, cheats, &c.,* 1699.

The new practice of piety; writ in imitation of dr. Browne's Religio Medici: or the Christian virtuoso: discovering the right way to Heaven between all extreams. to which is added, a satyr on the house of lords for their throwing out the bill against occasional conformity, 1704.

A new reciept of ye fanaticks, diascordium, n.d.

A new song. being a second part to the same tune of Lillibulero, 1711.

Edward Hatton, *A new view of London; or, an ample account of that city, in two volumes,* 1708.

The new way of selling places at court. in a letter from a small courtier to a great stock-jobber, 1712.

Daniel Defoe, *No queen: or, no general. an argument, proving the necessity her majesty was in, as well for the safety of her person as of her authority, to displace the d[uke] of M[arl]borough,* 1712.

(John Arbuthnot), *Notes and memorandums of the six days, preceding the death of a late right reverend* etc., 1715.

Notes conferr'd: or, a dialogue betwixt the groaning board, and a Jesuite: demonstrating the ambiguous humour of the one, and curiousity of the other, bs. 1682.

Daniel Defoe, *Not*[tingh]*am politicks examin'd. being an answer to a pamphlet lately publish'd intitul'd, observations upon the state of the nation*, 1713.

Occasional poems on the late Dutch war, and the sale of Dunkirk. to which is added, a satyr against the Dutch, 1712.

On the church's being in danger (1705?).

On the jewel in the Tower, bs. 1712.

(Thomas Burnet), *Our ancestors as wise as we: or ancient precedents for modern facts, in answer to a letter from a noble lord*, 1712.

The Oxford almanack of 1712, explain'd: or, the emblems of it unriddl'd. together with some prefatory account of the emblems of the two preceding years, 1711.

A pacquet from Parnassus: or, a collection of papers, 1702.

The parliament of ladies. or divers remarkable passages of ladies in Spring-garden; in parliament assembled, 1647.

A particular description of the famous town and cittadel of Dunkirk, with all its fortifications, viz. rice-bank, forts, harbour, peere, the bason, the number of ships in the harbour, and canon in each fort, as it is now in possession of the queen of Great Britain, 1712.

Gilbert Burnet, *A pastoral letter writ by the right reverend father in God, Gilbert, lord bishop of Sarum, to the clergy of his diocess, concerning the oaths of allegiance and supremacy to k*[ing]. *William and Q*[ueen]. *Mary*, 1689.

(Jonathan Swift) *Peace and Dunkirk; being an excellent new song upon the surrender of Dunkirk to general Hill*, bs. 1712.

Humphrey Mackworth, *Peace at home; or a vindication of the proceedings of the house of commons on the bill for preventing danger from occasional conformity*, 1703.

The peace-haters: or, a new song, for the illumination of those that won't see, 1711.

Daniel Defoe, *Peace, or poverty. being a serious vindication of her majesty and her ministers consenting to a treaty for a general peace. shewing the reasonableness, and even the necessity, there was for such a procedure*, 1712.

(John Howell), *A perfect description of the people and country of Scotland*, 1659.

The perquisite-monger: or the rise and fall of ingratitude. being one of the stories, which the monks of Godstow were formerly wont to divert fair

Rosamund with, and which may serve to clear up several absurdities in the history of prince Mirabel, 1712.

The petticoat plotters, or; the d[uche]*ss of M*[arlboroug]*h's club,* bs. 1712.

Pharmacœpia Radcliffeana: or, dr. Radcliff's prescriptions, faithfully gather'd from his original recipe's. to which are annex'd. useful observations upon each prescription, 1716.

The picture of a low-flyer (1704?).

The picture of the first occasional conformist (Job I. 6) drawn in little, 1705.

Alexander Pennecuik (or William Forbes), *A pil for pork-eaters: or, a Scots lancet for an English swelling,* Edinburgh, 1705.

(Daniel Defoe), *Plain English, with remarks and advice to some men who need not be nam'd,* 1712.

A pleasant discourse by way of dialogue, between the old and new Jack Catch, occasioned upon the latters being whip'd from Rosemary-lane to the Hermitage, on Thursday the 21th. of January, 1685 etc., 1685.

Edward Ward, *The poetical entertainer: or tales, satyrs, dialogues, &c. . . . III,* 1712.

Poor England bob'd at home and abroad by N. F. G. Gent., bs. 1712.

A postscript to John Bull. containing the history of the Crown-inn, with the death of the widow, and what happened thereupon, 1714.

William Oliver, *A practical essay on fevers. containing remarks on the hot and cool methods of their cure. wherein the first is rejected; and the last recommended. to which is annex'd a dissertation on the Bath-waters,* 1704.

Lewis Bayly, *The practise of pietie, directing a Christian how to walke, that he may please God,* 1613 (3rd edn.).

Presbyterian loyalty, in two letters: one directed to the moderate-church-men; to which is annexed the ballad of the cloak, or, the cloak's knavery. the other to a tacking member of the late house of commons. giving an account of the history of dissenters loyalty . . . part II, 1705.

Daniel Defoe, *The present negotiations of peace vindicated from the imputation of trifling,* 1712.

The present state of the court of France, and city of Paris: in a letter from Monsieur ——, *to the honourable Matthew Prior esq; one of the commissioners of her majesty's customs,* 1712.

Daniel Defoe, *The present state of the parties in Great Britain: particularly an enquiry into the state of the dissenters in England, and the presbyterians in Scotland; their religious and politick interest consider'd, as it respects their circumstances before and since the late acts against occasional conformity in England; and for the tolleration of common-prayer in Scotland,* 1712.

The press restrain'd: a poem, occasion'd by a resolution of the house of commons, to consider that part of her majesty's message to the house, which relates to the great licence taken in publishing false and scandalous libels, 1712.

Prince Eugene not the man you took him for: or, a merry tale of a modern heroe, 1712.

P[rince] *Eugene's memorial in the name of the emperor: deliver'd to mr. secretary St. John, Feb. 18*, 1712.

John Arbuthnot, *Proposals for printing a very curious discourse in two volumes in quarto, intitled ψευδολογια πολιτικη; or, a treatise of the art of political lying, with an abstract of the first volume of the said treatise*, 1712.

The protestant joyners ghost to Hone the protestant carpenter in Newgate. with his confesssion, bs. 1683.

The pulpit-fool. a satyr, 1707.

The queen's and the duke of Ormond's new toast, bs. 1712.

Daniel Defoe, *Reasons against fighting. being an enquiry into this great debate, whether it is safe for her majesty, or her ministry, to venture an engagement with the French, considering the present behaviour of the allies*, 1712.

Reasons for restoring the whigs, 1711.

Daniel Defoe, *Reasons why a party among us, and also among the confederates, are obstinately bent against a treaty of peace with the French at this time*, 1711.

Reasons why the duke of Marlborough cannot lay down his commands, deduced from the principles of loyalty, gratitude, honour, interest, &c. in a letter from the country to a friend in London, 1710.

Daniel Defoe, *Reasons why this nation ought to put a speedy end to this expensive war; with a brief essay, at the probable conditions on which the peace now negotiating, may be founded. also an enquiry into the obligations Britain lies under to the allies; and how far she is obliged not to make peace without them*, 1711.

The re-representation: or, a modest search after the great plunderers of the nation: being a brief enquiry into two weighty particulars, necessary at this time to be known, viz. I. who they are that have plundered the nation. II. why they are not detected and punished, 1711.

The reward of ambition: exemplified in Aesop's fable of the courtier; with reflections, bs. 1712.

The rights and liberties of Englishmen asserted. with a collection of statutes and records of parliament against foreigners. shewing, that by the constitution of England, no outlandish man, whether naturaliz'd or not, is capable of any office in England or Ireland etc., 1701.

Daniel Defoe, *R[ogue]'s on both sides. in which are the characters of some r[ogue]'s not yet describ'd; with a true description of an old whig, and a modern whig, an old tory, and a modern tory; high-flyer, or motley; as also a minister of state*, 1711.

William King, *Rufinus: or an historical essay on the favourite-ministry under Theodosius the great and his son Arcadius. to which is added, a version of part of Claudian's Rufinus*, 1712.

Charles Leslie, *Salt for the leach. in reflections upon reflections*, 1712.

Sauce for an English gander is excellent sauce for a Scotch goose: or a demonstrative proof that this present parliament has not broke the union by tolerating the episcopal people in Scotland, to worship God their own way etc., 1712.

Scotland characteriz'd: in a letter written to a young gentleman, to dissuade him from an intended journey thither, 1701.

A search after Dutch honesty: or, the old use and custom of that nation to their friends and allies ever since they have been a common-wealth; faithfully taken from their own histories and authentick records, 1712.

The second part of the locusts: or, chancery painted to the life, and the laws of England try'd in forma pauperis, 1704.

The secret history of Arlus and Odolphus, ministers of state to the empress of Grandinsula. in which are discover'd the labour'd artifices formerly us'd for the removal of Arlus, and the true causes of his late restoration, upon the dismission of Odolphus and the quin-quinvirate etc., 1710.

Edward Ward, *The secret history of clubs: particularly the kit-kat, beef-stake, vertuosos, quacks, knights of the golden fleece, florists, beaus, &c.*, 1709.

Mary de la Riviere Manley, *The secret history of queen Zarah, and the Zarazians; being a looking-glass for —— in the kingdom of Albigion. faithfully translated from the Italian copy now lodg'd in the Vatican at Rome, and never before reprinted in any language*, 1705.

The secret history of the calves-head club, complt. or, the republican unmask'd. wherein is fully shewn, the religion of the calves-head heroes, in their anniversary thanksgiving songs on the thirtieth of January . . . with reflections thereupon, 1705 (5th edn.).

Daniel Defoe, *The secret history of the white staff, being an account of affairs under the conduct of some late ministers, and of what might probably have happen'd if her majesty had not died. Part III*, 1715.

The secret intrigues of the duke of Savoy. with a faithful relation of the ill treatments which monsieur de Phelippeaux, ambassador of France, receiv'd from his royal highness, against the law of reason and the right of nations, 1705.

Mary de la Riviere Manley, *Secret memoirs and manners of several persons of quality, of both sexes. from the New Atalantis, an island in the Mediterranean. written originally in Italian*, 1709.

Seldom comes a better; or, a tale of a lady and her servants, 1710.

(Benjamin Hoadly), *Serious advice to the good people of England: shewing them their true interest, and their true friends*, 1710.

John Arbuthnot, *A sermon preach'd to the people, at the Mercat Cross of Edinburgh; on the subject of the union*, 1706.

William Bromley, *Several years travels through Portugal, Spain, Italy, Germany, Prussia, Sweden, Denmark and the United Provinces*, 1702.

A short abstract of the behaviour of the occasional communicants, towards the members of the church of England, since the revolution (1702).

Daniel Defoe, *A short narrative of the life and actions of his grace John, d[uke]. of Marlborough, from the beginning of the revolution, to this present time. with some remarks on his conduct,* 1711.

A short treatise of the epidemical diseases of these times (1701 ?).

Daniel Defoe, *The shortest way with the dissenters: or proposals for the establishment of the church,* 1702.

Charles Davenant, *Sir Thomas Double at court, and in high preferments. in two dialogues between sir Thomas Double and sir Richard Comover, alias mr. Whiglove: on the 27th of September, 1710,* 1710.

A sober vindication of the reverend dr. and the harmlesss board. lately glew'd together in a profane pasquil etc., bs. 1682.

Some conjectures, concerning the causes of the difficulties which the German branch of the house of Austria meets with, at this time, in their way to the crown of Spain, 1705.

Gilbert Burnet, *Some letters. containing, an account of what seemed most remarkable in Switzerland, Italy, &c. written by G. Burnet, D.D. to t[he]. H[onourable]. R[obert]. B[oyle]. at Rotterdam,* 1686.

William Pittis, *Some memoirs of the life of John Radcliffe M.D. interspersed with several original letters: also a true copy of his last will and testament,* 1715.

Gilbert Burnet, *Some passages of the life and death of the right honourable John earl of Rochester, who died the 26th of July, 1680. written by his own direction on his death-bed,* 1680.

Mary Pix, *The Spanish wives, a farce, as it was acted by his majesty's servants at the theatre in Dorset-garden,* 1696.

Daniel Defoe, *A speech without doors,* 1710.

Star-board and lar-board: or, sea-politicks. an allegory written by a gentleman that has made himself merry on board the fleet, ever since it has been got off from the shelves of the late ministry, thro' the means of the present parliament, who have generously resolv'd to pay the debts of the navy, 1711.

William Paterson, *A state of Mr. Paterson's claim upon the equivalent; with original papers and observations relating thereto,* 1712.

William Wagstaffe (with John Arbuthnot?), *The story of the St. Alb[a]n's ghost, or the apparition of mother Haggy. collected from the best manuscripts,* 1712.

The strange and wonderful apparition: or, the advice of Colledge's ghost to the new plotters, bs. 1683.

Strange news from Newgate: or, a relation of how the ghost of Colledge the protestant-joyner appeared to Hone the joyner since his condemnation: being an account of the whole discourse that past between them, bs. 1683.

The stumbling-block from Claudian against Rufinus, 1711.

Suffragium: or, the humours of the electors in chusing members for parliament. a poem, 1702.

A summons from a true-protestant conjurer, to Cethegus's ghost to appear Septemb. 19. 1682, bs. 1682.

William Atwood, *The superiority and direct dominion of the imperial crown of England, over the crown and kingdom of Scotland, and the divine right of succession to both crowns inseperable from the civil, asserted*, 1704.

A supplement to the history of the Crown-inn, for the first three years under the new landlord. with additional characters of some of the chief servants, 1717.

John Stow, ed., *Survey of the cities of London and Westminster . . . brought down from the year 1663 . . . to the present time by J. Strype. to which is prefixed the life of the author by the editor*, 1720.

The tackers toss'd in a blanket: or, the humours of elections, in a dialogue between a freeholder and a country-farmer, 1705.

The taxes not grievous, and therefore not a reason for an unsafe peace, 1712.

They are all mad, and bewitch'd. or, the devil to do at Westminster, and at St. James's, bs. 1712.

Charles Hornby, *A third part of the caveat against the whiggs, in a short historical account of their transactions since the revolution*, 1712.

The thoughts of a country gentleman upon reading dr. Sacheverell's tryal. in a letter to a friend, 1710.

Benjamin Hoadly, *The thoughts of an honest tory, upon the present proceedings of that party. in a letter to a friend in town*, 1710.

The thoughts of an honest whig, upon the present proceedings of that party. in a letter to a friend in town, 1710.

(Charles Davenant), *Tom Double return'd out of the country: or, the true picture of a modern whig, &c.*, 1702.

Bernard Mandeville, *A treatise of the hypochondriack and hysterick passions vulgarly call'd the hypo in men and vapours in women; in which the symptoms, causes, and cure of those diseases are set forth after a method intirely new . . . in three dialogues*, 1711.

The trimmer catechised: or, a serious discourse between Trueman and Trimmer, bs. 1683.

The trimming court-divine. or reflexions on dr. Sherlock's book of the lawfulness of swearing allegiance to the present government, 1690.

A trip lately to Scotland, with a true character of the country and people: also reflections on their proceedings to disturb the present reign: to which are added several remarks, on the late barbarous execution of capt. Green, Mr. Madder, Mr. Simpson, and several others, 1705.

A trip to Spain: or, a true description of the comical humours, ridiculous customs, and foolish laws, of that lazy improvident people the Spaniards. in a letter to a person of quality from an officer in the royal navy, 1704/5.

Daniel Defoe, *A true account of the design, and advantages of the South-Sea trade: with answers to all the objections rais'd against it. a list of the commodities proper for that trade: and the progress of the subscription towards the South-Sea company,* 1711.

A true and exact character of the Low-Countreyes; especially Holland. or, the Dutchman anatomized, and truly dissected. being the series of three moneths observation of . . . the people, 1652.

A true and faithful account of the last distemper and death of Tom. Whigg, esq; who departed this life on the 22d day of September last, anno domini 1710. together with a relation of his frequent appearing since that day in town and country, to the geat disturbance of her majesty's peaceable subjects (Parts I and II), 1710.

The true-born-English-woman, in a letter to the public, 1703.

The true characters of, viz. a deceitful petty-fogger vulgarly call'd attorney. a know-all astrological quack . . . a female hypocrite . . . a low-churchman . . . a trimmer, or, Jack of all sides, 1708.

The true danger of the church. in a letter to a friend in the country, bs. 1707.

The true, genuine modern whigg-address. to which is added; an explanation of some hard terms now in use, for the information of all such as read or subscribe addresses, 1710.

Charles Davenant, *The true picture of a modern whig, set forth in a dialogue between Mr Whiglove & Mr. Double, two under-spur-leathers to the late ministry,* 1701.

The true picture of an ancient tory, in a dialogue between Vassal a tory and Freeman a whig, 1702.

Charles Davenant, *The true picture of the modern whig reviv'd. set forth in a third dialogue between Whiglove and Double, at Tom's coffee-house in Covent-garden,* 1707.

John Denham, *The true presbyterian without disguise; or, a character of a Presbyterian's ways and actions,* bs. 1680.

Mary de la Riviere Manley, *A true relation of the several facts and circumstances of the intended riot and tumult on queen Elizabeth's birth-day. gathered from authentick accounts: and published for the information of all true lovers of our constitution in church and state,* 1711.

The true spirit and elixir of cant, bs. 1684.

The tryal, examination and condemnation of occasional conformity. at a sessions of oyer and terminar, held at Troynovant, before Mr. Justice Upright, and baron Integrity. at a common-hall of the said city on T[uesday] the 26th of J[anuar]y 1703, 1703.

The tryal of Dr. Henry Sacheverell, before the house of peers, for high crimes and misdemeanors; upon an impeachment by the knights, citizens and burgesses in parliament assembled, in the name of themselves, and of all the commons of Great Britain, Published by Order of the House of Peers, 1710.

The ungrateful world, or; the hard case of a great g[enera]l, bs. 1712.

The very case, or the story of John the Butler, bs. 1712.

Daniel Defoe, *The villany of stock-jobbers detected, and the causes of the late run upon the bank and bankers discovered and considered*, 1701.

A vindication of the present m[inistr]y, from the clamours rais'd against them upon occasion of the new preliminaries, 1711.

Humphrey Mackworth, *A vindication of the rights of the commons of England*, 1701.

Thomas Shadwell, *The volunteers, or the stock-jobbers. a comedy, as it is acted by their majesties servants, at the Theatre Royal*, 1693.

Edward Ward, *Vulgus Britannicus; or, the British Hudibras*, 1710.

We are bravely serv'd at last, by the q[uee]n and p[arlia]m[en]t, 1712.

The Westminster combat, bs. 1710.

Westminster projects: or, the mystery of iniquity of Darby-house discovered, 1648.

Where's your peace now? or, the tories are all untwisted, 1712.

Whig and tory: or, wit on both sides. being a collection of poems, by the ablest pens of the high and low parties, upon the most remarkable occasions, from the change of the ministry, to this time, 1712.

The whigs feast: or, a protestant entertainment design'd by the city for a popish general, 1712.

The Whitson-fair: rary-show. lately brought from the flaming isle of moderation, all alive, bs. (1703?).

Who plot best; the whigs or the tories. being a brief account of all the plots that have happen'd within these thirty years, 1712.

White Kennett, *The wisdom of looking backward, to judge the better of one side and t'other by the speeches, writings, actions, and other matters of fact on both sides, for the four years last past*, 1715.

Daniel Defoe, *Wise as serpents: being an enquiry into the present circumstances of the dissenters, and what measures they ought to take in order to disappoint the designs of their enemies*, 1712.

Charles Leslie, *The wolf stript of his shepherd's cloathing, in answer to a late celebrated book intitul'd moderation a virtue, wherein the designs of the dissenters against the church: and their behaviour towards her majesty both in England and Scotland are laid open. with the case of occasional conformity considered*, 1704.

Thomas D'Urfey, *Wonders in the sun, or, the kingdom of the birds; a comick opera. with great variety of songs in all kinds, set to musick by several of the most eminent masters of the age*, 1706.

Daniel Defoe, *Worcestershire-queries about peace. by Tom Flockmaker, clothier of Worcester*, 1711.

'A word in season to England's representatives in parliament', 1701, *A collection of state tracts, publish'd during the reign of king William III*, vol. iii, 1707.

A word to the wise: or, some seasonable cautions about regulating the press, 1712.

Edward Ward, *The world bewitch'd. a dialogue between two astrologers and the author. with infallible predictions of what will happen in this present year, 1699. from the vices and villanies practis'd in court, city and country*, 1699.

3. Principal secondary sources

ADDISON, Joseph, STEELE, Richard, and others, *The spectator*, ed. Donald F. Bond, 5 vols. (Clarendon Press, Oxford, 1965).

ARBUTHNOT, John, *The history of John Bull for the first time faithfully re-issued from the original pamphlets, 1712, together with an investigation into its composition, publication and authorship*, ed. Herman Teerink (H. J. Paris, Amsterdam, 1925).

—— *The life and works of John Arbuthnot M.D., fellow of the royal college of physicians*, ed. George A. Aitken (Clarendon Press, Oxford, 1892).

——, GAY, John, and POPE, Alexander, *Three hours after marriage*, ed. John Harrington Smith (Augustan Reprint Society, 91–2, Los Angeles, 1961).

AVERY, Emmett L., ed., *The London stage 1660–1800. part ii. 1700–1729* (Univ. of Southern Illinois Press, Carbondale (Ill.), 1960).

BARNETT, Corelli, *Marlborough* (Eyre Methuen, 1974).

BEATTIE, Lester M., *John Arbuthnot mathematician and satirist* (Harvard Univ. Press, Cambridge (Mass.), 1935; reissued, Russell & Russell, New York, 1967).

BENSE, Johan F., *A dictionary of the Low-Dutch element in the English vocabulary* (O.U.P., London; Martinus Nijhoff, The Hague, 1926–39).

BIRKS, Michael, *Gentlemen of the law* (Stevens & Sons, 1960).

BOND, Richmond P., *English burlesque poetry, 1700–1750* (Harvard Univ. Press, Cambridge (Mass.), 1932).

BOYCE, Benjamin, *The polemic character, 1640–1661: a chapter in English literary history* (Univ. of Nebraska Press, Lincoln (Nebr.), 1955).

BROWN, Peter Hume, *The legislative union of England and Scotland* (Clarendon Press, Oxford, 1914).

BRUNETEAU, Claude, 'John Arbuthnot (1667–1735) et les idées au début du dix-huitième siècle', 2 vols. (offset thesis, Université de Lille, Lille, 1974).

BURNET, Gilbert, *Bishop Burnet's history of his own time: with notes by the earls of Dartmouth and Hardwicke, speaker Onslow, and dean Swift*, 6 vols., 2nd edn. (Univ. Press, Oxford, 1883).

—— *A supplement to Burnet's history of my own time*, ed. Helen C. Foxcroft (Clarendon Press, Oxford, 1902).

BURTON, Ivor F., *The captain-general: the career of John Churchill, duke of Marlborough, from 1702 to 1711* (Constable, 1968).

CARSTENS, Patricia J. (now Köster), 'Political satire in the works of Dr. John Arbuthnot', Ph.D. thesis, London Univ., 1958.

CARTWRIGHT, James J., ed., *The Wentworth papers 1705–1739: selected from the . . . correspondence of Thomas Wentworth, lord Raby, created in 1711 earl of Strafford* (Wyman & Sons, 1883).

CHURCHILL, Sir Winston, *Marlborough, his life and times*, 2 vols. (Harrap & Co., 1947).

CLARK, Sir George N., *The Dutch alliance and the war against French trade 1688–1697* (Univ. of Manchester, Manchester, 1923).

—— *The later Stuarts 1660–1714* (Clarendon Press, Oxford, 1934).

CLARK, Henry W., *History of English non-conformity from Wiclif to the close of the nineteenth century*, 2 vols. (Chapman & Hall, 1911–13).

CLARK, J. Kent, 'Swift and the Dutch', *Huntington Library Quarterly*, xvii (1954), 345–56.

CLARKE, Thomas E. S., and FOXCROFT, Helen C., *A life of Gilbert Burnet bishop of Salisbury* (Univ. Press, Cambridge, 1907).

COOK, Richard I., *Jonathan Swift as a tory pamphleteer* (Univ. of Washington Press, Seattle and London, 1967).

COOMBS, Douglas S., *The conduct of the Dutch: British opinion and the Dutch alliance during the war of the Spanish succession* (Martinus Nijhoff, The Hague & Achimota, 1958).

COOPER, Anthony Ashley, 3rd Earl of Shaftesbury, *Characteristics of men, manners, opinions, times, etc.*, ed. John M. Robertson, 2 vols. (Grant Richards, 1900).

CUNNINGHAM, Peter, *A handbook for London, past and present* (John Murray, 1850).

CUSHING, Harvey W., *Dr. Garth, the Kit-Kat poet 1661–1718* (Friedenwald Co., Baltimore, 1906).

DAVIES, Godfrey, 'The seamy side of Marlborough's war', *Huntington Library Quarterly*, xv (1952), 21–44.

DAVIES, Reginald Trevor, *Spain in decline 1621–1700* (Macmillan, 1957).

DEFOE, Daniel, *Defoe's review reproduced from the original editions*, ed. Arthur W. Secord, 23 vols. (Columbia Univ. Press, New York, 1938).

—— 'Defoe's true-born Englishman', ed. A. C. Guthkelch, *Essays and Studies*, iv (1913), 101–50.

DICKINSON, Harry T., 'The October club', *Huntington Library Quarterly*, xxxiii (1970), 155–73.

—— 'The tory party's attitude to foreigners: a note on party principles in the age of Anne', *Bulletin of the Institute of Historical Research*, xl (1967), 153–65.

DICKSON, Peter G. M., *The financial revolution in England: a study in the development of public credit 1688–1756* (Macmillan, London; St. Martin's Press, New York, 1967).

DOBRÉE, Bonamy, *Alexander Pope* (Sylvan Press, 1951).

DRYDEN, John, *Essays of John Dryden*, ed. William P. Ker, 2 vols.

(Clarendon Press, Oxford, 1899; reprinted, Russell & Russell, New York, 1961).

ELLIOTT, John H., *Imperial Spain, 1469–1716* (Edward Arnold, 1963).

ELLIS, Frank H., ed., *Poems on affairs of state: augustan satirical verse 1660–1714*, vols. vi and vii (Yale Univ. Press, New Haven & London, 1970, 75.)

EVERY, George, *The high-church party, 1668–1718* (S.P.C.K., 1956).

FEILING, Sir Keith G., *A history of the tory party 1640–1714* (Clarendon Press, Oxford, 1924).

FLEEMAN, John D., '18th-century printing ledgers', *The Times Literary Supplement*, 19 Dec. 1963, 1056.

FRISCHAUER, Paul, *Prince Eugène. a man and a hundred years of history*, trans. Amethe Smeaton (Victor Gollancz, 1934).

FRYE, Herman Northrop, *Anatomy of criticism: four essays* (Univ. Press, Princeton, 1957).

GAY, John, *The plays of John Gay*, 2 vols. (Abbey Classics, 1923).

GEIKIE, Roderick, and MONTGOMERY, Isabel A., *The Dutch barrier 1705–1719* (Univ. Press, Cambridge, 1930).

GOLDGAR, Bertrand A., *The curse of party, Swift's relations with Addison and Steele* (Univ. of Nebraska Press, Lincoln (Nebr.), 1961).

GREEN, David, *Sarah Duchess of Marlborough* (Collins, 1967).

GREENHOUGH, Chester N., 'Characters of nations', *Collected Studies by Chester Noyes Greenhough*, ed. F. W. C. Hersey (Harvard Cooperative Society, Cambridge (Mass.), 1940).

GWATKIN, Henry M., *Church and state in England to the death of Anne* (Longmans & Co., 1917).

HAYMAN, John G., 'Notions on national characters in the eighteenth century', *Huntington Library Quarterly*, xxxv (1971), 1–17.

HENDERSON, Nicholas, *Prince Eugen of Savoy* (Weidenfield & Nicolson, 1964).

HERTZ, Gerald Berkeley, *English public opinion after the restoration* (T. Fisher Unwin, 1902).

HOLMES, Geoffrey S., *British politics in the age of Anne* (Macmillan, London; St. Martin's Press, New York, 1967).

—— *The trial of doctor Sacheverell* (Eyre Methuen, 1973).

—— and SPECK, William A., eds., *The divided society: parties and politics in England 1694–1716* (Edward Arnold, 1967).

HONE, Campbell R., *The life of Dr. John Radcliffe, 1652–1714* (Faber & Faber, 1950).

HORWITZ, Henry, *Revolution politicks: the career of Daniel Finch second earl of Nottingham, 1647–1730* (C.U.P., 1968).

JOHNSON, James W., *The formation of English neo-classical thought* (Univ. Press, Princeton, 1967).

JOHNSON, Samuel, *The Yale edition of the works of Samuel Johnson, volume ii: the idler and the adventurer*, eds. W. J. Bate, J. M. Bullitt, and L. F. Powell (Yale Univ. Press, New Haven & London, 1963).

JONES, James R., *The first whigs: the politics of the exclusion crisis 1678–1683* (O.U.P., 1961).

JOWITT, William A., Earl JOWITT, and WALSH, C., eds., *The dictionary of English law*, 2 vols. (Sweet & Maxwell, 1959).

KNOX, Norman, *The word irony and its context, 1500–1755* (Duke Univ. Press, Durham (N.C.), 1961).

KÖSTER, *see* CARSTENS.

KRAMNICK, Isaac, *Bolingbroke and his circle: the politics of nostalgia in the age of Walpole* (Harvard Univ. Press, Cambridge (Mass.); O.U.P., London, 1968).

LAPRADE, William T., *Public opinion and politics in eighteenth century England to the fall of Walpole* (Macmillan, New York, 1936).

LEADAM, Isaac S., *The history of England from the accession of Anne to the death of George II, 1702–1760* (Longmans & Co., 1912).

LEYBURN, Ellen D., *Satiric allegory: mirror of man* (Yale Univ. Press, New Haven, 1956).

—— 'Swift's view of the Dutch', *PMLA* lxvi (1951), 734–45.

LIVERMORE, Harold V., *A history of Spain* (Allen & Unwin, 1958).

LODGE, Sir Richard, *The history of England from the restoration to the death of William III, 1660–1702* (Longmans & Co., 1905).

LOFTIS, John, *Comedy and Society from Congreve to Fielding* (Univ. Press, Stanford, 1959).

—— *The politics of drama in augustan England* (Clarendon Press, Oxford, 1963).

LUTTRELL, Narcissus, *A brief historical relation of state affairs from September 1678 to April 1714*, 6 vols. (Univ. Press, Oxford, 1857).

MACAULAY, Thomas Babington, Baron Macaulay, *The history of England from the accession of James the second*, ed. C. H. Firth, 6 vols. (Macmillan, 1913–15).

MCINNES, Angus, *Robert Harley, puritan politician* (Gollancz, 1970).

MACKINNON, James, *The union of England and Scotland. a study of international history* (Longmans & Co., 1907).

MCLACHLAN, Jean O., *Trade and peace with old Spain, 1667–1750: a study of the influence of commerce on Anglo-Spanish diplomacy in the first half of the eighteenth century* (Univ. Press, Cambridge, 1940).

MANLEY, Mary de la Riviere, *The novels of Mary Delariviere Manley*, intro. Patricia J. Köster (Univ. of Florida Press, Gainesville (Fla.), 1971).

MAZZEO, Joseph A., ed., *Reason and the imagination: studies in the history of ideas, 1600–1800* (Columbia Univ. Press, New York; Routledge & Kegan Paul, London, 1962).

MITCHELL, William F., *English pulpit oratory from Andrewes to Tillotson: a study of its literary aspects* (S.P.C.K., 1937).

MOORE, John R., *A checklist of the writings of Daniel Defoe* (Indiana Univ. Press, Bloomington (Ind.), 1960).

MOORE, Sir Norman, *The physician in English history* (Univ. Press, Cambridge, 1913).

MORGAN, William T., *English political parties and leaders in the reign of Queen Anne, 1702–1710* (Yale Univ. Press, New Haven; Humphrey Milford, London, 1920).

—— and CHLOE, S., *A bibliography of British history 1700–1715* (Indiana Univ. Press, Bloomington (Ind.), 1934–42).

MUNRO, Neil, *The history of the royal bank of Scotland* (R. & R. Clark, Edinburgh, 1928).

NICHOLS, John. *Illustrations of the literary history of the eighteenth century. consisting of authentic memoirs and original letters of eminent persons,* 8 vols. (Nichols, Son & Bentley, 1817–58).

NICHOLSON, Thomas C., and TURBERVILLE, Arthur S., *Charles Talbot duke of Shrewsbury* (Univ. Press, Cambridge, 1930).

OGG, David, *England in the reigns of James II and William III* (Clarendon Press, Oxford, 1955).

PASTON, George (pseud. Emily Morse Symonds), *Social caricature in the eighteenth century* (Methuen & Co., 1905).

PAULSON, Ronald, *The fictions of satire* (Johns Hopkins Press, Baltimore, 1967).

—— *Satire and the novel in eighteenth-century England* (Yale Univ. Press, New Haven & London, 1967).

PETRIE, Sir Charles, *The Jacobite movement,* 3rd edn. (Eyre and Spottiswoode, 1958).

PLUMB, John H., *The Growth of political stability in England 1675–1725* (Macmillan; published as 'The origins of political stability . . .', Houghton Miflin, New York, 1967).

—— ed., *Studies in social history: a tribute to G. M. Trevelyan* (Longmans, 1955).

POPE, Alexander, *The correspondence of Alexander Pope,* ed. George Sherburn, 5 vols. (Clarendon Press, Oxford, 1956).

—— ARBUTHNOT, John, and others, *Memoirs of the extraordinary life, works and discoveries of Martinus Scriblerus,* ed. C. Kerby-Miller (Yale Univ. Press, New Haven, 1950; reissued, Russell & Russell, New York, 1966).

—— *The poems of Alexander Pope: a one-volume edition of the Twickenham text,* ed. John Butt (Methuen & Co., 1965).

POSTON, Lawrence, 'Defoe and the peace campaign, 1710–13: a reconsideration', *Huntington Library Quarterly,* xxvii (1963), 1–20.

POTTER, Lee H., 'The text of Scott's edition of Swift', *Studies in Bibliography*, xxii (1969), 240–55.

PREBBLE, John E., *The Darien Disaster* (Secker & Warburg, 1968).

PRIOR, Matthew, *The Literary Works of Matthew Prior*, ed. H. Bunker Wright and Monroe K. Spears, 2 vols. (Clarendon Press, Oxford, 1971).

RICHARDS, James O., *Party propaganda under queen Anne: the general elections of 1702–1713* (Univ. of Georgia Press, Athens (Ga.), 1972).

RILEY, Patrick W. J., *The English ministers and Scotland 1707–1727* (Athlone Press, 1964).

ROGERS, Pat, *Grub street: studies in a subculture* (Methuen, 1972).

ROLLINS, Hyder E., ed., *The Pepys ballads*, 8 vols. (Harvard Univ. Press, Cambridge (Mass.), 1929–32).

ROSCOE, Edward S., *Robert Harley, earl of Oxford, prime minister 1710–14: a study of politics and letters in the age of Anne* (Methuen & Co., 1902).

ROSS, Angus M., 'The correspondence of Dr. John Arbuthnot, first collected together and edited, with a biographical introduction, notes and a dissertation', Ph.D. thesis, Cambridge Univ., 1956.

ROWSE, Alfred L., *The early Churchills, an English family* (Macmillan, 1956).

RUBINI, Dennis A., *Court and country 1688–1702* (Rupert Hart-Davis, 1967).

ST. JOHN, Henry, Viscount Bolingbroke, *Letters and correspondence, of the right honourable Henry St. John viscount Bolingbroke*, ed. Gilbert Parke, 2 vols. (G. G. & J. Robinson, 1798).

SCHILLING, Bernard, *Dryden and the conservative myth: a reading of Absalom and Achitophel* (Yale Univ. Press, New Haven & London, 1961).

SCHNEIDER, Ben R., *The Ethos of Restoration Comedy* (Univ. of Illinois Press, Urbana (Ill.), 1971).

SCOUTEN, Arthur H., *A bibliography of the writings of Jonathan Swift: second edition, revised and corrected by Dr. H. Teerink* (Univ. of Pennsylvania Press, Philadelphia, 1963).

SMOUT, Thomas C., *A history of the Scottish people 1560–1830* (Collins, 1969).

—— *Scottish trade on the eve of the union 1660–1707* (Oliver & Boyd, Edinburgh, 1963).

SNYDER, Henry L., 'Daniel Defoe, Arthur Maynwaring, Robert Walpole, and Abel Boyer: some considerations of authorship, *Huntington Library Quarterly*, xxxiii (1970), 133–53.

—— 'Daniel Defoe, the Duchess of Marlborough and the advice to the electors of Great Britain', *Huntington Library Quarterly*, xxix (1965), 53–62.

—— 'The reports of a press spy for Robert Harley: new bibliographical data for the reign of queen Anne', *Library*, 5th ser. xxii (1967), 326–45.

SPENCE, Joseph, *Observations, anecdotes, and characters of books and men, collected from conversation*, ed. James M. Osborn, 2 vols. (Clarendon Press, Oxford, 1966).

STANHOPE, Philip Dormer, 4th Earl of Chesterfield, *The wit and wisdom of the earl of Chesterfield: being selections from his miscellaneous writings in prose and verse*, ed. William Ernst Browning (1875).

STANHOPE, Philip Henry, 5th Earl Stanhope, *History of England, comprising the reign of Anne until the peace of Utrecht*, 2 vols., 4th edn. (1872).

STEELE, Richard, and others, *The Tatler*, ed. George A. Aitken, 4 vols. (Duckworth & Co., 1898).

STEEVES, Harrison R., *Before Jane Austen: the shaping of the English novel in the eighteenth century* (Holt, Rinehart & Winston, New York, 1965).

STEVENS, David Harrison, *Party politics and English journalism (1702–1712* (George Banta, Menasha (Wis.), 1916; reissued, Russell & Russell, New York, 1967).

SUTHERLAND, James R., *Background for queen Anne* (Methuen, 1939).

SWEDENBERG, Hugh T., ed., *England in the restoration and early eighteenth century: essays on culture and society* (Univ. of California Press, Berkeley, 1972).

SWIFT, Jonathan, *The correspondence of Jonathan Swift*, ed. Sir Harold Williams, 5 vols. (Clarendon Press, Oxford, 1963–5).

—— *A discourse of the contests and dissensions between the nobles and the commons in Athens and Rome with the consequences they had upon both those states*, ed. Frank H. Ellis (Clarendon Press, Oxford, 1967).

—— *Journal to Stella*, ed. Sir Harold Williams, 2 vols. (Clarendon Press, Oxford, 1948).

—— *Miscellanies in prose and verse 1711*, ed. C. P. Daw (Scolar Press, Menston, 1972).

—— *The poems of Jonathan Swift*, ed. Sir Harold Williams, 2nd edn., 3 vols. (Clarendon Press, Oxford, 1958).

—— *The prose writings of Jonathan Swift*, ed. Herbert Davis, 14 vols. (Basil Blackwell, Oxford, 1939–63).

—— *A tale of a Tub: to which is added the battle of the books and the mechanical operation of the spirit*, ed. A. C. Guthkelch and D. Nichol Smith, 2nd edn. (Clarendon Press, Oxford, 1958).

TILLEY, Morris P., ed., *A dictionary of the proverbs in England in the sixteenth and seventeenth centuries: a collection of the proverbs found in English literature and the dictionaries of the period* (Univ. of Michigan Press, Ann Arbor, 1950).

318   BIBLIOGRAPHY

TREVELYAN, George M., *England under queen Anne*, 3 vols. (Longmans, 1930–4).

TROYER, Howard W., *Ned Ward of Grubstreet: a study of subliterary London in the eighteenth century* (Harvard Univ. Press, Cambridge (Mass.), 1946).

TURNER, Francis McD., *The element of irony in english literature* (Univ. Press, Cambridge, 1926).

UFFENBACH, Zacharias von, *London in 1710: from the travels of Zacharias Conrad von Uffenbach*, trans. and ed. W. H. Quarrell and Margaret Mare (Faber & Faber, 1934).

WALCOTT, Robert, *English politics in the early eighteenth century* (Clarendon Press, Oxford, 1956).

WARD, Edward, *The London spy*, ed. Kenneth Fenwick (Folio Society, 1955).

WILLIAMS, Sir Harold, *The text of Gulliver's travels* (Univ. Press, Cambridge, 1952).

INDEX

Italicized numbers refer to the text of *John Bull*; roman numerals which immediately follow these refer to a note on the subject.